Theatres of Memory

Theatres of Memory

Volume 1:
Past and Present in
Contemporary Culture

RAPHAEL SAMUEL

VERSO
London · New York

First published by Verso 1994
©Raphael Samuel 1994
Paperback edition published by Verso 1996
Reprinted 1996
All rights reserved

Verso
UK: 6 Meard Street, London W1V 3HR
USA: 29 West 35th Street, New York, NY 10001-2291

Verso is the imprint of New Left Books

ISBN 0 86091 209 4
ISBN 0 85984 077 9 (pbk)

British Library Cataloguing in Publication Data
A catalogue record for this book is available from the British Library

Library of Congress Cataloging-in-Publication Data
A catalogue record for this book is available from the Library of Congress

Typeset by Solidus (Britol) Limited
Printed and bound in Great Britain by
Biddles Ltd, Guildford and King's Lynn

Endpapers:
Philip Ranger's Almanac, 1618 (left)
and
An Almanac for 1758 (John Johnson Collection,
Bodleian Library, Oxford) (right)

Contents

Preface: Memory Work   vii

Acknowledgements for Illustrations   xiv

INTRODUCTION

Unofficial Knowledge   3

PART I   Retrochic

Retrofitting   51
Retrochic   83
The Return to Brick   119

PART II   Resurrectionism

Resurrectionism   139
Living History   169

PART III   Heritage

Semantics   205
Genealogies   227
Sociology   242

PART IV   Flogging a Dead Horse

Heritage-baiting   259
Pedagogies   274
Politics   288

PART V   Old Photographs

The Eye of History   315
The Discovery of Old Photographs   337
Dreamscapes   350
Scopophilia   364

PART VI   Costume Drama

Modern Gothic: *The Elephant Man*   381
Doing the Lambeth Walk   390
Docklands Dickens   401
'Who Calls So Loud?' Dickens on Stage and Screen   413

AFTERWORD

Hybrids   429

Index   448

Preface: Memory Work

'The past is not dead. It is not even past yet.'
WILLIAM FAULKNER

Memory, according to the ancient Greeks, was the precondition of human thought. Mnemosyne, the goddess of memory, was also the goddess of wisdom, the mother of the muses (conceived in the nights she passed with Zeus on Mount Helikon), and therefore in the last analysis the progenitor of all the arts and sciences, among them history (Clio was one of her nine children). By the same token mnemonics, the science of recollection allegedly discovered by the poet Simonides of Ceos, was the basis of the learning process. Aristotle gave it a no less privileged place in the disciplines of thought. He distinguished between conscious and unconscious memory, calling the first – the memory which comes unbidden to the surface – *mneme*; and the second, the deliberate act of recollection, *anamnesis*. What Frances Yates, its first historian, called *The Art of Memory*, was taken over intact by the Romans. For St Augustine at the end of the Empire, as earlier for Cicero, memory was the mother of all the pedagogies and the *fons et origo* of thought. In a well-known passage of the *Confessions* he likens it to a 'vast hall' or 'palace' in which 'the whole treasure of our perception and experience is laid up'. The art of memory was revived by the medieval schoolmen (there is an authoritative statement of it by St Thomas Aquinas); and it had a last great flowering in the Renaissance, when it gave an occult underpinning (Frances Yates argues) to both art and science.

The 'art of memory' as it is practised today, whether in psychoanalysis, oral history, or 'heritage', arguably owes more to the Romantic movement in poetry and painting than it does to Greek mnemonics or Renaissance science. The 'spots of time' in Wordsworth's 'Lines Written above Tintern Abbey' or the commemorative passion of his essay on epitaphs are here more germane than Rosicrucian rhetoric or Hermetic iconography. Scott's *Minstrelsy of the Scottish Borders* and his Waverley novels, *Heart of Midlothian* in particular, bringing folk speech and folk ways into the very heart of historical narrative, would be another crucial set of texts. Still more pertinent would be the notion of 'resurrectionism' developed, in the 1840s, by the social-romantic French historian, Jules Michelet, a history which aimed to give a voice to the voiceless and speak to the fallen dead. E.P. Thompson's notion of history as a gigantic act of reparation, rescuing the defeated from the 'enormous condescension' of posterity, could be said to fall within this ambit. So also do those 'hands-on' museum exhibits, which use animatronics to simulate the sights and sounds of the past and turn material artefacts or relics into 'living history' displays.

The art of memory, as it was practised in the ancient world, was a pictorial art, focusing not on words but on images. It treated sight as primary. It put the visual first. Outward signs were needed if memories were to be retained and retrieved: 'Something is not secure enough by hearing, but it is made firm by seeing.' The primacy of the visual was even more apparent in the Middle Ages, when images were systematically mobilized to fix sacred narrative in the minds of the unlettered and when emblems, such as pilgrims' badges, or the heraldic devices adopted as a measure of genealogical descent, were a kind of universal currency. Mary Carruthers, in her very interesting book on medieval memory, argues that the illuminated manuscript, the stained-glass window and the church gargoyle were all there, in the first place, because of their mnemonic usefulness, and that it was by the exploitation of 'synaes-thesia' – the appeal to all the senses – that religious propaganda was effective.

In Simonides' mnemonics, place was coeval with imagery as a focus of memory-work. This had nothing to do with the anthropomorphizing of landscape, as in romantic ecology; nor yet with that sense of territorial belonging which underpins a modern politics of identity and the swelling literature on 'roots'. It involved rather a species of mental mapping in which space rather than time provided the significant markers, and ideal qualities were given symbolic abodes. Less abstractly, memory places were represented by sarcophagi and shrines, the sites of the earliest form of historical record. Mnemonic landscape was quite fundamental to the Western Christendom of the Middle Ages, with its far-flung network of pilgrim routes and landmarks – 'grottoes, springs, and mountains' – conveniently sited for commemorative worship. Sacred geography, secularized in the service of the state, was to play an even more vital part in nation-building and the geopolitics of colonial expansion.

In the Renaissance 'theatre of memory', wonderfully described by Frances Yates in her book, sacred geometry took the place of sacred geography. Here the act of recollection was conceptualized as a kind of ascent to the stars. In the Hermetic–Cabbalistic tradition of occult science, the theatre was built up layer by layer, like a pyramid, to capture the astral currents pouring down from above and use them for life and health. It also uncovered the hidden harmony between the earthly and the transcendental spheres. The tower – square or rounded – was crucial for the Rosicrucians, as it is in Tarot cards, since the bearers of enlightenment were cast in the role of visionaries: the higher they could mount the further they could see. Likewise the lofty designs of Giulio Camillo – the most famous of the Renaissance memory theatres, and among the originals, it has been argued, for Shakespeare's 'Globe' – offered (in Frances Yates's words) 'a vision of the world and of the nature of things seen from a height, from the stars themselves and even from the supercelestial founts of wisdom beyond them' (p. 148).

The romantic 'theatre of memory' was altogether more introspective, not scaling the heights but following the inner light. It was uninterested in the cosmos, but focused instead on the family circle and the individual self. Its landscapes of the mind or memory places were, as often as not, like those of Wordsworth's 'Intimations of Immortality', the childhood home. Romanticism built on time's ruins. Its idea of memory was premised on a sense of loss. It divorced memory-work from any claim to science, assigning it instead to the realm of the intuitive and the instinctual. It pictured the mind not as a watchtower but as a labyrinth, a subterranean place full of contrived corridors and hidden passages. Instead of anamnesis, the recollection that resulted from memory-training and conscious acts of will, imaginative weight fell on what Proust called 'involuntary memory' – the sleeping traumas which spring to life in time of crisis.

It is perhaps a legacy of Romanticism that memory and history are so often placed in opposite camps. The first, according to Maurice Halbwachs, one of its more impressive twentieth-century delineators, is primitive and instinctual; the second self-conscious. The first comes naturally to the mind, the second is the product of analysis and reflection. Memory was subjective, a plaything of the emotions, indulging its caprices, wallowing in its own warmth; history, in principle at least, was objective, taking abstract reason as its guide and submitting its findings to empirical proof. Where memory can only work in terms of concrete images, history has the power of abstraction. Where memory is time-warped, history is linear and progressive. History began when memory faded. Jacques Le Goff, in *History and Memory*, barely modifies these antinomies. 'Just as the past is not history but the object of history, so memory is not history, but one of its objects and an elementary level of its development.' (p. 129)

It is the argument of *Theatres of Memory*, as it is of a great deal of

contemporary ethnography, that memory, so far from being merely a
passive receptacle or storage system, an image bank of the past, is rather
an active, shaping force; that it is dynamic – what it contrives symptomatically to forget is as important as what it remembers – and that it is
dialectically related to historical thought, rather than being some kind
of negative other to it. What Aristotle called anamnesis, the conscious act
of recollection, was an intellectual labour very much akin to that of the
historian: a matter of quotation, imitation, borrowing and assimilation.
After its own fashion it was a way of constructing knowledge.

It is also my argument that memory is historically conditioned,
changing colour and shape according to the emergencies of the
moment; that so far from being handed down in the timeless form of
'tradition' it is progressively altered from generation to generation. It
bears the impress of experience, in however mediated a way. It is
stamped with the ruling passions of its time. Like history, memory is
inherently revisionist and never more chameleon than when it appears
to stay the same.

On the other side of the divide, history involves a series of erasures,
emendations and amalgamations quite similar to those which Freud sets
out in his account of 'screen memories', where the unconscious mind,
splitting, telescoping, displacing and projecting, transposes incidents
from one time register to another and materializes thought in imagery.
On the one hand, history splinters and divides what in the original may
have presented itself as a whole, abstracting here a nugget of descriptive
detail, there a memorable scene. On the other hand, history composites.
It integrates what in the original may have been divergent, synthesizes
different classes of information, and plays different orders of experience
against one another. It brings the half-forgotten back to life, very much
in the manner of dream-thoughts. And it creates a consecutive narrative
out of fragments, imposing order on chaos, and producing images far
clearer than any reality could be.

Theatres of Memory is meant to be an open text, one which can be read by
different readers in different ways and used for different purposes. But
without wanting to claim too much for these volumes, or to force a unity
which they do not have, it seems worth pointing out that the essays
return again and again to the idea of history as an organic form of
knowledge, and one whose sources are promiscuous, drawing not only
on real-life experience but also memory and myth, fantasy and desire;
not only the chronological past of the documentary record but also the
timeless one of 'tradition'. This first volume – sub-titled 'Past and Present
in Contemporary Culture' – is object-centred, and is about the ways in
which history is being rewritten and reconceptualized as a result of

changes in the environment, innovations in the technologies of retrieval, and democratizations in the production and dissemination of know-ledge. The second volume – 'Island Stories' – is about the wildly different versions of the national past on offer at any given point in time, depending on whether the optic is that of town or country; centre or periphery; the state or civil society. It begins with a series of pieces on 'The Spirit of Place'; continues with 'The War of Ghosts' (politics and memory in the 1980s); and concludes with a series of arguments on 'History, the Nation and the Schools'. A final chapter addresses the question of post-colonial history. The third volume, 'Memory Work', is about the commemorative arts, and the ways these give expression to the idea of progress, the sense of loss and the glamour of backwardness. It concludes with some chapters on the interplay of memory and myth in oral testimony, drawing, self-critically, on the writer's own use of it; and argues that subjectivity, like history itself, is socially constructed, a creature or child of its time.

I have relied heavily on oral history for leads on the resurrectionary movements of the last thirty years and thank the following: Patrick Fridenson of *Movement Social* and Gene Lebovics for guidance on *son et lumière*; Michael Wildt, Dagmar Engel and Lyndal Roper for 'barefoot' historians in Germany; Alessandro Triulzi and Carlo Poni for introduc-ing me to the Museum of Peasant Life in Emilia – one of my starting points for self-critical reflection on the practice of 'history from below'; Daniel Walkowitz and Eric Foner on public history in the United States; Sallie Purkis, editor of *Teaching History*, on 'learning by doing' in primary schools; Elizabeth Wilson for help on retrochic; Simon Traves, editor at Alan Sutton, for a state of the art account of the local publication of photographs; Ruth Richardson on the Rose Theatre campaign, necro-philia, and Victoriana; Dan Cruikshank, Andrew Saint, Jane Priestman, Jules Lubbock, Ken Powell, Mark Girouard on matters architectural; Su Clifford of 'Common Ground' for material on environmentalist cam-paigns; George Nicholson of the old GLC and Mr Pollard of Westminster City Council for the 'light up the Thames' movement of the 1970s; Pippa Hyde of the Council for the Protection of Rural England for anti-ivy campaigning in the 1930s; Michael Stratten, programme director at Ironbridge Institute, for guidance round the museum; John Naylor and Brian Southam for the history of Batsford; Peter Addyman, Dominic Tweedie and Linda James for acting as guides at Jorvik and the York Archaeological Society projects; Peter Windett of Crabtree and Evelyn for details of that firm's global outreach; Su Tahran of 'American Retro' for explaining her shop to me; John Seale of 'Past Times' for the history of that firm's growth; Jon Gorman Jr of G and B Arts and Chris Edmonds for material on steam traction rallies; Malcolm Gliksten of Relic Designs for the history of the pub mirror craze, and Richard Gomme of Hugo Russell for showing me round his warehouse – one of the great sources of both pub and flea-market kitsch. On the history of bricks, Bob Lloyd-Jones of the Brick Development Association, B.J. Taylor, managing director of Blockleys, and Sir Andrew Derbyshire, architect of the Hillingdon centre. Georgina Boyes, author of *The Imagined Village*, Vic Gannon and Alun Howkins, singers and historians, for the second folk song revival; Mr Amos and Les, of LASSCO, for the architectural salvage trade; Denis Severs and Jim Howett for some of its by-ways; Joe Laurie for the Sevington School project; Richard Boston for the cuttings file of his 'real ale' campaign in the 1970s; Eileen Carnaffin of Gateshead Public Library for the Derwent Valley Trail; Sarah Quaile of Portsmouth Record Office for materials on the town's naval memorials; John James of 'Jason's Trip' for the photographs on pages 141 and 142 of this book, and for the hospitality of himself and his family on their boat; Robert Thorne for materials on the London property market; Bill Holbrook of Kentish Ironworks for the early days of stone cleaning; George Matthews, librarian of the Communist Party archive, for the 'March of History' brochure reproduced here; Gordon House, Richard Hamilton and Clive Barker for guidance on Pop Art. Jennie Pozzi gave me a fine autobiographical account of the early days of picture research; Audrey Linkman introduced me to the Manchester photographic archive; and Roger Taylor of the National Photographic Museum was a mine of information on photographic retrieval programmes. Peter Gathercole, of Darwin College, Cambridge, has been an excellent guide on matters archaeological; James Mosley, the learned librarian at St Bride's Institute, was a *vade mecum* on printed ephemera; David Webb at the Bishopsgate Institute used his librarian's magic to discover all kinds of out-of-the-way sources, as did David Horsfield of Ruskin College, Oxford; Bernard Nurse, librarian at the Society of Antiquaries, dug out some eighteenth-century conservationists; Malcolm Taylor of Cecil Sharp House produced a complete file of *Ethnic* and issues of *Heritage*, the cyclostyled journal of a 1950s folk club. Stella Beddoe of Brighton Art Gallery sent me the excellent material on Henry Willett and his collection of chimney-piece ornaments; Andy Durr introduced me to the world of historical ceramics. Olivier Stockman of Sands Films, in spite of our disagreement about *Little Dorrit*, was kind enough to help in getting permission to reproduce the still included here. Andrew Byrne of Spitalfields Trust, hunting through debris, came up with the picture which is on the front cover of this book; Jinty Nelson helped me with the Bayeux tapestry.

My students at Ruskin, who originally initiated me into the folklore of

British industry, have latterly been my guides to such contemporary mysteries as New Ageism; in particular the megalithic standing stones of Avebury have been made a vivid presence in my thought by Brian Edwards, who has the good fortune to live there. Gareth Stedman Jones, with his Enlightenment suspicion of anything which smacks of the irrational, and his fastidious disdain for what he thinks of as Arts-and-Crafts sentimentality, has been an unspoken point of address in many of the arguments of this book; while at the opposite end of the epistemo-logical spectrum, Anna Davin, a tireless champion of the extra-curricular sources of knowledge, has encouraged me to think of the learning process – what happens to children in the class-room, the street and the home – as a kind of ultimate test of worth. Another invisible point of address in these volumes is postmodernism and the attempt to escape from the abstracted empiricism of social-science history. Here my mentors and fellow-travellers have been Carolyn Steedman, Sally Alexander and Alex Potts, experimenting with new forms of historical narrative, while at the same time trying to keep faith with older ones.

Alison Light was one of my original spurs for undertaking this work, and she has been my wife and long-suffering companion throughout the writing of it, as well as a severe and exemplary critic. John Barrell gave a most helpful critical reading to the pieces on photography; Richard Gott, of the *Guardian*, Paul Barker of *New Society*, and Gordon Marsden of *History Today* were my editors for the pieces on film.

My publishers, Verso, must take the blame, or (if it is to the reader's taste) the credit, for the fact that a book which began life as a collection of reprinted pieces has now swollen into three volumes which make quite ambitious claims. The bulk of the chapters here, and in the subsequent volumes, were written for Verso, and specifically for my editor there, Lucy Morton. Dealing with a difficult author who alternated between crab-like progress and paralysis, she showed a remarkable tolerance for changes of direction, and by a judicious combination of enthusiasm and criticism contrived both to enlarge and to contain the project. Without her patience and tact, few of the writings in these volumes would have seen the light of day. Dusty Miller, also of Verso, strongly supported the idea of making graphics integral to the book. In these days when conglomerates swallow up everything in sight and independent publishing houses are the exception rather than the rule, it is a pleasure to have a house in Soho where authors can drop in, make themselves a cup of tea, and be assured of someone who really wants to talk about their work.

Spitalfields, London E1
November 1994

Acknowledgements
for Illustrations

The Death of Harold, from the Bayeux tapestry, eleventh century (page 33). Musée de la Tapisserie, Bayeux/Bridgeman Art Library, London. With special authorization of the city of Bayeux/Giraudon Bridgeman Art Library.

The Practical Householder, November 1956 (page 53).

The Smiths record sleeve (page 108), reproduced by kind permission of Warner Music UK Ltd.

Regents Canal photographs (pages 141–2), courtesy of John James Private Collection.

Flogging a Dead Horse cover (page 258), photograph by Paul Reas, courtesy of Cornerhouse Publications.

Family photographs (page 326), courtesy of Audrey Linkman and Documentary Photography Archive, Manchester.

Photograph of boy navvies (page 327), courtesy of Greater Manchester County Record Office.

Engraving of child labourers (page 327), courtesy of Mary Evans Picture Library.

'Worktown People' by Humphrey Spender (page 368), courtesy of Humphrey Spender.

Walker Evans photograph (page 370), courtesy of Walker Evans.

Walker Evans photograph (page 372), courtesy of Walker Evans.

'The Lambeth Walk' sheet music cover (page 391), courtesy of The Raymond Mander & Joe Mitchenson Theatre Collection.

Great Expectations still (page 403), courtesy of BFI Stills.

Little Dorrit still (page 408), courtesy of Sands Films and BFI Stills.

Nicholas Nickleby still (page 415), photograph by Clive Davies.

Introduction

Unofficial Knowledge

1 Popular Memory

History, in the hands of the professional historian, is apt to present itself as an esoteric form of knowledge. It fetishizes archive-based research, as it has done ever since the Rankean revolution – or counter-revolution – in scholarship.[1] When matters of interpretation are in dispute, disagreement may turn on such apparently arcane questions as the wording of a coronation oath,[2] the dating of a royal portrait[3] or the correlation of harvest yields with fluctuations in peasant nuptiality.[4] Argument is embedded in dense thickets of footnotage, and lay readers who attempt to unravel it find themselves enmeshed in a cabbala of acronyms, abbreviations and signs.

The historical discipline encourages inbreeding, introspection, sectarianism. Academic papers are addressed to a relatively narrow circle of fellow-practitioners. In thesis work, the problematic is likely to come from within. Often it is suggested by 'gaps' which the young researcher is advised to fill; or else by an established view which he or she is encouraged to challenge. Fashion may direct the gaze of researchers; a new methodology may excite them; or they may stumble on an untapped source. But whatever the particular forms, they will be working within an existing form of inquiry and respecting its limits (however much they chafe). History in any of these cases is its own measure of significance and touchstone of worth.

The Balkanization of the subject and the multiplication of sub-disciplines, a phenomenon of the last twenty-five years, has produced a crop of new specialisms, each with its own society, its schisms and secessions. Intended to take scholarly inquiry into hitherto untravelled terrain, and to create a space for subjects which have been 'hidden from history' in the past – as, say, women's history, 'folk' medicine or occult science – it can also have the unintended effect of staking out proprietary claims to knowledge, and locking it up in academic publication and seminar circuits.

3

The enclosed character of the discipline is nowhere more apparent than in the pages of the learned journals, where young Turks, idolizing and demonizing by turn, topple elders from their pedestals, and Oedipal conflicts are fought out. The mere fact of publication turns the novice at a stroke into an authority, and articles are referred to, within a year of publication, as 'path-breaking', 'seminal' or 'classic'. Academic rivals engage in gladiatorial combat, now circling one another warily, now moving in for the kill. In the seminars such conflicts serve the function of blood sports and are followed with bated breath. Surnames quite unknown outside a coven of initiates become shorthand expressions for arguments, and are bandied back and forth as if they were household words.

These autarchic tendencies are reflected in a quite tribal sense of who is, and who is not, a historian. Biographers do not count, either because their subjects are literary rather than historical, or because they opt for narrative rather than analysis. Antiquarians, to judge by the frequency with which the 'ism' is used in a pejorative sense, are a different species-being, though they were the pioneers of record-based research in the New Learning of late Elizabethan England and the 'discovery' of Anglo-Saxon history.[5] Local historians are disqualified by their parochial outlook from being more than second-class citizens. Oral history is even more dubious: critics accuse it of practising a naïve empiricism in which the facts are supposed to speak for themselves.

Behind such negativities lies the unspoken assumption that knowledge filters downwards. At the apex there are the chosen few who pilot new techniques, uncover fresh sources of documentation, and formulate arresting hypotheses. These are the practitioners of what Professor Elton calls 'real' history, the heavyweights of the profession, who bring their trained minds to bear on an apparently disorderly assembly of material.[6] Their findings are rehearsed in academic papers, published in the learned journals, and amplified in scholarly monographs. Then at a lower level there are the textbooks, which relay the findings of higher research to the student public. Below them come the enthusiasts, 'amateur brain surgeons' as they have been disparagingly described; at best 'antiquarians' – the plodding accumulators of inconsequential facts – at worst the purveyors of myth. They may assemble some of the raw materials from which serious history can be constructed – transcribing parish registers, or digging up archaeological remains – but as mere fact-grubbers they are condemned to tunnel vision.

Hovering on the sidelines there are the commentators and communicators, who will present garbled accounts of the current state of scholarly controversy to the general public. As for the writers of historical romance, or the illustrators of the 'Ladybird' books, they might exist on another planet for all the attention they receive in the tea-room circles at the Institute of Historical Research.

All of this involves a very hierarchical view of the constitution of knowledge, and a very restricted one. Fetishizing the act of research while ignoring its conditions of existence, it takes no account of that great army of under-labourers, handmaidens and scribes who, in any given period, are the ghostly presence in historical work; nor yet of those do-it-yourself retrieval projects, such as barrow-hunting in the sixteenth century or family reconstitution today, which give new directions to writing and research, and create new landscapes for the historically minded to explore. So far as pedagogy is concerned, it allows no space for the knowledge which creeps in sideways as a by-product of studying something else: geography, for example, with whose fortunes history, ever since the Elizabethan 'discovery' of England,[7] has been umbilically linked; or literature, with which – in the days when the great historians were anthologized as stylists – history was freely bracketed.

Children's theatricals are also overlooked, the historical knowledge which a child acquires gratuitously and unconsciously in the course of play or as a result of trying out adult roles – impersonating a historical character, as, say, Lord Nelson, squinting down the end of a telescope; dressing up as a sheriff; taking on the part of the executioner;[8] or – a TV-bred fantasy of the 1960s – pretending to be Soames and Irene in *The Forsyte Saga*.[9] 'Bring out your dead!', re-enacting the horrors of the Plague, seems to have been a favourite with those who fell under the spell of Harrison Ainsworth's *Old St. Paul's*[10] while in army games Saxons and Normans or Roundheads and Cavaliers was a standard line-up if there was a pitched battle in the offing.[11] A more solitary 'pretend' game – one castaway, as it were, acting out the predicament of another – is recorded by Kipling in *Something of Myself*. He is describing the loneliness of a very unhappy seven-year-old in Southsea, two thousand miles from home:

> When my Father sent me a *Robinson Crusoe* with steel engravings I set up in business alone as a trader with savages (the wreck parts of the table never much interested me), in a mildewy basement room where I stood my solitary confinements. My apparatus was a coconut shell strung on a red cord, a tin trunk, and a piece of packing-case which kept off any other world. Thus fenced about, everything inside the fence was quite real, but mixed with the smell of damp cupboards. If the bit of board fell, I had to begin the magic all over again.[12]

Another great absence in conventional accounts of historiography – despite periodic reminders of the great part it played in medieval and early modern perceptions of the past, and a now quite extensive anthropological commentary – is oral tradition.[13] It wells up from those lower depths – history's nether-world – where memory and myth intermingle, and the imaginary rubs shoulders with the real. As a form of knowledge it is acquired higgledy-piggledy, in dibs and dabs, as in the proverbs or jokes which children learn from one another in the playground, or the half-remembered incidents and events which are used to fill in the missing link of a story.[14] It draws its sustenance from the spoken rather than the written word, though often, as with legendary histories of all kinds, there will be some chap-book, or chronicle original.

Popular memory is on the face of it the very antithesis of written history. It eschews notions of determination and seizes instead on omens, portents and signs. It measures change genealogically, in terms of generations rather than centuries, epochs or decades. It has no developmental sense of time, but assigns events to the mythicized 'good old days' (or 'bad old days') of workplace lore, or the 'once upon a time' of the storyteller.[15] In place of the pedagogue's 'causes' and 'effects' or the scholar's pursuit of origins and climacterics, it deals in broad-brushed contrasts between 'now' and 'then', 'past' and 'present', the new-fangled and the old-fashioned. So far as historical particulars are concerned, it prefers the eccentric to the typical; the sensational to the routine. Wonders and marvels are grist to its mill; so are the comic and the grotesque. George III is remembered because he went mad; Edward VII because he had mistresses; Henry VIII because he married six times and executed his unwanted wives. The South Sea Bubble, the speculative mania and financial disaster of 1720, is the one event in English economic history which everyone has heard of; George Hudson, the railway king who crashed, is perhaps the best-known nineteenth-century capitalist; while Horatio Bottomley, the War Bonds swindler, is still a vivid presence in the Valhalla of posthumous fame. As the sceptical Lovel puts it in *The Antiquary*, 'The events which leave the deepest impression on the minds of the common people' were not 'gradual progress' but some period of fear and tribulation: 'They date by a tempest, an earthquake, or bouts of civil commotion.'[16]

In the nineteenth-century schoolroom, where before the 1890s subject-based teaching was the exception rather than the rule,[17] a little history might be taught, and examined in the Standards, as a memory test – the reason for those genealogical tables of the English monarchy which figure so largely in the primers and cribs; and it might also be taught as part of what came to be known as 'general knowledge', as, say, the origins of the national flag, or the names and dates of famous painters.[18] But history, anyway secular history – matters were different with sacred history, which was systematically taught both in the Sunday Schools and in Scripture lessons[19] – was typically a knowledge acquired in the process of studying, or being trained in, something else. At the earliest age children were given historical story-books as a way of teaching them their letters, rather as horn-books had been used in earlier times. Thus for instance the *Story Book of English History* (1885), in a chapter on the Act of Union between England and Scotland ('a great blessing to both countries'), gives 'Edinburgh', 'Newcastle' and 'Carlisle' among the new words; singles out 'un-ion' and 'e-qual' both for new vocabulary and for elocution; and feels obliged to define the meaning of 'Parliament' ('national assembly for law-making and ruling'). The following chapter, on the Black Hole of Calcutta, introduces such novelties as the words 'jailer' and 'agonies'.[20] For a slightly older age-group, histories might be excerpted for models of style, rather as the speeches of Burke, Chatham and Canning – or Cicero – were read as pearls of oratory. Historical ballads, or 'lays', as they were sometimes called – one of the great discoveries of the nineteenth century, so far as the writing and teaching of history was concerned[21] – were a staple fare in those readings and recitations which brought the breath of romance into the classroom; indeed, even so severely instrumental a primer as Pinnock's *Catechism of English History,* first published in 1822 and constantly reprinted, prefaced each section with a ballad.

It was outside the classroom that the historicism of the nineteenth century imposed itself. In the newly medievalized churches and chapels, and the Gothicized railway stations and town halls, the high Christian architecture of the thirteenth century supposedly prevailed. At Astley's amphitheatre, re-enactments of the Battle of Waterloo, together with Dick Turpin's ride to York and an equestrian version of Shakespeare's *Richard III*, were for half a century the high points of the repertoire.[22] In Guy Brett's *Boys of England* – the first and the most successful of the penny dreadfuls – serialized drum-and-trumpet histories, adorned with lavish displays of military antiquities, competed for popularity with such swashbuckling stories as the adventures of Jack Harkaway;[23] while Agnes Strickland's multi-volume histories of the Queens of England (and her six-volume life of Mary Queen of Scots) performed something of the same service for court biography, a female version of monarchical history which was to inspire generations of romantic novelists.[24] At a humbler level, secular hagiography, detailing the pursuit of knowledge under difficulties, or the *Lives of the Engineers*, was the staple of the self-help manual.

One particular piece of unofficial learning which seems worth remarking on, if only because it shows the place of history in nineteenth-century platform oratory and its popularity as a vehicle for moral and political argument, is the set-piece historical debate. As a dramatic device, or educational resource, this must have already been well established in the 1820s, because the Oxford Union chose as the subject for their opening debate, in 1829, the motion 'Was the revolution under Cromwell to be attributed to the tyrannical conduct of Charles, or to the democratic spirit of the times?'.[25] At the other end of the social spectrum the working men radicals of Birmingham, who maintained a Sunday evening Debating Society at the Hope and Anchor Inn, Navigation Street (it met continuously from the mid 1850s to 1886) were debating the motion, in June 1861, 'Was the motive of Henry the 8th, at the reformation, of a religious, political or libidinous character?' (four votes were cast for the first, two for the second and twelve for the third).[26] At the Winchester School debating society, the one place where modern-side history had a recognized place at the time when the young Charles Oman was a pupil, the first oration which he made was in hot justification of the execution of Mary Queen of Scots, 'whose death, I appear to have argued, was absolutely necessary for the cause of Protestantism in Europe'. His next harangue was to the motion – lost by eighteen votes to thirteen – that 'the good effects of the French Revolution enormously exceeded the bad'.[27]

The starting point of *Theatres of Memory*, hardly a controversial proposition but one which, with the return to subject-based disciplines in the schools and the multiplication of specialisms in higher research, bears repeating, is that history is not the prerogative of the historian, nor even, as postmodernism contends, a historian's 'invention'. It is, rather, a social form of knowledge; the work, in any given instance, of a thousand different hands. If this is true, the point of address in any discussion of historiography should not be the work of the individual scholar, nor yet rival schools of interpretation, but rather the ensemble of activities and practices in which ideas of history are embedded or a dialectic of past–present relations is rehearsed. From this point of view textual exegesis, of the kind practised by Hayden White in *Metahistory*[28] or Stephen Bann in *The Inventions of History*, i.e. the close reading of a limited number of well-thumbed books, would be less germane than a study of readership, or what is called in literary criticism 'reception theory'. Still more pertinent would be an attempt to follow the imaginative dislocations which take place when historical knowledge is transferred from one learning circuit to another – as, say, in screenplay adaptations of the literary classics, where the written word is translated into imagery; or in comic-strip versions of grand narrative, such as those potted histories of great events which were displayed on the back cover of *The Eagle* in the 1950s.

Tapping into popular memory requires a different order of evidence, and a different kind of inquiry.[29] One possible starting point would be autobiography, which is rich in family lore, as also in the stories, legends

THE
HISTORY

OF

SIR RICHARD WHITTINGTON

THRICE

Lord Mayor of London.

PRINTED AND SOLD IN ALDERMARY CHURCH YARD,
BOW LANE.

THE

HISTORY

OF

JACK OF NEWBURY

CALLED

THE CLOTHIER
OF ENGLAND.

PRINTED AND SOLD IN LONDON.

and songs which a child might learn at a grandmother or grandfather's knee. John Aubrey, the genial seventeenth-century antiquary who, though a royalist, has some claim to being the originator of the idea of 'people's history' (as well as being in his native Wiltshire, the discoverer of Avebury), claimed that he could construct a consecutive history of England from the Norman Conquest onwards, on the strength of the ballads which he had learned from his nursemaid. But it was to the influence of his grandfather that he attributed his 'strong and early impulse to Antiquitie'. He was a man, as Aubrey described him, of the 'old time'. He still wore a doublet and hose and carried a dagger, in the Elizabethan style. He had been to court, and provided his grandson with snippets of information about it; such as that of the 'delicate, clear voice' of Sir Walter Raleigh's brother, Carew. When a boy, Aubrey tells us in a brief self-portrait, 'he did ever love to converse with old men as Living Histories'.[30]

Another possible starting point is local lore. Pierre Nora's multi-volume work, *Les Lieux de Mémoire*[31] shows how public history can be gleaned from civic ritual, street nomenclature and literary or political statuary. But so far as unofficial knowledge and popular memory are concerned, the peculiarities of the landscape might be a better place to begin. Woods are famously the haunt of spirits; caves are smugglers' lairs. Standing stones (menhirs as they are known in Cornwall and the Derbyshire Peak) invariably have legends attaching to them, rather as castles and monastic ruins do. Blasted trees, like empty houses, are often thought to be haunted. What is interesting here is the tremendous desire to turn fragments into mysteries and signs; lore is not so much passed on or transmitted as made up and amplified, until there is not a stone without a story attaching to it. Alfred Williams's *Villages of the White Horse* (1920), the remarkable ethnography of a Swindon factory worker turned folklorist and musicologist, is a wonderful collection of local lore, illustrating the ways in which such stories can take wing. Here, he stumbles on the remains of Arthurian romance, in those places which were supposedly the real-life originals of Camelot; there, it is a matter of ancient rights of way supposedly won by the pre-Reformation monks on behalf of the local cattle drovers.[32]

Place-names, and the legends and histories which grew up, often in the guise of etymology, around them, have produced a vast literature from which it would be possible in some cases to trace stories back to their original source, as with the supposedly 'Huguenot' origins of Spitalfields street nomenclature;[33] in others, to see how fragments were turned into narrative wholes.

Place-names were the great enthusiasm of the comparative philologists and Saxonists of the nineteenth century, and a perennial subject of controversy and dispute in that great monument of local scholarship, *Notes and Queries*.[34] Later, the Place-Name Society, founded by Stenton and Maurer in 1922, carried the study to new heights; it is currently being given a fresh boost by the archaeologically based study of early English colonization and settlement. Natural history, pioneered by Plot in his *Oxfordshire* (1677) and *Staffordshire* (1686),[35] is another vast depository of local lore. As in the case of place-names, nineteenth-century commentary is particularly rich, with *flora* and *fauna* as a normal section of the local history; and the county archaeological societies doubling in the role of field clubs.

One splendid source for local lore, and for those 'remarkable' occurrences and sensational events which engrave themselves on popular memory, is the nineteenth-century date book. Gleaned, largely, from the local newspapers, though sometimes with an admixture of oral testimony and eye-witness recollection, and dignified quite often with the title 'Annals' or 'Chronicle' of the place in question, they offer a whole new landscape of public events. Thus in Mayhall's three-decker *Annals of Yorkshire* the great landmark of the 1860s is the Sheffield Flood of 1864, which occupies inconceivably more space than any general election. The Sayers–Heenan contest, a celebrated prize-fight of 1860, here gets star billing as it does in other date-books and diaries of the time.[36]

The 'hidden curriculum' in the schools – if one extends that term to include the whole spectrum of learning experiences which have no part in the official syllabus – might be another fruitful way of inquiring into the unofficial sources of historical knowledge. The focus here might be, as in the studies of the Opies and Lady Gomme, the scraps of lore which children learn in the corridor and playground, and on the fossilized remains of the past embedded in rhymes, riddles and tongue-twisters. Or it might be such rudimentary exercises in historical role-playing as the 'Greeks' and 'Trojans' of an 1890s hoop game, or the 'Germans' and 'English' of its 1916 equivalent.[37]

Within the school syllabus it might turn out that the significant history which children learnt came not from the timetabled hours, or reading devoted specifically to the subject, but rather from other kinds of scholastic exercise. Modelling a Roman trireme, building a Saxon hut or pretending to be an Arawak – which might be the primary-school child's first initiation into the idea of a historic past – will come under the generic heading of 'topic' work.[38] Period costume may be the subject of a drawing lesson; later the précis given out as a class exercise in English may be an introduction to the orotundities of Victorian prose or platform rhetoric. History – 'the linear study conducted through comprehension exercises and dictated notes' – came a poor second for one who traced her engagement with the subject to a Dorset village schooling in the 1950s:

> My overriding memory is of being inspired by the somewhat eccentric . . . tall, silver haired, inordinately energetic schoolmistress who invoked an insatiable appetite for making sense of the world – a world entirely rural but which often looked out to the exotic world of myth and legend. I cannot impose any semblance of order upon what we learned – save to say this exceptional teacher exploited the potential of any and every opportunity that presented itself. Dorset as a whole presented a treasure trove of historical stimulus – hill forts and earthworks abound, fossils surface everywhere, country houses, large and small, evocative place names, ancient ridges and ridgeways, flint tools and implements turning up in the flower beds . . .[39]

In the present day, television ought to have pride of place in any attempt to map the unofficial sources of historical knowledge. Quite apart from drama documentaries, and such long-running series as 'Timewatch', it is continually travelling down memory lane and using the past as a backdrop. Replaying old films – a staple fare – it has turned dead film stars, such as Humphrey Bogart, and Marilyn Monroe, into cultural icons, as appealing and as well known, so far as mannerisms and looks are concerned, as today's heart-throbs. Television is also continually returning viewers to studio re-creations of the past. It chooses period settings, as often as not, for its sit-coms (twenty-five years after *Dad's Army*, war-time Britain is still a favourite location). It uses anniversaries as the occasion for retrospectives, and obituaries as the excuse for revisiting old celebrities and recycling old film footage. Not only does it personalize great events through the medium of the biopic, it also brings personal time into line with historical time, as in that most successful and exportable of television blockbusters, the family saga. Some indication of the sheer mass of historical material appearing on television and of the variety of soubriquets under which it is disguised, can be seen from the following selection of BBC 1 programmes on offer on a 1981 weekend:[40]

Saturday

10.55	**Down Memory Lane**
	A 1949 film largely using clips from famous silent movies.
12.00	**Trouble Brewing**
	A 1939 George Formby film.
6.10	**Hi-De-Hi!**
	A comedy show set in Maplin's Holiday Camp 1959.
6.40	**Taras Bulba**
	A 1962 film. An eccentric 16th-century period epic set in the Ukraine, filmed in Argentina and starring Yul Brynner and Tony Curtis.

8.55   **Roots**
            Episode 7 of Alex Haley's 13 part saga of one man's search for his
            roots. Set in Henning, Tennessee, 1882.

Sunday
2.00   **Pool of London**
            A 1950 film from Ealing Studios, continues the season of British
            films from the 40's and 50's. Romance, a daring robbery and a
            portrait of post-war London are all interwoven with the racial
            theme which proved way ahead of its time.

3.30   **Travellers in Time**
            The first of six films of early exploration. Part one: 'South with
            Shackleton 1914'.

4.00   **Centennial**
            Part 5 of a 12 part saga of a land and its people, set in 1860s
            Colorado.

6.40   **Your Songs of Praise Choice**
            The third of 7 programmes with Thora Hird. The short film
            Thora includes this week is of a beautiful chapel on Orkney, built
            by Italian prisoners-of-war.

7.15   **Inside Daisy Glover**
            A 1965 film about a 1939 movie star on the make.

10.15   **We're Not Savages – We are People**
            This 'Everyman' report, filmed in the Amazon jungle, examines
            the impact the missionaries have had on an Ecuadorean tribe.

11.30   **Discovering English Churches**
            The 4th of a 10 part series. 4: 'The Church Builders', in Medieval
            times the skill of the mason was so respected that God himself
            could be portrayed as the divine Architect of the Universe.

In one register, television offers us a past that is completely static: a
time when family was the backbone of society, when 'old-fashioned'
virtues were unquestioned and everyone knew their place; an indeterminate past, a retrospective haven of stability to which we can escape from
the disorders and uncertainties of the present. In another, all is
movement and we are whirled about in a kaleidoscope of change: a
hundred years of American history are rushed through in a dozen
episodes; inter-war Britain is encapsulated in six one-hour slots; Glasgow
rises and falls in a series. In a third, the past is presented as a chamber
of horrors, a sequence of catastrophic events from which we can count
ourselves fortunate to have escaped: slaves are whipped in the Middle
Passage; the tumbrils roll through the Paris streets; convicts endlessly
pace the prison yard; families flit from country to town with their
household belongings piled high on rickety carts; ragged children play
in the dirt, cloth-capped men stand dejectedly at the street corners and
queue up at the Labour Exchange. Smoking ruins signify Guernica or

the blitz, gas-masks the First World War, barbed wire and brick chimneys the concentration camps. Ideologically, too, the mix is promiscuous. On the one hand television exalts the role of the individual in history – great artists, famous inventors, war leaders, newspaper barons, movie moguls. On the other – anti-heroically – it insists on the primacy of ordinary everyday life and resilience of the family in face of outside pressures.

Historians who, ever since the advent of nineteenth-century realism, have made the recovery of the past 'as it was' (Ranke's deceptively simple term) the watchword of their vocation, and who, in the last analysis, depend for their professional existence on the talismanic importance attaching to antiquities, are in no position to despise the taste for bygones and memorabilia, the popular appetite for costume drama, or the fashion for retrochic. As teachers we cannot be indifferent to those extra-curricular sources of knowledge which subvert the learning process, change its direction or create alternative histories of their own. As historians, too, we might be expected to be interested in the conditions of existence of history itself, and the reasons for the wildly different versions of it on offer. The sense of the past, at any given point of time, is quite as much a matter of history as what happened in it; if the argument of *Theatres of Memory* is right, the two are indivisible.

If the subject of history is the record and residues of the past, then legendary history is as legitimate a field of inquiry as, say, Elizabethan foreign policy, or the relations of church and state.[41] Dick Whittington, the poor boy made good, or Tom Hickathrift, his Anglo-Saxon predecessor,[42] are as much a part of British history as, say, Cardinal Beaufort with his red hat, or the Duke of Newcastle and his pocket boroughs – indeed more so, from the point of view of the formation of character ideals. So is Jack-the-Giant-Killer, originally it seems a Cornishman, and according to legend a very incarnation of that recurrent figure of national myth, the free-born Englishman. Similarly in the case of the outlaw heroes of medieval legend, what matters, as a generation of historical commentators has shown, is not so much the precise location of the original story, even if it could be identified, but the protean character of the myth.[43]

By the same token a ballad or song, a novel or a poem, is as much a historical document as a cartulary or a pipe roll. If literature was made integral to the study of history, children could be given a quite different set of benchmarks when considering, say, the idea of the monarchy, or the history of the nuclear family. Faced with panegyrics on the development of constitutional liberties they might pause on the fact that there is barely a mention of Parliament in Shakespeare's Chronicle plays, and in his *King John* no word of the Magna Carta. Is not *Robinson Crusoe* as good a starting point as any for the study of English individualism, 'enterprise culture' or overseas colonization and settlement? And might not *Black Beauty* serve as a basic text for the study of gender and class in nineteenth-century England,[44] and as pertinent a way of approaching 'Victorian values' as Samuel Smiles's *Self-Help*? If *The Pilgrim's Progress* is no longer to be a set book in school English, could not historians think of adopting it?

Popular memory, if we were to study it as closely as we do more conventional historical records, looking at the ways in which a story crystallizes around a particular personality or event, might put in question the notion, so dear to the 'new-wave' social history of the 1960s and 1970s, that history is fulfilling its democratic vocation when it takes as the object of its inquiry 'ordinary' people and 'everyday' life. Popular memory suggests almost the reverse of this, that it is the remarkable occurrence and the larger-than-life personality which stirs the interest of listeners, readers and viewers; just as 'true romance' (Carolyn Steedman has argued) is the escapist version of history likely to capture the imagination of the young. When 'ordinary' life does appeal as a historical subject it may be, as in the long-running TV series 'Yesterday's Witness', because it has become, retrospectively, exotic.

Nineteenth-century history readers, and even the primers and cribs, seem often to be closer to popular memory than their latter-day successors. They were alive to the human side of politics, and indeed, like the tabloid newspapers today, personalized everything they touched. They set enormous store by character, and entered with zest into the private lives of monarchs. They were hungry for stories and snapped them up, irrespective of whether they were apocryphal or true. The spectacle of suffering moved them, and they were ready, if need be, to side with this country's enemies in matters of honour – as with Mary Queen of Scots and Joan of Arc,[45] the doomed heroines of nineteenth-century history's Gothic romance, who enjoyed a cult following, it seems, among both boys and girls; or Saladin, the great protagonist in one of its favourite epics.

The nineteenth-century history 'readers' also bear out the truth of Sir Walter Scott's dictum that it is disaster rather than the record of progress which leaves the deepest impression on the public mind. They are full of macabre episodes and atrocious deeds. The Black Death, the Plague and the Great Fire of London are, next to the Norman Conquest, the greatest events in national history. The murder of the little princes in the tower usually gets a chapter to itself, along with an affecting engraving showing them peacefully asleep. The French Revolution is described in terms of Grand Guignol, with the tumbrils and the guillotine as a kind of apocalypse of blood.[46] Ever since the 1978 *Past and Present* conference on 'the Invention of Tradition', and the publication of Hobsbawm and Ranger's influential collection of essays drawn from it, historians have become accustomed to thinking of commemoration as a cheat, some-thing which ruling elites impose on the subaltern classes. It is a weapon of social control, a means of generating consensus, and legitimating the *status quo* by reference to a mythologized version of the past. The heritage critics have followed suit, treating nostalgia as a contemporary equivalent of what Marxists used to call 'false consciousness' and existentialists 'bad faith'; they are at pains to show the deceptions involved in retrieval projects, and the ways in which the received version of the past is sanitized so as to exclude any disturbing elements.

A more ethnographic approach, such as the one adopted by the Gottingen school of micro-history, might think of the invention of tradition as a process rather than an event, and memory, even in its silences, as something which people made for themselves. Rather than focusing on state theatricals, or the figures of national myth, it might find it more profitable to focus on the perceptions of the past which find expression in the discriminations of everyday life.

II   Invisible Hands

If history was thought of as an activity rather than a profession, then the number of its practitioners would be legion. In the present day they might well include – if one was concerned to map the unofficial sources of knowledge – the writers of that new and flourishing sub-genre in which scholars themselves have begun to dabble,[47] the historical who-dunnit. Reference might be made to Peter Lovesey, the master of the Victorian detective novel, whose explorations of London by gaslight draw heavily on nineteenth-century descriptions of low-life deeps;[48] or Ellis Peters who covers page after page of her Brother Cadfael books with gobbets of Anglo-Norman history – e.g. the 'anarchy' of Stephen's reign in the recently televised *One Corpse Too Many* – and uses illuminated manuscripts for her book-jackets.[49]

In any archaeology of the unofficial sources of historical knowledge, the animators of the Flintstones, the stone-age family who were rehear-sing the rudiments of palaeolithic living for 1960s TV viewers and who have now been given the accolade of a feature film, surely deserve, at the least, a *proxime accessit*. Stand-up comics, such as Rowan Atkinson, whose *Blackadder* series re-animated the legendary moments of British history for a generation of television addicts, might get as much attention as the holder of a Regius chair. The impresarios of the open-air museums, and their ever-increasing staff, would be seen to have made a far more substantial contribution to popular appetite for an engagement with *t* past than the most ambitious head of a department. Space might e be found for those electronically equipped cowboys of archaeological excavation, the metal detectorists, whose finds have done so much to enlarge the map of Romano-British settlement.[50]

Even as a form of literary production, history is the work of a thousand different hands. The books, monographs and articles in the learned journals draw on a whole army of ghost-writers. Quite apart from the indexers, the copy-editors, and the proof-readers – and in the old days the typist – without whom a book could hardly exist, one might refer to scholars' wives who, even if they have been through every line of the text, are likely to be recognized by no more than a single acknowledgement. F.J. Furnivall, the historical philologist and founder of the Early English Texts Society, who seems to have married or attempted to marry not once but twice for the sake of an amanuensis, and who enlisted a platoon of lady helpers for his philological enterprises, is one example;[51] James Murray the Saxonist and the first editor of the *Oxford English Dictionary* another.[52]

Clio's invisible hands in the 1920s might include the musicologists employed on the Tudor Church Music Project, transcribing from cathedral part-books, and scouring the minster archives for manuscripts.[53] There may well have been some, too, in the women readers whom George Gissing describes in *New Grub Street*, buried in the darker recesses of the British Museum, employed as copyists on behalf of the scholars and writers.[54] More skilled, but only slightly less anonymous – they are credited neither on the title page nor in the individual entries – were the young history graduates, all of them female and most of them medievalists, who undertook the work of record-searching and making up slips in the early years of the *Victoria County History* – 'wonderfully plain girls' as they were jocularly referred to by J.H. Round, the cantankerous old Tory who set them to work on their tasks.[55] By the same token, a discussion of nineteenth-century medievalism, if it were to do justice to its anonymous hands, would need to refer not only to the propaganda of Ruskin and Pugin and the church restoration work of Morris and Co., but also to the sewing women, briefly discussed by Roszicka Parker in *The Subversive Stitch*, who produced altar cloths, tapestries and embroideries for the newly ritualized church interior.[56]

If attention was focused, as it should be, on the infrastructure of research, and all those whose labours have gone into the making of archives and sources, then reference might be made to the palaeographers who give names to the anonymous and dates to the undated; the archive staff who calendar solicitors' accumulations and index leases and wills; the cataloguers who make library deposits accessible to the reading public; the conservation officers who perform miracles of invisible repair.

Librarians, though sometimes treated as the Poor Bloody Infantry of the profession, have some claim, historically speaking, to being thought of as among its strategists. They often double in the function of bibliographers, signposting hitherto untravelled terrain. They serve as honest brokers when arranging for the transfer of a collection into public hands. Often, too, they have acted as principals where matters of local history are at stake. The 'Record and Survey' movement of the 1890s and 1900s, to which we owe a great mass of old photographs and the topographical record of now vanished townscapes, is a case in point.[57] City and borough librarians seem to have been instrumental in putting the movement on the map; their libraries were the repositories of the collections; very much later, in the 1960s and 1970s, they played a leading role in bringing them, through exhibition and publication, into the public sphere. The post-war renaissance in local history was similarly beholden to the county record offices. If there is reason to be anxious for the future of historical scholarship, the run-down in library services, the break-up of local history collections, the disappearance of the post of local history or borough librarian and the impending reorganization of the county record offices, are at least as much a threat to research as cuts in postgraduate funding.

Bibliographers might also be classed among Clio's invisible hands. Partly because of the revolution in information technology, partly because of the multiplication of subject specialisms, recent years have seen an explosion in the number and reach of bibliographies, while under the influence of the antiques boom there has been an extraordinary proliferation in collectors' handbooks and guides. Whereas thirty years ago bibliography lagged behind research, bringing up the rear with occasional worthy tomes, such as those produced by the Royal Historical Society of writings on British history, today's bibliographers are typically pro-active, bringing the resources of learning to bear on subjects and specialities which researchers have not yet begun to tackle: Martin Hoyle's volumes on garden history are a case in point.[58]

A more generous definition of the historical profession might also include that great army of collectors who, whether in the field of material culture or that of the written word, have so often anticipated the directions which scholarship was later to take. In the seventeenth century one might instance George Thomason the London stationer who, starting in 1641 and continuing to 1662, contrived to collect some 23,000 Civil War tracts, broadsheets and books, snapping them up as they came off the printing press and then binding them up into 1,983 volumes, the ultimate authority for all twentieth-century commentaries on the Levellers and the Diggers;[59] Samuel Pepys, whose collection of black-letter ballads and broadsides, deposited at Magdalene College,

Cambridge, seems to have been one of the original inspirations for Lord Macaulay's version of 'history from below';[60] and that group of royalist antiquarians, such as Thomas Hearne and Edward Rymer, who produced the collectanea on which generations of medievalists were to draw.[61]

The discovery of printed ephemera and its incorporation into library holdings and museum display – a phenomenon of the 1960s – has sensibly enlarged the notion of the historical, turning the spotlight of inquiry on to subjects which would have fallen beneath the dignity of the subject in the past. Who could be interested in a *laundry* list?, the eminent Edwardian historian Sir Paul Vinogradov allegedly exclaimed, giving to the term something of the scorn which Lady Bracknell visited on the idea of someone being spawned in a *handbag*. If such condescension is rarer today, it is partly because feminism and gay history have put body politics on the agenda of higher research, and also because, under the influence of the antiques boom of the 1960s, the notion of the collectable has now been extended to the humblest artefact of everyday life.

Collectors are routinely accused of being obsessive, human magpies or carrion indiscriminately swooping down on everything which falls within their chosen field. Yet, like the Tradescants, whose natural history curiosities were the original nucleus of the Ashmolean Museum, Oxford,[62] their madcap enthusiasms often turn out to be prophetic. Scavenging among what others are busily engaged in throwing out or consigning to the incinerator, they have been the true architects of our libraries, galleries and museums, and, if only at second or third remove, the Svengalis of historical research.

Henry Willett, whose collection of chimneypiece ornaments, or Staffordshire figures, is the pride of Brighton Museum, was a popular educator, as well as a self-made museologist. He collected biological specimens and chalk fossils with the same enthusiasm as he did industrial art. He seems to have been quite conscious of the sociological significance of his collection of porcelain figures, and when he put them on show to the public for the first time, in 1879, offered them as a kind of people's history: 'On the mantelpieces of English cottage homes may be found representations which its inmates or their forefathers admired, revered and trusted in; an evidence of real worship perhaps more accurate than external religious observances and of a truer faith than their lip confessions; a kind of unconscious survival of *lares* and *penates* of the ancients.' Still more ambitiously, and presciently, he made his collection, as he told those who visited it, 'to illustrate the principle, or rather in development of the notion, that the History of a Country may be traced in its homely Pottery.'[63]

John Johnson, whose collection of printed ephemera – a million separate items – has a place of honour in the Bodleian Library (by a symptomatic irony, Bodleian throw-outs in the 1930s were one of his principal sources) also seems to have known exactly what he was about. A trained Egyptologist, he would have known how the obscurest hieroglyphic could be translated into substantive historical fact. His collection, assembled over a period of forty years, is an *omnium gatherum* illustrating every phase in the history of the printed word, and the commercial use of graphics. The classification of items, when it was handed over to the Bodleian in 1968, prefigures some of the main new lines of research in subsequent years – thanatology, for instance, in such category heads as 'death' and 'funerary', while in other cases such as body politics, it is only now that it is beginning to be used in its own right.[64]

Aesthetes rather than historians are responsible for constituting our notions of 'period'. Thus the term 'Regency', a profitable one for the writers of historical romance, and for the manufacturers of reproduction furniture, seems to have been a neologism of 1920s interior decorators, and it is only now, with the renewed interest in Holland House Whiggery, that professional historians are beginning to show some interest in taking it up. A camp taste for Victoriana was an aristocratic sport – and a metropolitan fashion – fully two decades before the social historians got 'Victorian people' and 'Victorian values' in their sights.[65] Kenneth Clark gave precocious expression to it in *The Gothic Revival* (1928); Cecil Beaton and the Bright Young Things of the 1920s experimented with it at their fancy dress parties; John Betjeman, pioneering time travel on neglected or forgotten branch lines, gave a taste of it to readers of the *Daily Herald*;[66] while at *Late Joys*, translating a well-worn literary conceit into a species of camp performance art, Leonard Sachs in 1937 began staging Old Time Victorian Music Hall.[67] More recently, the 1960s Art Deco revival, and the brisk trade in Clarice Cliff tea-sets has been not the least of the subliminal influences in buttressing the argument of those revisionist historians who stress the modernity of inter-war Britain rather than its *ancien régime* conservatism.

Antiquarian and archaeological illustrators, such as those who adorned the guide-books of the later eighteenth century, were the avatars of Victorian medievalism, making the bare ruined choirs of the monastic remains as familiar a spectacle as the gentleman's seat. Thomas Pennant, anticipating the discovery of geology and the invention of pre-history, had his text illustrated with megalithic drawings.[68] Later, the antiquarian illustrators were among the most effective popularizers of the romantic medievalism of Sir Walter Scott. They monopolized attention in such influential works as Gough's *Sepulchral Monuments of Great Britain* (1786–99) as also in Stothard's *Monumental Effigies*.[69] The ecclesiologists of the Camden Society, launching their propaganda for a return to the church furnishings of the high middle ages, made extensive use of them. The county histories of the early and middle years of the nineteenth century also bear their mark, while transactions of the record Societies were by the 1850s and 1860s making a feature of their engravings of fonts, naves, and effigies.

Popular illustrators also played a large part in the mid-Victorian turn to the Elizabethan, and the creation of an alternative, more Protestant (and more nationalist), 'Merrie England' to the medieval one of Cobbett, Carlyle and Pugin.[70] W.P. Frith's 'A Coming of Age in the Olden Times' – a crowded canvas showing an Elizabethan squire surrounded by gaggles of his frolicsome tenantry, from which the Art Union, in 1852, extracted the plate 'An English Merry Making in the Olden Time' – was one of the most popular of Victorian prints.[71] 'Archaeological' revivals of Shakespeare, such as those of Charles Kean,[72] and John Gilbert's wood engravings (831 of them) for Boydel's *Shakespeare*, 'one of the most memorable English illustrated works', established a distinctly Victorian idea of the Elizabethan age which has proved remarkably tenacious.[73] Most pertinent of all in creating an appetite for the Elizabethan were the multi-volume works of the architect John Nash, a pupil of Pugin. His *Historic Mansions*, published between 1840 and 1844, and his *Baronial Halls of England*, elevated the stately home to a pinnacle of romantic esteem while at the same time making the Elizabethan the morning star of the indigenous.[74]

Another memory-bank which would repay attention in any attempt to draw up a genealogy, or archaeology, of the unofficial sources of historical knowledge, would be music. The first histories, in medieval Europe as in ancient Greece, were the ballads, which, starting with Ulysses, made gods and heroes of ordinary mortals. They also served as war memorials, in the case of the Battle of Roncevaux, as also perhaps that of Maldon, giving an epic quality to what in the original event may have been a comparatively minor skirmish. Ballads served as mnemonics in recitations of genealogy and (to follow John Aubrey's account) the learning of dynastic history. They could also be – if radical readings of the Robin Hood legend are accepted – repositories for what Professor Tawney once called 'the doctrineless communism of the open field village'.

From a historiographic point of view, one of the more remarkable instances of the power of the ballad, in consciousness-raising and creating a historical narrative, would be that of the Jacobites, who earned their place in history and romance quite largely on the strength of Lady Nairne's songs. Written and composed in the 1820s – the high point in pan-European Romanticism, and the moment of the Highland tartan's coming-of-age – the songs turned Culloden into a modern Thermopylae and made Charles Edward Stuart into a romantic fugitive ('Over the Sea to Skye' was written by Sir Harold Boulton in 1908). At the present time, music seems even more potent as a period signifier. 'The White Cliffs of Dover' has firmly established itself as a kind of alternative national anthem in any account of Britain during the Second World War, and it is perhaps indicative of this that in the recent controversies over the celebrations of the fiftieth anniversary of D-Day it was neither the Queen nor the Prime Minister who spoke for the soldierly dead, but Dame Vera Lynn. For the cult followers of *Casablanca*, a gravelly-throated rendition of 'As Time Goes By' evokes bitter-sweet memories of the anti-fascist resistance. 'Goodbye Dolly Gray' is famously a kind of signature tune for the Boer War; already well-established, it seems, in 1931, when Noël Coward adapted it for the English family saga of *Cavalcade*. In France it seems that *Le Temps des Cerises* played a similar part for those who wanted to honour the martyrs of the Paris Commune.

Music has also played some part in creating the resurrectionary enthusiasms of our time. The playing of early Baroque music, and the use of original instruments, pioneered by a small group of musical archae-ologists in the 1950s, was already able to support an alternative concert circuit in the 1960s; today such performances can command a full house at the Royal Albert Hall. The restoration of old film scores – starting with the mega-musical experience of Abel Gance's exhumed *Napoleon* – is another widely imitated example, while in rock music revivals are so thoroughly mixed up with the production of new music that it is often impossible to know where an old track ends and a new one begins.

Any account of history as a social form of knowledge would need to admit, and rejoice in, the motley character of its following. In the Middle Ages, R.W. Southern writes in his account of the twelfth-century historical revival, it embraced all those who were caught up in the process of collecting and arranging charters, transcribing documents, studying monastic buildings and inscriptions, assembling ancient texts, writing estate history, compiling saints' lives and chronicles. For each surviving work there may well have been many hundreds of constituent fragments.

Clio's under-labourers would also need to include those who worked as visual memory-keepers, in the pictorial representation of the past. One might instance those anonymous ladies – according to some commentators, Anglo-Saxon, and attached to St Augustine's, Canter-bury, rather than to a French monastery, or William the Conqueror's court – who sewed the Bayeux tapestry, that incomparable pictorial narrative; or the ecclesiastical painters who turned sacred history into stained-glass windows and frescoes; or the heraldic engravers who inscribed the family coat of arms on seals, banners and fortified keeps. At the crossing-point between the sacred and the secular, pride of place would go to the masons, carvers and goldsmiths who made lifelike statues in churches – a kind of medieval Madame Tussaud's is how they are described by one commentator – and who reproduced, in the *misericordia*, scenes from provincial life. Reference should be made, also, to the members of the artisan guilds, involved in the production and performance of the miracle plays, the moralities and those folk dramas and carnivalesque floats which in the later Middle Ages turned civic ritual into street theatre and an early form of the Elizabethan stage.

Memory-keeping in the Middle Ages, to follow Marc Bloch's admirable pages on it in *Feudal Society*, or the more extended and complex account given of it in M.T. Clanchy's work on the transition from orality to written record, was a public activity in which almost everyone might find themselves involved, if only as witnesses or – in the case of the sermon *exemplum* – silent listeners. This was above all the case in matters of custom and the law where, even after the advent of written documents, a quite special credence was given to the testimony of the elders. In another sphere, there were the members of the parish guilds and fraternities who kept up the *libri memoriales* and prayers for the departed; those who dramatized Bible stories on liturgical feast-days; and that vast number who gave credence to the miracle stories by prostrating themselves before saints' and martyrs' relics.

In the nineteenth century, when history emerged as a great public art, and when its leading practitioners enjoyed the status of men of letters – if not on a par with the poets, then certainly the superior of the novelists – attention might be focused on those new literary forms which shaped the character of historical work and the direction of historical inquiry. Sir Walter Scott, with his anti-heroic heroes, his scenes from everyday life, and his play with vernacular speech would appear as one of the great architects of historical realism, while at the other end of the scale attention might be drawn to that literary underworld where the penny-a-liner, writing drum-and-trumpet histories for one of the boys' monthlies; the poor schoolmaster writing heroic biography for Sunday School prize-books; and the literary lady trying to carve out a corner in the history of philanthropy or the diffusion of useful knowledge lived out a precarious existence.

No less pertinent for nineteenth-century historical awareness would be that small army of popular educators who by means of public lectures and exhibitions, or printed primers and guides, turned nineteenth-century Britain into a showcase of natural history – 'fossilizing' when they went on holiday to the seaside, 'archaeologizing' or 'geologizing' when they visited historic sites, collecting samples of flora and fauna when they went on country walks, and setting up museums of natural history in the home. A genealogy here would range from the pedigree-obsessed country squire to the self-educated stonemason or wool-sorter, who week by week took up the 'Notes and Queries' columns of the newspaper and periodical press, either on account of their literary and biographical discoveries, or because they helped to establish a foundation for local research.[75] Numismatists, such as the great Roach Smith of London, a City tradesman who contrived to establish a Roman museum and to publish a small library of Romano-British studies on the strength of workmen's scavengings, might be seen retrospectively as archivists for the future;[76] so might those working-man botanical societies and Saturday afternoon naturalists whose excitements included the discovery of prehistoric remains.

Today history is no longer regarded as a branch of literature, if only because historians themselves harbour quite other ambitions, connecting their work with 'theory' or quantifying their findings in the manner of science. There is no longer, as there was in the nineteenth century, a historical school of painting. Memory-keeping is a function increasingly assigned to the electronic media, while a new awareness of the artifice of representation casts a cloud of suspicion over the documentation of the past. Despite this, history as a mass activity – or at any rate as a pastime – has possibly never had more followers than it does today, when the spectacle of the past excites the kind of attention which earlier epochs attached to the new. Conservation, whatever the doubts about the notion of 'heritage', is one of the major aesthetic and social movements of our time. Family history societies fill the record offices with their searchers. We live – *Theatres of Memory* will argue – in an expanding historical culture, in which the work of inquiry and retrieval is being progressively extended into all kinds of spheres that would have been thought unworthy of notice in the past, the whole new orders of documentation are coming into play.

In any more pluralist notion of the historical profession, or one which paid due respect to those under-labourers without whom historical enterprises would founder, some small space ought to be given, I argue in my chapters on the 'discovery' of old photographs, to the picture researchers – a new breed of Cliographers who owe their existence to the photo-litho revolution of the 1960s, so far as popular historical publication is concerned, or those coffee-table books and Sunday colour supplements which have been the principal medium for the reproduction of 'period' photography. Then there are the television technicians who have the job of synchronizing sight and sound for television docudrama, the writers of screenplays who adapt the literary classics, the film archivists who splice in and select old footage; the independent

THE People's Show Festival
SUMMER 1994

Venues all over Britain are holding a "Peoples Show" inviting local peoples collections in to the exhibitions
Over 5,000 collections will be on display

Springburn Museum
Glasgow

LEEDS
Leeds City Museum
Leeds Industrial Museum
Abbey House Museum
Thwaite Mills Museum

Falkirk   Edinburgh
Callendar House   People's Story Museum

Hexham   Newcastle-upon-Tyne
Prospect House   The People's Gallery

Middlesborough
Dorman Museum

Darlington
The Arts Centre

Lancaster
County Museum

Harrogate
Museum & Art Gallery
Service

LONDON
The Museum of London
Harringay Museum
Croydon Museum
Islington Museum
Museum of Richmond

Bradford
Cartwright Hall

Manchester
Museum of Science & Industry

Bangor   Warrington
Museum &   Museum & Art Gallery
Art Gallery Chester Grosvenor Museum

Tipperary
S. R. Museum

Nottingham Castle Museum

Burton on Trent
Bass Museum

Welshpool   Hednesford Valley Heritage Centre
Powysland Museum   Cannock

WALSALL
Museum
& Art Gallery

Leicester Museum & Arts Gallery

Kidderminster   Nuneaton Museum
Hereford & Worcs County Museum
Aberystwyth   Bewdley Museum   Market Harborough Harborough Museum
Ceredigion Museum

Droitwich Spa   Daventry Museum
Heritage Centre

Hereford
City Museum & Art Gallery

Milton Keynes
Museum of Industry & Rural Life

St Albans Museum

Rhonda
Heritage Park

Swansea   Swindon
Museum   Museum &   High Wycombe
           Art Gallery   Museum

Whistable
Museum & Art Gallery

Salisbury
Salisbury & South
Wiltshire Museum

Walsall
Leisure for all

companies bidding for *Timewatch* slots. In another sphere, where do-it-yourself projects have transformed the map of knowledge, family history is a whole industry unto itself, with a bizarre databank at one end of the spectrum – IGI (the International Genealogical Index), the Mormon-funded archive of dead souls which is a first port of call for those in search of lost ancestors.

One of the more remarkable additions to the ranks of Britain's memory-keepers – or notable recent augmentation of them – would be the multiplication of do-it-yourself curators and mini-museums. Business houses, goaded into an action by an enthusiast on the staff (quite often, it seems, the Principal), have incorporated these into the machineries of self-presentation, putting up display cases in the reception area. The conversion of the home into a kind of miniature historical shrine is even more common, with old photographs – blown up and framed – doing duty for the family portraits and Victorian stuffed squirrels serving as make-believe family heirlooms. Then reference would need to be made to the legions of bargain-hunters who through the medium of the flea market and the car-boot sale have created whole new classes of collectables, or made archives of the future out of the ephemera of the everyday. Walsall Museum discovered dozens of them in 1991, when it staged its first 'People Show', inviting the town's collectors to take up the museum's exhibition space. 'Memorabilia' here appeared in pluralist guise, starting with the veteran jazz musician and his collection of vintage drums and ending up the bedroom culture of the adolescent boy or girl with their collection of football scarves, fanzines or Madonnas.

III Graphics

A historiography that was alert to memory's shadows – those sleeping images which spring to life unbidden, and serve as ghostly sentinels of our thought – might give at least as much attention to pictures as to manuscripts or print. The visual provides us with our stock figures, our subliminal points of reference, our unspoken point of address. When we think of eighteenth-century politics we see Hogarth's Wilkes. The bubonic plague brings skeletons out to dance. The Crimean War is Florence Nightingale with her lamp. The retreat from Moscow is Napoleon on a horse looking downwards. The Viking is a man wading ashore from a long-boat; dressed in a horned helmet, and grasping a broad-sword in his right hand: he is off to sack a village.[77] Likewise, in a well-worn iconographic tradition, the picture that comes to mind of the ancient Britons may well be that of a caveman wielding a club – long-haired, bare-chested, and protected from the cold by nothing but a primitive sarong. The earliest visual portraits of ancient Britons, Stuart Piggott tells us in *Ruins in a Landscape*, date from about 1575, when a Dutchman, Lucas de Heere, in a description of Britain, made a drawing of a couple of wild-looking naked men, tattooed or woad-painted, carrying long shields, spears and a sword.[78]

The iconography of war would be particularly rewarding to study from the point of view of the visual sources of historical consciousness. Wall panels commemorating famous victories, such as those to be found in the Valley of the Kings, and vase paintings celebrating legendary heroes, are among the earliest historical records, while war memorials are among the most ancient of the public arts. The Bayeux tapestry (Napoleon's rediscovery) is probably most people's idea of the Norman Conquest, and we are no less indebted to monumental effigies and ecclesiastical statuary for our idea of the crusades (the nineteenth-century rediscovery of the Knights Templar seems to be responsible for the visual cliché which has the crusader wearing a surplice over his armour).[79]

The nineteenth-century romanticization of war – a subject which awaits its historian – owed a great deal to historical illustration, and to the taste for military antiquities which it was one of Sir Walter Scott's achievements to have made into a pan-European enthusiasm. The knight in chainmail, mounted on a horse, and with his pennant pointing upwards to the sky, was a heroic figure in public statuary (Richard Coeur de Lion outside the Houses of Parliament,[80] Westminster, and the Black Prince in the City Square, Leeds are well-known examples). Engraved pictures of naval encounters were another nineteenth-century favourite, as for example in the pubs, where marine subjects such as Horace Harral's illustrations to Southey's *Life of Nelson* competed for attention with hunting and racecourse prints. In the pleasure gardens, such as Belle Vue, Manchester, there were also 'living history' firework displays – a kind of Hollywood epic before its time, in which with the aid of the pyrotechnicist's art, the Siege of Gibraltar was symbolically lifted and the Battle of Trafalgar refought.[82]

In the Middle Ages spectacle had been quite fundamental to the dissemination of sacred history. Here the street theatre of the Corpus Christi procession, with its banners, tabernacles and crosses,[83] and the open-air perambulating stages where the miracle and morality plays were performed, dramatically re-enacted the Passion.[84] Legendary history was disseminated in a similar fashion. The Gog–Magog procession in London, celebrating the giants who were supposedly the city's founding fathers, is a well-known example.[85] Then there were those annual turn-outs and open-air demonstrations of the artisan trades, such as the Bishop Blaize procession of the wool-combers, or the St Crispin's Day celebrations of the shoemakers, which seem to have had their origin in a civic ritual. Robin Hood, though he has his origin in medieval ballad, was given a whole new life through the late medieval and early modern development of civic pageantry and ritual; Maid Marian – a great figure at Foresters' and Hospital Sunday demonstrations in the nineteenth century – seems to have been the brainchild of some sixteenth-century parish organizers of May games, who believed the Robin Hood story might show to better advantage if it was played as a drama of young love.[86] In a more carnivalesque vein reference should be made to those folk devils of the popular imagination, in the first place the Pope, later Guy Fawkes, annually consigned to a ceremonial bonfire.[87]

How often has the visual been the original prompt for an historical inquiry? A famous if possibly apocryphal example is that of Edward Gibbon who, according to his own retrospective account, was moved to embark on his *Decline and Fall of the Roman Empire* by the spectacle of the ruins at the Colosseum.[88] A more recent example would be Philippe Ariès whose inquiry into the history of childhood seems to have been sparked off by a portrait of Louis XIII, painted when he was still a child of seven, but in which he is depicted as a grown-up.[89] It seems to have been the spectacle of Père Lachaise, and those November migrations which brought flocks of pilgrims to the cemeteries, 'in the cities as well as the country' which set him off on the thanatological inquiries which eventually produced *The Hour of Our Death*.[90] Ruth Richardson, whose *Death, Dissection and the Destitute* has given a bizarre twist to debates about the New Poor Law, traces her life's interest in the subject to some 'frightening' woodcuts of the Black Death which she saw in a book as a little girl of three, a year or so before she learnt to read. (The book was Johannes Nohl's *The Black Death*, translated from the German, and it has as the frontispiece a skeleton riding on a chariot.[91])

More indirectly, it might be instructive to inquire into the part played by the topographical illustrators in treating, or ministering to preservationist instincts and historicist tastes. Chorography, the Elizabethan name for the mapping and description of place, was one of the earliest forms of local history.[92] The maps themselves, pictorial in character and very often bordered with county heraldry and sketches of local scenery and seats, were intensely graphic. The 'many cuts' which adorned Dugdale's *The Antiquities of Warwickshire* (1656) – the greatest of the early county histories – marked in some sort topographical illustration's coming of age;[93] henceforth it formed part of the normal repertoire of antiquarian research. Maurice Barley's bibliography of topographical prints shows etchings, mezzotints, copper and steel engravings, photos and lantern slides as well as artists' impressions of buildings and views.[94] When, in the late seventeenth century, Edward Lhuyd (1660–1709) began his topographical researches in Wales – or West Britain as it was then often called – 'he made large collections of drawings of megaliths', and much the same was true of the tragic J.T. Blight's illustrations of Borlase's *Antiquities of Cornwall.*[95]

One of the leading subjects of the topographical illustrators has been that of environments at risk, and one of their recurring inspirations – already a nostalgic subtext in the Elizabethan 'discovery' of England – has been that of creating a graphic archive of disappearing worlds. This was the inspiration of the *Recording Britain* project launched in the dire days of 1940 – the 'pictorial Domesday' for which Sir Kenneth Clark mobilized a galaxy of talents to preserve, in watercolour and gouache, tokens of the civilization which an enemy invasion might be expected to destroy.[96] It was also the urgent impulse behind Sir Thomas Dugdale's frantic journeyings on the eve of Civil War, the one-man crusade of an obsessive antiquarian 'to make notes of those ecclesiastical memorials which might be destroyed in the political storm he saw approaching'.[97] Topographical illustration in the eighteenth century, though less driven by an emergency sense of change, was, if anything, even more seized by the symptoms of decay. 'Drawing ruins' was one of the passions of the eighteenth-century antiquary,[98] as it was of William Stukeley before he converted to an obsession with Druids, and it was also quite central to those picturesque travellers whose late-eighteenth-century writings were in some sort heralds of the Gothic turn in architecture and design.[99]

If one wanted to look for a single figure who would represent the 'new wave' social history of the 1960s, or the turn to those user-friendly, interactive and informal displays which were such a feature of that decade's 'new museology', David Gentleman, the wood engraver and illustrator, would be as strong a candidate as any. He is the man who put living-history pictures on British postage stamps, among them a series on Ironbridge and some of the monuments of industrial archaeology.[100] His Eleanor Cross mural at Charing Cross underground station – a tapestry of medieval labour, with spare, skeletal figures simplified in the manner of an Arts-and-Crafts frieze – is a successful essay in the kind of modernist pastiche which the conservation movement was to make the quintessence of refurbishment.[101] His illustrations to *Ask the Fellows Who Cut the Hay* (1966) or, later, *David Gentleman's Britain* (1982) are very much in line with those of Edward Bawden, Eric Ravilious and John Piper before him – pen and ink with flat washes of watercolour, but without neo-romantic hints of apocalypse or darkling intimations of gloom.[102] His woodcuts to the 1964 Oxford edition of *The Shepherd's Calendar* are also quite strikingly up-beat, indeed positively fecund when it came to August harvest-sheaves, September apple-picking and even the labours of 'beamless and pale' November.[103]

Pedagogically, pictures have usually been the child's first introduction to the idea of the past, from the tiny woodcuts which decorated the early horn-books to the large-format historical illustrations in today's children's pictorials. In the days of mnemonics, pictures were frequently used as visual aids – as for example in those history cards of the kings and queens of England 'showing ... a remarkable family likeness ... from William I to William IV'[104] which were a great standby of the Victorian governess; or the board game of 'Sovereigns' in which genealogical information was the counter.[105] Later, with the advent of 'learning by doing' – a phenomenon of the 1920s in go-ahead and progressive junior schools – modelling a Tudor house, drawing an Elizabethan ruff, or mapping the three-field system were fiercely and successfully championed as a modernist and progressive alternative to rote-learning.

Graphics were of course quite central to the chap-books, those 'penny histories' which took as their subject legendary heroes, and which owed their street credibility to the juxtaposition of vivid engraving and crude black-letter text.[106] It was the 'horrid and awful-looking woodcuts at the head', which drew the young Samuel Bamford, a workhouse master's son and an apprentice hand-loom weaver, to the legendary histories on sale at a Manchester printer–stationer–bookseller of the 1780s:

> Every farthing I could scrape together, was now spent in purchasing 'Histories of Jack the Giant Killer,' 'Saint George and the Dragon,' 'Tom Hickathrift,' 'Jack and the Bean Stalk,' 'History of the Seven Champions,' tale of 'Fair Rosamond,' 'History of Friar Bacon,' 'Account of the Lancashire Witches,' 'The Witches of the Woodlands,' and such like romances; whilst my metrical collections embraced but few pieces besides 'Robin Hood's Songs,' and 'The Ballad of Chevy-Chase.' Of all these tales and ballads I was soon master, and they formed the subjects of many a long study to me, and of many a wonder-creating story for my acquaintance both at the workhouse and elsewhere. For my part I implicitly believed them all, and when told by my father or others that they were 'trash' and 'nonsense,' and 'could not be true,' I, innocently enough, contrasted their probability with that of other wondrous things which I had read in books that 'it were a sin to disbelieve.' So I continued reading, and doubting nothing which I read until many years after, when a more extended acquaintance with men and books, taught me how better to discriminate betwixt reason and unreason – truth and falsehood.[107]

The nineteenth century was a great age of historical illustration. It was through the medium of the visual that nineteenth-century versions of medievalism imposed themselves, and that the Gothic side of Scott was amplified. While written history moved in a definitely Whig direction, and in the schools parliamentary sympathies in the Civil War were almost unresisted, in the visual a high Tory romanticism prevailed, represented by a whole series of doomed and tragic monarchs, from Lady Jane Grey to Bonnie Prince Charlie. Cheap printing encouraged an astonishing proliferation of educational toys – such as the paper ship game where a very young Eleanor Farjeon waged war, on the nursery table.

One major nineteenth-century addition to the repertoire of visual aids was the Bayeux tapestry. Almost unknown during the first eight hundred years of its existence, and disappearing entirely from view at the end of the fifteenth century, it was discovered by Napoleon in the course of his preparations for the invasion of England, and exhibited for the first time outside Bayeux in 1803, when the preparations for the invasion of England were at their height.

> The exhibition was a great success, with Napoleon himself spending some time studying the Tapestry. The parallel between the comet which was seen in France and southern England in November 1803 and the comet shown in the embroidery adjacent to the scene of Harold's coronation was not lost on the audience. A description of the phenomenon was included in the first edition of the handbook which was prepared for the exhibition: 'Dover, December 6, 1803. Last night about five o'clock we observed a superb comet which rose in the south-west and moved towards the north: it had a tail about thirty yards long. The whole countryside was lighted for many miles all around, and after it disappeared, one smelled a strong odour of sulphur.' There was also a story, without foundation, circulated by later English writers, that Napoleon was so struck by the coincidence of the comet that, inter- preting it as a bad omen, he abandoned his plans for an invasion of England! The modern propaganda value of the Tapestry was realized for the first time with its Paris exhibition.[108]

It was the enthusiasm of British Gothicists which led to the tapestry's second migration and its return, in the form of imitation and print, to the country where it had originally been embroidered, and whose history it purported to tell. Charles Stothard, whose *Monumental Effigies*, published between 1822 and 1829 were (Mark Girouard tells us) a kind of visual equivalent to the Waverley novels in stirring medievalist sympathies, took up the cause of the tapestry. In 1816, on assignment from the Society of Antiquaries of London, he set about producing a full- size, full-colour reproduction of the tapestry, an undertaking which took two years to complete. 'By closely studying the needle-holes and thread traces Stothard was able to "restore" much of the damaged area and produce drawings of what he considered to be the tapestry's original appearance.'[109]

Historical illustration is, on the face of it, one of the most conservative of art forms. The same stock figures seem to appear in an astonishing variety of contexts, as though there were some puppet-master pulling the strings. Often it seems that archetypal images are involved, even when a picture is ostensibly drawn or painted from life – one could refer to the

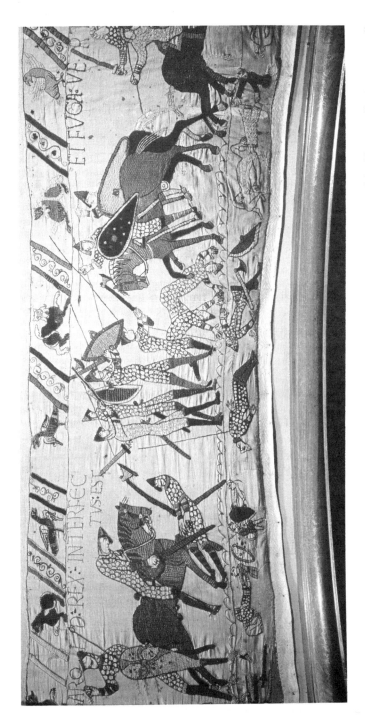

Almost unknown during the first eight hundred years of its existence, today the best-known image of the Norman Conquest, as well as a capital source for the study of the material culture of Anglo-Saxon England, its ploughs and harrows, its waggons and barrels and glassware as well as its shields and battle-axes. The Bayeux tapestry owes its discovery and nineteenth-century renown to Napoleon's plans for the invasion of England.

pietà grouping of Daniel Maclise's enormously popular *Death of Nelson*, as of its predecessor and the original of a long line of military martyrologies, Benjamin West's *Death of Wolfe*; the killing fields, in the outstretched hand of G.W. Pabst's *All Quiet on the Western Front*, or Matthew Brady's well-known photographs of the carnage at Gettysburg, in the American Civil War.

Perhaps the most remarkable example of iconographic longevity is that of the woodcuts to *Foxe's Book of Martyrs*, those 'realistic engravings of the horrible tortures inflicted on the faithful Protestant' – as they appeared to a young Spitalfields apprentice of the 1860s[110] – which held their own, almost unchanged, for some three hundred years. John Day, the original illustrator, was an ardent Protestant who had himself been a Marian prisoner, and his woodcuts were re-cut and re-copied, with remarkably little modification, right down to the last popular edition in 1875. They were, writes Hodnett, in his history of book illustration, 'the earliest examples of graphic journalism in England'. The martyrs were pictured being scourged, burned, hanged and stretched on the rack. The horror of the scene was enhanced by the grim but matter-of-fact bearing of the executioners.[111]

Historical illustration today, in popular educational publishing, such as Kingfisher, Usborne and Dorling Kindersley – the 1990s successors to the 'Ladybird' books – are, in their own way, equally conservative, alternating between extravaganzas of the kind which drew the young Samuel Bamford to the chap-books – e.g. 'How to Draw Ghosts, Vampires and Haunted Houses' – with a 'realistic battlegame' of *Fighting Ships*, in which Viking boats alternate with four-masted Spanish galleons; and a 'time-travelling' series which moves from 'Knights and Castles' to 'Famous Inventors and Explorers'.

The heroic biography which was offered to 1950s and 1960s readers of *The Eagle* – Charlemagne, Alfred the Great and Joan of Arc among them – would not have looked out of place in the self-help manuals and Sunday School prize books of the nineteenth century;[112] while the comic strip serials in the girls' magazines – often with a period setting – loyally continue in the idiom of the Evangelically inspired 'waif' novels. Ringing the changes on court biography and royal romances, the girls' comics have worked a rich vein in little-girl-lost or orphanhood stories, set sometimes in Victorian England, sometimes in Regency times, and typically involving both aristocratic patronage and profiles of people in need. Thus for instance 'Sophie Sixpence' (*Mandy*, 3 March 1984) tells the story of a twelve-year-old, rescued from a life of poverty, the workhouse and begging by wealthy Sir John Fielding, who bought her from an unscrupulous couple for sixpence – hence her name. When Sir John goes away on business the wicked step-parents try to snatch her back, rather in the manner of the Artful Dodger in *Oliver Twist*. 'Angel' (*Mandy for Girls*, 26 January 1985) has a Victorian miss, the only child of a wealthy banker, who, stricken by an illness for which there is no known cure, devotes what she thinks are her last days by setting up as a good Samaritan in the London slums. *Nikki for Girls* (27 April 1985) has a bonneted villainess scheming to starve a Victorian orphan to death on behalf of a wicked guardian; while in *Judy and Tracy* (5 July 1986) Hetty Dean, a flower seller in Victorian London, is magically translated into a Moldanian princess.

Closer inspection of any of those images, however, makes them seem a good deal less timeless. The queens who look out from the 'Ladybird' books seem to have been drawn from Julie Andrews or Anna Neagle – fresh-faced or statuesque according to the role in which they are cast. Likewise in the *Royal Story Book of English History* – a popular reader published in 1883 – all of the pictures, whatever the period to which they ostensibly refer, look like those to be found in Victorian moral tales. Except for the inscription 'Lord Have Mercy on Us', the 'Street in London during the Plague', with its tottering, dilapidated tenements, is pure Gustave Doré (after his *London, A Pilgrimage*, 1872). The young King Alfred absent-mindedly burning the cakes, though ostensibly a boy, is a dead ringer for Sir John Tenniel's (and Lewis Carroll's) Alice. Geoffrey Chaucer, the poet, and Edward III, his sovereign, are both pictured as Pre-Raphaelite Merlin-like figures, with long beards reaching down almost to the ground. Forty years earlier, in the illustrations with which Charles Knight used to swell the sales of the Penny Magazine, the philosophers and poets, so far from being hirsute, have barely a whisker or a superfluous tuft of hair between them.

It is the genius of television, and especially perhaps television directed at children, that it can reinvent historical characters in such a way as to make them speak in the authentic accent of the here-and-now. Indeed it was under the aegis of that long-running favourite, *Dr Who*, that the idea of back-to-the-future and time travelling – a leitmotif of post-modernism – was born. In the 1970s, children's serials celebrated the feats of Richard the Lionheart and the Crusades (*The Talisman*), brought Anglo-Saxon England to life in *Hereward the Wake*, and featured medieval swordplay and chivalrous knights-in-armour in *Ivanhoe*. More recently, through the medium of its eco-friendly and popular *Robin of Sherwood* children's television has created a kind of New Age outlaw hero, one who was on friendly terms with a Celtic wizard, and a dab hand at conducting Druidic ceremonies. A still more striking case is the recent cult serial *Sharpe*. Set in the period of the Peninsular War, and with some haunting songs of the period to suggest that this really happened, Sean Bean, the male lead, is a cross between a swashbuckling Errol Flynn-type hero, putting cowardly and treacherous enemies to flight, and a more sensitive Lawrentian figure: he falls in love with a Spanish guerrilla who proves her emancipation by knifing someone in every episode; and he cuddles his baby daughter with all the rapture of an Islington-trained 'new man'.

The art of memory as Frances Yates describes it, following a trajectory which leads from ancient Greece to Renaissance Italy and Shakespeare's England, had a very strong graphic side.[113] Beginning as a rhetorical device, it came to be practised, in the Middle Ages, as a kind of visual analogue to thought. It was associated both with the production and storage of images, and with the location of memory places – as, say, burial grounds and shrines.[114] Memory of words becomes memory refracted through the iconography of things, and finally, when it is caught up in occult philosophy, astral figures.[115]

Medieval scribes, with their delight in such mnemonic devices as the visual alphabet, had a genius for discovering the pictorial equivalent of verbal utterance. Words, in the illuminated manuscripts, double in the character of things; while the flora and fauna of the marginalia and the animal heads and facetious figures offset the mysteries of religion or the formalities of the charters by being rooted in the humours of everyday life.[116] Knights announced themselves through heraldry, 'an alternative language of signs, which was peculiar to the knightly order, and distinguished their names'.[117] The merchant class of later medieval London followed suit, 'choosing the same predatory creatures for their emblems as had traditionally appealed to noble families as symbols of power', though the London fishmongers (Sylvia Thrupp tells us) preferred to draw on Christian iconography.[118] Stained-glass windows told the story of the Bible in the form of pictorial narrative and represented saints' lives in gilded tabernacles where the incidents of their sufferings, and their miracles, were rehearsed. Frescoes and friezes depicted scenes of combat and made effigies of the knightly dead.[119]

It is then fitting that Matthew Paris, whose *Chronica Majora*, compiled between 1230 and 1251, is one of the finest medieval histories, should have combined the role of historiographer with that of artist. His text is richly illustrated with relevant scenes, sketched in many cases (it seems) by himself, and he also devised a system of pictorial reference signs, both as an ornament and as a kind of allegorical index. 'We find in one place a fish, in another a stag's head ... elsewhere ... two halves of an animal's body.'[120] 'He had such skill in the working of gold and silver and other metal', a fellow monk wrote in 1400, 'and in painting pictures, that it is thought that there has been none to equal him since in the Latin world.'[121]

Antiquarians, with their eye for eccentric and quirky shapes, their love of curiosities and their often very strong aesthetic preference for the archaic, have been much more alert to the visual than historians.[122] Taking their original inspiration, quite often, from exotic objects or the evidence of ruins and relics; using bronze and pottery inscriptions rather than the written or printed word as primary sources; and calling on burial goods or coin hoards to reconstitute the track of ancient settlement, antiquarians have often been concerned to exhibit and display, as well as to write about, the object of their inquiries, while illustration, if only for the purposes of exegesis, has often been a necessity of their published work.[123] In nineteenth-century publication, title pages would often make a feature of Gothic typefaces and archaic words, while decorative borders and end-pieces would simulate some of the effects of the medieval illuminated manuscript.[124]

Architectural history, heraldry and ecclesiology, the leading pre-occupations of the county archaeological and record societies, also put a premium on illustration, while the illustrated lecture, using 'dioramic views' of monastic ruins or magic-lantern slides of old English churches, was a firm favourite, it seems, with that large public interested in ecclesiastical antiquities.[125] In the case of popular publishing, such as that of William Hone, Robert Chambers and the egregious S.C. Hall, it was the very basis of their appeal to the reading public.[126] Hone's three-decker *Every-Day Book* was illustrated with 436 engravings, drawn quite often, it seems, by the antiquaries themselves.[127] Charles Roach Smith, the city-of-London chemist who assembled a whole museum of Roman remains, contributed his own etchings in the publication and populariza-tion of his work, improving on the original so that the Roman inscriptions have every letter in place, the mosaic pavements every tessera.[128] His fellow-antiquary Thomas Wright illustrated his wander-ings and finds with quantities of engravings and vignettes, drawn (it seems) by his own hand. He enjoyed 'rude forms', and was something of a humorist[129] (one of his drawings shows the barrow diggers, sheltering under an umbrella from the storm);[130] but like Roach Smith he seems to have been unable to prevent himself from improving on the original when making his on-the-spot sketches. Wright's triple-decker *History of Ireland* was illustrated with engravings by the President of the Watercol-our Society – 'Death of Brian Boru', 'Richard Earl of Pembroke Taking Leave of his Brother', 'Henry II Presenting the Pope's Bull'.[131] His very influential *History of Domestic Manners and Sentiments in England during the Middle Ages* drew on scenes in illuminated medieval manuscripts to illustrate his account of houses, furniture, dress, food and recrea-tions.[132]

Historical illustration was the cutting edge of the introduction of social history into the elementary schools – a phenomenon of the 1920s. The Board of Education, in its *Suggestions* for 1918, argued that children needed 'the picturesque element'.[133] Material culture – in the form of houses, food, dress and means of locomotion – was easier for children to understand than more abstract political and constitutional questions; material artefacts were also – as progressive teachers showed – ideal candidates for 'handwork' (e.g. modelling and drawing), for 'playway' forms of education, and for what was called, after Froebel and Dewey, 'learning by doing'. A model of Stonehenge, 'period' rooms and history friezes were, it seems, among the most popular exercises in junior classes at the time; and the books which catered to them, such as the 'Piers Plowman' histories, were richly illustrated with historical engravings and prints.[134]

By contrast the Historical Association, which established itself in the same period as the gazetteer of masters and mistresses in the senior schools, offered unrelieved acres of print, both in its much-thumbed pamphlets and in its quarterly journal. The university presses – a growing presence in these years – were no less severe, though when Oxford University Press published the Orwins' *Open Fields* it was illustrated by one of the archaeological excitements of the 1920s – aerial photographs.[135]

In an increasingly image-conscious society, and one in which children are visually literate from a very early age, the learned journals stand out as one of the very few forms of publication on which historical illustration has yet to leave its mark. Except for art historians, pictures do not count as a source, nor is there any call for seminars and lectures to be turned into slide-shows. For some, such as those who condemn the open-air museums and theme parks, the visual seems to be disqualified because of its association with the popular. Easy on the eye but undemanding, it is also thought of as being in some sort morally dubious – a kind of pedagogic equivalent to the fling.

'History from below' – the 'new-wave' scholarship which dedicated itself to rescuing England's secret people from the 'enormous condescension' of posterity – stopped short of any engagement with graphics. Caught up in the cultural revolution of the 1960s it nevertheless remained wedded to quite traditional forms of writing, teaching and research. E.P. Thompson's *The Making of the English Working Class* (1963) has not a single print to leaven the 800 pages of a narrative which covers some of the most brilliant years of English political caricature. Nor has Peter Laslett's *The World We Have Lost* (1965), the book which offered a more domestic version of people's history. 'New-wave' social history did take photographs on board, in ways discussed in Part V of the present volume, but it was for their reality content rather than their pictorial value or interest – in short, because they were thought of as being of a piece with documentary truth.

It seems possible that history's new-found interest in 'representation', and its belated recognition of the deconstructive turn in contemporary thought, will allow for, and even force, a more central engagement with graphics. It is possible that politics will be studied as a species of performance art, religion as a liturgical drama. Photographs, if in the spirit of postmodernism they are dissevered from any notion of the real, might be studied for the theatricality of social appearances, rather than as likenesses of everyday life.

Whatever historians choose to do, graphics are likely to come more and more insistently on to the agenda of reflection and research. For one thing, there is the fact that more and more information is coming to us in the form of visual display, from cashpoint machines to CD Rom. Then there are the ways in which historical illustration and historical reconstitution are becoming, with the aid of information retrieval and advanced technology, inconceivably more sophisticated than they were in the past. With the aid of laser-beam cutting it is possible to produce, in the built environment, brilliant copies for which there is no original; while animatronics have advanced to the point that it is possible to make a flesh-and-blood figure of a tenth-century Viking skull. Archaeologists, using deonchronology, allow us to sup, metaphorically speaking, with the Beaker people, while in another sphere the new biogenics – it is believed – can bring long-extinct species back to life.[136]

Finally, and perhaps as a result of the collapse of ideas of national destiny, there is the growing importance of 'memory places' in ideas of the historical past. Landscape, and in particular those vast tracts of it which now come under the administration of the National Trust, is now called upon to do the memory work which in earlier times might have been performed by territorial belonging. The historicization of the built environment – discussed in this volume of *Theatres of Memory* – is an even more striking case in point, ministering to an appetite for roots at the same time as it often involves dishousing the indigenous population. Old houses, formerly left to decay, are now prized as living links to the past, a kind of visual equivalent to what used to be known as 'a stake in the country'. Even when houses are brand new, they cultivate a lived-in look, as epitomized by the universality of those neo-vernacular styles in which local materials, 'mature trees' and well-etablished shrubs give a mellow look to starter homes. Conversely, as Rachel Whiteread showed in her 1993 installation, the deserted mid-Victorian house, cut adrift from its moorings, shuttered, blind and empty – a house you could go round but not enter – is perhaps the most disturbing monument to the urban diaspora.

Notes

1. Peter Burke, 'Ranke the Reactionary' in George G. Iggers and James M. Powell, eds., *Leopold von Ranke and the Shaping of the Historical Discipline*, Syracuse 1990, pp. 36–44.

2. For some of the debates on the coronation oath of Henry IV, a *locus classicus* for discussion of the alleged 'constitutionalism' of the Lancastrian Kings, see S.B. Chrimes, *English Constitutional Ideas of the Fifteenth Century*, Cambridge 1956.

3. Margaret Aston, *The King's Bedpost: Reformation and Iconography in a Tudor Group Portrait*, Cambridge 1993, is a wonderful exercise in forensic skills and shows how the religious propaganda of state Protestantism was by the reign of Elizabeth turning to the retrospective painting of supposedly historical events.

4. Peter Laslett, ed., *Household and Family in Past Time: Comparative Studies in the Size and Structure of the Domestic Group over the Last Three Centuries*, Cambridge 1972; Pierre Goubert, *Beauvais et les Beauvaisis, de 1600 à 1730*, 2 vols., Paris 1960; Emmanuel Le Roy Ladurie, *Les Paysans de Languedoc*, 2 vols., Paris 1966.

5. T.D. Kendrick, *British Antiquity*, London 1950; Stuart Piggott, *Ruins in a Landscape*, Edinburgh 1976, pp. 33–76; F.J. Levy, *Tudor Historical Thought*, San Marino 1907, pp. 124–66; A.B. Ferguson, *Clio Unbound: Perception of the Past in Renaissance England*, Durham, NC 1979, pp. 3–27, 78–125.

6. G.R.Elton, *The Practice of History*, Glasgow 1976.

7. A.L. Rowse, *The England of Elizabeth*, London 1951, pp. 31–65; E.G.R. Taylor, *Late Tudor and Early Stuart Geography*, 1583–1650, London 1934. Richard Helgerson, *Forms of Nationhood: The Elizabethan Writing of England*, Chicago 1992.

8. Daphne du Maurier, *Myself When Young*, London 1977, p. 29.

9. Alison Light, remembering a 1960s Portsmouth girlhood.

10. 'Then a neighbour who had bought a bundle of old books for a few pence at a sale lent them *Old St Pauls* and the outhouse door was soon chalked with a cross and the wheelbarrow trundled round the garden to the cry "Bring out your dead!"' Flora Thompson, *Lark Rise to Candleford*, Oxford 1961, p. 371; for an almost identical memoir. Daphne du Maurier, *Myself When Young*, p. 30.

11. James Williams, *Give me Yesterday*, Llandysul 1971, pp. 33–4, for such a battle.

12. Rudyard Kipling, *Something of Myself*, Harmondsworth 1992, p. 38.

13. In a vast literature, Elizabeth Tonkin, *Narrating our Pasts: the Social Construction of Oral History*, Cambridge 1992; David Henige, *Oral Historiography*, London 1982; Ruth Finnegan, *Oral Tradition and the Verbal Arts*, London 1992; Jan Vansina, *Oral Tradition as History*, London 1985.

14. Iona and Peter Opie, *The Lore and Language of Schoolchildren*, Oxford 1959; *Children's Games in Street and Playground*, Oxford 1969.

15. For some examples, Linda Degh, *Studies in East European Folk Narrative*, Bloomington 1978; Albert Bates Lord, *Epic Singers and Oral Tradition*, Ithaca 1991.

16. Lovel adds: 'the ferocious warrior is remembered, and the peaceful abbots are abandoned to forgetfulness', Scott, *The Antiquary*, Chapter 17.

17. 'History was often taught in voluntary schools for the poor towards the middle of the nineteenth century, until the Revised Code of 1861 led to it being regarded as superfluous in comparison to the three Rs for which a government grant was received. In the 1870s history was once again reinstated in favour as a subject for the upper standard, and since the teaching of it was found to be unsatisfactory, the aid of history reading books was usually made compulsory in Board Schools (LCC Report on the Teaching of History 1911, p. 11). In the Code of 1900 the subject itself was made compulsory for the first time.' Valerie E. Chancellor, *History for Their Masters: Opinion in the English History Textbook, 1800–1914*, Bath 1970, p. 28. In Flora Thompson's North Oxfordshire village school of the 1880s, 'History was not taught formally; but history readers were in use containing such picturesque stories as those of King Alfred and the cakes, King Canute commanding the waves, the loss of the White Ship, and Raleigh spreading his cloak for Queen Elizabeth.' Flora Thompson, *Lark Rise to Candleford*, p. 192. Marion Johnson, *Derbyshire Village Schools in the Nineteenth Century*, Newton Abbot 1970, pp. 208–11 for some mid-Victorian history teaching.

18. Henry Smith, *1,000 Questions on General Knowledge*, London 1919. Mr Smith was headmaster of Chester Road Council School (Senior Boys), New Ferry, Birkenhead.

19. See C.R. Attlee, *As It Happened*, London 1954 for the use of mnemonics as a way of learning by heart the genealogical descent of the Kings of Israel. See also *The Life of Joseph Barker, Written by Himself*, London 1885, pp. 53–4, for learning the Bible as literal truth, on a par with other histories.

20. *The Royal Story Book of English History*, Nelson Royal School Series, London 1885.

21. See Thomas Wright, *Political Poems and Songs Relating to English History*, London 1859, for one historian's awareness of the importance of the ballads. The publications of the Early English Texts Society brought Anglo-Saxon ballads within the corpus of the national literature.

22. On Astleys, A.H. Saxon, *Enter Foot and Horse: A History of Hippodrama in England and France*, New Haven 1968.

23. *The Boys of England* began publishing in 1866. I am very grateful to Louis James for lending me some of the volumes.

24. On Agnes Strickland, as well as her own voluminous historical works, and her romantically Cavalier poetry, there is a good biography by Una Pope-Hennessey published in 1940. What is lacking is any sense of the literary world (or literary underworld) in which she and other writers moved; Norma Clarke, *Ambitious Heights*, London 1990, a portrait of the Jewsbury sisters, Felicia Hemans, Jane Carlyle and their relationship to mid-Victorian publishing, is one possible model which would be worth following.

25. H.A. Morrah, *The Oxford Union 1823–1923*, London 1923, p. 10. I am grateful to Brian Harrison for this reference. At the Watlington Mutual Improvement Society in February 1852, after what the enthusiastic secretary declared was the most momentous debate which had ever taken place in the town's history (it went on for seven successive nights) the young men, after taking a vote (in the most advanced manner of the day) by ballot, decided by a large majority that 'with the exception of sometimes allowing his religion to degenerate into enthusiasm and consenting to the death of the King . . . a better Christian, a more noble-minded spirit, a greater warrior, a more constant man (than Oliver Cromwell) had hardly ever appeared on the face of the earth.' *Oxford Chronicle*, 4 February 1852. For some discussion of the place of such debates in nineteenth-century historiography, Raphael Samuel, 'The Discovery of Puritanism, 1820–1914: a Preliminary Sketch', in Jane Garnett and Colin Matthew, eds., *Revival and Religion Since 1700: Essays for John Walsh*, London 1993.

26. Brian Harrison, 'Pubs' in H.J. Dyos and Michael Wolff, eds., *The Victorian City: Images and Reality*, vol. 1, London 1973, p. 180. This was a very radical club which had the courage – in a debate of 11 June 1871 – to support the Paris Commune.

27. Sir Charles Oman, *Memories of Victorian Oxford and of Some Early Years*, London 1940, p. 67. Philippa Levine, *The Amateur and the Professional: Antiquarians, Historians and Archaeologists in Victorian England, 1838–1880*, Cambridge 1986.

28. Hayden White, *Metahistory*, Baltimore 1973. Through an extended study of what he rather grandiosely called 'the historical imagination in nineteenth-century Europe', and by an analysis of modes of 'emplotment', he offers a fourfold typology, in which histories are assigned to the Romantic, the Tragic, the Comic and the Satiric – Michelet being labelled by the first, Tocqueville by the second, Ranke (somewhat improbably) by the third; Burckhardt – in a reading singularly at variance with commonsense usage of the word – is aligned with the satiric. In another fourfold classification the writer argues, on the basis of his textual exegesis, that the narrative strategies of the historian can be resolved into metaphor, metonymy, synecdoche and irony – i.e. the four recognized tropes of classical rhetoric. So far from being, as one of White's English admirers puts it, 'a uniquely comprehensive view of the nineteenth century historical imagination', *Metahistory* confines itself to a limited number of well-thumbed texts. White has nothing to say about the scholarly community or the reading public, or – a matter now quite well documented so far as Victorian Britain is concerned – of the chequered career of history in the schools. Having set out his formulae, and proved, at least to his own satisfaction, that Ranke, Michelet, Tocqueville and Burkhardt fit the bill, he does not attempt to test his scheme on works which might resist it. Curiously for an American, he has nothing to say about the

Epic, which in the nineteenth century found in the conquest and settlement of the New World one of its grand subjects. There is no discussion of the historical novel, on any count one of the moving forces in nineteenth-century perceptions of the past (throwing off the influence of Sir Walter Scott was an important stage in the intellectual formation of Ranke), nor of nineteenth-century medievalism. The discovery of pre-history, an event on a par with *The Origin of Species* so far as geological time was concerned, goes undiscussed. White does not refer to the nineteenth-century debates about free will and determinism, nor the challenges to the 'great men' theory of history, a flashpoint of popular controversy in the 1850s and 1860s, nor the interplay of ideas of nation and race – all of them important growing points for new historical work. In short, White is uninterested in what nineteenth-century histories were *about* or where they came from: 'tropological strategies' are all. White's idea of 'metahistory', a master narrative which underpins the individual work, is a genial one, but if the object is to analyse (as White claims for his work) 'the deep structure of the historical imagination', or to identify 'the artistic components of historical work', attention would need to be extended to the ensemble of nineteenth-century historical practices, and their relationship to literature and art.

29. Keith Thomas, *The Perception of the Past in Early Modern England*, London 1983, is a pioneering attempt to bring oral tradition within the ambit of cultural history; see D.R. Woolf, 'The "Common Voice": History, Folklore and Oral Tradition in Early Modern England', *Past and Present*, 120, 1988, pp. 26–54 for some further illustrations. The writer suggests that oral tradition disappears once a scholarly mode of historical inquiry had been established. For medieval use of the oral see, above all, M.T. Clanchy, *From Memory to Written Record: England, 1066–1307*, 2nd edn., Oxford 1993; Antonia Gransden, *Legends, Traditions and History in Medieval England*, London 1992 for the spin-offs of a lifetime's engagement with medieval chronicles. James Fentress and Chris Wickham, *Social Memory*, Oxford 1992 has a medieval and ethnological focus. For the ancient world, see Rosalind Thomas, *Oral Tradition and Written Record in Classical Athens*, Cambridge 1989.

30. David Tylden-Wright, *John Aubrey, A Life*, London 1991, pp. 15–16. For his nurse's ballad-singing, Leslie Shepard, *The Broadside Ballad: a Study in Origins and Meaning*, London 1982, p. 54.

31. *Les Lieux de Mémoire*, ed., Pierre Nora, 7 vols., Paris 1984–1993.

32. Alfred Williams, *Villages of the White Horse*, London 1920.

33. Of the alleged 'Huguenot' place-names in Spitalfields, Fleur-de-Lys Street (a royal not a Huguenot symbol) was named after a pub, Fournier Street after an early nineteenth-century builder of that name; while Wilkes Street seems to have been the initiative of some right-on, liberal-radical member of the Whitechapel Board of Works. For the evidence, London County Council, *Names of Streets and Places in the Administrative County of London*, London 1929, p. 199; Adrian Room, *The Street Names of England*, Stamford 1992; F.H. Harben, *London Street Names: Their Origin, Significance and Historic Value*, London 1896.

34. For *Notes and Queries*, see the memoirs of its founder, J. Thom, the man who also coined the term 'folk-lore'.

35. Plot, who seems to have modelled his work on Pliny, published his *Natural History of Oxfordshire* in 1677. The plan of his work specified first, 'animals, plants and the universal furniture of the world'; second, nature's 'extravagancies and defects'; lastly, artificial restraints. In 1686 Plot published his *Natural History of Staffordshire*. Plot was the first custodian of the Tradescant's collection of natural curiosities when it was brought to Oxford to form the original nucleus of the Ashmolean museum.

36. John Mayhall, *The Annals of Yorkshire from the Earliest Period to the Present Time*, Leeds 1866, vol. II, pp. 196–231.

37. Eleanor Farjeon, *A Nursery in the Nineties*, pp. 385–6. Norman Douglas, *Street Games*, London 1916, p. 135.

38. Carolyn Steedman, 'True Romances', in R. Samuel, ed., *Patriotism: The Making and Unmaking of British National Identity*, vol. 1, London 1989, p. 28.

39. Kate Moorse, 'A Dorset Village School', in R. Samuel, ed., 'History, the Nation and the Schools', cyclostyled papers, Oxford 1989. Oral tradition also had its place in this child's precocious sense of the past, both in 'chats over the railings with village elders' and in her own family lore: '. . . My maternal grandmother had been born the youngest of 18

of a Purbeck quarry owner who drank his quarries away. She'd gone into service at 12, moved to London and experienced a vast array of situations and dilemmas which she talked about quite freely ... until her death at 94 she vividly recalled the turn of the century and the personal tragedy associated with the First World War.'

40. The material used here was prepared by Susan Barrowclough and Raphael Samuel for 'Television History', *History Workshop Journal*, 12, Autumn 1981.

41. Jennifer Westwood, *Albion: A Guide to Legendary Britain*, London 1985; *The Quest for Arthur's Britain*, ed. Geoffrey Ashe, London 1972; *The New Arthurian Encyclopedia*, ed. Norris J. Lacey, 2nd edn. London 1991; Ralph Merrifield, *The Anthology of Ritual and Magic*, London 1987, is by a former curator of the London Museum. Iona Opie, *A Dictionary of Superstitions*, Oxford 1989.

42. Margaret Spufford, *Small Books and Pleasant Histories; Popular Fiction and its Readership in Seventeenth Century England*, Cambridge 1981, pp. 4, 29, 59, 247–9.

43. J.C. Holt, *Robin Hood*, London 1982; Maurice Keen, *The Outlaws of Medieval Legend*, London 1961.

44. Raphael Samuel, 'Black Beauty' in Norma Clarke and Adam Lively, eds., *Nineteenth Century Children's Literature* (forthcoming).

45. At random, in a vast literature, reference might be made to Moncrieff's 1872 historical drama, *Mary Queen of Scots*; to a chap-book history published in Newcastle in 1860; and to the *Life and History of Mary Queen of Scots* published in Clarke's Juvenile Histories, 1850. For an Eton schoolboy smitten with the queen, L.E. Jones, *A Victorian Boyhood*, London 1965.

46. See Valerie Chancellor, *History for Their Masters*, p. 63, quoting an 1872 book by W.S. Ross. 'Crunch went the knife on the beautiful Marie-Antoinette' wrote the author; he went on to describe the 'sweet lips pale' and the glorious ringlets 'heavy with gore-gouts ... When the head of Louis fell with a dull thud upon the scaffold, Europe awoke with a shriek from her reverie of horror.'

47. John Bossy, *Giardano Bruno and the Embassy Affair*, London 1991. Long ago, in a typically compressed but resonant passage, R.G. Collingwood, the historian and philosopher, pointed to the affinities between research and the detective fiction of the day. R.G. Collingwood, *The Idea of History*, Oxford 1946.

48. The description of 1870s Pedestrianism in *The Detective Wore Silk Drawers*, London 1971, one of the most successful of Lovesey's novels, might have come from the pen of James Greenwood or J. Ewing Ritchie.

49. The title pages of the Brother Cadfael series say that a portion of the royalties will be devoted to rebuilding Shrewsbury Abbey. An account of the origins of the series runs as follows: 'In 1977, Peters, a lifelong fan of the history of her small corner of the world, began thinking about an historical incident involving the translation of the bones of St Winifred to the abbey in Shrewsbury. What if someone were to use this as an opportunity to hide another body. Who would do such a thing and why? Who would be able to detect such a crime? And so Brother Cadfael was born, a medieval renaissance man who can give Mr Holmes a run for his money in a contest of the clearest and cleverest eyes. Soldier, sailor, crusader and lover, come to the cloistered life late, and of his own volition, the native Welshman forms a small company of monks going to Wales to secure Winifred's relics,' ed. Lesley Henderson, *Twentieth Century Crime and Mystery Writers*, 3rd edn., London 1991, p. 849.

50. Patrick Wright, 'The Man with a Metal Detector', *A Journey through Ruins: The Last Days of London*, London 1991, pp. 139–51.

51. '"Missy", as F. calls the girl, is his amanuensis and transcribes; takes long walks too with him and others, of ten and twenty miles a day', A.J. Munby wrote of Eleanor Dalziel, the pretty young lady's maid whom Furnivall married in 1862. Derek Hudson, *Munby: Man of Two Worlds*, London 1972, pp. 123–4. Twenty years later Furnivall abandoned his wife in favour of his twenty-one-year-old secretary and co-worker, Teena Rochfort-Smith. The story of their tragic romance is told in William Benzie, *Dr. F.J. Furnivall: Victorian Scholar–Adventurer*, Norman, Okla. 1983, pp. 29–31.

52. Elizabeth Murray, *Caught in a Web of Words: James Murray and the Oxford English Dictionary*, New Haven 1977.

53. Claire Harman, *Sylvia Townsend Warner: A Biography*, London 1991, pp. 38–43.

54. George Gissing, *New Grub Street*, London 1891, Chapter 7.

55. Victoria County History Archives, correspondence of J.H. Round with H.A. Doubleday, 1900–1901. R.P. Pugh, 'The Victoria County History, its Origin and Progress', in *Victoria County History*, General Introduction, 1970, pp. 4–5; W.R. Powell, 'J. Horace Round', in *Essex Archaeology and History*, vol. 12, 1980, p. 30.

56. Roszicka Parker, *The Subversive Stitch*, London 1984.

57. For the 'Record and Survey' movement see Part V of this book.

58. Martin Hoyles, *Gardening Books from 1560 to 1960*, vol. I, London 1994. A second volume, covering political themes in gardening literature, is promised for 1995.

59. G.K. Fortescue, ed., *Catalogue of the Thomason Collection*, 2 vols., London 1908. The Thomason tracts seem to have been little used before the upsurge of interest in the Levellers – and the discovery of the Diggers – at the end of the nineteenth century. G.P. Gooch, *The History of English Democratic Ideas in the Seventeenth Century*, Cambridge 1889, was a pioneering work in this field. In the 1850s, when David Masson made some use of them for his splendid life of Milton, Thomason's collection was known in the British Museum as 'the King's Tracts'. David Masson, *Life of Milton*, London 1859, vol. 1, p. 456.

60. *Catalogue of the Pepys Library at Magdalene College, Cambridge*, vol. III, Cambridge 1980; *The Pepys Ballads*, ed. W.G. Day, Cambridge 1987.

61. David C. Douglas, *English Scholars*, London 1939 is an affecting account of them.

62. Mea Allan, *The Tradescants, Their Flowers, Gardens and Museum, 1570–1667*, London 1964.

63. Henry Willett, *Introductory Catalogue of the Collection of Pottery and Porcelain in the Brighton Museum lent by Henry Willett*, Brighton 1879, p. 3. Willett, a lifelong supporter of Liberal 'not to say Radical' causes, was a friend of Richard Cobden, whose books and papers he donated to Brighton reference library in 1873. An ardent friend of popular education, he conducted public readings at Brighton's open-air forum, The Level. His earliest collecting passion was geology, and the first of a series of privately printed catalogues was one in 1871 on cretaceious fossils (the volume was dedicated to his friend John Ruskin). A precocious ecologist, his next collecting venture was in the field of natural history – he even found dinosaurs and the bones of an iguanadon at Cuckfield, Sussex. Willett's ceramic collection, designed to provide illustrations of popular British history, included masses of militaria (one of Willett's more unlikely enthusiasms) and such up-to-the-minute specimens as the coloured plaster sculptures made by Randolph Caldecott, the well-known *Punch* illustrator, for the Tichborne case. Stella Beddoe, 'Henry Willett (1823–1905): Brighton's Major Benefactor', Brighton Museum, October 1933.

64. *The John Johnson Collection. Catalogue of an Exhibition*, ed. Michael L. Turner, Oxford 1971. Tom Laqueur, 'The John Johnson Collection in Oxford', *History Workshop Journal*, 4, Autumn 1977; Louis James, *Print and the People, 1819–1951*, London 1976, draws heavily on the collection.

65. On early 1930s Victoriana, Robert Graves and Alan Hodge, *The Long Week-End: A Social History of Great Britain, 1918–1939*, London 1950; on Victoriana and the Bright Young Things, Christopher Sykes, *Evelyn Waugh, A Biography*, Harmondsworth 1977.

66. Bevis Hillier, *Young Betjeman*, London 1989.

67. Archie Harradine, 'The Story of the Players' Theatre' in *Late Joys*, London 1943. Originally the brain-child of Peter Ridgeway and Regency in inspiration, an attempt to recapture the flavour of the 1830s supper rooms, the Players' Theatre evolved into a pastiche of late Victorian music hall performance.

68. Glyn Daniel, *A Hundred and Fifty Years of British Archeology*, London 1975, pp. 30–31; John Michel, *Megalithomania: Artists, Antiquarians and Archaeologists at the Old Stone Monuments*, London 1983.

69. Charles Alfred Stothard, *The Monumental Effigies of Great Britain*, London 1811–33. Thomas Stothard, Charles Alfred's father, was a leading painter of medieval subjects and was instrumental in making the Bayeux tapestry known in this country.

70. For an excellent brief discussion of the Victorian turn to the Elizabethan, Alun Howkins, 'The Discovery of Rural England', in Robert Colls and Philip Dodd, eds., *Englishness, Politics and Culture, 1880–1920*, London 1986, pp. 70–71; Georgina Boyes, *The Imagined Village: Culture, Ideology and the English Folk Revival*, Manchester 1993, pp. 34–5, 39,

70–71, for later stages in the Elizabethan revival. For its influence on architecture, Mark Girouard, *The Victorian Country House*, Oxford 1971, pp. 33–5, 55, 65. For typography, Cyril Baxter, 'Andrew Tuer and the Leadenhall Press', *Print in Britain*, XI/8, December 1963, pp. 31–2; on the reinvention of old English types, Talbot Baines Reed, *A History of Old English Letter Foundries*, London 1952, p. 249. The St Bride's Institute has some examples of 'Ye Olde Englishe Fayre' events, staged for charitable purposes in the 1880s, and making a feature of his English fonts. The Holbein Society's facsimile reprints (the first was published in 1876) also helped to propagate the charms of Tudor type.

71. Hilary Guise, *Great Victorian Engravings, A Collector's Guide*, London 1980, p. 8.

72. For 'archaeological' revivals of Shakespeare in the 1840s and 1850s, Michael Booth, *Victorian Spectacular Theatre, 1850–1910*, London 1982, pp. 34–5, 47–59; J.W. Cole, *The Life and Theatrical Times of Charles Kean*, London 1859.

73. For Gilbert, Forest Reid, *Illustrators of the 1860s*, New York 1975, pp. 20–23; Edward Hodnett, *Five Centuries of English Book Illustration*, Aldershot 1988, pp. 123–5; John Jackson, *A Treatise on Wood Engraving*, London 1861, p. 561.

74. Michael Twyman, *Lithographers, 1800–1850*, Oxford 1970, pp. 213–17.

75. W.J. Thoms, 'Gossip of an Old Bookworm', *Nineteenth Century*, 1881 for autobiographical notes by the founder of *Notes and Queries* (he was also the man who coined the term 'folk-lore').

76. Charles Roach Smith, *Catalogue of the Museum of London Antiquities*, London 1854; *Illustrations of Roman London*, London 1859; *Collectanea Antiqua*, 7 vols., 1848–1880. Smith's *Retrospections* combine memoirs of his forays and friendships with notes on Roman fragments. Brian Hobley, 'Charles Roach Smith (1807–1890): Pioneering Archaeologist' in *The London Archaeologist*, vol. XIII, no. 22, 1975, pp. 328–33. There is brief reference to Roach Smith in Philippa Levine's *The Amateur and the Professional*.

77. See Victor Ambrus's brilliant illustrations to R.J. Unstead, *The Story of Britain: Before the Norman Conquest*, London 1971.

78. Stuart Piggott, *Ruins in a Landscape: Essays in Antiquarianism*, Edinburgh 1976, pp. 66–7. Piggott suggests that the drawings were closely related to contemporary drawings of native Americans. John White, who accompanied Sir Walter Raleigh on his 1585 Virginia expedition, not only drew native Americans, but a series of ancient Britons, Picts and 'Neighbours unto the Picts', whose characteristics were profoundly influenced by the New World peoples he had seen and drawn. Ibid., p. 67.

79. On the nineteenth-century rediscovery of the Knights Templar, James Stevens Curl, *The Art and Architecture of Freemasonry*, London 1992.

80. Benedict Read, *Victorian Sculpture*, London 1983, pp. 13, 59, 31–4. For a contemporary review of Maruchetts's 'Richard Coeur de Lion', *The Times*, 15 January 1862.

81. John Jackson, *A Treatise on Wood Engraving*, London 1861, p. 583.

82. Marshall's 'Grand Historical Peristrephic Panorama' in Spring Gardens, Lambeth, was an early form of this particular spectacle, using moving pictures and a light show to re-enact the different stages of the Battle of Trafalgar, and following this up with a series of views of the Battle of Waterloo, Horace Wellbeloved, *London Lions for Country Cousins . . . A Display of Metropolitan Improvements*, London 1826, pp. 57–8. For a magnificent history of the dioramas, cosmoramas and pyrotechnic spectacles on offer in early Victorian times, R.D. Altick, *The Shows of London*, Cambridge, Mass. 1978.

83. Miri Rubin, *Corpus Christi: The Eucharist in Late Medieval Culture*, Cambridge 1991.

84. Glynne Wickham, *Early English Stages*, vol. 1, London 1959, is a superb account – the subsequent two volumes of the work take the story of the processional stage to the Bankside theatre of Shakespeare's London and beyond. See also Richard Southern, *The Seven Ages of Theatre*, London 1962.

85. Frederick W. Fairholt *Gog and Magog, The Giants in Guildhall, Their Real and Legendary History*, London 1859.

86. R.B. Dobson and J. Taylor, *Rymes of Robin Hood: an Introduction to the English Outlaw*, London 1976, pp. 39–42, 147, 209, 223–36.

87. O.W. Furley, 'The Pope-Burning Processions of the late 17th Century', *History* 45, 1959, pp. 16–23. See Roger Tilley, *Playing Cards*, London 1967, pp. 103–5 for 'No Popery' playing cards in 1678–1681.

88. *The Autobiography of Edward Gibbon.*

89. Philippe Ariès, *Centuries of Childhood*, London 1962, pp. 52–3, 66 ff.

90. Philippe Ariès, *The Hour of Our Death*, Harmondsworth 1981.

91. Ruth Richardson, in conversation with the writer, April 1994.

92. As Helgerson points out, whereas Elizabethan 'histories' were a story of kings and their line of descent, the chorographers offered an England of counties, towns, villages and even wards. Richard Helgerson, *Forms of Nationhood: the Elizabethan Writing of England*, Chicago 1992, pp. 132–3.

93. *Life and Times of Anthony Wood*, vol. I, p. 209, quoted in T.D. Kendrick, *British Antiquity*, London 1950, p. 167.

94. M.W. Barley, *A Guide to British Topographical Collections*, British Council for Archaeology, London 1974.

95. Stuart Piggott, *William Stukeley, an Eighteenth Century Antiquarian*, Oxford 1950, p. 8; Frank V. Emery, *Edward Lhuyd FRS, 1660–1709*, Cardiff 1971 for a fuller account.

96. David Mellor, Gill Saunders and Patrick Wright, *Recording Britain, A Pictorial Domesday of Pre-War Britain*, Victoria and Albert Museum 1990.

97. David C. Douglas, *English Scholars*, London 1939, pp. 36–7.

98. J.L. Nevinson, 'Antiquarian', *Museums Journal*, vol. 59, no. 2, May 1959, p. 34.

99. Michael Twyman, *Printing, 1770–1970*, London 1970, p. 88; *Lithography, 1800–1850*, Oxford 1970, pp. 29–32, 169–74.

100. See 'Resurrectionism' in this volume for this episode.

101. David Gentleman, *A Cross for Queen Eleanor*, London 1979, is his interesting justification, by reference to medieval sources, of the Charing Cross mural.

102. David Gentleman, *A Special Relationship*, London 1987, for this illustrator's quite fierce radicalism.

103. John Clare, *The Shepherd's Calendar*, ed. Eric Robinson and Geoffrey Summerfield, with wood engravings by David Gentleman, Oxford 1964.

104. Lady Peck, *A Little Learning*, p. 22; Eleanor Farjeon, *A Nursery in the Nineties*, Oxford 1960, p. 263 for autobiographical reference to being taught by these cards. Thomas Arnold, in his scheme for historical study, had favoured for young children, 'a series of lessons as pictures or "prints" of scenes from universal history portraying remarkable events in striking fashion. Their main object is to give vivid centres of association around which to group the stories', Thomas Arnold, 'Rugby School – Use of the "Classics"', in *Miscellaneous Works*, London 1845. Dean Stanley, in his *Life of Dr Arnold* (chapter 3, p. 100) tells us that 'In examining children in the lower forms he would sometimes take them on his knee and go through picture-books of the Bible or English history, covering the text of the narrative with his hand, and making them explain to him the subject of the several prints'.

105. Jigsaw puzzles made a feature of chronological tables of English history, Linda Hannas, *The English Jigsaw Puzzle, 1760–1890*, London 1972, plates 6, 17, 25; pp. 23–4, 28–32. The book has an inventory of historical jigsaws on pp. 93–7; an introduction which links them to the 1740s rise of children's publishing; and some fascinating pages on the way the writer tracked her quarry.

106. See Margaret Spufford, *Small Books and Pleasant Histories: Popular Fiction and its Readership in Seventeenth Century England*, Cambridge 1981 for a fine history. John Ashton, *Chapbooks of the Eighteenth Century*, has recently been reprinted facsimile by that excellent second-hand bookshop, Skoob's of Sicilian Avenue.

107. Samuel Bamford, *Early Days*, London 1849, pp. 90–91.

108. Shirley Ann Brown, *The Bayeux Tapestry, History and Bibliography*, Woodbridge 1988, pp. 11–12. Cf. also David M. Wilson, *The Bayeux Tapestry*, London 1985.

109. Mark Girouard, *The Return to Camelot, Chivalry and the English Gentleman*, London 1981.

110. Thomas Okey, *A Basketful of Memories*, London 1930, pp. 17–18. 'Granny had a lot of books very old and worn. One was *Foxe's Book of Martyrs* with all the esses printed like effs and many pictures of poor men and women being tortured'; *Shop Boy*, p. 24. The grandmother in question kept a small grocer's shop in Morriston, near Swansea.

111. Edward Hodnett, *Five Centuries of English Book Illustration*, Aldershot 1988, p. 31.

In an extensive literature reference might be made to J.F. Mozley, *John Foxe and His Book*, London 1940; William Haller, *Foxe's Book of Martyrs and the Elect Nation*, London 1963. E.R. Norman, *Anti-Catholicism in Victorian England*, London 1968, p. 13, points out that the 1875 edition of Foxe included a print depicting the St Bartholomew's Day Massacre which took place after the original edition. Warren J. Wooden, 'John Foxe's Book of Martyrs and the Child Reader' in *Children's Books of the English Renaissance*, Kentucky 1986, pp. 73–87. I am grateful to Carolyn Steedman for this reference.

112. Frank Hampson, the creator of *The Eagle*'s Dan Dare, brought his career to a climax with a strip cartoon life of Jesus Christ. In his autobiography, *Before I Die Again*, London 1992. Chad Varah, who went on to be the founder of the Samaritans, has little to say about his authorial role in the *Eagle* back-cover histories. In a more satiric vein, and enjoying a cult following in the Fourth and Fifth forms, is *Asterix* which, brilliantly translated from the French and with a heady mix of the topical, the antiquarian and a theatre of the absurd, has made Roman Gaul – and a tiny unoccupied part of it – a kind of paradigm for the emancipatory movements of today. (The footnotes at the back keep Asterix within the ambit of education; R. Goscinny and A. Uderzo, *French with Asterix: The Complete Guide*, London 1993, recycles it for schools).

113. Frances A. Yates, *The Art of Memory*, Harmondsworth 1978, pp. 124–7, 129–30.

114. Ibid., pp. 74–6.

115. Ibid., pp. 210–12, 217–18, 225–6.

116. M.T. Clanchy, *From Memory to Written Record, England 1066–1507*, First edn., London 1979, p. 229.

117. Ibid., p. 230.

118. Sylvia Thrupp, *The Merchant Class of Medieval London*, Michigan 1962, pp. 252–3.

119. George Henderson, *Early Medieval*, Harmondsworth 1977, pp. 155–7.

120. Richard Vaughan, *Matthew Paris*, Cambridge 1958, p. 211.

121. George Henderson, *Gothic*, Harmondsworth 1978, p. 22.

122. 'The idea of archaeology as fundamentally connected with artistic values was widely held', writes Philippa Levine in her interesting account of some of its nineteenth-century practitioners. 'Birch rounded off his descriptions by asserting that the value of archaeology was that it "aids in the formation and cultivation of public taste" ... John Marsden on his appointment to England's first Chair of archaeology at Cambridge, talked of "the close connection between the antiquaries and the poet".' Philippa Levine, *The Amateur and the Professional*, p. 90.

123. Glyn Daniel, *A Hundred and Fifty Years of Archaeology*, London 1950, p. 31.

124. Anastatic printing, a facsimile process invented in the 1840s, was widely used in antiquarian publication, as for example in illustrations of Old English churches. Geoffrey Wakeman, *Victorian Book Illustration*, Newton Abbot 1973, pp. 51–5.

125. Archives of St John the Baptist Church, Bridgwater, cuttings book of the Rev. C. Bazell, 1998–90, has the Town Hall crowded for a series of such lectures. I am grateful to Rev. C. Pidoux for exhuming this and other records from the parish chest.

126. Hall's *Book of British Ballads*, London 1842, contained upwards of four hundred wood engravings 'and was the first work of any consequence that presented a combination of the best artists of the time'. John Jackson, *A Treatise on Wood Engraving*, London 1861, p. 564. Hall, a very successful literary impresario, is said to have been the original of *Martin Chuzzlewitt*'s Mr Pecksniff.

127. William Hone, *The Every-Day Book and Table Book: or Everlasting Calendar of Popular Amusements*, 3 vols, London 1839.

128. Charles Roach Smith, *Catalogue of the Museum of London Antiquities*, London 1854; *Illustrations of Roman London*, London 1859; *Collectanea Antiqua: Etchings and Notices of Ancient Remains, Illustrative of the Habits, Customs and History of Past Ages*, 7 vols, London, 1848–1880.

129. Wright was an admirer and friend of George Cruikshank. One of his many compilations was *A History of Caricature and Grotesque in Literature and Art*, London 1875. For an interesting but too brief profile of Wright, Richard M. Dorson, *The British Folklorists, A History*, London 1968, pp. 61–6.

130. Thomas Wright, *Wanderings of an Antiquary*, London 1856, pp. 186–7.

131. Thomas Wright, *The History of Ireland from the Earliest Period . . . to the Present Time*, London 1854, 3 vols.

132. Thomas Wright, *A History of Domestic Manners and Sentiments in England during the Middle Ages*, London 1862.

133. R.D. Bramwell, *Elementary School Work, 1900–1925*, Durham 1961, quoting the Board of Education's *Suggestions for the Considerations of Teachers*, London 1918.

134. 'The Exeter Exhibition of Handwork Illustrative of History', *History*, 7, 1923–4; L. Logie, *Self-Expression in a Junior School*, London 1928, pp. 57–9.

135. C.S. and C.S. Orwin, *The Open Fields*, Oxford 1938.

136. Michael Crichton, *Jurassic Park*, London 1991.

PART I

Retrochic

Retrofitting

I The Aesthetics of Light and Space

Forty years ago, when 'Do-It-Yourself' first caught on as a national enthusiasm, modernization and home improvement were interchangeable terms, just as 'ugly' was commonly coupled with the old-fashioned, and 'Victorian' with the out-of-date. The ruling ideology of the day was forward-looking and progressive, the ruling aesthetic one of light and space. Newness was regarded as a good in itself, a guarantee of things that were practical and worked. Modern heating was efficient ('In ... the open fire ... only about 17 per cent of the heat finds its way into the room; the rest goes up the chimney'[1]); modern plumbing, as house-hunters were advised, 'sound'. The Victorian mansion, though it might be converted into maisonettes or flats was, left to itself, large, draughty and wasteful of space – 'crumbling, decaying and totally uneconomic'[2] was the verdict on those cleared away at Roehampton when the LCC put up its much-admired 'point-blocks'. The by-law terraced street, with its poky houses and absence of light and space, was ripe for demolition. Like the 'Dickensian' tenements and the basement dwelling, it was thought of as a breeding-ground for TB.

In the domestic interior, new materials – man-made fibres especially – were routinely preferred to old. 'Scientifically up-to-date' carpets – in the words of the *News of the World* 'Better Homes' book – had rubberized backings to make them moth- and damp-resistant.[3] Plastic lavatory seats were more hygienic than wooden ones, which collected germs. Traditional upholstery, 'with its daily accumulations of dust',[4] was much less serviceable for soft furnishings than Pirelli webbing, fibreglass covering and latex foam rubber – 'light', 'hygienic' and 'almost everlastingly resilient'.[5] Latex foam was also recommended as a hygienic filling for children's toys[6] and as an alternative to the interior-sprung mattress ('Latex foam mattresses ... do not gather fluff or dust, and can be washed if necessary'[7]). Candlewick bedspreads were recommended for the same reason: 'easy washing, no ironing, no trouble'.[8]

For the handyman (Do-It-Yourself, then, was still regarded as a masculine province) home improvement was largely a matter of making surfaces seamless. Doors were hardboarded to cover up dust-collecting panels and give them a streamlined look. Dados and picture-rails were taken down so that the walls could be painted in one colour: 'the unbroken surface ... will make your room seem much larger'.[9] Bathroom pipes were boxed in as unsightly and the bath itself, if the household budget ran to it, replaced by modern 'non-chippable and rust-proof' fibreglass, recommended on the grounds of both hygiene and looks. 'The gleaming, streamlined bathroom is a modern invention ... a fine spick-and-span affair.... Bathrooms in old houses can look incredibly dreary.'[10] Fireplaces were removed as dust-traps and replaced by convectors or radiators. The cast iron, as *Do It Yourself* explained to readers in October 1958, could be cracked away with a club hammer:

> Before bringing in any materials, remove the unwanted cast iron surround. First take away all parts that are normally removable, then use the club hammer to crack the cast iron plate that fits behind the overmantel. Although the thin plate usually breaks fairly easily with a few hard sharp blows with the hammer take care ... Many of these plates are composite castings, having ... ornamental mouldings attached ... by hidden nuts and bolts ... These mouldings can be extremely dangerous when struck with the hammer, as they are apt to fly in any direction, and can cause serious injury. I am very cautious to crack these off carefully first, and then attack the main thin plate.[11]

In the kitchen – regarded, in those days, as a menial workplace, and occupying much less space than it does in houses and flats today – the great object of improvement was 'labour saving'. The *News of the World* 'Better Homes' manual advised 'gradual modernization'.[12] The old-fashioned sink could be replaced by a stainless steel unit. The cupboards could be fitted with 'flush' doors. Above all there should be a washable and continuous working surface. Formica – 'the surface with a smile' – was vigorously promoted in this way, an easy-to-fit domestic improvement which could transform the housewife's lot: 'More leisure, more colour, less work are yours from the day "FORMICA" Laminated Plastic comes into your kitchen. You can do a busy morning's cooking on a "FORMICA"-topped table – and wipe away every trace, in seconds. The satin-smooth surface thrives on hard work and is impervious to stains or marks.'[13]

Windows, too, ideally were seamless. Glazing bars were dispensed with to produce a deadpan, streamlined surface which was easily cleanable and maximized the light. 'The outside coming in' was one of the architectural ideals of the period. One frequent device was the horizontally pivoted window, framed in metal; another, sliding sheets of glass which could be pushed back into a cavity. 'The south wall of the living

This wash-off mark distinguishes all FORMICA surfaces

FORMICA
LAMINATED PLASTIC
DE LA RUE

FORMICA for me!

When you discover how easy it is to cover up old-fashioned wooden surfaces with FORMICA laminated plastic, you'll get ambitious. It brings such a wonderful feeling of light and cleanliness into your home. FORMICA laminates won't stain, chip or crack; they resist heat up to 310°F and wipe clean in a flash; stay new and fresh for years.

Why not start on the kitchen table? In less than an hour, with the help of De La Rue adhesive, you'll have a spic-and-span FORMICA-topped table, a joy to look at, to eat off and work on. A 3 ft. x 2 ft. table need not cost you more than 35/-. You can buy 1/16″ panels in any of the thirteen popular patterns at 5/- a sq. ft. or, cut to size, at 5/9 a sq. ft.

Write for the free 'Do it Yourself' leaflets to Thomas De La Rue & Co Ltd (Plastics Division) Dept 39C, 84/86 Regent Street, London W1

FORMICA *is the registered name for the laminated plastic made by Thomas De La Rue & Co Ltd* room is ... of glass', runs an admiring report in *The Country Life Book of Houses* of 1963, 'the upper part comprising three frameless sheets of glass which slide very sweetly on a brass track.'[14] When the replacement window boom began in the early 1960s, it followed a similar pattern. Sash windows were dispensed with, on account of the frequency with which they needed to be repainted and the likelihood that the wood would rot. Metal-framed windows, in steel or aluminium, were much in vogue for the kitchen. Double-glazing units came in seamless sheets of glass; 'picture windows' in giant panels.

One of the delights of the handyman of this period was making old furniture look new. Tables could be made to look 'contemporary' by taking off their legs and substituting screw-on splays;[15] the shabby old dresser could be smartened up with a colourful coat of Robbialac – 'the quick-drying easy-to-use finish which gives a diamond-hard gleaming surface'[16] and the addition of bright plastic handles to the drawers. A little modernizing of this kind could transform the old-fashioned bathroom: 'A new bath or basin may be too costly for the family budget, but modern fittings, particularly chromium taps, can save a great deal of the housewife's time and add to the general appearance of the bathroom. Few women have time nowadays to polish brass taps every day.'[17] Under influences like this, children's rooms of the period were given a sunshine look. 'Old Furniture Made Smart' is the heading of an article in the 'Fatherhood' section of *Parents* in April 1955:

> An increasingly popular home handicraft is the use of gaily coloured plastic veneers for renovating and transforming what is practically junk furniture into useful and attractive fittings. For example, this old cupboard, shown opposite, was bought for a few shillings at a sale, and easily converted into a nice looking toy cupboard capable of withstanding all the hard wear it is likely to meet in the nursery. The doors and sides were surfaced with panels of plastics in a bird's eye maple reproduction, while the top, shelves and base were covered with blue stardust patterned plastics.[18]

The early gentrifiers taking up residence (rather nervously) in run-down Victorian terraces, and the architects and developers converting multi-occupied rooming-houses into self-contained flats, acted in a similar spirit when doing up old properties to give them a contemporary look. Interiors were systematically gutted to remove every trace of the past. In large houses suspended ceilings covered up cornices and mouldings; in smaller ones partition walls were removed to give rooms a see-through look. Floors were sanded and sealed to give them a modern feeling, 'spare yet gay'. 'Off-white' here served as the equivalent of the bright colours of the working-class interior, cantilevered shelves as the space-savers. Curtains were dispensed with, in defiance of the English laws of propriety, allowing the light to stream in by day and at night transforming dining-rooms into stage-sets. Furniture was minimalist – futurist pieces, in glass or metal, being regarded as the perfect foil to older surroundings. Lighting was futurist too – fluorescent tubes in the kitchen[19] and on the desk a swivel-joint anglepoise lamp with perforated metal reflectors.[20] Taps, handles and coat hooks, knives and forks and crockery were all ideally rimless, 'designed for easy handling and cleaning, with no ridges to collect soap and dirt'.[21] If there was an extension at the back of the house – as was often the case when houses in erstwhile industrial terraces were transformed into bijou residences – it might be finished off with floor-to-ceiling glass walls in the form of 'patio' sliding doors.

In the property columns of the newspapers, as in the *House and Garden* interior, modernization, where period properties were concerned, was treated as an absolute good. Roy Brooks, the fashionable left-wing estate agent, whose advertisements in the *Sunday Times* and the *Observer* – Jimmy Porter's 'posh Sundays' – were a delight of the cognoscenti, and who has some claim to being a pioneer of gentrification in the scruffier parts of London, treated new gadgetry as a selling-point where period property was at stake – even a Tudor farmhouse was recommended on account of its 'luxury tiled bathrooms' and its 'super kitchen' with 'double sink unit'. Here are some representative examples of his style.

> CHELSEA. Reconstructed under the eagle eye of a capable surveyor, this small Period house has a really decent Drawing rm, 2 rms thrown into one.... 4 proper bedrms, a mod lux bathrm, & good sized lab-sav kit.

> LADY OF TITLE ... must sacrifice one of the loveliest of modernised PERIOD HOUSES in CHELSEA'S BEST GDN SQ ... 4 perfect bedrms, 2 mod bathrms, mod lab-sav kit, super stainless steel sink unit, cks, & frig.

> *L*SD**R M*LN* of top tely, 'To-Night' ... outgrown KENSINGTON SMALL NEW (1953) HOUSE ... 3 b'rms, lovely large 24ft. drawing rm ... mod b & k. Superb Formica working surface and serving hatch.[22]

One moment to pause on, in any archaeology of changing attitudes to the past, would be the 1951 Festival of Britain. Taking its occasion from the centenary of the Great Exhibition of 1851, it was determinedly modernist in bias, substituting, for the moth-eaten and the traditional, vistas of progressive advance: 'a great looking forward after years of rationing and greyness'. The past was present only in the form of anachronism. The model of Stephenson's Rocket which graced the Dome of Discovery was a primitive original of more streamlined successors; the Emmett Railway in the Battersea Pleasure Park, with its whimsical title ('The Far Tottering and Oyster Creek Railway') was a phantasmagoria of backwardness, showing that the British had a sense of humour; old-time music-hall, one of the Festival's evening entertainments, showed that they could let their hair down and engage in 'knees-up' frolics. The things that one was expected to admire were the novelties – the bright new towns of the future, represented by the Lansbury estate; the products of industrial design, proudly displayed on the trade stands; the labour-saving kitchen units; the clean lines of 'functional' architecture; the gay colours of 'contemporary' style. 'The Homes and Gardens' pavilion, a major influence on design, was a showcase for the new; as visitors were informed as they entered, it took the past 'as read'.[23]

The themes of the festival were amplified by the 'Do-It-Yourself' movement of the 1950s. They were vigorously promoted by the Council of Industrial Design with passionate moderns at its head – first Gordon Russell and then Paul Reilly. They were taken up by go-ahead manufacturers such as Hille, and embraced by avant-garde designers. Enthusiasm for the modern was to a remarkable degree cross-class. Up-market design magazines such as *House and Garden* embraced it as enthusiastically as those like the *News of the World* or Odhams Press whose guides were directed at working-class readers. Most striking of all – in the light of its later contributions to conservationism and, as critics complain, the revival of aristocratic fantasy – was the endorsement of *Country Life*, the taste leader of the gentrifiers. Its 1963 *Book of Houses for Today* has not a single period conversion or period property but is given over entirely to a celebration of the flexible, the transparent and the new. In a doctor's house in the Cotswolds 'everything is ... uncompromisingly contemporary' and even the Cotswold stone is synthetic.[24] A country house in Yorkshire – built on the site of a demolished farmhouse – is open-plan and see-through, 'so much more comfortable, convenient and easy and economical to run than the Edwardian house it replaces as the family home'.[25] A solar house in Rickmansworth is dedicated to refracting natural heat.[26] An architect's house in Surrey is 'the last word' in glass walls: 'Mr Lovejoy decided that the living room should have two glass walls, opposite each other, making this part of the house as transparent as an aquarium.'[27]

The appetite for modernization – with its opposition between the old and dirty and the new and clean, and its enthusiasm for the labour-saving or space-saving device – was to be found, during the 1950s, in every department of national life, and was indeed a mainspring of popular consumerism. Washing powders, intensely competitive products, and pioneers of the TV commercial, advertised themselves as soapless detergents, substituting chemicals for the greasiness of old soap. There was a real excitement about the appearance of new synthetics – Pyrex

unbreakable ovenware, Bri-Nylon fitted sheets ('wrapped in protective polythene'), Vynair ('the fabric that breathes'). The shirt manufacturers, making a corner in Terylene, manufactured drip-dry non-iron shirts, which took the labour out of washing day. Carpets manufactured in tufted nylon blossomed out in multi-coloured geometrics and brought lightness and brightness into the home.

The modernizing aesthetic, embraced wholeheartedly by progressives in Britain as in the United States and Western Europe, and an offshoot of the social architecture and radical aesthetic of Bauhaus, was also – it was perhaps its Achilles' heel – masculine in its biases, and it may not be an accident that it flourished in a decade which may now retrospectively be seen as the Indian summer of the working man: a time when overtime earnings and new domestic opportunities for the handyman seemed to be advancing hand-in-hand. Architects praised each other for their 'bold, uncompromising lines', their 'courageous' minimalism, the 'crisp elegance' and 'clean-cut' 'orderly' resolution of space problems, their ruthlessness in dispensing with clutter; and it may not be an accident that, as visitors to late 1950s and early 1960s housing developments will know (or those who have lived in the ship-like conversions of the time) one of their most distinctive achievements was the near-abolition of the kitchen.[28]

'Pretty' was, in the language of the design writers of the time, an almost pejorative term; the 'decorative', whenever it raised its head, a corruption of taste. Thus one finds Mary Gilliatt in search of the quintessence of English design, praising the young Terence Conran's Suffolk residence for being 'wholesomely rural without a shadow of the usual ubiquitous old world cottage charm';[29] while at Jaynes Court, Bisley, Glos., 'a remarkably lyrical old stone house' she praises the lack of curtains 'so that there is no encroachment of softness', 'the orderly row of spotlights trained on the paintings', the 'deliberately brutal shape' of the pewter-coloured steel chairs 'designed by Roy Wilson'.[30]

The obverse of this enthusiasm for the new was that almost anything old was suspect and ripe for development. 'Only comprehensive reconstruction to a new design will do', wrote Geoffrey Moorhouse in *The Other England*, a Penguin Special of 1964, 'When the question is asked of the manufacturing towns of the North and the Midlands, few people would suggest that it would be anything but beneficial to raze potentially everything and start all over again, as they are virtually doing with great patience and foresight in Sheffield.'[31]

Country houses, which have since the 1960s been vigorously promoted as the quintessence of Englishness and treasure-houses of the nation's art, were regarded in the 1950s as, if anything, even more moribund than the decaying Victorian mansions of the 'twilight' zones. In British films of the period they appear – like Satis House in *Great Expectations* – as sepulchres of decay, while in real life they seemed – as in Evelyn Waugh's *Brideshead* – to be doomed to takeover by the state. Here is how W.G. Hoskins described them in his 1955 book, *The Making of the English Landscape*:

> The country houses decay and fall: hardly a week passes when one does not see the auctioneer's notice of the impending sale and dissolution of some big estate. The house is seized by the demolition contractors, its park invaded and churned up by the tractors and trailers of the timber merchant. Down comes the house; down come the tall trees, naked and gashed lies the once beautiful park. Or if it stands near a town, the political planners swarm into the house, turn it into a rabbit-warren of black-hatted officers of This and That, and the park becomes a site for some 'overspill' – a word as beastly as the thing it describes. We may indeed find the great house still standing tidily in a timbered park: but it is occupied by what villagers describe detachedly as 'the

atom men', something remote from the rest of us, though not remote in the sense they themselves like to think. And if the planners are really fortunate, they fill the house with their paper and their black hats, and open-cast mining of coal or iron ore simultaneously finishes off the park. They can sit at their big desks and contemplate with an exquisite joy how everything is now being put to a good use. Demos and Science are the joint emperors.[32]

II Neo-vernacular

If the leading aesthetic of the 1950s and 1960s was one of light and space and its decorative motifs hard-edged – 'clean-cut' concrete slabs, 'stark' lines, 'flush' walls with right-angled corners, 'bold' colours, geometric patterns – that of the 1970s and 1980s was one of warmth, softness and enclosure; a feminine rather than a masculine style. Where the first gave a privileged place to seamless surfaces, sliding doors, window walling and open-plan layouts, the second took as its leading idiom what Oscar Newman, in an influential tract, called 'defensible space'.[33] Where the first made a virtue of plainness, and prided itself, moralistically, on 'pure' white, 'clear' glass, 'honest' design, the second had a distinct hankering for dreamscapes, discovering decorative possibilities in the most unpromising settings, aestheticizing the most humdrum objects of everyday life and beautifying kitchens and bathrooms.

Designers, in retreat from international style, adopted an altogether more English palette, exchanging Mediterranean and modernist primaries – the hard, bright colours of the 'contemporary look' – for more rustic shades, reminiscent of the old-fashioned vegetable dyes. Homes took on a mellow look, as stripped pine made its way from the floorboards via the kitchen dresser to the dining-room table, and crept upstairs to invade the bedrooms. Shopfitters, cultivating a clubland or country-house look for the new up-market boutiques, were no less enamoured of 'rich', 'dark' mahogany, praised for its 'warmth', 'dignity' and 'seasoned' character. (Sheila Pickles, the founder of Penhaligon's, the bogus-traditional perfumier, and something of a pioneer in these matters, furnished her premises with old chemists' cabinets.)

Lighting softened and became more intimate, exchanging the high-pressure glare of the mercury lamp and the naked transparency of the fluorescent strip for an apricot or amber glow – the lighting equivalent of the 'honeyed look' of pine floors and furniture. Neon suffered an almost complete eclipse, banished from the kitchen in favour of noiseless, recessed lights at about the same time as it was abandoned by the signwriters and disappeared from shop and advertising displays. Metallic reflectors, such as those used in the anglepoise lamp, also lost favour. In the sitting room centre lights gave way to floor and table lamps. In the bedroom lamps, instead of being functional, took to wearing period dress – the mob cap being a great favourite with the mail-order catalogues.

The revival of candles, though a minority enthusiasm or fad, deserves mention in this context. Emanating, it may be (the aetiology deserves investigation), among simple-lifers and counter-cultural craftspeople, they were by the late 1970s a fast-selling item as presents in the gift shops – chunky, novelty or 'advent' candles, latterly with the addition of candle-making kits for children and Wee Willie Winkie candleholders.[34] Candles were by the 1980s *de rigueur* at the dinner parties of the rich. Restaurateurs adopted them to turn each table into a snug, tailor-made, or purpose-built, for romantic coupledom; while in newly restored 'period' property, where candle-sconces were installed in the dining room and hallways, they also entered the repertoire of the retrofitter's arts.

In furnishing fabrics, textures went from hard to soft, and patterns from the sharp, clear lines of modernism to the decorative borders and floral motifs of more traditional design. Fibreglass furniture coverings 'hard to the touch' gave way to printed cottons and revived 'archive' chintz. William Morris and, after she began producing them,[35] Laura Ashley wallpapers reflected the colours of 'Victorian' chairs and sofas. Curtains, which in the modernist interiors of the 1950s and 1960s had been discarded in favour of bare picture windows, or metal-slatted blinds, staged a spectacular comeback, first in the form of the Victorian swag, later – the 'country house look', pioneered by John Fowler at National Trust properties and popularized by *World of Interiors* – in the festoon or 'knicker' blind, an adaptation of eighteenth-century costume which framed windows in the manner of a ballgown.

Clean-cut lines also beat a retreat in landscaping and garden design, where arched trellises and trailing plants were as representative an enthusiasm as concrete flower-beds had been in the 1960s.[36] Trees, which in the 1950s and 1960s had been ruthlessly pollarded, for fear that they would grow into light-traps,[37] were now, on the contrary, positively encouraged to show off their foliage. Shrubs, which in the early 1960s were still being routinely cleared away as 'unsightly', were now encour-aged into rampant growth – quick-growing Russian vine and virginia creeper being especially favoured, on that account, in new-build deve-lopments.

Where the style of the 1950s and the 1960s was built out of plastics, using man-made, chemically-based fibres for clothes, fabrics and furnish-ings, the style leaders of the 1970s made a fetish of the 'natural', the 'organic' and the home-grown; indeed to follow the range of hand-made

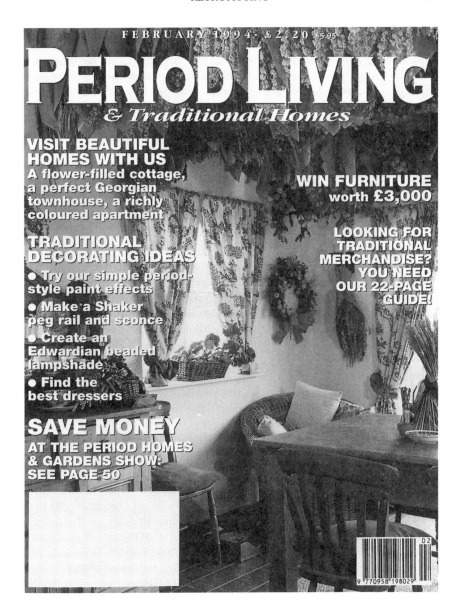

goods advertised in the Sunday colour supplements, on offer at the gift shops and galleries, or displayed at the home furnishers, one might have imagined that the economy had reverted to pre-industrial times. Anita Roddick at the Body Shop, championing 'environmentally sound' products and making war on the cosmetics industry, built a multinational fortune out of 'traditional natural substances', offering henna as a herbal alternative to peroxide, herb-pillows as sleeping aids, and turning such exotica as jojoba, neroli ('distilled from the blossoms of bitter oranges') and sweet almond oil into toners, moisturizers and shampoos.[38] Laura Ashley, using cotton as a fashion fabric – 'fine natural cotton' 'freshly starched'[39] – was no less insistent on using nothing that was not one hundred per cent natural fibre. 'No mixes. No compromises', she told her shop managers, when they pleaded for just the occasional stiffening of synthetics.[40]

'Back to Nature' – the pastoral turn of the late 1960s and 1970s – also had its echo in the built environment, where the country look established itself at the very heart of the urban dream. New techniques, such as the marketing of container-grown shrubs, allowed gardens in newly renovated industrial terraces to take on an established look, while hanging baskets in the front doorway, festooned with trailing lobelia, allowed erstwhile slums to take on an Arcadian air and to become, in the property advertisements, 'artisans' cottages'. 'Charming little jungles of greenery'[41] sprouted from the area steps of grey eighteenth-century houses, while wall-to-wall foliage transformed backs into outdoor sitting rooms. The advent of central heating allowed for a massive revival of Victorian houseplants and 'Victorian style' conservatories. The atria of new office buildings doubled as nursery grounds or even – following the example of Coutts Bank in the Strand – miniature botanical gardens. Newly renovated warehouses sported penthouse or roof terraces. Pubs turned their yards into garden rooms. In the suburbs ivy, virginia creeper and wisteria, banished as Victorian horrors in the great streamlining of the 1950s and 1960s, wound their way around the windows of the inter-war semi; back gardens, formerly the province of the lawnmower and the paviour, blossomed out in arbours; while mature trees and well-established shrubs were a feature of those village-like clusters which the quantity housebuilders adopted, in the 1970s, as an alternative to the new estate. It was indicative of the strength of all this that in the urban regeneration schemes of the 1980s, the 'greening' of the city should have been the ideal object of job-creation schemes, and Garden Festivals (the first was held in 1984) one of the grand remedies for urban blight.

A rejection of synthetics, and a return to traditional, or supposedly traditional, materials – 'mellow' brickwork, 'solid' wood, 'natural' stone – was no less well advertised in building and construction work than it was in commodity marketing and design. Buildings, according to the new orthodoxy, were to be 'human' in scale rather than, like the tower blocks of the 1960s, 'soulless'. They should be visually interesting rather than repetitive and monotonous. According to a frequent conceit they should aim to look not 'contemporary' but timeless. The pioneers here were those local authority architects – the last generation of them, it seems – who made the 1970s an Indian summer of council housing. In flight from the machine aesthetic – 'hygienic, puritan styles, stripped of ornament and ... reference to the past'[42] – they turned back to that homespun and vernacular style which Philip Webb at the Red House, Norman Shaw at Bedford Park, and Raymond Unwin at Letchworth and Hampstead Garden Suburb, had established as 'old English'. They championed the use of brick as 'warm', 'friendly' and, by comparison with concrete, durable. As Sir Andrew Derbyshire wrote of Hillingdon Town Hall (1977) – a flagship of the new turn, and one immediately copied in Post Office architecture as well as in municipal housing – 'The use of cladding materials indigenous to the Borough – hand-made bricks and tiles – gives the building a familiar colour and texture, adds the infinitely variable surface which is characteristic of hand made things, and is incidentally almost maintenance free'. These architects were no less committed to the cottagey look: 'kindly sloping roofs, friendly front doors, homely gardens with trees and shrubs'. Their new estates – the last generation of council housing – were built as urban villages, laid out irregularly to secure privacy. A mixture of low-rise flats and three- and four-bedroom houses made for 'interesting variations' in roofscape. Small courtyards, linked by arched openings and liberally planted with shrubs, provided usable open space.[43]

Conservationism, which began to establish itself, in the 1970s, as a leading idiom in new development, as well as a rallying cry for the defence of what was increasingly seen as a heritage under threat, put a premium on the indigenous and the home-grown. Buildings, according to the new aesthetic, should look organic. Instead of making 'bold', 'uncompromising' statements, in the manner of New Brutalist architecture, they should rather be dignified and restrained, showing respect for their older neighbours, and minimizing the visual intrusion of the new. They should look as though they had grown up naturally, using 'regional' materials, and 'blending' with or 'echoing' the local environment. Thus in the British Architectural Design Awards of 1984, a new estate at Conwy, North Wales (a suburban development of houses, bungalows and flats) was praised on the grounds that it captured 'a flavour of Welsh indigenous cottage architecture'; its two-tone roof (in 'concrete tiling') was particularly admired on the ground that the colours reflected 'the bracken on the hills beyond'.[44] A swimming pool at Elswick, Newcastle, was honoured in similar fashion. A postmodernist construction, resting on steel supports with a 'regular geometry of profiled metal sheet' as its roof and huge Bauhaus lettering to warn bathers when they were out of their depth, it was nevertheless seen by the Royal Institute of British Architects, when they gave it one of their six awards, as 'a continuation of the English tradition of winter gardens, conservatories, or arcades'.[45]

Office developers, with Colonel Seifert in the lead, latched on to these conceits – or, mindful of the need to secure planning permission, deferred to them. They adopted brick as an overcladding, or outer skin – 'rustic facing brick' with terracotta-coloured mortar was by the early 1980s a visual cliché – and used stone (or stone-effect concrete) for ornamentation. As well as returning to traditional materials they also reverted to traditional forms. Windows, instead of disappearing into curtain walling, were arched and pedimented, as they had been before the advent of prefabrication. Entrances were heavily profiled instead of presenting a blank face to the world. In the hands of postmodernists, in revolt against the monotonies of blank walls, or neoclassicists, simulating the glories of the Palladian, these buildings were full of visual interest, making a feature of Romanesque arches or classical pillars where the high modernists would have made a spectacle of column-free open space; landscaping the cobbled forecourt as gardens; disguising water towers as medieval turrets.

One measure of the progress of retrofitting would be the rise of the architectural salvage trade which by 1988, when *Refurbishment*, a supplement to *Building News*, published its first directory, numbered some 181 firms. Charles Brooking, who established his collection of architectural antiques in 1968, 'as an exercise in pure and applied preservation', seems to have been the first in the field. The London Architectural Salvage Company was established in 1976. By 1982, the local authorities, emboldened by conservation legislation, were taking a hand in it:

> Planning authorities will often insist on the use of second-hand materials wherever possible and a number of District and County Councils have established Materials Banks open to potential restorers. There are good examples in Abingdon, Birmingham, Brighton, Cardiff, Dartmoor National Park, Lewes and Salisbury. In Derbyshire applicants for listed building consent are asked if they would be willing to donate fabric and features retrieved from demolition to the bank run by the county. Listed building consent will often be accompanied by conditions about the salvage of important items, although as it is impossible to condition a third party by such a consent particular new locations have to be specified in a roundabout way. In some counties like Cambridgeshire builders are so alive to the advantages of storing second-hand materials that a municipal store is regarded as superfluous. Most demolition contractors are well aware of the value of salvage and will sell ... either to builders or exchange of cash on the site. The professional salvager will normally have the items in which he is interested entered as credits in a demolition contract with an agreement to purchase at a certain price. This gives the owner a return and the contractor an interest in their retention. It is important to remember that retrieval of materials from a demolition site without authorization is, strictly speaking, illegal. At the

more sophisticated end of the market there is a flourishing export trade to
America, Japan and Europe in everything from stained glass to Victorian bar
fittings and reclaimed bricks. Indeed such is the discrepancy between the
demand and supply that the supply to the legitimate market is being
supplemented by a spate of thefts particularly of Georgian fireplaces, even
doors, from houses in use. Some salvage firms are not known for the
scrupulous observance of listed building consent procedures.[46]

Another striking 1970s testimony to the appeal of retrofitting was the
success of the new 'old world' pub, re-Victorianizing what in earlier years
had been almost modernized out of existence. Precociously advocated,
as early as 1949, by the *Architectural Review*[47] (who also built 'The Bride
of Denmark' in the basement of their premises);[48] championed,
nostalgically, by a galaxy of writers in *The Saturday Book*; promoted, in a
small way, by Roderick Gradidge, in his capacity as architect to the
brewers, Ind Coope;[49] the traditional pub was nevertheless a minority
enthusiasm, and more regarded, it seemed, by aesthetes than by serious
drinkers.[50] In the early 1970s, when the Campaign for Real Ale was
launched, it seemed to many to be on its last legs. 'What has been
happening in the past few years is an appalling desecration of pub
interiors', wrote Bevis Hillier in *The New Antiques* (1977), 'As groups with
a mania for "house style" take over the pubs, the old richness of engraved
glass and "Queen Anne" style mahogany is replaced with plastic and blue
leatherette.'[51] Within a matter of a very few years these procedures had
been reversed, and by the time Nicholson's published their *London Guide*
(1981) 'pub Victoriana' was a visual cliché. Crimson plush took the place
of the plastic and blue leatherette as the approved 'house style' of the Big
Twelve. Newly installed curtaining and drapes, hung on glistening brass
rungs, made liberal use of 'that most Victorian of fabrics – velvet'.[52]
Mahogany or mahogany-veneer fittings ('a trademark of Victorian
pubs') were lovingly restored to the bar and kept in a state of high polish.
Heavy hand-pumps staged a comeback too, taking the place of fibreglass
taps even when, in reality, the beer was gassed, rather than drawn from
the casks. Wall sconces and table lamps replaced the overhead glare.

Neo-vernacular came into its own in the property boom of the 1980s.
The quantity house-builders adopted a 'cottagey' style for their starter
homes, and a neo-Georgian one for those of the executive class. Indeed,
to follow the advertisements in the property monthlies – as remote as
could be from the architectural controversies which raged in the quality
press – the 'battle of styles' in the dormitory towns and outer suburbs was
not between 'modernists' and 'postmodernists' but between 'traditional', 'cottage' and 'Tudor'.[53] 'Traditionally built' (though they were
almost invariably chimneyless) and 'period' in design (though promising all mod cons), these houses, according to the prospectuses, brought

a breath of Old England. Roofs were steeply pitched, with dormer windows peeping out of them and 'tile-covered' (with concrete tiles) if only more occasionally tile-hung. Brickwork was often featured in the advertisements, 'reclaimed' or second-hand bricks at the upper end of the market, where an element of refurbishment was involved. Two-tone bricks were widely adopted for the wharfside developments in London docklands, to blend in with and reflect 'the characteristic style of the traditional riverside architecture in the area', 'red brick detailing' providing an 'interesting contrast' to the yellow. Wood, too, sometimes features in the advertisements: 'mahogany timber-framed hardwood front doors with brass fittings' runs one such.[54] On greenfield sites, where the quantity house-builders adopted country names for their new developments, and made a feature of such cottage features as inglenook fireplaces, *genius loci* was much insisted on. Ideal Homes, number four in the list of Britain's top house-builders, claimed to run the gamut of tradition in their 'County' range, launched onto the market in 1986, featuring 'Oriel bay windows, corbelling at eaves level, arched window-heads, special sill details, projecting rafters, dormer and circular windows, attractive porches, colour wash rendering'. They also promised to mirror or echo regional tradition: 'It was felt vital that elevational styles of new homes should relate to their county locations. [So] while Ideal Homes might build a "County Range" home in Wiltshire finished in brick, it might build one in Yorkshire which is virtually identical, but clad in local stone; in East Anglia, it might be decorated with the kind of white weather-boarding which has been popular in that area for some centuries.'[55]

It was not only on the built environment that the 'cottagey' look left its imprint, but also on commodity marketing and design, where festoons of flowers, issuing in long tendrils, delicate petals and gently opening buds were as ubiquitous as geometric abstracts had been in the heyday of modernism. One influence here was *The Country Diary of an Edwardian Lady*, a world bestseller, which made its fortune on the strength of pressed flowers. It provided the motifs for a whole series of matching co-ordinates, set a fashion in herb- or flower-sprigged 'country' kitchens, and confirmed *broderie anglaise* as a more or less mandatory decorative frill. A rustic romanticism, typified by lots of trailing patterns, deep silks and damasks, a little aged and faded, was successfully marketed in the 1980s as the 'country house' look, while its 'Hedgerow' or cottage alternative offered wild flowers in pastels.[56] Hi-tech manufacturers followed suit. Russell Hobbs adorned its electric kettles 'country style' with wheatsheafs; its market rivals, Swan, opted for trailing lobelia.[57] In the mail-order catalogues, where even alarm clocks appeared with flowered borders, such motifs were ubiquitous. The 'period' telephones which sprang up after 1988, in the wake of denationalization – gold-plated, to add a touch of luxury, and made of Wedgwood, bone china or Galway crystal – offered themselves as 'Cottage Garden', 'Wild Tudor', 'Country Meadow' or 'Moss Rose', as well as (for those who preferred marble) 'Florentine' and 'Milano'.

III Modernization in Disguise

In the 1960s, the heyday of streamlining and systems-building, virtually anything old was at risk: Doric arches (as in the rebuilding of Euston station) hardly less than Dickensian tenements and slums. City planners, intent on building tower blocks – what Le Corbusier had called 'the vertical garden city' – believed that demolition was a good in itself, both on account of the 'obsolete' buildings and 'out-of-date' layouts which it did away with and because it prepared the way for comprehensive redevelopment – a 'surgical operation' (as it was conceived by Graeme Shankland, the butcher of Liverpool 8) designed to put a knife to the dead and decaying.[58] The property speculators, buying up whole streets for their office developments, trading planning permissions for planning gains, and using cloak-and-dagger methods to winkle out unwanted tenants and assemble vacant sites, made a fetish of building brand-new, and on the largest possible scale. Local authorities, with their slum-clearance programmes, were even more hungry for space, putting acres of housing to the bulldozer and condemning the twilight zones of the city to what was known at the time as 'planning blight'. They were impatient with anything which stood in their way. When road-widening schemes were canvassed, compulsory purchase orders were served on anything which impeded the free flow of traffic. The new flyovers and roundabouts – 'spaghetti junctions' as they were to be called when the public turned against them – were seized upon by go-ahead councils as catalysts of modernization, and even praised as sculptural beauties. Lightness and airiness – 'the sensation of open space' – were the great object pursued in the building of the tower blocks, and it was also fetishized in environmental improvement schemes.

In the following years these priorities were progressively reversed, in recoil from what were seen as the planning disasters of the 1960s. The revulsion from high-rise flats, and the simmering resentment at council housing policy which came to a head after the Ronan Point disaster of 1968 (the collapse of a tower block in which thirty-three people lost their lives) was followed by a much more widespread disenchantment with the modernism which the motorway boxes of the civil engineers, the sodium lights of the highway departments, as well as the 'deck-access' walkways and concrete canyons of the New Brutalist architecture all represented. Clearance areas, the 'twilight zones' of the 1960s, were elevated by degrees into 'conservation areas', subsidized by the local authorities, and protected by a legislation in which the old, far from being regarded as obsolete, took on the mantle of the historic. 'Planning gains', which in the 1960s had been measured in terms of releasing land for road-widening schemes, were now on the contrary assessed in terms of the 'period' features which the prospective developer undertook to retain or to restore. Face-lifts, in schemes of environmental improvement, were likewise a matter of bringing out, emphasizing or restoring period detail rather than, as in the 1950s and 1960s, attempting to give the old-fashioned a modern face. Comprehensive redevelopment gave way to a decided preference for rehabilitation, renewal and infill. Even where mega-developments were embarked on, as they were on the waterfront, the whole point of the operation, to follow the rhetoric of the architects and the developers, was to maintain or indeed 'enhance' the character of the local environment.

The local authorities, though universally blamed for the planning disasters of the 1960s, were in the 1970s to play a leading role (though one hardly acknowledged either at the time or in the present day) in establishing conservationism as a practical alternative to wholesale destruction and clearance. Prompted, in the first place, by pressure from the newly formed amenity societies and local pressure groups and influenced, no doubt, by the groundswell of conservationist sentiment which by the 1970s was becoming apparent in every sphere of national life, the planning officers began to call a halt to clearance schemes, and to explore the possibilities of piecemeal alternatives. Increasingly starved of funds by central government, and dependent for environmental improvement on attracting the interest of the property developers, or the enthusiasm of the homeowner, they discovered a whole new field for municipal enterprise. Under the Civic Amenities Act of 1967 they had the power to designate 'conservation' areas, where traditionalizing, rather than modernizing, the townscape became the first of the local authority's appointed tasks. Planning powers, legislated for in the same act, encouraged the local authorities to set down restrictions on new development, such as those issued by Essex County Council in 1973, and widely imitated elsewhere, which made the use of 'vernacular' regional styles mandatory. Local authority improvement grants, originally intended to bring substandard properties up to scratch, followed the same pattern: from the late 1960s they were being freely called upon to restore 'period' features, and to bring 'listed' buildings into a habitable state. Where their 1960s predecessors,

deferring to the borough engineers, had built traffic roundabouts and
multi-storey car parks, the municipal authorities of the 1970s bent their
ingenuities to the creation of traffic-free zones. Street furniture, which
in the aftermath of the Festival of Britain had been made to look

'contemporary', with tubular steel, fibre-glass fittings, multi-coloured plastics and fluorescent lighting to give brightness to the urban scene, was now, on the contrary, no less systematically antiqued, leading in the 1980s to such solecisms as Regent Street's 'Georgian' traffic lights and Monmouth's cobbled car parks.

Old property, under influences like these, was simultaneously modernized and antiqued. The terraced house, when it blossomed out as a 'period' residence, would have an indoor loo instead of an outside lavatory, would install a luxuriously appointed bathroom where earlier generations of occupants might have had to make do with a zinc tub, and would have gas- or oil-fired central heating fitted. At the same time it served as a showcase of the restorer's arts, making a feature of those nooks and crannies which the modernizers of the 1950s feared as dirt-traps; resurrecting, as architectural treasures, those artefacts which had been put to the hammer. When old houses were done up it was to 'enhance' their original features and make them look more traditional. In the vernacular of *World of Interiors*, the style leader of the 1980s, they were 'lovingly', 'sympathetically', 'sensitively', 'charmingly' restored. Arched window frames were repointed and window shutters re-installed, wooden beams exposed, dados and picture rails made good, skirting boards repaired, fireplaces, where they had been removed, recast and blackleaded. Ceiling roses which in the 1950s, when Victorian ceilings were regarded as 'ugly' and 'disproportionately high', might have been covered up with Polystyrene, were singled out for decorative treatment, with contrasting colours or 'dragging' to highlight the filigree work. Cornices, machine-made in mid-Victorian times, when ornamental plasterwork began to be mass-produced, were treated as reverentially as Adam brothers ceilings. In the hallways, if the house was Edwardian, stained-glass panels returned to the doorway and encaustic tiles – albeit reproduction ones – to the floor. In the bathroom chromium-plated taps, sleek and rimless, were discarded in favour of bulbous 'period' castings, ceramic-topped or brass according to means and taste (repro-duction ones could be bought from the architectural ironmongers, in 1988, for as little as £20 a pair).

For the gentrifiers, that adventurous section of the middle class who, for some thirty years, had been buying up working-class property in the inner city, 'bringing back the style' was by the 1980s automatically assumed to be a matter of restoring a house to its former glories. 'If you are lucky', *South Circular*, the Battersea-based property magazine advised its readers, 'features which you think have been removed may simply have been covered up. Original turned-wood banisters, panelled doors, even fireplaces are often found lurking under panels of painted hardboard. If not, few missing features are irreplaceable and few so-called improvements are irreversible.'[59] 'Classic' builders sprang up to service them. In the property boom of the 1980s restoration and refurbishment emerged as a distinct, highly prosperous branch of the building trade, with its own press and trade suppliers, and a range of local shops offering 'expert period advice' and 'period' fittings. The tell-tale signs of occupancy were to be seen not only within the newly refurbished houses, but also without – in the newly cast 'Regency' numerals on the doorway, the 'Victorian' door knocker in cast iron or the 'Georgian' one in lacquered brass and, if there was a forecourt, the newly restored 'period' railings.

Estate agents, though slow off the mark – the mortgage societies were for a long time reluctant to take on period property – emerged in the 1980s as connoisseurs of retrofit, attaching a talismanic importance to anything which could be plausibly labelled 'period'. In their portfolios, 'original features' were described as fulsomely as if they were landmarks on a Heritage Trail and the customers not clients but culture-vultures and sightseers visiting historic homes. The most commonplace domestic appointments were treated as infinitely precious. The cheapskate cup-board gave 'character' to an otherwise featureless room on account of its 'period' mouldings. The stained-glass panel in the doorway was singled out as a mark of distinction – though for Robert Tressell in *The Ragged Trousered Philanthropists* it was a very epitome of Edwardian shoddy. The cast-iron fireplace, newly installed, it may be, by the developer or the vendors, shot-blasted and blackened at the architectural salvage yard, was spoken of as excitedly as if it were the Elgin marbles. 'A beautiful period room with twin floor-to-ceiling sash windows . . . working shutters, ornate balcony, features marble fireplace with mantel, two double radiators, original cornicing and skirting, double doors into en suite bathroom' runs the specification for a master bedroom in Islington (the accompanying photograph also shows an 'original' brass bed).[60] 'A spectacular room with high ceiling and high skirting boards', runs another, this time referring to a dining-room. 'Large sash window with original shutters, original period fireplace, with tiled surrounds. Dado rail, chandelier on dimmer switch.'[61]

'Original' features were perhaps less important in all this than a range of brand-new period effects. One might instance the 'Georgian' door furniture and 'Georgian' power-points installed in new conversions and 'Georgian' dimmer switches (Hollywood masquerading as Hanoverian) which controlled the candelabra – 'Georgian' because they were made in brass rather than plastic and had a little bit of beading round the rims; the replica window-shutters with clover-leaf cut-outs to testify to their authenticity; the 'Victorian' sanitaryware in the bathroom, the 'Victo-rian' hardware in the kitchen. Some of these features figured so frequently and so prominently in houses which had been 'sympathetically' restored that they became, in some sort, iconic. The 'Victorian style' bathroom, and the 'country' kitchen routinely appeared in the property columns of the newspapers as though they were original features, as did the 'stripped' floors and the 'top quality fittings'.[62] The enthusiastic Islington estate agent who advertised an 'elegantly restored Victorian terrace house in original Georgian style'[63] may have been going a little over the top, but he was doing no more than a rival who featured a 'farmhouse-style' kitchen in a 'well-restored' Canonbury town house.[64]

In working-class home improvement, the taste for period effects is no less pronounced than in the middle class, as can be seen from the four- or six-panelled Georgian doors, with built-in fanlights, which are a near-universal sign of owner-occupancy on the newly privatized council estates. But the aesthetic is unashamedly one of embellishment and it is much more apt to run to extremes – 'Tudor-style' door furniture, for instance, and fibreglass cottage beams, to take the example of two popular lines at Texas Homecare; 'Sheraton-style' TV cabinets in the mail-order catalogues. It also has to compete with an unstaunchable appetite for fantasy and glitz, which has more to do with the magic of holidays than with a taste for vernacular effect – whence perhaps the Spanish archways, 'Algarve' doors and Californian sun-beds. One of its most vivid contemporary expressions is the leaded lights craze, which with the aid of squeeze-on tubes, seems to be giving a latticed look to everything in sight in the outer suburbs, not only bay windows but also hall panels and even garage doors.[65]

Do-It-Yourself, a movement which began life as a modernizing force, registers these changes of taste. The home improvement centres, such as B & Q and Texas Homecare, are full of archaicizing aids. There are self-assembly kits of spindles, newels and rails for the maker of traditional staircases, off-the-peg window frames, with clip-on bars, for the amateur glazier. The vinyl wallpapers are fashioned to look like damask, the walling tiles – often there is a whole bay of them – take their cue from Victorian ceramics (tiling ranks among the top three DIY enthusiasms). The ornamental plasterwork manufacturers, such as Aristocast, offer ceiling roses and cornices, niches and columnettes. There are tie-backs for the 'swagged' curtains, arched mirrors for the hallways, Grecian urns – in fibreglass – for the patio, and in the rooms devoted to self-assembly bedroom furniture a display of period prints. Likewise *The Practical Householder* these days is full of regressive tips, counselling readers to put back what their 1950s predecessors would have cheerfully consigned to the scrap-heap, and there is a full-blown periodical, now in its third year of publication – *The Traditional Woodworker* – exclusively devoted to retrofitting. 'Picture rails, dados and cornices add style to the humblest of dwellings' runs an article in the March 1990 issue of *The Practical Householder*:

> Dado rails are an ideal means of breaking up an otherwise bland and uninspiring expanse of wall. In a cramped modern hall, there's simply no room for furniture or plants. Add interest instead by fitting a dado rail at waist height and using contrasting wallpapers above and below. For a grand effect use a deeply textured paper like Lincrusta below the rail.... Sponging or ragging the wall below the rail can also add interest. In a living room timber panelling below the dado can create a warm and intimate atmosphere, or add period charm to an older property. A picture rail allows you to hang pictures around the room from elegant brass chains.[66]

In the form of Victorian street furniture, or that born-again and aestheticized version of it which prestige developments, such as the new up-market shopping precincts, helped to establish as traditional, 'retrofitting' helped to give shape and definition to a new vernacular of public space in which the tree- or shrub-lined enclave, the sheltered awning and the railinged enclosure replaced the wide-open vistas of modernism. The municipal authorities embraced it with all the enthusiasm they had shown in the 1960s for yellow salt bins, mushroom seats and concrete flower beds, installing it in conservation areas as a kind of talisman of historicity, and using it in high-street facelifts as a kind of herald of urban regeneration. By the end of the 1980s it was as inescapable a feature of the townscape as skylon-like verticals had been in the wake of the Festival of Britain. One might instance those 'Victorian-style' litter bins – octagonal, hexagonal or pedestal according to municipal taste, and sometimes embossed with the municipal coat-of-arms – which serve as vandal-proof waste receptacles in newly pedestrianized shopping streets; or the cast-iron bollards, 'canon' or fluted, and sometimes fibreglass in disguise, which serve as the boundary-posts in newly refurbished town centres (Leicester Square, with its Hampton Court-like maze of 'amenity' spaces, has a myriad of them).

Cobblestones, still something of a discovery when the GLC architects set about their refurbishing work in Covent Garden,[67] and for the modernizers of the 1950s and 1960s (as for the social realist photographers of the 1930s) a byword of urban squalor, were in the 1980s routinely incorporated into the repertory of what the municipal authorities called 'environmental improvement', marking no-go areas for the motorist, and returning previously run-down streets to what Kensington Council, in its plans for the prettification of Portobello Road market, fondly refers to as 'Victorian grandeur'.[68] Originally invented, in the 1820s, as a road surface for horses to get a grip on with their hooves, they are now freely requisitioned for pedestrian walkways, regardless of the obstacles to prams and wheelchairs or the hazards they present to high heels. In mews and precinct developments they serve as landscaped 'gardens' or forecourts. On the waterfront, bordered by chains or rails, they turn former industrial docklands into make-believe fishermen's quays. In heritage towns, or conservancy areas (such as the one I live in) they even give a vernacular look to the car-parks.

A still more conspicuous period signifier is the Victorian street-lamp, ostensibly made of cast iron (though many of the replicas are steel or aluminium coated black), and with a hooded lantern allowing electricity to masquerade as gas (in one of the versions currently on offer, the manufacturers have even contrived to incorporate a make-believe flicker).[69] The Civic Trust, pioneers in the campaign against concrete gibbets and high-pressure sodium glare, preferred recessed lights as an alternative;[70] while the Design Council, as late as 1976, was condemning Victorian street-lamps as 'twee'. Far better, they argued, pointing to the example of a riverside walk at Eton where modern lamps offset a refurbished period street, to rely on contrast rather than chocolate-box replicas.[71] The 1978 battle to keep the gas-lights in Covent Garden, won by the traditionalists after a mighty public controversy and a spate of celebrity representations, seems to have been some kind of watershed. Westminster City Council who, along with Camden, had been the advocates of electrification, caved in. Three years later, with a newly established 'Urban Design' unit in tow, the Council embarked on an ambitious programme of refurbishment, in which 'co-ordinated street furniture', with Victorian street-lamps in the van, complemented the restoration of period façades, the installation of ornamental archways, and the transformation of shopping streets into shopping 'villages'. By the mid 1980s what D.W. Windsor, the market leaders in the field, called 'heritage' lighting enjoyed an unchallenged hegemony. Lighting engineers and planning officers were adopting it as a matter of course, 'to recapture the charm and elegance of early street lighting'; while in newly gentrified conservancy areas, residents' associations were clamouring for it. In Westminster itself, the borough engineers, having transformed Parliament Square into a kind of stage-set for Charlie Chaplin's *Limelight*, and South Molton Street into a *fin de siècle* colonnade, have now set about Georgianizing Soho, using wall brackets and pendant lanterns to give a cloistered look to newly reclaimed alleys and passages.

A recent addition to this repertoire of period effects has been York stone paving, or at any rate that cut-price version of it, machine-sawn rather than cut down the natural vein and perfectly squared rather than irregular, which is currently favoured in refurbishment schemes. Westminster Council, who became the leaders in 1980s municipal retrochic, seem to have been the first to use it when, in 1981, they set about repaving Queen Anne's Gate; later they adopted it for their road-narrowing schemes, with enlarged pavements, lined by trees or shrubs, to provide 'small restful places'. By 1986 York stone paving seemed to have overtaken cobblestones as a style-setter. Thus when Bradford City Council ('in conjunction with developers and local industrialists') set about rehabilitating 'Little Germany', the town's historic 'merchant quarter', a total of £4 million (a grant, it seems, from English Heritage) went into the renewal of the street-lamps, 'in a design more sympathetic to the area's Victorian character', and in re-laying the pavements in York stone. A specially created Festival Square, flagged in York stone paving, acted as a catalyst in the regeneration of the quarter. Buildings were cleaned 'to give an immediate cosmetic lift' and even the car park (at a cost of £150,000 for 120 spaces) was aestheticized: 'It has planted beds, brick paved-surfaced parking bays and dwarf stone boundary walls topped by iron railings.'[72] Westminster City Council used a similar strategy when, in 1988, it set about reclaiming Soho from the vice-shops.[73] Peter Heath of the Council's Urban Design Division explained, 'We use York stone for the pavement and granite blocks for the roadway and have them both at the same level so it looks like a pedestrian street. It makes cars feel they shouldn't be there, as well as giving the street a much-needed face-lift.'[74]

Beneath the period dress, a great deal of what passes for restoration is modernization in disguise, a continuation and extension of the 1950s ideals of open-plan living, rather than a reversal of them. It involves changes of occupancy, transformations of function, and physical surgery which effectively make a rehabilitated property brand-new, even when its period features have been emphasized. The re-traditionalized pubs would be a prime example. They have not brought back sawdust to the floor, spittoons to the bar or snob-screens to divide the serious drinkers from the saloon bar or the jug-and-bottle. On the contrary, they are associated with a wholesale change of clientele, in which working men in 'soiled clothes' or 'dirty boots' (as the notices delicately put it) have been excluded, along with the dominoes and the darts. The period look here, with its soft carpets, velvet half-curtaining and subdued, intimate lighting could be seen as a rather successful attempt to *feminize* – or bourgeoisify – the interior. It coincides with the invention of the ploughman's lunch and the rise of the office-based luncheon trade; it has broken down many all-male preserves, and enabled the brewery trade to beat off the competition of the wine bars.

Retrofitting also bears the mark of that revolution in expectations which in the 1950s and 1960s changed the living environment from a fixed property into one on which individuals could make their mark. It reflects, in an obvious way, the vast increase in owner-occupancy – 29 per cent of all householders in 1952; 64 per cent today. It has also been the beneficiary of advanced technology. Indeed the very idea of rehabilitation and refurbishment would have been unthinkable without the advent of central heating, which at a stroke turned large rooms into comfortable living spaces and transformed the servantless, uneconomic mansion into a potential family home. Similarly the Victorianizing and periodizing of the bathroom has gone hand-in-hand with the introduction of new technologies, transforming a chilly space into a kind of sauna, and introducing an astonishing variety of water jets. The advent of 'Victorian Style' conservatories – very popular in the housing boom of the late 1980s, especially in the suburbs, and a new field for do-it-yourself – would have been difficult to imagine without double-glazing, and its promise of all-the-year round, room-temperature heat.[75] Another modernization which helped to make the legacy of the past exploitable was the Clean Air Act of 1958, which retrospectively can be seen as the original impetus to those stone-cleaning and brick-pointing schemes which have been the *terminus ad quem* of refurbishment. Just as the 'period' conversion of Victorian mansions would have been unthinkable without central heating, so the restoration of 'period' façades – and the invention of sand-blasting and shot-firing as a way of clearing away dirt and grime – was premissed on the ending of coal-fired boilers and coal-warmed homes.

'Period' conversions are as ruthless in dispensing with traditional limitations on space as the open-plan office or the see-through shops and stores. Basements are opened up and extended with the aid of sun-roofs. Load-bearing walls are removed to turn the front and the back rooms of terraced houses into 'through rooms' – those vast reception rooms which have pride of place in the estate agents' brochures. In the kitchen there is no attempt to reinstate the pantry, the scullery or the copper – on the contrary, internal partitions are systematically removed and storage spaces made transparent. 'Doors and windows had to be swapped round' runs an ecstatic account in *Period Living*, describing the ways in which a traditional kitchen had been made out of three tiny rooms at the back. 'What is now the back door used to be the pantry window'.

Loft conversions, with windows front and back where previously there was at best a skylight, are even more obviously the product of an aesthetic of light and space. Similarly conservatories, though marketed as 'Victorian' and quite often Gothic in style, could be seen as lineal descendants of the picture windows of the 1950s and 1960s, of Eric Lyons's 'Span' flats, and of the glass-walled primary schools of modernist architecture – that is, they are an attempt to bring the outside in and abolish the division between interior and exterior space. Whereas the Victorians had a horror of sunlight and kept it out of the conservatory by a profusion of plants, as well as by choosing shady locations, the modern 'traditional' conservatory is marketed as an oasis of natural light – 'a Victorian sun-lounge' is how one of the manufacturers advertised their offering in *Ideal Home*,[76] while 'light without light fittings' according to *Traditional Interior Decoration* was the design ideal.[77]

Where the 1950s and 1960s were good at making the old look new, the 1970s and 1980s were no less resourceful at establishing what was called, in relation to the masthead of the *Independent* when the newspaper was launched in 1986, 'instant oldness'.[78] Retrofitting depends as much on concealing the evidence of modernity as in multiplying period effects. It banishes its thermostatically controlled boilers to the utility room. Electric lights masquerade as candelabra, or hide themselves in tasselled shades. RSJs (rolled steel joists), the supports inserted in place of partition walls when two rooms are knocked into one, were in the early days of conversion left untouched; today it is more common for them to be disguised by 'feature' arches, ruched curtains or columnettes, turning the living room, with its divider, into a kind of proscenium stage. The progress of double-glazing has followed a similar course. First intro-duced when modernism was in the ascendant, it exemplified a stream-lined look. Today it is more apt to appear in period dress, with neo-Gothic arched frames and glazing bars in the manner of the traditional English sash window. Indeed it is quite common for double-glazing and Victorian sash windows to be marketed in tandem.

The 'country' or 'country-style' kitchen is a triumph of these arts, banishing the evidence of modernity, as it were, to outer space, even though – in the new ecology of domestic order – it is the most expensively equipped room in the house, and can cost as much as £70,000 to install.[79] Modern appliances such as dishwashers are hidden away behind ingenious, custom-made doors – panelled in the more expensive 'Georgian' or 'Regency' kitchen as though they were the wainscotting of a library. A floor-to-ceiling cupboard – in one extravagant case, modelled on a medieval manor – conceals the fridge and freezer. Food-processors are discreetly hidden in niches. Only the worktop – in 'antiqued' pine, 'traditional ash' or terracotta tiling – advertises its functional presence. The waste-disposal unit and the trash compactor, electrically operated, are hidden beneath the sink; and the sink itself, in the more expensive fitted kitchen, dresses itself up as copperware or ceramic. In the advertisement even the cooking is invisible, and there is not the faintest sign of washing-up.

The country kitchen, manufactured and marketed in Britain under a variety of local names – 'the Woodstock', 'the Chartwell', 'the Balmoral' in the case of the grand; 'the Elizabeth Ann' in that of the coy and twee

– and a choice of period, ranging from Renaissance to Art Deco,[80] was originally a *German* invention; an offshoot, it seems, of the fitted kitchen revolution of the 1950s, and more generally of that streamlined 'modern living', the promise of which had been one of the great excitements of the Festival of Britain. It began its career as a modernist phenomenon, and though its units have been given traditional cabinet work and its continuous surfaces are now made up of wood, the basic principle of the continuous working surface – the 'flush' surface – has remained untouched. The compositional principles are modular and futuristic, carrying the idea of built-in, space-saving furniture to the limit.

The success of the country kitchen – a pan-European and transatlantic phenomenon – may serve as a reminder that retrofitting, so far from being a throw-back to the past, is a fulcrum of economic change. The more nomadic business becomes – it sometimes seems – the more it affects a homespun look, recycling old trade names, refurbishing old properties, and laying claim to the production of classics. Multinational companies franchise their operations or trade as local firms. The regions may be robbed of their distinctive economies, but their image is intensively marketed on the strength of an aestheticized version of their past. A government ruthlessly intent on modernizing (and American-izing) British society nevertheless calls for a return to traditional ways. Neo-vernacular architecture, though an international style with look-alike features in every shopping mall and office precinct, is passed off as home-grown and indigenous.

On a wider plane it is possible to see retrofitting as part of a new enclosure movement in which there is a transfer of population and resources from one sector of the economy to another, and a new social division of living space.[81] Conservation appears here as the epicentre of a whole new cycle of urban and, it may be, rural development. Like the Highland clearances of old, it dishouses entire populations; like the enclosure movement it changes patterns of settlement. It is, in one aspect, the cutting edge of the business recolonization of the inner city, and indeed in the property boom of the 1980s it sometimes seemed that for a really grand work of destruction to be set in hand the developer needed the imprimatur of the Fine Arts Commission or English Heritage for an 'imaginative' scheme.

Retrofitting could also be seen as a force for renewal, creating social and public space, discovering concealed corridors and hidden passages, reoccupying vacant lots, revitalizing redundant plant. The new Liverpool Street railway terminal, a brilliant success from the point of view of the creation of social space, and a fascinating combination of old and new, may serve as a corrective to the notion that the hybrid is necessarily inferior to the pure. Its crown, now spectacularly visible to the travelling public, is a glazed Victorian canopy, modelled on Liverpool Street's old railway sheds but covering the entire surface of the station. Laser-cut and bolted into place in the manner that has become a cliché of postmodernism, it nevertheless contrives to look like one of the soaring structures of Isambard Kingdom Brunel, or a Crystal Palace *redivivus*. The spandrels which serve as roof trusses have been picked out in buttermilk and blue to emphasize the intricacy of the Gothic fretwork, and they are reproduced as a kind of unifying thread in the station's lesser ironwork. Yet, whatever the period detail, the ruling aesthetic is thoroughly contemporary, closer in spirit to an air terminal than to a railway. The station looks inward rather than outward, making a feature of its shopping mall rather than the platforms. In place of a cavernous gloom, dedicated to the mysteries of travel and reflecting the power of coal and steam, it gives us an atrium flooded with light. In place of nooks and crannies, it gives us a unified concourse. Where the old Liverpool Street was a labyrinth of dark places, the new one is comprehensible at a glance.

Notes

1. *News of the World Better Homes*, ed. Roger Smithells, London 1954, pp. 135, 165.

2. 'The Crisis in Town Planning', *Universities and Left Review*, I, no. 2, Summer 1957, p. 38. 'A Victorian interior with everything from aspidistra to whatnot, in what to us is the worst of taste', *Everybodys*, 10 February 1951; Alexandra Palace, 'a Victorian architectural monstrosity', ibid., 1 September 1951; 'the dreariness that is the legacy of the last hundred years', Mary Gilliatt, *English Style*, London 1967, p. 100. When eighteenth-century houses were praised it was because of their contemporary or proto-modern characteristics – lightness, simplicity, self-discipline and restraint.

3. *News of the World Better Homes*, p. 184.

4. Ibid., p. 73 (advertisement).

5. *The Practical Householder*, November 1956.

6. *Do It Yourself*, October 1958 (advertisement).

7. *House Beautiful Guide to Better Homes*, London 1961, p. 101.

8. *House Beautiful*, February 1956.

9. *News of the World Better Homes*, p. 44.

10. Ibid., pp. 106–7.

11. *Do It Yourself*, October 1958. An editorial note in the same issue draws attention to the Clean Air Act. 'When you think of the crippling effects of smog, the illness it causes and the gradual destruction of historic stonework – to say nothing of our ugly black towns, you should sympathise with the new Act. It is now in force, though it may take time to catch up with you.'

12. *News of the World Better Homes*, pp. 102–3.

13. Ibid., p. 91 (advertisement).

14. H. Dalton Clifford, *The Country Life Book of Houses for Today*, London 1963, p. 15.

15. 'Contemporary Table Legs', *Do It Yourself*, October 1958.

16. 'A New Dresser for 2/9', *Practical Householder*, November 1956.

17. *News of the World Better Homes*, p. 107.

18. *Parents*, April 1955, p. 44. I am grateful to Sheila Rowbotham for lending me a copy of this journal.

19. *News of the World Better Homes*, p. 64.

20. *House Beautiful*, February 1956.

21. *House and Garden Small Houses*, p. 162; *House Beautiful Guide to Better Homes* (advertisement).

22. *Mud, Straw and Insults: A Further Collection of Roy Brooks' Property Advertisements*, London 1971.

23. Festival of Britain, *Exhibition of Architecture*, London 1951, p. 69. 'The "Homes and Gardens" pavilion takes the past as read, and the visitor follows the British people straight into their homes – the houses of the present time.' *A Tonic to the Nation: The Festival of Britain, 1951*, ed. Mary Bonham and Bevis Hillier, London 1976, is a fine retrospect, with memoirs by many of the leading spirits, but it plays down the modernizing spirit of the time and perhaps makes rather more than the Festival itself of British whimsy.

24. *Houses for Today*, pp. 14–15.

25. Ibid., p. 24.

26. Ibid., pp. 36–9.

27. Ibid., p. 80.

28. H. Dalton Clifford, in later years author of the 1963 *Country Life Book of Houses Today*, advising readers of *Homes and Gardens* to get rid of overgrown trees and shrubbery, compared the 'ornate' and 'fussy' late Victorian house, or the 'old-world' suburban one, to a scarlet woman. 'A house which is overloaded with awnings, wrought-iron grilles, plaques, lanterns, vines, hanging baskets and trellis is like an overdressed woman. One suspects that all these trimmings are necessary to distract attention from serious defects.' H. Dalton Clifford, 'Put the Best Front on Your House', *Homes and Gardens*, August 1953.

29. Mary Gilliatt, *English Style*, London 1967, p. 14.

30. Ibid., p. 99. Her sympathies are equally modernist where town conversions are featured. 'The nineteenth century cornice is the only reminder of the house's origins', she writes, when praising an architect's conversion of a house in Fulham Road.

31. Geoffrey Moorhouse, *The Other England*, Harmondsworth 1964, p. 59. 'Twilight zones' – 'the decaying inner rings of Victorian housing, commerce and industry' – were also earmarked for the bulldozer. 'Here, although many of the houses are not slums, the atmosphere is down-at-heel, the layout is obsolete, factories and houses are jumbled together, there is an oppressive ugliness and a discordant mess that cannot be cured by piecemeal rebuilding. Only comprehensiive reconstruction to a new design will do.' 'The Face of Britain, a Policy for Town and Country Planning', *Socialist Commentary*, 1961 reprint, p. xii.

32. W.G. Hoskins, *The Making of the English Landscape*, Harmondsworth 1971, pp. 298–9.

33. Oscar Newman, *Defensible Space*, London 1973. See Alice Coleman, *Utopia on Trial: Vision and Reality in Planned Housing*, London 1985 for the sociological attack on modernist architecture; Jane Jacobs, *The Death and Life of Great American Cities*, Harmondsworth 1964, and Robert Venturi et al., *Learning from Las Vegas*, Cambridge, Mass, 1986, for the defence of 'eccentric spaces' and 'vital mess'.

34. Wee Willie Winkie Candleholder feature in the Save the Children Christmas Catalogue, 1992.

35. Anna Sebba, *Laura Ashley, A Life by Design*, London 1990, p. 104. Sanderson, the wallpaper manufacturer, began to print coordinating William Morris designs on fabrics and wallpapers in 1965. Ibid., p. 65.

36. *British Architectural Design Awards, 1984*, Macclesfield 1985, gives approving mention to: 'semi-mature trees create a conservatory within which the restaurant and meeting rooms are sited' (a new civic centre) (p. 43); 'luxurious planting' (Covent Garden housing project) (p. 103); 'planting ... to soften the junction of buildings with the ground', 'generous landscaping', 'wide variety of shrubs' (sheltered housing project) (p. 111); 'fully grown trees' (atrium of a new office building) (p. 208); 'a garden courtyard', 'balcony planters' (an office block) (p. 253).

37. 'Improvements and Conversions', *Housing Review*, vol. X, no. 6, November–December 1961, pp. 177–8, has 'before' and 'after' photographs of council 'improvements' at some old property in Leeds. 'Before conversion and landscaping', two pairs of old Victorian houses face the street with straggly entrances and a generous display of

overgrown bushes; 'after conversion', the greenery has vanished and a geometric walkway has replaced the wiggly paths.

38. Anita Roddick, *Body and Soul*, London 1991; Gilly McKay and Alison Cooke, *The Body Shop: Franchising a Philosophy*, Pan Books 1986; Lynn Barber, 'Fruitful Fidget', *Independent on Sunday*, 3 March 1991; 'Anita Roddick', *Observer*, 26 February 1984.

39. Sebba, *Laura Ashley*, pp. 93, 106.

40. Ibid., p. 114.

41. Roddy Llewellyn, *Beautiful Backyards*, London 1985.

42. Andrew Derbyshire 'Hillingdon Civic Centre', typescript, 22 November 1977. I am grateful to Sir Andrew for a copy of this paper.

43. Colin Ward, *When We Build Again: Let's Have Housing that Works*, London 1985, p. 118, for the Lillington Street Estate, Pimlico; *British Architectural Design Awards 1984*, p. 107, for Colbeck Mews, Islington.

44. *British Architectural Design Awards 1984*, p. 120.

45. Ibid., p. 11.

46. Saunders, *Historic Houses Companion*, 1982, pp. 144–5.

47. In October 1949, the *Architectural Review* published a special issue devoted to the qualities of the Englsh pub, and in the following year its press brought out Maurice Gorham and H. McG. Dunnett, *Inside the Pub*. The *Review* also sponsored a competition, 'Pub Tradition Recaptured', in 1950 (reported in the June 1950 issue); it returned to the issue in 1955 when it hailed the new interior of The Champion, Wells St W1, as 'the first example of the creative refitting of an existing pub', *Architectural Review*, February 1955, p. 135.

48. The book jacket of Andrew Saint, *Towards a Social Architecture: the Role of School Building in Post-War England*, London 1987, has a fine picture of a caucus-meeting of public-sector architects at the Bride of Denmark.

49. For the group of architects who at Ind Coope in the early 1950s set about re-creating the pub's lost intimacies, see Ben Davis, *The Traditional English Pub*, London 1981, pp. 12–13. Gorham and Dunnett's book, he tells us, was 'their bible'. I am grateful to Roderick Gradidge for answering queries about his own work.

50. On the Society for the Preservation of Beers from the Wood, the immediate predecessor to the 1970s Campaign for Real Ale, see Christopher Hutt, *The Death of the English Pub*, London 1973, pp. 25–7; Richard Boston, *Beer and Skittles*, London 1976, pp. 95–6.

51. Bevis Hillier, *The New Antiques*, London 1977, pp. 202–3; Boston, *Beer and Skittles*, pp. 170–1.

52. Jim Kemp, *Victorian Revival in Interior Design*, New York 1985, p. 23.

53. 'Homes in Formby', *What House?*, June 1988.

54. 'Traditional Design', *The House Buyer*, February 1990.

55. *The House Buyer*, May 1988.

56. 'Past Perfect', *Hertfordshire Countryside*, June 1988.

57. For some cordless 'traditional' electric kettles, with floral motifs, *The Kitchen*, March–April 1990, p. 112.

58. Graeme Shankland, 'The Crisis in Town Planning', *Universities and Left Review*, vol. I, no. 1, Spring 1957, p. 40. See also p. 57, '... our Victorian urban encampments remain at the centre of our twentieth century conurbations. They are our dead centre'. See also James MacColl, *Policy for Housing*, Fabian Society 1964, p. 27.

59. 'Putting Back the Style', *South Circular*, March 1989, p. 21.

60. Folkard and Hayward, portfolio for a house in Gibson Square N1, October 1989.

61. Ibid., specification for 'a property of genuine distinction and character' in Parkholme Road, Hackney.

62. *Observer*, 18 October 1987.

63. *Observer*, 20 August 1989.

64. *Observer*, 22 June 1986.

65. 'Let There Be Light', *Practical Householder*, March 1990, for the replacement garage door; *South Side*, March 1989, for an elegant leaded lights style seecurity grille. For the replacement window boom generally, *Home Improvement*, no. 8, 1988, pp. 28–32.

66. 'Do-It-Yourself', *Practical Householder*, March 1990, p. 28. An advertisement in the same issue runs: 'Recognising the current vogue for all things Victorian, W.H. Newson has now developed a complete range of ornate skirtings, picture rails and dados.'

67. Gordon Cullen in *Townscape* (London 1961), a book which happily combined the *Architectural Review*'s commitment to modernism with its feel for the texture of town life, was a persuasive advocate of the decorative use of cobbles, 'to landscape promenades and squares, to draw attention to the dramatic scenery of the floor' – and to deter motorists (pp. 128–131 for some illustrations). They were to be used, however, to add 'variety' to the urban scene, rather than, as in the 1980s, to give instant maturity. Pseudo-cobbles – imitation or 'simulated' stone made from concrete – had not yet been invented.

68. 'The Prettification of Portobello', *Independent*, 22 November 1989.

69. For some early examples of re-traditionalized street lighting, Konrad Smigielski on the Leicester Art Gallery improvement scheme of 1967 in Civic Trust, *Conservation in Action*, 1972, pp. 42–3; The Mound, Edinburgh 1959, in Department of the Environment, *New Life for Historic Areas*, 1972; also Poole, Dorset, '20 early local street lights rescued, converted to electricity, repainted and installed in Precinct Area'.

70. Civic Trust, *Pride of Place*, p. 88: 'Bear in mind the possibility of commissioning new designs for special circumstances (but *not* please "rustic" and ... "period")'.

71. Design Council, *Street Furniture*, 7th edn, 1976, p. 40, praises the approach to Windsor Bridge in the newly completed restoration scheme. 'Old fashioned street lamps were eschewed in favour of simple modern design'.

72. 'Bradford Darns', *Building*, 18 November 1988, pp. 40–2.

73. For some protests, 'Save our Soho', *Evening Standard Magazine*, January 1989.

74. Oral information, Peter Heath of Westminster City Council, 1990.

75. 'Conservatories', *Practical Householder*, May 1988, pp. 83–4.

76. *Ideal Home*, July 1986 (advertisement).

77. 'Outside In', *Traditional Interior Decoration*, June–July 1988, p. 71.

78. Michael Crozier, *The Making of the Independent*, London 1980.

79. Arena of Oxford, who claim to have been manufacturing fitted furniture since 1772, have the following advertisement, which may stand for a thick wad of cuttings on this point. It is taken from *The Kitchen*, March–April 1990:

CLASSIC HAND-MADE KITCHENS

We have been creating kitchens for over 25 years. This scheme was designed to look as though it had always been there – a lovely room is seldom enhanced by self-conscious fittings. The furniture was made in old pine, great care being taken to sympathise with the surrounding patination, the best of today's technology being discreetly hidden away. Interesting and practical features such as the wine store were worked into the design, enabling us to echo the pleasing contrasts between polished wood and the hewn stone of the original floor. We work in many old houses where our sensitivity and experience in conservation are particularly relevant.

80. At random: 'Kitchen in Scottish Renaissance Style' hand-made and hand-painted by Smallbone, *Observer*, 3 October 1987; 'Victorian "pickled" English oak ... Trevor Moore ... caring for tradition', *The Kitchen*, March–April 1990; 'Georgian' Mahogany, Kitchens Direct, *Observer*, 27 July 1986; The Country Diary Kitchen ('captures the classic charm and elegance of the Edwardian era') *County Homes*, May 1986; 'Traditional Period Kitchens ... Harpers', *House and Garden*, August 1986; 'Paula Rosa Kitchen ... traditional Victorian Design', *County Homes*, May 1988; Elizabeth Ann 'the warmth of Cognac oak', *Country Living*, June 1988; The National Trust Kitchen, *Stately Homes*, May 1988.

81. Michael Wallace, 'Reflections on the History of Historic Preservation', in Susan Porter Benson et al., *Presenting the Past: Essays on History and the Public*, Philadelphia 1986, p. 196.

Retrochic

I

Retrochic enjoys an uncertain place in the cartography of taste, making a fugitive appearance in a whole succession of style wars and taking its bow now on the catwalks of the fashion trade, now on the stalls of the flea markets (like retrochic itself, a term imported into this country from France in the 1970s), now in the installations of pop art. Aesthetically it is double-coded: 'olde worlde but ultimately modern', in the words of a 1988 fashion guru, the London dressmaker John Galliano.[1] It plays with the idea of the period look, while remaining determinedly of the here-and-now – as with the fitted carpets and soft lighting of the newly re-Victorianized pubs, or the air-conditioned modern offices which hide themselves behind supposedly classical, or neo-classical, façades. Janus-faced, it looks both backwards and forwards in time, using the most up-to-date technologies to age or 'distress' what would otherwise appear brand new, such as 'antiqued' pine and 'stonewashed' jeans; to re-mix 'classic' rock albums or tracks; to recycle archive prints. More futuristically, as in the punk style of installation sculpture, retrochic gives free play to some of the more utopian elements in national life, or what a recent writer has called 'England's Dreaming'.[2]

Unlike other forms of revival, retrochic has been technology-led. One might refer to the advent of litho printing, which brought facsimile reproduction within the reach of millions, or more recently to colour photocopying, which allows the manufacturers of giftware to turn out period labels at minimum cost. The pub mirror craze, which brought the humours of the old curiosity shop and the Portobello Road stallholders to the gift trade (at the height of the boom, in 1977, the mirrors were being turned out at the rate of a hundred thousand or more a week)[3] was based on an application of silkscreen or transfer printing to the simulation of cut glass. Electronically driven laser-cutting has allowed the architects of the new railway terminals to achieve a Crystal Palace effect (at the new and brilliantly successful Liverpool Street Station it is

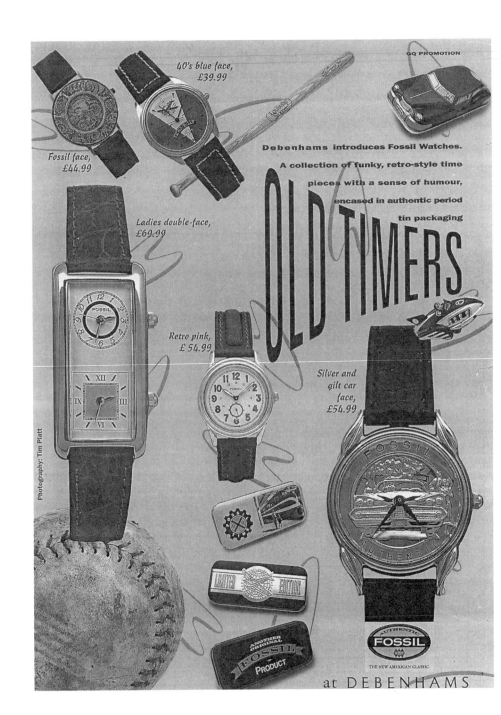

impossible for the onlooker to tell where restoration ends and new-build begins);[4] while in a more low-tech sphere, 'Paint Magic' or stencilling, the invention of Jocasta Innes,[5] allows do-it-yourself gentrifiers to simulate the pleasing decay (or faded elegance) of what *World of Interiors* dubs 'The Country House look'.

Retrochic trades on inversion, discovering hitherto unnoticed beauties in the flotsam and jetsam of everyday life; elevating yesterday's cast-offs into antique clothes and vintage wear; and treating the out-of-date and the anachronistic – or imitations of them – as though they were the latest thing. It will turn inkwells into what the gift catalogues call 'desk jewellery'; and pay four- and five-figure sums at the auction houses for old teddy bears[6] – along with pop memorabilia, one of the very few classes of antiques not to have suffered a drop in price, or loss of public, during the recent recession. It will make a cult of Hollywood B-movies, 'space-age' wrist watches, Dan Dare comics, flying ducks. It will revive Busby Berkeley (or Ziegfield Follies) showgirl waistcoats as executive-style costume; promote dungarees as fashion garments (in the Paris collections of 1989 they were supposed to represent the 1940s 'concierge' look); and manufacture road-sweepers' donkey jackets or sailors' pea-coats as evening wear for city slickers.

The big stores and the mail-order firms latch on to these conceits. Woolworth's now have a collection of natural, country-born, and allegedly herb-based, cosmetics and shampoos; their fashion wear, which thirty years ago would have been in Terylene and Bri-Nylon today boasts of being 100% cotton. Debenhams are currently launching 'Fossil', a brand name for a range of watches which they call 'New American Classics': 'a collection of funky, retro-style time pieces with a sense of humour, encased in authentic period tin packaging'; among them is a '40s blue face' decorated with an aeroplane and bearing the date 1953, and a Louisville Slugger.

Lexically, according to the dictionaries of neologisms, 'retrochic' was a critical term originating in the Paris avant-garde. It was one of the names given in the early 1970s to the rapidly growing taste for the revival of period styles – a vogue no less apparent, it seems, in the French cinema of the time than in the fashion trade. With the enormous expansion of the *marché aux puces*, today perhaps the largest assemblage of bric-à-brac in the world, *le mode rétro* came to encompass, by metaphorical extension, any aspect of tradition 'from the grandeur of Louis XIV to tubular steel furniture'.[7] The term was quickly adopted in this country, where there was a shop bearing the name 'Retro' as early as 1974; and also in the United States, where it seems to have coexisted, somewhat uneasily, with the slightly older term of 'vintage chic'. Malcolm McLaren, the Svengali of The Sex Pistols and the original architect of punk, was fiercely determined to avoid anything 'retro', as were the singers and songwriters of The Clash.[8] Yet the word seems to have been a difficult one to escape in pop music circles, as it is today. In 1979 the feminist and avant-garde New York art critic Lucy Lippiard defined it as a 'reactionary wolf in countercultural sheep's clothing'; punk was not iconoclastic but atavistic; retro, whatever form it took, was backward-looking.[9]

According to the fashion writers, retrochic takes its cues from the styles of the recent past, but this is not necessarily so. Under the influence of New Ageism crystals have been making their appearance as fashion accessories, and zodiacs are amongst the best-selling lines at Hugo Russell, the replica-ware supermarket which supplies period bric-à-brac to the pubs. Country copperware and horse-brasses, copied from Victoriana and produced at Moradabad in India, are old staples; a more recent craze, also taken from nineteenth-century originals, is the phrenological head.[10] A Viking amulet (the replica of an original in the Statens Historika Museum, Stockholm), a 'tree of life' brooch based on a seventh- or eighth-century cross at St Paul's, Jarrow, and a compact disc of medieval Christmas music, including wassail carols and nativity songs, are among the offerings in the current catalogue of Past Times, the rapidly expanding mail-order firm and 'historical collections' chain of upmarket gift shops. The catalogue plays with what is conventionally regarded as retro (one current offer is a reproduction 1930s wireless; another a *Picture Post* scrapbook); but it begins with the Romans and if the owner had had his way would have started with replica Neolithic arrowheads. Past Times draws its originals from museums and art galleries, and makes a fetish of facsimile: 'Generally our items are authentic replicas or based on actual period designs.' Thus, for instance, the Celtic jewellery, though a 'contemporary interpretation', follows 'traditional Celtic knotwork'; the 'Mille Fleurs cardigan' takes its detail from medieval tapestry; the 'Roman Fresco' silk scarf ('Printed in Italy exclusively for Past Times') takes its decorative motifs from Pompeii and Herculaneum.

Past Times began life in 1986, opening its first shop in Oxford. A product of graduate entrepreneurship (it is said that all the buyers have History or History of Art degrees), it is presided over by John Beale, whose 'Early Learning Centres' carried the principle of 'learning by doing' into the high-street shops. Past Times, though targeted at a very much older age group, is also intended, after its own fashion, to be improving. It is geared to the niche market for what the firm calls 'historical gifts', but it aims to be (and is) 'a bit more intelligent than the National Trust'. In place of kitsch, it offers what the catalogue calls 'thoughtful presents' to give to family and friends, accompanying each item with 'carefully researched descriptions', and taking as originals the best possible example in the field. Saxton's County Maps are reproduced from the edition of 1579, Churchill's war speeches – on cassette – from his BBC broadcasts. The playthings and toys are intended to be authentic even though they are new. Among those currently on offer are the Victorian parlour game of Anagrams ('You win tiles by making words'); the Roman game of 'Tabula' ('enormously popular throughout the Empire from the beginning of the 1st century AD'); and 'The Viking Game', a 37-piece forerunner of chess (The Jorvik Museum at York also makes a great feature of Viking games).[11]

Su Tahran, the proprietor of American Retro, the stylish and success-ful shop which has been one of the temples of gay consumerism, and not the least of the reasons for Old Compton Street's revival as Soho's Champs Elysées, is more interested in novelties than antiquities, needing to keep one step ahead of a youthful and fashion-conscious following. When she started the shop in 1986 there was a small section of second-hand clothing, the 'tail end' of an earlier version of retrochic. Today what she sells is either old factory stock or brand new. 'Retro' does not connote any particular period, but serves as a term interchangeable with 'classic', a label which the shop gives to anything which has stayed the course – Ivy League button-down shirts, symbolizing the nice boy or 'Preppy' look; heavy lumberjack shirts; John Smedley's traditional English knitwear, manufactured at Matlock in the Derbyshire Peak; sailors' pea-jackets; 'classic' Y-front underpants and vests (American Retro is famous for them, according to Paul Hallam's *The Book of Sodom*[12]) as well as more esoteric bondage wear. Matt black in the 1980s, and cultivating the cold hard look of Art Deco, the shop has just been given a major re-fit and, possibly under the influence of New Ageism, has adopted a more natural look. Old here will often stand for camp, something which serves simultaneously as a subject of ridicule and an object of desire – as in a Joan Crawford glamour photograph, a cult crucifix or the fantasies of aberrant art.[13]

A very different form of retrochic, ministering to a much more historicist fantasy, as well as providing a watering hole for the more impecunious members of the republic of letters, can be found round the corner from American Retro, at Black's, the semi-private literary club in Dean Street. As at Hazlitt's, the recently opened hotel which has added a touch of eighteenth-century urbanity to nearby Frith Street, the club is pioneering a new version of the Georgian, a masculine alternative to the ruched curtains and soft furnishings of the country house look. Here there is nothing dainty, nothing soft, but bare, pitted floorboards, curtainless windows, scattered, hard-back chairs. There are tables on which you can (if you are minded to do so) bang down a fist in an argument, or plonk a beer mug; a real log fire in the basement lends its atmospheric smells to the gas log fire substitutes on the floors above. A few good pictures hung on chains, original Hogarth prints which mirror the appearance of the interior, and a soup of light in which candle-sconces contrive to disguise the concealed electrics (at Denis Severs's house in Spitalfields, one of the inspirations for Black's, only real candles are used), produce an aura of pastness in which detail and chronology seem irrelevant. Stunning marble fireplaces, the fruits of architectural salvage, invite you to lean against them and indulge in a quite urban poetics where literary and historical fantasy have free rein.[14]

A more modernist reincarnation is to be found on the eastern side of Charing Cross Road, a few hundred yards from Hazlitt's and Black's, where Denmark Street, the 'Tin Pan Alley' of the 1940s and 1950s, deserted by the music publishers and the song writers about the time of the advent of pop, has suddenly started to sprout music shops. With the exception of a barber's and a Greek publisher, they now occupy both sides and either end of the street. In May 1990, under the chairmanship of Andy Preston, whose vintage guitar shop is a cornucopia of 1960s electronics, the traders formed themselves into a Tin Pan Alley Associa-tion and are campaigning to have the street designated 'Music land' rather as Drury Lane is dignified by Westminster City Council as 'Theatreland' and Gerrard Street as 'Chinatown'. In anticipation of success, the local pub has been renamed Tin Pan Alley Bar, while Andy's folk and blues club, an offshoot of the vintage shop, recruited from musicians who began their life as buskers, serves to make live perform-ance a real presence.[15]

An older, more comprehensive version of retrochic, masterminded by the historic buildings division of the old Greater London Council, can be seen a quarter of a mile away, on the other side of Charing Cross Road, in Covent Garden, the prototype of the up-market shopping precincts of the 1980s. The shops, though for the most part brand-new enterprises, cultivate the air of throw-backs to an earlier past, with their small-paned windows and carefully calligraphed hanging signs. Here one finds food shops and even restaurants pretending to be English rather than, as in the old days, French; and offering 'country' salads, 'traditional' cheddar cheeses and 'old-fashioned' trifles for all the world as if they were national delicacies. Culpepper's, survivors of an earlier phase of simple lifeism, sell traditional herbal remedies, and the Body Shop more cosmopolitan ones. In Neal's Yard, Plunket's the organic farm shop sells organically grown vegetables; the Neal's Yard Dairy 'organic' English cheeses (tough as old boots compared with Camembert); the Neal's Yard apothecary shop (surely one of the originals for Crabtree and Evelyn, the bogus-traditional perfumery), country-born shampoos.[16]

Retrochic has progressively up-dated the notion of 'period' clothes, as well as creating a market for them among the young and adventurous. Granny Takes a Trip, the jokily named progenitor of the secondhand fashion trade in London (Harriet Love opened her Vintage Chic store in New York, the first of its kind, a year earlier in 1965),[17] sold 'Naughty Nineties' memorabilia – ostrich-feathered hats, genuine old 'granny shoes', Army redcoats at £3 a time and, as a descriptive guide to 'Swinging London' put it in 1967, 'other historical garments'.[18] Under the influence of the Art Deco revival (the term was a 1960s neologism) the floppy hats of the 1920s replaced Marie Lloyd headgear; while in menswear the joke Hussar uniforms of 'The Charge of the Light Brigade' and 'I Was Lord Kitchener's Valet' gave way to Oxford bags, and (as some have argued) the seriously reactionary, *Forsyte Saga-* or *Brideshead*-derived three-piece suit.[19] The architects of punk, in the years immediately preceding 1977, were attempting to revive 1950s drainpipes and drapes (a pastiche of the very earliest essay in pop retro);[20] while in the 1980s, under the influence of *Dallas* and *Dynasty*, the Utility clothes of the 1940s were brought out of mothballs and revived as precocious instances of 'power dressing'. As an aggrieved, or puzzled, London antique dealer put it in 1985, 'Old-fashioned and ultra-modern have become almost the same thing – antiques are barely old, and contemporary fashion is barely new.'[21]

Quite the most remarkable example of this instant historicization is in the world of rock and pop, where the hunger for new sounds is only matched by the constancy with which older ones are recycled, re-invented and re-mixed.[22] Here, there is a vast and it seems ever-extending retro market, with its own shops and stalls where records are assigned to their respective class (Rockabilly, Pop, Psych, Rock, Prog, Indie, Goth, Metal Hardcore) and its collectors' fairs, where vinyl junkies drool over the forgotten beauties of seven-inch singles. There are now half-a-dozen specialist companies reissuing vintage records and rare, early DJ tapes; while the major record companies like EMI produce albums of classics on CD. On Virgin's round-the-clock music marathon, 'classic' albums and 'classic' tracks enjoy parity of esteem with new releases, while the new records themselves will often turn out to be remakes of older ones. Clubs, the principal venue for dancing, almost inevitably become a musical journey back in time: at Button's, Great Russell Street, 'a right groovy happening' according to the *Guardian*, 'mid-'80s classics' are the current offering.[23]

In a more necrophiliac vein, there is the cult of the living dead. Pop's own history – 'three decades of great music'[24] – is endlessly re-rehearsed, and its legendary singers and performers enjoy a more active following in many cases than current stars (a macabre example would be the division among the Marc Bolan groupies, recently publicized in the national press, with rival fanclubs – one calls itself the Marc Bolan Liberation Front[25] – picking over the bones of their dead hero). Tribute records are cut for them. Biopics are made of their often tragically short, doomed lives. The advertisers will raid them for sound bites and video clips.[26] Through the medium of rock tourism they are perhaps the most prolific source of new historical shrines, as well as giving new life to older ones (at Père Lachaise cemetery, Jim Morrison's grave has far more visitors and flowers than the Mur des Fédérés where the martyred dead of the Paris Commune are buried).[27] Bob Marley presides over the Notting Hill carnival, as he has done for many years; while among current releases attracting attention is a brand-new Jimi Hendrix album 'containing in excess of 50 Hendrix samples and previously unheard solos'.[28]

Whereas retrochic, on the catwalks, is a relatively superficial affair, a matter sometimes of no more than accessories, or the slant of a revere, in the world of pop music it is systematic, built into the technology of recording, the tastes of the public and the life-cycle of a hit. Musically it draws its energies from the juxtaposition and assimilation of wildly dissonant lexicons (Afro and Eastern as well as American and European) and calls on centuries of songwriting, as well as echoes and half-echoes of its own more recent past. Technically, electronic synthesizers – its chosen instrument for the mechanical reproduction of art – put at its fingertips every conceivable musical idiom, allowing the heavenly choir to serve as a foil to the urban beat of rap.

So far as sentiment or what Raymond Williams called 'structure of feeling' is concerned, pop follows well-worn poetical tropes. Its lyrics – a kind of adolescent, or pre-pubescent keening – record the pain of moving on. They remember the good times – 'back in 1957', 'back in 1963', 'the days of the Ford Cortina' – and offer a whole music of exile and growing up. In another register they echo the Elizabethan love sonnet and the poems of courtly love ('Please Forgive Me, I Can't Help Loving You' was Top of the Pops when the above lines were written). The faithless lover is another recurring figure, while the outlaw hero taking 'a walk on the wild side' – the affecting character of one of pop's often-repeated talking Blues – might have been drawn from some transsexual version of the *Iliad*. Something of the same might be suggested for such other stock figures as The Little Boy Lost, the Lonesome Traveller, the Jilted Lover. Mary Hopkin's 'Those Were the Days My Friend' which stayed in the charts throughout the long hot summer of 1967 – as concentrated an expression as one could hope to find of the wistful dream of a land of lost content – took its sentiment from centuries of pastoral and cribbed its melancholy air, note by note, from a Russian

folksong. 'Love, frustration, post-adolescent angst, encroaching madness, the richest, loveliest sonic textures ever committed to Vinyl' runs
a *New Musical Express* hype for a 'completely beautiful' pressing of a
Beach Boys album of 1966.[29]

II

Retrochic began life as an anti-fashion, winning a cult following by
allowing for a return of the repressed. It wanted to be outrageous,
shocking the salons by its irreverence towards the pretensions of high
art, flouting public decorum by ignoring the conventional boundaries of
sex or class. For the poster artists and the record sleeve designers of the
1960s the swirling lines of Art Nouveau and the dayglo colours of
psychedelia served as an invitation for the pleasures of the perverse. The
idea of outlaw fashion was even more appealing to the architects of punk,
reviving Teddy Boy quiffs and drapes, or their more proletarian cousins,
the skinheads, making a style of Doc Marten boots and granddad
collarless shirts.

At the same time, by a whole series of dialectical reversals, retrochic
contrived to keep in step with or even ahead of its time, reflecting sea-
changes in popular taste, and anticipating or prefiguring new depar-
tures. The counter-culture of the 1960s was famously the nursery of a
new, more ecologically sound consumerism – 'pine' furniture, 'health'
foods, 'herbal' medicines, 'natural' shampoos. The allegedly outlaw
punk within the space of three years had conquered the catwalks of the
world. And it is no accident that today the influence of retrochic is
paramount in those urban fairgrounds such as Portobello Road and
Camden Lock – the largest open-air markets in the metropolis – where
youthful stylists cut their teeth and musical cults are born.

According to writers on the fashion trade[30] 'retrochic', or what they
sometimes call 'the nostalgia industry', was a phenomenon of the late
1960s and 1970s. They date its advent to the wistful turn in late 1960s
counter-culture, and draw attention to a whole series of short-lived
period revivals which followed the Art Nouveau craze of the late 1960s.
Yet each of these revivals has its pre-histories which are both analytically
and chronologically distinct. Neo-vernacular, for example, *the* style of the
1980s so far as the quantity housebuilders were concerned, and perhaps
the major influence on commodity marketing and design, traces one of
its origins to the *cottage ornée* of the 1790s; another to the Arts and Crafts
movement of William Morris and C.R. Ashbee; and yet another to post-
war British modernism.

So far as period graphics are concerned, attempts to revive or to

pastiche traditional lettering were well under way at the time of the
Festival of Britain, and were indeed one of the chief enthusiasms of the
book illustrators, the typographers and the avant-garde art teachers of
the time. The Festival itself quite deliberately chose Egyptian and Gothic
typefaces for its displays – 'fun' or 'fairground' lettering in preference to
the sans-serif severities of Helvetica.[31] At St Martin's School of Art,
according to one who was a student there in 1950–53, all the avant-garde
teachers were experimenting in Egyptian and Gothic faces, imitating the
humours of the Victorian playbill.

So far as product marketing is concerned, it would not be difficult to
find anticipations of retrochic in the 1950s. Laura Ashley, whose
'romantic escapist clothes' perfectly suited the back-to-nature mood of
the seventies, was printing her tea-towels ('with a characteristic Victorian
motif') as early as 1953: the first batch sold so quickly at John Lewis, the
Oxford Street store, that by the time she returned to her Pimlico flat
(according to trade legend) the telephone was ringing for repeat
orders.[32] It was about the same time that Roy Brooks, the fashionable
left-wing estate agent, was pioneering a new market in run-down period
properties.[33] Sanderson's began marketing (or more properly re-
marketing) William Morris wallpapers about the same time, while
William Morris fabrics began to establish themselves as a favourite
curtain for the discriminating. The craze for vintage ephemera seems to
have started a little later. It was only, it seems, 'in the late 1950s' that
Portobello Road began its climb to fame, as a style-setter for the
advertisers and the interior decorators, and as a grand emporium of
Victoriana.[34]

These early retrochic enthusiasms were self-consciously *minority* tastes,
even a kind of eccentricity. They acquired a wider resonance in the
prosperity of the 1960s as an alternative version of consumerism,
pandering to the nostalgia for a simpler life. It was then that 'the great
surge of public interest in antique collecting' began;[35] that the dealers
began to set up in the Cotswolds (in 1955 there was not a single pot-
pourri shop to be seen at Burford; they are now more numerous than
butchers or bakers);[36] and that in Islington Camden Passage was
founded as 'London's antique village'.[37] In the same period product
labelling began to adopt vintage logos; 'yesterday's advertisements'
made their appearance, as tradesmen's signs, at Oodles and Cranks, the
new health food restaurant. The late 1960s also seems to have been the
time when the serious production of heritage ware began; when 'vintage'
photographs established themselves in the card trade, and when
'stripped' pine furniture, originally promoted for its modernism, began
to be marketed for its 'cottagey' look.

In its play aspect, its love of dressing up, and its taste for histrionics retrochic rejoins, and could be seen as a late offspring of, that self-indulgent strain in British national taste which design historians see as a kind of antiphon to the austerities of post-war Britain – the Battersea Pleasure Gardens side of the Festival of Britain, as it were, rather than the Dome of Discovery. At the Festival itself there were such wayward exercises in the aesthetics of the absurd as the 'Lion and the Unicorn' pavilion, which celebrated the greatness and 'whimsicalities' of the British national character; in the Battersea Pleasure Gardens there were the Nell Gwyn orange girls who were supposed to recapture the vanished delights of Ranelagh, Vauxhall and the Cremorne. Outside the Festival, but closely related to it, one might instance the opening, at Whitsun 1951, of the first pretend Victorian railway; the 'revival' (after a gap of some four hundred years!) of the York Mystery plays; and the White-chapel Art Gallery's celebration of the 'Unsophisticated Arts', those of the fairground and the seaside in particular.[38]

Another genealogy which would repay attention would be the middle-class cult of childhood, with its celebration of the time-warped and its sentimentalization of the nursery. It is brilliantly represented in theatre by the annual revivals of *Treasure Island* and *Peter Pan*; in ethnography by the Opies' *Lore and Language of Schoolchildren* (1960), and in the auction rooms by the extraordinary prices paid for such vintage juvenilia as dolls' houses and toy theatres. The National Trust gift shops – a phenomenon of the last twenty years – also subscribe to it. Here Beatrix Potter receives far more attention, as a writer, than Shakespeare, Dickens and Scott, or as an illustrator, than Hogarth or Blake. For long the preserve of the ladylike (she has been called 'the Disney of the Middle Classes') Beatrix Potter has gained a vast new constituency of admirers following the recent video release of her *Tales*. Working-class three-year-olds, it seems, are among the new addicts, and it is perhaps in recognition of this that 'Peter Rabbit' cookies are among the giant boxes of confectionery on offer at Woolworth's,[39] and that Jemima Puddleduck has been annexed for potty training, a grimacing figure on nursery toilet rolls.

In retro advertising, the past is there to humanize the present, and substitute a personal for a corporate image. In the current series of Levi ads, harking back to 1920s hillbillies, as in the 1974 Hovis 'bike ride' commercial directed by Ridley Scott which helped to make soft-focus nostalgia a leitmotiv of TV commercials, sepia is there to sentimentalize the image. But period is also widely used for comic, or serio-comic effect, as in those parodies of old masters currently being used by Vodaphone in the cordless communications war. An old film clip from Harold Lloyd's *Safety Last*, showing the comic clinging for dear life to the clock-face at the top of the Empire State Building, was for many years a very

popular insurance ad. A recent Heineken series contrived to parade Marilyn Monroe (from *Some Like it Hot*), John Wayne from a western, and Humphrey Bogart. A much admired current effort is Mercury's pastiche of a 1950 Pathé newsreel in which words and image are out of synch and a nincompoop of the officer class tries to rally the other ranks.[40]

As the foregoing may have suggested, retrochic, when it imitates or appropriates the past, often does so tongue-in-cheek. It is playful and theatrical in the way it appropriates artefacts and uses them as icons or emblems. According to the theorists of postmodernism, retrochic differs from earlier kinds of period revival in that what it does is parodic. It is irreverent about the past and only half-serious about itself. It is not concerned with restoring original detail, like the conservationist, but rather with decorative effect – choosing objects because they are aesthetically surprising, or 'amusing', rather than because they are authentic survivals of the past. Indeed retrochic seems often to prefer remakes to originals, cheerfully engaging in the manufacture of replica-ware without any attempt to disguise the modernity of its provenance. When it imitates or cribs, it draws attention to its own piracies; when it borrows it puts its loans, metaphorically speaking, in quotation marks; when it takes on a part it makes a point of advertising its own artifice. In short, it does not want to deceive anyone into a hallucinatory sense of oneness with the past but, on the contrary, cultivates an air of detachment and ironic distance. Retrochic, on this view, involves not an obsession with the past but an indifference to it: only when history has ceased to matter can it be treated as a sport.

All this is certainly true of pop art, one of the crucibles of the cultural revolution of the 1960s, as also, if more obliquely, of retrochic. Breaking with both figurative painting and abstraction and creating new art forms out of debris, it juxtaposed past and present iconoclastically – using historical pop-ups or parodies of Old Masters as well as more contemporary images, to cock a snook at the pretensions of the salons and show high art's affinities to kitsch. Pop art showed a precocious appetite for the decorative use of old product labels and advertising enamels, and of printed ephemera generally; Alice peeped out from Peter Blake's montages rather as classical busts had been wont to do in the lunar landscapes of the Surrealists. In a more vampiric mode (as Elizabeth Wilson aptly calls it[41]) old movie stills, showing the stars of the silent screen, were recycled as poster art; while dead movie stars of the 1940s and 1950s enjoyed a vigorous after-life in the mugshots of Andy Warhol and the record sleeve of *Sergeant Pepper*.

It was the notion of fun antiques – objects which sold because they were colourful, garish or bizarre rather than because they were valuable, or, in any more conventional sense, *objets d'art* – which made the fortunes of Portobello Road, turning Victorian trinkets into 'with-it' jewellery, and coronation mugs into collectables. Taken up in the 1950s, by the impecunious young and the denizens of London's bedsitterland, Portobello Road profited, in the 1960s, from the advent of new and more opulent lifestyles, as well as the insatiable demand of fashion photographers and the film and TV studios for period props. By the end of the 1960s there were some two thousand mini-shops and stalls in the complex. Many of them were in the hands of part-time or Saturday dealers, connoisseurs of 'off-beat' and 'found-in-the-attic' Victoriana, and making a speciality of such previously unregarded bygones as Second World War gas-masks, old trade signs, Edison gramophones and – as the Art Deco craze gathered pace – chromium-plated ashtrays. 'They do not take themselves very seriously', runs a 1967 Portobello Road guide, which gives a stall-by-stall account of the market, 'and are more likely to sell a bargain or a fake without knowing it in either case.'[42]

Kinky clothes and joke ceramics – though for the most part replica rather than originals, and manufactured as souvenirs – also helped to make the fortunes of Carnaby Street and to establish it, for a brief but brilliant period, as a fashion centre of the world. Indeed its most celebrated shop, selling joke militaria and accessories – I Was Lord Kitchener's Valet – had first made its home at the freakier end of Portobello Road.

There was a very strong camp element in the late 1960s vogue for dressing up in period clothes, one which gave free play to fantasy and fetishism, while at the same time caricaturing or sending up class and gender stereotypes. It allowed male narcissism to disguise itself as macho, while women could vamp it up as *femmes fatales* in the slinky clothes of 1920s Mayfair or Manhattan. Terence Stamp's performance as Sergeant Troy in *Far from the Madding Crowd* seems to have been as influential on male fashion as Julie Christie's Bathsheba in the same film, making the scarlet tunic and tight pantaloons of the gay hussar a kind of alternative lifestyle uniform.

Kinky clothes seem to have graduated very quickly from being freaky to being fashionable. By 1967, according to a guide to Portobello Road, Art Deco was already high style:

> There's nothing like a street market for finding thirty-year-old clothes which need little alteration to make you the smartest woman at the party. Now the 1920 look is back, keep an eye open for the beaded and fringed creations which are so fashionable at present. If the couturier's label is still inside, it will add to the price now just as it did in the original sale. Look out too for the accessories which went with them – the long necklaces, the eighteen-inch

cigarette holder, or the ostrich-feather fan. Men can also be the centre of attention if they are lucky enough to find a period waistcoat. An eighteenth century one will be thigh length and embroidered in brightly coloured silks ... Victorian ones are shorter and will have lapels; black and yellow stripes, paisley pattern or *petit point* embroidered waistcoats are just a few of the designs you may find.[43]

Alice's, the celebrated Portobello Road emporium for Victoriana, with its strategically placed premises on the corner with Denbigh Close and its old-fashioned trade sign, was among the very first shops in London to make a speciality of Victorian brass bedsteads and stripped furniture, 'both of which emerge free of paint and rust from brother Pete's caustic soda bath'. Along with its counterparts in Church Road, Marylebone, it might be accounted an original of that 'pine' look – originally Scandi-navian and modernist, later 'country kitchen' or 'Victorian' – which replaced walnut and mahogany veneers as the incarnation of British national taste.

Portobello Road, as well as being a vast emporium of Victorian bric-à-brac and inter-war kitsch, was also, in the later 1960s, a world capital of hippiedom, an early stomping ground for the Hare Krishna cult and one of the original nurseries of New Ageism. The Macrobiotic restaurant in Ladbroke Grove, and Ceres Whole Grain shop were as much a part of the scene as the jokily named Chip and Dale or Dodo Designs. Elizabeth Wilson, in her fine autobiographical sketch, *Mirror Writing*, has described the dream-like druggy scene, as it presented itself in the heyday of flower-power and on the eve of the campus risings of 1968:

> In the peeling shells of those enormous, pompous houses a new culture spread like a golden lichen, a new growth which was actually a symptom of decay. Every Saturday long-haired men and women, in flappy, droopy clothes thronged the pavements of the Portobello Road, a fluctuating crowd edging past the old clothes stalls, the stall with yams and plantains, the health food stores, the 'head' stores – the shops for hippies – which smelt of joss sticks and patchouli.[44]

Retrochic set a whole style for the alternative culture of the 1970s and 1980s. John Lennon's wire-framed 'granny' glasses, a passing fancy adopted, in 1967, along with his Astrakhan coat, had become Trotskyist wear by the early 1970s and later still – the position they have retained – the standard spectacles for the studious and the owlish. The droopy Zapata moustache which George Harrison sports on the cover of *Sergeant Pepper* was taken up by working-class heroes (among them the celebrated soccer star, George Best); by West Coast Chicanos in the United States; a more aggressive toothbrush version of it in combination with workwear and shaven heads, was the clone look, affirmative and up-front, adopted

in the early 1970s by many gay men. More generally, by the licence which
it gave to cross-dressing, and camp styles of putting on a front, the new
taste for dressing up in period clothes might be thought of as one of the
invisible influences subverting sexist ideologies.

Retrochic has also sensibly influenced the business corporation. The
swirling lines and decorative lettering of Art Nouveau, still an eye-
catching novelty when they were used to adorn the shop-front of Granny
Takes a Trip, have proved serviceable to every kind of marketing,
ranging from the Body Shop at the 'green' end of the new consumerism
to Mr Kipling's 'exceedingly good' cakes at the bogus-traditional end.
Art Deco, taken up by the business corporations, has gone straight –
as with the sprite-like figure ('the dancing pooftah' according to unkind
critics) who decorates the kiosks of British Telecom, or the Matisse-like
Apollo who makes the Prudential Insurance Company's property
operations seem warm, friendly and human. Likewise in the sphere of
mass communications the dayglo colours of psychedelia, originally an
invention of the light-show and later a hallmark of the underground
press, are now becoming *de rigueur* in both the quality press and the
tabloids.

III

Economically, retrochic could be described as a child of the post-war
boom. It makes its first appearance in Festival of Britain year as a kind
of whimsical gesture against the severities of utility fashions and
rationing. It was closely tied, in the 1960s, to the rise of an alternative
consumerism in which free time counted for more than money, and
style leaders were drawn from the culturally privileged rather than the
wealthy. In its later development it reflects the growth of niche
marketing and what was variously termed, in the 1980s, 'leisure',
'festival' or 'speciality' shopping. Retrochic has notably profited by and
indeed quite largely fuelled the great explosion in fashion accessories
– for example, the waist jewellery, armlets and bondage-wear,
recommended on the catwalks as reviving a 'medieval' look.[45] In its
feminine aspect (women account for 82 per cent of the customers of
Past Times,[46] and they are the chief purchasers at the 'bygones' stalls
on Portobello Road and at Camden Lock) retrochic might be related
to the growth of women's earning power and perhaps to the increasing
gender segmentation of markets, with the growth of whole new classes
of feminine commodities. Social stationery – hardly less in evidence at
commercial stationers like Ryman's than in the card shops and fancy-
goods stores – is an obvious case in point, a kind of retrochic equivalent

of the scented notepapers of the nineteenth-century miss. Quite apart from greetings cards themselves, the busy secretary can hardly avoid seeing the twee boxes of notelets, with country cottage, wildlife or furry animal illustration; the birthday diary, intended to keep the present-giver, or the party-pooper, up to the mark; the nameplate with scrolled or illuminated lettering – the office worker's answer to the gentleman's *ex libris* book-plate. Interesting here is that recently minted modern classic, the Art Nouveau photo frame, which sits as comfortably, it seems, in the teenage bedroom as it does in the attic of the *House and Garden* or *Period Interiors* cottage. Past Times are currently marketing 'Celtic Art Notecards', a 'Celtic sword paper knife', Lindisfarne Gospels 'illuminated notepaper', and – a striking extension of the notion of late Gothic – 'Fleur-de-Lys' ballpoint pens.[47]

'Classic' sportswear, much of it, like Doc Marten boots, newly manufactured, is some kind of male equivalent to female potlatch, though it seems to function more as a self-given present than as a gift for others. A case in point would be the 1970s club football shirts, dating from the pre-sponsor days, which have a sale at the record shops along with the fanzines and pop memorabilia; the limited edition T-shirts reproduced from testimonial matches (that of Matt Busby, the Manchester United manager, has the hero of the day in a top hat); the David Twydell videos of defunct football clubs (Accrington Stanley is apparently the most popular); and the new high-fashion market in 'vintage' or replica 1960s trainers (there is a whole shop devoted to them in Soho).[48]

Americana, another contemporary growing point in 'retro', is also distinctively masculine. So far as James Dean and Marlon Brando uniform is concerned – white T-shirt, black leather jacket, blue jeans – it seems to descend from the Gay Liberation movement of the early 1970s, and the adoption of a 'clone' or 'macho' look as a way of breaking away from effeminate stereotypes of the 'queer'. In 'performance clothing', manufactured as new 'vintage' wear or 'modern classics' as well as selling second-hand at the flea markets, it is associated with the rugged, outdoor, 'he-man' look. Indeed to follow some of the advertisements for Timberland or Rockport workwear one would imagine that the British male was about to take off for the Arizona desert or Louisiana's alligator-infested swamps.

> Take the three pieces of rugged, versatile footwear shown on these pages. One is our ... timeless waterproof boot for all-around rugged use. Two is our handsewn Trekker.... And three is our well-known Weatherbuck, which combines classic casual shoe styling with ... no-compromise waterproof technology.... Equally versatile is our Blue Ridge Mountain Parka. Whether you're pounding through icy Arctic mud or puddle-jumping through warmer

climes, you'll find its composition ideal for fending off the extremes of turbulence found in much of the Northern Hemisphere.[49]

A recent addition to British Americana, translating vintage chic into the chromium-plated modernities of the 1950s, is Fatboy's Diner, the Worcester, Mass., lunch car which has successfully gone native in Spitalfields (another version of it can be seen in Covent Garden). Dreamed up by Mark Yates, a young entrepreneur who served one of his business apprenticeships in 'events catering', it invites customers to 'eat a piece of history', and offers, along with early rock 'n' roll music, such exotica as paprika-sprayed chips, Hillbilly Fatburgers, and New Young Hound, with root beer as the speciality drink to wash it all down.[50]

The rise of retrochic, and especially of the female end of it, might be related to the emergence of a mainly office-based, or schoolgirl-oriented, gift culture.[51] A great deal of retrochic is manufactured as giftware, and might be considered as a kind of contemporary equivalent of the Victorian, and pre-Victorian 'fairing'.[52] This is obviously the destiny of those hexagonal soaps, as also those cameos and lockets, shaped as Victorian miniatures, which are a staple fare at the National Trust gift shops. The Body Shop moved into the gift business in a big way when it added cosmetics to its herbal soaps and oils. As one of the firm's admiring chroniclers records: 'Gift baskets were made up to a customer's specifications, with an assortment of the products and sundries displayed prettily in baskets with dried flowers, and then cling-film wrapped.'[53] 'For the best in china, glass and giftware' runs an advertisement for Lawleys of Regent Street, a metropolitan showcase for Wedgwood china, Royal Doulton porcelain and Limerick glass. Novelty teapots, offered by the mail-order firms as well as at some of the museum shops, seem to have a similar destination: 'Most are given as gifts.... Choose one to match the recipient's hobby, like fishing or gardening; a cat teapot for cat lovers; a balloon teapot for a high flyer.' The British Museum shop, once a little corner, now an entire gallery, offers 'great little gifts' – a replica ancient Egyptian cat, selling at £8 a time, being an all-time favourite. 'Country kitchen' jams – such as Wilson's, 'the gift with a taste of history', or Cartwright and Butler's 'conserves' ('hand-made in Norfolk') – are manufactured as tokens, selling as much for their gingham-covered tops and period labels as for the preservative-free spreads within.

Retrochic in the 1970s and 1980s was one of those fields where enterprise culture came into its own, ministering not only to the tourist trade but also to the 'alternative' consumerism of the counter-culture; to teenage 'outlaw' fashions (notably punk); and to the new narcissism of health, epitomized by the Body Shop. In the case of the giftware trade,

ACCRINGTON STANLEY

FOR THE BEST IN LIVE MUSIC

Any remaining doubters may wish to heed that The Beatles also had a dreadful name. And I hear they did all right.

Melody Maker, April 1993

Thursdays at

the Black Lion
Kilburn High Rd   7.30-12pm

From Elvis to REM and back again

where some four thousand firms occupy thirteen miles of exhibition space when the annual trade fair is held at Birmingham (there are two other national fairs, as well as international ones at Frankfurt and New York), there are no big companies but for the most part small one-off shops and studios.[54] The rise of 'charity shops', an offshoot of the new-wave philanthropy of the 1960s, brought the humours of the flea market to the shopping parade, allowing a 'concerned' middle class to experiment with style and at the same time perform a simulacrum of social service. In a more commercial vein, retrochic's exploitation of old factory stock – the fashion trade's equivalent of publishers' remainders – has produced many profitable new lines.

Charity shops, it seems, are a pan-European and transatlantic phenomenon, indeed in the United States the vintage clothes trade seems to have been, in the first place, an outcrop of mid 1960s Third Worldism. Flea markets too are an international phenomenon. Street market antiques are represented in Amsterdam by Waterlooplein, where 'together with more or less new surplus goods, you will also find old crockery, storage tins, seventy-eights, grandma's furniture, grandpa's clothes, hats and caps, and who knows, if you look closely, ladies' corsets';[55] in Paris, the *marché aux puces*, already a focus of artistic attention in the early days of surrealism, is now the emporium for a far-flung international trade, a place for off-loading newly produced Americana as well as Provençal ovenware or Breton ceramics. Madrid's flea market, the Rastro, is – to judge by the photographs – second cousin to Oxford's Gloucester Green, while Camden Lock, with its great stock of Americana, seems to be a favoured outlet for transatlantic retro surpluses.

Starting life in quite impromptu ways, often in the pursuit of an individual whim, retrochic nevertheless prepares the way for big business, pioneering the advent or smoothing the passage of new classes of commodity and new forms of trade. It moves by degrees from the world of the flea markets to that of franchises and contracts. Andy Thornton's, for instance – a husband-and-wife team who set up as architectural salvage merchants in 1975 – now find themselves manufacturers of replica ware for hotel groups and brewery chains right across the country, as well as for the theme parks and open-air museums: among their clients, as well as McDonald's, the hamburger chain, and the Metro Centre, Gateshead, are the House of Lords, the National Museum of Photography, and Eurodisney.[56] Christopher Wray the lighting contractors, who began life with a stall in Kensington Market, now supply newly minted traditional fittings to a vast range of travel and leisure groups, as well as to the Victorian Inn at what is fancifully called 'Gatwick Airport Village'. They maintain a whole factory in Birmingham 'using the traditional drop stamping processes' to produce brass fittings; and a glass works at Wakefield, Yorks, using 'state-of-the-art modern technology' to produce traditional old-style uplighters and shades.[57]

Retrochic made some contribution to the snacks explosion of the 1980s, minting a range of brand-new vintage products – 'hand-made' crisps, 'traditional' tortilla chips, and a great mass of nutty bars and munchies which sold in the shops as health foods. The sauciest of these new promotions, and to judge by the brave show they make at both the supermarket and the chemist, one of the most successful, would be the Phileas Fogg collection of snacks, manufactured in an industrial estate on the outskirts of Gateshead, but bearing an image of Uncle Sam on the packet. Jordan's 'frusli bar',[58] issuing, if the packaging is to believed, from a country mill in Hertfordshire, Sainsbury's Grain Crackers, produced, apparently, at an Art Deco farmhouse, and Tesco's 'harvest brunch' are current examples.

Commercially, retrochic shows no signs of having exhausted its impetus. In textiles and the clothing trade it is busy promoting a series of self-styled 'modern' or 'timeless' classics which serve in some sort as an alternative to the fickleness of fashion, and offer a stylish realization of the old middle-class belief in 'sensible' clothes. There is currently the extraordinary proliferation of so-called 'country wear', in which the brand name – as with Barbers – confers a kind of honorary baronetcy on the wearer. In a more urban pastoral, the donkey jacket – variously recommended as a throw-back to eighteenth-century elegance, naval mufti or proletarian chic – is nowadays being snapped up by the style-conscious. 1960s trainers, now reproduced by the English manufacturers as 'vintage', have recently been elevated to this status.

Then retrochic, for all its vernacular and local appearance, continues to be a multinational business. Make-believe Victorian lamp-posts are exported to the four corners of the globe. Merchant–Ivory films, like the costume dramas of Goldcrest in the 1960s, are among the British film industry's few successful exports. Crabtree and Evelyn, the bogus-traditional perfumers, selling 'traditional English products' – toiletries and 'comestibles' especially – to the international rich, and using a liberal display of make-believe apothecaries' cabinets, have three hundred shops in the United States (the country where the idea of the shop was born), eight in France, and three in the United Arab Emirates.[59]

At Camden Lock – now by far the biggest open-air market complex in London, and ministering almost entirely to the young, sixth-formers, art college students and hard rock followers especially – the past has almost caught up with the present. A nursery of the Art Deco revival of the 1960s and in its early days the home of 'ethnic arts', it is today, when not given over to the very latest in streetwise fashion, quite largely taken up with

1960s and 1970s collectables. 'Yesterday's luggage' makes a brave display of duffel-bags; the music stalls have rare tapes of early disc-jockeys; a Boy George mannequin stands proudly by a chromium-plated tea-cosy; Batman curios are displayed as though they were Stevengraphs; psyche-delic Poole Pottery of the 1960s as though it were early Spode. The 'vintage' clothing snapped up by teenage stylists includes such near contemporary items as Biba tops and Mary Quant scarves.[60]

In the fashion trade, where platform shoes are adopted as the latest thing, and Lycra as the newest of materials, past and present trip so closely over one another's heels that it is difficult to know where one begins and the other ends. On the catwalks, where the 'army surplus' look is apparently enjoying a small vogue,[61] the utilitarian clothing of the 1940s, which in the 1980s provided one of the models for power dressing, has now been annexed in the service of make-believe fatigues. Paul Smith, the Covent Garden style leader, has latched on to this for menswear. In his recent venture in designer-led retailing he has taken over a 'Heath Robinson-like' Victorian factory – R. Newbold of Derby, founded in 1885 and long-time clothiers of the uniformed working class – and is trawling through its old pattern-books and samples to produce, under the firm's old label, an English answer to American denim and Australian workwear. His first, not inexpensive, collection includes a shirt originally made for agricultural workers in Lincolnshire, a donkey jacket (price £120) based on the City of Westminster roadsweeper's uniform, and a GPO shirt. 'With his love of British history and good basic design, Smith seems to be finding this new venture fun', writes a fashion journalist.[62]

In pop music, the re-release of many older albums on CD, the discovery of hitherto unused recordings and tapes such as those of Jimi Hendrix, and not least the progressive ageing of many hard rock and heavy metal followers, is producing a veritable explosion of nostalgia. In the clubs a seventies revival is in full swing, and when it comes to new releases, a piece of recycled New Romantica or Glam Rock can be as much of an excitement as the latest Acid House. 'The best of Boy George and Culture Club' runs a huge new advertising panel at Marble Arch tube station, showing the androgynous face of the star in a fade-away yellow etching: 'nineteen timeless hits. You will love every word and every note ... CD and Tape.'[63] *Q,* the bestselling rock magazine for adults – a nineties hit – might fairly be described as a style leader in retro; and the same is going to be even more true of its stablemate *Mojo,* aimed at 'the vintage forty-something rock fan'. Long articles are promised on such esoteric names as Blind Faith, the short-lived supergroup founded by Eric Clapton and Steve Winwood in the 1970s, and ideal-typical readers are those who – with the aid of the latest hi-fi equipment – want to re-live the great moments of punk. 'They're still going to get excited by the Clash, and not by Andrew Lloyd Webber', says one of the new editors.[64]

In costume drama, too, as represented in cinema and TV, the past is continually breathing down the neck of the present, with a progressive up-dating of the notion of period and a new-found delight in the supposed modernity of the past. In *Tales of the City*, a serial of the cult novel recently screened on Channel 4, the 1970s appeared as an age of lost innocence in which twenty-somethings cut their teeth and drug-taking and homosexuality were colourful novelties. Here is the trailer which appeared in *The Independent*:

> The hairdos are remaindered from *Cagney and Lacey*, the medallions come courtesy of *Saturday Night Fever*, and the shirt-collars are built by Pan Am. People say things like 'far out', 'fantabulous' and 'mellow out' with a straight face. For TALES OF THE CITY (9 p.m. C4), a new five-part serial, Seventies San Francisco has been recreated with a meticulousness formerly seen only in BBC adaptations of George Eliot.[65]

The recent BBC documentary on the London Underworld in the 1950s had a similar reception:

> [The show] has to pretend to disapprove of the criminals it profiles but is actually beside itself with excitement at their presence. It opens with rain-soaked streets, a vintage Jag and plenty of dramatic backlighting, and the *Long Good Friday* feel is accentuated by the decision to have Bob Hoskins do the voice-over. In other words, the irrepressible appeal of the outlaw is reinforced by plenty of retro-chic – police cars with bells on front and Ealing Film wrong 'uns. There was certainly more than a whiff of nostalgia for the days when good honest criminals only carried coshes and did their porridge without whining to the Appeal Court. Try as he might, Hoskins never found a tone of voice which sounded convincingly disdainful – 'He prides himself on never having won even a day's remission for good behaviour' he said of 'Mad' Frankie Fraser, and he couldn't extinguish the little thrill of respect for the hard man that the remark contained; he even talked at one point about 'the post-War generation of British thieves', as if they were an artistic movement due for re-appraisal on *The Late Show*. They were undoubtedly more innocent times. 'Quantities of discard chewing-gum have been discovered', said a Cholmondeley-Warner voice from the BBC archives, 'leading the authorities to believe that the crimes are the work of a band of foreigners – possibly Americans'. They were, in fact, the work of Eddie Chapman, a charming safe-cracker who introduced gelignite to the trade in Britain.[66]

The spread of green consumerism also seems to be giving retrochic a new lease of life. Part of this trend is the growing association between the idea of heritage and the protection and maintenance of wildlife reserves. Like the restoration and featuring of 'period' façades, and the role of 'retrofitting' and 'refurbishment' in the building boom of the 1980s, this has now been built into the machinery of new development. Here for example is the prospectus for Chafford Hundred, an 'exciting new homes development', near Grays, Essex, currently promoted by a consortium of quality housebuilders:

> The foresight that went into the planning stages of Chafford Hundred has succeeded in making this a very special place indeed. A community where a genuine concern for the environment and its preservation will provide the future generations of Chafford Hundred residents with a privileged blend of quality homes and an outstanding landscape.
>
> The concept of Chafford Hundred has been to create a new beginning for man and nature. A major part of this concept is the provision of over 250 acres of landscaped open space. This helps to create a balanced, self-contained community that is in sympathy with nature whilst giving residents a sense of place and belonging . . .
>
> Chafford Hundred Limited realised that on this site they had a unique opportunity to retain and improve the ecology of the area and forge a balance between the needs of people and wildlife.
>
> The rare chalk grassland, native to Essex, has not fallen victim to the development. Chafford Hundred have taken positive steps not only to protect, but also to translocate some of the most important areas of chalk grassland. Seeds of the wildflowers and grasses have been collected and stored for future use. Uncommon orchids have been individually lifted and replanted in safe locations such as Warren Gorge to ensure their future survival. It is intended that these ecologically interesting areas will be accessible to the people of Chafford Hundred for nature walks and trails.
>
> Home of Chafford Hundred's rarest plants and animals is Warren Gorge. It is hoped that Warren Gorge will be a declared Local Nature Reserve with a public park and picnic area in the middle for the pleasure of both residents and visitors . . .
>
> The plan has been created by Chafford Hundred's landscape and ecology consultants and both the Nature Conservancy Council and Essex Wildlife Trust. Schools will be encouraged to use this wildlife asset as a valuable supplement to children's education . . .
>
> Chafford Hundred is also one of the few sites to contain active badgers within the development. Landscaped areas have been carefully designed and located to provide corridors and foraging areas for the Chafford Hundred badgers, and every contingency has been considered in the purpose made under-passes provided under roads which were previously crossed by bad-gers.[67]

Green consumerism provides business with a new environment-friendly heraldry. At Sainsbury's, the tuna steaks, so the label informs the customer, have been caught with a pole and line rather than netted: 'thus avoiding danger to other marine life'[68]. A quite remarkable number of commodities now wear a vernacular dress. The paint manufacturers blossom out in country colours, with pastel shades in place of Mediterranean (or modernist) primaries – 'Harvest Beige', 'Rose White', 'Bracken Leaf', 'Wild Primrose', 'Sweet William', 'Hydrangea', to name some of those currently in vogue. 'Rich garden colours' are likewise a favourite with the soft furnishers. The shelves of the supermarkets are full of newly-minted traditional goods – 'ploughman's' pickles, 'country' ales, 'Wiltshire' mustard, 'Norfolk' turkeys, and an astonishing range of technicoloured English cheeses in which county is distinguished from county by its speckles. Sainsbury's offer 'harvest slims' crispbread and 'all-fruit preserves'. Tesco market their own farmhouse brunch. Heinz have turned from the vivid oranges and browns of their 1960s tins to the yellowy-greenery of their 'ploughman's' pickles.

'Eggs laid in Shakespeare's country' – the current boast of Alden's butchers in Oxford's covered market[69] – may seem a bit excessive, but not more so than the Sainsbury labels which contrive to associate bacon with every element in the pastoral idyll – ivied church, village green, babbling brook, even the haystack (something which disappeared from the English fields about thirty years ago) – but never the sight of a pig, let alone a carcase. Indeed if one were to take product labelling seriously one would imagine that the country had reverted to spade husbandry, such is the cornucopia of baskets of fruit, wheelbarrows of vegetables and cow-bred dairy produce confronting the shopper.[70] Whereas commodities, in the 1950s, were advertised in such a way as to make a feature of their chemical additives or synthetics ('RINSO washes WHITER THAN NEW – contains SOLIUM'), today, on the contrary, they will make a feature of being 'pure', 'fresh' and 'natural': in the case of jams, 'unsweetened'; in that of pickles, 'free of preservatives'. Where nineteenth-century manufacturers made a visual feature of their modernity and progressiveness – the 'steam' flour-mill, and gigantic, multi-storey warehouse or factory – their more ecologically sound, or commercially bashful, successors prefer to suggest that the produce is both literally and metaphorically 'farm-fresh'. The Sainsbury artist has a team of two horses dragging a plough to illustrate a bottle of pickled onions; their butter puffs seem to have come from a thatched cottage.

Another and more bizarre growing point of retrochic, drawing on pre-history and archaeology, ley-lines and crystals rather than polystyrene or bakelite, would be New Ageism. Interesting is the emergence of the Glastonbury Festival, in the twentieth year of its existence, as a style leader in both pop music and the fashion trade. Its influence is very apparent in jewellery, where belly chains and necklaces sport zodiac and runic signs, earrings are fashioned after Celtic crosses and 1960s hippy

beads are reactivated for 1990s karma, while on the principle of 'sleeping with the enemy' giant crucifixes are appropriated from the Jesus freaks and sported on pagan breasts. At Glastonbury itself, 'Gothic Image' – a combination of emporium, mail-order business and resource centre – has been for some fifteen years a headquarters of the town's alternative culture, as well as the unofficial tourist office for mystical trails.

> A large proportion of the shop premises is given over to books on … Glastonbury, Arthur, the Celts, myth and legend, earth mysteries, the Goddess, shamanism and native astrology, personal growth and transformation, divination and healing. In addition there are Glastonbury souvenirs (such as candles decorated with Glastonbury 'Thorn leaves'), children's toys and books (for this is 'a family shop'), Celtic silver jewellery, reproduction neolithic objets d'art, Celtic and New Age cards, dowsing implements, tarot cards, New Age music, a selection of pendulums … the Global flag, incense, crop circle T-shirts and 'Tao – the Game of the Way to Divine Harmony'.[71]

It is possible that the rise of gay culture will give an even more extravagant twist to retrochic. Even in the days of its clandestinity, when, so far as the general public was concerned, it was barely distinguishable from 'the bright young things', it was the first nursery in which – through the instrumentality of Cecil Beaton's high camp fancy-dress parties – a taste for Victoriana was formed. With the coming-out of the late 1960s, such gay fashions as cross-dressing, or the wearing of male jewellery, began to feed into the wider culture. The more sado-masochistic delight in leatherwear and black also found a resonance in the wider culture. More recently the gay imagination, with its delight in visual artifice and decorative excess, has begun to leave its mark on the built environment, pioneering some of the most adventurous lines in period decor. In Manchester the city council, desperate for some sign of the green shoots of urban regeneration, looks on with a benevolent eye, as *Gay Times* reported when describing the success of the recent Pink Festival:

> There is no doubt that Manchester's gay village is the near-perfect location to stage a daytime gay festival, but luck has played some part in creating this setting. Gay bars and businesses originally sprung up in Bloom Street at a time when nobody else was interested in the slum buildings and derelict warehouses found in the area. This road is now effectively gay run from kerb to chimney pot, and the straights don't get much of a look-in. The Bloom Street car park provided the space for Saturday's pub sports day and late-night impromptu parties which lasted until breakfast time. Monday's midnight Candle-Lit Aids Vigil was held there too, attracting some 2,000 participants.
>
> In recent years, the gay village has spread its boundaries into Canal Street, and bars like the Manto and the New Inn are allowed to put tables and chairs out onto the street, continental cafe-style. Even the city council were happy to help the Pink Pound clean up what had been a tatty haunt for prostitutes – the street has been re-cobbled and new street lamps carry colourful hanging baskets in the summer months. At the other end of Canal Street there's also Sackville Park, which provided the ideal space for the Pink Weekend's Sunday afternoon picnic and concert.
>
> Police co-operation in the Pink Weekend was also remarkable and, under Chief Constable David Wilmot, in marked contrast to the city policing of James Anderton's days. With police approval, magistrates granted gay pubs and clubs late licences for the weekend, and the roads around the gay village were blocked off to traffic to create a safe space. Indeed, the police were so impressed by Saturday's colourful carnival procession through Manchester's city centre that they're talking about their own brass band taking part next year.[72]

IV

How new is retrochic, and how far is it a throwback to, or re-working of, earlier forms of pastiche? What used to be called 'copyism' had an honoured place in the grammar of ornament as practised by the goldsmiths and lapidaries of ancient Egypt, the Minoan vase painters, and the medieval illuminators and scribes, while the fabrication of replicas has always been a mainstay of the decorative arts.[73] Revivalism, the recycling of old images, the taking up of lost inheritance, has been a leitmotiv of European culture ever since the quattrocento's discovery (or rediscovery) of classical antiquity; later, the imitation and emulation of Old Masters was at the heart of salon painting; while for Winckelmann and the patrons of what has come to be known as neoclassicism, the revival of 'true art' took the form of a return to the supposed austerities of Graeco-Roman taste.[74] Even more apparent are those short-term crazes which are today called retrofads, such as the 'Chinese' taste which crossed exotically with the medieval one in the early days of the Gothic revival, or the vogue for the Egyptian which took off in the 1820s following the pioneering work of Napoleon's archaeologists. Aesthetically, in short, it is modernism, with its fetishization of the new, which is the exception; revivalism, whether in the form of cultural borrowing or variations on a classical theme, has more often resembled the norm.

The idea of making something beautiful, or bizarre, out of bric-à-brac is also a venerable one, though it seems the term *objet trouvé* was only coined in the 1920s. It was used by Dada iconoclastically, and by surrealism as a token of the visual unconscious, long before it was adopted, in the 1960s, by pop art.[75] In another line of descent it could be seen as a late realization of what is perhaps the fundamental principle of poor people's art, that of making something out of nothing – as in the sailors' art of scrimshaw; or the tatting of thrifty housewives.

Architectural salvage has its precedents too, though I think it is only in the past twenty years that old materials have come to be thought of as almost by definition superior to anything new. At South Molton, Devon, the splendid eighteenth-century assembly rooms are said to have been taken lock, stock and barrel from a manor house in Cornwall which had fallen into decay, while the sixteenth-century manors famously profited from the plundering of the monasteries and the chantries after the dissolutions of 1536, 1539 and 1549. According to Dan Cruikshank it was quite normal for eighteenth-century building contracts to specify that, where an old building was taken down, the materials should be re-used (Queen Anne's Gate, Westminster, rebuilt in 1770, was one of the beneficiaries).[76] In the great rebuildings of the nineteenth century, more especially towards the end of the century with the early stirrings of protectionist sentiment, there are plenty of individual examples of the venerable being relocated or incorporated rather than destroyed. One of the most piquant is the case of Swanage, where John Mowlem, a local boy made good (in the 1860s he emerged as the principal demolition contractor in the metropolis) filled his native town, then in a rapid stage of expansion as a seaside resort, with some of the choicer bits and pieces which came his way – among other things the lamps from London Bridge, an illuminated clock made for the Great Exhibition of 1851, and the Cheapside entrance to the Mercers' Company,[77] re-erected as the town hall for Swanage in 1881.

So far as commodity marketing and design are concerned, it seems possible that revivalism has been the obverse side of the mania for novelty. No one made more use of it than Josiah Wedgwood, one of the great popularizers of neo-classicism as well as perhaps the factory system's best-known pioneer. As if by osmosis, at first, and then through the systematic study of classical statuary and urns, Wedgwood took on the classical simplicities of the most advanced artistic and aristocratic taste of his day, giving to his ceramics some of the shapes still retained today. 'I only pretend to have attempted to copy the fine antique forms, but not with absolute servility', he wrote. 'I have endeavoured to preserve the style and spirit or if you please the elegant simplicity of the antique forms, and so doing to introduce all the variety I was able, and this Sir W. Hamilton assures me I may venture to do, and that is the true way of copying the antique.'[78] In the mid nineteenth century – the epoch of the railway boom, the rebuilding of the Houses of Parliament, and the laying out of Trafalgar Square – the battle of styles was waged between Gothicists and Classicists. A designer-led architecture, with elements of retrochic ineluctably clinging to it, was very much to the fore in inter-war Britain. Art Deco, celebrated today as a modernism, was much influenced by the Egyptian mania which followed Howard Carter's discovery of Tutankhamun; the suburbs made a fetish of being vernacular, using Tudor half-timbering like mad; while the metropolitan and the sophisticated adopted what Colefax and Fowler called 'Regency' style.

Revivals were until recently top-down affairs; the property to begin with of small circles of connoisseurs who, aided by wealthy patrons, could indulge eccentric tastes. Neo-classicism was the work of aesthetes and scholars. The Gothic revival famously began as a kind of aristocratic folly. Regency style was a 1920s invention of Mayfair interior decorators, Margaret Jourdain, the authority on eighteenth-century furniture,[79] and not least Georgette Heyer, whose Jane Austen pastiche gave generations of schoolgirls a superior class of heart-throb. The taste for Victoriana, too, was in its early days, the 1920s, a kind of upper-middle-class sport;[80]

not until the 1950s, when the craze for 'below-stairs Victoriana' caught on, did it begin to enter the realm of the popular.

Retrochic, on the other hand, starting perhaps with the Teddy Boy phenomenon of the early 1950s, welled up from nowhere. It profited from the boom in, and democratization of, new classes of collectables. Its new businesses have typically been in the hands of absolute beginners, like Gordon and Anita Roddick; image pirates and plagiarizers, like Malcolm McLaren and the youthful Vivienne Westwood; cowboy operators, like some of the architectural salvage merchants. Where earlier revivals made a point of imitating the grand, retrochic has been more apt to make a fetish of the vernacular and the demotic. Bankrupt factory stock has been a standby in the street-wise fashion trade. Junk, too – things which survive by default – has been a major resource, and the interior decorators are apt to pride themselves on getting their best pieces out of skips.

Another way in which retrochic does seem to differ from earlier forms of revival – and one reason perhaps why it causes such offence – is the absence of sentimentality about the past. It is deficient in what the Victorians called high seriousness, drawing much of its pleasure from the play of the incongruous or the bizarre. Its tastes are cavalier and eclectic, syncretizing ancient and modern, and accommodating a promiscuous mix of different styles. It slips easily in and out of period costume, and passes lightly across boundaries which others have found insurmountable. It approaches its work in the spirit of the beachcomber, or the snapper-up of unconsidered trifles, rather than that of the antiquarian or the connoisseur collecting gems, treasuring relics and worshipping at time-hallowed shrines. It does not thrill to the glamour of backwardness, like the late-eighteenth-century Gothicists, taking their inspiration from the mossy ruins of old abbeys; nor, like the neoclassicists of the time, does it dream of restoring Hellenic harmony and perfection. It differs, too, from the pioneer preservationists of the late 1940s, drooling over the spectacle of pleasing decay. When it does go in for 'distressing', as in retro advertising, pub Victoriana and gift-shop kitsch, it does so quite often for the purpose of a visual joke.

Unlike restorationism and conservationism, the cultural phenomena with which it is frequently bracketed, retrochic is untroubled by the cult of authenticity. It does not feel obliged to stay true to period; on the contrary, it is never happier than when turning the old-fashioned into the up-to-date. It blurs the distinction between originals and re-makes. It prides itself on being proactive, not so much slavishly imitating the past as reinventing it, making up for the original detail which has gone missing. Like magic realism it abolishes the category differences between past and present, opening up a two-way traffic between them. Objects can be transferred from one sphere to another, as though they were so many pieces on a chessboard. As in a video game, they can be moved fast-forward or backward in time. A medieval tapestry can provide 'an elegant Gothic touch' to giftwrap; a 'richly evocative' Renaissance design provides a swagged and tasteful cover for 'Florentine' Christmas crackers, which come packed with silver charms; or – a favourite solecism in this current marketing of 'vintage' radios – a 1930s bakelite case dignifies a modern mini-cassette.

It is argued against retrochic that it is dazzled by surface appearances; that it is more interested in style than in substance, and that it is obsessed with the language of looks. It is also charged with fraud – creating copies, as Baudrillard puts it in *Simulations*, for which there are no originals, using hyperreality to camouflage the absence of the real.[81] Then – in a residue of 1960s jeremiads against consumerism – retrochic is charged, like heritage, with 'commodifying' the past, instrumentalizing it for the purposes of commercial gain, exploiting the sacred in the interests of the profane.

Fastening on objects because they are amusing or bizarre or pretty, it offends the traditionalists by its frivolity. Aesthetes are appalled by its readiness to play fast and loose with styles. Conservationists accuse it of using period survivals for merely cosmetic effects, separating form from function, and encouraging a general resort to 'façadism'. It is no less offensive to modernists, who accuse it of being backward-looking and atavistic, the resort of a culture at the end of its tether.

A more positive reading of retrochic might register its successes in animating the inanimate. It would look with interest at the way in which it ministers to the appetite for objects of fantasy and desire, and in particular at the excitement which it generates from the juxtaposition of old and new – according to one school of pedagogy the crucial element in awakening an interest in the past.

In its flea market or car-boot sale aspect, retrochic has helped to form Britain into a nation of collectors, and in so doing has done some of the spadework not only for the retrieval of the recent past, but also for its interpretation. The historical instinct of those who have created a market in pop memorabilia, and a whole industry out of classic albums and tracks, may be different in kind from that of the bibliophile or the scholar, but if the 1960s and the 1970s come to be seen in the future as the rock 'n' roll years rather than, say (to take two current favourites) 'political de-alignment' or 'the collapse of British power', it will be to the vinyl freaks that future historians of this country will need to turn.

Part of the genius of retrochic is that it can create an aura of pastness even when the documentary record – or the archaeological one – leaves us with no more than a few shrivelled tissues in the hand. Like performance art, it can bring paintings to life and create – as Sally Potter does in her film *Orlando* – a whole gallery of flesh-and-blood characters, or at any rate persuasive celluloid simulacra of them. In the built environment, retrochic, though cavalier about detail – and indeed, in the eyes of the purist, destructive – can be truer to period atmosphere, or at any rate more interesting in attempting to evoke it, than mere replica. 'Thomas Gent's coffee house', York, a recent installation of the Jorvik Trust, is a case in point: with its robust, no-nonsense tables, its painted floorboards (not a touch of stripped pine), its curtainless windows and its dun-coloured walls, it is the very reverse of that twee and dainty look which has been palmed off, for some fifty years or more, as 'Georgian elegance'. A more fantastical example, marrying a gay or Californian taste for fantasy and excess with a wonderful feel for the power of miniatures, would be Denis Severs's house in Spitalfields, where parties of visitors are invited to eavesdrop on a 'roads to ruin' ghost story. Here, Hogarth's scenes step out of the frame and create the substance of period rooms, while a Dickensian attic forms the servants' quarters. Historically speaking, the narrative which accompanies this is fanciful; aesthetically though – if only as a provocation to a historical engagement with the arts – it is a brilliant success, a magical mystery tour which dazzles the visitor with a succession of scenes more crowded with memorable incident than the mere facsimile of what passes in the museums as a 'period' room.

Professional historians are poorly placed to condescend to retrochic since, whether we acknowledge it or not, it is one of the currencies in which we deal. We too put the past in quotation marks, as a way of marking our distance from it, and often as a way of extracting some quaint or comic effect. We too want to make our writing evocative, and the more adventurous or self-confident, when the evidence runs out, will go in for imaginary conversation or even fiction. In any event our work is always an imaginative reconstruction of the past, never – for all the elaboration of our footnotage – mimesis.

If it is true, as Oscar Wilde aphoristically puts it in *Lady Windermere's Fan*, that only the really serious can be frivolous, then we might look more tolerantly at the ways in which retrochic makes a plaything of the past. The 'camp' and the 'kitsch' of 1960s pop art did a great deal to create the imaginative space for the sexual revolution of the 1970s, and the 'coming-out' of previously stigmatized minorities. It seems possible that retrochic may have similarly prepared the way for a whole new family of alternative histories, which take as their starting point the bric-à-brac of material culture, the flotsam and jetsam of everyday life.

Notes

1. 'Vivat Victoriana', *Guardian*, 6 June 1988.

2. Jon Savage, *England's Dreaming: Sex Pistols and Punk Rock*, London 1991.

3. Richard Gomme of Hugo Russell, the retrochic wholesalers whose giant warehouse off Western Avenue is one of the sources of the bric-à-brac which decorates the period pub told me that it was the pub mirror craze which made his firm's fortunes. I am also grateful to Mick Marshall, a pioneer of the pub mirror craze, and Malcolm Gliksten of Relic Designs, for their memories of the rise and fall of the trade.

4. As if shamefaced about the boldness of its new design, Liverpool Street Station has just added ornamental gates with the words 'Great Eastern Railway' inscribed in a cast-iron, multi-coloured medallion. It is as though the station were turning its back on not only half a century of BR (the 'British Railways' of nationalization) but also on the amalgamation of 1922 which produced the LNER (London and North Eastern Railway).

5. Jocasta Innes, *Paint Magic: The Home Decorator's Guide to Painted Finishes*, London 1981.

6. 'Scarce German Steiff teddy bears have monopolised top auction prices for so long that demand has overflowed into British teddies – they have doubled in value in the past two or three years. Bonhams has two toy, doll and teddy sales (both also strong on doll's house furniture). The teddies are mostly at Bonhams Chelsea on Wednesday (1pm) where a 1907 Steiff in tip-top condition is estimated at £1,800–£2,500 and a British bear by Farnwell of 1920 in superb condition is £800–£900.' *Independent*, 4 September 1993. See also 'Teddy Bears are Big Business', *Collectables*, October 1993; Pauline Cockrill, *The Teddy Bear Encyclopedia*, London 1993. Teddy bears seem to have taken over Oxford. 'The English Teddy Bear Company' occupies the double-fronted shop next to the Examination Schools (in an earlier phase of retrochic it was tenanted by Frank Cooper's 'Oxford' marmalade); and teddy bears occupy the entire Market Street window space of Clinton's the Cornmarket card shop (quite a lot of the cards are given over to teddies too).

7. Nonie Niesewand and M. Lawrence, *Encyclopedia of Interior Design and Decoration*, London 1988, pp. 94–5: 'Retro' is defined as 'ways of dressing based on resurrected style' in R.J. Herail and E.A. Louatt, *A Dictionary of Modern Colloquial French*, London 1984.

8. *England's Dreaming*, pp. 61, 66, 232.

9. Lucy Lippiard, 'Reflecting in Retrochic', in *Get the Message? A Decade of Art for Social Change*, New York 1984, pp. 173–8.

10. I am grateful to Alan Taylor for showing me round the stock of Hugo Russell's and accounting for its provenance.

11. Past Times Catalogue, Autumn 1993. I am grateful to John Beale, the founder of the firm, for a great deal of information about it.

12. Paul Hallam, *The Book of Sodom*, London 1993, p. 85.

13. I am grateful to Su Tahran of American Retro for showing me round her shop and explaining it to me.

14. I am grateful to the founder and proprietor of Black's for a sample of its hospitalities.

15. I am grateful to Mr Preston for a copy of the manifestos of the Denmark Street traders' association.

16. I have taken this passage from 'Exciting to be English', my introduction to Volume I of *Patriotism: The Making and Unmaking of British National Identity*, London 1989.

17. *Harriet Love's Guide to Vintage Chic*, New York 1982.

18. Piri Hallazz, *A Swinger's Guide to London*, New York 1967, p. 119; Jonathon Green, *Days in the Life: Voices from the English Underground, 1961–1971*, London 1988, pp. 219–21.

19. Elizabeth Wilson, *Adorned in Dreams: Fashion and Modernity*, Berkeley 1987; Elizabeth Wilson and Lou Taylor, *Through the Looking Glass: A History of Dress from 1860 to the Present Day*, London 1989.

20. *England's Dreaming*, pp. 45 et seq.

21. Jeremy Cooper, *Dealing with Dealers: the Ins and Outs of the London Antiques Trade*, London 1985, p. 128.

22. *Record Collector,* the monthly 220-page glossy 'for all serious collectors of rare records, CDs, videos, Pop memorabilia etc.', features a vast range of record fairs and second-hand record stores. Two pages of reviews are given over to newsletters and fanzines, e.g. *Head,* 'a welcome addition to the current array of Monkees 'zines on the market', *Record Collector,* October 1993, p. 158; there are some fifty pages given over to sales and auctions and the rear is brought up by '25 Years Ago', listing the singles and albums of the time.

23. 'The Guide', *Guardian,* 18–24 September 1993.

24. Virgin Radio, 22 September 1993. J.M. Richards, *Introduction to Modern Architecture,* Harmondsworth 1946.

25. 'Museum Exhibition Makes its Mark', *Hackney Gazette,* 10 September 1993; 'Glam-rocker or great artist?', *Independent,* 17 September 1993.

26. 'Elvis. Germany. The Missing Years. For the first time ... newly discovered unseen film footage of the rock legend as a soldier on and off duty. Sound track by ... the Jordonaires', Poster seen at Holborn Underground station, 23 December 1993.

27. Christine King, 'His Truth Goes Marching On: Elvis Presley and the Pilgrimage to Graceland', in Ian Reader and Tony Walker, eds, *Pilgrimage in Popular Culture,* London 1993, pp. 92–106.

28. 'Rilly Groovy', *New Musical Express,* 1 September 1993.

29. *New Musical Express,* 11 September 1993.

30. Kennedy Fraser, 'Retro, a Reprise', in *The Fashionable Mind: Reflections on Fashion, 1970–1982,* New York 1982; Wilson and Taylor, *Through the Looking Glass;* Lucy Lippiard, 'Reflecting on Retrochic' in *Get the Message?*

31. Charles Hasler, 'Preface', *A Specimen of Display Letters Designed for the Festival of Britain,* London 1951; Nikolaus Pevsner,'Lettering and the Festival on the South Bank', *Penrose Annual* 1952, pp. 28–33; Geoff Weedon and John Gorham 'English Fairground Decoration', *Penrose Annual* 1973, pp. 41–5.

32. 'Laura Ashley: Inspiration that founded an Empire', *Daily Telegraph,* 18 September 1985.

33. Roy Brooks was a passionate Bevanite and member of the Chelsea and Kensington Labour Party, using his advertisement columns to forward his political causes as well as to insult his rather fashionable clients. His celebrated advertisements for run-down period property have been gathered together in *Mud, Straw and Insults: A Further Collection of Roy Brooks Property Advertisements,* London 1971, and *Brothel in Pimlico,* London n.d.

34. Jeremy Cooper, *A Complete Guide to London's Antique Markets,* p. 13.

35. Ibid., p. 68.

36. For an account of the colonization of Burford by the antique dealers, 'Face to Face', *Traditional Interior Decoration,* June–July 1988, pp. 39–43.

37. 'The Camden Passage market started in the mid-sixties, the brain-child of a local music shop owner', Ronald Pearsall and Graham Webb, *Inside the Antique Trade,* London 1974, pp. 115–16; Cooper, *Guide,* pp. 59–68; 'Camden Passage', *Collectors World,* April–May 1968.

38. William Feaver, 'Festival Star', Barbara Jones, 'Popular Arts', James Gardner, 'Battersea Pleasures', John Piper, 'A Painter's Funfair', in Mary Banham and Bevis Hillier, eds, *A Tonic for the Nation: The Festival of Britain, 1951,* London 1976.

39. September 1993.

40. The Post Office, with Mercury telephone and other new-born competitors yapping at its heels, has revived the telegram, and in a rather desperate bid for the retro market is currently running a black and white poster advertisement showing two telegraph boys in pill-box hats. 'There's nothing like a telegram for getting a message across' is the legend. Poster seen at Liverpool Street Station, 20 November 1993.

41. Elizabeth Wilson, 'Second-Hand Films', *Hallucinations: Life in the Post Modern City,* London 1988, pp. 97–104.

42. Ray Curtis and Amoret Scott, *Portobello Passport,* London 1968, pp. 15–16.

43. Curtis and Scott, *Portobello Passport,* pp. 37–8.

44. Elizabeth Wilson, *Mirror Writing: An Autobiography,* London 1982, p. 115.

45. 'Exotic, Soft Mixture adds a Medieval feel to Martine Sitbon' *Independent,* 13 October 1993. Joanne Dubbs Ball and Dorothy Hehl Torem, *The Art of Fashion Accessories,* New York

1993, provides a pictorial history of fashion accessories in the twentieth century.

46. Information from John Beale, founder and proprietor of Past Times.

47. Past Times Catalogue, Autumn 1993.

48. On 'vintage' sports shoes, 'A Step-by-Step Guide to Trainers', *Independent*, 23 October 1993; 'Puma vs. Adidas', *Sky*, October 1993.

49. 'Our Name is Mud', *Independent*, 25 September 1993.

50. Information and brochures from Mark Yates, November 1993.

51. David Cheal's *The Gift Economy* (London 1988) seems to be almost the only book written by a sociologist on what to the anthropologist is a venerable theme. Like others he remarks (pp. 176–83) on the fact that the gift givers are typically, and often exclusively, women.

52. Photographs of these appear in *Victorian Fairings and their Values*, ed. Margaret Anderson, 2nd edn, Galashiels 1978.

53. Gilly McKay and Alison Corke, *The Body Shop: Franchising a Philosophy*, London 1986; see also Anita Roddick, *Body and Soul*, London 1991.

54. Information from John Beale at Past Times and Alan Taylor of Hugo Russell's, plus trade catalogues.

55. For Waterlooplein, Klaartje Schweizer 'Nostalgia Like ... A Fly', cyclostyled paper, Amsterdam Conference on National Identity, 30 September 1993.

56. Andy Thornton, Catalogue 10, 1990.

57. Christopher Wray Lighting Catalogue, n.d. (1992?).

58. Visit to Sainsbury's, Islington, 21 September 1993. Jacobs grain crackers by contrast 'baked with kibbled wheat, barley flakes and bran' seem from the logo to have been fired in a village church; while McVitie's Abbey Crunch ('light and oaty') seem, from the medieval motif, to have been baked before the dissolution of the monasteries.

59. Information from Peter Windett, creative manager. The firm began life in 1970, in Cambridge, Massachusetts, trading in the US with products commissioned in England.

60. Notes on a perambulation, 12 September 1993. Camden Lock does not figure in London guides of the 1970s. Charles Kean (*Fight Blight*, London 1977, p. 142) speaks of the 'splendid scheme of having craft shops and stalls on the canalside', but says the site is under threat of imminent redevelopment. *Time Out Directory* 1990–91 and *Time Out*, 7 July 1993, for Camden Lock's huge volume of transactions.

61. Milan Fashion Show, *Guardian*, 7 October 1993.

62. 'Yesterday's Style Worn with Today's Attitude', *Independent*, 11 September 1993; 'Sense of History in the Making', *Observer*, 12 September 1993; 'Elements of Style', *GQ*, October 1993, pp. 26–8.

63. October 1993, advertising a Virgin release. 'In further celebration of one of the genuine vocal talents of the early '80s British pop boom ... there's also a BBC2 documentary on George scheduled for November, and his autobiography, *Take It Like a Man*, is due to be published next year', *I-D*, October 1993.

64. '"Mojo" Working to Capture Lucrative Market', *Independent*, 29 September 1993. *Q*, now in its seventh year, sells 172,000 copies a month.

65. 'Case the Joint', *Independent*, 28 September 1993.

66. Tom Sutcliffe review, *Independent*, 17 February 1994. See also editorial 'Giving Gangsters a Touch of Glamour', in *Independent*, 18 February 1994.

67. *Tower Hamlets News*, 5 August 1993.

68. Notes on a visit to Sainsbury's, Islington, 21 September 1993.

69. 'Reid's 12 Farm Fresh Shakespeare Country eggs. Laid in Britain', runs the label. I am grateful to Jackie Cameron for a copy.

70. Sainsbury's made their name as the leading supermarket of the 1960s because they were modernizers – not least in a coordinated use of Bauhaus style and Helvetica lettering to give an ultra-modern appearance to the labels and packs. Peter Dixon, the designer responsible for this, is astonished at the volte face.

71. Marion Bowman, 'Drawn to Glastonbury' in *Pilgrimage in Popular Culture*, ed. Ian Reader and Tony Walter, London 1993; cf. also 'Love at the Fest Site', *Sunday Times*, 4 July 1993.

72. 'A Tale of Two Cities', *Gay Times*, October 1993.

73. George Henderson, *Early Medieval Art*, Harmondsworth 1977, pp. 15, 20, 38–9, 57, 59–63.

74. David Lowenthal, *The Past is a Foreign Country*, Cambridge 1985, pp. 80–85, 100–105, 301–5.

75. Maurice Nadeau, *The History of Surrealism*, Harmondsworth, 1928, p. 107.

76. Dan Cruikshank and Neil Burton, *Life in the Georgian City*, London 1990.

77. Fascinating detail of this bizarre story is in David Lewer and J. Bernard Calkin, ed., *Curiosities of Swanage: or, Old London by the Sea*, Yeovil 1986.

78. Adrian Forty, *Objects of Desire: Design and Society, 1750–1980*, London 1986, p. 24.

79. On Margaret Jourdain, see Alison Light, *Forever England: Feminists, Literature and Conservatism between the Wars*, London 1991, pp. 34–6, 56, 61.

80. For 1920s Victorian follies and dressing up, Christopher Sykes, *Evelyn Waugh: A Biography*, Harmondsworth 1977; Harold Acton, *Memoirs of an Aesthete*, London 1948; Alan Bott, *Our Fathers*, London (1932?), p. 4.

81. Jean Baudrillard, *Simulations*, London 1984; Umberto Eco, *Travels in Hyperreality*, London 1987.

The Return to Brick

I

All over London early Victorian terraces and 1870s by-law streets, newly sandblasted, are gleaming with yellow stock bricks. Grey eighteenth-century houses, stripped of their rendering and repointed, blossom out as period residences. Office blocks which twenty years ago would have made a feature of curtain walling now disguise themselves in skins of neo-Gothic reds. 'Exposed original brickwork' is a feature of those warehouse conversions in which Grade II listed buildings are refurbished as studios, apartments or offices, while 'herringbone' or multi-coloured brickwork serves as a kind of rustication for the new-build property rising alongside them.[1] 'Mellow grain facing bricks' are likewise a leading attraction in those mews and courtyard developments now favoured for luxury housing in the inner city, 'with red string courses and arches over doors and windows' in the case of Roland Way, South Kensington, 'and ... sills in Portland Stone'.[2] Quinlan Terry, the neo-classicist, has carried this kind of development to some kind of *ultima Thule* at Tarrant Place, Marylebone, 'a unique courtyard of distinctly grand houses quietly located by St Mary's Church': the courtyard is cobbled and the houses look for all the world as though they had been transported from Downing Street.

In the philosophy of conservation as it has crystallized in recent years, brickwork occupies the sacred space which Ruskin and the early Victorian Gothicists gave to stonework. It combines rugged good looks with exquisite, if unobtrusive, detailing; picturesquely irregular walls with perfectly cut arches and soffits. Bricklaying, regarded in the nineteenth century as one of the lowlier of the building crafts, distinctly inferior to that of the mason and only doubtfully conferring artisan status, becomes the proof of authenticity. The bricks themselves – hand-wrought, hand-thrown, hand-fired, and varying in colour, texture and shape – are treated as art objects: under the influence of conservation they are now the subject of one of the more flourishing branches of the architectural salvage trade. The fact that the two great ages with which modern conservation has concerned itself – the Georgian and the Victorian – were also the two great ages of building in bricks makes it possible to knock stone off its pedestal and to treat other building materials as sidelines; while the preoccupation with period frontages – preserving them is often the limit, if not the summit, of conservation's ambition – means that an extraordinary amount of attention is lavished on external walls.[3]

In run-down districts the major effort of the conservationists is devoted to restoring brickwork to what are imagined to be its former glories. Crumbling courses are repointed, bulging walls tied back, fault lines pinioned, spalling remedied. When new bricks have to be stitched in, they are chosen from old stocks to match the existing ones and create the illusion of a seamless web. Infilling, too, follows the principles of invisible repair, with period frontages preserved intact even when there are more new houses than old. Home extension follows suit: in many conservancy areas it is a condition of council planning permission that additions and alterations should be faced with old stock bricks.

For partisans of 'neo-vernacular' 'community' architecture – influentially represented to the wider public by the Prince of Wales[4] – brick represents a craft material in an age of mass production. In recoil from the 'faceless' buildings of functionalist architecture, they invest brickwork with almost human qualities. It is tactile, textured and grainy where modernism's surfaces are flat. It is individual and quirky where modernism is uniform, 'warm' where glass and concrete are cold. It breathes easily and naturally where breeze blocks are apt to sweat (not the least of the advantages claimed for brick is that it makes air-conditioning unnecessary). It grows old gracefully where curtain walling stains. Brick matures and improves with the passage of the years: modernism goes to seed.

For the quantity housebuilders, the great practitioners of 'neo-vernacular' architecture, brick serves a symbolic function somewhat akin to that of Tudor half-timbering for their 1920s and 1930s predecessors, the speculative builders of the inter-war 'semi'.[5] It is 'mellow' and 'traditional', giving to a new house what Heritage Potton in one of their advertisements call a 'welcoming charm'.[6] It lends itself to crenellation and variety. The return to brick here is not only a matter of building material, but also of shape and style, or what are advertised in the newspapers and the brochures as 'features'. 'Inglenook fireplaces' (in 'natural' brick) are a current favourite, or more grandly (where 'country-house style', is aspired to), a neo-baronial open-brick fireplace.[7] 'Tile-hung eaves'[8] are a frequent feature in 'cottage-style' starter homes, 'double-gabled roofs' in neo-Georgian 'executive-style' residences.

The quantity housebuilders also make use of old brick, both as a source of symbolic capital and as a form of borrowed prestige. 'Antique stocks' or 'reclaimed' bricks are a feature of their prestige developments. Thus at Dulwich Gate, the neo-Georgian estate where the Thatchers bought their retirement home, all the houses are faced with recycled London stocks supplied by a well-known East London salvage merchant.[9] Church's 'Quality homes of character' at Queen's Acre, Windsor, combine 'old-stock bricks' with a variety of ageing effects – flint facings, roof tiles, beams of Douglas fir.[10] Berkeley Homes' 'Regency style' development at St Mary's Square, Brighton, adds 'irregularly placed doors and windows', to 'ensure the period character is maintained'.[11] More ambitiously, in establishing an imaginary pedigree, these estates often take their name and character from some tumbledown piece of brickwork which provides a focal point around which the new-build houses cluster. Old barns and farmhouses, renovated and refurbished, are a feature of those 'courtyard-type' developments favoured for 'greenfield' sites in the countryside; in town and suburb, it seems that any old piece of brickwork will do – in the case of the Fairbriar development at King George's Square, Richmond, where gold-plated finials proclaim an air of elegance, the remnants of an old workhouse.[12]

For the office developers, clothing their steel and concrete structures in films of cladding, the return to brick, though less universal than in the field of domestic house-building, is first and foremost cosmetic. Brick here takes its place, along with stone and marble, as something which gives an air of dignity to new developments, masks fast-track methods of construction with a patina of rusticity. The more ambitious – following the example of the fire-stations and post-offices of the 1970s – go in for neo-Gothic turrets and pitched roofs or make their dramatic statements in Victorian reds. As in up-market housing developments, period façades are incorporated into new-build projects; abandoned warehouses serve as the shell within which air-conditioning plant and computer terminals can be accommodated without interference to either the frontage or the skyline. Quinlan Terry, in the Richmond Riverside development, has carried this line of thought to a neoclassical extreme, hiding a complex of air-conditioned offices behind arched entrances; disguising cooling towers as campanile and waste-disposal units as turrets.

The rehabilitation of old brickwork has swelled the estate agents' portfolio with entire classes of building which ten or twenty years ago would have been routinely consigned to the bulldozer, turning warehouses into hot properties,[13] fire stations into restaurants,[14] and conjuring studios, apartments and offices from the entrails of the most unlikely

WHERE TO FIND HANDMADE AND AUTHENTIC BRICKS

Whether it's bricks fired to your personal colour specification or ones that have been reclaimed, our list of suppliers should be able to help

THE ASHBOURNE BRICK AND TILE COMPANY
The Green Road, Ashbourne, Derbyshire DE6 1EE, tel: 0335 342809.
This company produce handmade bricks, and will try to match customers' existing bricks.

BULMER BRICK & TILE CO
Bulmer Brickworks, Bulmer, nr Sudbury, Suffolk CO10 7EF, tel: 0787 269232.
Bulmer's hold nearly 4,000 different moulds for handmade bricks and can match a wide variety of patterns.

BUTTERLEY BRICKS
Wellington Street, Ripley, Derby DE5 3DZ, tel: 0773 570570.
Butterley has 11 brickworks across the country producing handmade and carved brickwork, and can match most brick types. ▶

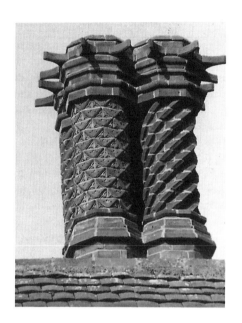

premises. The developers have added it to their repertoire, making imaginative restoration – or creative adaptation – a flagship of their mega-schemes. 'Refurbishment', a category unknown to the trade directories of the 1950s, is now a major sector of the building industry, with a trade journal to itself. The cleaning firms, giving facelifts to old buildings, are another new arrival on the scene. Thirty years ago, when grit-blasting and high-pressure water jets were first introduced, the number of them could be counted on the fingers of one hand: today there are some eighty firms in the metropolis alone. An offspring of all this is the trade in secondhand bricks, which has made windfall profits for the demolition contractors, and provided cowboy operators (and wide-awake labourers) with a nice little earner on the side.

The building materials industry also bears testimony to the revival of traditional brick. In recent years they have developed sophisticated technology of 'tumbling' and 'distressing' which enables new bricks – somewhat in the manner of 'stonewashed' jeans – to simulate the colours, the textures and even the broken surfaces of old ones. Blockleys of Telford, one of the market leaders, have carried this to a fine art, reproducing not only the colours of old-fashioned bricks but also the faults. Kiln-dried bricks are tumbled and distressed before they have time to settle. Computer-designed bricks have the faults built into them from the start. Blockleys' popular 'Ironbridge' model not only contrives to look chipped and cracked, with the corners rubbed off, it also bears the stain of soot marks. Apparently mildewed bricks are also included, to give variety or surprise and to enhance the vernacular effect. Builders who buy this range are offered 'the rugged good looks and special character of reclaimed brick without having to put up with all the drawbacks of that material ... by choosing the Ironbridge brick, you can combine the authentic reclaimed appearance with all the durability, weather resistance, and other outstanding technical qualities which are synonymous with the Blockleys name'. Blockleys' 'Heritage' bricks, 'thrown not by hand but by computer ... in the country's most sophisticated plant', bear an almost equally 'distressed' appearance, pockmarked, as it seems, by wear and tear and rain, and coming in heather mixtures and harvest colours.[15] Redland's 'Olde English Range' – specially designed for 'conservation work' and 'urban renewal' in northern and central England – trade under county names.[16] Nottingham Brick plc, not content with the success of their Georgian brick – 'coloured like Oakham and textured with a fine rustication' – have gone back to the times of the heptarchy with their 'Mercia' facing brick which claims to take its inspiration from Anglo-Saxon burial mounds.[17]

II

In the 1950s, by contrast with today, brick was held in the lowest possible esteem.[18] Labour-intensive, it was expensive to lay and an obstacle to modern building methods and the use of prefabricated parts. Cumbersome and heavy, it was the enemy of light and space. In an aesthetic for which the very idea of façade was anathema, the decorative use of brickwork was particularly despised and one of the great objects of functionalist architecture was to get rid of it. Gables and dormers were unnecessary, if high-pitched roofs were replaced by flat ones. Lintels and arches could be dispensed with, along with the traditional sash – a 'debased' form which modernizers discarded in favour of metal-framed windows or glass panels.[19] Concrete, the wonder material of the age, was dynamic, upholding vast weights on the slenderest of podiums. Glass was an invitation to the sun.[20] Brick, on the other hand, was claustrophobic, trapping a building in its interior instead of letting the outside in.

Brick was in no way redeemed by its historicity, but rather condemned by it. It was associated, in the nineteenth century, with prison-like factories and warehouses, dank walls and narrow passageways, back-to-back houses and 'mean' by-law streets. The legacy of the industrial revolution, according to J.B. Priestley in *English Journey*, was 'a wilderness of dirty bricks'.[21] The rubble of the bomb-sites seemed to mark the end of that particular story, and the housing reformers of the time, brilliantly aided by the photographers, were never happier than when contrasting the 'Dickensian' squalor of the tenements and the slums with the brave new world of gleaming white apartment blocks, sun-kissed gardens and abundant open space.

Neo-vernacular brickwork was also in disrepute. Revived by Norman Shaw and the Arts and Crafts movement, and representing, in the early days of the garden city movement, a vision of New Jerusalem, it had been utterly debased, according to the critics (they included the entire architectural profession) by the 'little red boxes' of the interwar years; the 'bungaloid' developments which were ruining the coastline, the 'ribbon' developments which, according to the rural preservationists, were desecrating the English countryside. Though free of the taint of poverty, they excited as much legislative attention as the tenement and the slum. The 'Green Belt' legislation of 1937 put a restraint on them. The Town and Country Planning Act of 1947 was intended, as far as the future was concerned, to put an end to them. In the writing of the 1950s the 'simplicity', 'good proportions' and 'dignity' of postwar housing was contrasted to the 'fussy bow windows, complicated gable and imitation timbering'[22] of the 1930s semi; the private developers, as can be seen from the columns of *Ideal Home*, and even *Country Life*, were no less anxious to minimize brick than were the public architects and planners.

The monumental use of brick was guaranteed to produce a well-bred sneer, not only on account of its 'useless' ornament but, at least so far as nineteenth-century public architecture was concerned, on account of its pretension. Stone ornament was permissible, even classical, provided the period was right. Brick, on the other hand, except when used for utilitarian and domestic purposes, was absurd. Thus St Pancras was the most despised of the London railway terminals, on account of its red-brick Gothic, while Euston, its neo-classical neighbour, with its portals of Portland stone, went unremarked. Likewise in Oxford University the red brick of Butterfield's Keble College was a standing joke (even the Fellows, it was said, made a point of chipping away at it) while the stone mullioned frontage of Balliol College – no less expressive of the fantasies of Revived Gothic – was an accepted part of the townscape.

Aesthetically, an appreciation of Victorian cast iron preceded that of Victorian brickwork by some two decades. It is symptomatic of this that when 'listing' was introduced in 1949, giving statutory protection to buildings that were deemed 'historic', King's Cross, a precocious example of functionalist architecture with cast-iron girders everywhere, was listed as Grade I while Sir Gilbert Scott's St Pancras, 'a hotch-potch of . . . Classical and Gothic', was listed as Grade III. As late as 1966 the architects at British Rail were proposing to demolish it in favour of a new concourse.[23]

The beauties of Victorian engineering were, it seems, being praised by young architects as early as the 1930s and when the propaganda for modernism got under way, the industrial architecture of the nineteenth century came to occupy the imaginative place which the Gothic Revivalists of the nineteenth century had given to medieval cathedrals. J.M. Richards, the editor of the *Architectural Review*, singled out the Victorian engineers as the morning star of the functional tradition, contrasting the 'simplicity' and 'honesty' of their work with the follies and pretensions of 'academic' architecture – i.e. the work of the Gothicists and classicists.[24] For Nikolaus Pevsner – perhaps the most influential of the propagandists for modernism, and in later years, after 1958, chairman of the Victorian Society – the work of the railway engineers epitomized the functionalist virtues: 'truth to materials', 'unbroken' lines of construction, 'bold', 'uncompromising' statements. English architecture in the nineteenth century, he wrote in *Pioneers of Modern Design* (1936), was largely based on the development of iron, 'first . . . cast iron, then . . . wrought iron'.[25] Brunel's Clifton suspension bridge was 'pure functional energy swinging out in a glorious curve to conquer the 700 feet between the banks of the deep valley';[26] Crystal Palace was 'the outstanding example of mid-nineteenth century iron and glass', 'as assertive a profession of faith in iron as the largest of the suspension bridges'.[27]

The taste for Victorian brickwork spread much more slowly, and although it was inspiring a small literature in the 1950s it took second place to iron in the discovery of industrial archaeology. The Victorian Society, founded in 1958, was, at least under the chairmanship of Pevsner, uninterested in Victorian villadom; concentrating its efforts on public and commercial buildings. Its early battles, like those of conservationists generally, were apt to focus on Victorian stonework, most famously in the 1962 battle to save the Euston Arch. Albert Dock,

Liverpool, was an early cause of the Victorian Society; in 1968 they succeeded in getting it elevated to a Grade I listed building, but it remained under threat in the 1970s, and was rescued from redevelopment only by the property crash of 1974. So far as the refurbishment of warehouses was concerned, it was not until the marina-like developments of the 1980s and the 'discovery' of the waterfront as a setting for the ideal home that the bulldozers and the incendiaries began to leave them alone (as recently as 1981 it was still quite normal for listed warehouse buildings to be mysteriously consumed by fire).

Brick cleaning was a comparative latecomer to the restorer's arts, though today it is almost as routine as stripped pine.[28] There was no sign of it when Canonbury, Islington, was 'discovered' in the 1950s; indeed one of the charms of that district today is that the buildings are as soot-grimed as they were when the comfortable classes began to move in. Not, it seems, until the gentrification of Georgian Lambeth (a phenomenon of the 1970s) was brick-cleaning adopted as a normal part of restoration's repertoire. Grit-blasting, today the most popular of the technologies used in brick cleaning, was originally invented to be used on stone – the initiative, it seems, of a firm which had originally specialized in ship's bottoms (it was first tried out in the early 1960s when Horseguards Parade was given a face-lift). High-speed water jets were also introduced in the first place for stone, an adaptation of an American device for car cleaning. The cleaning of St Paul's (1960–61) served here as the laboratory experiment, the jets being used on the 'frilly bits' of the cathedral, where wire brushes might have harmed the stone. It was not until the cleaning of the Albert Hall (1971–73), an expensive work made possible by a generous grant from the Historical Monuments Commission, that a major Victorian piece of brickwork qualified for a treatment which for some ten years had become quite normal in the case of stone. Once adopted, however, the procedure spread rapidly. In the north it was aided, in the mid 1970s, by government grants to distressed areas and was taken up not only by local conservationists, but also by cowboy operators. In Leeds it had so sensible an effect that the local Victorian Society, in 1977, felt moved to sound a note of alarm, observing that, as a result of cleaning jobs, there were very few black buildings left in the centre of the town. 'Greater public awareness of the quality of the city's older buildings' had been gained but, especially where sandblasting had been employed, at a cost to the fabric, which in some cases had assumed 'a rather ghastly hue'.[29]

So far as conservation is concerned, a landmark might be the upgrading of St Pancras from Grade III to a Grade I listed building, something which happened, after agitation from the Victorian Society, in 1968. But it seems that the revaluation of Victorian brickwork was more a collateral effect of the 'gentrification' and rehabilitation of erstwhile slum terraces of the inner city by a culturally ambitious if somewhat impecunious stratum of the middle class. It was the local estate agents, the stripped-pine merchants, even the dealers in architectural salvage who established its leading idioms and offered models for the uninitiated to follow. Conservation areas reflected these efforts rather than initiating them; typically they have involved a local council giving the imprimatur of municipal authority to a process already near complete.

So far as new-build 'period' brickwork is concerned, the great fillip was the revival, or discovery, of neo-vernacular architecture. It seems to have been the work, in the first place, of repentant modernists, and though associated today with the quantity housebuilders, was pioneered in the first instance in public-sector housing. A justly influential example was Lillington Gardens, Pimlico, a deliberate attempt to create a domestic architecture of enclosure, as opposed to the windswept estates of the 1950s.[30] The Hillingdon Civic Centre (1976) was a landmark so far as public architecture is concerned, creating an idiom which has latterly been exploited by the supermarkets (notably Sainsbury's and Tesco's), the office developers and the shopping malls. And it was the design guide issued by Essex County Council in 1973 which laid down the pattern followed by the quantity housebuilders. It may be no accident that two of the 1980s brand-new vernacular villages, South Woodham Ferrers[31] and Chafford Hundred – reproducing not only the detail of 'traditional' cottage building, but pretending to be seventeenth- or eighteenth-century villages in their own right – come within or near that county.

III

The age of brick began in this country with the Fire of London in 1666,[32] and its hegemony was undisturbed until the 1940s when, under the impress not only of modernist, or 'functionalist', architecture, but also of post-war shortages of labour and raw materials, prefabricated surrogates took its place. It was only with the development of systems-buildings in the 1950s and 1960s – a process which computer-operated design is carrying to new heights – that its future was seriously in doubt. Nevertheless, it has gone through many vicissitudes in the course of a long career and it has always had its more prestigious competitors – masonry in church-building, stone copings and porticoes in public buildings and commercial offices. Even in the eighteenth century, brick was seldom trusted as a loadbearer and in the cheaper kind of hovel it could not compete with such makeshift materials as mud and thatch. In Regency times brick was generally covered up with stucco; in high Victorian times, so far as commercial architecture was concerned, it played second fiddle to Portland stone. Even with the Arts and Crafts revival of vernacular its place was definitely restricted to the domestic. Edwardian classicism was generally stone even if, like Lutyens, the architect was sympathetic to brick when it came to cottage style; and much the same duality prevailed in the inter-war years as can be seen from the neo-Georgian banks and post offices of the 1920s.

The philosophy of building, in any given period, follows circuitous paths. It reflects changes in notions of hygiene as well as in the poetics of space; ideals of the domestic order as well as principles of design. As critics and commentators have long insisted, it is the spirit of the age incarnate, bearing the impress of the dreams and dilemmas of its time. Something of the same might be suggested for the revival of brick. It is related to a sea-change in environmental politics, with the gravitational shift from public-sector to private-sector development, and from tenancy to owner-occupation – no less a feature in the erstwhile bed-sit districts of the inner city than on out-county estates. It corresponds to a more widespread reversal of taste, which has rehabilitated the decorative and the picturesque at the expense of the functional and the utilitarian. But it could also be said to be bound up with such exogenous factors as containerization, which at a stroke turned docklands into development areas.

The revival of brick possibly owes more to sociological changes than it does to aesthetics. It is the business recolonization of the inner city which has turned warehouses into hot properties and made the preservation of period façades the first of the developer's arts. Likewise it is the formation of new housing classes – 'gentrifiers' in the inner city, long-distance commuters on greenfield sites in the countryside – which has turned conservation and preservation from an aesthete's dream into a profitable investment. There is nothing 'historic' in any archaeological sense about many of the districts, or enclaves, now designated conservation areas. What marks them out is the class of people which has moved into them, and the idiom of their ambition. Conservation is the currency with which they deal, in upgrading their houses and themselves. It turns the humblest dwelling into a period residence; façades into 'historic' fabrics. In a triangular exchange of prestige it invests property with a pedigree and newcomers, if only by proxy, with roots, while allowing council officers to notch up 'environmental' gains for what might otherwise be a deteriorating locality.

Brick may also be the beneficiary of those compensatory mechanisms which have made cultural nationalism a feature of the designer-led consumerism of the past twenty years. It is opposed implicitly, and sometimes explicitly, to the cosmopolitan impurities of modernism. For the promoters of neo-vernacular architecture, brick is the most 'English' of the building materials: honest and down-to-earth, plain and unvarnished, it reflects the national virtues. It is not flashy like marble, which comes from Italy or places even further afield; not artificial like concrete which, perhaps from its associations with Bauhaus, perhaps because of memories of the Second World War, is thought of as vaguely German. Timber may come from Scandinavia or the tropics, but brick is indubitably British, or more specifically – since the Scots build in granite, and the Welsh in stone – English. No other country in the world, it seems, has such a variety of building clays, or so many distinctive stocks.

The discovery (or rediscovery) of vernacular architecture, and the democratization of notions of 'heritage' (a feature of the 1960s), also helped to give a new dignity to brick. It shifted attention from the monumental and the grand to the local, the regional and the domestic. By a strange alchemy of taste, the present age has come to admire precisely those features of the built environment which in their own time were neglected or despised. The warehouses, today blossoming out as luxury apartments and penthouses, were a byword for drudgery and dirt in early Victorian England, as readers of *David Copperfield* will recall. The barns singled out for up-market conversion are the erstwhile domain of cowmen, swineherds and farmhands. The brickwork 'exposed' as a gauge of authenticity, and subject to conservationism's admiring gaze, was in the nineteenth century, for those who had the means, disguised as stone. When an old workhouse – the one-time prison of the poor – can provide the symbolic focus of an executive-style housing complex, as has happened at King George's Square, Richmond;[33] and when a public lavatory can be refurbished as a design studio, as has happened in Fulham, it is evident that we are entering a world turned upside down, where oldness is all and class discrimination, retrospectively at least, irrelevant.

The Clean Air Act of 1958 and the spread of smokeless zones created the conditions of existence for the rehabilitation of period brick, even if it cannot be hypothesized as a cause, and it may also have helped to focus conservationist attention on historic fabrics and façades rather than on the preservation of interiors. The Clean Air Act has also helped to give brick a competitive edge over curtain walling when it comes to new-build property, allowing the first, as in 'warehouse-style' developments, to appear in fairground colours – reds, yellows and oranges – while making the second appear, by comparison, fly-blown and dowdy.

The revival of brick could also be seen as the nether side of comprehensive clearance and redevelopment. It took shape at a time when acres of Victorian terracing and generations of industrial building were being put to the bulldozer. It stepped into the ecological vacuum created, in the countryside, by the disappearance of the farm labourer and the demise of labour-intensive agriculture; in the towns, by the exodus of the indigenous population and the haemorrhage of tradi-tional occupations and trades. Grasping originally at the survivals of disappearing worlds, it now seeks to recreate the simulacrum of an environment which, within recent memory, has been transformed out of all recognition, and at the same time to return to an older past. A similarly inverse relationship might be suggested between the revival of brick and the triumph of fast-track methods of building construction: it staged its comeback at the very time when systems-building was making it redundant.

Another way of approaching this matter would be in terms of urban eugenics, and the ways in which the return to brick dovetails with contemporary social phobias. For the housing reformers of the 1950s, as for the social hygienists when the idea of slum clearance was first launched, the ruling fear was overcrowding and tuberculosis, and the grand solution was fresh air, whether in the form of tower blocks ('cities in the sky') or low-density, out-county estates. The ruling fears today are those of insecurity, and the grand specific, vigorously canvassed since the early 1970s, is that of 'defensible' or 'protected' space. The revival of brick has gone hand-in-hand with a move from large- to small-scale developments, and the creation of new forms of urban space or, as the architects and developers prefer to think of them, the revival of older ones – the Elizabethan almshouses,[34] the Jacobean Inns of Court, the 'Georgian' mews or square.[35] Interestingly it is not the traditional terraced street which is favoured – in these days of security anxiety it seems no longer to be trusted – but the guarded precinct, a courtyard-type development, protected from the outside world by iron railings, electronically operated gates and an imitation watchtower or keep.[36] Such are the 'wharfside villages' springing up in docklands;[37] the walled estates appearing in the outer suburbs; even, in Storrington, Sussex – a development by Wates, the quantity housebuilders, in association with Courtyard Historic Proper-ties – 'village style flats'.[38]

In any of these instances one seems to encounter what Charles Jencks, the theorist of postmodern architecture, has famously termed 'double-coding'; meanings which could be said to point simultaneously to the future and to the past.[39] Thus by means of new techniques of cleaning and refurbishment old buildings can be marketed as if they were new; while on the strength of 'distressing', or make-believe weathering, brand-new buildings can be palmed off to the public as though they were traditional. Frontages, in either of the two cases, are flagrantly at odds with the interior; the apparently hand-tooled façade camouflaging hi-tech appointment within. The walls, even if they have the solid appearance of masonry, are not load-bearing but decorative; the cottagey look conceals a battery of electronics.

'Double-coding' might also help to resolve the mystery of how it is that neo-vernacular, though marketed as regional and local, is international in character. The high-pitched roofs, though supposedly indigenous, have more in common with Dutch gables or Tyrolean chalets than with any known English townscape. Clay paving – brick-effect concrete – was introduced here, it seems, in imitation of the German; the manufacture of 'heritage' bricks was started in the United States; and it was from Australia that Blockleys of Telford took their example when, in 1985, they launched the first of their antique lines.[40] 'Warehouse' conversions were pioneered in the SoHo district of New York, and had been a feature of Greenwich Village lifestyles for a decade or more before they began to be adopted in London,[41] while marina-style developments are to be found in every erstwhile docklands. Reference might be made, finally, to the 'Mas Provençal', a bestselling line in French period kitsch – allegedly the revival of a traditional Provençal farmhouse, though in fact, with its 'exposed' timbers and masses of decorative tiles, a very modern pastiche. It has spread like wildfire, not only in Provence where it made its appearance in the 1970s, but all over southern France: sightings have even been reported from the Paris suburbs.[42] Neo-vernacular brickwork, in short, has some claim to being the international style of our times, even though it taps sentiments which are regional and claim to be indigenous.

Notes

1. 'Leaded light windows, timber beams ... herringbone brick panels and cottage style tile hanging all add to the character appeal of the properties', *New Homes*, March 1989. 'Inside, the original honey-coloured London bricks have been carefully sand-blasted ...' 'Dockland Shock', *Traditional Interior Decoration*, October–November 1987, p. 136. 'Retention of the arched multi-pane warehouse style windows, exposed original brickwork and sturdy metal pillars echo the building's historic past', 'Bronze Award', *What House*, March 1989.

2. 'Silver Award ... The Gilston', *What House*, March 1989.

3. For the restoration of terracotta at the Hackney Empire – as earlier at the Royal Albert Hall – see Shaw's of Darwen Catalogues and portfolio. For the use of new-old brick

in refurbishing industrial monuments and commemorative plaques, Ibstock, *Decorative Brickwork*, 1985.

4. Prince Charles's longstanding preference for the 'homely' as opposed to the grand, his belief in the 'privacy' and 'elegance' of courtyard developments, and his strong support for the use of local and county materials and 'recognised vernacular styles' are well set out in his *Vision of Britain*, London, 1984, pp. 15, 41, 72, 88, 113, 124–5.

5. For a graphic conspectus of new-build projects using traditional brick, see Douglas Wise, 'Urban Regeneration', in *Brick Bulletin*, 2/84, 1984. On the feast of brick at Lillington Street, Pimlico and the matching development at Marquess Road, Islington, *Brick Bulletin*, January 1975. For Odham's Walk, Covent Garden, an admired late development by the Greater London Council, *Brick Bulletin*, 4/83, October 1983. On another Darbourne and Darke scheme – this time for a housing trust in Richmond, Surrey – *Brick Bulletin*, 2/86 (the same issue has a spectacular example of new red brick at Reading Central Library). I am most grateful to Bob Lloyd-Jones of the Brick Development Association for a mass of such material on brick's recent advances.

6. 'Exposed brick' features prominently in 'Heritage Potton' self-build house-types; notably in the inglenook, 'the heart of a heritage home', where it is topped by a beam for hanging pots. Heritage 'Rectory' portfolio, *Daily Telegraph* Period Homes exhibition, 26 February 1989.

7. 'Home is Where the Hearth Is', *Building Homes Supplement*, 2 December 1988, p. 37; 'New Design Unveiled', *Home Buyer*, February 1990; 'West Midlands . . . Lovell Homes' *Home Finder*, 1989, p. 26.

8. 'Sussex' in *What House*, June 1988; East Kent *House Buyer*, February 1990. 'Teddington', *Home Finder*, 1989; *Daily Mail* National Housebuyers Exhibition, 25 February 1990.

9. I am grateful to Carol Clark of Lasdun for this information, as for much other detail about the secondhand brick trade.

10. 'Where Nostalgia Finds a Home', *Independent on Sunday*, 4 March, 1990.

11. 'Sussex', *Home Finder*, 1989. 'Much consideration is given to the choice of materials. It is not unusual to use old stock bricks and clay tiles to ensure the period character is maintained and around the country where appropriate they (Berkeley Homes) will use local materials: Purbeck stone in Dorset, Cotswold stone in Bath, Flint and brick in Hampshire whilst in Sussex the indigenous farmhouse style is carefully recreated', Berkeley Homes stand at *Daily Mail* National Housebuyers Exhibition, February 1990.

12. 'Past Historic, Future Perfect at King George's Square, Richmond', *Observer*, 3 October 1987; and oral information from Fairbrother Homes.

13. It would be interesting to know when 'fine historic warehouses' (as Prince Charles calls them in *Vision of Britain*, p. 31) first began to be listed. Oliver's Wharf, Wapping, is said to have been one of the first to be converted to residential or studio use, around 1971.

14. Or, in the case of Oxford, a performance space and arts centre.

15. Blockleys Heritage Brick Collection Catalogue and Portfolio 1990.

16. Redland Olde English Range, portfolio 1990. Redland used 'Cambrian' slate-tile roofs in a prestige development at Brighton marina. 'Good old Sussex by the Sea', *What House*, March 1989, p. 13; also *House Improvements Journal* no. 8, 1988.

17. 'Facing Bricks', *Building*, 18 July 1986.

18. It says something of the low repute of brick that even W.G. Hoskins, one of the great champions of vernacular building, found himself tricked into publicly disparaging it. 'Redbrick is irredeemably commonplace and nothing will hide its meanness', he wrote in 1950, commenting on 'the little boot-and-shoe towns of Northamptonshire and Leicestershire'. By contrast, 'There is a certain dignity about a stone building which brick can never approach, and when it is blackened by generations of smoke its dignity is enhanced', W.G. Hoskins, *Chilterns to the Black Country*, London 1951, p. 41.

19. For 'extruded aluminium sections' and 'extreme transparency' of a new office block at Poole, *Architectural Review*, March 1955, p. 160.

20. 'A striking example of the decorative value of glass is provided by many cinemas in the Odeon circuit. Here, ¼" thick, cream opaque glass with 1" cover strips of black glass covers the building, accenting the contemporary styling by day, while at night, reflected light produces an effect of interior illumination that is both arresting and attractive.

Structurally sound in every way, glass used in this manner offers valuable economies. Speedily erected, it eliminates the need for costly redecoration, while its smooth, hard surface, resistant to dirt, fumes and smoke, requires no attention other than very occasional washing to maintain it in perfect condition.' (advertisement), *Architectural Review*, May 1955. Cf. 'The Soho Project' by the Glass Age Development Committee – a horrifying scheme to turn Soho into a glass city to which the *Architectural Review* gave much space (March 1955, LXIV–LV, April 1955, LXIX–LXXX).

21. J.B. Priestley, *English Journey*, London 1934, p. 400. Labour's 1945 election programme, *Let Us Face the Future* was quite as severe about ribbon development as the CPRE.

22. *News of the World Better Homes Book*, ed. Roger Smithells, London 1954, p. 12.

23. The Victorian Society, *Annual Report*, 1966, p. 7. Dr Curtis, architect to British Rail, apparently contrasted the 'pioneering' train shed (King's Cross) with the 'reactionary' hotel (St Pancras).

24. J.M. Richards, *Introduction to Modern Architecture*, Harmondsworth 1946, pp. 36–7.

25. Nikolaus Pevsner, *Pioneers of Modern Design*, Harmondsworth 1984, p. 118.

26. Ibid., p. 128.

27. Ibid., pp. 132–3.

28. I am grateful to Ian Clayton of Haywards Heath for a great deal of information about the development of the brick cleaning trade.

29. Victorian Society, *Annual Report*, 1977, p. 21.

30. Here is Nikolaus Pevsner's remarkable tribute to the estate (Victorian Society, *Annual Report*, 1972–3, p. 3):

ELECTIVE AFFINITIES

If you can spare the time, sample the new south extension of the Victoria Line. Get out at Pimlico, and walk for five minutes – but what a walk – and you'll find yourself face-to-face with G.E. Street's St James the Less, built in 1860–61 by private munificence in the slums of Westminster. You may not be able to get in, but the exterior alone is worth a walk, even if it were much longer. Eastlake, in his famous *History of the Gothic Revival in England*, which came out in 1872, called it 'one of the most original and remarkable churches in London'. But I would not have sent you all the way to St James's if what you found there were the church alone. In fact what you see from Pimlico station or – much better – from Vauxhall Bridge Road is Street plus, and the plus is a large housing estate by the young partnership of Darbourne and Darke, and this estate (called, by the way, Lillington Gardens), is designed in such a way that its climax is Street's church. The first designs were done in 1961, precisely a hundred years after St James's. So here is the architectural style of 1960 proclaiming its appreciation of the style of 1860. This is, I need hardly say, very gratifying to us committed Victorians. Nor should we really be surprised to see this sympathy. After all, the Gropius–Mies–SOM style went with clean-shaven faces, but both 1860 and 1970 are bearded generations. But this is only by the way. What I want to do now is to document this sympathy, and the best way in which I can do that is by quoting from Eastlake and from a paper on town churches by Street, printed in *The Ecclesiologist* in 1850 (XI, 227ff.). So first, St James's is brick, Lillington Gardens is brick. Street wrote that town churches are often 'hedged in with myriads of bricks on all sides'. So, now, is this one. Eastlake points at St James's to a 'dazzling distribution of stripes'; Lillington Gardens has a rhythm throughout of horizontal concrete bands across the brick walls. But the bands are plain buff, the church stripes are more colourful, and as colourful are its geometrical patterns. In order to secure superiority for the church, Darbourne and Darke decided not to compete with it. But they have projections and recessions and sudden diagonals to answer the closer geometry of the church walls and especially the church spire. A 'restless notching of edges' Eastlake points out (inside St James's): the very words could refer to a favourite motif of the 1960s. And if Eastlake sums up Street as 'incapable of insipidity', that is exactly what I would say of Darbourne and Darke. Street himself, à propos town churches in general, sums up with these words: 'there are cases in which irregularity is obviously necessary; it then becomes admirable'. And so let me end by proclaiming Lillington

Gardens as admirable – admirable in itself and admirable for its understanding of High Victorian values.

31. South Woodham Ferrers, Essex, 1977–9, by the Holder and Mathias Partnership, opened by the Queen in 1981, is approvingly described by David Watkin (*The English Vision: The Picturesque in Architecture, Landscape and Garden Design*, London 1982, p. 199) as 'one of the most thoroughgoing of the many recent attempts to produce a kind of picturesque folk-architecture in reaction to the lack of historical resonance in modern architecture'. A more critical account is by Sutherland Lyall (*Dream Cottages: From Cottage Ornée to Stockbroker Tudor*, London 1988, pp. 150–51) who after detailing its 'almost Tolkeinesque' charms, and describing it as one of the most sensational British neo-vernacular developments, comments tartly on the 'impossible-to-vernacularise car-park' off to one side of the shopping area, the supermarket masquerading as an Essex barn and the 'Georgian' roof to the petrol filling station.

32. R.W. Brunskill, who helped to pioneer the 1960s rehabilitation of vernacular architecture, has made the gazetteering of this subject his own. *Brick Building in Britain*, London 1989; *An Illustrated Handbook of Vernacular Architecture*, London 1987; *Traditional Buildings of Britain*, London 1985; *Vernacular Architecture of the Lake Counties*, London 1978. Dan Cruikshank and Peter Wyld, 'Brick', 'Stucco' and 'Stone' in Brunstone, ed., *The Art of Georgian Building*, London 1975, pp. 178–197 for the eighteenth century. Among earlier works, Nathaniel Lloyd, *A History of English Brickwork*, London 1925, is worth mentioning.

33. Advertisement in *Observer*, 3 October 1987 and oral information from Fairbrother Homes.

34. 'The English Courtyard Association have a well earned reputation for high quality developments and currently have eight schemes throughout the country. The Company's developments are based on the traditional courtyard plan of almshouses and comprise terraces and courts of two storey cottages and flats', 'A Round-Up of the Latest Sheltered Housing Schemes', *Home Finder*, June 1988.

35. 'Plans by Bovis Retirement Homes to construct 23 retirement homes have been approved by West Oxfordshire planners … Located within Burford's conservation area, the development will be fully landscaped, combining new foliage with mature trees and shrubs, many of which are subject to preservation orders. An impressive archway will mark the entrance to the courtyard in the style of an 18th century stable block', *Oxfordshire Property Weekly*, 15 February 1990. 'Enjoy the elegance of our Georgian courtyard' runs a Lovell Homes advertisement for Stapleton Hall, a refurbished Grade II listed building – with two new wings attached – in London N4. 'You'll sense a Georgian feel here, with sash windows and six-panel front doors. Stapleton Hall itself remains stuccoed. Perched on the far end of the roof is an ancient bell tower, now fully restored, like the early Victorian porch', *Midweek*, 15 February 1990.

36. For Sutton Square, Hackney, with its Georgian arch looking for all the world like the gateway to a gentleman's park, though it also serves the more utilitarian function of concealing television security cameras, see *Country Life*, 6 April 1989, which describes it as 'one of the earliest schemes where younger architects have led speculative builders to a more restrained Georgian style'.

37. For the Trafalgar House developments in Paddington Basin, see 'The Pleasure of Living by the Water', *Daily Mail*, 23 February 1990.

38. 'Set just off the High Street in this pretty village, 31 two-bedroom flats and cottages will be built by Wates in association with courtyard Heritage Properties. The new homes are to be built on the site of Chanctonbury House, former council offices, and are next to the Abbey and church of St Mary … The properties will be laid out to form small, intimate courtyards with a blend of Georgian and cottage-style details. Parking spaces will be provided and the whole development will be landscaped with additional shrubs and trees', 'Sussex', *Home Finder*, 1989.

39. Charles Jencks, *The Language of Postmodern Architecture*, London 1984; *What is Postmodernism?*, London 1986.

40. I am grateful to Mr B.J. Taylor, Deputy Chairman of Blockleys, for this information. *Blockleys Clay Paving: The Total Concept*, Telford n.d., impressively illustrates the extent of

local authority and business corporation take-up. See also 'Clay Tile Revival', *Building*, 17 January 1986.

41. Sharon Zukin, *Loft Living: Culture and Capital in Urban Change*, London 1988, pp. 58–81.

42. I am grateful to Bertrand Taithe of Manchester University for documentation and reference to the 'Provençal' farmhouse.

PART II

Resurrectionism

Resurrectionism

I

The last thirty years have witnessed an extraordinary and, it seems, ever-growing enthusiasm for the recovery of the national past – both the real past of recorded history, and the timeless one of tradition. The preservation mania, which first appeared in reference to the railways in the early 1950s, has now penetrated every department of national life. In music it extends from Baroque instruments – a discovery of the early 1960s, when concerts of early music began to be performed for the *cognoscenti*[1] – to pop memorabilia, which bring in six-figure bids when they are auctioned at Christie's or Sotheby's. In numismatics it has given trade tokens the status of Roman coinage. Industrial archaeology, a term coined in 1955, has won the protective mantle of 'historic' for abandoned or salvaged plant. The number of designated ancient monuments (268 in 1882, 12,900 today) also increases by leaps and bounds: among them is that brand-new eighteenth-century industrial village – product of inspired scavengings as well as of Telford New Town's search for a historical identity – Ironbridge. Country houses, on their last legs in the 1940s, and a Gothic horror in British films of the period, attract hundreds of thousands of summer visitors and have helped to make the National Trust (no more than a pressure group for the first seventy years of its existence) into the largest mass-membership organization in Britain. New museums open, it is said, at a rate of one a fortnight and miraculously contrive to flourish in face of repeated cuts in government funding: there are now some seventy-eight of them devoted to railways alone.[2]

One feature of the historicist turn in national life – as of the collecting mania – has been the progressive updating of the notion of period, and a reconstruction of history's grand narrative by reference to the recent rather than the ancient past. Thus in TV documentary, the British Empire is liable to be seen through the lens of 'The Last Days of the Raj', as it is in Paul Scott's trilogy, or the films of Merchant–Ivory. The year

1940 – replacing 1688, 1649 or 1066 as the central drama in the national past – becomes, according to taste, 'Britain's finest hour' or a privileged vantage point for studying the national decadence. Twentieth anniversaries, these days, seem to excite as much ceremony and rejoicing as for centenaries or diamond jubilees. Very pertinent here is what Fredric Jameson calls 'nostalgia for the present'[3] – the desperate desire to hold on to disappearing worlds. Hence it may be the growth of rock pilgrimages and the creation of pop shrines. Hence too, it may be – memorials to the fragility of the present rather than the past – the multiplication of commemorative occasions, such as 40th and 50th birthdays, and the explosive growth in the production of commemorative wares. The past under threat in many retrieval projects, as in the mass of 'do-it-yourself' museums, and self-made or family shrines, is often the recent past – the day before yesterday rather than as, say, in nineteenth-century revivalism, that of the Elizabethan sea-dogs, medieval chivalry or Gothic architecture.

British postage stamps, which ever since the Benn–Gentleman revolution of 1965–6,[4] have set out to represent this country pictorially rather than, as previously, regally and symbolically, seem finally to have caught up with the car-boot sales, the flea markets and the private collection of bygones and memorabilia. A recent set of greeting stamps falls firmly within the category of what is known in the auction rooms as juvenilia. Designed by Newell and Sorrell, they feature characters from children's literature, with Dan Dare, the comic superhero of the 1950s, enjoying parity of esteem with Biggles, the famous fighter pilot invented by Captain W.E. Johns. The Three Bears, who first appeared in Robert Southey's *The Doctor* (1837) are matched by Rupert Bear, from the *Daily Express* comic-strip, and Paddington Bear, who first appeared in 1958. Among the female role models, a rather vexed Alice, still bearing the traces of Tenniel's Gothic, offsets the sweetness of Little Red Riding Hood and Orlando the Marmalade Cat.

At the other end of the chronological spectrum, the New Agers and the organic farmers, proclaiming a spiritual and material kinship with the earliest inhabitants of these islands; the environmentalists, calling themselves 'Friends of the Earth'; and the ecologists, pondering the question of whether the Iron Age or the Dark Ages were the last time when Man and Nature were still in balance, have each in their own way helped to make prehistory much more vividly present. Taking legend seriously, and arguing that it represents oral tradition and oral history, at many generations remove, they set out to discover its lost and hidden landscapes. Summer solstice celebrations, such as the mass open-air festival at Glastonbury, or the 'New Age' travellers' rave-ups, resuscitate the memory of ancient shrines, and create a whole network of new ones.

A photograph from John James's student days, just before he ran the first 'Jason's Trip' on the Regents Canal.

Camden Lock as it was circa 1951, another photograph from Mr James's private album.

The 'Little Venice' stretch of the Canal circa 1951.

A picture of 'Jason's Trip' circa 1956.

Through the medium of ley-lines, or what one of New Age's more critical writers calls 'Astro-Archaeology', every old footpath is liable to be the vestige of some ancient British trackway.[5] By the same token ecologists, anyway the self-styled 'Merlin' ecologists, argue that Celtic and druidical place names are clues to aboriginal settlement.[6] Old landmarks, under an optic like this, become the survivals of an ancient civilization, on a par with Pompeii and Herculaneum. The standing stones at Land's End, if we interpret them rightly, are the cabbala of what one writer calls 'megalithic science',[7] while Cheesewring on Bodmin Moor is 'one of the wonders of prehistoric engineering.'[8]

New Ageism has a huge cult following among the young. It finds echoes in rock music, and outer circles of influence in fringe medicine, holistic therapies and radical feminist activism. More recently it has emerged as a potent new force in environmentalist campaigning, bringing its own sacred geography into the arena; calling up a pharaoh's curse on those – like the motorway builders – who disturb the bones and the spirit of the dead; and using the occult, in the form of chants and charms, to give demonstration and protest a runic edge. Thus the Dongas tribe (white witches) and the Elfs,[9] (the eco-saboteurs or the Earth Liberation Front) backed by such New Age outriders as 'cyclists from Mother Urf'[10] made the running in the Battle for Twyford Down, a Greenham Common-like action directed against the extension of the M3, with hundreds of protesters invading the construction site. In the brilliantly successful battle for Oxleas Wood in southeast London, 'the biggest victory for environmentalists for several years', it was the People of Dragon, 'a pagan group that brings together witches, odinists, druids, magicians and the many other elements of the neo-pagan revival now taking place in Britain' who led the way in the resistance:

> For the past two years members have been gathering here to throw a protective ring of magic around the wood, which is threatened by a proposed six-lane motorway, part of the East London River Crossing. They are relying on the natural forces and earthly spirits they believe still survive in the wood's ancient heart. As the legal battle to save the area becomes increasingly desperate, members of Dragon plan to step up their efforts. They have been encouraged by the recent defection of a transport industry lobby group, the British Road Federation, to the side of the dissenters. This has left the Department of Transport isolated.
>
> Dragon's members have tried to keep a low profile in the Shooter's Hill area, where Oxleas Wood stands, for fear that their pagan activities could damage the campaign to stop the motorway. Now, however, they are becoming less circumspect, and on Saturday they will gather under a full moon to hold an energy-raising session and candlelit procession. They

assemble at a boarded-up café on top of a hill overlooking Oxleas Meadow; a high-spirited, straggling group of men, women, children and the inevitable dogs. A few crusties with army greens and muddy boots mingle with grannies in bobble hats, young mothers with pushchairs, youngsters with names such as Cherokee, and a core of slightly intense, baggy jumpered people in their thirties. Some have drums, one man has brought an electric guitar with portable speakers, one woman has a flute.

Among the crowd is John, who sells magical artefacts and jewellery from his 'holistic' bookshop in nearby Dartford. He joined Dragon after seeing the devastation at Twyford Down in Hampshire, where an extension to the M3 is destroying another sacred site. 'They dug up ancient graves containing seven-foot skeletons, and there is a definite magical aspect coming into effect,' he says. 'Already four of the building workers and security guards have died of heart attacks. I don't think people should discount the ancient forces they have disturbed.'

John played in Oxleas Wood as a child, and says he wants to preserve the area for future generations. 'As a pagan, I see all life and nature as sacred, yet I live in a society which views the Earth as a plunderable resource,' he says. He believes that Dragon's magic can influence people, including John MacGregor, the Secretary of State for Transport, but only if it is backed up by other, non-magical action. 'It's like if you were out of work, you could sit down invoking all sorts of magic, but if you don't then get yourself down to the Job Centre, it won't work. You have to link your magic with practical work, which is what Dragon is doing very well.'[11]

Environmentalists, after their own fashion, can be quite as ecstatic about Neolithic times as New Agers. Thus Richard Mabey, in his interesting credo, *The Common Ground*, conjures up that Arcadian time, 'about 7,000 years ago, when the wetlands were still undrained', the climate was 'agreeably warm', and about two-thirds of the land surface was thickly wooded.[12] Like the New Agers, too, though for different reasons, environmentalists, oppressed by the knowledge of disappearing or endangered species, are apt to make a fetish of relics and survivals – 'old' grasses, 'vintage' herb-rich meadows, 'semi-natural' or 'ancient' woods. Nature Conservancy officers follow suit, keeping inventories of species at risk, making a shrine of wildlife reserves – 'Nature's Heritage' is the generic title given to them in Scotland – and waymarking them with interpretive panels where their history is set out.

Under the influence of the new arboriculture ancient woodland, which in the 1960s seemed on the point of extinction, is now treated as if it was a historic monument and promoted as one of Nature's antiquities: 'prehistoric wildwood', 'relics of the original forest'.[13] By 1989, as a result of careful management and a revival of the ancient forestry arts of coppicing, as well as the formation of local and national woodland trusts, there was actually more surviving 'ancient' woodland than there had been in 1975.[14] Oliver Rackham, who had some part in this expansion, as well as being its chronicler, comments as follows:

Problems of the 1990s

With diminished pressure on land, the survival of ancient woods is no longer in question. They will continue to be nibbled at by the forestry interest, though much of this damage is self-reversing; they will occasionally be taken for roads and perhaps development. But a sign of the times is the change in emphasis within the Nature Conservancy Council – the State conservation service – from Sites of Special Scientific Interest to the Inventory of Ancient Woodland. In the desperate 1960s, it seemed possible, at best, to try to schedule and protect about one-tenth of the ancient woods. In the 1980s, although the SSSI system is still in use, the listing of *all* ancient woods is by no means an impossible goal. It is also more objective: most woods either are or are not ancient, but who can say whether a wood has just enough scientific interest to qualify it as an SSSI? A first Inventory is almost complete, although it will doubtless continue to be revised over many years as the list of historic buildings has been.[15]

The idea of re-enacting, or establishing a living connection with, pre-historic Britain seems also to have been one of the inspirations behind the long-distance walkers' routes developed by the Countryside Commission.[16] Thus the South Downs Way, in the long stretch from Eastbourne to Petersfield, 'follows the ancient path used 5,000 years ago by early travellers'; while on the Cotswold Way, 'many hill forts are passed'.[17] The Ridgeway, 'one of the best used of all the prehistoric long-distance trade routes' was one of the models. In Wiltshire it ran round the Marlborough Downs to the Iron Age hill fort of Barbury Castle. In Oxfordshire it became the Icknield Way. In Norfolk it ended up at Grimes Graves – 'the Neolithic flint mines which seem to have produced the principal trade commodity for the route'.[18]

More generally there is a strong historical element in the nature trails – or 'nature heritage' trails – developed, since the 1960s, as an educational device, and latterly as a tourist or visitor attraction. 'As you walk along the sandy rides, sharp eyes may see worked flints discarded by Neolithic hunters' runs the brochure for Thetford Forest Park, 'a cradle of British history'.[19] The interpretation panel at Reydon Wood, a little stretch of ancient woodland near Southwold currently being coppiced by a local trust, is equally insistent in drawing attention to the medieval earthworks. The Derwent County Park, Gateshead, includes the remnants of old ironworks, mill dams and waterways on its Nature Detective Trails.[20]

Conservation, a minority cause in the early 1960s when the term entered common currency, and restricted at the outset to the protection – or attempted protection – of well-known historic landmarks, is today the most favoured outlet for the reformist impulse in national life, mobilizing a vast amount of voluntary effort and enjoying the nominal support of politicians of all stripes. In schemes of environmental improvement, it occupies the ideological space accorded in the 1940s to modernization and planning; under the influence of ecology it has extended its activity from the built environment to bird sanctuaries and wildlife reserves. In the countryside, the Woodland Trust, which began its life in 1972, now has some three hundred woods in its care. The Council for Small Industries in Rural Areas designates priority areas for the revival of traditional crafts. 'Enterprise Neptune' fights to protect the 'heritage' coast from pollution; while the National Trust, to judge by the tastefully lettered signposts which confront the modern rambler, has contrived to take every beauty spot in the country into its care.

No less symptomatic than the protection of the countryside is the 'historicization' of the towns, which has nowadays replaced streamlining and modernization as the great object of municipal idealism and civic pride. Glasgow's 'Merchant City' is an apparently successful example, the restoration and refurbishment of a run-down district of sweatshops and warehouses into one that is simultaneously pre-industrial and post-modern, exorcizing memories of the shipyards by resurrecting the commercial glories of the age of Adam Smith, while at the same time providing a showcase for modern fashion and a new business head-quarters for information technology. A more macabre example would be the Rhondda Heritage Park, built on the corpse of the recently closed pits, occupying a site where less than ten years ago miners were staging a sit-down strike. 'Operation Groundwork', a partnership between government, local councils and private enterprise first established in south west Lancashire in 1981, is now generalizing such refurbishments. Landscaping and recycling old industrial plant serves to attract new investment and development, providing new office blocks with a 'heritage' core, and associating them, through museums and concert halls, with both history and the fine arts.

The historicist turn in national life may be dated to the 1960s, when it appeared as a pole of opposition to the modernizations of the time, though it also bore their impress. It was then that the museums movement got under way, and that projects for 'folk' museums, or 'industrial parks', were widely adopted by county and municipal author-ities, though the newly appointed curators, painstakingly relocating and reconstructing old buildings and plant, were so thoroughly engaged in the work of site assembly that it was not until the 1970s that they began to reveal their potential. Beamish Hall, the open-air industrial museum which today attracts some three hundred thousand visitors a year to its 'Northern Experience' theme park, was adopted by Durham County

Council in 1965, and Frank Atkinson, the curator whose inspired scavengings brought it about, was outlining the idea of it as early as 1961, in the first issue of *Industrial Archaeology*, but it was not until 1971 that it opened its gates to the public. As the admissions figures show, once opened, the new museums attracted a large following. At the end of the 1970s, the *English Heritage Monitor* commented on them as follows:

> One type of historic building which weathered the storm rather better than average in 1979 was the industrial monument. Taking into account industrial museums such as Beamish, and steam railways, the number of visits to these attractions increased by 3% in 1979. This result is based on a sample of 77 sites, of which the Black Country Museum, North Yorkshire Moors Railway, Peak District Mining Museum, Sutton Windmill, Ellesmere Port Boat Museum, the Midland Railway Centre, the Mid-Hants Watercress Line, and Otterton Mill all increased their customers by over 20% last year. Since 1975 visits to industrial monuments, taking a constant sample of 31, have increased by 12%, compared with a 7% increase to all historic buildings. During that period the number of visitors to the Hull Town Docks Museum, Wedgwood Visitor Centre, and National Railway Museum in York has more than doubled.
>
> Between 1975 and 1979 the number of known admissions to industrial monuments rose from 2,576,000 at 49 sites to 6,567,000 at 113 sites. Altogether, 7,879,000 most recent admissions to 149 sites have been identified during that period. The most numerous type of industrial monument is the windmill and watermill, 48 of which have supplied admission figures. However, the Society for the Protection of Ancient Buildings publishes a list of 180 mills open to the public in England, so that there are likely to be considerably more than the ½ million visits identified. The most visited type of industrial monument is the steam railway, 34 of which attract a total of 2,880,000 passengers yearly. In addition there are at least 17 railway museums or railway centres attracting 1,717,000 visitors. Open air museums which preserve redundant industrial buildings are becoming increasingly popular. Beamish attracted as many as 316,000 visitors in 1979, an increase of 8% on 1978. The Black Country Museum and the Amberley Chalk Pits Museum are recent examples of this type. Mine works and historic ships are also attracting large numbers of visitors.[21]

Environmental education, or 'field studies', promoted by the Schools Council and progressive education officers as a species of 'discovery learning' and an ideal framework for 'project' work, took on a historical hue, and indeed in the primary schools of the 1960s and 1970s was perhaps the main agency through which a 'new-wave' social history made itself felt. In either case, there was a well-developed faith in the local and the immediate. 'Hedges and Local History' was a favourite topic – a subject which (as in synaesthesia) could be simultaneously seen and touched and yet which opened up on to the largest questions of land use and settlement. In 1969 Nature Conservancy initiated a hedgerow project, with the aim of introducing field studies into the schools and testing out deonchronology, its new method of dating:

> The substance of the project is concerned with surveying throughout the country the different types of hedgerow, their management and the kinds of shrub in them. And the type of questions which it is hoped will reveal the kind of information required range from asking recorders to give the age of a hedge where known, to note whether it serves as a parish boundary hedge, whether the hedge is managed by clipping or layering, and what shrubs comprise the given length of hedge chosen for study. From the point of view of the schools, they have much to gain from building up over a period of time details concerning the history, biology, geography and geology of the hedges in their own parishes. The results so obtained could be translated into a set of coloured maps showing the ages of hedges, their flora and birds' nests, and these could be used as wall charts for classrooms and serve as demonstration material.[22]

Family history was one of the most striking discoveries of the 1960s. Towards the end of the decade, when the family history societies began their growth, it was giving rise to quite the most remarkable 'do-it-yourself' archive-based scholarship of our time – a movement which started literally on the doorstep and owed nothing to outside influence. In the early 1960s family history was, it seems, an unknown subject so far as university historians were concerned (Keith Thomas, addressing a *Past and Present* conference in 1962, casually remarked on its absence[23]); and it was still sailing under the aristocratic and heraldic flag of 'genealogy' when it was practised by amateurs and part-timers. Yet already Peter Laslett, a historian who had cut his teeth on the popular when working during the war in the Army Bureau for Current Affairs, and later on the BBC Third Programme, was launching the Cambridge group for the study of population, an extra-mural enterprise which made 'family reconstitution' the heart of its work, and enlisted the labour of hundreds of volunteers in transcribing parish registers.[24]

So far from wanting to construct an ideal pedigree, these new-wave genealogists can take a perverse pleasure in the transgressive. Thus Orpington, Bromley and North-west Kent family historians, maddened perhaps by the respectability which surrounds them on all sides, seem to be fastening on murder and mystery as a means of keeping their ancestry up to the mark. Recent issues of the society *Bulletin* are positively ghoulish. 'Murder or Suicide' is the title of an article in which the author, not content with a coroner's inquest on one of his great-aunts, follows the death by TB of his grandfather's first wife. Another article, melodramatically titled 'Crushed to Death: Kiln Collapse at Swanscombe' chronicles the untimely death of a researcher's great-grandfather.[25] 'Killed in the Blitz' is a third which gives an inventory of an aunt's personal clothing ('white blouse, blue skirt, pink corset') and even of her dentures.[26]

In another area, reflecting 1960s pedagogic enthusiasm for project-work and 'learning by doing', the idea of family history was being taken up by progressive teachers in the schools. David Sylvester, later an HMI, devoted a long chapter to it in *History for the Average Child* (1968)[27] and another HMI, R. Wake, defending the worth of history as a separate discipline, recommended it in an early issue of *Teaching History*:[28] 'Two unfailingly rewarding topics are: The day I was born; My great-grandfather/mother'. Primary and secondary school teachers in Berkshire and Hampshire collaborated in the scheme outlined by Don Steel and Lawrence Taylor in *Family History in Schools: An Interdisciplinary Experiment* (1968). By 1971 the new pedagogic enthusiasm was sufficiently well established for it to get BBC 2 airtime.

The 1960s take-off of 'living history' and the new appetite for 'living' nature were in Marxist (or Freudian) terms, overdetermined. In the case of the museums movement, a concurrence of different causes might be hypothesized: in one aspect it can be seen as a by-product or analogue of the antiques boom of the 1960s, and the collecting mania which sent scavengers and detectorists on the trail of the humblest artefacts. In another sense, it was the beneficiary of the local government reforms of 1962, under which the county councils were empowered to appoint their own archaeologists and take charge of the museum services. In yet another – the turn to 'hands-on', interactive display, and living, working exhibits – it could be seen as a museological or historical parallel to that very 1960s excitement, the 'happening'.

Urban conservation was sparked into being, in the first place, as an alarmed response to the automobile revolution of the 1950s (car ownership tripled in the course of the decade) and the grandiose road-building programmes which followed in its wake. It was given a further fillip by the great rebuilding of the 1960s, and the destruction of old neighbourhoods which prepared the way for it. In quite another direction – the politics of the environment and the way it relates to changes in occupancy – reference might be made to the spread of home-ownership to 'period' properties, and the middle-class colonization of previously run-down streets. Here the rise of the amenity societies would be related to the influx of newcomers to the older Victorian suburbs, just as the spread of wildlife trusts in the same period – notoriously with 'townies' in the lead – might be explained in part by the growth of weekend commuting and the multiplication of 'second' (i.e. country cottage) homes. The enthusiasm for voluntary associations – reflected in the membership figures, and the readiness to undertake part-time

volunteer work, as well as the protective nature of the causes themselves
– has evident affinities with the 'new-wave' charities of the 1960s, such as
Shelter and Oxfam, while the campaigning spirit in face of threat seems
of a piece with the middle-class radicalism which, in Britain as in the
United States, did so much to shape the politics of the decade.

As for the parallel rise, especially towards the end of the decade, of
do-it-yourself history, a rather different set of causes might be hypothesized; one in which past–present relations were reworked as a way of
taking refuge from the here-and-now. It cannot be an accident that
labour history makes its appearance in the very decade which saw the
start of a secular withdrawal of the working class from politics; that local
history, so far as writing and often even readership was concerned, was
so often in the hands of newly settled residents (the local amenity
societies derived much of their energy from the same source); and that
family history seems to have had a particular appeal to the geographically and socially mobile – i.e. those who, without the aid of
history, were genealogical orphans. 'Feelings of rootlessness', as the
family history societies themselves acknowledge, animated the new
enthusiasm.[29] It gave to the territorially mobile the dignity of ancient
settlement, to the limited nuclear family a far-flung kinship network, and
to the urban and suburban a claim to 'country' origins.

One impetus for the historicist turn in national life, as also for the
multiplication of retrieval projects and the growth of environmental
campaigns and fears, was a vertiginous sense of disappearing worlds – or
what was called in the early 1960s, when a V & A exhibition on the subject
toured the country, 'Vanishing History'.[30] It was amplified in the 1970s
by a whole series of separation anxieties which affected now one sector
of national life, now another; by the destruction or run-down of regional
economies; by threats to the living environment which put the taken-for-
granted at risk; and not least by the rise of a cultural nationalism which
spoke to a lost sense of the indigenous.

Many of these projects were born out of a sense of emergency, and
they have been sustained by the belief that, whatever their achievements, they are fighting a losing battle against the erosions of time.
From this point of view, Gordon Winter, compiling his *Country Camera*
and discovering old glass slides in a cottage lettuce-bed, or John
Gorman the printer-historian, rescuing old trade-union banners from
the incinerator,[31] belong to the same imaginative universe as the high-
level lobbyists of Save Britain's Heritage, even if there are very few other
affinities between them. Retrieval projects are typically carried out, in
the first place, as rescue operations, and indeed in the 1970s what was
called 'Rescue' archaeology – a Houdini-like operation in which the
scholars and diggers bargained for a species of time-share, snatching

their findings from the very jaws of the excavators – turned every dig into a crusade and every clearance site into a potential battleground. In industrial archaeology there is a terminal sense of recording something which is crumbling into ruins; in wildlife sanctuaries and nature reserves, of protecting endangered species; in rural conservation of defending a dwindling patrimony in which hedges are disappearing at a rate of knots and even the remotest wetlands threaten to become things of the past.

In the built environment, the working ideology of the conservationists was bleakly Malthusian, picturing an overpopulated landscape in which scarce resources were constantly being depleted and forces of destruction were on the march. There were the office developers hovering like vultures and swooping down whenever there was a vacant space. There were the lax council officials, unwilling to use the protective legislation available to them; the selfish householders who carried out alterations regardless of the building's character. There were the traffic engineers, churning up the few remaining cobblestones, and putting asphalt patches in their place. Horror stories abounded: of demolition contractors doing their destructive work by dead of night, or even, where a preservation order was immovable, setting fire to historic buildings; of country-house owners threatening to turn their properties into theme parks; of priceless panelling put out to grass in a skip; of residential houses illegally converted into offices.

II

Under influences like these, the notion of 'heritage' has been broadened and indeed transformed to take in not only the ivied church and village green but also the terraced street, the railway cottages, the covered market and even the city slum; not only the water-meadows, such as those painted by Constable, but also the steam-powered machinery lovingly assembled in the industrial museums. Historic Scotland and the Argyll and Bute Regional Council have recently voted some £200,000 for the refurbishment of a gentlemen's urinal on the island of Rothesay: 'The porcelain in the pierhead pissoir is an outstanding example of the work of Twyford Cliffevale Potteries. The urinals, called the "Adamant", are made of white porcelain with black fake marble surrounds. They are flushed via brass pipes from overhead tanks with bevelled glass panels.'[32]

Archaeology has extended the work of preservation and retrieval to objects which previous generations would have ignored or despised. A brilliant example is the application of radiocarbon dating to the analysis of waterlogged detritus. Extending their inquiries from geological remains to biological leavings, archaeologists have been able to pass from the material culture of everday life to the intimacies of the meal-table. Thus the latrines of the forts on Hadrian's Wall have yielded dietary details of the Roman soldier, including the relative proportions of meat and veg, while the fossilized shit of a seventeenth-century Provost of Oriel College, Oxford, has revealed an entire menu of gastronomic delights, including mustard, plums, black pepper, apples, grapes or raisins, figs, raspberries, black mulberries, wild or alpine or hautbois strawberries, walnuts, and hazels or filberts.[33]

By encouraging thousands to try their hand at museology, the collecting mania has also contributed, albeit subliminally, to an enlargement of the notion of the historical. So have the inspired scavengings of the numismatists – a great source of the medieval pilgrims' badges now on display in the Museum of London. The rage for Victoriana which took off in the 1950s (and made the fortunes of Portobello Road) has raised the humblest items of household furniture to the status of antiques. Commercial ephemera are, if anything, even more highly prized. Old enamel signs are collected as 'street jewellery'.[34] Old pot-lids have their own price guide (including 'copious notes on how to distinguish modern reproductions from the genuine article').[35] At Gloucester Robert Opie has a whole museum devoted to vintage labels and decorative printed tins;[36] Buckley's Shop Museum in Battle is 'a unique collection of packaging'.

As well as enlarging the notion of the historical, and bringing within the reach of scholarship (or connoisseurship), ephemera which earlier generations would have despised, the collecting mania has also served progressively to update conventional notions of 'period'. 'Suburban style', for so long an object of ridicule to snobs, now has its cult followers, with coffee-table books devoted to the inter-war semi, and exhibitions which celebrate them as 'little palaces'.[37] The Bakelite Museum in East Dulwich memorializes – along with inter-war kitchenware – the vanished glories of polystyrene; the Trerice Museum has an exhibition illustrating the history of the lawnmower. Clarice Cliff tea-sets, which took Metro-land by storm in the 1930s – a mass-produced pastiche of modernism, decked out in suburban style – can sell at over £100 a piece in the salerooms, and she has been given the accolade of an exhibition at the National Theatre.[38] In another sphere, 'classic' pre-war wirelesses, the subject of a notable exhibition at the V & A, now realize anything up to £20,000 when they get into the hands of the specialist dealers, and (as readers of *Collectors Fayre* will know) there is also a vigorous sub-trade in spare parts.

This updating of the idea of the past has allowed for and been encouraged by a multiplication of historical shrines. The Colman's mustard shop (with a Colman's museum attached) may not have had the accolade of being classed as a Grade I historical monument, but for many visitors to Norwich it enjoys parity of esteem, as far as sight-seeing is concerned, with the fifteenth-century cathedral.[39] World War II memorabilia insinuate themselves in the most unlikely places – the otherwise medieval Dover Castle, for instance. They crop up as visitor attractions at some country houses and there is a whole class of newly established museums and shrines devoted to them, starting with the recently opened Cabinet War Rooms, which have joined the Houses of Parliament and the Abbey as one of the sights of Westminster. World War II is also a great favourite for 'living history' or 'shared experience' displays at the theme parks – partly no doubt because of the ready availability of sound recordings and film footage which can be used to animate the display of relics with 'reality effects'. Pop pilgrimages are among the more recent additions to this country's heritage trails. The museum devoted to the comics, Laurel and Hardy, at their Cumbria birthplace, has recently doubled in size. The Abbey Road zebra crossing outside the recording studio, remembered from the record sleeve of one of the Beatles' albums, is, it seems, a Mecca for Japanese tourists (Kenneth Baker, in a populist moment of his secretaryship at the Department of Education, had himself photographed there); the Cavern, Liverpool – a replica of the original musical cellar destroyed by a fire, on the other side of the road – is visited as excitedly as if it were the real thing.[40] The Granada Studios tour, opened in the summer of 1988, offers visitors 'a walk down the hallowed cobbles of Coronation Street' and the chance of being photographed outside, if not having a drink in, the Rovers Return.

The most remarkable updating of the national past has been in the field of domestic architecture, where almost anything built before 1960 is liable to be labelled as 'period' – even, it seems, Second World War air-raid shelters.[41] Forty years ago the great stock of the nation's housing was regarded as obsolescent. Terraces, unless they were 'Georgian', were almost automatically designated as slums, 'unfit for human habitation'; while Victorian mansions, 'dilapidated, unsightly ... and totally uneco-nomic', were either consigned to the bulldozer or converted into modern flats. As Stanley Alderson wrote in *Housing*, a Penguin special issued in 1962:

Eighty years is a fair life for an ordinary house – even a good house. Most of the houses built before 1880 were not good ones. Not only had no minimum housing standards been laid down, until the Public Health Act of 1875 there were no effective building regulations. It is a safe assumption that there are

3,000,000 houses we ought to pull down right away. It is almost unthinkable
that we should not have pulled them down before they are a hundred years
old.[42]

In the modernizing hour of the 1960s, as earlier at the time of the
Festival of Britain, ideas of domestic comfort were taken from abroad –
central heating from the Continent; dream kitchens, with their streamlined surfaces and electric gadgets, from the United States. Scandinavia
set the pace in open-plan layouts and teak-handled tableware. Chianti
bottles provided the artistically inclined but hard up with their table
lamps; Chinese rush matting was a modernist alternative to carpets.
Simple lifeism, too, took its cues from abroad, as in the Le Creuset
kitchenware and Provençal casserole dishes which launched Habitat on
its brilliant career. Pine kitchens, marketed today as 'Victorian', 'Georgian' or 'farmhouse', were in their earlier version promoted as the latest
Swedish thing.

Conservationism has invented an English version of the ideal home,
one which draws its decorative styles from the national past, and its idea
of comfort from the cluttered Victorian interior. 'Old-fashioned', so far
from being a term of opprobrium, as it was in the 1950s, is here a gauge
of authenticity. It may be indicative of the influence of this aesthetic
that in the interiors featured in the *Observer*'s voyeuristic series, 'A Room
of My Own', hardly a single one has new furnishings. The number of
listed buildings (i.e. 'Buildings of Special Architectural and Historical
Interest') increases by leaps and bounds: it has more than doubled since
1982, and now approaches half a million (1920s council houses in
Edinburgh are among those which have recently been added).[43]
Victorian buildings which quaked before the bulldozer are listed for
preservation as a matter of course, and the very features which
condemned them in the 1960s as dust-traps are now advertised as
'original'. Erstwhile slums, lovingly rehabilitated, are exhibited and sold
as 'period' residences – rather as mews cottages were in 1920s Mayfair
and Chelsea. The terraced house – the *English* terraced house as it is
called by a recent and admiring historian[44] – could be said to enjoy
parity of esteem with the stately home. No less striking is the renaissance
of the farm labourer's cottage – minus, of course, the farm labourer.
In the 1940s these houses were thought of by many – even by country
writers such as Geoffrey Grigson, and certainly by many of the
inhabitants, who were only too anxious to secure a council house – as
rural slums, by-words for darkness and damp.[45] For the Labour Party
in particular, campaigning against 'tied' cottages, they were physical
emblems of servitude. Today, expensively refurbished and emptied of
their original inhabitants, they are a talisman of the Englishness

projected in the tourist brochures, charming traditional homes.

It is not only individual houses which have been rehabilitated but, more pertinent to ideas of national heritage, 'townscape'. A term coined by the architectural writer Gordon Cullen and adopted by the Civic Trust in their town improvement schemes of the late 1950s and 1960s, it was given legislative recognition by the Civic Amenities Act of 1967, which empowered local authorities to designate conservation areas. The first of these to be declared, the historic centre of Stamford in Kestven, fell within a quite traditional preservationist aesthetic: the refurbishment of the late medieval and Tudor heart of an old market town, given a face lift under the guidance of the Civic Trust.[46] But by the mid 1970s, when conservation areas began to increase by leaps and bounds (today there are some 7,000 of them), the most ordinary Victorian estate developments were being given statutory protection as a matter of course, while the planning officers of the local councils were bending over backwards to please the local amenity societies.

In the countryside, as in the town, there has been a vast metaphorical extension of the notion of 'heritage'. Under the influence of the environmental movement, as also of ecological fears, 'scenery', the great enthusiasm of the rambler of yesteryear, and 'beauty spots', the great object of picnickers and motorists, now take second place, as a focus for conservationist anxiety, to wildlife habitats and wilderness sites. Protective legislation, which under the National Parks Act of 1949 was restricted to twelve 'areas of outstanding natural beauty', has been progressively extended in scope until it can be routinely (though not always successfully) invoked in the case of the humblest bird-pecked mud-flat or orchid-bearing meadow. Otter-rich riverbanks, which the water authorities of the 1960s – like their counterparts, the traffic engineers, in the municipalities – were intent on straightening out and freeing of unsightly encumbrances, are now allowed to grow their trees again. 'Ancient woods', which in the 1960s were succumbing to the onward march of the conifer – and which so late as 1976 could still be felled at the farmer's whim – are now systematically coppiced, both to weed out intruders, and to give the hardwoods space to grow.

As in the case of the built environment, there has been a progressive updating of the notion of the historical. In the case of 'Save Our Orchards', the campaign launched by Common Ground in 1989, the indigenous strain of apple under threat (the *English* apple as opposed to multinational hybrids) seems to be largely the fruit of Victorian horticulture. The 'ancient woodlands', which the arboriculturists, the local wildlife trusts, and conservancy-minded local authorities have been rather successfully saving from the Forestry Commission and the farmers, are in some cases no more than two hundred years old, though to follow the signboards and the information panels one might imagine them to be prehistoric relics. The hedges and ditches which farmers are now being bribed, or subsidized, to retain, must in some cases be a legacy of the enclosure movement which peaked at the time of the Napoleonic wars. The wetlands, flashpoint of some of the fiercest controversy and sustained environmental campaigning, are often more recent still, a chance result of disindustrialization. Thus a National Trust wetland site in County Durham which is a great favourite with ornithologists was produced by the flooding of a former open-cast mine; Lavender Pond, the ecological park on the Southwark side of Tower Bridge, was formed out of a former timber-wharf (its projects have included the re-creation of wildflower meadows and wetlands, an urban windmill, a butterfly sanctuary and Britain's first 'fungi garden').[47] One newly formed bird sanctuary in Suffolk seems to have originated as a kind of conservationist *quid pro quo* for extensions to Felixstowe docks.

Archaeological exploration, extending its inquiries to the chemical analysis of biological remains and discovering history-bearing deposits in the most improbable locations – waterlogged ditches seem to have been the source of some of its most spectacular recent finds – has served simultaneously to enlarge received notions of the recoverable national past, extending it both backwards and forwards in time, and to intensify the notion of landscape as an environment at risk. It has identified, for instance, some three thousand deserted villages – the 'lost' villages of medieval and early modern England, depopulated by the Black Death and the enclosure movement – where ridge-and-furrow, the visible remains of open-field farming, are at the mercy of deep ploughing, while new roads or housing developments threaten to pour concrete over the surviving footings. The draining of the wetlands, though a disaster for wildlife sanctuaries, has yielded such treasure-trove for archaeological digs as, for instance, the hurdles of a prehistoric trackway;[48] while the analysis of animal remains has enabled them to map old sheep walks and drove roads.

It is in relationship to the industrial landscape that the influence of archaeology in updating and enlarging the notion of the historical is most apparent. Forty years ago the industrial was a by-word for squalor, a dead weight of the past which the environmentalists of the day – as well as the planners – dreamed of grassing over (rather as London, in the utopian dream of William Morris's *News from Nowhere*, was given over to pasture and forest). W.G. Hoskins, the pioneer of 'history on the ground', recording one of his post-war itineraries, pictured the Black Country as a dark planet, stretching out beneath a canopy of smoke and inhabited by prisoners or madmen: 'factory chimneys and cooling-towers, gasometers and pylons, naked roads with trolley-bus wires everywhere, canals and railway tracks, greyhound racecourses and gigantic cinemas; wide stretches of cindery waste-land, or a thin grass where the hawthorn blooms in May and June – the only touch of the natural world in a whole vast scene.' The Potteries, 'demonic' in their ugliness, were worse: 'hundreds of bottle-shaped kilns, black with their own dirt of generations, massed in groups mostly on or near the canal, with square miles of blackened streets of little brick houses – tall chimneys or iron and steel works, steam from innumerable railway lines that thread their way through the incredible tangle of junctions.'[49]

The discovery of industrial archaeology, a term coined by Michael Rix and quickly adopted by local historians, did not immediately change these perceptions: steam-powered factories were conspicuously absent from the major projects and initiatives of its early years, whether in the field of recording or of preservation. Windmills were the great passion of Rex Wailes, the official at the Ministry of Public Works charged with responsibility for industrial monuments in the 1960s. Canals, dating from the earliest years of the industrial revolution, were the favourite subject of early publications in the new subject. The local historians who took up industrial archaeology seem to have treated it at first as an extension of preindustrial history, rather than as a historical and aesthetic reality in its own right. When the East Yorkshire Local History Society and the East Riding Archaeological Society Joint Industrial Archaeology Group came together in 1966 their first project was a survey of the watermills in the district.[50] The Lincolnshire Local History Society's Industrial Archaeology Sub-Committee, in the same year, were making an inventory of turnpike roads and tollhouses. It is perhaps symptomatic of this that most of the local societies active within the field in its early years came from the southern counties (i.e. those which had escaped the factory system: Poole, Salisbury, Cambridge and Rickmansworth were among those who came to the fore), and that the southern counties were heavily over-represented in the early years of the National Record of Industrial Monuments.[51] The decline of smoke-stack industries, pit closures, and the haemorrhage of jobs in manufacturing employment changed all this. By 1971 it was possible to publish a coffee-table book with the expressive title *Our Grimy Heritage*, 'a fully illustrated study of the factory chimney in Britain'.[52] In the same year Durham County Council, which only three years before had come almost bottom of the list in the Industrial Monuments Record, opened its industrial and open-air museum dedicated to conveying 'the northern experience'. With its exciting tram-rides, lifelike Co-op stores, and pit-head winding gear, it was attracting two hundred thousand visitors a year by the end of the decade – more than Durham Cathedral. At the other end of the kingdom, on the western approach to London, the destruction of the

Firestone factory – a brilliant example of Trading Estate Art Deco – was
exciting as much outcry as if it had been the Rollright Stones or
Cleopatra's Needle.

III

The past in question – the 'heritage' which conservationists fight to
preserve and retrieval projects to unearth, and which the holiday public
or museum visitors are invited to 'experience' – is in many ways a novel
one. Though indubitably British, or at any rate English, it departs quite
radically from textbook versions of 'our island story'. It has little or
nothing to do with the continuities of monarchy, parliament or British
national institutions as it would have done fifty years ago, when, in the
heyday of the Army Bureau of Current Affairs, Westminster was still
regarded as the mother of parliaments, and 'the British Way' was seen,as
the envy of the world. Overseas colonization and settlement hardly figure
in it, though the family history societies, ransacking army records[53] (or
convict registers[54]) for the trace of forgotten ancestors, are laying some
of the foundations for the study of the British diaspora. International
relations, one of the great subjects of the school histories of yesteryear,
are apt to appear only intermittently and in terms of their domestic
repercussions – as, say, women's work in the First World War, or the
experience of the evacuees in the Second. Under the influence of
ecology, and of pioneering works by Keith Thomas[55] and Oliver
Rackham,[56] the history of the countryside has been reconceptualized in
terms of the relations of man and the natural world; the time does not
seem far distant when pit ponies will figure as largely as parish
apprentices in the history of the industrial revolution. The physical
remains of the past enjoy a new salience, even though they are still
largely ignored in higher research; and under the influence of conservationism, as also perhaps of lifestyle politics, there is a new interest in the
record of vernacular architecture and the evolution of domestic space.

It is the little platoons, rather than the great society, which command
attention in this new version of the national past; the spirit of place
rather than that of the common law or the institutions of representative
government. In one influential version, propagated by W.G. Hoskins and
carried forward by the amateur topographers of 'history on the ground',
the making of the English landscape becomes the grand subject of 'our
island story'; the palimpsest on which the national past is inscribed and
the genius of national life and character revealed. Archaeologists study
it in terms of ancient deposits, distinguishing between scattered and
nucleated settlement. Agrarian historians, identifying the pattern under

the plough, ground local economies in the chalk and the clay, upland
and lowland, field and forest. Local historians, conjuring villages out of
suburbs, rediscover the fields beneath the streets. Family historians,
tracing their ancestry back to some original parish or settlement, identify
locality with 'roots'. Conservationism seizes on these conceits, interpreting the built environment in terms of the spirit of place, imbuing
localities with personalities which it is the duty of the planning
authorities to protect.

The holiday industry follows suit – indeed, to follow the emphasis
on regional difference in the tourist brochures, or to historical
geography in English Heritage's guide to the properties in its care, one
might imagine that England was still living in the times of the heptarchy
and that the Act of Union with Scotland had never happened. The local
authorities, desperate to attract investment, and turning back to the past
to promote a new corporate image, amplify these effects with fancies
of their own. County Durham, as motorists discover if they drive in on
the A1, is 'the land of the Prince Bishops' (i.e. a palatine jurisdiction);
while South Shields (more modernistically), for those who follow that
town's heritage trail, is Catherine Cookson country. Middlesbrough, the
home of ICI, impudently promotes itself as 'Captain Cook's country',
with a heritage trail which ends up on the cliffs at Whitby;
Peterborough, in the post-war years expanding on the strength of
London 'overspill', is now revived as 'one of the great Roman towns',
Glasgow, with its newly sandblasted warehouses and tenements, is 'the
Victorian Bath'.

This new view of the national past allows for, and even builds upon, an
urban Britishness. The terrace enjoys parity of esteem with the country
house or the cottage, the vintage tram excites as much affection as the
show of shire horses. The fairground organ competes with the madrigal
as the sound of national music. In the heroic moments of the national
past 'the Blitz experience' – a light-show sensation at the Imperial War
Museum, and a great favourite at the theme parks – seems to count for
more than El Alamein or Trafalgar. Even when it comes to pastoral the
city gets a look-in, with disused shunting-yards serving as bird sanctuaries, deserted railway tracks taking on the character of urban
meadows, back-yard ponds supporting wildlife and suburban bee-
keepers producing a better class of traditional honey than their rape-fed
country rivals.[57] It is a testimony to the imaginative appeal of all this that
the biggest victory for environmentalists for several years, recorded as
this chapter was going to press, was the battle for a wildlife site in
southeast London.

Shopping enjoys an altogether new visibility in representations of the
national past. In pictorial histories (such as those reproduced from old

postcards by the Hendon Publishing Company: *Bolton As It Was,
Blackburn As It Was*) pride of place is given to the high street scene. In
the mock-ups and pop-ups of the 'traditional' village, the general stores
– or village post office – occupy the symbolic space once given to the
parish church. 'Period' shopping is a leading attraction at the open-air
museums and theme parks. At the York Castle Museum, a pioneer in this
field, a cobbled Victorian street has been reconstructed, with complete
shopfronts rescued as architectural salvage. 'Here are intriguing windows of a pewterer, a haberdasher, an apothecary, tobacconist, china
shop and a pawnbroker. A hansom cab stands in the street and across the
way is a fire establishment, a coaching house, a tallow-candle factory, a
general store and a bank.' Shops of a more recent vintage are also the
centrepiece of the open-air and industrial museums. At Beamish visitors
are transported from place to place in enamel-encrusted trams. Shop
assistants in 1920s costume serve them. At the Annfield Plain co-operative society store, everything is added up on the National Till: 'A big jar
of stoned damson jam, 1/4d; a quarter of co-op economy tea, 9d; a dozen
eggs, 1/-; 1 lb of Wensleydale, 1/5d; 2 lb of granulated sugar, 6d (most
people bought it by the half stone); and 1 lb of finest mild cured bacon
10½d.'

The new version of the national past, notwithstanding the efforts of
the National Trust to promote a country-house version of 'Englishness',
is inconceivably more democratic than earlier ones, offering more
points of access to 'ordinary people', and a wider form of belonging.
Indeed even in the case of the country house, a new attention is now
lavished on life 'below stairs' (the servants' kitchen) while the owners
themselves (or live-in trustees) are at pains to project themselves as
leading private lives – 'ordinary' people, in 'family' occupation. Family
history societies, practising do-it-yourself scholarship and filling the
record offices and the local history libraries with searchers, have
democratized genealogy, treating apprenticeship indentures as a symbolic equivalent of the coat of arms, baptismal certificates as that of title
deeds. They encourage people to look down rather than up in
reconstituting their roots, 'not to establish links with the noble and
great' – as in the days when blue blood ruled the roost – but, on the
contrary, to celebrate humble origins.[58] To discover ancestors who were
weavers or drovers, or to find oneself 'an eastender once removed', far
from being a matter of shame, as it would have been when families were
haunted by the fear of losing caste, is a matter of pride.[59] 'My
grandfather committed a murder in the Commercial Road', an expatri-
ate old Londoner told me after I had given a talk on London history to
the West Surrey Federation of Family History Societies: he had tears in
his eyes as he spoke.

Labour, so far from being despised, as it was so often in the real historical past, is retrospectively dignified. Its artefacts are lovingly preserved at the industrial museums, and subject to 'hands-on' interactive displays with aproned artisans plying their trades, and machinery moving on its wheels and pulleys; while at the farm museums butter is churned and horses plough a lonely furrow. It is not only labour which has been rehabilitated and given an honoured place in this new version of 'our island story', but also the shopkeeper. He is no longer the obsequious figure of nineteenth-century caricature, fawning on the carriage trade, nor yet a melancholy Mr Polly, teetering on the edge of bankruptcy and communing (or squabbling) with his fellow-failures, nor yet the vulgar commercial of Matthew Arnold's *Culture and Anarchy*, but rather, like the old-fashioned draper, an emblem of 'knowledgeable and friendly service'. In the books of sepia photographs, he is a figure of authority, flanked by respectful assistants, and backed by mountains of produce. In the trade catalogues, often reproduced in facsimile in recent years, shopkeepers figure, as in Whiteleys of Queensway, as 'universal providers'. In oral history's childhood memories they are fondly remembered as the purveyors of broken biscuits and spotted fruits.

This new version of the national past is not only more democratic than earlier ones but also more feminine and domestic. It privileges the private over the public sphere, and sees people as consumers rather than – or as well as – producers. Hearth and home, rather than sceptre and sword, become the symbols of national existence; samplers and patchwork quilts the tradition-bearers. In the hands of the historical demographers, the grand permanences of national life are no longer those of altar and throne, nor, as in the 'Whig' interpretation of history, constitutional government, but rather those of the nuclear family, as representative a feature of sixteenth-century Ealing, it seems, as of any London suburb today. Oral history, 'the spoken memory of the past', has been centrally concerned with motherhood. Starting, in the 1970s, with autobiographies of occupation – mainly male – it has increasingly come to concentrate on profiles of family life, adopting a child's-eye view of the past, and a home-centred view of sociability.

Nature has been feminized too. Wild nature is seen as a habitat, warm and life-giving rather than – as in the Wordsworthian apostrophes or Byronic tropes – rugged mountains and rocky eminences. Historical romance reinforces the feminine strain. In the hands of its most popular practitioner, Catherine Cookson, it takes the form of a family saga. Even when high politics is ostensibly the subject, as in the novels of Jean Plaidy, it is transposed into a drama of everyday life in which the most illustrious figures in national history turn out to have been made of the common clay. Costume drama, too, promotes an intimate view, making the empire-builders accessible to us by reason of their marriages and amours.

A bizarre but, perhaps for this reason, symptomatic expression of this imaginative shift, would be the recent poster campaign of the Tower of London, which contrived to present even that emblem of Kingly power as a haven of domesticity:[60]

EDWARD I HAS 14 CHILDREN AND A 3 ROOM PALACE.
HOW HE MUST HAVE WISHED IT WAS THE OTHER WAY ROUND

Nowadays even an Estate Agent would be amazed to learn that Edward I's Palace was once considered 'fit for a King'.

With only 3 modest sized rooms it must have been an incredibly tight squeeze for a monarch with a country to run, and 14 children to boot.

Since Edward's death in 1307 the Palace has been used as quarters for Henry VIII's servants, as an infirmary, even as home to the Crown Jewels.

Now at last it has been restored and opened to the public. So you can now go where your counterparts in 1280 never could – Edward built the Tower of London's moat and outer wall specifically to keep Londoners out.

They were angered by his nasty habit of raising taxes. Shame on them, didn't they realise that as well as financing his conquest of Wales, the King had to keep 14 growing children in shoes? . . .

Your visit begins in the Lanthorn Tower, where period manuscripts, artefacts, decor and music will give you a feel for the daily going-on in the Palace. As you cross the 'Wall Walk' see if you can spot the difference between today's views, and the panels illustrating what the same views looked like in 1280. Now on to the Medieval Palace itself.

First the Wakefield Tower where, sat upon his throne, the King hatched his plot to conquer Wales. Take in the oratory and stained glass windows as the Chancellor brings the scene to life. Then on to St. Thomas' Tower, where the King ate and slept.

Ask the Lady in Waiting how the Tower got its name and you may get to hear a ghost story.

Here you can also see examples of medieval pursuits. Calligraphy and quill making, perhaps royal seal making, maybe even a chess game (the board and pieces are medieval, but what about the tactics?) Then it's King Edward's bedchamber, which has been carefully preserved as an archaeological site . . .

The Tower of London. It's alive with history.

It is for anyone, like the present writer, who is a socialist, an unfortunate fact that these resurrectionary enthusiasms, emanating very often from do-it-yourself historical projects, popular in their sympathies and very often radical in their ancestry or provenance (even the Society for the Protection of Ancient Buildings was founded by a socialist, and the National Trust, in the early days of its existence, was a kind of Liberal front) have been subject to Conservative appropriations, and have strengthened the Right rather than the Left in British politics. Nor is this an accident. The historicist turn in British culture coincided with the decline of Labour as a mass membership party, with the demise – in Britain as in other countries – of socialism as a worker's faith, and with the Labour Party's loss of historic confidence in the necessity and justice of its own cause – a disillusion compounded by a growing alienation from, and disenchantment with, its own electorate. At the same time the break-up of the two-camp 'us' and 'them' divisions in British society, the fragmentation of class into a thousand different splinters, the crumbling of the barrier between 'high' and 'low' culture and the growth of a two-way traffic between them, robbed the 'popular' of its subversive potential and even allowed it to be annexed to the Conservative cause. It is perhaps indicative of this that the restoration of History to the core curriculum in the schools was the work of a Conservative government, and that while, in the subsequent debate radical voices were very much to the fore in the schools and universities, there was barely a squeak out of the Labour front bench at Westminster.

In the built environment, the turn against comprehensive clearance and high-rise flats, the rise of conservationist sentiment, and the discovery of 'heritage' in what had previously been designated slums, removed at a stroke what had been, ever since the birth of the Labour Party and in the imagination of its Fabian and ILP predecessors, the very essence of the socialist vision: a transformation of the built environment, the physical burying of what was conceived of as the nightmare legacy of Victorian industrialism and unplanned urban growth. In other countries such matters were secondary to the socialist cause; in Britain they were of its essence.

People's history may also unwittingly have prepared the way for more Conservative appropriations of the national past. Its preference for the 'human' document and the close-up view has the effect of domesticating the subject matter of history, and making politics seem irrelevant – so much outside noise. Its very success in rescuing the poor from the 'enormous condescension' of posterity has the unintended effect of rehabilitating the past, opening the nation retrospectively to the excluded. The focus on 'domestic budgeting' and poor people's survival strategies underwrites the values of good housekeeping. The recycling of old photographs – a feature of the 'new' social history – also provides subliminal support for Conservative views of the past. It is difficult to think of the family in terms of oppression and insecurity when photographs testify to its stability and grace.

'Victorian values' were being rehabilitated in the public mind, or at any rate in the public taste, for some twenty years before Mrs Thatcher, in the run-up to the 1983 general election, annexed them to her political platform – not least through the efforts of radical historians such as Asa Briggs, who offered a positive reading of the ideas and institutions of self-help, reminding us that Samuel Smiles, so far from being an apologist for Gradgrind and Bounderby, was a radical doctor and even, in 1839 when he was editor of *The Leeds Times*, a Chartist sympathizer. Victorian slums took on a new lease of life as refurbished cottages – in an age of tower blocks, the very emblem of building to a human scale. Beam engines and pit-shafts painstakingly reassembled in the new museums of industrial archaeology served as a vivid reminder of the time when Britain had been workshop of the world. In another, more sentimental vein, the antiques boom of the 1960s encouraged a positive revaluation of Victorian family life. Mangles, from symbols of toil, were turned into *objets d'art*; samplers and decorative fire-screens replaced Thomas Hood's *Song of the Shirt* as emblems of Victorian stitchwork.

It seems that a comparable revaluation is now taking place in relation to the inter-war years. A time in Labour mythology, as in the collective memory of the older working class, of mass unemployment and the means test, of Colonel Blimp and 'love on the dole', it now appears as the epoch when modernity took root in British society, when progressive ideas inched forward in the schools, when the aircraft industry and precision engineering gave British technology a claim to world leadership. The inter-war semi – for so long derided as jerry-building – is now seen as a child of the Arts and Crafts movement and a pioneer of the labour-saving home. Even the sentiment which Mr Chamberlain mustered in support of Munich and Appeasement is now seen in the light of the recoil from the barbarities of the Great War.

I do not think radicals ought to press their objections to all this too closely since, as the public controversy about 'Victorian values' suggests, there are no historical propositions which are insulated from contrary readings. If radicals are fearful that resurrection domesticates the past, and by making it too familiar robs history of its terrors, there are others, at the opposite end of the political or pedagogical spectrum, who are no less convinced that the new history is turning out a nation of subversives. Here is the aggrieved letter of one of them. It appeared in a recent issue of the *Daily Telegraph*:

PUT NELSON BACK ON HIS PEDESTAL

Sir – I have recently visited HMS Victory in Portsmouth Dockyard, and was both perplexed and disappointed by the commentary given by the guide.

As a child I remember being fascinated by the description given by the sailor who was then our guide, not only of the function of the ship's equipment and weapons and the duties of all who sailed in her, but of the battle of Trafalgar and its place in our history.

But now Victory is presented simply as an ancient artefact. The guide dwells mainly on the dreadful conditions suffered by the men below deck and the punishments meted out to them by the officers, who enjoyed great comfort on the deck above.

No mention is made of the fact that all these officers, including Nelson, would have gone to sea as midshipmen, aged as young as 10; they would have lived and worked on the same decks as the men, going aloft with them to handle the sails. There was no purchase of commissions in the Royal Navy, so they would have risen to become officers only if they had mastered the skills of seamanship required to sail and fight.

Nelson's death is now presented as little more than an incident at the battle of Trafalgar. Anyone without historical knowledge might think he died just because he was standing carelessly on deck at the time. There is no explanation of why Nelson and his flagship have been held in such esteem by the nation. No reference is made to his genius, the signalling innovations he used, or his new tactics which enabled him to win his great battle.

This is deplorable today, when so little history is taught in many schools. We need our national heroes as never before.

Jean Gordon, Petersfield, Hants.[61]

Notes

1. For some of the difficulties and excitements of this, Harry Haskell, *The Early Music Revival*, London 1988; Tess Knighton and David Fallows, eds., *Companion to Medieval and Renaissance Music*, London 1992; Christopher Page, *Discarding Images: Reflections on Music and Culture in Medieval France*, Oxford 1993.

2. For the way these museums have become national monuments in their own right, see Ronald Maddox's 'Industrial Archaeology' postage stamps of 1989 – with pictures of Ironbridge; St Agnes tin mine, Cornwall; New Lanark mill, and a Clwyd viaduct. They are reproduced in *The Stanley Gibbons Book of Stamps and Stamp Collecting*, London 1990, p. 76.

3. Fredric Jameson, *Postmodernism, or the Cultural Logic of Late Capitalism*, London 1992.

4. The philatelic revolution, to follow the numerous diary entries Benn devotes to it, was undertaken in a modernizing spirit. He wanted to get the Queen's head off the postage stamps (an object in which he was defeated by the guile of the Palace, and the outrage of the Establishment); to democratize, or broaden, the iconography of national life; and to reflect best practice contemporary design. David Gentleman, his fellow worker, or conspirator – 'about my age and ... undoubtedly one of the best ... stamp designers in this country' – shared Benn's radicalism, but artistically he was a late offspring of English neo-romanticism, having trained under Edward Bawden. In his postage designs, as in his 'Eleanor Cross' mural, which give Charing Cross tube station a striking medieval motif, or his illustrations to the Suffolk oral histories of George Ewart Evans, he seems closer in spirit to the book illustrations of Walter Crane or Thomas Bewick than to either Festival of Britain modernism or 1960s pop art. In any event, from Benn's time onwards postage stamps have been resolutely historical, pouncing on commemorative occasions, and giving a public platform for such historicist enthusiasms as industrial archaeology. For the struggle with Buckingham Palace, see Tony Benn, *Out of the Wilderness: Diaries 1963–7*, London 1987, pp. 218–20, 229–32, 234, 237, 279–82, 284–5, 287–8, 296–300, 313, 316–17, 364–5, 391–3, 408–9, 411–15, 420, 428–31. For David Gentleman's historicism, see his *Britain* (1982); his *London* (1988) and the *pièce justificatif* for his design on the Northern Line platform at Charing Cross, *A Cross for Queen Eleanor: the Story of the Building of the*

Medieval Charing Cross, London Transport 1979. *Design in Miniature*, London 1972, is an autobiography; and *A Special Relationship*, London 1987, an unexpectedly fierce little portfolio of sketches directed against Mrs Thatcher and President Reagan.

5. *Early British Trackways* (1922) was the first book of Alfred Watkins, the original creator of the idea of ley-lines. Jennifer Westwood, *Albion, A Guide to Legendary Britain*, London 1985 is a place by place inventory of such legends.

6. John Michel, *A Little History of Astro-Archaeology – Stages in the Transformation of a Heresy*, London 1979.

7. John Michel, *The Old Stones of Land's End: An Enquiry into the Mysteries of Megalithic Science*, London 1974, quoted, with suitably critical commentary, in Tom Williamson and Liz Bellamy, *Ley Lines in Question*, Tadworth 1983.

8. Williamson and Bellamy, *Leylines*, p. 149 quoting Michel, *A Little History*.

9. For the role of Elfs in the battle for Twyford Down, see 'Explode a Condom, Save the World', *Guardian*, 10 July 1993.

10. *Catalyst*, May–June 1993.

11. 'If You Go Down to the Wood Today', *Independent*, 27 May 1993.

12. Richard Mabey, *The Common Ground: A Place for Nature in Britain's Future*, London 1980, pp. 69, 142. This book, written for the Nature Conservancy Council, uses photography quite brilliantly. The writer is also keenly aware of the historicity of the landscape.

13. The Arboricultural Association was formed in 1964 at the same time as a group of tree surgeons formed the Association of British Tree Surgeons and Arborists. Ten years later the two societies merged to form the Arboricultural Association. *Environment World*, March 1992.

14. Oliver Rackham, *Trees and Woodlands in the British Landscape*, London 1990, p. 198.

15. Ibid., p. 205.

16. Hugh D. Westacott, *The Walker's Handbook*, London 1979; *Long Distance Footpaths and Bridleways*, Countryside Commission 1975. I am grateful to Alun Howkins for this reference.

17. Senlac Travel, 'Long Distance Walk', 1992.

18. Martin Robertson, *Exploring England's Heritage: Dorset to Gloucestershire*, London 1992. Old packhorse bridges and drovers' tracks also seem to be favoured for these long-distance walkers' routes.

19. Thetford Forest Park brochure 1991.

20. Derwent Walk Country Park brochures, 1993.

21. *English Heritage Monitor*, 1980, p. 25. The museums explosion, though it took a decade to get under way, was greatly facilitated by the Local Government Act of 1964, which empowered county councils and town hall administrations to start their own museums, and to resource them with services and staff. This also seems to have been the act under which county councils began to employ archaeologists, and later to form archaeological units.

22. A 'Hedgerow Project for Schools', *Amateur Historian*, vol. 7, no. 7, 1969, p. 269.

23. 'The Study of the Family in England has simply not begun', Keith Thomas, conference address on 'History and Anthropology', reproduced in *Past and Present*, April 1963, p. 15.

24. Institute of Historical Research, interviews with historians, Peter Laslett interviewed by Keith Wrightson. Also *The World We Have Gained – Essays Presented to Peter Laslett*, ed. Lloyd Bonfield, Oxford 1986.

25. *North-West Kent Family History*, vol. 6, no. 9, April 1984.

26. *North-West Kent Family History*, vol. 6, no. 4, December 1992.

27. P.J.H. Gosden and D.W. Sylvester, *History for the Average Child*, Oxford 1968.

28. Roy Wake, 'History as a Separate Discipline', in *Teaching History*, vol. 1, no. 3, 1970.

29. Royston Gambier, president of the Federation of Family History Societies, quoted in 'Digging Your Family Roots', *Morning Star*, 7 July 1979.

30. The 'Vanishing History' exhibition, which later went on tour, was designed 'to draw public attention to the need for the recording of old buildings due for demolition', *Amateur Historian*, vol. 5, no. 6, Winter 1963, p. 197. It is interesting that the summit of conservation ambition, in 1963, was to *record*; there was as yet no idea that the threatened

buildings might be *saved* – i.e. listed and statutorily protected against clearance and vandalism.

31. John Gorman, *Banner Bright, An Illustrated History of the Banners of the British Trade Union Movement*, Harmondsworth 1976. 'Disappearing Battlefields' is currently the focus of a great deal of campaigning, both by the recently formed Battlefields Trust and by individual causes, such as the Friends of Naseby Battlefield. 'Our Backyard', *Observer*, 10 July 1990; 'Objectors Fight to Save the Site of a Yorkist Victory' *Independent*, 6 August 1993.

32. '£300,000 Facelift for Historic Gents', *Independent*, 10 May 1993.

33. *Environmental Ecology, A Regional Review*, ed. H.M.C. Keeley, vol. 2, London 1987, p. 71.

34. Christopher Baglee and Andrew Morley, *Street Jewellery: A History of Enamel Advertising*, London 1978; and *More Street Jewellery*, London 1982. Also see *The Ephemerist*, the quarterly journal of the Ephemera Society.

35. *Yesterday's Junk, Tomorrow's Antiques*, ed. James Mackay and John Bedford, London 1977, p. 124; A. Ball, *The Price Guide to Potlids*, London 1970; David Griffith, *Decorative Printed Tins*, London 1979.

36. For a description, Debra Shipley and Mary Peplow, *The Other Museum Guide*, London 1988, p. 210.

37. The title of a splendid exhibition at the Church Farm House Museum, Hendon, 22 August–4 October 1987. It used the 'Silver' collection of inter-war furnishings, but had the wit to see that many of the pieces in an inter-war semi would have been second-hand or inherited.

38. See Leonard Griffin and Louis J. Meisel, *Clarice Cliff: The Bizarre Affair*, London 1988; and Pat and Howard Watson, *The Colourful World of Clarice Cliff*, London 1992, for her difficult personal life. Art historical or collecting interest in her work seems to have started with an exhibition in Brighton in 1973.

39. A feature on weekend breaks in the *Wigan Evening Post*, 30 June 1993, summarizing the attractions of Norwich, features Colman's mustard shop and museum while omitting the cathedral entirely.

40. Brian Southall, *Abbey Road: The Story of the World's Most Famous Recording Studios*, Cambridge 1982; Granada Studios Tour brochure, 1991.

41. One of them is on display at the Brewhouse Yard Museum, Nottingham. For an example of a preservation order, *Preservation: Dawn of the Living Dead*, Cumbernauld 1986.

42. Stanley Alderson, *Housing*, Harmondsworth 1962, p. 43.

43. See *Traditional Homes*, May 1988, for Northfield Gardens, 'a classic inter-war council housing scheme'.

44. Stefan Muthesius, *The English Terraced House*, London 1982.

45. 'The council houses with their means of pleasanter living'; Geoffrey Grigson, introduction, George Bourne, *Change in the Village*, London 1955, p. xv. 'The tied cottage is rightly regarded by agricultural workers as one of the most serious evils of rural life', Labour Party, *Our Land, The Future of Britain's Agriculture*, London 1943.

46. *Amateur Historian*, vol. 7, no. 8, 1963, p. 282.

47. David Nicholson-Lord, 'Dockland Nature Reserves Under Threat of Closure', *Independent*, 12 May 1993.

48. Geoff Wainright, 'Archaeology and the Green Movement', *English Heritage Magazine*, December 1992.

49. W.G. Hoskins, *Chilterns to the Black Country*, London 1951, pp. 26–7.

50. *Amateur Historian*, vol. 8, no. 4, 1968–9, p. 157.

51. The National Record of Industrial Monuments, Fourth List, May 1990.

52. Walter Pickles, *Our Grimy Heritage*, Fontwell 1971.

53. Simon Fowler, *Army Records for Family Historians*, Public Record Office, 1992; Michael and Christopher Watts, *My Ancestor was in the British Army: How am I to Find Out About Him?*, Society of Genealogists, 1992; Norman Holding, *More Sources on World War One*, 2nd edn, Birmingham 1991.

54. David T. Hawkings, *Criminal Ancestors: a Guide to Historical Criminal Records in England and Wales*, Gloucester 1992.

55. Keith Thomas, *Man and the Natural World: Changing Attitudes in England, 1500–1800*, Harmondsworth 1983.

56. Oliver Rackham, *The History of the Countryside*, London 1986.

57. 'Wild Life in the City' *Green Magazine*, October 1989; Bob Gilbert, *The Green London Way*, London 1991. More generally, Oliver Rackham argues that these woods – a limb of ancient royal forest – 'have almost certainly fared better under urbanisation than they would have done had they remained rural.... They have been loved and appreciated by a large population, and have been managed by a succession of sympathetic people ... urbanization has brought its problems of dogs, rubbish, horses, and minor encroachment; but these are small matters compared to the destruction of replanting which have been the fate of many rural woods.' Oliver Rackham, *The Ancient Woods of England: The Woods of South-East Essex*, Rochford 1986, p. 108.

58. Don Steel, *Discovering Your Family History*, London 1980; Stan Newens 'Family History Societies', *History Workshop Journal 2*, Spring 1981.

59. *Cockney Ancestor*, Summer 1980, p. 29; Spring 1982, p. 3.

60. I am grateful to Mark Lunn of Collett, Dickenson, Pearce and Partners Ltd, who devised the poster, for the text of the Tower of London advertisement.

61. 'Letters to the Editor', *Daily Telegraph*, 14 March 1994.

Living History

As well as the recovery of the real historical past, there is also the creation of imaginary ones – 'Tudor' gardens, Victorian steam fairs, Edwardian shopping streets. In the new and burgeoning field of applied archaeology, there have been the ever-growing extensions to Hadrian's Wall (a new stretch has recently been opened outside Newcastle) and the building of replicas such as the brand new Roman Gateway at South Shields, which now supports its own legion, the Quintagalorum, a locally recruited re-enactment society which makes a speciality of fourth-century drill.[1] A more recent example would be the Tower Hill Pageant, the latest of those 'dark ride' museums which bring the excitements (and terrors) of the Ghost Train to the exhibition of archaeological finds. Here scholarship of the kind more familiar in the cabinet of curiosities has joined hands with the new styles of showmanship generated by Disneyland and the American theme parks. The inspiration, it seems, of curators of the Museum of London, who have used it to display some of the more recent findings of their archaeological digs, the Pageant is a systematic exercise in time-travelling, starting with a descent which marks a journey back in time, and then underground offers a series of *tableaux vivants* recapturing, in artist's impression or models, London's evolution as a river crossing, a port town and a capital city.[2]

The taste for 'living history' also finds expression in the creation of make-believe historical settlements, improving on the original where there is a nucleus of material remains to create what Barrie Trinder, a moving spirit at Ironbridge, calls 'a hypothetical industrial community'[3] or assembling historical artefacts on a greenfield site and threading them with a narrative. One such model settlement is Cockley Cley, the prehistoric hamlet which a Norfolk landowner-turned-archaeologist has opened on the grounds of his estate;[4] another is Warrham Percy, the reconstituted 'lost' medieval village discovered by Maurice Beresford and now a visitor attraction for those who want to fathom the mysteries

of three-field farming. Then there is a crop of Saxon hut settlements (the one erected at Battle, Hastings, for the nonagentenary of the Domesday Book was so popular with visitors that it was retained in subsequent seasons).

On a much more extravagant scale there is Jorvik, the lost Viking metropolis, 'England's most celebrated museum or gallery outside London', where the waterlogged remains of tenth-century York and the stunning finds of a five-year archaeological dig have been turned into an underground spectacle of urban squalor. Aided by the peculiarity of the soil, which had preserved the underground remains of the town in an anaerobic cocoon, Jorvik offers – along with the humours of the fairground – an affecting gallery of the archaeological arts. Miraculously preserved footwear competes for attention with slender and elegant locks, household and personal jewellery and a mass of basketry and trugs. A life-size model of a Viking man on an outside toilet was one of Jorvik's early sensations, along with the period stinks which served as a gauge of multi-sensory authenticity. A more recent one is the skull reconstruction of the head of Eymund the Fisherman, whose deep-set eyes stare back at the spectators in their time-cars – a pioneering collaboration between archaeologists, laser and computer technology, sculptural skill and artistic teamwork, it draws on a technique developed at a London hospital to enable an excavated skull to take on a flesh-and-blood appearance.[5]

The newly established 'nature reserves', creating bird-rich habitats, quite often on wasteland sites, and restoring species which agribusiness or environmental pollution had driven away, could be thought of as second cousin to the newly invented historical settlement, and indeed in some way their senior. 'Nature trails' were being marked out in 1963, a dozen years before town-trails and heritage walks were adopted by the municipalities, while wildlife sanctuaries precede town conservancy areas by about the same number of years. After their own fashion, nature reserves are a form of 'living museum',[6] creating a protected environment where animal and plant life can flourish, while allowing visitors to get as close as possible through observational trails, hides and safaris. In the case of the country parks and the wildlife centres, established as an educational resource and devoted to the interpretation of what is called sometimes 'living nature' and sometimes 'nature's heritage', 'touch and try' is the user-friendly curatorial motto, with every encouragement to persuade children to try their hand at pond-dipping, butterfly spotting, moth trapping and nature study.

Nature reserves, or 'Sites of Special Scientific Interest' as they are also designated, are typically artificial, 'created habitats'. They may involve re-seeding old grasses, 'managing wilderness',[7] irrigating flats. Rare birds flock to the Somerset Levels, because they are flooded in winter and kept moist in summer.[8] Minsmere, the first and best known sanctuary of the Royal Society for the Protection of Birds, was the result, initially, of war-time counter-invasion strategy – the flooding of potential landing strips. It has been extended by turning erstwhile arable acres into a wilderness state and involves electronic fences and even guns to keep the avocets safe.[9] Here, from another part of Suffolk, is a notice about a more recently completed reserve:

TRIMLEY NATURE RESERVE NEARLY FINISHED
The creation of the Trimley Nature Reserve on the north bank of the River Orwell is now nearly complete. After 18 months of careful development work the Suffolk Wildlife Trust has succeeded in designing and constructing a first class wetland nature reserve. The Trust's Trimley Project Officer Roger Beecroft said: 'The whole area has been transformed from arable farmland, some 2 years ago, into a patchwork of pasture, grazing marshes and lagoons surrounding a large central reservoir. Trees and shrubs have been planted and reedbeds are fast developing. We've even created a sand cliff to provide breeding areas for Sand Martins'. A Nature Reserve Visitor Centre was officially opened on May 1st and this along with 5 bird hides provides visitors with the best possible facilities to view and appreciate wildlife.[10]

In some cases, 'living history' is a matter of using electronically

operated devices to animate what would otherwise be inert – as in the
Gregorian chant which, for those who opt for the Walkman commentary,
accompanies those latter-day Wordsworthians who make the pilgrimage
to Tintern Abbey;[11] or the 'gurgling sounds and ... din of workmen
handling barrels' which apparently accompany visitors to the Scotch
Whisky Heritage Centre, Edinburgh, on their tour.[12] The 1994 Tower
Bridge exhibition entitled 'The Celebration Story, 1894–1994' makes a
feature of its monster-engines, but also – possibly tongue-in-cheek –
offers the visitor the sensation of 'all manner of ANIMATRONICS, HOLO-
GRAPHIC GHOSTS, SPECTATROPIC PARAPHERNALIA' as well as 'ACTUAL ARTE-
FACTS'.[13]

In other cases living history is a matter of improving on the original
by installing, in replica and facsimile, what ought to be there but is not
– as in the furnishing of monastic cells, a current favourite in ruin
interpretation. The restoration of such 'historic ponds' as the old
monastic fishery near Bruisyard Hall, Suffolk;[14] or the re-created
nineteenth-century flower garden opened in 1993 at Audley End,[15] the
result of a decade of research and construction by English Heritage,
perhaps fall into this category.

Then there is the matter of 'stabilizing' or 'consolidating' what
otherwise threatens to disintegrate, or to fall into a state of decay. Here,
as on Hadrian's Wall, stabilization is apt to metamorphose into a process
of embellishment, and even invention. An outstanding example would
be the treatment meted out to one of this country's rare monuments to
fertility:[16]

> For decades, motorists have marvelled at the Cerne Giant, the 180-foot-long
> chalk etching of a man engraved in the Dorset hills near Cerne Abbas, not
> least because of its colossal anatomy, particularly impressive in the area of the
> loins. Now, I can reveal, there is something else to look at. A nose. 'People
> have become so used to seeing the face without a nose that they have been
> beguiled into thinking he was created noseless,' says Ivan Smith, a spokesman
> for the National Trust, which looks after the landmark. 'In fact, the organ –
> traditionally one of the more obvious parts of the giant, since it sticks up – got
> eroded away.' Led by Martin Papworth, the trust's archaeological surveyor for
> Wessex, a team has rebuilt the nose, raising it nine inches by lifting the turf
> in the area around it and remodelling it with chalk. Most historians agree that
> the ithyphallic giant – thought to be over 2,000 years old – is a fertility symbol.
> The figure, which carries a club in its right hand while stretching out its left,
> is probably Hercules, who presumably had a big nose.

The open-air and industrial museums go to great lengths to show their
exhibits in action. At the working farm museums and countryside
interpretation centres, where old barns and period cowsheds are
re-erected or reassembled on site, the fields are treated as an extension

of the exhibition space: heavy horses drag their ploughs; stationary engines perform their threshing. The industrial museums are no less eager to show off the capabilities of belt-and-pulley-driven machinery. The artefacts themselves – often, by present-day standards gigantesque – are typically originals, rescued from the scrapheap and restored to vigour and life. But they will usually have been transplanted from somewhere else. The Museum of Rural Life, Reading, one of the first of the working museums, was a kind of *omnium gatherum* – a collection of plant, tools, waggons and domestic articles assembled from all over the country (the historical farm records at the museum have the same character). The example provoked others into activity – notably in Lincolnshire and Essex.[17] And it was followed by the industrial museums. Beamish, with its 'colliery', 'farming' and 'urban' areas, its working shops, its crowded trams and throngs of visitors, treats buildings and plant as if they were so many props on a stage set, gathering them in from the far corners of north-east England and relocating them on what was previously a greenfield site. The engine-house, winding-engine head-stock and winding-gear came from Beamish Colliery No. 2 Pit, a few miles distant. The coal sorting screens are from Ravensworth Park Drift, Gateshead, and the small powder-house is from Houghton Colliery, near Sunderland. The terrace of six miners' cottages come from Francis Street, Hetton-le-Hole.[18]

A still more celebrated example of historical bricolage is the open-air museum complex at Ironbridge, which opened to the public in 1973 and now enjoys the status of a United Nations World Heritage Site and a Grade I historical monument.[19] Beginning life with no more than a small company museum,[20] a bridge and a run-down industrial plant, it accreted to itself, under the entrepreneurial directorship of Neil Cossons, not only a matching ironworkers' hamlet, but also five additional 'living history' museums, including a Museum of the River, 'which examines the influence rivers have had on the industrial process' and – the great visitor attraction – Blists Hill, a re-created Victorian village, now growing into a town, of transplanted nineteenth-century buildings. Period and place are promiscuously mixed. The make-believe clay mine, on the site of Madeley Wood Pit, has a gigantic wheel for its pit winding-shaft, as gross and primitive as in a late-eighteenth-century engine house. The pharmacy, with shelf upon shelf of mysteriously labelled phials, looks like the fantasy of some high Victorian poisoner; while the Lloyd's Bank, kindly donated by the corporation – the place where you change your decimal coinage into coppers – would not look out of place in one of our surviving Edwardian high streets.

The relocation of historic ships – or, in the case of the *Mary Rose* at Portsmouth, the excavation of shipwrecks – is in some sense a maritime equivalent of the re-siting of agricultural machinery and industrial plant. They have allowed every port in the country to lay some special claim to maritime heritage. They also give a kind of instant antiquity to even brand-new marina-like developments. Thus the SS *Great Britain*, the world's first ocean-going, propeller-driven iron ship, designed by Isambard Kingdom Brunel, built in Bristol and launched in 1843, had been abandoned in the Falklands and used as a storage hulk. It was towed back to Bristol in 1970 and restored to an 1843 appearance with some twenty years of craftsmanly labour. She now graces the waterside development. A small fleet of privately owned vintage craft is moored in the marina (alongside them the Maritime Heritage Centre introduces the theme of shipbuilding in Bristol over a period of two hundred years, 'as illustrated by the important collection of models, paintings and archive material assembled by the Bristol shipbuilders, Charles Hill and Sons, and their predecessor, James Hilhouse').[21] In London the 'Historic Ship Collection' formed by the Maritime Trust dignifies St Katherine's Dock, a marina-like development opened in 1977 and built on the corpse of Thomas Telford's warehouses and quays. 'Discovery Point', Dundee, a £60-million heritage centre built around the ship which took Scott to his death in the Antarctic (the ancillary exhibits include an Antarctic iceberg), is a more recent example of such developments. It was opened by Prince Philip on 30 June 1993.[22] (Not to be outdone, Aberdeen is building a new maritime heritage port housing the last ship built in Aberdeen, a costume museum and a new film theatre.[23])

In quite another sphere of national life one could point to the current vogue for historical re-enactment, as for example in restaging the sieges and battles of the Civil War.[24] The National Association of Re-enactment Societies, an umbrella organization set up in 1991, attempts to promote co-operation between the different fight societies (the Dark Age societies, 'the wild ones of the re-enactment world' tend to keep themselves to themselves, as do the local groups who make a speciality of being Celts or ancient Britons). The Jousting Federation of Great Britain is the official body representing the medievalists; it is affiliated to the Sports Council. The Nonagentenary Year of the Battle of Hastings was the occasion for some rudimentary exercises in this vein, with the government footing the bill for a military and festive display.[25] The event was so successful, it seems, that it was re-enacted twenty years on, for the nine hundredth anniversary of the Domesday Book. The events this time were organized by Battle Promotions Ltd, in association with English Heritage, the government-funded quango which took over the functions of the Historic Buildings Commission in 1984. At Battle, 'the town where Norman rule was first established', and near the abbey founded on the site of William's victory, 'a specially constructed Anglo-Saxon village', had craftsmen and labourers demonstrating the peaceful arts, 'living daily life as they would have done in Anglo-Saxon times'. A Saxon fair amplified these effects. The Leek tapestry ('a remarkable piece of embroidery made in the 1880s from tracings of watercolour drawings from the original Bayeux tapestry') provided an artistic representation of the battle scenes. Each day, during the period of the festival, the Norman commissioners arrived to make their Domesday survey, while nearby there was a camp of Norman mercenary soldiers, a Norman horse race and tournament, falconry displays and battles.[26]

Here is an epitome of some of the historical re-enactments offered by English Heritage at its properties during the 1993 summer season:

Gisborough Priory, Cleveland (Sunday July 18). Falconry – spectacular flying displays demonstrating the training and exercise of magnificent birds of prey – together with a talk about the history of using hawks and falcons for hunting, the different breeds and their conservation.

Beeston Castle, Cheshire (Saturday and Sunday, August 7–8). The castle fell to the Royalists in the English Civil War in 1643. Watch soldiers on guard, at drill and firing musket and cannon while camp followers cook and go about daily life.

Corbridge Roman Site, Northumberland (Bank Holiday weekend, August 28). The imperial Roman army – armoured legionaries and auxiliaries on parade, demonstrating the battle tactics that made Rome invincible.

Richmond Castle, North Yorkshire (Sunday and Bank Holiday Monday, August 29–30). Life in a medieval castle – recreates life in a military garrison of the late fifteenth century and reveals how the household carried out domestic duties 400 years ago.

Carlisle Castle, Cumbria (Saturday and Sunday, September 18–19). Wellington's Redcoats – superbly uniformed and highly trained soldiers demonstrate light infantry drill, tactics, musket firing and off-duty life during the Napoleonic Wars.

If there is a unifying thread to these exercises in historical reconstruction it is the quest for immediacy, the search for a past which is palpably and visibly present: 'stepping back in time', for those who sample the sights and sounds of the Great Fire at the Museum of London; 'taking a walk with history', for those who follow the old packhorse trail along the Pennine Way. In a phrase which has been adopted by a whole succession of retrieval projects, from canal restoration and steam preservation in the 1950s to the Heritage centres and town trails of today, it is 'living history'. Objects must be seen and felt and touched if they are not to remain inanimate, and restored to their original habitat, or some lifelike replica of it, if they are to be intelligible in their period setting. Events should be re-enacted in such a way as to convey the lived experience of the past. Country houses should be in family occupation, if visitors are to sample their true quality.[27]

'Living history' owes a great deal to the do-it-yourself enthusiasm of mechanical fanatics who spend their weekend breaks, or their summer holidays, resurrecting some long-lost skill – be it getting up steam on the footplate, negotiating the sluices of a canal lock, messing about in boats or trying their hand at steam ploughing. In a kindred vein, dating from the 1950s, there are the tall ship regattas, which mobilize a veritable armada of full-rigged vessels and attract huge crowds of onlookers when they sail up an estuary or anchor in a port.

More theatrically, there is the staging of historical pageants and spectacles, in which the living impersonate the dead and onlookers are invited to take a walk-on part in the drama. Reference might be made here to the medieval and Victorian 'fayres', which now rank with the shire horse shows and the cathedral town concerts in the listings of summer spectacles; to the summer carnivals and street festivals (Notting Hill's has developed into the largest open-air carnival in Europe); and to the multiplication of anniversary and commemorative events. Thus, for instance, the centenary of Wandsworth and Putney Common in 1971 (the remote origin of one of today's Roman legions) began with a representation of iron-age man, and after its central tableau – the mid-Victorian rifle volunteers – passed on to such remembered pleasures as the Walls Ice Cream 'stop-me-and-buy-one' vans and concluded with the dug-outs of 1938.[28] Armada 400, in which beacons were lit on the clifftops and Plymouth was crowded with make-believe Elizabethan sea-dogs, seems to have given a great fillip to the vintage boat runs.[29]

'Living history' – despite, or perhaps because of, the oxymoron – is a trope which shows no sign of exhausting its imaginative appeal. Schoolteachers continue to champion it, as they have done ever since the Schools Council History Projects of the 1970s, as an example of learning by doing. It has been incorporated into the machineries and strategies of 'heritage interpretation',[30] rather as 'living nature' and nature trails are used in wildlife conservation and management. The stately homes mount their falconry displays and jousting tournaments in its name. And it has been adopted as a kind of motto by the open-air and working museums, dedicated to giving visitors a first-hand experience of the past and priding themselves on life-like detail: 'Crawl through a coal and clay mine and wander the street of Halifax of 1850', runs the brochure for one, a former textile mill 'lovingly converted to recreate the working conditions, sounds and smells of Halifax's proud industrial past'.[31]

Children seem to be the principal consumers of these exercises in historical make-believe. At the White Cliffs 'experience' in Dover they are encouraged to board a Roman galley, clamber up the rigging of an old ferry and pick their way through the glowing embers of a 1944 street.[32] At the May Day chimney sweeps' procession, newly reinvented by the leisure and arts department of Rochester town council, and a national exhibition space for the morris dancers, they black up their faces to act the part of climbing boys.[33] At Kentwell Hall, Long Melford, Suffolk, a Mecca for Tudor freaks, school parties have the lion's share of the open days – about thirty thousand come each year – trying out Tudor costumes, enjoying themselves (or frightening themselves) in the stocks, and watching the humours of a Tudor feast, solemnly performed by a local cast who are now so thoroughly identified with their act that they seem oblivious of onlookers.[34]

At the museums where 'living history' has been adopted as a watchword by go-ahead curators it takes the form of audio-visual display, using artists' impressions, photographic blow-ups or replicas to exhibit what ought to be there but is not and contextualize the artefacts in a narrative whole. Instead of being temples for the worship of the past, these museums make a fetish of informality, discarding glass cases in favour of free-standing exhibits which ideally can be handled and touched, encouraging visitors to hob-nob with the demonstrators, and replacing galleries with intimate 'rooms'. Instead of a solemn hush, the visitor is assailed by a cacophony of sounds. In the working exhibit, the machinery moves ponderously on its belts and wheels; enginemen wind the shafts; shopkeepers stand in their doorways. Tape recordings are often used to amplify the reality effects – old hands explaining the complex processes at work. The domestic gallery of the Science Museum adopted this technique some years ago: 'As you gaze at the reconstructed nineteenth-century kitchen, you can hear the voice of a domestic servant describing her duties.' Similarly in the Museum of Oxford, 'transcripts of conversations with retired workers are included in the displays of the places where they worked and the tools they used.' A more elaborate exercise in reincarnation – pioneered by (of all people) the Public Record Office when, in 1986, they mounted an exhibition to mark the nonagentenary of the Domesday Book – is the use of animatronics, which makes the models move and appear to come alive, even (in the case of one of the Domesday scribes) to address the visitors. The newly opened museum of science at the Wellcome Institute has gone one better, by animating replica skeletons.

Immediacy is even more strenuously insisted on in the theme parks, where 'living history' displays take the form of *tableaux vivants* and are offered as a form of shared experience. The 'Edwardian Experience' is the central attraction at the Dobwalls' Theme Park in Liskeard, Corn-wall, winner of the 1987 Sotheby's Award for the best fine-art museum in England. 'Turn-of-the-century Jermyn Street comes alive with shops, lamps and cobblestones underfoot. Round the corner scenes of country life.... Imagine a whole street like it was in grandad's time. Real shops and everything! Magic'.[35] At Flambard's Theme Park, Helston, the comparable attractions are a 'Victorian Village' ('undercover, authenti-cally reconstructed life-size with shops, carriages and fashions'), and 'Britain in the Blitz', a tableau opened by Vera Lynn ('a life-size wartime street' with a 'wealth of genuine artefacts of those perilous days').[36]

At the war museums – widely imitated in the theme parks – smoke generators supply the acrid fumes of battle, hi-tech lighting the search-lights, blue flares the shell-fire. At the Imperial War Museum visitors queue up for the experience of cowering in the trenches, where they are bombarded with electronically operated audiovisual effects. At the Second World War gallery in the Museum of London visitors are positioned as targets of the blitz, wakening to the wail of the sirens, listening to the ack-ack of the anti-aircraft batteries and the whine of the high explosives. At Jorvik, the Vikings land to the sound of synthesizers. At Chepstow Castle, where the Royalists are annually besieged by Roundheads, electronically operated batteries simulate the sight and sound of the Cromwellian cannonballs.

The example of the tall ships races, which began as a Torbay to Lisbon run in 1956, with Swedish, Norwegian, Danish, Dutch, French and Italian ships – and even an Argentinian cutter – may serve as a reminder that 'living history', though it builds on a sense of place, is a transna-tional phenomenon, and that many of the leading initiatives have come from abroad.[37] Thus, for instance, Robert Birley's inspiration for his Hadrian Wall replicas at Vindolanda seems to have come from the example of such places as Saalburg 'on the Roman Rhine frontier', and the simulated Roman Fort at South Shields is attributed to a similar influence.[38] At Jorvik, Peter Addyman, the director and original begetter of the spectacle, claims to have taken his original inspiration from a visit to that monument to American preservationism, make-believe eight-eenth-century Williamsburg.[39] The Welsh Folk Museum, opened in 1958 at St Fagan's was no less beholden to the Scandinavian example of Skansen. More generally, the idea of the 'hands-on', interactive display – the leading idea of the new museology – is modelled on the practice of the Deutsches Museum established at Munich in 1903.[40]

AUGBUT, the preservation societies which fill Stockholm harbour with reclaimed and refurbished steamboats, are, it seems, as representa-tive a historicist enthusiasm in contemporary Sweden as canal restora-tion or the preservation of narrow gauge railway lines have been, for the past forty years, in Britain.[41] The Dutch shipyards are apparently the great source of newly made vintage boats. The Scandinavian ports, it seems, are full of pretend Vikings (last April, some of them attempted to stage an 'invasion' of Grimsby); and perhaps one should recall too, that it was an intrepid Norwegian seaman, Thor Heyerdahl, whose celebrated raft, the *Kon-Tikki*, navigating the perils of the South Pacific and attempting to establish the ancient sea-routes of the Maoris, provided, quite as much as Drake's *Hind*, the original for *Gipsy Moth* and those round-the-world British yachtsmen who, in the late 1960s, set a new fashion in deep-sea historical re-enactments.

The revival of historic ports, and the 'heritage' rehabilitation of abandoned waterfronts – whether at the docks or on the canalsides and canal basins – is also a transnational phenomenon. There is an elective affinity, here, between Albert Docks, Liverpool, now a Grade I listed building, and the centre of a museum, art gallery and leisure complex which attracts more visitors than Blackpool Tower – and such developments as Fishermen's Wharf, San Francisco. In the case of the new 'living museum' at Chatham, where the former royal dockyard has been transformed into shopping malls, waterside offices and a marina, with the refurbished Georgian buildings of the dockyard as its imaginative heart, the model was that of Baltimore harbour, a spectacular example of a city on a downward spiral brought back to life by the resurrection of derelict warehouses, now attracting, it is claimed, 'more visitors than Disneyland'. 'The Rocks', Sydney, an erstwhile docklands refurbished as 'the birthplace of Australia' in preparation for the bicentenary celebrations of 1988, nicely illustrates the Janus-faced character of such developments, a twilight zone which serves both as a shrine to the national past and a new frontier to a post-industrial future.

In another sphere, the floodlighting of historic buildings and later of town-centre conservation areas, the original model was French: *son et lumière*.[42] The genial invention of the radio celebrity, Pierre-Arnaud de Chassy-Poulay, vigorously promoted as a form of 'museum without walls' by André Malraux in his years as de Gaulle's minister of culture, it combines the visual sensation of the light-show with an al fresco dramatic entertainment highlighting great moments in a building's past – for example, in the case of St Paul's, the Great Fire of 1666 and the funeral of Lord Nelson. It was imported into Britain as early as 1958, and in the subsequent decade was staged at the old royal palace of Hampton Court and at half a dozen cathedrals (Durham, Canterbury, York, Hereford, Westminster Abbey and St Paul's). This is possibly the origin of the floodlighting of historic churches today – such a dramatic feature of the nightscape in East Anglia, and also, during its year as European City of Culture, of Glasgow's illumination of the Gothic skyline of the Necropolis. In 1994 *son et lumière* formed the centrepiece of the extravaganza marking the centenary of Blackpool Tower.[43] One can speculate on whether it was a subliminal influence in the 1970s and 1980s floodlighting of re-Victorianized town halls and pubs. What is beyond question is that the 'light up the Thames' spectacular, which embraced a two-mile stretch of the river from Vauxhall Bridge to Lambeth and left as its substantial legacy the night-time illumination of Big Ben and the Houses of Parliament, the Victoria Embankment and the Southwark riverside, was devised as London's contribution to European Architectural Heritage Year of 1975, and more specifically to the London meeting of the Commission Internationale d'Eclairage.

> When London decides to celebrate and put itself on show, the whole world knows of it. The plan to 'light up' London's Heritage had been formulated about 1974 and became known as 'Light up the Thames'. The object was to bring light and life to the river at night, to enhance it, and to give pleasure to residents and tourists. The energy crisis, which was at a peak at the time, caused the enthusiastic organisers some embarrassment and gave rise to major difficulties. However, when the Queen's Jubilee drew near, it became clear that London must be illuminated after dark, as part of the general celebrations which, as a whole, were expected to attract a vast number of tourists. One by one, the riverside buildings were floodlit, and parks and gardens were prepared for night enhancement, until a week before the event, all were switched on and the river in the centre of the City was transformed from a black water causeway to a ribbon of light, with every building, bridge and ship brilliantly illuminated. The tourists came, as expected, in their thousands and went home spellbound after seeing the *new* London by night.[44]

II

As well as anticipating the 'virtual reality' of computer games, 'living history' could be seen as a reincarnation, or new incarnation, of quite ancient forms of play. In particular, historical re-enactment is one of the oldest of the mimetic arts, and a perennial favourite in children's make-believe. It was the centrepiece of civic ceremony and procession in early modern Europe,[45] as it had earlier been in Corpus Christi.[46] The Primrose League, the first mass political organization of women in this country, practised it on a grand scale; so did the nineteenth-century friendly societies with their elaborate processions and floats. Impersonating the legendary figures of the past has always been fundamental to rituals of resistance and rebellion. As an aristocratic folly or sport, and possibly as a popular taste – the latter awaits historical investigation, and piecing it together would require a formidable deployment of forensic skills – it has

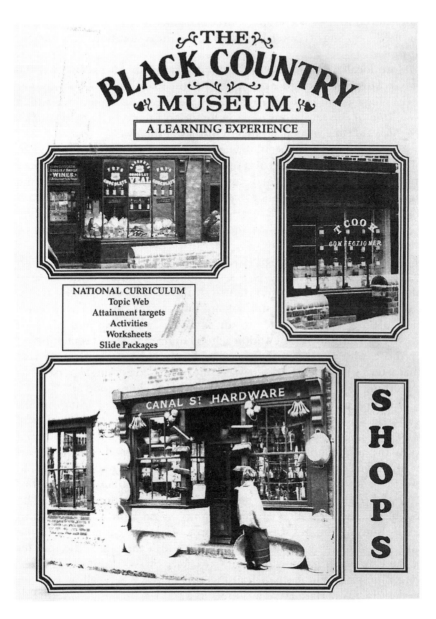

been a recurring fashion in English life. One could point to the frolics of the Hell-fire Club at Medmenham Abbey,[47] one of the originals of the Gothic Revival; or to the 1840s Eglington Tournament which Mark Girouard, in *Return to Camelot*, takes as his text for the Victorian cult of chivalry.[48] Ritualism – the nineteenth-century 'Catholic' revival in the

Anglican church – was a prolific source of historical re-enactments, both in the medievalizing of church buildings and in the restoration of the ancient liturgies.

More locally, the 'simulation' exercises so brilliantly executed at the Jorvik Museum, though making use of the most advanced computer technology, recall nothing so much as the spectacular dioramas which were one of the sensations of early Victorian London (Richard Altick's *The Shows of London* is a magnificent history of them).[49]

As a watchword or conceit, 'living history' was a coinage of the 1960s, but it had been anticipated and prefigured in a series of resurrectionary movements, each concerned, after its own fashion, to animate the inanimate and bring tradition back to life. The idea of what Margaret McMillan called 'education through the imagination'[50] goes back to the 1920s, so far as schooling is concerned, and it was being taken up by wide-awake museum curators, like Marjorie Quennell, in very much the same spirit as it was by progressive teachers in the schools. In the 1940s and 1950s Molly Harrison, the very adventurous curator of the Geffrye Museum, Hackney, and the inventor of the idea of the 'period' room, was taking up arms against the 'solemn hush' of the 'huge marble halls', and turning her museum into an extended workshop and place of activity learning for East London schoolchildren.[51] She is remembered by those who worked with her as 'a lovely lady', 'a battler', 'a real character', whose heart's desire was education. ' "Every single person has something to give", she would say, "something they are good at" '.[52]

The idea of the 'period' street – a favourite form of living history spectacle in today's theme parks – is often attributed to the Castle Museum in York, opened in 1938 to display in dramatic and pictorial form the remarkable collection of bygones assembled, over a period of fifty years, by John L. Kirk, a country doctor. But it had a remarkable precursor in the make-believe medieval and Elizabethan 'Old London' street fabricated for the International Health Exhibition of 1884. The exhibition itself – a kind of 'Ideal Home' *avant la lettre* – was held in South Kensington, but it was in Bishopsgate, at the eastern end of the City, that visitors were invited to step back into the past – the one bit of the City which had escaped the Great Fire of 1666, and where there were clumps of Elizabethan housing still in place, as well as the late medieval Crosby Hall. Here was erected a papier-mâché life-size replica of the old 'Bishop's Gate', the eastern entrance to the old walled city; 'Whittington's House', built Elizabethan style with latticed windows; and the stocks and whipping post which one of the souvenir photographs of 1884 has complete with a bearded figure in place.[53]

The idea of the historical walk is as old as antiquarianism itself. Leland's *Itinerary*, compiled in the 1530s and extended by later

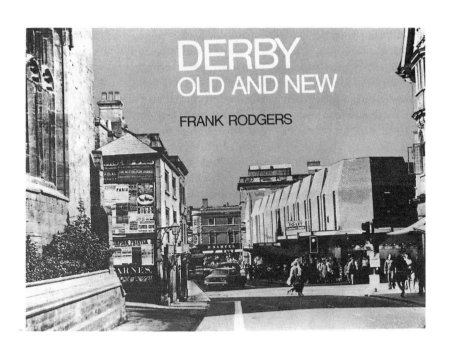

DERBY
OLD AND NEW

FRANK RODGERS

Jack Hulme

A PHOTOGRAPHIC MEMORY

Elizabethan travellers, is one original; Stow's *Survey of London* another,
Camden's *Britannica* (and the 'discovery' of England by the early county
historians) a third. In mid Victorian times, when it was known as an
'archaeological walk', it seems to have been a favourite pastime of the
more historically minded Oxford undergraduate, and had its counterpart in those who spent their seaside holidays hunting up vestiges of
creation among the rocks. But the change from ancient monuments
to modern, or comparatively modern, townscapes, and from antiquities
and curiosities to more contemporary themes, is quite recent. The
itineraries of the London Appreciation Society, founded by a
schoolmaster in 1935 and still quite active today, made no pretence at
interpreting the historical environment, still less at presenting the walk
as living history. When Bill Fishman, the newly appointed head of
Bethnal Green Evening Institute, began his East End walks in 1955, the
high point of the itinerary was the spot where Edward I, in 1297, ceded
the right of taxation to the nobility. There was no tour of the Jewish
East End, in later years the great object of his walks as also of his
historical work; mesmerized by an earlier past, he preferred to focus
on such gentile figures as General Booth of the Salvation Army, who
began his mission outside the London Hospital, and Dr Barnardo.

The idea of a historical ride, or journey back in time – today perhaps
the most popular form of historical re-enactment and certainly one with
great appeal to the juvenile section of the holiday public – seems to have
crystallized as a form of entertainment in 1951, the year of the Festival
of Britain.[54] Jason's Trip – a canal trip from Camden Town to Edgware
Road which in subsequent years was to serve as the unofficial ambassador
of the Inland Waterways Association, carrying its message into the very
heart of the metropolis – was launched in May 1951, as a contribution
to the Festival, attracting immediate attention on account of the
celebrities associated with it. May 1951 also saw the opening of the Tal-
y-llyn railway, the first of those narrow-gauge lines which, in the space of
a very few years, were to make 'the romance of steam' a term to conjure
with.

Railway preservation caught the public imagination in a very big way,
calling up childhood memories of seaside holidays, and offering
historical rides in the most picturesque parts of the country, notably
Snowdonia, the 'spiritual heartland' of the movement's early years. The
railway preservation mania was the first mass historical enthusiasm of the
post-war years. In its reliance upon volunteers, and its emphasis on
shared experience, it prefigured the 'living history' movements of more
recent times. It involved not only the resuscitation of abandoned or
moribund branch lines, but also a quite elaborate exercise in historical
re-enactment, with passengers cast in the role of Victorian excursionists

or Edwardian day-trippers, while the volunteer staff manned the foot-plate and the signal boxes, or (dressed in company canonicals), acted as ticket collectors, stationmasters and guides. The closure of lines and stations under the Beeching Plan for streamlining and modernization released a flood of railway memorabilia which were relocated at other sites – platform and waiting-room seats, station signs, lamps, clocks. Some four thousand pieces were assembled at the Bleadon and Uphill station, Weston-super-Mare, among them 'a magnificent, century old, cast-iron lavatory'.

The romance of steam may have been a discovery of the 1950s – a counterpoint to the dieselization of locomotives and the rationalization of branch lines. But the romance of sail, with all its attendant ecstasies and terrors, is possibly as old as the coming of iron shipbuilding. As readers of *The Riddle of the Sands* will know, it was thoroughly in place during the run-up to the First World War, even though the nation's maritime interests were supposedly monopolized by 'Dreadnought' battleships; while in a more pacific vein, where sailing appears as the greenest, the most natural and the most co-educational of the manly sports, reference might be made to the ultra-liberal *Swallows and Amazons*.[55] *Coral Island* is one possible starting point, if one wanted to follow the line of sea romance which ends up with Captain Hornblower, and which turned the *Cutty Sark*, even in the days when it was only a training ship, into a symbol of national greatness. In the 1950s the romance of sail produced not only the Duke of Edinburgh's 'outward bound' schemes, but also the building of the first marinas; the filling of the southern fishing ports with thousands of make-believe mariners; and the preparation for those round-the-world voyages which in the 1960s were supposed to prove that the spirit of adventure was not dead.

Canal restoration, which made its debut in 1946 with the formation of the Inland Waterways Association, was the work, originally, of a small band of enthusiasts. It quickly took on a life of its own, introducing the primitive delights of the narrow boat to a widening circle of initiates. By 1950, it attracted some fifty thousand visitors to a display of boats at Market Harborough. In the following years it was able to enlist the weekend and holiday labour of an army of volunteers in repairing locks, stabilizing embankments, and reopening disused waterways. By 1960, when the National Trust took over management of the restoration work on the Stratford and Avon Canal, the public authorities were ready to take a hand in it – even, in the last stages of this ten-year effort, the War Office.[56]

Tramway rides, today one of the best-loved features of the open-air museums, might fancifully be traced back to 1955, when lovers of the old Aldwych tram, which ran down the middle of Holborn Kingsway, sounded the last post – and took a last ride – on the day that the line was discontinued. A more substantial origin would be the activities of the Tramway Museum Society founded in the same year. In 1959 the society took over Crich quarry, between Matlock and Derby, as the site for a museum, assembling some forty tramcars 'with examples of horse, steam and electric tramcars', and using track from many different parts of the country 'laid by the society's supporters'. In the summer of 1964 it began carrying passengers.

It seems, too, that historical walks – retracing the footsteps of the past, or using them as a vantage point to read the landscape – were in the air in the 1950s. Local historians, enjoined by Professor Hoskins to put on a stout pair of boots and exchange the seclusion of the library carrel for the rugged freedom of the open fields, went out in pursuit of deserted villages (in 1935 only three had been identified; by 1960 some three thousand had been found). The pioneer industrial archaeologists, drawing up their inventories, trudged from site to site and attempted to identify old tramroads. The Ramblers' Association, in the agitation which led to the opening of the Pennine Way, began to canvass the idea of reopening ancient tracks as a means of enlarging access to the countryside, and it was of a piece with this that when long-distance trails were established they were given historic names: the 'Pilgrim's Way', no more than a dream when Powell and Pressburger made *A Canterbury Tale* (1944), is now open to the public.

In the towns, the rise of the local amenity societies, a feature of the late 1950s, and the growth of conservationist sentiment, produced a remarkable proliferation of architectural and historical walks, focusing on lost townscapes and highlighting buildings and environments at risk. The Society for the Protection of Ancient Buildings began promoting walks in 1958; the Victorian Society, founded in the same year, adopted them almost at its inception – a membership-led initiative which in the subsequent three decades produced a vast portfolio of town trails.[57]

The post-war renaissance of local history which got under way in the 1950s (from 1952 local history had its own learned journal,[58] and from 1960, with the foundation of David & Charles, its own publishing house) also had the effect of bringing resurrectionism into play, first in relation to the written records, then to material artefacts, and finally, with the advent of oral history, to 'living memory'. It was here that a new attention to the visual began to make itself felt, notably towards the end of the 1950s, with the discovery and use of old photographs – in later years a mainstay of local publication. Still more pertinent to the 'living history' movement of later years was the attention given to the domestic order – as for instance in W.G. Hoskins's use of probate inventories to determine the level of household comfort, the quantity (or paucity) of bed-linen and the division of domestic space:

Written for the most part in a homely style, with many a struggle over the spelling, these documents provide a mass of information for the economic and social historian, throwing light upon many aspects of life in a way no other class of records can do. We may trace from them the development of the simple domestic architecture of town and village, room by room, over a period of two and a half centuries, and the evolution of furniture and other household goods of all kinds, or observe the farming methods of different generations – the crops that are sown, the animals kept, the implements and the farm buildings; walk into the craftsman's workshop and see his tools or into the shop in some little Elizabethan country town and inspect the stock-in-trade. The inventories provide, too . . . a mass of miscellaneous information that is full of interest for its very minuteness: the changes in fuel in lighting, the clothing of different generations, and of different classes of people, the titles of books read in the parson's study or the farmhouse kitchen, the various sorts of drink in the tavern cellar, sometimes even the names of the cows that grazed in the ancient fields.[59]

'History on the Ground', the first of those 'do-it-yourself' enthusiasms which enlisted the energies of the part-time or 'amateur' historian, prefigured the 1960s fascination in the visual. It mapped out the making of the landscape and the study of vernacular architecture. Applying an archaeological approach to agrarian systems and a topographical one to patterns of settlement, it invited attention to a past that was palpably present: in the lie of the land, the slant of the roofs, the eccentric shapes of boundaries, paths and villages. It entered into the intimacies of farm layouts, believing that vernacular building (a term which it helped to popularize) presented 'a tremendous body of evidence' for the local history of every parish. It studied field-systems from the biological evidence of plant life, dating hedge-banks from the number and variety of shrub-species contained in them. Scholars were asked to apply their forensic skills in deciphering the visible remains of the past. The pattern under plough and the fields beneath the streets (such as those which Professor Hoskins studied at Wigston Magna) could be treated as a kind of parchment on which the dead generations had left their mark, a manuscript 'written on again and again' which secreted hidden meanings. Every stone, Professor Hoskins argued (and demonstrated), could tell a story:

Even a hedge far out in the fields may have a long history, going back to the great age of English colonisation of woodland and waste in the twelfth or thirteenth century.... The smallest pool or spring far away from the village will have an ancient name that, could we but know it, illuminates its special quality today, the name over the village shop may be one that is written in the Domesday Book (perhaps even older than that): there are depths beyond depths in the simplest scene.[60]

'Industrial archaeology', a term first coined in 1955, and a movement which grew with astonishing speed in the following years, transposed these preoccupations from the farm to the factory, and from agrarian history to that of mining, mineral-working and manufacture.[61] It also updated the notion of disappearing worlds. Whereas 'history on the ground' had been devoted to medieval and early modern history, industrial archaeology ended up by putting the imprimatur of 'heritage' on such monuments to modernism as the electrically powered factories of the 1920s. Seized with the idea of a history that could be, as one of them wrote, 'seen, touched and photographed'[62] as if it were a living presence, industrial archaeologists, like the canal restorationists before them, soon turned their hand to reincarnation. Thus, for instance, the Council for the Conservation of Sheffield Antiquities, founded in 1957, set about saving the Shepherd Wheel which the City Corporation was planning to demolish. Volunteer effort allowed this remarkable little eighteenth-century grinding establishment to be completely re-conditioned and it was opened to the public in the summer of 1962.[63] They followed up this success with a much more ambitious project, 'the most important single task yet undertaken within the field of Industrial Archaeology': the restoration of Abbeydale, a complete eighteenth-century industrial hamlet, which contained 'a Huntsman's crucible furnace, a water-driven tilt-forge and grinding wheel, and blacksmith's forge, workshops and warehouses'.

Another 1950s progenitor of resurrectionism – this time in the field of oral history – was George Ewart Evans, a schoolmaster-turned-ethnologist whose *Ask the Fellows Who Cut the Hay* (1956) presaged a cumulative and collective biography of the East Anglian farm labourer. Here was a work quite as local in scale as that of Beresford and Hoskins. But the preoccupation was with people rather than place, and with occupational rather than material culture. Whereas Hoskins and Beresford had made their starting point the medieval settlements abandoned under the impact of plague, depopulation and enclosure, Evans, even when he wanted to reconstitute some more ancient past, took his evidence from living memory, that of the Suffolk horsemen and labourers who provided him with his eye-witness accounts. Like Hoskins he was a man of the Left (indeed more so, having served his writerly apprenticeship in Communist circles), and he remained a fierce radical to the end of his days. Like Hoskins, too, he was concerned with recovering the memory of disappearing worlds, but the point of reference was not the yeoman farmer, as it had been for Hoskins when he returned to the world of his sixteenth- and seventeenth-century forebears, but rather that of his septuagenarian and octogenarian neighbours.[64]

A precursor of resurrectionism from a female perspective, anticipating many of the preoccupations of the 'new-wave' social history of the 1960s, was Flora Thompson's three-decker *Lark Rise to Candleford*, a memoir of Victorian village life written in an elegiac strain, and conveying a most delicate sense of both people and place. Publication in the World's Classics series in 1954 marked its acceptance as a primary text on the nineteenth century; a Penguin edition in 1974 made it available to a wider audience; and publication of an 'illustrated' *Lark Rise*, complete with pressed flowers, associated it, however illegitimately, with what by the 1970s had come to be known as the Laura Ashley look. Using memory not as a distancing device but rather as a way of allowing the reader to eavesdrop on the past and treat the inhabitants of the village as familiars, it brought a child's-eye view to bear on a world which in the writings of previous historians, as of contemporaries, had been unrelievedly harsh and deprived.

Each of these resurrectionary enthusiasms has a pre-history which it would be instructive to piece together. So far as industrial archaeology is concerned one might follow the extra-mural activities of Rex Wailes, an official at the Ministry of Public Works who enthusiastically backed the new movement. For some thirty years he had been single-handedly conducting a crusade recording, and where possible rescuing, old windmills – an expertise which he brought to the service of the new movement when he used his official position to launch the National Record of Industrial Monuments in 1962.[65]

Reference should also be made to the transactions and proceedings of the Newcomen Society, founded in 1921; pioneer historical studies of British engineering drawing in many cases from the industry itself. Its summer meetings, held in some place of historical technological interest, were spent in visiting works and sites. In the 1950s, anticipating the advent of the 'living' or 'working' museum, it began to establish trusts:

> One of these maintains at Stretham, in the Fens near Ely, a beam engine and its scoop wheel, the last of many such installations that were once the principal means of raising water from the fenlands to the drainage canals. The other trust has accepted from the Inland Waterways Commission a Newcomen-type engine erected in 1821 (after use elsewhere) to pump water into the Coventry Canal at Hawkesbury. The engine has been re-erected in a prominent site in Dartmouth to serve as a permanent memorial to Thomas Newcomen in the place of his birth.[66]

III

It was at the end of the 1960s that these various movements, so heteroclite in their origins, began to converge and that – partly as a result of their intermingling, partly under the impact of new techniques of retrieval and display – the idea of 'living history' started to take shape. At the end of the decade, in line with the rise of conservationist sentiment, it began to move from the peripheries of society, or its eccentric fringes, to the centre of the national stage. The idea of the historical walk was adopted by go-ahead museums, such as the Geffrye, to promote local trails, and it was taken up as a form of activity-learning by the schools. The municipal authorities began to adopt walks in 1975, as a contribution to European Architectural Heritage Year (in the case of Chester, with the aid of costumed guides; in that of the City of London with pictorial interpretative plaques). In 1977, the year of the Silver Jubilee, many new walks were opened – among them the Jubilee Walk on the South Bank, with its London poems engraved in the paving stones. In 1980s London the 'cowboy' operators moved in, as well as hard-up historians, unemployed archaeologists and retired taxi drivers. Today London walks take up nearly a page of the listings magazines. A May 1993 issue of *Time Out* included the following: 'Beatles Magical Mystery Tour', 'George Orwell and Islington', 'Spitalfields before the Change', 'Charlie Chaplin's Lambeth', 'Gallows, Gardens and Goblins', 'The London of Bertie Wooster and Jeeves', 'Jack the Ripper Haunts', 'Death's Dark Angels: Plagues, Pestilence and Panaceas', 'The Southwark Story – Starring Shakespeare, Dickens, Chaucer and John Harvard', 'The Angel, Joe Orton and Camden Passage'.

Old photographs, a delight to the picture editor, the TV documentarist and boutique shopfitters, as well as to the compilers of local albums and nineteenth- and twentieth-century researchers, helped to give history a human face, as well as to whet the public appetite for Victoriana and the visual artefacts of the recent past. They were a discovery of the 1960s so far as the general public and local researchers were concerned – though connoisseurs, and picture-postcard fanatics, had been collecting them for some years, and local libraries turned out to have caches of them in the storerooms. The schools were amongst the earliest to take them up, incorporating them in classroom learning packs and slide shows, while publishers adopted them as cover illustrations or plates in the place of period engravings. Museum curators used period photographs as blow-ups to contextualize objects in real-life settings. By 1969 the taste for period photographs was sufficiently well established for 'Victorian' photography booths to open up at the seaside and in the fairground.

Another 'living history' enthusiasm which caught on in the 1960s was the facsimile reprint of texts. Production was greatly facilitated and cheapened by the reprographic revolution of the decade, the diffusion of photo-litho in particular. By the middle of the decade, after the example of David & Charles, who established a market niche for railway and canal books, and Adams & Dart, who performed something of the same function for nineteenth-century autobiography ('working-class autobiography' as it was usually referred to at the time), this was a standard offering in publishers' lists. A number of houses made a speciality of facsimile reprints, notably Dover Publications of New York, whose paperback reprint of Mayhew's *London Labour and the London Poor* helped to make it a central text of 'new-wave' social history. The facsimile reprint of individual documents, popularized by Jackdaw publications and packs, was a fundamental classroom aid to project work and curriculum innovation in the primary school and the lower forms of the new secondary schools.

'Living history' was also facilitated by the spread of the portable tape-recorder. Like the facsimile reprint it gave a privileged place to the verbatim and encouraged those who used it to make a fetish of authenticity. Variously canvassed as 'living memory' or 'the voice of the past', and collected as an archive for the future as well as a new form of historical record, oral testimony emerged at the end of the decade not only as an alternative form of historical documentation, but also as one which, by its very nature, would give a central place to 'lived experience'. Surfacing in an astonishing variety of different quarters in the years from 1967 to 1971, it was taken up enthusiastically in do-it-yourself publishing projects and local history groups, such as 'The People's Autobiography of Hackney'; while nationally the Oral History Society, founded in 1970–71 by a mixed group of writers, broadcasters and younger historians, attempted to popularize it in the universities and the schools. One of its early conquests was the BBC, which began to trawl in its own sound archives for the 'voice of the past'; which mounted Stephen Peet's *Yesterday's Witness*, a long-running TV series; and which on the model of *The Long March of Everyman* (1971) began to incorporate oral testimony as a kind of radiophonic foil to its documentaries and commentaries.[67]

A more histrionic 1960s addition to the repertoire of 'living history' was the staging of historical pageants and the birth (or rebirth) of the taste for historical re-enactment. It had been anticipated by the railway preservationists of the 1950s, dressing up in company livery, and impersonating, or taking on the part of, the Victorian railway servant. The Sealed Knot, the first of the re-enactment societies, was founded in 1968, and it seems to have been about that time that the taste for dressing up in period costume caught on. In 1971 the Ermine Street Guard, the first of the Roman army groups, was formed, originally an ad hoc group of locals brought together for a village festival and pageant at Whit-combe and Bentham, a Gloucestershire parish which stood on the Roman Way.[68] The annual Levellers Day pilgrimage to Burford, a great rallying point of the Labour Left, got under way in 1974; 'Dickens Week' – a catalyst for the historicization of Rochester-upon-Medway[69] – in 1979.

IV

'Living history', though practised in the name of verisimilitude, has its hidden aesthetics. Its emergence – as a watchword and as a practice – in the 1960s could be seen as an expression or analogue of that decade's cult of immediacy. Here the new museology's insistence on accessibility and its use of audio-visual aids to position the spectator as an eaves-dropper on the past, an eye-witness to everyday transactions and events, has obvious affinities with TV docudramas and 1960s *cinéma-vérité*. Likewise the 'hands-on' interactive displays, breaking down the barriers separating the object and the viewer by taking exhibits out of the prison of the glass case, seem very much of a piece with the more generalized revolt against formality and such characteristic 1960s cultural (or counter-cultural) enthusiasms as 'theatre in the round', with its rejection of the proscenium stage in favour of free-floating space. It anticipated those promenade productions pioneered at the National Theatre by Bill Bryden's adaptation of *Lark Rise to Candleford* and *The World Turned Upside Down*, and brilliantly realized in Tony Harrison's version of the Mystery Plays where the audience, instead of being passive spectators, were invited to fraternize with the actors. Reference might also be made to the parallels with installation art, the 1960s revolt against the tyranny and formality of the salons, which took pictures out of their frames and removed sculpture from its pedestal, creating art objects instead as freestanding exhibits which could be walked around and touched.

Likewise the use of 'voice-over' to interpret and animate museum display both anticipated and then actually drew on the 'living memory' which oral history, when it crystallized, claimed as its special province. The new museology's insistence on 'real-life' working environments and the intimate detail of the domestic interior has its analogue in those 'human' documents of the industrial revolution (or of Edwardian England) which it was the pride of the new-wave social historians of the 1960s to have discovered,[70] and the primacy given (as critics were to complain) to 'lived experience'. In another aspect – the use of black-and-white photography to provide a living setting and backdrop for the objects on display – the new museology was perhaps touched by the visual excitements of the 'new-wave' fashion photographers, with their appetite for grainy realism and blow-ups, and their discovery of an urban picturesque.

The craze for historical re-enactments which seems to have taken off in the late 1960s has a family resemblance to the street theatre and counter-culture 'happenings' of the time, though since the fight societies were recruited, like the Ermine Street Guard, from deepest England, the parallel may seem far-fetched. Less fanciful are the parallels between the 'living history' exhibition as it was developed in the new museology and the synthesizers, amplifiers and flashing lights of the pop concert. Those attempting to bring the excitements of history to the young and uninitiated were only too anxious, in the idiom of the time, to prove themselves 'with-it', and to use up-to-date methods of display. As the passage below – taken from a 1966 number of *The Amateur Historian* – may suggest, they were even ready to adopt that transatlantic neologism of 'the teach-in':

> *Pop History*: Another ninth centenary – that of the Battle of Hastings – is being celebrated with archery, regattas, singing, dancing, a teach-in and other commemorative events. The Government is providing £12,000 of the costs.
>
> Additionally, a 288ft square scale model of the battle is being housed at Hastings, in a specially constructed circular hall at a cost of more than £200,000. At Pevensey, where William is said to have landed, a mock invasion by a fleet of sailing dinghies is taking place.[71]

The success of 'living history' in the schools – where slide-shows and audiovisual displays were seized upon as classroom aids, while such groups as 'Theatre in Education' popularized the idea of historical re-enactment – owed a great deal to the progressive movement in English education. Under the influence of the 'new history' as it developed in the teacher-training colleges and in the new GCSE examination, instituted in 1965, the quality required of the child in the GCSE was first of all 'empathy', seeing things in terms that would have been familiar to the real-life historical actors. History was no longer the biography of great men but rather the record of everyday things. Historical make-believe also caught on in the schools, especially the primary schools where the interests of the new history happily coincided with the age-old love of dressing up, and acting out an adult role. 'Grandmother's Washing Day' was one favourite project which developed under the influence of oral history, with dollymops and peg-boards brought in by the children; another was 'A Day in the Life of a Victorian Schoolchild'. This last was taken up by go-ahead museums, who dressed the children up in sailor-suits and pinnies, set them to work on slates, and demonstrated the rigours of Victorian classroom discipline.

'Living history' was also caught up in 1960s retrochic and indeed at the end of the decade, when 'yesterday's advertisements' began to appear as the latest thing in poster art, and when the replica production of Victoriana took off (Dodo Designs Ltd, founded in 1966, produced an eclectic mixture of revivalist kitsch, ranging from Victorian fob-watches to eighteenth- and nineteenth-century insurance company enamels)[72], the overlap showed every sign of becoming a convergence.[73] The late 1960s craze for 'granny clothes'[74] which put a premium on Victorian lace, must have done a great deal to create that taste for period dress which was not the least of the visual pleasures of the historical re-enactment, and which museums incorporated into their living history displays when making a feature of costumed attendants and guides. And one might speculate on how far living history's preoccupation with the recent past was beholden to the Art Deco revival pioneered by the avant-garde boutique Biba.[75]

Another set of parallels was with the world of interiors. Here museums, in pursuit of 'living history', made some contribution to what became the ruling belief of conservation-minded renovation, restoration and refurbishment work: namely that if 'period' properties are to be true to themselves they need 'period' interiors (and 'period' street furniture) to match. The idea of the 'period' shopping street – the inspiration of today's up-market shopping precincts, as well as a great visitor attraction at the open-air museums and theme parks – was born in the museum world (one original, still very popular today, was 'Kirkgate', the make-believe Edwardian shopping street in the York Castle Museum). It was taken up by the Civic Trust in its town improvement schemes of the 1960s; by the GLC architects in their designs for Covent Garden; and in the 1980s – when Victorian street furniture became ubiquitous – by the conservation officers of the local authorities. The museums may also have played some part in popularizing the idea of the 'period' interior – one model being the period rooms at the Geffrye Museum, Hackney; another those assembled by the Museum of London when it moved into its new and enlarged premises in London Wall. In a related historicist enterprise John Fowler's designs for the restoration of National Trust properties provided the original for that 'country house' look which emerged in the late 1970s and 1980s as a market leader in soft furnishings, competing for public favour with the 'cottagey' look of Laura Ashley and William Morris prints.

Conversely, one could point to the way in which museum directors and curators have drawn on the arts of the interior decorators and designers – 'distressing' in particular – to give a lived-in look to their period rooms and displays. Particularly interesting here is the current fashion for kitting out 'historic' buildings – often no more than an empty shell when they come into the hands of the museum authorities – with all the accoutrements of hearth and home. In the name of 'living history', ruin-interpretation turns by degrees into retrofitting. Whether the space at issue is a 'restored' Tudor kitchen, a 'reconstituted' farmhouse, or a 'recreated' monastic cell, the whole effort is to restore the building to a domestic state, with homely touches as a gauge of period authenticity. When for instance, in 1988, English Heritage opened the Medieval Merchant's House at French Street, Southampton – an 'amazing survival', carefully restored over a period of six years, 'after centuries of modification and neglect' – it was furnished with newly crafted items, 'made in accordance with the methods and materials of the late thirteenth century' (to complete the *trompe l'oeil*, the custodian was equipped with medieval costume).[76] The York Archaeological Trust is currently engaged, as it has been for some years, on a similar endeavour with 'Barley Hall', the name given to a group of medieval buildings in Coffee Yard. Archaeologists have established where the long-lost walls ran and where the central hearth and other fittings stood. Conservation architects have devised a scheme for restoring one of the buildings as a merchant's house. The historical records have provided it with a fifteenth-century tenant. It is being furnished with craftsman-made replicas of the items which appear in a 1478 probate inventory: chests and a dining table are already in place, and there are even newly made and richly coloured wall-hangings dyed in woad and madder – to the untutored eye they would not look out of place in the haberdashery department of Liberty's or the Shaker Shop in Chelsea.[77]

Another and more democratic aesthetic crossover is in relationship to the poetics of the ordinary. Here 'living history' shared in the 1960s taste for the vernacular, as expressed in aestheticized kitchenware, windswept hair and the 'natural' look. Its ethnographic enthusiasm for the recovery and display of the commonplace had its counterpart in 1960s pop art, which treated the spectacle of the everyday as a matter of wonder, and elevated the most ordinary articles of commerce and consumption – famously, Warhol's tin of Campbell's soup – to the status of cultural icons. Its poetic of manual labour was of a piece with the crafts revival and back-to-nature movements of the late 1960s, which were one of the counter-culture's more enduring contributions to British national life.

In other aspects, 'living history', so far from representing a throw-back to the past, might be thought to have prefigured some of the favourite conceits – or genial tropes – of postmodernism. In place of facts it offers us images – 'hyperrealities' – in which the old is faked up to be more palpable than the here-and-now.[78] It involves a quite conscious exercise in make-believe, not so much trading on our credulity as inviting us to connive at the subterfuge and give ourselves up to its pleasures. It eschews epic and grand narrative in favour of personal observation and local knowledge. It invites us to play games with the past and to pretend that we are at home in it, ignoring the limitations of time and space by reincarnating it in the here-and-now. It pins its faith in surface appearances, visible artefacts, 'evidence ... which can be seen, touched and photographed', rather than aggregates and abstractions. For a history of master narratives, or evolutionary theories of growth, it substitutes one of moments which can be intercepted, and arrested – as in the postmodern novel – at any point in time. Instead of being an alp on the brain of the living, the past dissolves into a thousand different views.

So far as the appeal of 'living history' to children is concerned some references should be made to the use of, and taste for, the Gothic. The showcase caverns, such as Wookey Hole, where hi-tech lighting brings stalactites and stalagmites into dramatic relief, aim to thrill.[79] Sensations of a more low-tech kind are in evidence elsewhere. At Epping Forest Museum 'the children's favourite exhibits include a gory mantrap and pictures of medieval punishments for poaching'.[80] The Edinburgh Dungeon Torture Museum 'recaptures the beheading of Mary Queen of Scots, and the howls of witches burned at the stake. Visitors can also watch mock executions.'[81]

'Living history' in the schools also seems to have an eye for the morbid. '"Horrible." That was the verdict of two nine-year-olds from Bermondsey after visiting the Livesey Museum's vivid recreation of a Victorian schoolroom' (among the objects on display were punishment bands informing the world that the wearer was 'A DUNCE' or 'A LIAR'; among the demonstrations, a visiting infants class, 'dressed in Victorian pinafores and sailor suits' was put through the paces of Swedish drill).[82] At Sudbury Hall Children's Museum, top juniors from a nearby school reported, the rigours of the Victorian schoolroom were the subject of horrified fascination; as was the fate of the climbing boys who 'suffered from deformation of the spine, legs and arms, from going up chimneys while their bones were in a soft and growing state'.[83]

'Living history' tells us as much about the present as it does about the past. In the spirit of the age – the here-and-now – it is centrally concerned not with politics or economics, the subjects of yesteryear's grand narratives, nor yet, except tangentially, with religion (typically absent in accounts of the recent past), but essentially with that great preoccupation of the 'Me' generation: lifestyles. It privileges the private over the public sphere. On stage, in Brian Friel's *Translations*, it turns the English conquest of Ireland into a love story gone wrong. At the cinema, in Kenneth Branagh's version of Shakespeare, it makes *Henry V* into a kind of *Hamlet*; a prince, in the manner of the current heir to the throne, wanting to be a private person even when he finds himself thrust into the role of king. At the Imperial War Museum, when it is not diverting us with 'Forces Sweethearts', it invites us to share the personal experience of shell-shock. Family fortunes rather than wars and diplomacy are the subject of its epics; when it seeks to reconstruct grand narrative it is through the medium of the history of the self.

'Living history' is offensive to the professional historian. It shows no respect for the integrity of either the historical record or the historical event. It plays snakes and ladders with the evidence, assembling its artefacts as though they were counters in a board game. It treats the past as though it was an immediately accessible present, a series of exhibits which can be seen and felt and touched. It blurs the distinction between fact and fiction, using laser-beam technology and animatronics to authenticate its inventions and produce a variety of reality-effects.

Yet the practice of 'living history' – or at any rate its ambition – corresponds at many points to quite traditional scholarly ideals. The 'controlled reconstruction of the past' on which (in G.R. Elton's phrase) professional historians pride themselves has evident affinities to the idea of historical reenactment; in either case it involves making flesh-and-blood figures out of fragments. What Michelet called 'resurrectionalism' – bringing the dead to life – was arguably the hinge of the nineteenth-century revolution in historical scholarship and the rise of archive-based research; while a romantic realism, in which talismanic importance is attached to the idea of authenticity, was not the least of the aesthetic components of the so-called 'scientific' history of Leopold von Ranke.

What Simon Schama, a fine practitioner of it, calls 'animated description' could be seen as an equivalent, or near equivalent, of animatronics, using a battery of literary devices to quicken the interest of readers, to dramatize the evidence and to heighten the reality-effects. We use dates as choreographic devices to assemble our cast of characters and move them hither and thither according to authorial (or directorial) whim. Analogy and comparison, one of the analytic historian's most frequent standbys, and quite often the very framework of monograph, positively forces the writer to go time-travelling, hurtling backwards and forwards across the centuries with the zest of a Dr Who. Nor are we averse to practising modern Gothic, inviting our readers to sup with the unfortunates in the condemned cell at Newgate (the subject of two major studies in the last five years); to take down the confessions of the heretics; to listen to the sexual fantasies of the would-be witch.

Attempting to improve on the original, or to make up for memory's silences, 'living history' goes further than mere inference in piecing together fragments. But as a watchword it was a good deal less megalomaniac than the idea of 'scientific' history – one of the ideas which it displaced – or indeed than that of history as a 'discipline'. It was much more attentive to the small details of everyday life than those different versions of 'total history' which were all the rage in the 1950s – the abstracted empiricism of the social scientists, with their geometrically plotted histograms and their social structure; the cliometrics of the economic historians, reducing mighty social changes to the squiggles of a graph; or the *longue durée* of those *Annales* historians who boldly declared that without quantification no serious history was possible. As a mobilizing cry, 'living history' has galvanized a far greater enthusiasm than those 'new' histories which periodically make a small stir in the graduate seminars and then disappear from view. As a pedagogy it emerged in the 1960s as an alternative to those Dryasdust forms of scholarship which in the name of modernization were carrying all before them. It served as a flagship for the emergence of the 'social history' museum – a transnational phenomenon of the 1970s; for a history which enjoyed a recognized, if contested, place in the public sphere; and for a preservation movement which commanded mass support.

Notes

1. Roger J.A. Wilson *Guide to Roman Remains in Britain*, 3rd edn., London 1988; Stephen Johnson, *English Heritage Book of Hadrian's Wall*, London 1989; 'Vindolanda', *Current Archaeology*, vol. 11, no. 8, March 1992, pp. 344–9; Robin and Pat Birley, 'Storm over Vindolanda', *Heritage Interpretation*, 45, Summer 1990, pp. 8–9. See also the locally published, Henry Russell Robinson, *What the Soldiers Wore on Hadrian's Wall*, Newcastle 1976; *The Armour of the Roman Legions*, Newcastle 1980; J.N. Dore and J.P. Gillam, *The Roman Fort at South Shields*, Newcastle 1979.

2. Clive Orton, 'Taking a Ride for the Past or the Past for a Ride', *The London Archaeologist*, vol. 6, no. 13, Winter 1991, pp. 351–2.

3. Barrie Trinder, 'A Philosophy for the Industrial Open-Air Museum' in *Report of the Conference of European Associations of Open-air Museums*, Claus Ahrens, ed., Hargen-Detmold 1985, pp. 94–5.

4. *Cockley Cley Iceni Village and Museums, A Comprehensive Guide*, n.p., n.d.

5. Jorvik Viking Centre, *Guidebook*, York 1992, pp. 22–3. For a detailed account of the Coppergate excavations, Richard Hall, *The Viking Dig*, London 1984; for Jorvik's place in environmental and educational archaeology, there are a number of papers by P.V. Addyman, director of York Archaeological Trust. See also his 'Reconstruction as Interpretation: The Example of the Jorvik Viking Centre, York' in Peter Gathercole and David Lowenthal, eds., *The Politics of the Past*, London 1990, pp. 257–64; also Peter Addyman and Anthony Gaynor, 'The Jorvik Viking Centre, an Experiment in Archaeological Site Interpretation', *International Journal of Museum Management and Curatorship*, vol. 3, no. 1, March 1984, pp. 7–18.

6. The phrase is used in Richard Mabey, *The Common Ground: A Place for Nature in Britain's Future?*, London 1980, p. 218.

7. 'The Butterflies Should have a Ball', *Independent*, 21 August 1993.

8. 'Peace on the Levels as Farmers see the Green Light', *Observer*, 20 June 1993.

9. Simon Barnes, *Flying in the Face of Nature: A Year on Minsmere*, London 1992, pp. 46–51.

10. *Coast and Heath, a Free Newspaper for the Suffolk Coastal District Council*, 1992.

11. Tintern Abbey Brochures and Guide, 1993.

12. *Sunday Times*, 10 July 1988.

13. Notice in the London Underground, 4 September 1993. 'Bridging a Gap in London's History', *Independent*, 3 November 1993, for a description.

14. *East Anglian Daily Times*, 2 July 1993.

15. Ibid., 30 June 1993.

16. 'Restored to Prominence', *Independent*, 26 August 1993.

17. *Amateur Historian*, vol. 1, no. 3, December 1952–January 1953.

18. John Weaver, *Exploring England's Heritage, Cumbria to Northumberland*, London 1992, pp. 108–9. At the Black Country open-air Museum, Dudley, a notice outside the Halahan Mill says 'No original furnaces survived, and the furnace on the right was built by the museum to an old design, with iron panels cast in Oldbury. The furnace was designed to use coal fuel but at present runs on oil'. Notes on a visit, August 1993.

19. Ironbridge was singled out as the cradle of the Industrial Revolution in the 1955 article which coined the term 'industrial archaeology'. Six years on, the site was still in a semi-wilderness state. See the affecting description in Ray Gosling, 'Ironbridge', *About Town*, vol. 3, no. 10, October 1962.

20. Kenneth Hudson, 'Country Museums', *Journal of Industrial Archaeology*, vol. 1, no. 1, May 1964, p. 20 for the 250th anniversary celebrations of 1959.

21. Martin Robertson, *Exploring England's Heritage, Dorset to Gloucester*, London 1992, pp. 108–9; Veryan Heal, *Britain's Maritime Heritage*, London 1988.

22. *Dundee Evening Telegraph*, 1 and 2 July 1993; *Dundee Courier*, 2 and 3 July 1993; *Glasgow Herald*, 30 June 1993.

23. *Aberdeen Evening Express*, 29 June 1993.

24. Kirsty Milne, 'Fighting a Very Civil War', *New Statesman*, 20 August 1993, for an account of the 3,000-strong English Civil War Society, an early 1970s breakaway from the first of the fight societies, the Sealed Knot. In September 1993 the Sealed Knot had the ultimate accolade of figuring in that everyday story of country folk, Radio 4's *The Archers*.

25. 'Pop History', *Amateur Historian*, vol. 7, no. 3, 1966–7.

26. *Out of Town*, August 1986.

27. For the idea of the 'lived-in' country house, Vita Sackville-West, *English Country Houses*, London 1941; Anna Sproule and Michael Pollard, *The Country House Guide*, London 1988; 'Over a Hot Stove', *Out of Town*, August 1986; Min Hogg and Wendy Harrop, *The World of Interiors: a Decoration Book*, London 1988; John Cornforth, *The Inspiration of the Past: Country House Taste in the Twentieth Century*, pp. 91 et seq.

28. Wandsworth Common, 1971.

29. *In Britain*, July 1988.

30. David Uzell, ed. *Heritage Interpretation*, 2 vols., London 1989.

31. *Pennine Yorkshire Country Holidays*, Holmfirth 1992.

32. *Observer*, 21 July 1991.

33. The Festival, held each year from May 1 to May 3, and bringing troupes of morris dancers to Rochester, is a very successful municipal invention of the 1980s, designed to make Rochester a historic town.

34. Adriana Caudrey, 'Through the Time Tunnel', *New Society*, 4 September 1987, for an observer's account.

35. The Dobwalls' Theme Park, *Brochure and Guide*, 1988.

36. Flambard's Theme Park, *Brochure and Guide*, 1988.

37. *Torbay to Lisbon International Sail Training Ships Race, July 1956*, London 1956. For some of the later history, *The Cutty Sark Tall Ships' Races, Official Programme, 1982*.

38. Robin and Pat Birley, 'Storm over Vindolanda', p. 9; Johnson, *Hadrian's Wall*, pp. 131–2.

39. Interview with Peter Addyman, September 1993. Cf. *Legacy from the Past, A Portfolio of Eighty-eight Original Williamsburg Buildings*, Williamsburg 1971.

40. Svante Linquist, 'An Olympic Stadium of Technology: Deutsches Museum and

Sweden's Tekniska Museet' in B. Schroeder-Gudehus, ed., *Industrial Society and its Museums, 1890–1900*, Paris 1992.

41. I am grateful to Sven Lindquist, doyen of Sweden's 'Dig Where You Stand' movement, as of much else, for this information. The boats are very visible indeed in Stockholm – as is of course Skansen, the open air museum which was set up in the very heart of the city.

42. I am grateful to Patrick Fridenson of *Le Mouvement Social* for knowledge of the politics of *son et lumière*; Robert Gittings, *Son et Lumière in St Paul's*, London 1969.

43. *West Lancashire Evening Gazette*, 29 June 1993.

44. R.W. Robson-Smith, 'Light Up the Thames', *International Lighting Review*, vol. 27, no. 2, 1975.

45. Glynne Wickham, *Early English Stages*, vol. 1, London 1959, for late medieval and early modern street theatre.

46. Miri Rubin, *Corpus Christi, The Eucharist in Late Medieval Culture*, Cambridge 1991, for a fine recent study.

47. Daniel Mannix, *The Hell-Fire Club*, London 1970.

48. Mark Girouard, *The Return to Camelot: Chivalry and the English Gentleman*, London 1981, pp. 87–110.

49. Richard D. Altick, *The Shows of London*, Cambridge, Mass. 1978.

50. Margaret McMillan, *Education through Imagination*, London 1928.

51. Molly Harrison, quoted in Kenneth Hudson, *A Social History of Museums*, London 1975, p. 76.

52. For her own account of this work, Molly Harrison, *Museum Adventure: The Story of the Geffrye Museum*, London 1950; *Changing Museums, Their Use and Misuse*, London 1967.

53. International Health Exhibition, 1884, *Official Catalogue*, London 1884; *A Souvenir Containing Six Permanent Photographs of the International Health Exhibition*.

54. The idea of the historic ride, as one can see from old holiday photographs, had a well-established niche in seaside entertainment, whether in the form of miniature railways, carriage-and-pair promenade trots, or donkeys on the sands. Another conceivable imaginative origin would be in the culture of the fairground, where memories of old coaching days served as a scenic backdrop to the carousels, the hurdy-gurdies and gallopers. A more immediate ancestry might be the vintage car rallies of the 1930s, where L.T.C. Rolt, the pioneer of canal restoration and later the ideologue of the railway preservation movement, served his conservationist apprenticeship. For 'vintage cars', Graham Robson, *Motoring in the 30s*, London 1979.

55. For 'messing about in boats' between the wars, E. Arnot Robertson, *Ordinary Families*, Harmondsworth 1947; Daphne du Maurier, *Myself When Young*, London 1977, for a girl learning to sail single-handed.

56. Ian Mackersey, *Tom Rolt and the Cressy Years*, London 1985, for the immediate pre-history; autobiographies of Tom Rolt and Robert Aickman for two rival accounts; Roger W. Squires, *Canals Revived, The Story of the Waterway Restoration Movement*, Bradford-on-Avon 1979 is a useful short history. For the natural history dimension, Peter H. Chaplin, *Waterway Conservation*, London 1989.

57. 'Since the first City of London Festival, the Victorian Society has organized annual Walks in the City of London to arouse interest in the best Victorian–Edwardian buildings that remain and to study new developments'. Victorian Society, cyclostyled paper, 1968. I am grateful to David Lloyd for sending me a file of Victorian Society walks in the years 1975–76. The Victorian Society has a large archive of them from all over the country.

58. This was *Amateur Historian*. It changed its name to *The Local Historian* with vol. 8, 1968 ('The Amateur Historian or Local Historian', vol. 7, pp. 78–83 discusses the reason for the change). For many years the journal was published under the auspices of the National Council for Social Service. The Department of English Local History at Leicester – the only university one in the country – was founded by W.G. Hoskins in 1948.

59. W.G. Hoskins, 'The Leicestershire Farmer in the Sixteenth Century' in *Essays in Leicestershire History*, Liverpool 1950, p. 124.

60. W.G. Hoskins, *Midland England, A Survey of the Country Between the Chilterns and the Trent*, London 1949, pp. v–vi.

61. In 1959 a national conference was organized by the Council for British Archaeology to launch the subject. In 1963 the first regional survey appeared, and in 1964 the *Journal of Industrial Archaeology*. In the same year the Ministry of Works set about its national survey of industrial monuments.

62. Editorial Statement, *The Journal of Industrial Archaeology*, vol. 1. no. 1, May 1964, p. 1. 'Touching the past' has been the very successful sales-pitch of the Archaeological Resource Centre at York (see the advertisement in *Museums and Galleries*, 1992).

63. *Industrial Archaeology*, vol. 1, no. 1, May 1964, pp. 68–9.

64. George Ewart Evans, *The Strength of the Hills, An Autobiography*, London 1983; Gareth Williams, *Writers of Wales: George Ewart Evans*, Cardiff 1991.

65. In 1964 the Ministry of Works began a national survey of the relics of industrial development, in cooperation with the Council for British Archaeology. In the same year 'in order to allow a wider range of material to be covered' it renamed the National Building Record the National Monument Record. On Rex Wailes, Kenneth Hudson, *Industrial Archaeology, An Introduction*, London 1964, pp. 34 et seq. As well as logging windmills, Wailes also published half-a-dozen books on them, starting with *Windmills in England*, London 1948, and *The English Windmill*, London 1954. Perhaps this was the reason why, as Neil Cossons and Kenneth Hudson remarked in their 1971 *Guide*, 'Wind and watermills have undoubtedly been the largest single group of "industrial" structures to enjoy widespread preservation' (*Industrial Archaeologist's Guide*, Newton Abbot 1971, p. 57).

66. Dr Stanley B. Hamilton, 'The Newcomen Society and Industrial Archaeology', *Journal of Industrial Archaeology*, vol. 1, no. 1, May 1964, p. 75.

67. Theo Barker, ed., *The Long March of Everyman*, Harmondsworth 1977, attempted to put some of this material in book form but the real point of the series – sound radio's equivalent of video games – was the use of 'radiophonics'.

68. I am grateful to Nick Fuentes of Cohors Octo and Charles Hayes of the Ermine Street Guard for information about the Roman legions.

69. Rochester in 1972 (see the *Official Guide* published in that year) was 'constantly growing' as a port and as an industrial centre. It was the home of some very well-known names in British engineering – the Metal Box Company, C A V, Aviation Electronics. The town's 'historical turn' began in 1975 when the rather run-down High Street was declared a Conservation Area 'in recognition of the outstanding historical significance of Rochester City'. About that time the town began to call itself Rochester upon Medway. It started the Dickens Festival – now a gigantic assembly which floods the town with visitors – in 1979. Later came the 'revival' of a three-day Rochester Chimney Sweeps Festival, May 1–3; a 'Dickens' Christmas week; a midsummer regatta; a 'Norman' historical walk; four more conservation areas; and a whole cluster of museums and monuments around Chatham dockyard.

70. Royston Pike, *Human Documents of the Industrial Revolution in Britain*, London 1966; *Human Documents of the Victorian Golden Age*, London 1967; *Human Documents of the Age of the Forsytes*, London 1969.

71. *Amateur Historian*, vol. 7, no. 3, 1966, p. 100.

72. Jennifer Harris, Sarah Hyde and Greg Smith, *1966 and All That: Design and the Consumer in Britain, 1962–1969*, London 1986.

73. Anna Sebba, *Laura Ashley, A Life by Design*, London 1990, p. 84.

74. Jonathon Green, *Days in the Life, Voices from the English Underground, 1961–1971*, London 1980, pp. 219–21; Jonathan Aitken, *The Young Meteors*, London 1967, pp. 23–5; Elizabeth Wilson, *Mirror Writing*, London 1982, p. 115.

75. Ibid., pp. 55, 59; Bevis Hillier, *The Style of the Century 1900–1980*, New York 1983, pp. 208–11. '"You could say Biba just about invented art deco" she says with some justification', article on Barbara Hulanicki in *World of Interiors*, August 1992, p. 20.

76. *Stately Homes*, May 1988.

77. *Barley Hall, Medieval Life in the Heart of Medieval York*. I am grateful to Charles Knightley, who is in charge of the restoration, for discussing the difficulties of the project and giving me copies of the inventories on which the reconstruction is based.

78. Umberto Eco, *Travels in Hyperreality*, London 1987; Jean Baudrillard, *Simulations*, London 1983.

79. Richard Fells, *A Visitor's Guide to Underground Britain*, London 1989.

80. Mike Levy, 'Epping Forest Museum' in *Let's Go With the Children to Essex*, Bournemouth 1988.

81. *Observer*, 21 July 1991.

82. 'Educational Drills; Liz Heron visits an exhibition on the History of Education', *Times Educational Supplement*, 11 February 1983; Wendy Cope, 'Straight Backs and Straight Down', *Guardian*, 8 October 1982.

83. Francis Farrer, 'Expedition through Victorian Childhood', *Times Educational Supplement*, 23 September 1977.

PART III

Heritage

Semantics

'Heritage' is a nomadic term, which travels easily, and puts down roots – or bivouacs – in seemingly quite unpromising terrain: the 'Gunnersbury Triangle', for instance, an ecological corridor, or stretch of wasteland which has emerged in recent years as one of London's principal wildlife sanctuaries;[1] or Liverpool 8, that erstwhile twilight zone, now peppered with Beatles memorabilia.[2] It sets up residence in streets broad and narrow, royal palaces and railway sidings, canalside walks and town hall squares. It stages its spectacles in a promiscuous variety of venues, turning maltings into concert-halls, warehouses into studio flats. It attaches itself to an astonishing variety of material artefacts – not only Adam Brothers ceilings but also, under the influence of the Art Deco revival, 'Marcel' wave machines and naked lady lampstands. Medieval castles automatically qualify for its protective mantle, as do Roman forts and Martello towers, and so, more recently (under the Military Remains Act of 1986), do Second World War gun emplacements and pill-boxes.[3]

Lexically, 'heritage' is a term capacious enough to accommodate wildly discrepant meanings. In one narrative, very much in evidence in the political rhetoric of yesteryear, it was a matter of God, King and the Law, the altar and throne. In another – the 'Whig' interpretation of history – it referred to freedom broadening out from precedent to precedent, and the development of representative government. In folk-life studies, as defined by Iorwerth Peate, the founder of the Welsh Folk Museum at St Fagans, language, the principal element in conveying tradition from generation to generation, was as important as material culture, 'a social heritage'[4] to be studied both as etymology and 'living speech'. 'Living memory' was one of the standbys of the 'new wave' social history of the 1960s, as also of that army of 'do-it-yourself' genealogists who went in search of family 'roots'. The antiquaries of the eighteenth century, by contrast, were fascinated by the moribund. Bishop Percy, in his *Reliques of Ancient English Poetry* (1765) prided himself on resuscitating a rude and barbarous tongue; William Stukeley, the pioneer archaeologist, was obsessed by Druidical and Celtic remains.[5]

In *Heritage*, Vita Sackville-West's rather sinister novel of 1919, pedigree is a measure of eugenic fitness, with 'that great uneasy heave of the uneducated' as the looming menace on the horizon and the racially pure country folk – 'strong, deep-rooted' – as the enduring strength of the land.[6]

In folk-song circles, where the term 'heritage' surfaces during the Revival of the 1950s,[7] it seems to have been taken up as an alternative to what Cecil Sharp and his followers had been wont to refer to as 'tradition'.[8] Those who took it up were *modernizers*, claiming to be the discoverers of the industrial ballad and the voice of the city, songs which echoed the throb of shuttle and cage. They adopted crowded smoky pubs for their performance venues instead of draughty church halls, and substituted a man on the washboard or the guitar for the lady at the piano. In place of the more decorous innuendoes of 'Oh, No John, No John, No John, No' they took up bawdy. At Oxford, where the 'Heritage Club', founded in 1956,[9] was one of the nurseries of the Revival, and a launching pad for some of its best-known singers, the notion of tradition was – by Cecil Sharp standards – eclectic, embracing jazz harmonica, American work-songs and what were then called 'negro' Blues, as well as such more indigenous offerings as the Headington Quarry wassailing song and Cheshire souling.

The Oxford Heritage Club, in the manner of the London 'Ballads and Blues' concerts, was cosmopolitan in its musical tastes. In its early days there were Indian members who sang and played sitars. There were lectures on Balinese and Cretan folk music. A.L. Lloyd – the singer-scholar whose discovery of the nineteenth-century coalfield ballads gave a historical dimension to 'industrial' song – spoke on Roumanian gypsy music, of which, following in the footsteps of Béla Bartók, he had been a first-hand collector. Paul Oliver was a frequent visitor, 'talking about various aspects of Blues and African music' (the international out-reach did not inhibit the group from making ethno-musicological trips to Oxfordshire and Cotswold villages to collect traditional English songs).[10]

One of the more improbable musics launched under the flag of 'Heritage' – and an important one because it was a progenitor of British pop – was Skiffle,[11] a 'do-it-yourself' combination of jazz, folk and work-songs, to the accompaniment of washboard and guitar. The 'heritage of democratic song' which was its original core was for the most part taken from American Union songs of the 1920s, with a leaven of country-and-western music from Woody Guthrie and the negro blues of Muddy Waters and 'blind' Sonny Terry. Within the space of two years, from the launching of Skiffle at a 'Ballads and Blues' concert in 1954, some 200 or more groups were playing at espresso bars and pubs up and down the country, and the 'two i's' in Old Compton Street, where Tommy Steele and later the Rolling Stones first found their feet, was beginning its pop career.

Another unexpected use of the term 'heritage', of some interest because of its influence on the second folk-song revival, as also on the formation of a British School of Marxist Historians, was that of the Communist Party.[12] Adopted in the epoch of the Popular Front, and taken up later in the period of the Cold War, it attempted to present Communism as English – a vernacular, indigenous force, the natural heir to centuries of radical struggle. John Milton and Oliver Cromwell, the epic heroes of nineteenth-century radical nonconformity, figure largely in those 'March of History' pageants which the Communist Party staged in the summer of 1936 at the time of the outbreak of the Spanish Civil War, while among the 'outstanding milestones in English history' depicted on the banners was the supposed thirteenth-century foundation of Parliament by Simon de Montfort. The concluding appeal for the London march (from Tower Hill to Hyde Park on 20 September 1936) is representative.[13]

Over England are gathering the black shapes of reaction, of would-be dictatorships, of that concentration of every thought and thing most alien to English life – Fascism! Fascism is the scientific organisation of tyranny with modern methods. It installs again the Inquisition, which English people hundreds of years ago chased out of the country. It idealises and enthrones violence, brutality, terror. The Divine Right of Kings, the use of torture, government by secret police, the Star Chamber, conscription, the press gang, all this foulness which our fathers drove from English life is to be brought back again if Fascism has its way. Freedom of thought, freedom of religion, freedom of women, Fascism plans to abolish all these, along with the freedom to organise trade unions and political parties. We, the Communists of to-day, remind you of the heritage of England's long struggle for freedom in order that you shall join with us in preventing that freedom being trampled under Fascist jackboots, and that out of to-day's Democracy shall come tomorrow's Commonwealth in which man shall no longer exploit his fellow. We Communists march with the very essence and spirit of the English tradition, we are out to carry forward English history to new achievements. We call on YOU, Londoner of 1936, to join us in the march to a Free and Merry England. By our struggle to maintain Civil Liberties, to revive the old fire and spirit of the Socialist pioneers, to give aid to the working people of the colonies, to resist the oppression of landlords, employers, large and petty dictatorial police bans and encroachments on public liberties, we carry on the fight of our forefathers ... By our great agitation in aid of the Spanish people in their fight for life and liberty we carry forward the English democratic tradition, which always rallied to those who fought for liberty, whether Garibaldi in Italy, or Abraham Lincoln in America. Fascism and reaction seek to bar the people's way. Fascism must not pass. With your help THEY SHALL NOT PASS. England shall go onward and forward, not downward and backward.

It was in the Second World War – 'the People's War' as it was proclaimed in 1940, at the time when enemy invasion seemed imminent – that a radical–patriotic version of the idea of 'heritage' seemed to enter into its own. Even the National Trust was affected by it, making a propaganda film of its activities, in the run-up to the centenary, under the title *The People's Land* and calling on the services of the mystic-radical, Ralph Vaughan Williams,[14] to compose the music for it. It informed, indeed inspired, the wartime films of Humphrey Jennings, as for example in *Words for Battle*, where RAF pilots are pictured assembling round a Spitfire while, in a voice-over, Milton's *Areopagitica* describes a 'mighty and puissant nation' shaking her locks, or where a plaque commemorating Blake's Soho birthplace is juxtaposed against the retreating footsteps of evacuee schoolchildren.[15] The neo-romantic, Communist-leaning *Our Time* – an influential war-time meeting place of writers, artists and educators – ran a regular 'Heritage' feature, using a suitably Gothic font for the heading and culling passages from Chaucer, Shakespeare and Wordsworth as well as such more obvious sources (from a radical point of view) as the Hymns of the Parliamentary Army. 'Heritage' was also called up by the Army Bureau of Current Affairs – the major adult education effort of the time – which took its leading texts, and notion of a citizen-army, from the Putney Debates of 1647.[16]

Metaphorically, 'heritage' has been subject to a vast inflation, being extended to environments and artefacts which in the past would have been regarded as falling beneath the dignity of history, either because they were too recent to excite scholarly attention, or because they were too trivial or common. When, for instance, Prime Minister John Major champions the 'invincible green suburbs', bracketing them with the 'warm beer' and afternoon cricket of an England that will never change, he is turning his back on some ninety years or more of obloquy.[17] Flying in the face of literary and social disdain (on the West End stage, the mere mention of a place liked Sidcup will bring the house down) he seems to be deliberately courting the unfashionable. But it may be that, as in the case of Mrs Thatcher and her 1983 adoption of Victorian values,[18] he has caught public taste on the turn. His dictum is of a piece with the popularity of 'Moderne' tableware in the flea markets; with the current revival of Richmal Crompton's *William* books; and not least, it may be, with the current craze for greening the city. In any event it cannot be an accident that it comes within a year of John Carey's *The Intellectuals and the Masses*, a brilliant essay in literary populism, which takes the battle for the suburbs into the enemy country, and pins the convict's badge on its Edwardian critics.[19] Perhaps too the Prime Minister, or his ghost writer, Gordon Reece, was drawing on memories of *Metroland*, either in its 1984 TV version (still available on video from the BBC) or in Betjeman's original poems.

'Bygones' and 'memorabilia', long relegated to Cinderella status in museum display,[20] and treated as mere appendages in archaeological study,[21] have emerged in recent years as market leaders in the auction room, bringing a whole new class of collectables into being. Bygones also enjoy pride of place in the new 'Heritage Centres' and local history museums. Thus for instance the Clare visitor centre, Suffolk, has 'memorabilia of the age of steam in Clare'. Dewsbury Museum, devoting its main galleries to the theme of childhood, has a 1940s school classroom, 'available for use by school parties'. East Carlton Heritage Centre, Market Harborough, features the history of Corby New Town. Fleur de Lis Heritage Centre, Faversham, Kent recreates an Edwardian barber's shop and a village telephone exchange of the 1950s. The Cater Museum, Billericay, is 'principally an exhibition of local bygones, and includes a large collection of late nineteenth and early twentieth-century photographs of the district. Two rooms are furnished as a mid-Victorian sitting room and bedroom. A special feature of the museum is its large collection of model fire-engines, from very early examples to the 1950s.'[22]

In the language of nature conservancy, 'heritage' is represented by unspoiled countryside and wildlife reserves. Sustaining and managing bog habitats – 'some of the very last remnants of truly primeval landscape in this country'[23] – is a problem currently exercising Scottish Natural Heritage; another is the protection of bottlenose dolphins and harbour porpoises in the Moray Firth.[24] Under the influence of the National Trust visiting schemes 'garden heritage' has come more to the fore, as it has apparently in other countries;[25] while on what Operation Neptune calls the 'Heritage Coast' – the 700 miles of shoreline now in the custody of the National Trust – it is represented by the absence of seaside tat. For the lovers of literary landscapes it is the artistic associations of place which make it sacred. Among them would be the sixty-odd literary and artistic celebrities who have recently gone on record to protest at the 'assault on literary and artistic heritage' and 'despoliation of a landscape with uniquely important literary associations' represented by the wind turbines in the vicinity of the Brontë parsonage at Haworth.[26]

In the countryside, as in the town, there has been an enormous inflation of the notion of heritage. The environment at risk, which nature conservationists and Friends of the Earth campaign for as the 'heritage' to be preserved, now extends to the entire land surface of the country, not only 'areas of outstanding natural beauty', the object of the National Parks legislation of 1949, as of the campaigns for access to countryside which preceded it, but also wetland sanctuaries for waders, herb-rich wastelands threatened by pesticides, the hedges and ditches grubbed up in favour of prairie-like farming, and such endangered species as barn owls and tunnel bats. And it is indeed on wildlife habitat rather than mountain peaks or wild headlands that today's scenic gaze is fixed.

Government has played a part in these extensions, though following in the wake of public agitation and voluntary action rather than, as in France, taking the lead.[27] Both legislative and executive instruments have served to enlarge the sphere of conservation. Thus archaeological remains, under the Act of 1979, now enjoy the protection of the Department of the Environment and are given the imprimatur and relative security, previously reserved for wildlife sanctuaries, of being government-designated Environmentally Sensitive Areas. English Heritage, the quango established in 1984 to take charge of historic buildings and monuments, has some 500,000 properties for which it is in some final sense responsible, among them not only whole villages but even, in the lead-mining district of Derbyshire, Wirksworth, an entire town. The Department of National Heritage, established on the morrow of the Conservative election victory in 1991, is even more wide-ranging in its brief, and indeed in its enthusiasm for entering into the fine detail of the built environment it is coming to have an uncanny resemblance to the machineries of post-war planning.

Patrimoine, heritage's French cousin, is even more ecumenical in its ambitions and catholic in its tastes.[28] It brings under the umbrella of legislative protection, and state or regional intervention, not only historic buildings and historic monuments, but also a great range of material and cultural artefacts – family albums, for example, which have inspired a rich literature of historical and critical commentary.[29] Ever since the establishment of the Musée des Arts et Traditions Populaires – a notable legacy of the Popular Front – it has attempted to take under its wing such intangibles as folk medicine, regional dialects and local song. 'Ethnology' was institutionalized in 1978, when the Ministry of Culture appointed a special Commission to oversee it.

The notion of *patrimoine* has been progressively broadened in the last thirty years, and as in the British case, this has involved modernizing and updating the idea of what constitutes the historical, as well as extending its social base. André Malraux, as Minister of Culture, inaugurating, in 1962, an ambitious programme of *patrimoine* in which the 'Museum without Walls' would make the past accessible, returned to the levelling spirit of his salad days, arguing that the *al fresco* bookstalls on the banks of the Seine were as 'historic' a part of the built environment as Chartres or Notre Dame. Rural buildings, such as village wash-houses, were brought within the category of historic monuments in the course of 1980 Heritage Year, while more recent extensions have made a feature of rescuing historic brasseries. The Musée d'Orsay, opened in 1987, is a pantheon to industrial art, above all that of the *belle époque*. The 'mission' charged with the preservation of photographic *patrimoine* holds international exhibitions and colloques on such artists as Willy Ronis and Eugène Atget, whose work takes one from the 1920s to the early years of post-war Paris, while under the modernizing influence of Jack Lang, Minister of Culture in the 1980s Socialist administrations, it set about an ambitious programme of preserving and restoring old film footage (the brilliant new prints of *L'Atalante* and *Les Enfants du Paradis* are among its fruits).[30]

Aesthetically, as well as historically, heritage is a hybrid, reflecting, or taking part in, style wars, and registering changes in public taste. The poetics of labour, which dignifies the 'living history' exhibitions at the open-air museums, and which, through the medium of Victorian work photographs, is a great favourite for book jacket illustrations, owes something to the Arts and Crafts Movement of the 1880s, with its fervent belief in artisan skills, and rather more perhaps in its celebration of the male body, and feats of muscular strength, to the 'poetic realism' of the 1930s documentary film-makers – Robert Flaherty and John Grierson. Indeed, to follow the period photographs currently in print – almost all drawn from scenes of outdoor labour – one would imagine that the Victorian workplace was inhabited not by tubercular tailors and shoemakers, or care-worn mill-hands, panting to keep up with the shuttle or the mule, but a race of giants.

In any given period, conservation, and with it ideas of 'heritage', will reflect the ruling aesthetics of the day. One might instance the new visibility of shops and markets in representations of the national past, and a romanticizing of trade which serves as some kind of historical counterpoint to contemporary consumerism. The current enthusiasm for climbers and shrubs, for instance, is very much of a piece with the rehabilitation of Victoriana. It had no place in the functional landscaping of the 1950s and 1960s. In the 1930s and 1940s, climbers and shrubs, ivy in particular, were hated as the enemies of space and light;[31] for those in revolt against the 'dim religious light' of the Victorian Church, they were a by-word for darkness and claustrophobia. The 'Georgian' enthusiasm of the 1930s – a minority taste epitomized by the foundation, in 1937, of the Georgian Group, and the campaign to save

Bath – went hand-in-hand with a belief in order and simplicity and a very strong taste for the uncluttered, or what was sometimes described as architectural good manners and restraint.

These cross-currents, laced by 1930s cultural nationalism, and perhaps a residual anti-Catholicism, may be seen in the following passage which appears in the Council for the Preservation of Rural England's *Monthly Report* for October 1933. Like Virginia Woolf in *Orlando* (or Queen Mary in the grounds of Windsor Castle) it treats ivy as the enemy of sweetness and light. Like Bloomsbury too, and 1930s progressivism, it is decidedly pro-Georgian; at the same time, taking its cue from the suburban lawn or privet hedge, it extols the virtues of the orderly. The text itself was originally issued, 'with the approval of the Archbishop', by the *Canterbury Diocesan Gazette*:

THE CARE OF CHURCHYARDS

The growth of trees or shrubs near the church should be checked, as they cause a green deposit on the walls of the fabric and the choking of gutters with dead leaves. Nothing destroys ancient tombs and headstones more than ivy, which should be ruthlessly destroyed. Grave mounds add much to the time and trouble involved in the regular cutting and trimming of the grass. Where possible they should be levelled, but in every case due care must of course be taken of the feelings and wishes of the relatives. A beginning may perhaps be made with graves no longer tended.... Lych gates and remains of old churchyard walls should be carefully preserved. New walls, fencing, and gates should be simple in design, solid rather than ornamental. The size of crosses and headstones needs special consideration. Large and incongruous monuments tend seriously to mar the beauty of a churchyard; therefore no order should be given for any form of monument for a churchyard until drawings showing its size and particulars of the text and character of the lettering have been submitted to, and approved in writing by, the incumbent. (Three feet six inches is a fair height for a headstone, and 4 feet for a cross.) Stress should be laid on the importance of making use of native stone or wood and British workmanship. Italian white marble for headstones and crosses is both distracting to the eye and destructive of the harmony and quiet dignity which should be the dominant features of a churchyard. Artificial flowers under glass covers, and also white marble chippings and shingle, are to be deprecated, and must not be introduced without permission....

More encouragement might be given to the study of the style and character of the eighteenth-century gravestones to be found throughout the country. Many of them are beautiful works of art. They afford scope for very refined treatment in low relief sculpture, in which, if desired, the cross could be introduced. This is preferable to the frequently ill-proportioned single cross now so common.

There was no such sympathy for the Georgian, ('that *ne plus ultra* of wretchedness'[32]) or for the eighteenth century among the church restorationists of the 1840s, and indeed it was the view of the Cambridge ecclesiologists, their public architectural voice, that 'from the beginning of the reign of George I to the year 1820, not one satisfactory church was built.' Classical, or neo-classical architecture, was, to the Gothic revivalist, 'pagan', and at the very best 'drawing room' or 'meeting house' and un-churchlike. 'Such a building may have been well-enough adapted for the exhibitions of gladiators or of wild beasts in ancient Rome, but it is totally unfit for a Christian church', wrote *The Ecclesiologist* of one of them, a 1797 church in Banbury, North Oxon.[33]

The dream of a return to the 'Christian architecture' of the high Middle Ages, a leitmotiv of the 1840s Gothicists, extended also to churchyard layouts. Here the ecclesiologists took up arms against the eighteenth-century practice of introducing graves with individual inscriptions, and upright monuments or obelisks. An article in *The Ecclesiologist* of January 1845, regretting that 'though so many ancient monuments remain inside our churches', churchyards had been stripped of them, conjured up the memory of old-time foliage.

> How do we suppose the church-yards, which we see thus disfigured, were laid out in the ancient days? Why, we all know that there was a great stone Cross high amongst the graves, a venerable weather-beaten yew-tree, a wooden lich-gate over the entrance, and, it may be, a spring rising within the precinct or a brook running through it. Probably too, beautiful foliage grew thick around, making the abode of the departed peaceful and secluded as it ought always to be.[34]

There is nothing neat and tidy about the churchyard in *The Old Curiosity Shop* (1841) where Little Nell and her grandfather find a point of rest – arguably as influential a scene for the formation of Victorian sepulchral taste as the Cratchits' dinner was for the Victorian Christmas.[35] The ground is overgrown with rank grass and sodden with autumn leaves so thick that Little Nell's footsteps are noiseless. The gravestones are 'venerable' and the church itself, carved out of a monastic ruin, impossibly old, 'a very aged, ghostly place', 'grey even in the midst of the hoary landscape'. The sexton is a Methuselah figure whose greatest pleasure seems to be raising a forest of shrubs and trees. He looks forward to the day when the canopy of foliage will be so dense that the sky will no longer be seen. Dickens is quite untroubled by the fact that the tombs in the church vaults are made of marble, rather than honest English oak, and far from regretting the ivy – like the long grass, it has had a free run of the churchyard – he has the villagers collect it, along with the holly and the winter berries, to make up Little Nell's funeral bower. Dickens makes no reference to that spirit of improvement which in other spheres – such as the Sanitarian movement of the 1840s

– he was very ready to champion. The churchyard, requiring the bleak midwinter to work its magic spells, is a place that needs to stay in a wilderness state.

The association of heritage and the arts – institutionalized and formalized in the amalgamation of the two government ministries devoted to them – is quite recent. With the interesting exception of Snape Maltings, the converted brewery and warehouse complex which became home to the Aldeburgh Festival, there were no 'historic' performance venues in the 1960s, nor any megalomaniac plans – such as those about to be realized at the Shakespearian 'Globe' on Bankside – to resuscitate them from the dead. The new theatres of the 1960s such as The Belgrade, Coventry, and The Crucible, Sheffield made a point of being ultra-modern. 'Theatre in the round' – an avant-garde excitement of the time – made no reference to possible originals in Greek or Roman amphitheatres, nor yet to early English processional stages, but were hailed as new and informal performance spaces. The Chichester Festival Theatre, with its Scandinavian pine interior, positively flaunted its modernity. The National Theatre, with its push-button revolving stage, its sets which came out of the flies or up from the floor, was one of the mechanical wonders of the age, making the Drury Lane theatres, with their laborious cranks and pulleys, seem prehistoric. The building itself, with its raw, untreated concrete, made no faint gesture to tradition. Decor was minimalist, dispensing with gilt and crimson, along with the proscenium stage. There was no museum of relics or interpretative plaques commemorating the vanished glories of Bankside; no historicist nomenclature offering a continuity with, or throwback to, Elizabethan or Jacobean companies of players. Not Elizabethan madrigals but jazz saxophone was the favoured music in the foyer, while modern-dress productions of Shakespeare had pride of place in the repertoire.

The association of 'heritage' with corporate image-building – epitomized by the Nelson memorabilia on display at the new Lloyd's headquarters, an otherwise ultra-modern edifice, as also perhaps by the Florence Nightingale exhibition which greets visitors to St Thomas's Hospital – is a recent development, though one which has spread like wildfire. Amongst City of London insurance brokers it is now apparently standard practice to grace the entrance lobby or foyer with a mini-museum rather as, in the old days, barbers would sport a pole, and tobacconists install a wooden highlander as a mascot outside their shops.[36]

Coutts, family bankers to the English aristocracy – some of their customers, they claim, go back 250 years – offer one of the most striking examples of these new mini-museums. It was established in 1977 when the bank moved into brand-new, purpose-built premises in the Strand, a kind of token of antiquity to set off the modernity of the atrium. As visitors can see, there are some twenty display-cases – and a Voysey tapestry – in the banking hall, and a further exhibition of portraits and silver in the fourth-floor Director's Suite. As well as displaying the firm's treasures – e.g. a letter from Lord Byron asking for an extension of credit – they have also used the resources of the new museology. Photographic blow-ups provide an eye-catching backdrop to the exhibits. There is a life-size model of a 1692 goldsmith's shop, with Madame Tussaud-like mannequins of an appren-tice, John Campbell, the founder of the firm, and the Duke of Argyll, 'our first and most important customer'. Another piece of simulated reality is a nineteenth-century clerk, seated at a partner's desk. Upstairs there is a life-size model of Countess Burdett-Coutts, based on a photograph of her in the Coutts's family house in Piccadilly.[37]

At the other end of the social scale, in one of the fastnesses of working-class England, there has been the remarkable rise in football club museums, the number of which seems likely to increase by leaps and bounds in the wake of current stand redevelopment. Glasgow Rangers have what an enthusiastic visitor describes as a 'fabulous, wonderful museum' – 'very old-fashioned, all wooden panelling and wooden frames, almost a musty smell'. Liverpool FC's museum has a range of players' memorabilia, Billy Liddell's old football, a section on Bill Shankly, Liverpool's manager in the 1960s, and a vast array of medals and presents. A supporter's rattle from the 1960s is one of the few trophies of the humours of the game, but in the new 'living history' museum, or 'visitor centre', planned to open in 1995 after the rebuilding of the Kop, the museum 'experience' will include a visit to the players' dressing room, and a walk down the players' tunnel, to the accompani-ment, it may be, of the recorded roar of the crowd. Arsenal's museum, which opened to the public last autumn, has Alf Kirchen's full match kit, the football presented to the Club when it won the cup in 1936, the shirt which allegedly belonged to Alex James (an Arsenal supporter paid £1,500 for it at last year's Christie's sale of football memorabilia); cigarette cases and medals from the Club's Plumstead days; and an old pair of 1950s player's boots.[38]

The 'heritage' of Routledge's long-running 'critical heritage' series drew its inspiration from Arnoldian notions of 'tradition'. Brian Southam, who adopted the series and gave a name to it, as well as editing the first volume (a selection of critical writings on Jane Austen), was a recent ex-don, well versed in literary theory (T.S. Eliot's *Tradition and the Individual Talent* was one possible influence, F.R. Leavis another). John Naylor, who dreamed the series up, was a Batsford editor, working at a publishing house whose 'bread-and-butter' had been 'heritage' for some forty years.[39]

The version of 'heritage' developed by Batsford in the 1930s was topographical in character, referring sometimes to the parish church, sometimes to old inns ('one of the most attractive features of English life') and often, as in Gertrude Jekyll's *Old English Household Life*, to the beauties of the vernacular. As the publishers of the Quennells's *History of Everyday Things*, the firm had also pioneered the teaching of an Arts and Crafts version of tradition in the schools. In another idiom – that of colour-coding – it challenged the stridency of red-white-and-blue, the primary colours of military and imperial heraldry, with the gentle pastels of Brian Cook's Fauvist book-jackets.[40]

Graham Wallas, the post-Fabian political scientist, who devoted a book to the subject in the aftermath of the First World War (*Our Social Heritage*, 1921) used the term in an altogether more abstract and capacious sense, marrying liberal and reformist notions of the public good with more Darwinian ones of heredity and environment. 'Heritage' was on the one hand the social instincts and behavioural norms, as embodied in, say the habit of co-operation or the acceptance of customary obligation and right. It was at the same time, more cerebrally, the influence of the arts and sciences, or cultural heritage. In the field of government it included both the rights of representation and the duty of social control; in that of the professions, it included trade unionism as well as medicine, the army and the law.[41]

For Canon Rawnsley, a co-founder of the National Trust, and one of its most prolific propagandists, 'heritage' was a matter of nature rather than culture. A passionate Wordsworthian, with a living in the Lake District, which he refused to leave for a bishopric, he loved the wild solitudes, and *The National Heritage* (1919), the book he compiled to celebrate the first twenty-five years of the National Trust's activity, faithfully reflects this. He begins the travelogue with a chapter on Dinas Oleu (the fortress of light) – the dramatic white rocks overlooking the Barmouth estuary which had been the Trust's first acquisition. He ends the book – amidst 'magnificent bursts of rain' – with the 'Arthurian' headland at Baras, Tintagel, on the wild North Cornish coast. Here he listens to the sharp, shrill cry of the clough, and watches the falcon swoop on its prey, while peering down from his rocky eminence he sees the black cormorants and the white gulls skimming the heavy seas. Rawnsley gives two whole chapters to National Trust properties on Exmoor, making a bee-line for the gorges and caverns, the sparsely-wooded heaths and plateaux. The only stately home he notices is one that has been 'gutted and destroyed inside'. Nor does he seem much interested in gardens and flowers, the great enthusiasm in National Trust visiting today: wildness is all.[42]

A Countryman's England (1935), one of the books contributed by

Dorothy Hartley to Batsford's 'British Heritage Library', was equally remote from more recent versions of pastoral. There are no ivied churches or village greens, nor yet, in the manner of, say, the 'Shell' guide books, scenic beauties. 'Life and work in the countryside' is her unifying theme. The photographs are there not to establish a poetics of labour – as in British documentary film – nor (as in picture postcards) to illustrate sweeping views, but rather to document everyday tasks; the line drawings – taken from the author's notebooks – bring tools into the heart of the text: 'mountain sledge for milk churns', 'old style shepherd's hoggin', 'bee-skeps'. Crops define countryside heritage. Kent and Hampshire are 'garden and orchard country', where, to follow the photographs, labourers walk on stilts. In East Anglia a row of crouching women are photographed 'hand-hoeing sugar-beet'. A word-picture of the wire-enclosed poultry farm vividly prefigures the battery-fed hens of today.

> There are most ingenious mechanical gadgets for feeding, sorting and gritting with automatic seed hoppers. There are weighing machines and dust-baths, and the number of eggs are ancestrally accounted for by trap nesting. In fact a fowl ceases to have any private life and becomes a paying proposition.[43]

In the 1930s version of heritage, landscape, though threatened with 'bungaloid' development, and disfigured, as preservationists believed, by such modern excrescences as advertising hoardings and electric pylons, was still thought of as a wild solitude. Past and present, even to the lover of antiquities, or the connoisseur of the natural and the unspoiled, were a seamless web. Thus Hilda Coley, in *Heritage of Wild Flowers* (1935), began her book by celebrating the longevity and tenacity of her subject: 'Just as we are descended from the people who lived here in the past, so the wild flowers we see to-day are descendants of those that lived here hundreds of years ago ... some ... are exactly the same as they were ... others have altered their shape a little.' She was comparatively untroubled by the prospect of urban growth:

> A hundred, or even fifty years ago, there were many more wild flowers in Great Britain than there are now. So much land upon which they grew has been built on, for there are many more factories, shops and houses than there used to be. Little, narrow, shady lanes, where rare and lovely wild flowers grew, have had their hedges cut down and the grass at each side taken away in order to turn them into proper roads. Only very strong plants can grow if they have very little shade and very little soil, and so we have not so many of the rare and delicate plants. It is no good growling about it, for that will not bring the old days and ways back again. Most of us like going out into the country for motor rides and we can all help to keep the country-side beautiful by picking

flowers very carefully and not tearing them up by the roots. Also we can gather the ripe seed of different wild plants and drop this into bare patches in the hedgerows. Then there will be more beauty for other people and ourselves to look at the next year.[44]

In 1940, Britain's 'finest hour', when the country stood alone against the forces of tyranny and darkness, when its very existence was suddenly in question, the notion of 'heritage' was freely extended to what a series of propaganda booklets called 'the spirit and framework of British institutions' and what in the handbooks and lectures of the Army Bureau for Current Affairs became 'the British Way'.[45] The British were a freedom-loving people with an 'innate dislike' of compulsion and a predilection to voluntary effort.[46] British liberties had been established by struggle as 'our national heritage'. Westminster, 'the mother of parliaments', was the cradle in which the idea of democracy had been born. *Habeas Corpus* gave every subject the right to fair trial. The jury system was the envy of the world, while in Britain itself, the rule of law was sustained by an unquestioning public commitment to fair play.[47] London, the nation's capital, 'Never ... so beautiful' as it was under attack from the fire bombers,[48] had a very special esteem, as the principal target of the enemy attack. Cockney heroism and good humour – the stoical indifference to 'Jerry' of Mrs Mopp, the working-class char, the 'business as usual' of the cabbies, the clippies and bobbies – were symbols of national courage, the miraculous survival of St Paul's a talisman of the nation's will.

To follow the films of the period, or Priestley's *Postscripts* (1940) – the broadcasts he made at the height of the invasion fear – or to take up Orwell's 1940s essays, is to see a country in love with itself.[49] A vast amount of attention was lavished on the beauties of national character: the alleged tolerance of the English; their kindness to others; their extreme modesty; their love of sportsmanship. In one favourite conceit, the country was inhabited by a race of amiable eccentrics, lineal descendants of those 'mad dogs and Englishmen' who, in Noël Coward's doggerel, rushed out in the midday sun. In another the country was in essence a family, squabbling over inessentials, but pulling together when there was trouble. Straightforwardness, simplicity, loyalty, truthfulness, reliability, conscientiousness were all, it seemed, quintessentially *English* virtues. So were idealism (though the English were shy of admitting it) and commitment to high principle (though they did not make a song and dance about it). Practical and down-to-earth, the English were nevertheless romantically attached to tradition, to the 'unchanging beauty' of the English countryside, to the 'cottages small' 'beside a field of grain'. Crack shots when it came to confronting the enemy, disciplined when need be, but for the rest a nation of individualists, they preferred to muddle through.

These images, by contrast with those conjured up in the First World War, were typically anti-heroic. The English were a domestic people rather than a master race, home-lovers rather than conquerors. Their patriotism was quiet; like Leslie Howard in his mystic–national roles, they found fighting, even when necessary, abhorrent. A sense of humour – the ability to laugh at themselves – was, it seems, the secret weapon of the English, a code which in *Pimpernel Smith* all the raving of the Nazis failed to crack. Gardening, according to a conceit which seems to have caught on in wartime Britain (possibly under the influence of the 'Dig for Victory' campaign), was a distinctively national virtue. It had established itself between the wars as the most widespread English leisure pursuit, aided on the one hand by the suburban explosion of the towns, and on the other by the decline of domestic service. Orwell characterizes the English as a race of flower-growers in *The Lion and the Unicorn* (1941) and makes gardening an example of its privateness of national life. Noël Coward – hardly, one would imagine, a grower of prize leeks – used a similar fancy in his patriotic broadcasts, and he returned to it in the screenplay of *This Happy Breed*, his fable of family life in Britain between the wars. For Frank Gibbons, the Clapham householder of his narrative, gardening is the great argument for conservatism. 'We don't like doing things quickly in this country', he tells his wife:

> FRANK It's like gardening. Someone once said we was a nation of gardeners, and they weren't far out. We're used to planting things and watching them grow and looking out for changes in the weather.
> ETHEL You and your gardening!
> FRANK Well it's true – think what a mess there'd be if all the flowers and vegetables and crops came popping up in a minute. That's what all these social reformers are trying to do, trying to alter the way of things all at once. We've got our own way of settling things, it may be slow and it may be a bit dull, but it suits us all right and it always will.

Fifty years ago, in the heyday of post-war productivism, and in the afterglow of 'Britain's Finest Hour', heritage, the subject of a vast literature which reached some kind of climax in the run-up to the 1951 Festival of Britain, was a matter not of ruins (though they had a place in it), nor yet of 'bygones' and 'memorabilia' (the growth sector of the historical souvenir industry today), but rather of what were then conceived of as the beauties of national life and character – the British genius for compromise, the British love of fair play. State theatricals – such as the Lord Mayor's procession and the Queen's opening of Parliament, even the playing of the national anthem at the close of theatre and cinema performances – counted for a great deal. The House of Commons was 'the shrine of the world's liberties'; the Houses of Parliament, 'the outcome of a thousand years of ... political history'.[50] Hedges were 'the most typical element in the landscape of Britain'; the cultivated fields testified to the fertility of British agriculture.[51] Britain was a progressive society, building on the solid foundations of a unique past. Thus, for instance, *Our Historical Heritage*, a three-decker work addressed to post-primary school pupils, presented national history 'in such a way that pupils are stirred to learn more of "the story of human achievement"' ('Looking Forward' is the expressively-named coda of the book).[52]

At the time of the Festival of Britain, to follow *Everybodys*, one of the illustrated weeklies of the time, faith in all things British was undimmed. London was still 'the busiest port in the world' and the Festival would allow Britain to present itself to the world again as 'a leader in commerce, invention and art'.[53] Tyneside had a 'proud industrial ancestry' which meant that a ship from Tyneside was 'recognised as the world's finest in shipbuilding today'.[54] Malcolm Campbell was 'the fastest man on earth'.[55] The annual overhaul of the liner 'Queen Elizabeth' was 'one of the world's major spring cleaning operations'.[56] British aeronautics, too, were unrivalled. 'Despite great drawbacks since the war' British aviation was still 'supreme' in design and achievement, runs an article in February 1951:

> when Sir Miles Thomas, bustling chairman of BOAC, recently returned to the country from an intensive study of American aviation methods he declared that Britain had at least a two year lead over the U.S.A., our main rivals in building jet air liners. For the past year and more America's own semi-official aviation circles have also expressed the opinion that Britain was outpacing her, and all other competitors, in the jet-age air race.[57]

The pioneer industrial archaeologists, discovering 'much of interest and sometimes of beauty' in what to others was derelict waste, seem to have been optimistic spirits. Writing in a time of economic boom and full employment, they linked 'the cultural heritage of the past' with the technological developments 'of the present and the future'. For Michael Rix, the Maltings of Ditherington, Shrewsbury, 'the oldest metal-framed building in the world' (a building which in 1955, when he coined the term 'industrial archaeology', had only recently been identified) was 'the ancestor of every metal-framed skyscraper'. Brunel and Stephenson's viaducts were symbols of the fact that 'industry is not always synonymous with ugliness', while the stations of the London Underground 'represent some of the handsomest buildings erected in England in this century'. Coalbrookdale, 'the cradle' of the Industrial Revolution, 'still thickly sown with monuments' should be given a special attention because of the momentous consequences to which it was still giving rise.

> Great Britain as the birthplace of the Industrial Revolution is full of monuments left by this remarkable series of events. Any other country would have set up machinery for the scheduling and preservation of these memorials that symbolise the movement which is changing the face of the globe, but we are so oblivious to our national heritage that apart from a few museum pieces, the majority of these landmarks are neglected or unwittingly destroyed.[58]

Today, by contrast, the past is seen not as a prelude to the present but as an alternative to it, 'another country', and 'heritage' is more typically defined in terms of relics under threat – the old tank blocks and Second World War ack-ack batteries, for instance, which the Fortress Study Group has taken under its wing; old battlefields such as Marston Moor, which the Battlefields Society is attempting to save from the road-builders. Dissevered from any idea of national destiny, it is free to wander at will, taking up residence and holding court at quite recently discovered historical locations and attaching itself to a promiscuous variety of objects: not only jewelled treasures, such as the recently discovered Roman hoard at Hokne, but also the prehistoric apple-seeds which archaeologists are miraculously extracting from time-warped and fossilized faeces.

In the vernacular of Nature Conservancy, 'heritage' is a generic term for environments at risk – endangered habitats, such as the shrinking wetlands, drained for arable cultivation, the orchid-bearing meadows destroyed by chemical pesticides, the disappearing hedgerows grubbed for factory-like, mechanized, farms. English Nature (formerly the Nature Conservancy Council), has been for some years now directing its major effort to protecting the shrinking wetlands. The Council for the Preservation of Rural England, an older campaigning body, is no less concerned with the fate of roadside verges:

> Britain's roadsides are a vital and living part of our heritage. They are home to many species of animals and plants.... Our environmentally rich roadsides are constantly threatened by destruction, mismanagement and downright thoughtlessness.

Notes

1. David Goode, *Wild In London*, London 1986, for an overview by the ex-GLC founder of the London ecology unit; David Pate, *Nature Conservation in Hounslow*, Ecology

Handbook 15, London 1990, and M. Game *et al.*, Ecology Handbook 16, *Nature Conservation in Ealing*, London 1991 for an account of this wilderness site.

2. Ian Forsyth, *Beatles Merseyside*, Seaford, Sussex 1991; David Bacon and Norman Mason, *The Beatles' England*, p. 93 for the Cavern Mecca, 'the closest thing to an official Liverpool Beatles' tourist centre'; John Platt, *London's Rock Routes*, London 1985, pp. 81–92 for the Beatles' London.

3. Timothy Darvill, *Ancient Monuments in the Countryside, An Archaeological Management Review*, London 1987, p. 38; 'Coastline Battle Launched to Save Wartime Relics', *Independent*, 31 May 1993 for the pill-boxes. English Heritage, *Report and Accounts 1987–8*, p. 23, for the Martello towers.

4. Iorwerth C. Peate, *Tradition and Folk Life. A Welsh View*, London 1972, pp. 134, 139.

5. Stuart Piggott, *William Stukeley, An Eighteenth Century Antiquary*, Oxford 1950.

6. Vita Sackville-West, *Heritage*, London 1919. Suzanne Rait, *Vita and Virginia, The Work and Friendship of V. Sackville West and Virginia Woolf*, London, 1993, pp. 41, 42, 46, 48, 49–53 has some good passages on the 'moral eugenics' novel.

7. It seems possible that the term 'heritage' was in occasional use earlier, as a synonym for what was more usually called 'tradition'. *Scrutiny*, in some sort a 1930s literary-critical counterpart to the Folk Song movement, referred to folk-song as 'a heritage of all classes'. Bruce Pattison 'Musical History' in *Scrutiny* iii: 4 (March 1935) p. 374, quoted in Georgina Boyes, *The Imagined Village; Culture, Ideology and the English Folk Revival*, Manchester 1993, p. 130. In the 1950s club movement, it seems likely that the term 'heritage' was transplanted from 'progressive' singers in the USA. It was in constant use in the New York Journal, *Sing Out*, as in their *Lift Every Voice. The Second People's Song Book*, New York 1953, where folk-song becomes 'the democratic heritage of song'. The fraternal letter from New York, printed in the second issue of *Sing* (July–August 1954), also uses the term in this sense.

8. Ailie Munro, *The Folk Music Revival in Scotland*, London 1984, is an excellent history of the movement north of the Border. David Harker, *Fakesong. The Manufacture of British 'Folksong' 1700 to the Present Day*, Milton Keynes 1985 is a relentlessly hostile account (cf. also the same writer's 'May Cecil Sharp be praised?', *History Workshop Journal* xiv, Autumn 1982). Georgina Boyes's *The Imagined Village* is a more nuanced critical commentary, and one with both historical and cultural depth. She is particularly interesting on the war-time BBC, and the *Country Magazine* origins of the second folk-song revival. Ewan MacColl's autobiography *Journeyman*, London, 1990 devotes chapter 22 to a bitter-sweet memoir of the revival, and the 'almost impenetrable pall of cigarette smoke that shrouded singer and audience'.

9. The 'Heritage' Club was founded by some members of the Oxford University Cecil Sharp Society 'who felt that not enough stress was being placed on folk singing as opposed to folk dancing'. See the potted history in *Heritage*, Michaelmas 1965. Richard Mabey, in later years an eloquent environmentalist writer, is remembered as being an American bluegrass singer at the club. Communication from Tony Rose, January 1994. Tony Rose remembers the club as being 'pretty eclectic', 'a bit of everything'. I have not been able to find out when it migrated from university premises to the 'Baker's Arms', Jericho, where it was happily ensconced in the mid 1960s. The Vaughan Williams Memorial Library, Cecil Sharp House, has some cyclostyled issues of *Heritage*, the club magazine and one issue has made its way to the British Library. Cecil Sharp House also has a file of the more Anglocentric, though no less radical *Ethnic*, a quarterly journal which began appearing in 1959. It attacked the 'overwhelmingly genteel and precious' atmosphere surrounding the Cecil Sharp style of traditional song performance, and celebrated the winds of change 'blowing in the direction of greater vigour and earthiness'. I am grateful to Malcolm Taylor, librarian at Cecil Sharp House, for drawing my attention to it.

10. The 'Ballads and Blues' concerts, which seem to have begun life as fund-raisers for the *Daily Worker*, featured the jazz clarinettist Bruce Tuner and the Calypso singer Fitzroy Coleman, the two Gormans ('Irish Fiddle and Flute') and the Scottish singer Isla Cameron. *Sing*, 1/2, July–August 1954, 1/5, January–February 1955.

11. For Skiffle John Hasted *Alternative Memoirs*, privately printed, Itchenor, Sussex 1992, is a mine of information. It is possible to follow its progress in *Sing*, originally, in 1954, the

organ of Hasted's London Youth Choir, and later, it seems, taken over by the folk-music faction at the Workers' Music Association. For the later evolution of Skiffle into Pop, Dave Laing, Karl Dallas, Robin Denselow and Robert Shelton, *The Electric Muse: The Story of Folk into Rock*, London 1975; and Charlie Gillett, *The Sound of the City*, London 1983.

12. For this take-up of what Gramsci had called the 'national popular' see Bill Schwarz, 'The People in History: The Communist Party Historians' Group, 1946–56', in R. Johnson et al., eds, *Making Histories*, London 1982; Harvey J. Kaye, *The British Marxist Historians*, Oxford 1984; and Raphael Samuel 'British Marxist Historians, 1880–1980', *New Left Review*, 120 (March–April 1980).

13. Communist Party Archives 'The March of English History. A Message to you'. The archive has the brochure of the Pageant of Chartism organized by the party under the title *1839 Chartism; 1939 Communism* for the centenary of the Chartist Convention; and a 35-pp. typescript, 'The Heirs to the Charter' produced for the occasion by the writer Montagu Slater. *Daily Worker*, 30 March 1939 for one of a series of centenary articles; T. Islwyn Nicholas, *One Hundred Years Ago*, Aberystwyth 1939 for a Welsh Communist essay in this vein. Geoffrey Trease, *Comrades for the Charter*, London 1939 was a successful children's novel inspired by the centenary. It contrives to combine revolutionary enthusiasm with a strong sense of place – in particular the ironworking villages from which the Newport Rising of 1839 was recruited. Ernie Trory, *Between the Wars, Recollections of a Communist Organiser*, Brighton 1974, pp. 112–13, 151 and 158–9 and *Imperialist War, Further Recollections of a Communist Organiser*, Brighton 1977, pp. 219–20 for the 'March of History' pageants in Brighton. Trory, at that time Sussex organizer for the party, claimed a county 'heritage' stretching back to the Protestant martyr Deryk Carver; he included the 'Sussex poet – Percy Shelley' (!) and reminded his listeners that Simon de Montfort had defeated the King on Sussex soil. 'Sussex Manuscripts' in the same writer's *Mainly About Books*, Brighton 1945, pp. 111–13 suggests that, as with some other Communists of his generation, the idea of a vernacular and local heritage took root. Ralph Fox, 'The Cultural Heritage' in his *Novel and the People* London 1948, published after the writer's death in Spain, for an interesting attempt to turn T.S. Eliot's notions of 'tradition' to political ends. In Fox's notion of heritage, a blend of modernism, radicalism and Yorkshire – the writer came from a Dissenting family in the West Riding – Cobbett writes the purest prose in the language, *Ulysses* is the supreme novel, *Wuthering Heights*, *Jude the Obscure* and *The Way of all Flesh* were the greatest books of their age, 'all . . . cries of suffering . . . manifestos of English genius that a full human life in a capitalist society was impossible. . .' For the Communist Party's rather more manipulative use of the notion of cultural heritage in the period of the Cold War, 'The U.S.A. Threat to British Culture', in *Arena*, June–July 1951 (interesting for E.P. Thompson's address on 'William Morris and the Moral Issues Today') and 'Britain's Cultural Heritage', ibid, 1952. At the latter conference Roy Sear, speaking on 'Youth and Heritage', reported with approval that in the East Midlands youth 'had formed a folk-dance group'.

14. Ursula Vaughan Williams, *R.V.W., A Life of Ralph Vaughan Williams*, Oxford 1964, p. 245. For a thoughtful discussion of the composer's ways of relating to tradition, Wilfred Mellers, *Vaughan Williams and the Vision of Albion*, London 1987.

15. Anthony W. Hodgkinson and Rodney E. Sheratsky, *Humphrey Jennings, More than a Maker of Films*, Hanover, USA 1982, pp. 55–6. Jennings was a man of many loyalties as well as of prodigious talents. 'English to his marrow' (*Our Time*, July 1944, p. 13), he also – in 1942, when making a film of the South Wales miners – apparently regarded himself as a Communist and a Puritan. Invoking Miltonic epic at one moment, he was at the next celebrating the carnivalesque – never more effectively than in his blitz film, *Fires Were Started*, where the firemen gather around a honky-tonk piano to belt out a chorus, as the floor, swaying to the impact of high explosives, shudders beneath their feet.

16. Brian Denny, 'The Army Bureau of Current Affairs', Ruskin College history thesis, 1994. The historian of army education, who seems to have served his pedagogic apprenticeship in the ABCA (Army Bureau for Current Affairs) interestingly dates his subject, in the title of his book, from 1643 – the year when the New Model Army began to form.

17. John Major, speech of April 1993, quoted in 'The Roots of "Back to Basics" unearthed', *Independent*, 12 January 1994.

18. R. Samuel, 'Mrs Thatcher's Return to Victorian Values' in T.C. Smout, ed., *Victorian Values, A Joint Symposium of the Royal Society of Scotland and the British Academy, December 1950*, Oxford 1992.

19. 'The Suburbs and the Clerks' in John Carey, *The Intellectuals and the Masses. Pride and Prejudice among the Literary Intelligentsia, 1880–1939*, London 1992.

20. Peate, pp. 134–5, 139.

21. Ibid., pp. 17, 20–1. At Somerleyton, Suffolk, a charmless country house open to the public in the summer months, pride of place is given to a display of the family silver – fat and mid-Victorian; to a library of apparently unopened books; and to the ermine gown worn at the Silver Jubilee of 1977. Visitors will see a 1953 *Vogue* photograph of a Miss Somerleyton – then a débutante modelling for Ponds face-cream – but they can easily miss the old hand-tools, 'still in use to c. 1950' which have been relegated to an outhouse bearing the label 'bygones' – the only faint recognition that the estate depended for its existence on the labour of servants, groundsmen and staff. In the front hall, visitors are welcomed by a show of tiger skins and the upright corpses of two polar bears, shot – visitors are told – during a turn-of-the-century expedition by one of the family ancestors. A photograph of Mrs Thatcher's Cabinet, who seem to have spent a weekend on safari at Somerleyton, adds another *End of the Day* touch to the scene.

22. Kenneth Hudson and Ann Nicholls, *The Cambridge Guide to the Museums of Britain and Ireland*, rev. edn, Cambridge 1989, cf. also *Museums and Galleries of Great Britain and Ireland*, East Grinstead 1994; and Debra Shipley and Mary Peplow, *The Other Museum Guide*, London 1988.

23. 'For Peat's Sake', *Aberdeen Press and Journal*, 2 July 1993.

24. 'Actor to Help Out Dolphins', *Dundee Courier and Advertiser*, 7 July 1993.

25. Dusan Ogrin, *The World's Heritage of Gardens*, London 1994.

26. 'Windmills Around Haworth', *Times Literary Supplement*, 18 February 1994.

27. *Britain, 1993. An Official Handbook*, pp. 189–97 for a complacent description.

28. The French literature on the subject is refreshingly free of the attitudinizing which marks British publications on this theme. It also has a stronger sense of the eighteenth- and nineteenth-century progenitors of heritage. Cf. Françoise Choay, *L'Allégorie du patrimoine*, Paris 1992; Jean-Michel Leniaud, *L'Utopie française, essai sur le patrimoine*, Paris 1992; Marc Guillaume, *La Politique du patrimoine*, Paris 1980.

29. Philippe Hoyau, 'Heritage and the "Conserver Society": the French Case' in Robert Lumley, ed., *The Museum Time-Machine; Putting Cultures on Display*, London 1988, p. 28; Ministre de la Culture, Direction du Patrimoine, *Programme d'action, 1984*, pp. 5–11, 17–21; *Regards sur le patrimoine*, pp. 7–11 (preface by Jack Lang) 111, 116–17, 144, 225–39; Yvon Lamy 'Patrie, Patrimoines', *Genèses*, 11, March 1993.

30. Ministre de la Culture, Direction du Patrimoine, Mission du Patrimoine Photographique, *Programme d'action, 1985*, pp. 247–9.

31. For the damp, dark chill which settled on England with the coming of the nineteenth century, and the ivy which grew in 'unparalleled profusion', cf. Virginia Woolf, *Orlando*, Chapter V. For Stevie Smith's use of the same conceit, *Novel on Yellow Paper*, Virago 1991, pp. 13–14 (I am grateful to Alison Light for this last reference). One great enemy of ivy was apparently Queen Mary, the Queen Mother. 'She had always had a hatred of ivy and she organised squads to clear the Badminton estate of the "enemy". In all during the war years she supervised the clearing of 120 acres.' David Duff, *Queen Mary*, London 1985, p. 225, quoting Marion Crawford, *The Queen Mother*, London 1951. 'Queen Mary was certainly obsessed by her enmity towards ivy. She felt it was a destructive element.' Anne Edwards, *Matriarch, Queen Mary and the House of Windsor*, Sevenoaks 1984, pp. 379–80. The same book gives the following extract from her diary: 'Lovely morning which we spent clearing ivy off the trees in the grounds' (25 September). 'Lovely morning which we spent clearing ivy off trees – we watched a whole wall of ivy of 50 years being removed. Most of it came down like a blanket' (26 September). I am extremely grateful to Pippa Hyde, librarian at the Council for the Preservation of Rural England, for drawing my attention to these references.

32. James F. White, *The Cambridge Movement; the Ecclesiologists and the Gothic Revival*, Cambridge 1967, p. 91.

33. Basil F.L. Clarke, *Church Builders of the Nineteenth Century, A Study of the Gothic Revival*

in England, Newton Abbot 1969, p. 78. Cf. also the same writer's *The Building of the Eighteenth-Century Church*, London 1963, pp. 1–3, and app. V, pp. 232–7.

34. 'On Monuments', *The Ecclesiologist*, January 1845, p. 16.

35. *The Old Curiosity Shop*, chapters XLVI, LII–LIII, LV, LXXII.

36. For 'Wooden Highlanders' see *Notes and Queries*, vol. 162, 1932, p. 404; ibid., vol. 163, 1932, p. 14; vol. 181, 1941, pp. 53–4.

37. I am grateful to Tracey Earl, archivist at Coutts, for information about the display cases at Coutts, and to John Keyworth, curator of the Bank of England Museum, for a guided tour and history of that interesting addition to the City. A more remote ancestor would be the display of old fire-marks and fire-fighting equipment at the Chartered Insurance Institution in Aldermanbury, set up in 1937, shortly after the establishment of the Firemarks Circle, and currently in the throes of refurbishment. It seems to have been the original of these mini-museums, or wall-displays, which are now it seems a feature of insurance brokers' headquarters. Visitors to Spitalfields may have noticed the display of old firemen's tunics at Frizzell International in Folgate Street; there is, it seems, an even more spectacular one at Sharp's, Lloyd's Avenue, where the senior partner is also a historian of the trade. Cf. Brian Wright, *The British Fire Mark, 1680–1879*, Thetford, 1982. I am grateful to Mr Wright for information about the spread of these mini-museums. Model ships – such as the one which fills the window of Ocean House, Elder Street, Spitalfields – are perhaps a near cousin at the marine brokers.

38. I am grateful to Ian Cook of Arsenal FC and Brian Hall of Liverpool FC for information about both their own and other football museums. *Tower Hamlets News*, 22 July 1993 for the Millwall FC museum, which is to make a little show of the tram tickets which carried spectators to the ground as well as players' kits.

39. I am grateful to Brian Southam and John Naylor for their memories of how the series was born. Brian Southam's volume on Jane Austen, 1968, was the first of the series.

40. Brian Cook, *The Britain of Brian Cook*, London 1987 is a fascinating account of how those pink and emerald green 'Fauve' book jackets came to be designed.

41. Graham Wallas, *Our Social Heritage*, London 1921; Martin Wiener, *Between Two Worlds, the Political Thought of Graham Wallas*, Oxford 1971.

42. H.D. Rawnsley, *A Nation's Heritage*, London 1920; for his refusal of the bishopric of Madagascar, National Trust archives, Acc. 6/17, letter of Octavia Hill, 25 November 1901; and *Canon Rawnsley, An Account of his Life*, by Eleanor F. Rawnsley, London 1923.

43. Dorothy Hartley, *A Countryman's England*, London 1935. Dorothy Hartley, who among many publications wrote a kind of miniature *History of Everyday Things*, and a book promoting Yorkshire cooking, is remembered by one who saw her coming into the Batsford office as a 'tall, hawk-like countrywoman', 'a chatelaine crossed with a prioress', wearing a long black cloak and speaking with a country burr. Information from John Naylor.

44. Hilda M. Coley, *Our Heritage of Wild Flowers*, London 1935, pp. 9–10.

45. The series of ten booklets was published under the title 'British Life and Thought' by Longman.

46. J.E. Hales, *British Education*, quoted in 'The British Way of Life', *Britain Today*, no. 38, February 1941, p. 16.

47. 'The Life of a Nation', *Britain Today*, no. 61, September 1941, pp. 2–3.

48. Vera Brittain, *England's Hour: an Autobiography, 1939–41*, London 1982, p. 120.

49. The following two paragraphs are taken from the present writer's introduction, 'Exciting to be in English', in *Patriotism, the Making and Unmaking of British National Identity*, London 1989, I, pp. xxiv–xxv.

50. *Beauty in Britain*, London, n.d., p. 10. The same book (p. 30) says that the Grand National is 'the most formidable and the most testing steeplechase in the world'; it also hypes those rather staid south coast seaside resorts, Eastbourne and Bognor Regis, as 'big names' in 'up-to-date' entertainment' (p. 38).

51. L.F. Easterbrook, 'Life and Work on the Land', *Our Way of Life, Twelve Aspects of the British Heritage*, Country Life, 1951, p. 122.

52. H.P. Wolstencroft and T. Davidson, *Our Historical Heritage*, University of London Press, 3 vols, 1950.

53. Hilda Marchant, 'Here's The World's Front Door', *Everybodys*, 14 April 1951 and 19 May 1951.

54. 'Today on Tyneside', ibid., 3 March 1951.

55. Ibid., 31 March 1951.

56. Ibid., 17 February 1951.

57. 'Britain's Strength in the Air', ibid., 10 February 1951; cf. '... Bristol ... one of the greatest manufacturing centres of aeroplanes in Great Britain today', R.D. Way, *Antique Dealer, An Autobiography*, London, 1956, p. 44.

58. Michael Rix, 'Industrial Archaeology' in *The Amateur Historian*, vol. 2, no. 8, October–November 1955, pp. 225–6. Of interest here is the message of the Newcomen Society printed in the first issue of the *Journal of Industrial Archaeology*, May 1964. It welcomed wholeheartedly the advent of the journal and looked forward to a 'feast' of interesting information 'particularly on the period that links the cultural heritage of the past with the technological developments of the present and the future'.

Genealogies

Quite where and when, and how and why, 'heritage' acquired its currently inflated status is, or ought to be, an open question. So far as the built environment is concerned, there is no continual line. The Society of Antiquaries,[1] which had a Conservation Committee in the 1850s, was largely concerned with the protection of Anglo-Norman church architecture, then disappearing under the heavy hand of the Gothic revivalists. The Society for the Protection of Ancient Buildings, founded by William Morris in 1878 and leading players in environmental controversies today, also confined itself in its early years, to church architecture, though its special enthusiasm was for a rather later period.

The National Trust, though taking the whole environment for their province, were preoccupied, in the spirit of their founders, with access to the countryside. A handful of country houses came the Trust's way, through the accident of bequest. But neither domestic buildings nor commercial premises came into their brief. Inter-war conservationist legislation was still largely concerned with the protection of ancient monuments and stopped short at 1714. Public sentiment, newly hostile to the Victorian, was also indifferent to Regency (a term only coined by the interior decorators in the 1920s) and – at least before the Georgian Group began campaigning for it in 1937 – the Georgian. When, in the 1920s, John Nash's Regent Street was consigned to the bulldozer, there was, it seems, barely a murmur of disapproval. A few years later Brighton Corporation was hoping to knock down that stateliest of pleasure domes, Brighton Pavilion.

So far as nature conservation is concerned a much longer and more continuous line can be hypothesized. In the royal forest, game preserving, and attempts to exclude the encroachments of would be squatters, go back to Anglo-Saxon times;[2] the ancient sport of falconry 'so popular with many monarchs', led to various laws for the protection of eyries and nesting sites;[3] while the history of inland fisheries is one long record of disputes about close seasons and river conservancy.[4] Anxieties about hard woods, and keeping up supplies of ships' timbers, are as old as those about the Royal Navy. John Evelyn, who as a Restoration Commissioner for Woods and Forests wrote *Sylva, a Discourse of Forest Trees*, is from this point of view a pioneer arboriculturist and a doughty defender of what today is so carefully nurtured as 'ancient' forest.[5]

Another and more explicitly conservationist line which can be pieced together is one that connects nature conservancy with the nineteenth-century passion for natural history. Botany in the nineteenth century, as also to some extent geology, had the character of a mass enthusiasm, mobilizing great armies of specimen hunters, holiday fossilizers and Sunday naturalists,[6] while in the second half of the century, the animal welfare agitation put species protection on the legislative agenda. The first wildlife protection act – the Sea Birds Preservation Act – was put on the Statute Book in 1869 and was followed by many others. Charles Waterton, the celebrated Yorkshire landowner–naturalist, whose home at Walton Hall was a great favourite with early nineteenth-century travellers[7] (there is a fine description of it in Sir George Head's *Home Tour of the Manufacturing Districts*) is credited with establishing the first wildlife reserve – a breeding site for barn owls and starlings, and a home to both rare domestic plants and South American exotica. In another sphere, the Thames Angling and Preservation Society, founded in 1838 and still functioning, has some claim to being the first of the organized conservation societies,[8] just as the fishery societies of the Scottish Highlands and Islands were among the first in the field of habitat management. Later in the century the first nationwide association for all forms of wildlife – the Selborne Society for the Protection of Birds, Plants and Pleasant Places – was formed in 1885.[9]

So far as flora and fauna are concerned, 1886 saw the formation of the Wild Flower Society – it has seventeen local branches today – and 1888, the year of the passage of the County Councils Act, also saw the first local by-laws and county orders to protect endangered plants. Nature conservancy and habitat protection seem to have been on the agenda of the National Trust from the start. One of the very first acts of the Council was to take steps towards acquiring Wicken Fen, 'the only undrained portion of the old Fen ... the haunt of much wild life and of the rare swallow-tailed butterfly'. (A Southampton entomologist, J.C. Moberley, sold the Trust a first strip 'for the nominal sum of £10'. By 1911 its Wicken Trust property, swollen by purchases and gifts, covered 600 acres.)[10]

A genealogy of heritage might try to connect nature conservancy with the idea of preservation in the built environment. Typically they have been agitated, or taken up, by different sets of people; legislatively they are treated as though they existed in entirely separate spheres. Yet the first arguably provides the original for the second. This has certainly been true in recent times when a neo-Malthusian gloom about dwindling natural resources, and ecological alarm about toxic wastes, acid rain and global warming have given an emergency sense to environmental campaigning, while at the same time defining heritage as something under threat. Nature conservancy was arguably even more to the fore in the 1920s and 1930s, when the Council for the Preservation of Rural England, with Sir Patrick Abercrombie, the planner, as its honorary secretary, was by a long way the most influential of the environmental campaigners. 'Preservationist' is defined in the *OED* as 'one who advocates the preservation of historic buildings or antiquities',[11] and is given a first citation in 1927; but as the frequent nineteenth-century references to the Game Laws suggest, preservationists must have had an earlier career in relation to wildlife reserves.

'Conservation' is defined in the first place in reference to natural resources, 'conservancy' in relation either to the official preservation of trees and forests or to the regulation of the fisheries and navigation (there is a reference to a 1490 Act of Henry VII). The concept of a Conservation Area was introduced into protective legislation under an act of 1932 designed to put a stop to quarrying or deep ploughing in the vicinity of places like Hadrian's Wall.[12] The earliest Ancient Monuments designated under the Act of 1882 were rural – they were defined as ruins, and in order to be protected they had to be deserted.

Another genealogy that would repay investigation, if only because it might take one into the intellectual underworld of our time, and the intersection of science, magic and religion, is that which connects heritage with pre-history. It is a line which might lead back to William Stukeley's Druidical imaginings at eighteenth-century Stonehenge,[13] or to Geoffrey of Monmouth's version of the Arthurian Camelot, or to the lands of the Celtic wizards and ancient British giants. For those 'New Agers' who use the megalithic stones of the West Country as their gridlines and zodiacs as their stars this is part of the search for the riddle of the universe, drawing on occult archaeology and linking ley lines in Britain with those of the Euphrates, the Nile, and the Ganges.[14] But it also has its roots in half a century and more of Nature mystics and visionaries – among them numbers of the neo-Romantic artists and writers of the 1930s and 1940s – for whom the primitive and the prehistoric was the real classical antiquity, the age of poetry as opposed to that of prose.

Heritage is a word which descends to us from Old Testament times (Cruden's *Concordance* gives no fewer than twenty-seven references) and it was perhaps these biblical associations that recommended it to the Imperial War Graves Commission when, at the conclusion of their labours, they commissioned a book to dignify their labours, and settled on the title *Immortal Heritage* for the soldierly dead of the Great War.[15]

It is possible to find residues of religious belief, if not in contemporary uses of the term, then in some of the rhetorics associated with it. One could refer to the notion of recovering a lost innocence, as in the purification of ancient woodland, where parasites, such as the sycamore, are grubbed up; the refurbishment of old buildings, where the original features serve as totems of authenticity; even – as in the current re-planting in Regent's Park – the restoration of nineteenth-century paths and grids and shrubs. Old tithe barns are renovated as lovingly – and as religiously – as if they were cathedrals;[16] old engine houses are restored as temples of Victorian engineering. In any of these instances the past is the invisible presence, the Host with whom we commune, and it is very much in the same spirit that 'Heritage Walks', whether threading their way through a man-made or through a natural environment, are conducted as though they were pilgrimages.

Ancestor-worship is arguably a potential element in any historical project, while the idea of keeping faith with the past, or being 'true' to it, is the driving force or animating spirit in restoration work of all kinds. Solidarity with the dead – or an act of reparation towards them – has been a leading motive in many of these do-it-yourself retrieval projects which have as their object honouring the hardship and sufferings of those who have been hidden from history in the past. It is also perhaps an element in the outrage which descends on the heads of those who attempt to disturb underground remains, a sentiment which at the extreme, as in the Rose Theatre agitation of 1989, can make any attempt to put up a new building, or sink new footings, a kind of sacrilege.[17]

A more recognizable religious element in heritage – though with Gaia, the earth mother, in place of Jesus Christ or God – can be seen in those radical versions of environmentalism which picture the eco-system or the planet as an absolute good – wise, beneficent, far-seeing – and humanity as the pollutant. The language of Greenpeace and Friends of the Earth is no less highly charged. In the words of a favourite epiphany, we do not inherit the earth, we borrow it.[18]

The religious idiom was, of course, quite central to the Cambridge Camden Society, the Catholic revival ecclesiologists of the 1840s, who arguably provided one of the paradigms on which later preservationists have drawn, transferring to ecclesiastical ornament those numinous qualities which others reserved for the Word of God.[19] Church restoration was their grand panacea for the spiritual and social ills of their day. Where their Evangelical opponents measured vital religion by the urgency and vehemence of prayer – or in the case of Lord Shaftesbury by philanthropic good works – the Cambridge ecclesiologists pinned their faith in the fabric of the Church itself, and believed that by going back to the purity of decorated Gothic – the Christian art of the high Middle Ages – they would be returning worshippers to the certainties of an age of faith. Victorian preservationism, though its leading voices, Ruskin and Morris, were stoutly Protestant rather than crypto-Catholic, reproduced and even amplified this bias, indeed it was never given more eloquent voice than by Morris himself when the Society for the Protection of Ancient Buildings was started. Writing to the *Athenaeum* in 1877, and launching his famous thunderbolt against the sham restorationists who believed they were carrying out some divine purpose in Gothicizing chancels or naves, he argued that churches were not 'ecclesiastical toys' but – the words would have sat easily in the columns of *The Ecclesiologist* – 'sacred monuments of the nation's growth and hope'.[20]

In another trope – still much in vogue in the political vocabulary of yesteryear – heritage is a high-flown term, or poetical word, for hereditary rights, as in the ancient constitution which Coke and the Common lawyers invoked in the 1600s, to challenge royal prerogative;[21] or the traditional British tolerances which Mr Baldwin was summoning up in 1934, to warn against the menace of fascism.[22] To follow the *OED* this was one of its major uses in Middle English times, when it served sometimes as a synonym for birthright, sometimes as a grandiose word for liberties, privileges and immunities, and more occasionally, in religious discourse, as the mark of the elect – 'the people chosen by God'.[23] In the Middle Ages, when burghal independence was jealously guarded both against the exactions of local magnates and the claims of royal power, such liberties and privileges were the subject of civic ritual,[24] and of those 'invented traditions' which it has been the delight of a generation of historians to study. In the case of London – the Commune of London, as it was called in the thirteenth century, after its right to self-government had been secured – the shades of Gog and Magog, the ancient giants who allegedly came here with the Trojans, were invoked to defend the city's liberties and laws.[25] In the medieval countryside immunities and rights, such as those of the East Anglian Sokemen, were claimed by virtue of special tenure or, in the case of freemen, hereditary descent.[26] Elements of heritage were also involved in those 'rights of common' which were still being vigorously asserted, as Jeanette Neeson has shown, long after enclosure had made them legally extinct;[27] or the liberties, franchises and rights claimed, on the strength of often mythic charters, by such tightly-knit brotherhoods of workers as the Purbeck marblers, the Isle of Portland Quarrymen[28] and the free miners of the Forest of Dean.[29]

As a literary trope, writerly conceit, and editorial flagship, heritage seems to be an entirely twentieth-century phenomenon. It makes no serious appearance, before 1900, either in the short title catalogues or the indexes to periodical literature, but thereafter it soars. Publishers began to adopt it as a title both for multi-volume series and for individual books. Figures taken from the cumulative indexes in the *English Catalogue* show only five uses of the term before 1900.[30]

In the 1920s the word was everywhere. Anthologists used it to dignify their selections from the writers and poets, as in the series launched by Sir John Squire and Arthur H. Lee in 1929. The 'aesthetic geographers', following in the footsteps of Vaughan Cornish, adopted it to discourse on the beauties of 'scenery' while Home Counties topographers, taking their rambles in country churchyards, or propping up the bar at a roadside inn, treated it as a synonym for olde-worlde charm.[31]

The 1920s pedagogues – a flourishing breed in the golden age of the grammar school and the swot – latched on to 'Heritage' as a camouflage for their primers, trapping the unwary with tasty morsels before subjecting them to a battery of comprehension tests, practical exercises and potted histories. Longman's 'Heritage of Literature' series was in its earlier years mostly selected by headmasters, with biographical notes about the authors at the end. Some 120 titles are credited to the series in *Books in Print*, 1960. Longman followed up the success of 'Heritage of Literature' by launching a 'Heritage of Books' series, directed, it seems, at the top end of the junior school, with riddles, puzzles, pictures and 'amusing questions' at the end of the stories, to test children's comprehension.[32]

The most interesting of these publishing sequences, and certainly the most intellectually ambitious was the 'Heritage of India' series, published in Bombay. Compiled by both English and Indian students of Sanskrit, and drawing not only on academics but also on scholar–administrators and scholar–missionaries (among them Edward J. Thompson, the novelist father of E.P. Thompson, the historian, and an ardent follower of Tagore) these books are a wide-ranging attempt to fathom the mysteries of Indian religion and philosophy, as well as being, obliquely, a tribute to the antiquity of Indian civilization by those who were its notional conquerors. Scholarship here, and respect for antiquity, provided a common ground where Hindu and Christian could meet.[33]

The 'Heritage of India' series may serve as a reminder that British India was one of the great laboratories in which conservationist practices were developed. India was, it seems, the first country to organize a system of forest conservancy – according to *Nature*[34] it was already complete in 1884 – and it was also involved in making an inventory of temples and ruins for some twenty years or more before the passage of the Ancient Monuments Act in England.[35] Well before the Cambridge ecclesiologists set about restoring the English churches it seems that servants of the East

India Company, with time on their hands, or succumbing to the lure of the East, were undertaking rescue operations on the architectural remains for the Mughal conquest, or bringing Hindu temples back to life. The museum at Lahore, which is the starting point for Kipling's *Kim* – 'The Wonder House' as it was apparently called by city-dwellers[36] – had been founded, in March 1857, by a wealthy Parsee, Sir Jamsetjee Jeesebhoy, but it seems to have been under the curatorship of Kipling's father that it acquired the collection of Buddhist sculpture that made it world famous.[37] There were hundreds of pieces: friezes of figures in relief, fragments of statues and slabs crowded with figures that had encrusted the brick walls of the Buddhist *Stupas* and *Viharas* of the North Country and now dug up and labelled 'the pride of the Museum'.[38]

Heritage's 'lost England', according to Patrick Wright, is aristocratic-reactionary in character, and represents the hegemony of what he calls the 'Brideshead complex' over the more progressive spirit of the post-war welfare state.[39] Treating the country house 'not as a dead relic but as a potent symbol of everything that was threatened by modernisation and reform', Waugh's novel, 'seen as an irrelevant joke by many readers at the time', posthumously triumphed. Through the instrumentality of the National Trust, which increased its ownership of houses from seventeen in 1945 to eighty-seven in 1990, the country house was able to rise, phoenix-like, from the ashes; to impose itself as the very quintessence of Englishness in the world of interior design; and to provide the leading idiom both for TV costume drama, and for the public museum's 'living history' displays.

But if one goes back to 1944–45, a time when war-weariness gave a wistful edge to dreams of post-war reconstruction, one finds that *Brideshead* was only one of the lost Englands on offer. Another, presciently outlined in A.L. Lloyd's *The Singing Englishman* (1944) was that of folk art. The haunting opening sequence of Laurence Olivier's *Henry V,* an aerial view of Elizabethan London, and a living history recreation of the humours of the Bankside groundlings, helped to put the idea of a national theatre on the map, as well as planting the seeds of that about-to-be-realized resurrectionary folly, the rebuilding of the hexagonal Globe theatre. Trevelyan's *English Social History*, one of the great publishing successes of 1944, transported readers to an England in which the dark satanic mills were no more than a speck on the horizon; while the Forshaw/Abercrombie County of London *Plan* (1943) offered a *rus in urbe* dreamscape in which the metropolis would emerge from its war-time ordeal as a city of restored villages. L.T.C. Rolt's *Narrow Boat*, another 1944 bestseller which owed its appeal to the idea of paradise lost, offered an England where heavy horses took the place of lorries, and tow-paths that of arterial roads. Cinema-goers took *Tawny Pippit* to their hearts – an essay in rural romanticism by the left-wing director Bernard Miles: a kind of filmic prelude to Nature Conservancy and a narrative of survival in which wildlife was restored to its ancient rights.[40]

A country house of sorts does figure in Powell and Pressburger's *A Canterbury Tale* (1944), a quite sinister and now largely forgotten Tory-romantic film in which an outraged landowner takes up arms against lipstick, and tars and feathers the local girls who fraternize with GIs.[41] But it is singularly absent in the same film-makers' *I Know Where I Am Going* (1947), a romance of the highlands and islands where, at the climax of the film, the young heroine abandons her plutocratic fiancé and opts for the simple life, settling down to live with her boatman-hero amidst the dogs and sheep. Catriona, another invention of Tory male fantasy, who makes periodic appearances in the film, accompanied by her hounds, is a creature of the night, wild, raggle-taggle and gypsy in her dark beauty, a figure as remote as it would be possible to imagine from a Home Counties matron in twinset and pearls or even from her sporty cousin, in jodhpurs and riding boots, show-jumping at the gymkhana.

The country house is also not much of a presence in *Recording Britain*, the remarkable water-colourists' project commissioned in the early days of the Second World War to preserve for posterity a pictorial topography of vanishing Britain.[42] Kenneth Rowntree, a Quaker and a conscientious objector, preferred country churchyards.[43] Barbara Jones, with her wonderful eye for the grotesque, made a speciality of follies, among them the life-size models of Jurassic reptiles in the ruins of Crystal Palace. Her one essay in the monumental – a prescient one from the point of view of conservationist campaigning – was a water-colour of the Euston Arch.[44] John Piper did contribute some pictures of country houses, but they are offered as instances of what he was later to call 'pleasing decay' and when it came to symbolizing the continuities of country life he opted, like others at this time, for the medieval or early modern barn. A bare, bleak landscape with a building in the distance is a recurring motif in his topographical pictures. His earlier water-colours feature such places as Dungeness (that lunar landscape in the Thames Estuary which is the oldest reserve of the Royal Society for the Protection of Birds, and which Derek Jarman was to turn into surrealist art) or in the drystone walling of Snowdonia. So far as domestic building was concerned his greatest enthusiasm, so he told a collaborator, was for the 'olde-worlde' country cottage:

> Half-timber was my first love in the world of English domestic architecture. Much bad English landscape art has been produced under the influence of it, though I still find Mrs Allingham's Victorian watercolours of thatched and

timber-framed cottages with flowery gardens appealing, as I do Anne Hathaway's cottage itself (even as reconstituted to face the twentieth century). When I was young three volumes in a series called *Old Cottages and Farmhouses* (one for Surrey, one for Kent and Sussex, one for the Cotswolds) appeared. They were handsomely bound and full of excellent photographs taken with a big plate camera, mostly under cloudy skies but in perfect focus, by W. Galsworthy Davie. The texts were by distinguished architects of the Lutyens and Jekyll period – E. Guy Dawber and W. Curtis Green, who adorned their texts with careful pen and ink sketches of hood-moulds and other details.... As a boy, I longed to live in a timber-framed house with an over-sailing upper storey, and brick chimneys set diagonally, in pairs, and with stone slabs or irregularly-weathered tiles on the roof.[45]

The country house does not figure at all – to judge by the numerous books which were a by-product of the series, as well as by such recordings as survive in the archives – in the radio programmes which, for children growing up in the 1930s and early 1940s, probably did as much as anything to make the countryside an object of desire – i.e. the 'Romany' feature on Children's Hour. Produced in the BBC's Northern Region studio in Manchester, it transported children into an imaginary gypsy caravan, and gave them nature study through the voice of a real-life Romany descendant – the Methodist minister and naturalist J. Bramwell Evens. It was far more concerned with capturing, through sound recording, the distinctive notes of bird-song – or the 'Wuf, Wuf' of Romany's inseparable companion Raq – than with any more peopled landscape. When human characters were introduced, they were, it seems, chosen – like Romany himself – because they were plebeian, as complete a contrast as it was possible to imagine to the starched voice of the BBC announcers of the time.[46]

In any genealogy of heritage, and of the agencies which created a climate of opinion favourable to it, some mention might be made of the BBC.[47] It was the midwife, at the end of the 1960s, to the birth of the oral history movement and the creation of a national sound archive. Then the hugely popular TV programme 'The Antiques Roadshow' did as much as anything to democratize the notion of the collectable, update the notion of the historical, and create a public for the flea markets. Stephen Peet's long-running TV series, 'Yesterday's Witness', first screened in 1968, gave a human face to industrial archaeology as well as introducing the idea of oral history to a mass audience. Earlier in the 1950s and 1960s, BBC schools broadcasting had made the so-called industrial ballad – the songs of shuttle and cage, recorded by Ewan MacColl and A.L. Lloyd – as familiar an icon of the national past as 'Greensleeves' or Kathleen Ferrier's 'Blow the Wind Southerly' had been for war-time Britain. The Home Service programme *Country Magazine*, launched in May 1942, has some claim to being the original progenitor of the second folk-song revival (in 'As I Roved Out' the programme made a feature of living traditional performers). The 1951 'Ballads and Blues' programmes,[48] bringing together American and British work-songs, signalled and prefigured the urban and industrial turn in the notion of 'tradition'; later the 'Radio Ballads' programmes made by Charles Parker and Ewan MacColl attempted to marry the idea of folk to that of modern epic.[49]

In the 1930s the BBC had been one of the public voices of the Council for the Preservation of Rural England. A series of eight talks on 'Vanishing England' given in November and December 1933 and reprinted in *The Listener* seems to have been devised with the aim of bringing CPRE planning policy before the local authorities; six years later the same speaker, Howard Marshall, a popular broadcaster, used 'The Week's Good Cause' to appeal for the CPRE.[50] The celebrated broadcaster Richard Dimbleby made his debut as a reporter, in October 1936, with an account of the annual conference of the CPRE at Torquay; his second broadcast was a programme about 'Cherry', a Hampshire cow.[51] The National Trust was another of the BBC's good causes, and it is remarkable how many of its most popular broadcasters – pre-eminently J.B. Priestley and C.E.M. Joad – were campaigners and preservationists.[52]

Chronologically, conservation crystallized as a reformist cause and campaigning cry when the post-war expansion of the economy was carrying prosperity to new heights. The railway preservation mania emerged in the wake of modernization and rationalization. It was a counterweight to the extinction of branch railways and narrow-gauge lines. Later, it was the dieselization of locomotives – a technical innovation of the mid 1950s – which gave rise to the 'romance of steam'. A more immediate flashpoint of conservationist anxiety – and the original fillip to the formation of local campaigning groups – was the grandiose motorway-building programme of the 1960s. Fuelled by the end of petrol rationing, facilitated by the rise of HP and the spread of new and more affluent lifestyles, car ownership tripled in the 1950s. It was already cast as one of the villains of the piece in *Outrage* (1955), the *Architectural Review*'s famous attack on the 'subtopia' which was allegedly obliterating the distinction between town and country, and threatening to turn England into a gigantic Los Angeles, with filling stations and advertising hoardings at every turn, and a forest of traffic signs in place of hedges and trees. In the 1960s, when the Campaign Against the Motorway Box got under way, the traffic engineers appeared as Satan's out-riders, swallowing whole streets in their road-widening schemes, girdling city centres with their roundabouts and flyovers, scything neighbourhoods in two with their throughways.

The 1960s, a decade when modernization was in the ascendant, when the pace of change seemed to quicken in every sphere of national life, and when giganticism seemed to be carrying all before it, was also the decade when conservationism stepped out of the shadows to challenge both private developers and public authority. Defeated in the Euston Arch controversy of 1961–62, and appearing as just another lost cause, it was powerful enough, five years later, to put environmental protection on the statute book in a Civic Amenities Act which made grants for the restoration of listed (i.e. historic) buildings a first call on the municipal rates, and the creation of 'conservation areas' a new vocation for municipal planning. The passage of the Nature Conservancy Act of 1970 effected a comparable boost for the idea of wildlife reserves.

The 1960s saw a rapid growth in the number and influence of local amenity societies, starting life, often, as single-issue campaigns, sparked into being by outrage at some demolition order or road-widening scheme and then broadening out to act as all-purpose ginger groups: there were 213 such societies in Britain in 1957; 1,167 in England alone in 1977. The same decade also saw the formation of regional wildlife trusts, and the transformation of high-level conservationist pressure groups into mass-membership organizations. The Royal Society for the Protection of Birds, which began life in 1899, campaigning against the international trade in plumage, and which only began to establish its reserves in post-war Britain, is a striking case. Its membership growth testifies to both the new appeal of wildlife habitats and a readiness to take part in what became a major national passion, increasing more than tenfold in the decade between 1960 and 1970 (from 10,579 to 117,963) and then rising steadily to its present level of 840,000.[53]

Economically, the growth of conservationist sentiment seems to relate closely to the remarkable spread of home ownership (29 per cent of the population owned their homes in 1961; 65 per cent do today), and to the property boom which continued almost uninterruptedly, so far as house prices were concerned, from 1960 to 1990.

Another source of conservationist energy was the counter-culture of the 1960s, and the 'back to nature' movements which were perhaps its most enduring legacy. Oodles, the vegetarian restaurant chain, which decorated the premises with farmhouse motifs and old advertisements, and helped to popularize chunky wooden furniture as both 'natural' and traditional, was founded in 1959; Cranks in 1963; Ceres, the first of the 'wholegrain' shops, in 1966. By 1968, 'organic' food co-ops and 'organic' farm communes had emerged as ideal-typical representatives of an alternative lifestyle politics.

So far from being the preserve of aesthetes or of minority groups of campaigners, as it had been in the earlier days of preservation, heritage, as it crystallized in the late 1960s, was a cultural capital on which all were invited to draw. When, in 1968, the Automobile Association adopted it as the new title for one of their annual publications (a motorist's guide to 'Castles, Houses and Gardens'), it seems to have been because the appetite for historic sightseeing was growing, and not only allowed for but actively encouraged a more democratic definition of antiquities. 'A quick glance through its pages will suffice to show that descriptions of not only castles, houses, gardens, but museums, archaeological remains, holy wells, windmills, almshouses and other places of interest, too numerous to itemize, justify the impress of its new title – *Britain's Heritage*'.[54] A more clearly democratic intention, couched in terms of 'access', rather than object, can be seen in the multiplication of public footpaths and coastal paths on the model of the Pennine Way, sometimes under the aegis of the local authorities, sometimes of the National Trust, and most recently through the vigorous efforts of the Countryside Commission.[55] Here one can see a late triumph of a century-old campaign for access to the countryside and rights of way: an assertion of public rights over private property.

If there was a single agency that transformed 'heritage' from an enthusiasm into an industry it was not the country house owners or the National Trust, intent on rescuing private property from confiscation or ruin, but rather the local authorities, many of them Labour, and the museum curators, many of them, after their own fashion, 'new-wave' social historians, and the environmentalist campaigns, all of them, in some sort, radical, who seized on Youth Training Schemes and the Manpower Services Commission to take on paid and extra hands. Thus the Iron-bridge Museum, at the height of unemployment, in 1981, had no fewer than 200 staff paid for in this way, while even so modest a project as 'Manchester Studies' – the brainchild of a social historian at Manchester Polytechnic – could employ some nineteen apprentice researchers.

Notes

1. Society of Antiquaries Archives, Executive Committee Minutes, 9 November, 7, 14, December 1854, 11 January 1, 8 February 1855; and Joan Evans, *History of the Society of Antiquaries*, Oxford 1956, pp. 309–12.

2. Cyril Hart, *Royal Forest, A History of Deans Woods as Producers of Timber*, Oxford 1966 is a history written by a verderer. The Crown Estate Papers at the Public Record Office have a mass of detail about these disputes in the eighteenth century which can also be followed in printed Parliamentary Papers.

3. George A. Goultry, *A Dictionary of Landscape*, Aldershot 1991, pp. 192–3.

4. Conservancy also became a big issue in the deep-sea fisheries with the development of the trawler industry in the nineteenth century. Before the Royal Commissions of 1863 and 1878, Paul Thompson tells us (*Living the Fishing*, London 1983, p. 23), inshore fishermen were demanding the imposition of limitations on trawlermen 'in terms which anticipate the conservationist measures ... being imposed today'. Cf. *Encyclopedia Brit-*

annica, 1922 edn, XXX, 102/2: 'The most ardent of the conservationists failed to recognize the urgent importance of conserving the salmon and halibut fisheries.'

5. The most recent edition of this book, which gets periodically rediscovered, is 1979.

6. Lynn Barber, *The Heyday of Natural History, 1820–1870*, London 1980 is an attractive account; David Elliston Allen, *The Botanists; A History of the Botanical Society of The British Isles*, Winchester 1986; Anne Secord, 'Science in Popular Culture', *History of Science*, September 1994.

7. Julia Blackburn, *Charles Waterton, Conservationist and Traveller*, London 1980.

8. Bob Smyth, *City Wild Space*, London 1987.

9. David Evans, *A History of Nature Conservation in Britain*, London 1991.

10. Gaze, *Figures in a Landscape*, pp. 71–2. J.C. Moberley of Southampton, who owned a two-acre strip of the Fen, sold it to the Trust for the round sum of £10. The property, augmented by many other gifts, now covers 600 acres.

11. *OED*, 'preserve' 'preservation', 'preservation order', 'preservationist', 'conservancy', 'conservation', 'conservationist'.

12. This was under the Ancient Monuments Act of 1931, Boulting in Jane Fawcett, ed., *The Future of the Past, Attitudes to Conservation, 1174–1974*, London 1974, pp. 17–18, 21. Cf. 'In Denmark the protection of ancient monuments . . . is regulated by the Conservation of Nature Act . . . the means of protection employed being in many ways similar', Kristian Kristiansen, 'Denmark', in *Approaches to Archaeological Heritage*, p. 21.

13. Stuart Piggott, *William Stukeley; an Eighteenth Century Antiquary*, Oxford 1950.

14. Cf. Tom Williamson and Liz Bellamy, *Ley Lines in Question*, Tadworth 1983 for a sympathetic account of this by two landscape historians who are also editors of *Rural History*. Peter Le Mesurier, *The New Age Business. The Story of the Continuing Quest to Bring Down Heaven on Earth*, Moray 1990.

15. *The Immortal Heritage. An Account of the Work and Policy of the Imperial War Graves Commission*, London 1937.

16. See the superb photograph of Harmondsworth Manor Barn in David Pearce, *Conservation Today*, London 1989, p. 159.

17. Rose Theatre Campaign, *Newsletter*, May–November 1989, published daily as the property developers drove their stakes through the Rose's residue, is both finely researched and combative in spirit.

18. James Lovelock, *Gaia, A New Look at Life on Earth*, Oxford 1982.

19. J.F. White, *The Cambridge Movement; The Ecclesiologists and the Gothic Revival*, Cambridge 1962.

20. *Athenaeum*, 5 March 1877, quoted in Charles Dellheim, *The Face of the Past; the Preservation of the Medieval Inheritance in Victorian England*, Cambridge 1982, p. 87.

21. J.G.A. Pocock, *The Ancient Constitution and the Feudal Law; a Study of English Historical Thought in the Seventeenth Century*, 2nd edn, Cambridge 1957.

22. Stanley Baldwin, 'Our Heritage of Freedom', *The Menace of the Dictatorships – Speech Broadcast 6 March 1934*, London.

23. *OED*, 'Heritage'.

24. Mervyn James, 'Ritual, Drama and Social Body in the Late Medieval English Town', in *Society, Politics and Culture, Studies in Early Modern England*, Cambridge 1986.

25. Gwyn Williams, *Medieval London, From Commune to Capital*, London 1963, for a learned and effervescent account. For the Gog and Magog procession, Frederick William Fairholt, *Gog and Magog*, London 1859.

26. A remarkable and moving account of how this issue was agitated before the royal courts is R.H. Hilton, 'Peasant Movements in England Before 1381', *Economic History Review*, 2nd series, vol. 2, no. 2, 1949.

27. Jeanette Neeson, *Commoners, Common Right, Enclosure and Social Change in England, 1700–1820*, Cambridge 1993.

28. Raphael Samuel, 'Mineral Workers' in Samuel, ed., *Miners, Quarrymen and Saltworkers*, London 1977.

29. Chris Fisher, 'The Free Miners of the Forest of Dean, 1800–1841', in Royden Harrison, ed., *Independent Collier, The Coal Miner as Archetypal Proletarian Reconsidered*, Hassocks 1978.

30. The decennial figures on which this graph is based run as follows: 1881–90, 1; 1891–1900, 4; 1901–10, 5; 1911–20, 11; 1921–30, 29; 1931–40, 18; 1941–50, 10; 1951–60, 25. The British Library 'on-line' computer catalogue, which records any use of 'heritage' in a title, has eighty-nine 'heritage' titles for the decade 1921–30.

31. J.B. Priestley, ed., *Our National Heritage*, London 1939, gives an indication of how the war-clouds gave a new edge to this kind of writing.

32. *Whitaker's Reference Catalogue*, 1938, p. 574.

33. As well as contributing a volume on *Bengali Religious Heritage* to the 'Heritage of India' series, Edward J. Thompson published independently his tribute to Tagore, under the title *Tagore, Literature and Heritage*. E.P. Thompson, *Alien Homage, Edward Thompson and Rabindranath Tagore*, Oxford 1993 is an affectionate account of his father's involvement with Indian literary and national movements of the time. The 'Heritage of India' series suggests that he was perhaps a less isolated and embattled figure than his son believed. For another, briefer account of his place in Indian studies, Richard Symonds, *Oxford and Empire, The Last Lost Cause*, Oxford 1986, pp. 61, 114, 117–19. See also this writer's good passages on the scholar–missionaries, pp. 152, 501, among them Verrier Elwin, who went out to India with the Christa Seva Sangha Mission, settled among the Gonds, married a tribal girl and set up schools, dispensaries, a leper home and cottage industries.

34. *Nature*, 26 June, 1884, 195/6 quoted in *OED* 'conservancy'.

35. G. Mitchell, *Guide to the Monuments of India*, vol. 1; and Philip Davies, *Guide to the Monuments of India*, vol. 11, Harmondsworth 1990.

36. Rudyard Kipling, *Kim*, chapter 1.

37. Robert Hampson, editorial note, in Rudyard Kipling, *Something of Myself*, Harmondsworth 1987, pp. 172–3.

38. Angus Wilson, *The Strange Ride of Rudyard Kipling*, Granada 1979, p. 59.

39. Patrick Wright, *A Journey through Ruins, The Last Days of London*, London 1991, pp. 45–68.

40. Jeffrey Richards, 'National Identity in Wartime Films', in Philip M. Taylor, ed., *Britain and the Cinema in the Second World War*, Basingstoke 1988, pp. 44–8.

41. 'Curious would-be propaganda piece with Old England bathed in a roseate wartime glow' is the thumbnail sketch of *A Canterbury Tale* in *Halliwell's Film Guide* (9th edn, London 1993, p. 193). The authorities, according to Basil Wright, 'showed some reluctance' in exporting the film, which is not surprising, since the landowner–magistrate is the hero, and the only good GI is the one who falls in love with Tudorbethan cottages and Canterbury Cathedral.

42. David Mellor, Gill Saunders and Patrick Wright, *Recording Britain. A Pictorial Domesday of Pre-War Britain*, Newton Abbot 1990 is a catalogue of the exhibition at the V&A; and a more nuanced account of the history of the project than the explanatory panels at the exhibition itself.

43. David Mellor, 'A History Outline' in Mellor et al., pp. 16–18.

44. Cf. the painting in ibid., pp. 41, 57, 65–6, 96, 112, 120–1, 134 and her *Follies and Grottoes*, London 1953.

45. Richard Ingrams and John Piper, *Piper's Places; John Piper in England and Wales*, London 1983, p. 53.

46. For 'Romany' there are brief portraits in Paul Donovan, *The Radio Companion*, London 1991, pp. 233–4; Denis Gifford, *The Golden Age of Radio. An Illustrated Companion*, London 1985, p. 247. The North-West Sound archive has the cassette of a brief programme about him; and Wilmslow Public Library has parked his caravan in its forecourt. Eunice Evens, *Through the Years with Romany*, London 1946, is a life; among his books are *Out With Romany* (1937); *Out with Romany Again* (1938); *Out with Romany by Meadow and Stream* (1942). Evens was a Romany by birth, a great-nephew of the well-known evangelist Gypsy Lee Smith, and a Methodist minister by training and vocation.

47. On sound archives, Jeremy Silver, '"Astonished and Somewhat Terrified", the Preservation and Development of Aural Culture' in R. Lumley, *The Museum Time-Machine, Putting Culture on Display*, London 1988, pp. 170–96. The National Sound Archive has a file on the founders of the oral history society and I am also drawing on my own vivid memories

of it. George Ewart Evans, 'Flesh and Blood Archives', *Oral History* no. 1, 1973 for BBC help in this writer's 1950s oral history recordings.

48. Georgina Boyes, *The Imagined Village*, for an excellent discussion of this; Francis Dillon, ed., *Country Magazine; Book of the BBC Programme*, London 1949; A.L. Morton, 'A.L. Lloyd, A Personal Memoir', in *History and Imagination*, London 1991, pp. 314–15.

49. Ewan MacColl, *Journeyman*, London 1990, pp. 331–6. There is a Charles Parker archive in Birmingham.

50. Council for the Preservation of Rural England, *Monthly Report*, November 1933, October 1934, February 1936, June and July 1939.

51. Jonathan Dimbleby, *Richard Dimbleby, A Biography*, London 1975, pp. 72–5.

52. National Trust Archives, Acc. 45 Radio Script, 10 August 1947.

53. P. Lowe and J. Goyder, *Environmental Groups in Politics*, London 1983.

54. Automobile Association, *Britain's Heritage*, London 1968, p. 5.

55. Bizarrely, but understandably, because it seems they were the only source of funds, the Countryside Commission is credited with the newly opened stretch of the Thameside walk below Southwark Bridge.

Sociology

When Patrick Wright launched his attack on 'heritage', he accused it of reactionary chic and argued that it represented the triumph of aristocratic and reactionary nostalgia over the levelling tendencies of the Welfare State: it was Evelyn Waugh's posthumous revenge on Clement Attlee.[1] Robert Hewison, more crudely, puts the appearance of 'heritage' down to an aristocratic plot hatched, it seems, by the beleaguered owners of country houses in 1975. Faced with the prospect of a wealth tax and an incoming and unsympathetic Labour government, they mounted a high-level lobby, raising the cry of 'heritage in danger', and enlisting the support of the House of Lords, the National Trust and the Victoria and Albert Museum (the V&A 1974 exhibition 'The Destruction of the Country House', according to Hewison, is the point at which 'the heritage industry' was born).[2]

If in one set of discriminations heritage is accused of being crypto-feudal – a vast system of outdoor relief for decayed gentlefolk – in another it is charged with being 'deeply capitalist',[3] albeit in a post-modern rather than a proto-industrial vein. In a consumer-led society, in which everything has its price, and market values are unchallenged, it 'traffics' in history and 'commodifies' the past.[4] It turns real-life suffering into tourist spectacle, while at the same time creating simulacra of a past that never was. Museums are particularly suspect. They are 'part of the leisure and tourist business', and thus intimately linked to the Disneylands and theme parks. They are also, it seems, property's *franc-tireurs*:

> A new museum is not only one of the convenient ways of re-using a redundant mill or factory. It is treated as a form of investment that will regenerate the local economy that has decayed as a result of the closure of that mill or factory. That is why it is relatively easy to find capital to set up a new museum. Museum projects are a useful means of cleaning up a derelict environment prior to commercial investment.[5]

In either of these two cases heritage is an expressive totality, a seamless web. It is conceptualized as systemic, projecting a unified set of meanings which are impervious to challenge – what Umberto Eco calls 'hyper-reality'. In essence it is conservative, even when it takes on, or co-opts, popular themes. It brings the most disparate materials together under a single head. It is what one critic defines as a 'closed story', i.e. a fixed narrative which allows for neither subtext nor counter-readings. Its biases are more or less consistent, its messages coded, its meanings clear. Politics, culture and economics are all of a piece, reinforcing one another's influence, reciprocating one another's effects.

Heritage is also seen by its critics as a 'project',[6] if not a conspiracy or plot then at the very least a strategy, 'a complex and purposefully selective process of historical recollection'. It is a 'bid for hegemony', a way of using knowledge in the service of power. It shores up national identity at a time when it is beset by uncertainties on all sides. It is a way of compensating for the collapse of British power.

Chronology alone would put these symmetries in doubt, quite apart from the fact that the country cottage has played an inconceivably greater part in the idea of 'lost England' than the country house. It might suggest that there was not one moment but many from which current retrieval projects and strategies could trace their origin. Using perhaps the Braudelian notion of 'conjuncture', the historian of heritage might want to distinguish between the vintage car rallies – originally, in the 1930s, when no one else could afford to run in them, an aristocratic sport, and later, to judge by the Ealing Studios comedy *Genevieve* (1953) an affair of Home Counties playboys, dressed in cavalry twill trousers and blazers – and the altogether more plebeian 'vintage' engine rallies today where steam ploughs assemble in muddy fields, fairground organs blare out their music, and hobby-horses whirl on the carousels.

Chronology would also call into question association of heritage with conservative reaction. It might suggest that the cry of 'Heritage in danger', or at any rate that sentiment, crystallized, in the first place, in a recoil from the modernizations of the 1950s, rather than as a reflex of economic decline. The post-war mechanization of agriculture, the dieselization of the tractor, and the disappearance of the horseman, might appear as the inspiration, albeit a negative one, for the growth of the idea of the 'folk' or 'working farm', museum – an innovation of the late 1950s and early 1960s. The steam preservation mania of the 1950s is more obviously related to the dieselization of railways, the rationalization of services and the diminution of branch lines. So far as the built environment is concerned, it was arguably the astonishing increase in car ownership – a feature of the 'affluent society' of the 1950s – which set the alarm bells ringing and changed preservation from a rural to an urban cause.

Many of heritage's enthusiasms were in place long before 1975, the year when in Britain, as in the other countries involved in European Architectural Heritage Year, the term entered general circulation. Railway antiquarianism is almost as old as the railways themselves; as Bevis Hillier shows in *Young Betjeman*, in the 1930s it was thoroughly familiar to readers of the *Daily Herald* and the Shell *Guides*,[7] quite apart from the railway modellers running replicas of Puffing Billy, or visitors to the Science Museum confronting – as they had done since 1875 – Stephenson's 'Rocket'. A taste for early industrial buildings and plant goes back at least as far as Nikolaus Pevsner's *Pioneers of Modern Design* (1935),[8] while the gypsy arts – or folk arts as they were called at the time of the Festival of Britain – have had their admirers among the expensively educated ever since, in the 1860s, Francis Groome ran off with his Esmerelda and went off to live with the gypsies on Headington Hill.[9]

Economics, and especially economic history, might also put the moment of 1974–5 into question, by drawing attention to the long gestation period of many conservationist projects, and the changes in the material conditions of existence which allowed them to enter the realm of the thinkable. Statistics of car ownership – 2 million in 1949, 17.5 million in 1980 – might help to account for the growth of historic tourism,[10] while attendance figures, if they could be gleaned from the records of places like the Wigan Pier Heritage Centre, or the statistics of school parties, might dispose of the absurd idea that open-air museums are a great magnet to foreign tourists. In another sphere the spread of that most labour-saving and comfort-making of modern household devices, central heating, which can be logged, quinquennium by quinquennium from 1960, might appear as the ghost-in-the-machine of restoration, and the extraordinary increase in the number of 'listed' historic buildings which began in 1967. At a stroke it converted draughty Victorian mansions, fit only for conversion to flats, into desirable period residences.

Economics, disaggregating such abstracts as 'capital' and 'consumerism' and inquiring into their heterogenous and promiscuous components, might also serve as a useful corrective to those top-down accounts of the heritage industry which see it as a kind of ruling-class conspiracy or plot, or imply that there is some directive intelligence at work. While paying due regard to the ways in which business has been able to profit from, or accommodate itself to, the rehabilitation of old property, or to latch on to notions of 'period' in commodity marketing and design, it might draw attention to those more molecular processes in which any cultural politics takes shape. In heritage-ware, to judge by those who take up the stands when the gift trade holds its annual fairs, the typical entrepreneurs seem to be one-man businesses, female-run franchises and husband-and-wife (or gay) partnerships; the business corporation is a conspicuous absence.[11] Heritage supports and is supported by chains of charity shops and armies of flea-market stallholders. Organic farms make some contribution to it; so do the health and whole-food co-operatives.

Heritage puts a premium on the labour and services of the craftsman-retailer, and the maintenance of artisanal skills – one reason why, in the 1970s, conservation of the old town was so vigorously promoted by Communist-led municipalities in Italy (Bologna was a much-quoted example);[12] and why, in Britain, conservation areas have rather a high complement of manual skills. It has often given short-life tenancies to craftsmen while properties are awaiting rehabilitation, or in the protracted period when building work is in progress. It has provided premises or work-space at peppercorn rents for absolute beginners, one basis for the crafts revival of the 1970s. And it supports, at any given moment, a mass of short-life businesses. As Bob West writes, in his hostile account of those who made their appearance in the shadow of the open-air museum at Ironbridge Gorge: 'Some die off, others return, others metamorphose into different dreams of an independent living.'[13] Cowboy operators deserve attention too, as, say the small army of 'distressers' who manufacture curios for the flea markets; the souvenir sellers who station themselves outside the British Museum, and nowadays drive a trade in quite elaborate facsimiles and replicas; or the image pirates who conduct the street sale of old photographs. Mention might be made here of those unemployed historians who scratch a small livelihood conducting historical walks, or those penny capitalists who have been developing murder tours. One could refer to the housebreakers and demolition men who, in the property boom of the 1980s, helped to keep the architectural salvage merchants supplied with period fittings;[14] the scuba-divers who get black-market prices for underwater booty which is, legally speaking, the property of the Receiver of Wrecks;[15] and the metal detectorists who have created a glut in Pilgrim's Medals, as well as being responsible for some of the most sensational Roman and Dark Age finds.[16]

Heritage also has its plebeian entrepreneurs. One could refer to Fred Dibner, the demolition contractor, whose collection was one of the great sources of the fairground engines exhibited at the Steam Fairs.[17] Or to Dai Woodham, the scrapyard boss, whose four acres of rusting metal were, in the 1970s, one of the great sources of locomotives for the steam preservation societies.[18] In a more commercial vein one could refer to the rise of the architectural salvage trade which now has a hundred or more names in its directories.[19]

A sociological perspective on heritage, which took into account the hybridization of contemporary social identities, the mixing and mingling of what were formerly class preserves, or a Marxist one which looked for a dialectical relationship between the imaginary and the real, rather than a reductive and reflective one, might be even more unsettling to currently accepted negative stereotypes than an economic one. It could begin by pointing out that the rise of the heritage industry, if one chooses to take 1975 as a significant date, so far from heralding an epoch of feudal reaction, coincides, rather, in Britain, as in other European countries, with political dealignment and a collapse of two-camp class divides. It is a period which saw a remarkable and, on the part of Mrs Thatcher, a quite deliberate de-gentrification of the Conservative Party. Where Mr Macmillan, only thirty years ago, made a great play of filling his Cabinet with old Etonians, today ministers with cut-glass accents are the exception rather than the rule and the 1992 Tory intake of MPs was the first in which the state-educated were a majority. The crumbling of the pillars of the establishment, with the Church of England, the ancient universities, the BBC and even the judiciary at loggerheads with government, has put de-gentrification on the agenda in other spheres. The stone-cleaning at the Palace of Westminster may have restored the beauty of the Gothic fenestration, but it has not saved the House of Commons from being associated with public corruption and sexual sleaze. Most remarkable of all is the newspaper-led attack on a monarchy which less than twenty years ago, at the time of the Silver Jubilee, still commanded a near-religious veneration. Perhaps one should add that even in relation to stately homes the record is a chequered one. Some twenty years after SAVE Britain's Heritage was launched to rescue them, it seems that 249 of the 1400 'family seats' featured in the V&A exhibition of 1974 had been sold.[20]

One way of attempting to account for the popularity of heritage, as also the rapidity with which it has spread, is to see it as an attempt to *escape* from class. Instead of heredity it offers a sense of place, rather as environmentalism offers the activist and the reformist an alternative to the worn-out routines of party politics. It may be indicative of this that Covent Garden, that preservationist Ruritania, which emerged in the 1980s as one of the style capitals of the world, is also a Sloane-free zone, where gays are more in evidence than would-be ladies and gents. Heritage allows the Colonel's lady and Judy O'Grady, or at any rate their daughters, to wear the same vintage clothes. It encourages white-collar workers and middle-class men, getting up steam from the boiler, to try their hand at being mechanics; landlubbers, sailing before the mast, to play at being mariners. Heritage offers an ideal home which is defined not by pedigree but by period, and which can be decked out with make-

believe family heirlooms. Still more pertinent, through the medium of
family history it gives us a second identity and allows the most humdrum
and ordinary, so far as present occupation is concerned, to indulge in a
romance of otherness.

Heritage might also be aligned with the emergence in the 1960s of
what Frank Parkin has called, in another context, 'middle-class radicalism'.[21] It is a familiar feature of the universities in the 1960s, of such
newly radicalized groups as social workers and of the new-wave charities
of the 1960s. But might it not be applied equally to the formation of
amenity societies and 'ginger' groups, the staging of single-issue campaigns, such as those who in London defeated the motorway box, the
growth of the country wildlife trusts, and not least the appearance, for
the first time, of mass membership environmental campaigning organizations?[22]

The saving of Covent Garden was originally the work of a post-1968
grouping of Architectural Association students and community activists,
taking up arms against what seemed to be a juggernaut of comprehensive clearance and redevelopment.[23] The architecture and planning,
right down to the specification of the small-pane, 'Dickensian' windows
for the shops in Floral Hall, the installation of Victorian street lamps, and
the re-traditionalizing of the roads and paving with cobbled forecourts,
was the work of the very left-wing architects' department of the Greater
London Council. (The same department was responsible for the
Dolphin lamps on the Embankment, the repainting and restoration of
the ironwork on the Thames bridges, and the construction of the Jubilee
Walk.)

The Globe Theatre project – i.e. the rebuilding of Shakespeare's
theatre at or near its original site – which promises to open to the public
in 1995, has been agitated for, off and on, since the 1890s, when William
Poel founded the Elizabethan Stage Society, dedicated to performing
Shakespeare in the original conditions. Taken up by the theatrical
progressives of the day, it re-emerged in the County of London Plan,
1943, which combined a utopian vision of the future with a dream of
recreating the vanished glories of Elizabethan and Jacobean Bankside. It
was at one point to have been part of the 1951 Festival of Britain. The
current project, which has been in gestation for more than thirty years,
was the pet scheme of a blacklisted Hollywood producer who began
canvassing support for it during his enforced exile in 1950s London,
after he had refused to testify before the House Un-American Activities
Committee.[24]

At the other end of the ideological and political spectrum, canal
restoration, the earliest post-war resurrectionary enthusiasm, and the
first to be given statutory recognition and protection, was the project,

initially, of a small group of rather right-wing cultural dissidents who functioned effectively as a pressure group. It was conceived as a way of calling on the old world to redress the balance of the new. Tom Rolt, whose bestselling *Narrow Boat* brought the movement into being, derived much of his adrenalin from the belief that the project, if realized, would give England back its imaginary heart. A man who married romantically not once but twice, eloping with a water gipsy, and who pursued for some fifteen years a double life – a professional mechanical engineer by day, and by night a carefree barge-dweller – he loathed industrialism, or what he called 'materialism'; espoused the cause of organic agriculture; and in *High Horse Riderless*, a philosophical work of 1949, advocated a return to civilization based on land. In *Narrow Boat* he pictured the canals not as industrial waterways, not yet as the secret arteries of the city, but rather as gateways to tranquillity. His boat, the *Cressy*, chugged along at a leisurely pace (an average of about seven miles a day), swinging now this way, now that in a voyage that contrived to be both peaceful and Arcadian, and adventurously picaresque. The boat moved through a 'green ever-changing landscape', with frequent stops, 'sometimes for several days', to explore villages and the countryside, churches, stately homes and the mysteries of innumerable locks and sluices.[25]

Local initiatives were needed to put conservation areas on the map, though without the Civic Amenities Act of 1967 it is doubtful whether they would have been strong enough to resist the pincer movement of the motor car lobby, the traffic engineers and the property developers, each of them ministering to the 1960s fantasy of urban clearways. 'Heritage walks' or 'History Trails', devised sometimes by museum curators, sometimes by schoolteachers, sometimes by the amenity societies, were also the fruit of local initiative, taken up by the municipal authorities as a contribution to European Architectural Heritage Year (1975) or the celebration of the Silver Jubilee (1977). By 1977, when the English Tourist Board began publishing its *Heritage Monitor*, no fewer than 300 had been staked out.[26]

Working farmers played the leading role in the genesis of the steam traction rallies, partly, it may be, because in real life they were used to working with Heath Robinson-like contraptions, partly because they had the space to store the engines, and partly because it was with steam ploughs and threshers, rather than fairground engines, that the movement began.[27] According to the received account, which has the accolade of a printed book, and the supporting proof of photographs of the event, showing both the contestants and a small knot of spectators, the founding moment was a race in June 1950. Arthur Napper, of Appleford, Didcot, the chief protagonist, was a small farmer whose people had been farmers and railwaymen for generations.

By 1948, the combine harvester had arrived on most of the larger farms and those that still used threshing machines sought the easier method of tractors to drive them ... Arthur quite vividly recalls the morning when he woke up and thought to himself, there won't be a traction engine left in Berkshire. There and then he ... went down to Wilder's yard. 'You can have any one you like for fifty quid' said John Wilder. 'I'll bid you forty-five', countered Arthur'. 'Done' ... He called her *Old Timer*.[28]

A firkin of ale was the stake when Arthur wagered *Old Timer* against a neighbour's machine. The contest was an almost private one, but it took the fancy of the neighbourhood and was later featured in the press. Showmen's engines – today one of the great features of the steam fairs – made a first appearance when a national rally was held in 1957, but the event was still staged at Appleford and the locomotives taking part in the contest were still classified according to agricultural tasks – a 'timber loading demonstration' being added to the obstacle race for steam tractors and the show of working threshing sets.

The farming element is still there in today's Steam Fairs which function, in some sort, as a rough-and-ready carnivalesque alternative to the county shows. At the Great Dorset Fair, Blandford, the largest of them, a rally spread over some 750 acres, continuing four days, and attracting a quarter of a million spectators, Michael Oliver, the farmer who owns the land and masterminds the event, runs a continuous demonstration of ploughing by steam in the neighbouring fields, as also steam threshing, sowing by steam and making up a road with a steamroller. Likewise at Keeting, Sussex, one of the largest of the lesser steam rallies, Richard Parrot, the impresario of the event, as well as setting aside 75 acres for the visiting engines, makes a point of threshing 7 acres of corn by steam.[29]

Sunday mechanics, enthusiasts for Victorian engineering tied down, in many cases, to desk jobs during the working days of the week, provided the labour, skill and voluntary effort that got the railway preservation movement off the ground. The more knowledgeable acted as volunteer engine-drivers and firemen, while the true buffs busied themselves in the sheds bringing moribund locomotives and rolling-stock back to life. Sunday mechanics are also, it seems, very much in evidence in the current craze for resuscitating and re-working old pumping stations, the nucleus in some places of a working and industrial museum, but in other places exhibited as spectacles in their own right – 'like a woman taking her clothes off', in the ecstatic words of one admirer of the Brighton 'Engineerium', an old waterworks engine which pumps the water from the valley to the Downs – 'It's outrageously beautiful ... classic'.[30] The Levant Beam Whim, the oldest Cornish-built beam engine in the world, and the sole surviving item of machinery from the famous tin-mine, has been the property of the National Trust since 1967, having previously been rescued from the scrapyard (at a cost of £25) by the Cornish Engines Preservation Committee, later the Trevithick Society. In 1984 the Society asked for volunteers to clean it and get it into running order. The challenge was taken up by Milton Thomas, a former hard-rock mining engineer who had worked in West Africa and later spent twenty-one years teaching in Peterborough before retiring and returning to his native Cornwall. A 'greasy gang' of twelve – 'all of us retired and most of us true Cornishmen' – spent some eight years bringing the engine back to working order and turning it into a prize exhibit of early mining technology.[31]

Independent museums – there are some 1,300 of them, and they are arguably the greatest single influence on the museology of the age[32] – typically begin life, as they always have done, ever since the time of the Tradescants, with the overflowing hoard of an individual obsessive.[33] A small band of supporters gather round, running the museum on their own, though as operations expand part-time labour is taken on. Later ownership may be vested in a trust, transferred to the county museum service, or taken on by the city authorities. Thus the Theatre Museum, Covent Garden, is based on the Enthoven collection – an accumulation which had lain fallow for some twenty years at the V&A, after being bequeathed to the nation by the owner; while the rival Mander-Mitchenson theatre collection is now housed by Lewisham Borough Council.[34]

The Norfolk Rural Life Museum, housed in an eighteenth-century workhouse, was set up on the impetus of a Society of Friends group, who were almost all farmers.[35] The Northern Mill Engine Society – a group of enthusiasts – provided one of the core collections of the Manchester Science and Technology Museum, while the site of the museum – designated in 1983 'Britain's first Urban Heritage Park' – was secured by a successful conservation campaign to save a railway terminus.[36] The Labour History Museum, which after itinerating for some thirty years is now being grandly re-launched by the Manchester city authorities, began life in a very hole-in-the-corner way. In 1963 the town council of Reigate held a series of commemorative events to mark the centenary of Borough status granted by Queen Victoria. Two Labour councillors proposed that the Trades Council should sponsor an Exhibition of Trade Union History and Henry Fry was asked to organize the event. The exhibition was opened on 1 May and for the first time items from Fry's collection were on public view. The publicity generated by the exhibition reached the attention of Walter Southgate, who read of it in *Reynolds' News* and immediately wrote to Fry and his colleagues telling them of his own remarkable collection. The outcome was a broadening of the objects of the society, a change of name to the Trade Union, Labour, Co-operative, Democratic History Society, and negotiations to establish a trust for the Walter Southgate collection, the basis for a future museum.

At this stage, TULC was very much a cottage industry, the collection being stored in a bedroom of Henry Fry's small and crowded home in Reigate and in the garage of Richard West, the chairman of TULC. Fry's house had no telephone, outgoing calls being made from a public call box at the end of the road and incoming calls being made to Richard West, who lived several turnings away. Henry Fry's wife Betty, apart from sharing the home with her husband, two teenage daughters and stacks of memorabilia, provided refreshment and hospitality for curious and inquiring visitors. With scanty funds, the mounting of a series of exhibitions posed enormous problems. The TULC exhibition panels were homemade and to the dismay of professional archivists and museum curators, exhibits were affixed to the panels with drawing pins and Sellotape. Nevertheless, the society flourished and in 1968 purchased a small suburban house in Cornfield Road, Reigate ... a home that claimed to be the 'first visual history centre of Labour'.[37]

The Shipwreck Heritage Centre, Hastings – one of a remarkable line of museums and preserved net-houses that line the front in the Old Town – is a fine example of a more recent do-it-yourself museum. It was started in 1987 by Peter Marsden, an archaeologist at the Museum of London who had made the rescue and reconstitution of ancient ships his speciality. Unable to find a secure home for the ancient timbers he had rescued from the river-bed, and oppressed by a knowledge that 'lots of marvellous things' were being brought up from the sea-bed which would be treated not as historic wrecks but as commercial salvage, he established his own museum to display some of them, to initiate children into the mysteries of marine archaeology, and to provide a repository for divers' or fishermen's finds (one of the Hastings contributions is a stone anchor thrown up on the beach, a 'Roman anchor' as it seems to be called in the town, though Mr Marsden is content to say that it is 'very old').[38]

The female equivalent of the one-man crusade in industrial archaeology seems to be the preservation or reconstitution of the period schoolroom or shop, numbers of which are the focus of 'living history' exhibitions, and 'historical role-play' exercises in the museums, while a few contrive to sustain themselves as museums in their own right. The Kate's Grove schoolroom, Reading, maintained as a 'living museum' within an existing primary school, is a well-supported example, 'a fine example of Board school architecture', whose buildings date from 1872 and 1892. It is the love-child of Wynne Frankum, a part-time primary school teacher. She started her collection, five years ago, with the throw-outs of the Newbury school where she was teaching, built it up by 'making a nuisance of myself' in other schools' attics and cellars, and augmented it by calling on private schools. 'One four-seater desk was found in an orchard. Much of what we have comes from under the tarpaulin.' Interestingly it is the make-believe Victorian school furniture and equipment, devised for projects on 'A Day in the Life of a Victorian School', which are the centre of the museum's activity – in particular the slates on which children are put through their paces in arithmetic, and the copy-books on which they exercise their dip-pens:

> Teachers are very keen on teaching history through role play . . . You have to be a bit of an actress to be a teacher. The children do things instead of just reading about them. They realise what it meant to be treated in this incredibly oppressive way.[39]

Most of those who come to the museum are doing a 'Key Stage' two project on Victorian schooling but there are also 'quite a number of infants' and a few secondary school pupils studying the nineteenth-century novel.

One of the finest collections of printed ephemera in the country – and one whose reproduction, in the 1960s, helped to popularize a taste for Victorian typography – comes from the lucky find of Robert Wood, a Hartlepool schoolmaster and history teacher who in 1958 happened on a number of spike files in an abandoned building: the posters, notices and billheads of John Proctor, one of the town's nineteenth-century printers, who had set up in trade in 1834.[40]

> The sight was almost indescribable. Spike files like Christmas trees, black as soot, had been thrown into a large room till it was full to a height of about four feet. Most of the tiles were off the roof and the rain had seeped through above and the plaster of the ceiling had fallen down. To add to the mess, seagulls had nested in the place and there were two or three dead seagulls lying about.
>
> It was a cold wet February morning, so I dragged the nearest file out and took it along the courtyard to the warmth of the boiler house, where I began to peel off the top layers of jet black paper until I could find something readable. Three or four layers down, the paper was clean and I found myself gazing at the proof sheets of the paper railway tickets issued on the Hartlepool Railway in 1837.

Mr Wood, a hero of British ephemerists, spent the next ten years of his time peeling handbills off the sodden files and separating the rescuable from the irretrievably lost.

It is a measure of the growing ambition of conservationism, as also of a growing belief that artefacts should be preserved, where possible, *in situ*, that a similar find some twenty years on led not to facsimile reproduction of the more appealing prints – the destiny of Mr Wood's collectanea – but to the setting up of a full-fledged working, or 'living history', museum. Discovered by Maurice Rickards, the ephemerist, in the course of his wanderings, and generously donated by the owner, a third-generation small-town printer, to the cause of local history, Smail's, the Scottish National Trust-owned printworks at Innerleithen, on the Scottish borders, has in its office a profusion of ledgers, order-books and files, including the local newspaper, *St Ronans Standard*, which ran from 1893 to 1916. The Guard books contain every invoice, bill-head and fly-poster bill printed by the firm from the day it was founded, to 1986, when it ceased trading. 'They were squirrels. They filed everything.' The machines – a 'Heidelberg' bought in London in the 1950s is the most recent, and a 1900s 'Wharfedale', the prize antique – are, with only one exception, those which Mr Smail was working with when he retired. 'Really it is an absolute time warp' says one who works there as a demonstrator–compositor. 'There was already a working museum because of everything that was there. The Trust [the National Trust of Scotland] had to do very little.'[41]

Notes

1. Patrick Wright, *On Living in an Old Country*, London 1985. For the 'Brideshead' argument, first developed in an article in the *London Review of Books*, see the same writer's *A Journey Through Ruins, The Last Days of London*, London 1991, pp. 45–67.

2. Robert Hewison, *The Heritage Industry; Britain in a Climate of Decline*, London 1987.

3. Richard Johnson, 'Heritage and History', cyclostyled paper and presentation, Amsterdam, 2 October 1993. Cf. Bill Schwarz, 'Historical Patrimony and Citizenship: The English Experience', cyclostyled paper at conference on Historical Patrimony, Sao Paulo, 13 August 1991, p. 8:

> Capital had never shown much interest in history, preferring where possible to destroy whatever inheritances it could lay its hands on. Now capital is into organising the past as well. There has been an extraordinary profusion of high-tech strategies to 'recover' the past – in museums, theme parks, restoration schemes and so on – and re-present it, or more accurately and profanely, sell it to the British and to the nation's visitors. There are now more people employed in Britain in the hotel and tourist trade than there are in coal mining and car production combined.

4. Wright, passim.

5. Robert Hewison, 'Commerce and Culture' in John Corner and Sylvia Harvey, eds, *Enterprise and Heritage; Crosscurrents of National Culture*, London 1991.

6. John Corner and Sylvia Harvey 'Mediating Tradition and Modernity: the Heritage/Enterprise Couplet' in ibid.

7. Bevis Hillier, *Young Betjeman*, London 1988.

8. Nikolaus Pevsner, *Pioneers of Modern Design from William Morris to Walter Gropius*, Harmondsworth 1984, chapter V, 'Engineering and Architecture in the Nineteenth Century', pp. 118–47.

9. Francis Groome, *In Gypsy Tents*, Edinburgh 1880.

10. John Blunden and Nigel Currie, eds, *A People's Charter? Forty Years of the National Parks and Access to the Countryside Act of 1949*, London 1990, p. 114.

11. International Spring Fair, 1990, NEC Birmingham, *Official Catalogue and Buyers' Guide*.

12. Mario Panizza, ed., *Interventi nel Centro Storico*, Bari 1978; Giovanni de Fransiscis, *Ricerca per una Metodologia d'Intervento nei Centri Storici*, Naples 1975; Donald Appleyard, ed., *The Conservation of European Cities*, Cambridge, Mass. 1979.

13. Bob West, 'The Making of the English Working Past: a critical view of the Ironbridge Gorge Museum', in R. Lumley, ed., *The Museum Time-Machine, Putting Culture on Display*, London 1988.

14. 'Thieves Who Are Stealing Our History', *Evening Standard*, 26 November 1990.

15. I am quoting the phrase of Peter Marsden, the marine archaeologist.

16. For the metal detectorists, see the fine portrait by Patrick Wright in *A Journey Through Ruins*, pp. 139–51. 'Roman hoard worth £1.75m', *Evening Standard*, 4 November 1993:

A retired gardener and amateur metal-detector today became a millionaire after learning his treasure trove was worth £1.75 million. Eric Lawes, 69, discovered the Hoxne Hoard, Britain's most important Roman find, last November in a Suffolk field. Today the National Heritage Department disclosed that value as Mr Lawes and wife Getha went into hiding.

17. I am grateful to Michael Stratten of Ironbridge Museum for this information.

18. 'Rust in Peace', *Daily Star*, 3 April 1981:

The edge of a muddy, desolate old deep water dock hardly looks like one of Britain's tourist hot-spots. But over two million people from all over the world have trooped down there for a great free show that rivals the Tower of London. It is a scrap yard: four acres of rusting old metal – waiting among the weeds for the breaker's torch and a fiery end in furnaces of British Steel. But this heap of junk is made up of old railway locomotives. Steam locomotives, pensioned off when British Rail completely turned over to diesel and electric power 14 years ago. One thousand have passed through Dai Woodham's hands at the Barry Yard in South Wales. The 61-year-old boss says: 'When I bought the first one I never realised what would happen.'

19. Adrian Amos, whose LASSCO trades out of a deconsecrated Shoreditch church, the source of some fantastical recent film and stage sets as well as of individual householders' follies, comes from a family of North London builders.

20. Giles Worsley, 'A False Dusk', *Country Life*, July 1993, pp. 88–91. Hugh Massingberd, 'Old Families in Old Houses is a Way to Preserve Them' *Daily Telegraph*, 3 July 1993. SAVE's own country house rescue work, to judge by the interesting account in Marcus Binney and Kit Martin, *The Country House, To Be or Not To Be*, London 1982, seems to have gone hand-in-hand with massive de-gentrification, as the old properties were converted into modern living spaces, very often flats.

21. Frank Parkin, *Middle-Class Radicalism: The Social Bases of the British Campaign for Nuclear Disarmament*, Manchester 1968.

22. Gordon E. Cherry, *The Politics of Town Planning*, London 1982, for the rise of amenity group campaigns; John Tyme, *Motorways versus Democracy*, London 1978 for the successful resistance to the motorway box.

23. Brian Anson, *I'll Fight You For It! Behind the Struggle for Covent Garden*, London 1981 is the interesting account by one of the activists. Terry Christensen, *Neighbourhood Survival*, Dorchester 1979 for another account. Judith Hillman, *The Rebirth of Covent Garden; a Place for People*, London 1986, was the last publication of the Greater London Council.

24. Andrew Gurr with John Orrell, *Rebuilding Shakespeare's Globe*, London 1989 for a valuable account of earlier twentieth-century theatre radicalism; Andrew Gurr and John Orrell, *The Bankside Globe Project*, Coventry 1983; and R. Mulryne and M. Shewring, eds, *The*

Bankside Project, Coventry 1987. For a more embattled view of what is happening on Bankside today, cf. the sixty-seven issues of the Rose Theatre Campaign *Newsletter*, printed daily between May and November 1989 (there is a file of these in Bishopsgate Library).

25. L.T.C. Rolt, *Narrow Boat*, London 1944; *High Horse Riderless*, London 1949; cf. also his later autobiographies, *Landscape with Machines*, London 1971; and *Landscape with Canals*, London 1977.

26. *English Heritage Monitor*, 1977.

27. Chris Edmonds, *A Wager for Ale, The Story of Arthur Napper and the Origins of the Steam Traction Movement*, Henley 1985, p. 26; *A Little and Often*, Henley 1984, for some personal reminiscences. *Old Glory, Vintage Restoration Today* is a monthly glossy on sale at W.H. Smith's and John Menzies. *Steaming* is the newsletter of the Traction Engine Societies. The movement is large enough to afford schisms – the partisans of stationary engines, principally threshing machines, stage their own separatist rallies at Peel Park, Manchester.

28. Edmonds, pp. 27–33, 60.

29. I am grateful to Jon Gorman for this information. Mr Gorman, the son of John Gorman, the printer-historian, and himself a silk-screen printer, makes a show at the fairs with agricultural machines, graduating from fire engines, his original enthusiasm, to work in the Huntingdonshire Fens. Jon Gorman, 'The Abbot's Reformation', *Old Glory*, no. 42, August 1993; 'Three Went to St Ives', ibid., no. 48, February 1994.

30. Oral information, Andy Durr, Brighton. Near Hastings the still more brilliant pumping engine at Brede has a newly-formed Trust to bring it back to life. The initiative here comes from John Loxley, water manager for Southern Water Services. See 'Go with the Flow', *Guardian* February 9, 1994, a picture of John Loxley with Brede pumping station. Mr Loxley is a lifelong steam enthusiast; he was a trustee of the Festiniog railway as far back as 1956 and comes from four generations of railwaymen.

31. Brian Jackman, 'Full Steam Ahead', *The National Trust Magazine*, 1993, pp. 34–6. I am grateful to Ella Westland of Gorrinhaven, Cornwall, for this reference. One point of sociological interest, hinted at in the foregoing, which seems worth taking up explicitly is the phenomenon of what is sometimes called 'The Third Age' and the emergence of environmental and retrieval projects as a new way of having something to pass on to posterity. What is one to make of that party of septuagenarian mechanics, toiling away, over ten years, to re-start a Cornish beam engine; of the retired teachers who act as schoolmarms in museum-based exercises in historical role play; of the retired union official and former firebrand activist, Eddie Frow, who, together with his wife Ruth, and travelling by caravan, has assembled one of the finest libraries of nineteenth-century historical sources in the country?

32. Simon Tait, *Palaces of Discovery, The Changing World of Britain's Museums*, London 1989, p. 33.

33. Mea Allan, *The Tradescants*, London 1964; Prudence Leith-Ross, *The John Tradescants, Gardeners to the Rose and Lily*, London 1984.

34. *The Oxford Companion to the Theatre*, Oxford 1983, p. 260; M.I. Williams, ed., *A Directory of Rare Books and Special Collections in the United Kingdom and the Republic of Ireland*, London 1985, pp. 280–1, 367.

35. Nick Mansfield, 'The George Edwards Celebration', in Society for the Study of Labour History, 'Labour History in Museums', *Papers*, Sheffield 1988.

36. 'The History of the Museum and Its Site', cyclostyled paper, 1993, and information from the curator, Gabriel Porter.

37. John Gorman, *Images of Labour*, London 1985, pp. 12–13.

38. I am grateful to Steve Peak, of the Hastings Fishermen's Protection Society, and to Mr Marsden for the information in this paragraph.

39. I am grateful to Wynne Frankum for this narrative. The Sevington School Project, near Marlborough, stages 'living history' exercises at a former village school, closed in 1913 and reopened, as a museum, in 1992. Joe Laurie, the museum's officer in charge of it, has joined with Wynne Frankum to produce *The Victorian School Day*, Wiltshire County Council 1992.

40. Maurice Rickards, *This Is Ephemera, Collecting Printed Throwaways*, Newton Abbott 1978, pp. 33–4; John Lewis, *Collecting Printed Ephemera, a Background to Social Habits*

and Social History, to Eating and Drinking, to Travel and Heritage, and Just for Fun, London 1976, p. 114.

41. Elizabeth Grieg, 'The Day We Looked in on the Printer', the *Ephemerist*, June 1990, pp. 344–5. I am grateful to Alison Cox, compositor–curator at the museum, for much information about it.

PART IV

Flogging a Dead Horse

Heritage-baiting

'Heritage' is a term which has been serviceable to the local authorities, who have used it to promote town improvement schemes and to extract government money for service sector jobs. It has been one of the flagships of nature conservancy and the environmentalist movements of our time. In cases like the campaign for Oxleas Wood, it is a rallying point for opposition to the property developers and a challenge to the powers that be. Heritage is also popular with the general public, who seem untroubled by the philippics launched against it. 'Historic' towns (including such newly historicized ones as Rochester-upon-Medway) ancient monuments (a category nowadays extended to industrial heritage sites), country parks, working farms and wildlife reserves, provide a natural focus for Sunday outings and weekend breaks – rather as the spectacle of the new, or the wonders of science and invention, used to do in the days when the promise of modernization was undimmed (on Whit-Monday, 1871, some seventy thousand visitors are said to have flocked to Liverpool to see the new warehouses). On summer holidays, nature 'mystery trails' and 'historic' walks minister to the romance of place; living history museums and theme parks offer a vivid encounter with the past – for some children it may be a first one; while steam railways offer a journey back in time – last year they carried some fifty million summer season passengers.

Intellectually, on the other hand, 'heritage' has had a very bad press, and it is widely accused of wanting to commodify the past and turn it into tourist kitsch. Aesthetes of both Right and Left, though especially perhaps the latter, have found it offensive, accusing it of packaging the past, and presenting a 'Disneyfied' version of history in place of the real thing. Purists have objected to the schemes promoted in its name, arguing that it blurs the line between entertainment and education and warning that, as with church restoration in the nineteenth century, it will replace real-life survivals with simulacra of an original that never was.[1]

Heritage has also emerged as one of the principal whipping-boys of

Cultural Studies, a prime example of those tutelary complexes which it is the vocation of critical inquiry to unmask. They cast it in the role of a 'project' designed at once to anaesthetize and 'sanitize' the record of the past while making it harmless and unthreatening in the present.

Heritage-baiting has become a favourite sport of the metropolitan intelligentsia, the literary end of it especially. Barely a week goes by without it being targeted for abuse in one or other of the 'quality' newspapers, and indeed *The Independent*, taking up arms against the restrictive covenants imposed on the owners of 'listed' buildings, has taken to calling conservation officers 'the heritage police'.[2] The arts columns of the newspaper follow suit. For Tom Paulin, never at a loss for expletives where Ukanian matters are at issue, and flagging a recent *Independent*-sponsored conference on the subject, 'The British heritage industry is a loathsome collection of theme parks and dead values'.[3] Even the television correspondent of *The Independent* weighs in: 'A medal to whichever TV critic it was who blew the whistle on Morse, saying, in effect, that he was a boring and pretentious middle-brow snob. The enormous, almost religious, following that John Thaw's detective amassed must have something to do with the comforting "Brideshead-effect" of the series' timeless Oxford back-drop'.[4]

Heritage is accused of wanting to turn the country into a gigantic museum, mummifying the present as well as the past, and preserving tradition in aspic. Exchequer grants to Environmentally Sensitive Areas – where farmers are subsidized to retain and enhance traditional features of the landscape and wildlife habitats – are currently under attack: according to the Whitehall correspondents they are potential targets for the next round of Treasury economies. In a kindred vein, though here the attack comes from the Left rather than the Right, the National Trust is accused of featherbedding the owners of historic properties, insulating them from the cost of maintaining their establishments, and allowing them, however impecunious, to continue in a life of pampered ease and upholstered luxury.

Local authority interventions in the field of heritage are routinely savaged, and treated with derision as though they were necessarily an exercise in bad taste (a recent article in *The Independent* lampooned the municipal authorities in York for building a neo-Georgian public lavatory; an earlier one ridiculed the City of Westminster for putting up 'heritage' traffic-lights in the West End).[5] This is one of the very few spheres of municipal enterprise in which public sector employment, instead of contracting, has actually contrived to expand, and it may be that the critics, though coming from the Left, have taken on, as if by osmosis, the authentic accents of that New Right for whom the very idea of the public is suspect.[6]

Heritage, according to the critics, is the mark of a sick society, one which, despairing of the future, had become 'besotted' or 'obsessed' with an idealized version of its past.[7] The historicist turn in British culture, which they date from 1975 – the year when the term 'heritage' began its inflationary career – corresponded to the onset of economic recession, the contraction of manufacturing industry and the return of mass unemployment. It testified to the collapse of British power. Heritage prepared the way for, or could be thought of as giving expression to, a recrudescence of 'Little Englandism' and the revival of nationalism as a force in political life. It anticipated and gave expression to the triumph of Thatcherism in the sphere of high politics. Heritage, in short, was a symbol of national decadence; a malignant growth which testified at once to the strength of this country's *ancien régime* and to the weakness of radical alternatives to it. It was an admission, according to Robert Hewison in *The Heritage Industry* (1987) that history was 'over'.[8] In Patrick Wright's *On Living in an Old Country* it was 'part of the self-fulfilling culture of national decline'.[9]

Historians have been only too ready to join in this chorus of disdain, accusing heritage of travestying the past and counterposing its ersatz and kitsch to the allegedly objective inquiries pursued in the world of higher research.[10] David Cannadine, who from his American fastness seems never to tire of deriding 'this heritage junk',[11] charges it with encouraging a bunker mentality and attempting to imprison the country in a time-warp. He was already sounding a warning note in 1983, on the eve of his departure from these shores. 'Not since the 1890s or the 1930s has the worship of wistfulness been so widespread. And there in part lies the explanation; then, as now, depression is the begetter of nostalgia, disenchantment the handmaiden of escapism. As before, when the shopkeepers go out of business, we become a nation of ruminators'.[12] Interestingly the History Working Party, drawing up their recommendations for the new core curriculum, and strongly committed to the study of both material culture and the built environment, nevertheless felt obliged to distance themselves from a word which had become contaminated, proposing to use instead – a distinction, surely, without a difference – 'inheritance':

> We have been careful to minimise the use of the word 'heritage' because it has various meanings and is in danger of becoming unhelpfully vague. For historical purposes the word 'inheritance' may be more precise in its meaning, implying 'that which the past has bequeathed to us'.... While all people in Britain partake to a greater or lesser extent of a shared 'inheritance' they also have their own individual, group, family, etc. 'inheritances' which are inter-related. The study of history should respect and make clear this pattern of inheritances.[13]

For many radicals, 'heritage' is a sore on the body politic, reinforcing, or imposing, a reactionary version of the national past; feeding on fantasies of vanished supremacies; ministering to nostalgia for a time that never was. Neal Ascherson gave eloquent voice to these doubts when, in an influential series of articles in the *Observer*, he characterized heritage as being 'right-wing' and accused it of pandering to what he was pleased to call – with fine disregard to the parallel developments taking place in relation to Historic Scotland – 'vulgar English nationalism'.[14] Heritage, he argued, was a consolatory myth, entropy in holiday dress; it was the tourist industry's answer to secular economic decay:

> Where there were mines and mills, now there is Wigan Pier Heritage Centre, where you can pay to crawl through a model coal mine, watch dummies making nails, and be invited 'in' by actors and actresses dressed as 1900 proletarians. Britain, where these days a new museum opens every fortnight, is becoming a museum itself.[15]

Ascherson's use of the word 'vulgar' when complaining of the effrontery, or 'vulgar arrogance', of living history's claim to have opened a hot-line to the past, is worth pausing on. It may seem a strange epithet to issue from the lips of one who is on public record as a socialist, a republican and a democrat, but it is not that strange. As moral aristocrats, waging war on the corruptions of capitalist society, socialists, like the radical nonconformists who preceded them, have often been at their fiercest when denouncing Vanity Fair, or what Aneurin Bevan called in his last great speech the 'vulgar materialism' of capitalist society.[16] And from the time of William Morris onwards they have been apt to rebuke the masses for what another great Labour leader, Ernest Bevin, called the 'poverty' of their desires. In Ascherson's case, those attitudes are compounded by literary snobbery, an apparent belief that the only true knowledge is that which is to be found in books. Heritage is a fraud because it relies on surface appearance; like colour television, it takes the people's mind off higher (or deeper) things:

> The Total Museum, though it can entertain, is a lie. Pretending to open a window into the past is a technique which weakens imagination much in the way that colour television weakens the intuition, whereas radio – by its incompleteness – so strongly stimulates it.... The claim to be able to 'recreate' history is a vulgar arrogance.[17]

'Heritage', then, is accused of displaying the ignorance and brashness of the upstart. It is also by definition flashy, as meretricious as the baubles of Vanity Fair.

> The heritage industry is a fraud. What happened to the people living in these

islands can't be dug up, polished and sold. The past is not recoverable like some diamond brooch from the Titanic, partly because it is alive within us. It follows that the 'here is the past' display of heritage is not only a deception, but – more dangerously – a wall built across our awareness of history, and across the links between past and present.

Given an initial impetus, in this country, by Robert Hewison's 1987 squib *The Heritage Industry*, and a more substantial one by Patrick Wright's *On Living in an Old Country*, heritage-baiting rapidly established itself as a steady earner for TV documentarists, journalists on safari, and the writers of features in the quality press. Academics – radical academics – weighed in, proving, at least to their own satisfaction and that of Cultural Studies course-designers, that museums were a prison-house of artefacts, and souvenirs and gift shops a way of commodifying the past. By 1991, as a programme note suggests, exposures of heritage were competing with one another for prime time on the airwaves:

> *Chronicle: Past for Sale?* (BBC-2, 8.10) and *Signals: Theme Park Britons* (Channel 4, 9.15). It's rotten luck on both parties that these two very respectable programmes on the same theme should be scheduled for the same night. Both are concerned about heritage, the country's largest growth industry, and with the way our past is packaged and dispensed like so much fast food in heritage centres and theme parks. Each highlights the concern that historical truth and local needs are sacrificed to profit as the entrepreneurs appropriate from the museums the role of informing us about our past.
>
> One loving shot of a perfect Georgian window in *Chronicle* sums it up – the house is to go to make way for a Roman Heritage Centre flogging imitation antiquities, conceived by its designer as a 'Roman EastEnders'.[18]

Flogging a Dead Horse, the recent exhibition at the Photographers Gallery – sponsored by the Arts Council and now reproduced as a coffee-table book with king-size colour reproductions and text by a presenter of *The Late Show*[19] – might be described as anti-heritage's coming-of-age, a kind of *pot-pourri* of its clichés. The work of a colour documentarist, it takes in all the familiar targets, following a well-worn itinerary – a kind of anti-heritage trail – first marked out by Robert Hewison. Starting with The Northern Experience in County Durham, moving on to The Way We Were heritage centre at Wigan Pier (always good for a metropolitan sneer), it ends up with some softer Home Counties target – in this case 'Edward Elgar' country at Worcester.

Flogging a Dead Horse, a photographic commentary on 'hyper-history', cast as a critique 'not simply . . . of heritage' but also 'of the very notions of Englishness', is a sustained essay in disgust, in the manner of Wegee and Diane Arbus, though in colour rather than black-and-white, and with ordinary people – Northerners especially – as the grotesques rather than midgets and freaks. The Northern Experience at Beamish Hall, County Durham, is represented by a middle-aged man squinting uncomfortably through the eyepiece of a video camera; the Brontë museum at Haworth by a fat man and his even fatter wife standing by the churchyard wall looking hot and bothered. Ironbridge – 'birthplace of the Industrial Revolution', now designated a World Heritage Site – is represented by, of all things, a white-haired man with a Rottweiler straining at the leash (just in case we miss the point, the text tells us that he looks 'like a gauleiter'). On an open-topped bus tour of Liverpool's Albert Dock, two elderly ladies gawp. At Eden Camp, the Second World War theme park at Malton, Yorkshire, an overweight grandad, shot from below in order to make him look sinister, bring out his double chin and exaggerate the size of his hands, stares sightlessly into space, while the little boy at his side clasps 'The Great War Play Set'. At Wigan Pier Heritage Centre a young boy with a Mickey Mouse tee-shirt watches a pit-brow girl pushing a coal-wagon. The Vintage Tram Museum at Crich, Derbyshire, is represented by the headless torso of a boy clad in lavender-coloured Bermuda shorts; Westminster Abbey by the rear view of a bald-headed man looking at nothing.

Though directed against the packaging of history, *Flogging a Dead Horse* is a slick production, using a series of stratagems to make its images repellent. Angles and frames are so manipulated as to make every picture out of joint; objects and viewers are juxtaposed so as to diminish the one and belittle the other. We are never once shown the objects themselves – they exist as a kind of mocking commentary on the sightseers. In the manner of 1980s avant-garde photography the people are pictured in a state of alienation, looking neither at each other nor at the objects they have ostensibly come to view. Even though most of the photography is in the open air it looks studio-lit, so that the people are unnaturally flushed; the interior scenes are cropped to look claus-trophobic.

Behind the critique of heritage lie residues of that conspiracy theory according to which historical change is engineered by ruling elites, and popular taste is at the mercy of what 1960s and 1970s radicals took to calling the manipulations of 'the media'. In France this took the sophisticated form of countercultural high theory, developed by Michel Foucault in relation to the tutelary complexes of knowledge and power, and more specifically in relation to museum culture by Pierre Bourdieu and Philippe Hoyau.[20] In the United States it was rather an extension of the 1960s radical critique of 'consumerism'.[21] In Britain, where the rise of heritage was identified with the victory of New Right politics, a more traditional notion of the ruling class came to the fore and 'heritage' was said to represent a kind of return of the repressed, a victory of feudal reaction. It was a 'project' or 'strategy' (so radical critics alleged) undertaken on behalf of the wealthy, the privileged and the powerful, and actively promoted by the ruling elites.[22] It deployed a dominant form of 'Englishness', played with reactionary fantasies, and threatened to make the country-house version of the national past (or even, as the Birmingham Centre for Contemporary Cultural Studies argued, the Warwick Castle one) hegemonic. For Neal Ascherson it heralded the advent of a permanent Conservative majority:

> The heritage industry, like the proposed 'core curriculum' of history for English schools, imposes one ruling group's version of history on everyone and declares that it cannot be changed. One of the marks of the feudal *ancien régime* was that the dead governed the living. A mark of a decrepit political system must surely be that a fictitious past of theme parks and costume dramas governs the present.[23]

The denigration of 'heritage', though voiced in the name of radical politics, is pedagogically quite conservative and echoes some of the right-wing jeremiads directed against 'new history' in the schools. Like the videos, slide-shows or classroom exercises in 'empathy' it is accused of taking the mind out of history, offering a Cook's tour or package-holiday view of the past as a substitute for the real thing.[24] It abolishes, or seems to abolish, the distinction between work and play, and turns potential learners into passive consumers. It invites spurious identifications, robbing the past of its terrors and turning it into an ideal home. Still worse – a kind of ultimate profanity in the eyes of the purists – is the use of the performing arts, as with the actors and actresses who dress up in period costumes and act as demonstrators, interpreters and guides. The 'hands-on', interactive 'living history' displays at the museums are almost equally suspect, offering a Pick-'n'-Mix approach to the past in place of a coherent explanation or progressive narrative.

The charge of vulgarity could be said to be a leitmotiv of heritage criticism, and may account for the frequency with which heritage is bracketed with theme parks, toytowns and Disneyland. The association with the world of entertainment is clearly a cause of great offence, inviting the scorn of the high-minded, mingling as it does the sacred and the profane, high culture and low. Heritage is accused of trivializing the past, playing with history, focusing on unworthy objects. Its predilection for dressing up is thought of as childish, while its association with the holiday trades is almost by definition demeaning. The scorn is no doubt spontaneous but it does not seem fanciful to point to the lineal descent from those ancient notions of the 'dignity' of history against which Lord Macaulay inveighed when calling for a recognition of the domestic and the demotic. Fact and fiction, the imaginary and the real, like the sacred and the profane, are supposed to be at war. In a context like this, the very idea of spectacle, with its undertones of the theatrical and its reliance on glitter, is offensive.

Heritage is also discredited, in the eyes of its critics, by its association with what used to be called, in the heyday of aristocratic snobbery, 'trade'; but which in post-1960 critical theory, or Cultural Studies, is more apt to be labelled 'consumerism' and conceptualized as the Emperor's New Clothes. It is accused of making history a selling point; of trading on nostalgia; of commodifying the past. Here, as elsewhere, *Flogging a Dead Horse* has it off pat. A Brechtian slogan: 'THE PAST IS UP FOR SALE' – given a full-page spread – interrupts the flow of images, and serves as a kind of black-and-white equivalent to the voice-over. Constable's 'Hay Wain' is overprinted with a magenta-coloured price flash suggesting that, at 99p a time, the treasures of the past can come cheap. In another ironical juxtaposition a studious-looking man is peering at a shelf-full of souvenirs in which regional types, such as the 'Geordie' and the 'Collier lass', are cased as mannequins and reduced to doll-like figures. The message is rammed home in the double-page spread which brings the book to a close. Taken from the 'Elgar Country', Worcester, it superimposes the 'M' of a McDonald's American diner over the moustachioed elegance of an Edwardian tailor's dummy, and juxtaposes a group of denimed modern youths with the flannelled fools of a period cricket photograph (the modern youths, photographed from behind, are faceless clothes-horses, meaninglessly gesturing in the empty air; the Edwardian cricketers, highly individuated, and no doubt among the first to volunteer in 1914, stare back at us with all the poignancy of the fallen dead).[25]

Arguably it is not the traditionalism but the modernism and more specifically the postmodernism of heritage which offends. Aesthetes condemn it for being bogus: a travesty of the past, rather than a true likeness, let alone – the preservationist's dream – an original. In other words, in spite of the charge that heritage is imprisoning the country in a time-warp, and the accusation that it is sentimentalizing the past, heritage is being attacked not because it is too historical but because it is not historical enough. It lacks authenticity. It is a simulation pretending to be the real thing. It is not because heritage is too reverent about the past that it provokes outrage, but on the contrary the fact that, in the eyes of the critics at least, it seems quite untroubled when it is dealing with replicas and pastiche.

Literary snobbery also comes into play: the belief that only books are serious; perhaps too a suspicion of the visual, rooted in a Puritan or Protestant distrust of graven images. Artefacts – whether they appear as images on the television screen, in costume drama, or as 'living history' displays in the museums and the theme parks – are not only inferior to the written word but, being by their nature concerned with surface appearance only, irredeemably shallow. Here Neal Ascherson's preference for wireless over television and his real hatred for open-air heritage displays is worth pausing on: reading a book is strenuous and demanding; spectacle – and here Ascherson is following a well-worn line in cultural criticism – is something which is passively consumed. The first is an intellectual activity; the second is mindless. The unspoken assumption is that people cannot be trusted with pictures; that images seduce where the printed word engages the full intelligence.[26]

Some of the hostility aroused by the idea of heritage may be misogynist, and it is perhaps indicative of this that in the attacks on the 'commodification' of the past so much animus is directed against what is almost entirely a female gift culture – pot-pourris and toiletries, of the kind on sale at the National Trust gift shops, earning particular derision.[27] In the case of *Flogging a Dead Horse*, however, it is not the tea-shop ladies, those ancient targets of macho abuse, but the spectacle of the Northern working class – young and old, men and women – which excites sexual disgust. In the camera's eye they are no less repellent when smiling than when scowling, and it is difficult to imagine them doing anything which might make them appealing, or earn them a modicum of dignity and respect.

Something might be said too about social condescension. The idea that the masses, if left to their own devices, are moronic; that their pleasures are unthinking; their tastes cheapo and nasty, is a favourite conceit of the aesthete – as it was of their predecessors, the moralists and philanthropists who, in the manner of Philip Stubbes' *Anatomie of Abuses*, took up arms against the meretricious attractions of Vanity Fair. Behind the radical rhetoric of such an exhibition as *Flogging a Dead Horse* it is not difficult to find echoes of the Arnoldian belief that anything connected with commerce was by definition 'vulgar', that provincials were necessarily Philistine, and the populace uncultured. Superimposed on this are the familiar Leavisite themes derived from the cultural criticism of the 1930s and 1940s, according to which mass civilization is by its very nature degraded, and popular tastes, as they succumb to it, debased.[28]

Reas, in line with the film-school teaching of the 1970s and 1980s, wants to challenge the illusions of authenticity and to offer, in place of fixed images, a free-floating assembly of shapes which refuse any simple reading. And he seems to want to subvert those sentimentalized ideas of 'The Northern Experience', which *Coronation Street* and the 'new-wave' realism of the 1960s did so much to popularize. But his alienated figures conform to current film-school orthodoxy, and they also rejoin an older iconography, memorably represented in the Margate funfair of Lindsay

Anderson's *O Dreamland* and the Piccadilly Circus of Alain Tanner's *Nice Time*, in which pleasuregoing is represented as repulsive. It also echoes the age-old belief of the high-minded that the masses are being culturally debased. His 'heritage industry' is a kind of 1990s version of those 'mechanized' and 'Americanized' amusements, 'standardized' shows, and 'passive' audiences which J.B. Priestley in his 1934 portrait of holiday-making, and John Osborne in *The Entertainer*, contrasted to the 'old roaring Variety turns' of the Edwardian music hall.[29]

Theme parks – doubly offensive because they seem to come to us from America, and because they link history to the holiday industry – are a particular bugbear for the critics. As engines of corruption, or seducers of the innocent, they seem to occupy the symbolic space of those earlier folk-devils of the literary imagination, jukeboxes and transistor radios, or – the particular object of Richard Hoggart's spleen in *The Uses of Literacy* (1957) – candy-floss and milk-bars.[30] In contemporary left-wing demonology they have become the latest in a long line of opiates of the masses, on a par with Butlin's holiday camps and bingo halls in the 1950s; 'canned entertainment' and 'Hollywood films' in the 1930s, or what J.B. Priestley feared was the 'Blackpooling' of English life and leisure.[31] Their appeals are by definition meretricious and mechanical; their pleasures mindless, pandering to the lowest tastes. As the science-fiction writer E.L. Doctorow has put it, these simulated environments only offer 'shorthand culture for the masses ... a mindless thrill like an electric shock, that insists at the same time on the recipient's rich psychic relation to his country's history and language and literature. In a forthcoming time of highly governed masses in an overpopulated world this technique may be extremely useful as a substitute for education and, eventually, as a substitute for experience.'

For the aesthete, anyway for the alienated and the disaffected, heritage is a mechanism of cultural debasement. It leaves no space for the contemplative or the solitary. It forbids discrimination and the exercise of good taste. Its pleasures are cheap and nasty, confounding high and low, originals and copies, the authentic and the pastiche. It brings 'crowd pollution', in the form of mass tourism, to sacred spots, surrounds art treasures with crocodiles of visitors, and turns ancient monuments into spectacles for the ignorant to gawp at.[32]

The hostility of historians to heritage, though different in kind from that of the aesthetes, is no less overdetermined. Our whole training predisposes us to give a privileged place to the written word, to hold the visual (and the verbal) in comparatively low esteem, and to regard imagery as a kind of trap. Books, from an early age, are our bosom companions; libraries rather than museums are our natural habitat. If we use graphics at all it will be for purposes of illustration, seldom as primary texts, and it may be indicative of this that, as with material artefacts, we do not even have footnote conventions for referencing them. The fetishization of archives – fundamental to the Rankean revolution in historical scholarship – reinforces these biases, giving a talismanic importance to manuscripts. Even when our point of address is material culture – as in, say, current preoccupations with consumerism or changes in the use of domestic space – our evidence is more likely to be drawn from manuscript remains: probate inventories or household budgets rather than museum exhibits or archaeological finds (a rare exception is Margaret Spufford's use of a cambric handkerchief to reconstruct the itinerary of a seventeenth-century pedlar).[33]

Modern conditions of research seem to dictate an almost complete detachment from the material environment – indeed, to follow the recommendations of some migrant scholars, it is a positive advantage to be writing English history from the other side of the Atlantic. We do not go out on archaeological walks, as our Victorians forebears did, or learn the lie of the land – as Marc Bloch and R.H. Tawney recommended – by putting on a stout pair of boots. We are unlikely to spend our summer vacations, as students, poring over the mysteries of numismatics, as the young Charles Oman did in his apprentice days as a scholar,[34] nor staking out positions on a battlefield, as Thomas Carlyle did when preparing his *Letters and Speeches of Oliver Cromwell*.[35] The computer-literate, calling up a transatlantic or Antipodean printout, or down-loading information from a terminal, may not even have to leave the study.

Retrieval work is no part of our scholarly brief. We do not have to rescue our evidence from the teeth of the bulldozer, as archaeologists do, or call in the aid of the scuba-divers or the aerial photographers in search of an elusive quarry. Nor do we need a preservation order to protect our sources from the depredations of agribusiness, as is the case with those archaeologically sensitive landscapes protected under the Countryside Act of 1979. Blessed (or burdened) with a superabundance of records, we see no need to augment their number but are content to wait on the archivists and librarians, devoting our energies instead to record linkage or the exploitation of hitherto neglected files. With the exception of pre-Conquest scholars who, like classical historians, are heavily reliant on such fugitive remains as monumental inscriptions and burial mounds, we are very little interested in the evidence of material artefacts: we may initiate our students in the mysteries of the record office, but hardly of the cemetery or the dig.

The idea of 'living history' is even more remote from our scholarly routines – as well as being, in the eyes of the fastidious, offensive. We do not devote our sabbaticals to reconstituting a period street, nor spend our weekend breaks, or summer holidays, getting up steam on the footplate. Demographic historians, testing out their theories, do not dress up as Victorian mothers and fathers or pretend to be overseers of the poor. Economic historians, weighing the pros and cons of the machinery question, do not feel obliged to join in a steam ploughing match or crank a fairground engine into life; nor, studying the statistics of overseas trade, are they likely to feel moved to test out the speed of a tea-clipper by sailing one in a tall ships regatta or entering it for a North Sea and Baltic or cross-Channel race. Seventeenth-century scholars, preoccupied with their own internecine warfare, do not join in the annual re-enactments of the siege of Chepstow Castle or the Battle of Marston Moor.

The hostility of historians to heritage is possibly exacerbated by the fact that they are in some sort competing for the same terrain. Each, after its own fashion, claims to be representing the past 'as it was'. Each too could be said to be obsessed with the notion of 'period', though the one renders it through zeitgeist; the other in terms of icons. Interpretation, the privilege of the archive-based historian, and 're-creation', the ambition of heritage, also share a common conceit; the belief that scrupulous attention to detail will bring the dead to life.

Does envy play some part? Heritage has a large public following, mass-membership organizations whose numbers run to hundreds of thousands, whereas our captive audiences in the lecture hall or the seminar room can sometimes be counted on the fingers of one hand. Heritage involves tens of thousands of volunteers. It can command substantial exchequer subsidies, and raise large sums by appealing to the historically minded public. It has royal patronage, and enjoys support from politicians of all stripes. It fuels popular campaigns and is at the very centre of current controversy about the shape of the built environment. It can mount festivals and pageants. It enlists corporate sponsorship and support for its retrieval projects. It is something which people care passionately about; where they are ready to enter the arena of public debate rather as, in the old days, they were ready to re-rehearse the rights and wrongs of the Norman Conquest or the English Civil War.

Whatever the reasons, history and heritage are typically placed in opposite camps. The first is assigned to the realm of critical inquiry, the second to a merely antiquarian preoccupation, the classification and hoarding of things. The first, so the argument runs, is dynamic and concerned with development and change; the second is static. The first is concerned with explanation, bringing a sceptical intelligence to bear on the complexities and contradictoriness of the record; the second sentimentalizes, and is content merely to celebrate.

If the parable of the motes and beams were followed, as it should be, few of the historians' practices would emerge unscathed. Are we not guilty ourselves of turning knowledge into an object of desire? And is it not the effect, if not the intention, of our activity as historians to domesticate the past and rob it of its terrors by bringing it within the realm of the knowable? Historians are no less concerned than conservationists to make their subjects imaginatively appealing. We may not prettify the past in the manner of English Heritage or the National Trust, but we are no less adept than conservation officers and museum curators at tying up loose ends and removing unsightly excrescences. We use vivid detail and thick description to offer images far clearer than any reality could be. Do we not require of our readers, when facing them with one of our period reconstructions, as willing a suspension of disbelief as the 'living history' spectacle of the open-air museum or theme park? Is not the historical monograph, after its fashion, as much a packaging of the past as costume drama? And do we not call on our own *trompe-l'œil* devices to induce a hallucinatory sense of oneness with the past, using 'evocative' detail as a gauge of authenticity?

The perceived opposition between 'education' and 'entertainment', and the unspoken and unargued-for assumption that pleasure is almost by definition mindless, ought not to go unchallenged. There is no reason to think that people are more passive when looking at old photographs or film footage, handling a museum exhibit, following a local history trail, or even buying a historical souvenir, than when reading a book. People do not simply 'consume' images in the way in which, say, they buy a bar of chocolate. As in any reading, they assimilate them as best they can to pre-existing images and narratives. The pleasures of the gaze – scopophilia as it is disparagingly called – are different in kind from those of the written word but not necessarily less taxing on historical reflection and thought.

Notes

1. David Lowenthal, *The Past is a Foreign Country*, Cambridge 1985, p. 341; Richard North, 'Welcome to the Smile Zone', *Independent*, 17 September 1988; George Hill, 'Are We Forging our History', *The Times*, 12 March 1992.

2. 'Pensioners Forced to Remove Windows', *Independent*, 24 August 1993; 'Do Not Pass Go', ibid., 31 July 1993; 'Who will Protect us From the Protectors', ibid., 1 December 1993; 'Can We Have our Square Back', ibid., 15 February 1994; 'Conservation, the Last Straw', ibid., 28 July 1993 is a cautionary tale about a Dorset householder who used what the county officers of English Heritage believed to be an unsuitable foreign thatch.

3. 'Question of Real Value', *Independent*, 5 October 1993.

4. Television programme notes, *Independent*, 1 September 1993. A mild protest seems in order here since part of the point of Inspector Morse is that he is indifferent to Oxford's charms, and indeed seems to have chosen the police career in recoil from them. In any event it would be difficult to imagine a world further removed from that of Zuleika Dobson or the young Charles Ryder than Inspector Morse's murderous square mile.

5. 'A New York but not a Better One', *Independent*, 7 July 1993.

6. Patrick Wright, 'Our Island Story', *Guardian*, 1 October 1993, and Common Ground, *Local Distinctiveness*, London 1993.

7. David Cannadine, 'The Past in the Present' in Lesley Smith, ed., *Echoes of Greatness*, London 1988, p. 10.

8. Robert Hewison, *The Heritage Industry, Britain in a Climate of Decline*, London 1987, p. 141.

9. Wright, *On Living in an Old Country*, London 1987.

10. David Starkey, 'A House fit to House our Nation's History', *Independent*, 28 February 1994, expressed alarm at a version of Gresham's Law in which, as he discerns it, the bad history is driving out the good. 'Certainly we can have too much history of the wrong sort; too many Merchant/Ivory British Country House films; too much Crabtree and Evelyn In-My-Lady's-Chamber smelly scent and soap.'

11. BBC Radio 3, 'Nightwaves', 5 January 1993.

12. David Cannadine, 'Brideshead Revered', *London Review of Books*, 31 March 1983; cf. also *The Pleasures of the Past*, London 1989.

13. National Curriculum History Working Group, *Final Report*, London 1990, pp. 10–11.

14. Neal Ascherson, ' "Heritage" as Vulgar English Nationalism', *Observer*, 29 November 1987.

15. Neal Ascherson, 'Why "Heritage" is Right-Wing', *Observer*, 8 November 1987. For this writer's more recent variations on the theme, 'Reminders from the Past to Suspend our Disbelief', *Independent on Sunday*, 26 April 1992; 'It May not be Art ...' *Independent on Sunday*, 2 January 1994; 'What Should We Preserve', *Independent*, 16 October 1993.

16. Michael Foot, *Aneurin Bevan*, vol. II, London 1973.

17. Ascherson, ' "Heritage" as Vulgar English Nationalism'.

18. Television Notes, *Independent*, 10 October 1989.

19. Paul Reas and Stuart Cosgrove, *Flogging a Dead Horse: Heritage Culture and its Role in Post-Industrial Britain*, Manchester 1993.

20. Philippe Hoyau, 'L'Année du Patrimoine ou la Societé de Conservation', in *Les Révoltes Logiques*, 12, summer 1980, translated in R. Lumley, ed., *The Museum Time-Machine*.

21. Sharon Zukin, *Landscapes of Power; from Detroit to Disney World*, Berkeley 1991.

22. Richard Johnson, 'Reading National Heritage as Social Politics', cyclostyled paper, 'The Making and Unmaking of the Patriotic Past', Amsterdam, 1–2 October 1993; and cf. more generally the work of the Birmingham CCCs popular memory group, 1980–86.

23. Neal Ascherson, 'Why "Heritage" is Right-Wing'.

24. Hugh Pearman, ' "Wider Still and Wider". Uproar over Extension to Elgar Shrine', *Sunday Times*, 9 May 1993.

25. *Flogging a Dead Horse*.

26. Ascherson, 'Why "Heritage" is Right-Wing'.

27. Heritage-baiting is an almost exclusively male sport, and one way – it might be suggested – in which literary men can prove themselves manly. It is remarkable how often it is the pot-pourri and toiletries side of 'heritage' which is singled out for ridicule. Is it that the manifestation of femininity compounds the offence, or was it in some cases the original cause of disgust?

28. Q.D. Leavis, *Fiction and the Reading Public*, London 1932, paid popular culture the compliment of taking it seriously; *Scrutiny* was more apt to treat it as a simple degeneracy.

29. J.B. Priestley, *English Journey*, London 1934.

30. Richard Hoggart's denunciation of an earlier import from the United States – milk-bars – seems worth reproducing as a caution against a too immediate hostility to what is alien and innovatory:

> Like the cafés I described in an earlier chapter, the milk-bars indicate at once, in the nastiness of their modernistic knick-knacks, their glaring showiness, an aesthetic breakdown so complete that, in comparison with them, the layout of the living-rooms in some of the poor homes from which the customers come seems to speak of a tradition as balanced and civilized as an eighteenth-century town house. I am not

thinking of those milk-bars which are really quick-service cafés where one may have a meal more quickly than in a café with table-service. I have in mind rather the kind of milk-bar – there is one in almost every northern town with more than, say, fifteen thousand inhabitants – which has become the regular evening rendezvous of some of the young men. Girls go to some, but most of the customers are boys aged between fifteen and twenty, with drape-suits, picture ties, and an American slouch. Most of them cannot afford a succession of milkshakes, and make cups of tea serve for an hour or two whilst – and this is their main reason for coming – they put copper after copper into the mechanical record-player. About a dozen records are available at any time; a numbered button is pressed for the one wanted, which is selected from a key to titles. The records seem to be changed about once a fortnight by the hiring firm; almost all are American; almost all are 'vocals' and the styles of singing much advanced beyond what is normally heard on the Light Programme of the B.B.C. Some of the tunes are catchy; all have been doctored for presentation so that they have the kind of beat which is currently popular; much use is made of the 'hollow-cosmos' effect which echo-chamber recording gives. They are delivered with great precision and competence, and the 'nickelodeon' is allowed to blare out so that the noise would be sufficient to fill a good-sized ballroom, rather than a converted shop in the main street. The young men waggle one shoulder or stare, as desperately as Humphrey Bogart, across the tubular chairs.

Compared even with the pub around the corner, this is all a peculiarly thin and pallid form of dissipation, a sort of spiritual dry-rot amid the odour of boiled milk. Many of the customers – their clothes, their hair-styles, their facial expressions all indicate – are living to a large extent in a myth-world compounded of a few simple elements which they take to be those of American life.

Richard Hoggart, *The Uses of Literacy*, Harmondsworth 1977, pp. 247–8.

31. Priestley, *English Journey*, Penguin edition, pp. 249–55, 376.

32. 'SoHo . . . Disneyland for the Aesthete', Sharon Zukin, *Loft Living: Culture and Capital in Urban Change*, London 1988, p. 20; and 'Disney World' in *Landscapes of Power*, pp. 221–41; 'Theme Park Britain', *Guardian*, 16–17 December, 1989; Mark Lawson, 'Taking the Mickey out of Euro Disney', *Independent*, 24 August 1994 for hostility in France. The venom of the normally rather gentle Lord Mayor of Oxford to a proposed 'Alice in Wonderland' theme park on the outskirts of the city nicely catches the outrage which the mere mention of the word 'theme park' provokes: 'Oxford's Lord Mayor John Power and former city planning chief said: "There are more than enough theme parks in this country. It's outside the city boundary, so it can't call itself an Oxford attraction: we have enough places exploiting our name as it is. The Alice theme is disgusting. Alice is a beautiful classic story which has entertained generations of children. To have it turned into a Hollywood-type theme park is unbelievable. I bet Christ Church will have something to say"', *Oxford Star*, 1 July 1993. It is perhaps symptomatic of the fear and loathing currently directed at theme parks – in the United States, it seems, no less than in Britain and France – that the bogey figure in Stephen Spielberg's *Jurassic Park* – the children's hit of 1992–3 and before then a cult novel – is a megalomaniac millionaire eager to make a financial killing with his reconstituted prehistoric monsters.

33. Margaret Spufford, *The Great Reclothing of Rural England; Petty Chapmen and their Wares in the Seventeenth Century*, London 1984.

34. Sir Charles Oman, *Memories of Victorian Oxford and of Some Early Years*, London 1941.

35. J.A. Froude, *Thomas Carlyle; A History of His Life in London, 1834–1881*, London, 1897 edn, vol. 1.

Pedagogies

Instead of condescending to heritage, or joining in the chorus of recrimination and complaint against it, it might be more profitable for historians to speculate on the sources of its energies and strength. We might begin by recognizing the enormous scholarly input involved in retrieval projects, saluting the courage of those who have risked their lives – and in the case of the scuba-divers occasionally lost them – to enlarge the domain of the historically known. We might recognize too that after its own fashion, and making use of a battery of forensic skills, heritage has shown quite as much intellectual curiosity as the archive-based historian. It has been ready to back hunches and take risks, extending its retrieval work and its inquiries over very long periods of time – more than twenty years, for instance, in the still continuing sub-aqua explorations connected with the raising from the Solent of Henry VIII's warship, the *Mary Rose*.[1] Tribute might be paid to those madcap enthusiasts, and magpie collectors, who have brought whole new classes of collectables into play – e.g. the metal detectorists whose activity is graphically and sympathetically described in Patrick Wright's *Journey through Ruins*, and who recently – to follow excited accounts in the newspapers – seem to be stumbling on hitherto unknown Roman conurbations, or ancient British settlements, every other week.[2]

Then, historians might consider those areas or practices where heritage has the edge on archive-based scholarship and research, as for example in visual awareness and the use of observational skills. Here, heritage could do something to offset or put in question that narrow preoccupation with the words on the page which is one of the legacies of the Rankean revolution in historical scholarship as well as a near-unbreakable convention in academic monographs or articles in the learned journals. Heritage, if we adopted some of its procedures, could begin to educate us in the language of looks, initiate us into the study of colour coding, familiarize us with period palettes. It could force us to become our own picture researchers, if only because in an increasingly image-conscious society, so many historical preconceptions are likely to be iconographic. As well as poring over burial registers, in the manner which historical demography has made the basis of family reconstitution, it might invite us into the charnel-house, to consider the evidence of the bones, as in the recently completed Spitalfields Project.[3] Or it might take us into the graveyards as a way of introducing children to life-and-death issues in the past,[4] – a project being taken up, it seems, by go-ahead teachers in primary schools – and one which has proved its solid worth to historians of Victorian values.[5] It might induce us to join those tens of thousands of our fellow citizens who make their acquaintance with the medieval through the medium of brass rubbings, and to see that one way of consolidating knowledge about the past is to attempt, quite literally, to picture it.

Heritage has been much more hospitable than history to archaeology, working in tandem with rescue operations and digs and profiting from subterranean discoveries and finds. It is from archaeology that heritage derives one of its most attractive appeals – that of what a current TV series calls 'history on the doorstep'[6] – and from rescue archaeology, as much as anywhere, that it takes its emergency sense, as in the current efforts of the Royal Commission on Historical Monuments (a race against time) to record the lamp rooms, coal screens, baths and canteens at British Coal's newly-closed pits.[7] In the museums explosion of the 1970s and 1980s these associations were institutionalized with the formation of museum-based archaeological units, and the addition of applied archaeology to the range of museological skills. Currently both the National Trust and English Heritage have taken to treating historic sites as archaeological laboratories, with viewing platforms to observe work in progress, and visitor centres – or 'heritage interpretation centres' – to exhibit specimens and finds.[8]

One instructive point of comparison between history and heritage would be the industrial revolution, where two different kinds of scholarship can be seen at work, the one archaeological in inspiration, the other statistical: two entirely different takes on the national past. Among academic historians, a generation of revisionist scholars, influenced, it may be, by the precipitous decline of smokestack industries, have been exerting themselves to show that the industrial revolution was a myth, and that British capitalism never ceased to be anything but a gentlemanly affair.[9] There was no great quickening in the British economy between 1760–1830; no leading industrial sector; no population explosion that was in any way peculiar to this country.[10] Britain, according to Mr Rubinstein, the boldest of the revisionist historians, was never an industrial and manufacturing society but always a service economy. It did not become the workshop of the world in the years

1760–1830. The 'factory system' and what Marx and the writers of the 1840s and 1850s called 'modern industry' were a kind of optical illusion: the great centres of wealth and enterprise remained, as they always had done, in the south-east – the tall factory chimneys were quite marginal to this country's economy. The north, even at the time of Dickens's Coketown or Arnold Bennett's Five Towns, was much less important than the south; no great fortunes were made there, the self-made man was a fiction: the Victorian rich were not cotton magnates or Bradford millionaires but southern bankers, rentiers and landowners.[11]

The instinct of those conservationists – they number tens of thousands – who believe that something momentous happened when the factory system came into being, and who recognize an even more momentous turning-point when, in the 1960s and 1970s, the haemorrhage of industrial jobs began, was surely sounder than that of those quantitative historians who delivered themselves up to tests of statistical significance or counter-factual analysis. It was not the economic historians but the steam fanatics – and after them the industrial archaeologists – who resuscitated the crumbling walls and rusting ironwork of eighteenth-century furnaces and kilns; who kept alive, or revivified, a sense of wonder at the miracles of invention which made mid-Victorian Britain the 'workshop of the world'; and who treasured those cyclopean machines and clanking monsters that dieselization or electrification consigned to the scrap-heap.

'Heritage', with its ear closer to the ground than the quantifiers, and with many more points of access both to common experience and to popular memory, has responded to the collapse of manufacture, and the disappearance of smokestack industries, in an exactly opposite sense, enlarging the notion of historic monument to take in such Victorian public utilities as the Abbey Mills sewage works, Sir Joseph Bazalgette's Gothic folly at West Ham; turning the 'Tiny Tim' steam hammer ('weighing 70 tons') and the Ruston 'steam navvy' into visitor attractions at open-air museums;[12] and making a sculptural feature of derricks and cranes in warehouse refurbishment and re-development. At Lindisfarne, Holy Island, and at Bredeln, on the Northumberland coast, the National Trust-owned lime-kilns stand as monuments for that period which economic historians have taken to calling proto-industrialization.[13] Canalside walks – a discovery of the 1950s – give one a backside view of the industrial revolution (at Oxford the towpath offers a Joseph Wright-like scene when the furnace lights up at Lucy's ironworks). The 'Lady Isabella', the world's largest waterwheel, installed in 1854, is one of the great spectacles for visitors to the Isle of Man.[14] Sightseers at the Greg family mill at Styal, Cheshire, a National Trust property, are faced with a hardly less gargantuan beam engine.

Thanks to the activities of the Thirties Society, and the influence of the Art Deco revival, the number of twentieth-century industrial monuments, nil when the 'Firestone' factory was destroyed, in the midst of fierce controversy, in 1979, slightly more than 100 by 1983,[15] when the Historic Monuments Commission began to take them under its wing, increases exponentially. At Orford Ness on the Suffolk coast – a recent National Trust acquisition – the visitor can see the test site for British radar, 'which played a crucial role in winning the Battle of Britain in the Second World War', and the out-station of the Atomic Weapons Research Establishment at Aldermaston.[16]

Another sphere where heritage could be said to have a definite edge over academic history, and to be giving a precocious lead where others may be expected to follow, is in the history of the environment. Here it shows signs of re-uniting natural history with archaeological inquiry – the original basis on which, in the 1840s and 1850s, the county history societies and Field Clubs were formed.[17] Land, river and sea rather than monarchical reigns or party caucuses are the elements with which it works, scattered or nucleated settlements are its building blocks, the alehouse or the parish church its houses of parliament. It necessarily gives a privileged place to local knowledge. Territorial attachments, both real and imaginary, are its stock-in-trade. Whether concerned with living legend, hereditary tradition or historical context, it opens itself up to the spirit and romance of place. In terms of human geography, it brings a new awareness of the historicity of both landscape and townscape, treating as contingent what used to be conceived of as the grand permanences of climate, vegetation and soil, and linking the evidence of human activity to that of flora and fauna.

Heritage has also helped to give a new centrality to habitat, both in the interpretation of the built environment and in that of the natural world. Obsessed with period detail, and fetishizing material artefacts, it brings an archaeological – or anatomical – imagination to bear on the design and technology of the home, giving to cooking utensils, goffering irons and lavatories (the cesspit seems to be the great visitor attraction at Sutton House, the newly-opened National Trust property in Hackney) the kind of concentrated attention that the historical demographers reserve for such relatively more abstract matters as bastardy rates, inheritance patterns or nuclear family size.[18] At its most indulgent, this can degenerate into a more or less uncritical celebration of the household arts, irrespective of the conditions of obligation and service under which they were performed. But if it takes its cue from current archaeology it is just as likely to find itself addressing such uncomfortable matters as the incidence of whooping cough, the history of false teeth, and the weakness or otherwise of porridge.[19]

Finally, one could say that heritage has created, or helped to create the space for, what the Americans and the Australians call 'Public History' – i.e. those community-based, work- or office-related, and institutional forms of historical self-presentation and display which serve alike for affirming minority identities and boosting corporate images.

Pedagogically, whatever the misgivings it arouses in cultural critics, heritage has been a brilliant success, making 'history on the doorstep' into a normal teaching resource, and opening up whole new terrains for those activity-based, or 'playway' forms of learning which have been, ever since the early 1920s, the unifying thread of the progressive tradition in English education.[20] Through the medium of town trails and nature trails, a species of project work first developed in the 1960s, it gives a privileged place to local knowledge. Reading an old building, starting with the date-stone, if one exists, or detecting, behind a modern façade, the tell-tale signs of earlier occupancy, becomes a first introduction to the historical idea, as well as an elementary training in deconstruction. In the manner which the Arts and Crafts Movement introduced into English junior schools, knowledge is tested not by chalk and talk but by observational drawing and model-building. Learning by seeing is also the great rationale of the countryside interpretation centres, where children, set on such tasks as pond-dipping, or asked to exercise their forensic skills on habitat-detection, become trained observers of natural history.[21]

Heritage and its near-cousin, the collecting mania, have facilitated the progress of object-related forms of study, and in some fields may have called them into being. 'Jackdaws', which brought original historical documents, in the shape of wallets of facsimiles, into the very heart of classroom practice, while at the same time fostering a taste for 'period' typography and display, are an interesting example. The creation of a freelance writer and historian who had served his time on the radical-progressive *Picture Post*, and who had a strong belief in the use of visual material for teaching, the series began publication in December 1963 and was so popular with teachers that by 1974 130 titles had appeared.[22] 'Jackdaws' were, in one aspect, of a piece with the ephemera craze of the 1960s, which made the fortunes of Portobello Road, and produced the poster mania of the time. They owed their visual impact to the shock – or quaintness – of the old. Choice of subject was quite conservative, as befitted a mainstream publisher ('The Battle of Trafalgar' was the first title). But the documents were taken up enthusiastically by the proponents of child-centred education, and widely imitated by museums, town libraries and county record offices for 'do-it-yourself' history and learning packs.

Ever since the museum explosion of the 1970s, the use of material artefacts, both replicas and originals, has become increasingly central to teaching practice, more especially in junior school, where flexible timetabling still allows the luxury of collective projects, cross-curricular studies in the environment, and experiments in learning by doing. Here the advent of the new 'core' curriculum, with its material culture study units, and emphasis on sight and sound and touch, has given a big boost to museum visiting, and to such site-related projects as the history of a local granary, brewery or mill. Schools themselves have increasingly been involved in setting up mini-museums, acting as their own collectors and curators, if only as a way of meeting the new attainment targets.[23] Local history study units by definition take their starting point from the visible remains of the past. 'Invaders and Settlers' is an invitation to explore archaeological sites;[24] while 'Ships and Shipping', a popular option with boys, gets much of its adrenaline from visits to maritime heritage centres.[25]

'Since the implementation of the National Curriculum primary schools have increasingly enjoyed visiting the museum to investigate life in Victorian England', runs an article on the Bass Museum of Brewing, Burton on Trent:

Secondary schools use the facilities more to investigate the industrial and transport revolutions or life in the First World War. . . . Maps, large models, pictures and the newly furnished coaching inn clearly demonstrate firstly, the evolution of the transport system in Burton from horses and waggons through canals to the railways and subsequently, in the twentieth century, to lorries and diesel engines; secondly, the significance of transport development for Burton's principal industry and, thirdly, the changing trade routes within Britain and overseas which affected the growth of brewing. Pupils could work out why the preference for the Baltic trade was transferred to India and Australia. . . . Bass appears to have turned up in many places – for example, in the museum pupils can discover that Bass beer was demanded in a message by balloon sent from the 1871 Siege of Paris; it was drunk at Balaclava, and at the *Folies Bergères*, as illustrated by the proud display of a reproduction of Manet's famous painting of the latter with bottles of Bass prominent in the front. . . . The 'impact of economic change on families and communities, working and living conditions . . .' can be worked out through the clear evidence of the various processes of brewing; the people employed in the industry (including the annual invasion of farm-workers from East Anglia); the wide range of jobs (Bass was a self-sufficient brewery in the nineteenth century, making everything it needed) . . . Changing social relationships can be traced too, for example there is much evidence on the growing presence of women in pubs and the resistance to this. The contrast of Bass trying to make pubs more welcoming to families in the 1930s with the Edwardian bar with its spittoon and girl collecting her mother's supper beer form just one of the many contrasts which can be drawn in 'then and now' exercises.[26]

Another heritage-related, and in the first place, it seems, museum-based addition to teaching practice, again mainly at the level of junior school, has been historical role-play. Thus, 'Doing the Victorians', a popular project at Key Stage Two, often has as its high point the performance of character parts – e.g. exercises in carpet-beating or blackleading if the topic is a day in the life of a Victorian Servant, dollymopping if it is 'Grandmother's Washing Day', stitching, quilting or bobbin-knitting if it is the make-do and mend of the household economy. 'A Day in the Life of a Victorian School' was an early and enduring favourite both because of the great range of activities – e.g. exercises in Swedish drill and callisthenics, as well as in the using of slates for basic arithmetic – and because of its appeal to the strongly developed juvenile sense of cruelty and injustice.[27] The severities of the discipline are much insisted on, complete with the mnemonics which kept the children in line:

> Good-Better-Best
> Never let it Rest
> Till your Good is Better
> And your Better's Best.[28]

Historical re-enactment – or what is sometimes called 'live inter-pretation'[29] – is a regular feature of the open-air or working museum. It is in the hands of a remarkable new breed of demonstrators, instructors and guides whose performance skills and ability to impart knowledge any teacher might envy. Locally recruited, often it seems from retired or part-time teachers, or redundant workers, and starting out as volunteers, they seem typically both to research their parts and create their own narrative, not only disseminating information, but also projecting a character. Drawing on personal experience and local knowledge,[30] schooled or trained through the medium of oral history, and with their presentation enriched by a constant exchange with old-timers, they are at once pedagogically and histrionically effective, wearing period cos-tume and handling historical objects with aplomb, and fielding visitors' queries. The pawnbroker at the Black Country Museum, Dudley, drawing on local knowledge of the three brass balls – not least that of the town's one surviving pawnbroker – had found a narrative for every object in his store, even the false teeth which, as he explained, could be pawned on the Monday and taken out on the Friday since there would be no fresh meat to chew on before Sunday roast came round. The 1920s storekeeper explaining the mysteries and signs of the grocery trade was a mine of information, most of it gleaned, she explained, from museum visitors. The schoolmistress, a young lady in her prime, had a classful of children scratching away at their slates. The chainmaker, speaking with effortless authority, busied herself at the back, and demonstrated the rudiments of the blacksmith's arts.

The Worcestershire and Herefordshire Museum, Hartlebury, funded by the county rather than a trust, is not able to employ paid demonstrators on a full- or part-time basis, but it contrives to maintain four of them (three are ex-teachers) both for role-play work in the museum itself, and in outreach to 'talk through' the objects on display (e.g. Second World War memorabilia) and construct an imaginary and personal narrative around them. 'They really do perform. They become the characters.' One takes the part of a Victorian sea captain (for 'Ships and Shipping', Key Stage 2); one of a Victorian school marm; one of a housekeeper (instructing would-be scullery maids and boot-and-knives boys in their duties); one of Doris Dinsdale, a Second World War housewife. A cosmopolitan addition – played by a man who in real life is a stonemason and graphic artist – is an Egyptian pyramid builder from the time of the Middle Kingdom.[31]

So far as subject matter is concerned, there is no evidence that the effect of either historical role-play or object-based study has been to make a country-house, or *Brideshead*, view of the national past hegemonic, and indeed to advance the claims of history from below, as some of heritage's left-wing critics do, or to demand more attention to class differences, is to push at some very open doors. The peasant and the artisan have normally been given pride of place at the folk museums. At some of the working farms and countryside interpretation centres it requires an effort of will to remind oneself that the parson and squire ever existed, let alone that they lorded it over the lives of tenants, labourers and parishioners. Mock battles, such as those of the Sealed Knot and the Civil War Societies, are fought out between infantry rather than cavalry, though it is true that in jousting displays – a feature at some of English Heritage's medieval properties – the combatants are mounted on horseback.

So far from heritage being the medium through which a Conservative version of the national past becomes hegemonic, one could see its advent as part of a sea-change in attitudes which has left any unified view of the national past – liberal, radical or Conservative – in tatters. Culturally it is pluralist. Everything is grist to its mill – the inter-war 'semi', the subject of a growing coffee-table literature, no less than the stately home. A lifesize replica of the *Mayflower*, the restoration of Edward III's medieval manor house, an East Indian Bazaar in the heart of Rotherhithe and a Scandinavian Centre in the Surrey Docks (once the home of the North Sea timber trade) were among the plans being canvassed by the Docklands Development Corporation in 1987, while in the fond eye of the speculative housebuilders, taking a cue from

Australian or Californian beach-boys, the Pool of London was to be given over to lunch-time surfers.[32] The winter programme of site-related education activities at Tatton Park, a National Trust property in Cheshire, is even more promiscuous:

> From October to March, when the Mansion, Old Hall and Farm are closed to the public, the estate takes on another guise and goes back in time with a series of living history days designed specially for schools. Options include digging for victory as evacuees, reconstructing Saxon life in the Park, taking part in a Manor Court as 13th-century peasants, or going behind the scenes as servants during Tatton's Victorian heyday.[33]

Aesthetically, too, these heritage-related pedagogies could be described as polyglot, drawing in one register on the quotidian and the familiar, while in another playing with the Gothic and the uncanny. At one extreme there are those ruins which have been so carefully manicured, or hedged about with car parks, that it is impossible to imagine them in a wilderness state. At the other extreme, perhaps, are those drear landscapes favoured as wildlife sanctuaries where sour grass and sedge, rushes and stagnant pools make up a habitat for waders.

The archaeologically-minded like to see their excavations in a raw, half-finished state, and part of the brilliance of Jorvik is that at the end of the ride the time-car deposits you in the laboratory where the remains are being sifted. Arboriculturists, restoring or 'coppicing' ancient woodland, seem to be animated by a similar taste, giving a site-like appearance to the properties in their care. The National Trust, on the other hand, intent on removing eyesores, or on making their properties user-friendly, are more inclined to smooth out wrinkles.

Ironbridge, according to its many critics, sanitizes the past, and transfers imaginative attention from the ruined furnaces and iron-workers' cottages – the original eighteenth-century nucleus of the site – to Blists Hill, the newly-transplanted, make-believe late Victorian shopping centre. The landscaping, too, is criticized. What to the apocalyptic artists of the 1830s and 1840s appeared as a hell on earth, where the hammers never ceased and the furnaces were given over to infernal fires, is now an almost Arcadian spot, while Ironbridge itself, thronged with sightseers, and enjoying the accolade of being a world heritage site, is as difficult to imagine in its original condition as present-day Stonehenge.[34]

Pumping stations, maintained in a working state by small bands of enthusiasts, like the so-called 'engineerium' at Brighton, are not like this at all, but owe their renown to the display of industrial muscle. Much the same is true, it seems, of the working power-looms, such as those in the industrial museums of Lancashire and the West Riding, where the whole effort is to recapture the noise and clatter of the original.

At Wheal Martyn, one of the first of the open-air industrial museums, the maintenance foreman is a former groundsman, and some curators detect a tendency to the picturesque ('One tank is so full of bulrushes we can't bring ourselves to change it'). But the Nature Trail, a recent addition to the industrial site, exhibits a variety of wildlife habitats, while the Adventure Trail allows the children, 'commando-style' to make the most of the overgrown tips, hanging upside down from a ladder being a kind of ultimate dare. The children, reports one of the curators, will seize on anything strange. They are very interested in the life of the kettle boy – the little one who was the dogsbody of the adult workers ('children can relate to that'); they are 'very impressed' with the giant waterwheel; with the slow hiss of the pumping engine; and with the sight of the abyss – a topside view of a still-working clay pit. The heat and humidity of the furnaces apparently registers itself, though red lights do service for the fires. The flat rod tunnel – 'very narrow, children have to walk single file through it' – is a particular excitement for the more imaginative or the more timorous ('a dragon's lair' is how it appeared in one child's account).[35]

The Black Country Museum, like Wheal Martyn one of the earliest industrial museums in the country, is, though twenty-five years old, quite dotted about with unfinished or half-finished projects, and when I visited it in August 1993 it looked very much like a building site in a half-finished or quarter-finished state. The rolling mill is surrounded by convincing piles of scrap and the canal basin seems full of working craft. A very urban tramcar, which orders passengers not to spit, rumbles incongruously but engagingly down a semi-rural track, while the National School, where the children are engaged at slates, is almost bereft of ornament. The chainmakers' yards, where the women black-smiths are supposed to have been at work, are represented as tips, full of rusty cast-offs; the décor in the public house is minimalist, eschewing the more obvious appeals of period enamels. It is the talk of the demon-strators that makes the place come alive.

At the steam fairs, a big visitor attraction whenever they are staged, the poetry is in the grime, and those who take their locomotives away for the weekend rough it, cooking breakfast on a shovel, and dinner in the smokebox. On the last night of the great Dorset fair at Blandford, the scene is described as phantasmagoric, a 750-acre site crowded with engines and fires, huge marquees, a line of one hundred showmen's engines 'all generating power', organs belting out 'tara-rah-rah-boom-de-ay' music, and a vast concourse of spectators (a quarter of a million people visit the site during the four days of the fair).[36]

Children bring their own aesthetics to these spectacles, their own time

horizons, their own memories, their own points of past–present comparison, in a word, their own sense of history. They will be making dramas
and stories out of material that is apparently inert. They may wonder at
the weight of the cannonballs they are invited to handle on board 'HMS
Victory' or the size of the giant waterwheels which confront them at a
mill dam. They will invest labyrinths and caves with sinister properties.

Wide-awake curators minister to these tastes, turning nature trails into
treasure hunts, historical walks into mystery tours. Some will make a
feature of the forbidden, as for example at Vindolanda, the much-visited
fort on Hadrian's Wall, where the soldiers' latrines are one of the
sensations of the 'living history' display. In a more macabre vein they
may, like the curators of Snibston, the new and apparently very successful
'discovery park' in Leicestershire, use human skeletons to animate the
exhibits.[37] At the Natural History Museum, South Kensington, the
highlight of the dinosaur display is a bloodthirsty exercise in animatronics in which a robotic Deinonychus devours a Tenontosaurus.[38] At
Iceni, the ancient British Village in Suffolk, much used, it seems, by
visiting school parties, the great sensation is the Iceni giant – a six-foot
skeleton excavated on the site, and perhaps its best claim to historicity;
the landowner/curator has added, for good measure, the model of a
Dark Age snake-pit, and imitation scalps of 'executed prisoners'.[39]

Living history, so far from domesticating or sanitizing the past, makes
a great point of its otherness, and indeed the brute contrast between
'now' and 'then' is very often the framing device of its narrative.
Whether the measure is life chances, social discipline, or the severities of
old-time penal codes, it is only too apt to come up with horrors. Thus the
maritime museums are apt to make a feature of the perils of the deep,
military ones the mortality of the battlefield. Jorvik builds its whole
excitement around the idea of tenth-century urban squalor, and if
Spitalfields-like archaeological excavations continue it seems likely that
the next generation of museums will make a speciality of mortality and
disease.

'Living history' bears the impress not only of pastoral versions of the
national past, but also of romantic primitivism and modern Gothic.
Hence, one might suggest, the popularity of the 'dark ride' underground
museums, which combine the excitements of the descent into the inferno
with eerie sounds and period smells. Hence too perhaps the frequency
with which 'the Blitz experience' is the centrepiece of the 'living history'
exhibitions at the war museums and theme parks. Is this perhaps, too, one
of the excitements of the 'Mary Rose' – a 'Flying Dutchman', as it were,
raised from the deep, the sepulchre of 450 Tudor sailors?

A taste for the gruesome is very much in evidence on London walks,
with the haunts of Jack the Ripper joining such ancient attractions as

Execution Dock, Tyburn or the dungeons at the Tower. 'Ghosts, Ghouls and Graveyards' – 'a spine-chilling look at historic London's dark side', conducted, it seems, by professional archaeologists or museum curators – is the title of one nightly tour, which leaves the Barbican at 8 p.m., 'on the trail of Jack the Ripper'; another, 'A Bus Trip to Murder' is the night-time offering of 'Tragical History Tours' which starts from the Embankment at 7 p.m., a round trip which makes a speciality of the supernatural and paranormal.[40]

Even the normally staid National Trust seems to be ready to dabble in sensation. As the largest custodian of haunted houses in the country the Trust is finding it serviceable to announce ghoul hunts – at Scotney Castle, Kent, the ruins of a fourteenth-century moat, a priest's hole, from the time of the Elizabethan persecutions, 'and the ghoulish legends that surround the castle' have provided pupils at Kent junior schools 'with a great stimulus for imaginative work'.[41] 'Smugglers' caves' seem to be no less serviceable to National Trust authorities devising educational programmes for the 'Heritage' coast (Dorset, as well as Cornwall, is rich in them);[42] and in a post-Christian age, with New Ageism taking root among the very young, ritual monuments, such as stone circles and burial mounds – or what the National Trust calls 'ritual sites' (it has the ownership of the most famous of them) – are recommended as an ideal starting point for school projects on environment and myth.[43]

Notes

1. Alexander McKee, *How We Found the Mary Rose*, London 1982 for a narrative of the twenty-year rescue operation; and Margaret Rule, *The Mary Rose; the Excavation and Raising of Henry VIII's Flagship*, London 1982, for a discussion of the ship's waterlogged contents, and their extreme interest to the marine archaeologist. For a hostile account, Patrick Wright, on *Living in an Old Country*, London 1987, pp. 161–92. The author, who in some 15,000 words on the subject gives the reader no faint indication of what was in the 'Mary Rose', or why it is such an astonishing addition to the gallery of historic ships, insists on treating its rescue as a melodramatic incident in the history of late imperialism, and aligning it to the Falklands expedition of 1982.

2. Patrick Wright, *A Journey Through Ruins*, London 1991, pp. 139–54. The metal detectors – there are some 10,300 of them in the National Council for Metal Detectors – are currently facing a bill promoted by the British Museum which would put an end to the 'finders keepers' tradition; *The Times*, 2 March 1994, p. 6. I am grateful to Kate Hobson for this reference.

3. Theya Molleson and Margaret Cox, *The Spitalfields Project, Vol. 2, The Middling Sort*, York 1993.

4. Oral information from Alice Prochaska of the National Curriculum History Working Group.

5. Stuart Rawnsley and Jack Reynolds, 'Undercliffe Cemetery, Bradford', *History Workshop Journal*, 4, Autumn 1977, pp. 215–21. Bradford mill-owners, not content with commanding prime space in the cemetery walkways, had themselves buried as Egyptian sun-gods.

6. *Time Team*, a popular archaeological series on Channel 4 at the time of writing.

7. 'Fears for Lost Industrial Heritage in Rush to Redevelopment', *Observer*, 17 October 1993.

8. Cf. English Heritage, 'Education on Sites' series. At Felbrigg Hall, the National Trust property in Norfolk, there is a viewing platform from which work in progress can be monitored very much in the same was as it is during a City of London archaeological dig.

9. N.F.R. Crafts, *British Economic Growth during the Industrial Revolution*, Oxford 1985; N.F.R. Crafts, 'British Industrialisation in an International Context', *Journal of Interdisciplinary History*, XIX, 1989; P.J. Cain and A.G. Hopkins, 'Gentlemanly Capitalism and British Expansion Overseas', *Economic History Review*, vol. 39, pt. IV, 1986, pp. 501–25; vol. 40, pt. I, 1987, pp. 1–26. For the most recent statement of the revisionist position, Joel Mokyr, ed., *British Industrial Revolution, an Economic Perspective*, New York 1993.

10. When Ironbridge Gorge Museum, in 1984, advertised for a senior research fellow, it claimed that the success of the museum was 'in response to a growing awareness of the significance of the Industrial Revolution in the history of this country and of the world', Bob West, 'Ironbridge', in Lumley, ed., *The Museum Time-Machine, Putting Culture on Display*, London 1988, p. 53.

11. W.D. Rubinstein, *Men of Property. The Very Wealthy in Britain Since the Industrial Revolution*, London 1981; *Capitalism, Culture and Decline in Britain 1750–1990*, London 1993.

12. John Gorman, 'Photo Archive at Beamish Open Air Museum', *History Workshop Journal*, Autumn 1978.

13. I am grateful to the Northumberland district of the National Trust for material on these kilns.

14. L.S. Garrad et al., *The Industrial Archaeology of the Isle of Man*, Newton Abbot 1972, pp. 58–9 for a photograph of the Lady Isabella, and a print of the opening ceremony in 1854.

15. Kenneth Hudson, *The Archaeology of the Consumer Society, The Second Industrial Revolution in Britain*, London 1983. Royal Commission on Historical Monuments, *Industry and the Camera*, London 1985.

16. 'Trust Buys a Slice of Military History', *Independent*, 23 June 1993.

17. For some very interesting perceptions on the ecclesiological roots of the early Victorian county history societies, Stuart Piggott, 'The Origins of the English County Archaeological Societies', *Ruins in a Landscape, Essays in Antiquarianism*, Edinburgh 1976, pp. 171–95.

18. Molly Harrison's *The Kitchen in History*, Reading 1972 seems to have been a product of the writer's curatorial work at the Geffrye Museum, Hackney – the pioneer of the exhibition and display of English domestic interiors, and the reconstruction of 'period rooms'. Marjorie Quennell, her predecessor at the Geffrye, was co-author of the four-volume *History of Everyday Things*. Lawrence Wright's trilogy, *Clean and Decent*, London 1960; *Warm and Snug*, London 1962; and *Home Fires Burning*, London 1964 seem to have come from nowhere. Christine Hardyment claims that her interest in the history of domesticity began when she spotted 'a curious G-shaped metal object' at a South London repair shop. (*Home Comfort, A History of Domestic Arrangements*, London 1992, pp. xii–xiii.) *From Mangle to Microwave, The Mechanization of Household Work*, Oxford 1989, is based on the collection of domestic appliances at the London Science Museum, trade periodicals and domestic magazines.

19. Crispin Keith, *A Teacher's Guide to Using Listed Buildings*, English Heritage 1991: Sallie Purkiss, *A Teacher's Guide to Using School Buildings*, English Heritage 1992.

20. Marjorie and C.H.B. Quennell, whose *A History of Everyday Things in England* did so much to popularize this in the 1920s, were ardent disciples of William Morris.

21. G. Binns, *Brownsea Island; an Activity Book for Teachers*, National Trust 1992; *Rural Landscapes; a Resource Book for Teachers*, National Trust 1992.

22. John Lewis, *Collecting Printed Ephemera*, pp. 97–8. The writer in question was John Langdon-Davies, and the occasion for his invention of Jackdaws was the 1962 publication (under a pseudonym) of *The Cato Street Conspiracy*, his contribution to the radical historiography of the Peterloo years.

23. Paula Shaw and Janet Matthews, 'Old and New – A Cross-Curricular Approach',

Remnants, No. 18, Autumn 1992; B.P. Fox, 'Accentuate the Positive', *Remnants*, No. 29, Summer 1993 for two fine accounts of self-made museums.

24. Peter Fowler, 'Anglo-Saxon Attitudes' in *National Trust Education Supp.*, 1992, and Nigel Spencer, 'Investigating the Invaders', *Remnants*, no. 17, Summer 1992 for teaching the unit by means of historical role-play.

25. The National Curriculum History Working Party, whose chair was a former naval commander, spent a day with Portsmouth's historic ships and submarines. 'Ships and Shipping' seems to have been one of the most successful of their recommended study units. Information from Alice Prochaska.

26. Ruth Watts, 'Museums, History Teaching and Economic and Industrial Awareness', *Journal of Education in Museums*, 1993, pp. 20–4.

27. Wynne Frankum and Jo Lawrie, *The Victorian Schoolday; A Teacher's Manual*, Reading 1992. I am grateful to these authors for the Teachers' Preparatory Folders given out in advance of visits by school parties, and for much information about historical role play at their re-created Victorian schoolrooms – one a board school in Reading, the other a hamlet school on a Wiltshire estate.

28. I am grateful to Tony Wood of the Sevington School project for this verse.

29. Andrew Robertshaw, '"From Houses into Homes", One Approach to Live Interpretation', *Social History in Museums*, vol. 19, 1992, pp. 14–20; Joy Anderson, *Time Machines; the World of Living History*, Nashville 1984; Warren Leon and Margaret Piat, 'Living History Museums', in Warren Leon and Roy Rozenzweig, eds, *Historical Museums in the United States; A Critical Assessment*, Chicago 1989, pp. 64–97.

30. Author's notes on a visit to the Black Country Museum, August 1993.

31. Information and brochures from Alyson Lloyd, Curator.

32. Quoted in Samuel, 'Introduction', *Patriotism*, vol. 1.

33. National Trust *Educational Supplement*, Autumn 1993.

34. West, 'Ironbridge', p. 54; Malcolm Chase and Christopher Shaw, 'The Dimensions of Nostalgia' in Chase and Shaw, eds, *The Imagined Past, History and Nostalgia*, Manchester 1989, p. 1.

35. Information and brochures from Charles Thurloe and Sarah Harbige of Wheal Martyn.

36. I am grateful to Jon Gorman Jnr., a prize exhibitor there, for this description of Blandford Fair.

37. 'Digging into the World of Discovery', *Independent*, 9 February 1994. For some other examples B. Gardner, 'History, Mystery and Suspense', *Junior Education*, 16 (11) 1992, pp. 26–7, 29. At Walsall Museum the most popular exhibit with children is the grisly 'Hand of Glory' – the alleged limb of an executed eighteenth-century criminal. At Jorvik, the latest underground sensation – genuinely spine-chilling – is the reconstituted face of a tenth-century skull.

38. *Time Out*, 2 February 1994.

39. Information from the Curator at Iceni, May 1993.

40. The Tragical History tours, still apparently flourishing, despite competition, were started by Mr Michael Jones in 1986. Information from Mrs Jones and brochure in Bishopsgate Library.

41. National Trust, *Educational Supplement*, Autumn 1993.

42. National Trust, *Rural Landscapes*, p. 39.

43. National Trust, *Educational Supplement*, Autumn 1992.

Politics

I

Historically, preservationism is a cause which owes at least as much to the Left as to the Right. The founders of the Society for the Protection of Ancient Buildings – William Morris and Philip Webb – were socialists. 'Green belts' – the exclusion zones around the city where property developers were forbidden to build – were a creation of the 1930s Labour-led London County Council. National Parks were legislated into being by the Attlee Labour government, which also laid the legislative groundwork for Nature Conservancy and wildlife reserves. From the point of view of the National Trust, as John Gaze, one of its land agents at the time recalls, the landslide Labour victory of 1945 was an unquestioned good.

> The advent of a Labour Government with a large majority in 1945 brought new influences to bear on the Trust. Governments had never been hostile to the Trust, some had been positively helpful and we have seen how Baldwin felt about it. Nevertheless, now for the first time there was a Government not only prepared but anxious to advance the Trust's interests. In part this was due simply to the feeling that the Trust was a Good Thing; its work had been very much in line with the attitude of middle-class Fabians whose influence was strong in the Labour Party. There was also a feeling that the old order really was at an end, that there were some pieces which needed to be picked up. It was thought that the organisation would be a useful instrument to do that and might later be taken over by Government when convenient.[1]

In Australia, though heritage came under attack, at the time of the bi-centenary celebrations of 1988, as giving a licence to racism, it seems on the contrary to have been serviceable to the coming out of hitherto stigmatized and inferior minorities. Indeed, the recovery and advancement of Aborigine culture seems to have been the fulcrum for the emancipatory movement which, on the issue of land rights in the Northern Territories, has just registered so signal a victory.[2] The conservation movement in Australia has at least one of its origins in the 'green' initiatives of the left-wing, semi-syndicalist building workers' union. The establishment of a Committee of Inquiry into the National Estate in 1973, leading in 1976, to the enactment of the Australian Heritage Bill and the subsequent compilation of a register of protected properties; and the establishment of a Committee of Inquiry on Museums and National Collections, leading to the Museum of Australia Act of 1980, were all measures of Labour administrations, while the environmental direct action groups – such as the one which involved itself in tremendous struggle over wilderness sites in Tasmania – were ultra-radical in character. A recent commentator ascribes the success of these campaigns to a fund of radical patriotism:

> ... the willingness of Labour administrations, state and federal, to preserve historic sites from threatened destruction by developers served as a key emblem of this 'new nationalism' and its commitment to representing the interests of 'all Australians' against what were seen as the socially destructive activities of both international corporations and domestic élites.[3]

In the United States 'heritage' is notoriously the name given to one of the New Right's best-funded foundations, dedicated, in the 1980s, to the global fight against Communism. But the term has been adopted, no less affirmatively, for black-power cultural initiatives in the field of museology while 'Afro-American', the term adopted since the 1960s by black consciousness movements of all kinds, highlights the tremendous preoccupation with historical roots.[4] In the sphere of conventional politics, conservation-led redevelopment, on the lines of Lowell, Mass., has been the grand Democratic Party panacea for disindustrialization in the rust-belt states. Preservationism in the United States may take one of its inspirations from such exercises in historical make-believe as the Rockefeller-funded Williamsburg (the old colonial 'living history' town established in 1928) or Henry Ford's Greenfield Village, but it also owes a good deal to the cultural initiatives of the liberal New Deal era, which legislated the first protection for historic buildings and set in train a remarkable project of federal-funded ethnography – notably in the recording of slave narratives, and in the collection of negro spirituals and blues.[5]

In France, the historical association of 'heritage' with the Left comes from the French Revolution itself. The term *patrimoine* was a Jacobin coinage, an inspiration of the egalitarian priest, l'Abbé Grégoire, who used it both to combat iconoclasts and wreckers (he invented the term 'vandal' to describe them) and to establish the nation's claim to the treasures of the châteaux, the monasteries and the palaces.[6] For a century and more the idea of *patrimoine* ran in tandem with that of republican education and the creation of republican consciousness, and this embraced *all* aspects of heritage, not only 'arts et traditions populaires' (in which a notable museum was set up in the period of the Popular Front),[7] but also the châteaux: when they were opened up to *son et lumière* historical displays in the 1960s, some at least of the promoters hailed it as a further triumph of the republican idea.

In Germany, where *Volkskunde* was appropriated wholesale by the Nazis,[8] and used to give historic credence to the idea of a racial soul, the 'new-wave' social historians of the 1960s, like Enlightenment-oriented radicals generally, steered clear of anything with a *Volkisch* taint. By the same token, because of Nazi instrumentalization of former movements, any idea of back-to-the-land was deeply suspect. Yet in practice, the Federal Republic of the 1970s and 1980s was second only to Britain in its enthusiasm for industrial archaeology; it was the Social Democratic *Länder* who took the lead in promoting working museums, just as it was Social-Democratic municipalities who were most generous in initiating and resourcing town heritage centres, oral history projects and 'people's exhibitions'.[9] Historical suspicions of Nature mysticism did not prevent the green movement from capturing the imagination of a whole generation of the student Left, and indeed of presenting itself, as it did to the dissident Rudolph Barho, as the alternative to a historically exhausted and ethically bankrupt Communism.[10]

II

In Britain, when 'heritage' first came under attack, in 1987, it seemed quite plausible to think of it as reactionary, and to argue that it fitted into, and could be seen as an expression of, the dominant ideology, and ruling politics, of the time. The Conservatives were riding high after three general election victories, and the Falklands War – politically popular as well as being a military success – seemed to mark the comeback of a know-nothing 'Little Englandism' in which dreams of vanished supremacies served as consolations for the collapse of British power. By the same token the museums explosion – and in particular the rise of the open-air industrial museum – was seen as consolation for decline of the British economy and the departure of manufacture and production from these shores. Likewise in the property boom of the 1980s, 'gentrification' – the name given to the middle-class led rehabilitation of the inner city – was thought to be creating a new *rentier* class. Heritage, in short, was Thatcherism in period dress. It represented a posthumous victory of the aristocratic spirit over the levelling tendency, and egalitarian potential, of the post-war settlement.

In the light of subsequent development, as well as perhaps a belated recognition of heritage's popular roots, these confident equations and (from a radical point of view) pejorative associations may seem overdone. For one thing the Conservatives' attachment to the notion of heritage seems quite shallow. Nicholas Ridley, at the Department of the Environment, was quite as ruthless in ignoring or overriding conservationist opinion as any modernizer of the 1960s, though doing so on grounds of the sanctity of private property rather than the imperatives of comprehensive redevelopment. The increasingly restrictive character of environmental legislation makes it obnoxious to the free-market right, while the Tory Party's 'Little Englanders' are offended by the European (or American) provenance of ecology.

There is no doubt that from a capitalist point of view, whatever the discomfort to the motorway lobby or the property developers, 'heritage' has been a success, or at any rate a project which it can accommodate. The rent-map of London shows far higher premiums for office accommodation in Mayfair – where Westminster Council has listed more than half the buildings, and where the Grosvenor Estate jealously protects the eighteenth-century street grid – than the City of London, where the Corporation, ever since the great rebuilding got under way in the 1950s, has been even more destructive than Hitler's bombers.[11] Then again, one could point to the way in which the property developers have learnt to incorporate an element of conservation in their clearances; indeed it sometimes seems that for a comprehensive work of destruction to begin (I am thinking of the business village which has been built on the corpse of the old East India Company offices in Houndsditch) it needs the accolade of English Heritage, or the Fine Arts Commission, to say that a really imaginative redevelopment is envisaged.

Nevertheless, among property owners, to judge by a stream of attacks on 'retrophilia' in the quality press, there is a rising tide of complaint about heritage officers – a bunch of crazed aesthetes, as they sometimes appear, attempting to regulate the shape of the last corbel; and when the motorway lobby resumes its onward march, as it is threatening to do, the chorus of recrimination seems likely to grow. The reversal of the conservation order on Mappin and Webb – the last block of Victorian building in the Golden Mile – and the refusal of one for the Bankside power station (the government has sold the site to British Nuclear Fuels) perhaps marks the turning of the tide (government-instigated cuts in the archaeological services point in a similar direction). Mrs Thatcher, a ruthless modernizer, though espousing 'Victorian values' was not averse to using the word 'Victorian' as a pejorative, and treating it as synonymous with the out-of-date.[12] Her successors follow suit. 'We are not in the heritage business', the Minister of Health declared, when, to the outrage of both medical and metropolitan opinion, she announced her determination to press ahead with the closure of London's most ancient and prestigious teaching hospital.

On the other side of the party-political divide, 'heritage' in the 1980s proved very serviceable to hard-pressed Labour authorities. Deprived of their building programmes (from 1918 onwards the lodestar of municipal idealism) they turned instead to consortium-led redevelopment, using 'historic' buildings as a bargaining counter to negotiate with would-be developers – as Glasgow City Council has done with its recreated 'Merchants' City'; or, like Southwark Council with its newly opened Thames Path – trading off planning permissions in exchange for schemes of environmental enhancement. Labour councils also turned to 'heritage', or heritage-related projects, as a new source of service-sector jobs. In a climate of spending cuts and Exchequer-imposed economies, it was one of the very few fields of municipal enterprise in which they could still attract outside support – if not from government itself, then from the county council, or from one of the Department of the Environment's burgeoning quangos. Faced, as many of them were in the recession of 1977–83, with the run-down of local industries and the near collapse of the local economy, they turned to conservation as the grand remedy for urban blight.

In ways such as the foregoing, heritage and its allies have arguably given a new lease of life – and a new visual form – to what used to be called, in the 1890s and 1900s, when it found expression in municipal libraries, swimming baths and bandstands, the Civic Gospel. It is one of the very few areas in which local government can still take a lead, and almost the only one where public-sector employment has increased.

Notionally backward-looking and apparently reactionary, conservation has been for some twenty years or more a magnet for cultural dissidents. It makes utopianism feasible. The cry of 'heritage in danger' has proved by far the most potent of mobilizing forces – and of networking – in environmental campaigns. It is a popular cause even if the activists get much of their energy from the self-conscious righteousness of minorities. 'Heritage' is in fact one of the few areas of national life in which it is possible to invoke an idea of the common good without provoking suspicion of party interest, and it is also one of the few where notions of ancestry and posterity can be invoked without embarrassment or bad faith. It has notched up real achievement – reclaiming streets from the motorist and creating traffic-free zones, greening the inner city, restoring, or creating wildlife habitats.

What distinguishes conservation from other kinds of public issue – and perhaps accounts for the radicalism of many of those who take up its causes – is its predilection for direct action. It does not wait for the tedious processes of representation or the often unalterable processes of the law, but, in the manner of the Oxleas Wood campaigners, pins its faith on interventions in the here-and-now. At a time when mass membership parties are in precipitous and secular decline, and party politics very largely the preoccupation of self-regarding élites, the politics of the environment are one of the few places where individual action, and collective participation, counts, and it is no doubt indicative of this that Greenpeace – or for that matter the Royal Society for the Protection of Birds – have much longer membership lists than the Labour Party, and a much more vivid life. Conservation also allows for some measure of the politics of the personal, giving space for the unilateral action of the individual, asking us to practise its precepts in our lives, and giving us some say on who our neighbours might be – a dangerous power, and one which can be turned to ethnocentric or class-exclusive ends, but at the same time one of the inescapable components of any folk radicalism.

Heritage could also be described as a residuary legatee of the planning idea.[13] It is by its nature interventionist – one reason perhaps why it is currently attracting such obloquy. Like planning in the 1940s – though on the strength of popular initiative rather than central authority – it is an attempt to make a new landscape, both indirectly, through the take-up of improvement grants, and directly, through schemes of environmental enhancement. Like 1940s town and country planning, too, it wants to control land use, restrict market forces, and to integrate old and new. Its conservation areas, though less strict in segregating occupational and residential use, could be seen as late offspring of that favourite child of the 1940s town planners, 'zoning', while its urban regeneration schemes could be seen as a lineal descendent of 1960s comprehensive redevelopment, albeit in the name of a traditionalizing rather than a modernizing aesthetic.

Though ostensibly concerned to protect a particular environment, preservation usually involves a more or less systematic attempt to improve it, and quite often to effect a total transformation, as in such brilliant inventions as Covent Garden's Floral Hall. It also has an affinity to the comprehensive redevelopment schemes of the 1960s. It subordinates private interest to what it conceives of as the public good. In its own way it is quite collectivist in spirit, believing that new buildings should 'blend' with their surroundings and be 'in keeping' with their neighbours,[14] and it is indeed this predilection for theming and integration which is the solid basis for the historical and aesthetic arguments which can be advanced against it.

Whatever the criticisms of conservation areas – widely attacked for being Disneyfied, historical toy-towns – they at least involve a recognition that the ideal home does not begin on the doorstep but involves a total environment; and that – as Ian Nairn and the authors of the Architectural Review's *Outrage* (1955–6) knew – street furniture, kiosks, benches, even tree-irons are involved in it.[15] In its own way 'heritage' thus raises questions about whether or not an environment is to be planned, and it seems possible that some of the hatred aroused by it, though voiced in the name of the Left, bears the impress of that recoil from planning which has not yet run its course.[16] Those who want to do dirt on heritage might pause on the fact that after a decade and a half in which privatization and monetarization have seemed to carry all before them, and when the very idea of public service has been poisoned at its source, the politics of the environment is one of the few spheres in which the idea of the public has been given radical new extensions. We are not so rich in counter-examples as to be able to jettison one in which there is a popular support for an extension of the public sphere.

So far from standing for entropy or stasis, heritage and conservation could be seen as growing points in the national culture. Economically, at a time when micro-electronics are making almost every form of human skill redundant, it is one of the very few forms of labour-intensive employment which is actually growing. Politically it rests on a broad base of do-it-yourself retrieval projects in which local initiatives serve, in some sort, as a surrogate for municipal enterprise or state intervention. It puts a premium on cultural innovation and experiment.

It is customary to counterpose futurism and resurrectionism, the one forward-looking, the other a throw-back to the past. Yet historically speaking – as in England's first modernizer, the Arts and Crafts Movement of the 1880s – they might be seen as symbiotic, complementary and antagonistic at the same time, or even as two sides of the same coin, each testifying to a felt absence in the present. Each, typically, arises as an expression of cultural dissidence, and involves a radical rejection of the present in favour of an idealized (or fantasized) other. Under an optic like this the rise of heritage might be seen as a vehicle for the pursuit of the visionary, an idiom for the expression of otherwise forbidden, or forgotten, desire. It allows utopia to occupy the enchanted space which memory gives to childhood, promising a new age which will be simpler and purer than the present. It joins the practical and the visionary, the future and the past. When, for instance, in the winter of 1993–4, the *Independent* offered a £30,000 award, inviting readers to submit a statement on how they would use the money to change their lives – 'by fulfilling a dream, perhaps, or liberating themselves to take on a new job, or complete a long-nurtured project' – the winning entry was that of a 28-year-old marketing manager who wanted to return with his brother to the small village of Grampound, in Cornwall, to run the business that has been in his family for 300 years – 'one of only two in Britain still using natural oak bark tanning methods, selling high quality leather to top-of-the-range shoemakers'.[17]

III

Heritage criticism in Britain has been particularly severe on notions of rusticity which it treats by turn as risible and sinister. A powerful influence was Raymond Williams's *The Country and the City* (1973), which argued that pastoralism was always an exercise in bad faith. In Ben Jonson's time ('To Penshurst' is his text) it was a cloak for the spoliation of the peasantry; in Raymond Williams's own day it had been a licence for 'unconscious reaction'. In either case it involved historical illusion, nostalgia for a past that never was.[18] Martin Wiener's brilliant squib, *The Decline of the Industrial Spirit,* amplified this for the nineteenth and early twentieth centuries, making ruralism the villain of the piece in a narrative of English decadence.[19] Then, in 1987, Patrick Wright and Robert Hewison accused the National Trust of aggrandizing country house owners while reducing the rest of us to a forelock-pulling deference.

In the light of the foregoing, it seems worth pointing out that rural preservation has often been associated with both social protest and cultural dissidence, as it was for Sir Thomas More and the sixteenth-century 'Commonwealth' opponents of enclosure, or, later, for Cobbett and Clare at the time of Captain Swing. From the 1860s, when it began to emerge as a continuous cause, down to very recent times, rural preservation and revival – or rural 'reconstruction' as it was called in the 1920s – was a 'progressive' cause, one which found many of its most ardent supporters and exponents at the radical end of the political spectrum. The Commons, Open Spaces and Footpaths Society, founded in 1865 – the remote ancestor of the National Trust – was a kind of Liberal front, championing the claims of villagers and commoners against the encroachments of landlords and property developers.[20] Robert Hunter, the lawyer, one of the three founders of the National Trust, had been fighting common rights cases for some thirty years, winning such famous battles as those for Hampstead Heath and Epping Forest. As a young man he had come under the influence of Christian Socialism, while his political affiliations, whether working on commons preservation with John Stuart Mill, or in the service of government with Henry Fawcett, placed him on the radical side of mid-Victorian liberalism.[21] Octavia Hill, the second of the Trust's founders, was proclaimedly

a disciple of John Ruskin, her mentor, and by the nature of her fresh air
and open space enthusiasms, a critic, even at times an enemy, of the idea
of private property. Canon Rawnsley, the third of the Trust's founders,
had also come under the influence of Christian Socialism as a young
man and he was a lifelong follower of John Ruskin, though in his
belligerent defence of the Lake District, where he spent his life, he owed
as much perhaps to the Tory-radicalism of Wordsworth.[22] William
Morris's 'anti-scrape' agitation seems to have been one of the influences
on the founding of the National Trust, and a letter from him to Canon
Rawnsley in the Trust archives datelined 10 February (1887?) and
written from Kelmscott House, Hammersmith, conveys something of the
combative spirit of organized preservationism's early years:

> As to the Commission on the rights of way; my firm opinion is that we shall
> be quite helpless against the landowners as long as there is any private
> ownership of land. If I lived in the Country I should rage against these pickers
> and stealers with the best: but if you will not think it too cruel a paradox I must
> say I am not sorry that well-to-do people should feel the tyranny of the system,
> as it will thereby be more likely to come to an end.
> From Dear Sir
> Yours faithfully
> William Morris[23]

The Arts and Crafts Movement, according to their own lights, and
their admirers and imitators abroad (among them the great American
architect Frank Lloyd Wright) were modernists and experimentalists,
avatars of light, space and freedom.[24] They were pioneers of both
'rational' dress and the labour-saving home, exalting the Simple Life
against the suffocating claims of convention, the freedom of the open air
against the claustrophobia of the Victorian interior. Baillie Scott and
Raymond Unwin – the latter a revolutionary socialist by formation – were
housing reformers as well as propagators of cottage architecture, the
virtual inventors, for the middle class, of the two-storey, servantless
home, and for working-class housing of the garden city ideal.[25]

Cecil Sharp, the discoverer of Morris dancing, and collector of
traditional song, was a Fabian, and in his folkloric work at Headington
Quarry contrived to combine musical notation with canvassing support
for the Liberal Party during the stormy period of the People's Budget
and the House of Lords crisis.[26] Percy Grainger, the musicologist who
was largely responsible for the popularization of folk-song in the schools,
was a socialist, albeit of a racist Nordic kind;[27] so too was Mary Neal, who
performed a similar function for Morris dancing. Ruralism between the
wars was also quite largely in the hands of progressives, notably in the
attempt to revive village crafts (Leonard Elmhirst of Dartington, a

disciple of Tagore, was a representative and influential figure);[28] and in the opposition to 'ribbon' or bungaloid development, of which Clough Williams-Ellis was the energetic co-ordinator,[29] gathering about him a formidable array of writers and artists. And it was very much of a piece with this that Labour in its propaganda should have treated ribbon developments as a capitalist atrocity, the very epitome of the evils of unrestricted competition.

The early promoters of the country house cult – very much a lost cause, it seemed, between the wars – were also, curiously enough, in their politics if not in their preservationism, 'progressives'; and indeed as late as 1936, when George Lansbury was Vice-Chairman of the National Trust,[30] the rescue of doomed country houses was thought to be more of a Labour than a Conservative cause. In the 1930s a quite remarkable amount of socialist business seems to have been transacted at country houses, either because they had been converted into conference centres – like those in which the ILP, the Fabians and the Liberals held their summer schools; or because, like Dartington Hall, or Garsington, or Hinton Manor (host, in the 1930s, to a large part of Labour's future cabinet),[31] they were a weekend home for the radical intelligentsia. Or because in the manner of the Countess of Warwick's Easton Lodge in the 1890s,[32] or of Lord Faringdon's Oxfordshire estate (watering-hole of Bevanism in the 1950s) there was a radical aristocrat in place.

Vita Sackville-West, who championed the 'organic' country house against the more grandiose, Palladian alternative, was no progressive, but via marriage her connections were as liable to be Labour as Tory, and even before her affair with Virginia Woolf, at least one of her existences seems to have been on the outer fringes of Bloomsbury. In any event her notion of the 'informal' country house seems to be closer in spirit to the cottagey look, affectionately caricatured in Osbert Lancaster's 'Home, Sweet Home' than to the Roman fantasies of Sir John Vanbrugh.[33] Sybil Colefax, whose celebrated shop in Mayfair was one of the nurseries of what today is known as 'the country-house look', was in her other persona (that of a literary hostess) the friend and patron of left-wing writers and artists: along with Nancy Cunard and the Duchess of Atholl she was one of those dissident aristocrats who subscribed to Spanish Aid, and championed the Republican cause in the Civil War.

In a more popular vein, National Parks were Labour policy;[34] hiking was a major, if unofficial component of the socialist lifestyle;[35] and 'freedom to roam' was a left-wing campaigning issue.[36] It had been given a mass basis, in Edwardian times, by the Clarion League, the 40,000 strong organization of the young who combined Sunday cycle meets with preaching the socialist message on the village green. In the inter-war years it was forwarded by the Woodcraft Folk – a kind of anti-militarist, co-educational version of the Boy Scouts and Girl Guides who combined pacifist advocacy and nature mysticism;[37] by the Youth Hostels Association, formed in 1930; and by that great army of hikers who on high days and holidays went rambling on the mountains and moors. Hiking had a particular appeal to working-class Bohemians, as a mainly intellectual alternative to the dance hall, and one that cost no money. They seem to have figured largely among those who poured out of Manchester, Sheffield and Leeds for the mass occupation of Kinderscout in 1934, one of the actions which heralded the long-drawn-out campaign for the opening of the Pennine Way.[38]

None of these left-wing enthusiasms survived the post-war years, though (as a correspondent to the *History Workshop Journal* remarked) septuagenarian cyclists, 'with their bums up and their pedals working like pistons,' could still be seen on country roads, while hikers with knapsacks on their backs turned out *en masse* for the Aldermaston Marches of 1958–62. The 1960s editors of the *New Statesman* no longer felt obliged to write on country matters, as Kingsley Martin had done, or to write an occasional column under the pseudonym of Mr Park; while Labour, when it began to take notice of conservationist matters, showed itself more interested in civic amenity than in rural integrity. The counter-culture of the 1960s was much more metropolitan in its enthusiasms than its inter-war predecessors ('Make London a 24-hour city' was one of the watchwords of *International Times*), and though it staged huge open-air pop concerts, rambling was hardly its scene. But the counter-culture did have its Arts and Crafts side. 'Ethnic' clothes stalls were the original kernel of today's mega-market at Camden Lock; the macrobiotic restaurants and 'whole-food' shops promoted the idea of 'organic' farming. 'Cranks', the health-food restaurant which opened at Carnaby Street in 1961 – using only '100% whole meal flour, raw Barbados sugar, free-range eggs, fresh fruit and dairy produce' – could be said to be the pioneer of some of the vernacular lines to be found on the supermarket shelves today, while the now familiar but then revolutionary surroundings – 'handthrown stoneware pottery, solid natural-coloured oak tables, heather-brown quarry tiles, woven basket lampshades and hand-woven seat covers' – prefigured the stripped-pine look. More generally, it was in the nature mysticism, transcendental meditation, wistful songs and droopy clothes of 1960s hippiedom, and in the communes, squats and settlements of the early drop-outs, that the idea of 'back-to-the-land' resurfaced, not only as an environmental panacea but also as a private utopia (A. Rigby, *Communes in Britain*, 1974, shows the movement in its earlier phase).

In this context it seems pertinent to point out that Edith Holden, the so-called 'Edwardian Country Lady' of *The Country Diary of an Edwardian*

Lady – an international best-seller when it was published in 1977, and one which, by judicious franchising, gave rise to a vast profusion of 'Edwardian Country Lady' products – was not in fact a country lady at all, but a Birmingham socialist, and an artist, somewhat akin, in origins, occupation and outlook, to the Miriam of D.H. Lawrence's *Sons and Lovers*.[39] On weekdays, at the time she was compiling her 'country diary', she was a mistress at a Birmingham elementary school; on Sundays, following in the wake of her socialist father, she was a teacher at the Birmingham Labour Church, Hurst Street. Along with her family she was also in the habit of attending Sunday evening services there at which (as the researcher who went in track of her life put it) 'a socialist spoke every week'. Like her older sister Effie, Edith was an ardent follower of Arts and Crafts, and the Birmingham Art College where she received an 'excellent' for her drawing had apparently been started by disciples of William Morris.[40]

The publishers' blurb of *The Country Diary of an Edwardian Lady*, concerned, perhaps, to defend his opportunistic choice of title, cunningly notes that the diary was found 'in a country house' but there is no evidence that Edith Holden herself actually stayed in a country house, still less that she wrote her diary in one, indeed the diary has no reference to any domestic interior at all: it is made up entirely of flower sketches juxtaposed against verse. Her 'diary' is in fact very much akin to those of the nineteenth-century working-men botanists who (as Sabbatarians occasionally complained) spent their Sundays collecting specimens or taking sketches from nature. There is not a word in her diary about, nor a visual hint at, any of those commodities which have been manufactured in her name, neither the 'Edwardian Country Lady' set of bedroom co-ordinates which Marks and Spencer were still featuring in 1987–8 (in the following year it was replaced by the 'Versailles look'); nor the 'Edwardian Lady's Country Kitchen' which competed for favour with the 'Balmoral' and the 'Elizabeth Ann' in the monthly glossies, still less the 'Edwardian Country Lady' notelets on sale in the stationery department of W.H. Smith's and John Menzies.

IV

In the 1930s the modern movement in architecture and design went hand-in-hand with the organization of preservationist lobby and pressure groups. The Council for the Preservation of Rural England, founded in 1926, was definitely an advocate of the planning idea – seeing rural reconstruction and the prevention of ribbon development as the only way of preventing a new expropriation of the countryside.[41] It was also an early friend of the idea of National Parks, and a supporter of the 'freedom to roam' of hikers. Inevitably, too, it was an early advocate of those ideas of land-use control which were collectivism's grand panacea for rural ills. Sir Patrick Abercrombie, Secretary of the Council for the Preservation of Rural England, was the most famous planner of his day, a disciple of Geddes, and author in 1943 of that most remarkable of the utopian blueprints for post-war reconstruction, *The County of London Plan*.

Aesthetically, too, in the inter-war years, modernism and revivalism were partners. 'Regency Style', an invention of the interior decorators which became fashionable in the early 1930s, was offered as a parallel to the Modern Movement (symptomatically it was popularized by the ultra-modern Chelsea department store, Peter Jones).[42] So was Georgian architecture, with its supposedly simple lines and predilection for a light airiness. No less influential – a ruling philosophy with the Design and Industries Association established in 1915 – was the combination of the Arts and Crafts tradition with a belief in machine aesthetics. It was anticipated in the mystic socialism of W.R. Lethaby,[43] at the Central School of Arts and Crafts; taken up in the 1930s by Nikolaus Pevsner in *Pioneers of Modern Design* (1935) and by Herbert Read in *Art and Industry* (1934); and found its apotheosis in the war-time 'Utility' schemes and the founding of the Council of Industrial Design.

J.M. Richards, a founder of the Georgian Group in 1937, and in later years the long-running editor of the *Architectural Review* and an influential popularizer of modernism, combined a belief in social planning with a whole series of very strong attachments to the old. His *Functional Tradition* (1958) is given over to the analysis and celebration of such early industrial buildings and plant as Albert Dock, Liverpool (then falling into ruin, today a Grade I listed building); Snape Maltings (later adopted by Benjamin Britten and Peter Pears for the Aldeburgh Festivals) and the fishermen's sheds at Hastings, recently secured for the fishermen after a sixty-year campaign.[44] 'Structures of this kind', he writes of nineteenth-century storage sheds, 'may seem too modest to deserve the name of architecture, but they demonstrate better than any others the unselfconscious rightness of taste – based on robustness and simplicity – displayed by nineteenth-century engineers and builders'.[45]

Another figure who seems worth pausing on, partly because he was the writer of preservationism's finest contribution to the history of the built environment, partly because he helped to marry love of the Georgian with the planning idea, is John Summerson, author of *Georgian London*, and in his later years curator of that remarkable memorial to late eighteenth-century antiquarianism, Sir John Soane's Museum. As Mandler shows in his new study, Summerson was an enemy of what he once called 'architectural Toryism'; he was a supporter of the refugee scholars and architects coming to England from continental Europe, and the neo-Marxism of his history has been ascribed to the influence of the Warburg. As well as being an exemplary marriage of economic history and aesthetics, *Georgian London* is also a tremendous vindication of the planning idea and in its own way as much a tract for the times as Clough Williams-Ellis's *Britain and the Beast* and *Britain and the Octopus.*[46]

Educationally, as well as architecturally, heritage arrived on the scene as a progressive force. Thus country dancing was introduced to the Edwardian school, by teachers like Mary Neal, as an early experiment in eurhythmics, a way of freeing the limbs from Victorian tight-lacing.[47] Likewise handicrafts, in the form of pottery and woodwork, were promoted as an example of education through art.[48] Scouts and Guides, or in the Labour and Co-operative movement the Woodcraft Folk, represented the principles of the New Hygiene as well as a return to Simple Lifeism (forest camps seem to have something of the same function for ecologically-minded children and parents today). Later, in the 1950s, industrial folk-song was taken up by the promoters of the New English as a way of introducing 'working-class experience' into the school curriculum, and bringing the language of the classroom closer to that of everyday life.[49]

The open-air museums, derided today by cultural critics as the quintessence of sentimentality and Little England conservativism, were at the outset, in the 1960s, in the hands of the museum profession's Young Turks – curators who wanted to untether the exhibits from their mooring and position them instead in free-floating open space. Barrie Trinder, one of the founders of Ironbridge Gorge, writes that they took their aesthetic models from best-practice Scandinavian design:

> The projects of the 1960s shared many aspirations, and used many of the same expressions in justifying their existence. All were concerned with the monuments of the Industrial Revolution, with providing opportunities for voluntary labour, with potential visits from educational groups and with encouragement of crafts. The expression 'Open-Air Museum' was used in much the same way as a term which was thought to command instant approval, although few people understood its implications. The enthusiasm for Open-Air Museums is best explained by the fashion for all things Scandinavian which was in vogue in Britain in the late 1950s and early 60s. Girl students adorned their rooms with smoky glass and gonks. Stainless steel dishes were universal wedding presents, and the Saab 96 was widely admired. A generation of student filmgoers regarded Wild Strawberries and Smiles of a Summer Night as peaks of cinematic achievement. Almost every primary school of the 1960s contained echoes of Munkegard School in Copenhagen, and its architect was invited to design what proved to be the finest twentieth

century building in the University of Oxford. Scandinavia meant good design, in buildings, furnishing and fabrics, a serious concern for the arts, and a life-style which, in England, seemed blissfully hedonistic. Open-Air museums were part of this general impression.[50]

Post-war preservationism, in its early phases, was a movement in which the Establishment had little or no part. The Body Shop emerged from Brighton counter-culture;[51] the Campaign for Real Ale from beer-swilling radicals.[52] Covent Garden, in its present form, sprang from a 'community' agitation in which the newly radicalized students of the Architectural Association played a big part. Impossibilists were no less prominent in the early agitation against the motorway box, as they have been, in recent times, in the mass trespasses which have blocked the way of the road-builders. The idea of 'heritage centres' was introduced into this country by an ex-journalist of the *Daily Worker* who, in his passage from 'red' to 'green', had become the press officer of the Royal Institute of British Architects. As he wrote in a letter:

> Heritage centres were, in fact, my brainchild. I got the idea of 'interpreting' the natural environment to an urban population that had lost its contact with nature from the US national parks, and developed the idea in 1973–4 when working on a Leverhulme Fellowship study of the crisis in architecture that people should understand both the history and the actual working (including the allocation of social space) of environments in which they live. As a member of the committee for European Architectural Heritage Year 1975 I persuaded the Arts Council to fund three experimental 'architectural interpretation centres', and I was personally involved in the development of the York centre. I still think it was a good idea, although I never liked the name 'heritage centre', which was given to it by Lady Dartmouth (now the Countess Spencer and, God help him, the Prince of Wales' step-mother-in-law). I always argued that the concept of a centre where people could learn about their environment should not be restricted to the special 'conservation areas' and in that sense I'm delighted that Wigan has one![53]

At the other end of the political spectrum, preservation owes a great deal to right-wing cultural dissidents. Here James Lees-Milne, the long-standing secretary of the National Trust, with his hatred of the levelling tendencies in post-war Britain, and his determination to bring the rescue of imperilled country houses within the ambit of the Trust's work, was clearly an influential figure (there is an illuminating discussion of him in Patrick Wright's *Journey Through Ruins*); so was the anarcho-Tory architectural correspondent of the *Daily Telegraph*, Ian Nairn, one of the very first to extend the notion of 'conservation' from the protection of wild nature to that of the built environment. Railway preservation, the first of the post-war resurrectionist crazes, and arguably the one with the largest mass following, owes little to either right-wing aesthetes or left-wing intellectuals, but seems to have prospered on its own.

V

One reason why heritage cannot be assigned to either Left or Right is that it is subject to quite startling reversals over very limited periods of time. Conservation is not an event but a process, the start of a cycle of development rather than (or as well as) an attempt to arrest the march of time. The mere fact of preservation, even if it is intended to do no more than stabilize, necessarily involves a whole series of innovations, if only to arrest the 'pleasing decay'.[54] What may begin as a rescue operation, designed to preserve the relics of the past, passes by degree into a work of restoration in which a new environment has to be fabricated in order to turn fragments into a meaningful whole. Nature reserves are by definition pretty fragile places, which only the most vigilant and interventionist management (using electronic fences to keep out potential predators and engaging in complex hydrographical exercises to maintain optimum mud conditions) can keep in a wilderness state.[55] Reconstituted ruins are if anything even more vulnerable, being exposed both to the press of the visiting public, and to the aestheticizing hand of heritage management. Heritage, in short, so far from being a stationary state, is continually shedding its old character and metamorphosing into something else.

Industrial archaeology, when the term was first coined, presented itself as no more than a natural extension of the traditional dig, mapping and identifying the visible remains of the past. It was concerned with relics rather than the environment. The advent of the 'working' museum, and the attempt to re-create a realistic and total 'period' setting – shops as well as factories, mill-streams as well as mules, hearths as well as tools – had the collateral effect of aestheticizing the labour process and animating what had been inert. At the 'living history' museums, the demonstrators, drawn from retired or redundant workers, are prize exhibits. The blacksmiths at their forge are monuments of manly strength; the shoemaker stitching away at his awl is the old-time craftsman incarnate. The little piecers, darting in and out of the machines, are miracles of survival. What had begun as a rescue operation, concerned with material remains, was thus elevated, by degree, into a celebration of manual labour. 'Hurrah for the Factory' was the expressive title chosen by Manchester Studies when, in 1979, they put on a photographic display of old-time mill interiors.

Museum display introduces a further set of displacements since, as with any exhibition, it must choose objects for their expressive quality, turning them into a public spectacle and investing them with a public, and very often a historical narrative. The Museum of Rural Life in Emilia is an example. It began life, some thirty years ago, in 1964, when Ivano Trigari, a former peasant employed in an agricultural co-operative near Bologna, found an old farming tool, half-covered by earth, and locally known as a *stadura*. Putting it on show, he set off a fever of emulation, with *festa della stadura* – demonstrations of old hand tools – spreading through the province. The humours it seems were carnivalesque. Institutionalized in a museum, and with captions provided by the economic history department of the University of Bologna, the objects looked quite different – not wonders or marvels or curiosities but documentary illustrations of a quite predictable narrative.[56]

The mere fact of preservation aesthetizes, turning warehouse walls into townscape, derricks and cranes into obelisks, alleys into picturesque lanes. It makes backwardness visually appealing and turns subjects of study into objects of desire. The 'dark satanic mills' no longer seem horrors when they are exhibited as historical monuments or reassembled in picturesque settings. No one who visits the Greg mill at Styal, Cheshire, a National Trust property, can fail to be impressed by the giant water wheel, a veritable cyclops of Vulcan's arts. But no cotton waste sticks to the factory walls; the ground has been lovingly landscaped; and the restored looms, though 200 years old, are producing modern designer-ware – in 1986 'beautiful cotton cloth, incorporated by top designer Pat Albeck into the Styal Calico Collection'. The same cognitive dissonance awaits visitors to Robert Owen's old mill at New Lanark; it has been turned into a conservation village and given over to modern craftspeople. A factory can no longer be associated with the machine age – still less with 'sweating' – when its manufactures appear as art products.

Then, the historical object, however scrupulously preserved, or, as critics sometimes complain, mummified, is as much subject to time's whirligig as any living organism. Canal restoration began as an attempt to resuscitate a dying culture. In 1946, when the Inland Waterways Association was formed, it was still plausible – just – to think of reactivating the canals for inland transport, and also (Tom Rolt's peculiar and intense vision when he was writing *Narrow Boat*) of preserving the 'indigenous working life' of the boatmen. Even the much more practical Robert Aickman, a joint founder of the IWA and its full-time president, dedicating himself to 'an all-consuming campaign to breathe life into a corpse', believed that they might be opening the way to a second front in inland trade.[57] Today, when the canal basins have become showcases of urban pastoral, sprouting conference centres, leisure complexes, luxury apartments and brand new cobbled walkways, and when the Inland Waterways Board declares itself to be the only nationalized leisure industry, the canals, though boasting more than a thousand listed buildings, seem more a pointer to the future than to the past.

Even when the objects have remained the same, we can be sure that they are seen with different eyes, partly because of changes in the environment, but even more, it may be, because of the lens through which they are perceived. Thus at a time when, under the impact of agribusiness, field names are becoming a thing of the past, the subject matter of 'history on the ground' threatens to become as remote as the 'lost villages of medieval England' were when Professor Hoskins and Professor Beresford set out on their muddy walks. Likewise the farm labourer – still neighbours when George Ewart Evans[58] took his tape recorder to them – is an endangered species. Canal boats, too, 'splendidly restored ... in traditional livery' and painted in the harlequin colours of the Victorian fairground rather than rotting on their hulls, are inconceivably more 'historic' than they were when Tom Rolt began campaigning for them.

The meaning of industrial archaeology has been transformed out of all recognition by the disappearance, or near disappearance, of heavy manual labour and the unexampled haemorrhage of industrial jobs. In its early years, despite the name, industrial archaeology was largely concerned with the forerunners of the industrial revolution, windmills and canals in particular. Later, the decline of smokestack industry put the Lancashire and West Riding textile mills on the conservationist agenda, while more recently the robotization and computerization of the labour process has turned even assembly-line work into a potential museum-piece. The saving of the Oxo tower on the South Bank, and the floodlighting of the Hoover factory – the first of the sights of London which greets travellers from the West – testifies to the remarkable updating in the archaeological agenda (the youngest listed buildings now date from the 1970s).[59]

The metamorphoses that have overtaken the folk revival, though less publicly visible, are hardly less striking in character. It was highly political in origin, the work initially, of two Communist singer-scholars, A.L. Lloyd and Ewan MacColl, who more or less singlehandedly uncovered a forgotten corpus of industrial song and at the same time established a particular style of performance art. Musically, it was quite closely allied to the New Orleans of 'revival' jazz, promoting concerts as 'Ballads and Blues' and using a jazz banjo or even clarinettist as a kind of modernist counterpoint to traditional song. Ethnically, it was quite *anti*-English, drawing much of its repertoire, and some of its most notable singers, from the Scottish ballad tradition and from Irish rebel song. The proletarian idiom, borrowed partly from American work-songs, partly from coalfield ballads, was pronounced: 'rough songs . . . made by rough men . . . as coarse and awkward as the day they were first sung'. It offered a heroic view of manual labour rather than an elegiac one, and indeed, like the Northern voice in 'new wave' British cinema, it was widely acclaimed as announcing the arrival of a working-class presence in the national culture.

The folk club movement of the 1960s, though drawing on many of the same singers, was quite different. It was still highly political, being closely associated with what were then known as 'protest' politics (in Scotland the revival ran in tandem with the campaign against nuclear submarines in Holy Loch), but the politics were those of middle-class radicalism rather than a socialism of the working class. The transatlantic influences were those of Joan Baez and Bob Dylan rather than the little red song book of the Wobblies. Jazz idiom was left to rock, the banjo to country-and-western, while in the clubs it was the unaccompanied purist who set the pace. The Critics Group, with Ewan MacColl as teacher, resuscitated eighteenth-century and pre-industrial song, while recordings from Sam Larner, a Yarmouth fisherman, and Harry Cox, a Norfolk farm labourer, helped to inspire the discovery of an alternative heritage of *English* country song. With the harmony singing of the Copper family – recorded in print as well as on disc and much imitated in the clubs – the revival put down its roots in deepest Sussex. The clubs themselves seem to have served as some kind of refuge for the sociologically orphaned – the ex-working class from whose ranks the new generation of singers were largely recruited.

VI

Politically heritage, like conservation, draws on a nexus of different interests. It is intimately bound up with competition for land use, and the struggle for urban space. Whether by attraction or repulsion it is shaped by changes in technology. It takes on quite different meanings in different national cultures, depending on the relationship of the state and civil society, the openness or otherwise of the public arena to initiatives which come from below or from the periphery. In one aspect it is a residual legatee of the environmental campaigns of the 1960s, the aesthetic revolt against 'gigantism', and the rediscovery of simple lifeism. In another aspect it could be seen as the epicentre of a whole new cycle of capitalist development; the spearhead, or cutting edge, of the business recolonization of the inner city, a style-setter for post-Fordist small-batch production. In Eastern Europe on the other hand, where the mobilization and use of tradition was at least as much a feature of the politics of the 1980s as it was in the West, cultural nationalism and the revival of religion seem more pertinent than the restructuring of the economy.

Ideologically, too, heritage is chameleon, being subject to startling reversals over comparatively short periods of time. Like conservation, with whose causes it is umbilically linked, it is incapable of remaining in a stationary state, but is constantly metamorphosing into something else. That is why the focus on the 'manufacture' or 'invention' of tradition – the only way in which the heritage-baiters and the deconstructionists seem able to engage with the commemorative arts – seems often wide of the mark. Focusing on the 'strategies' of supposedly all-powerful and far-seeing elites, it cannot begin to address the great mass of pre-existing sentiment which underpins sea-changes in public attitudes and revolutions in public taste.

The notion that nostalgia is a peculiarly British disease, and that the rise of 'heritage' in the late 1970s and 1980s represented a recrudescence of 'Little Englandism' is not one which could survive comparative analysis intact. Conservationism is a global phenomenon, and the notion of heritage as an environment under threat, and as a cultural asset to exploit, has been a feature, for some thirty years, of the advanced capitalist economies of the world. Landmarks Conservancy in New York has been systematically 'listing' historic buildings for some twenty-five years, while the Environmental Protection Act of 1969 laid the groundwork for US industrial archaeology. The Garden Festival idea was German in origin. The historicist preservation and adaptive re-use of old commercial and industrial premises has been for some thirty years the cutting edge of the business recolonization of the inner city, as familiar in Lakeside Zurich as it is in Southwark Bankside.[60]

Nature conservancy is even more strikingly transnational, and it was indeed in recognition of this that, when Peter Scott in 1961 launched the initiative to which, more than any other, we owe the preservation of our ancient woods and surviving wetlands, it took as its name the World Wildlife Trust. As the ecological disasters in Russia and Eastern Europe painfully demonstrate, a preoccupation with wildlife habitat and eco-system balance, is – like the preservation of industrial monuments – prosperity-led, a privilege of the advanced, or relatively advanced, economies. It was at the very height of the post-war boom, when in the EEC countries talk of 'economic miracles' was giving way to fears of 'over-heating', and when in Britain the government was struggling with the problems of 'brimful' employment, that, in 1970, European Conservation Year was celebrated, 'the closest that the nature conservation movement has yet come to embracing all aspects of conservation'.

Friends of the Earth was founded in the USA in 1969, the World Heritage Convention – under which European Architectural Heritage Year of 1975 was promoted – was held in 1971, the year that TB was first identified in British badgers, and that the Otter Trust was formed. The International Convention on Wild Flora and Fauna, which Britain ratified in the Endangered Species Act of 1976, was held in the following year.

Heritage is also proving quite crucial in the construction of post-colonial identities, and indeed the demand for the restitution of national art treasures – for some two or three centuries plundered by the metropolitan powers – is not the least of the effects of the coming-of-age of newly independent states. Through the medium of cultural tourism it is allowing, and indeed encouraging, a whole new class of historic nations to emerge, e.g. Sicily, which now appears as an outer limb of Hellas, or a detached province of Byzantium, rather than as the place which Christ forgot. Building on cultural difference – as in the celebration of Native American art, or the nations within a nation which have been the high point of the exhibition year at the Smithsonian Intitute, Washington, since 1976 – heritage helps to support both a multi-ethnic vision of the future and a more pluralist one of the past.

Australia, currently re-making itself for the second or third time this century, and on the eve of becoming a republic and throwing off the imperial British legacy, is a particularly striking, indeed exciting, case in point. Here the creation of a post-colonial society, in which both historians and heritage have been quite decisive as consciousness raisers, has gone hand in hand with a wholesale revaluation and indeed discovery of the pre-colonial past. Instead of *terra nullius* – before the Mabo judgement of 1993, the formal status of the pre-European Antipodes – there is now a 20,000-year history of 'dreamways' for which archaeologists, geologists, ecologists and Aborigine campaigners are creating a whole new narrative.

Notes

1. John Gaze, *Figures in a Landscape, A History of the National Trust*, London 1988. In 1946 Hugh Dalton, as Chancellor of the Exchequer, introduced the National Land Fund to resource National Parks, one of his great enthusiasms – legislated into being in the Town and Country Act of 1948 – and the National Trust. This was the Fund which SAVE called on in its late 1970s battle to rescue Mentmore. In *Practical Socialism for Britain* (1935) Dalton had described the National Trust as 'Practical Socialism in Action'. Like many Socialists of his generation he was an enthusiastic walker, and had been in the habit of walking the Pennine Way for some years before, as Minister of Town and Country Planning in July 1951, giving it state protection. Ben Pimlott, *Hugh Dalton*, London 1985, pp. 218, 455–6, 553–4, 578–81.

2. The recent exhibition of Aborigine art, ancient and modern, at the Hayward Gallery gave the clearest indications of the role of art, history and heritage in consciousness-raising

movements among native Australians. Peter Sutton, ed., *Dreamings, the Art of Aboriginal Australia*, New York 1988 is a fine catalogue.

3. Tony Bennett, 'Museums and "the People"' in Robert Lumley, ed., *The Museum Time Machine*, pp. 76–82.

4. Geoffrey C. Stewart and Faith Davis Ruffins, 'A Faithful Witness: Afro-American Public History in Historic Perspective, 1828–1984' in Susan Porter Benson et al., eds, *Presenting the Past, Essays on History and the Public*, Philadelphia 1986. For Malcolm X's advocacy of the lost Afro-American identity, *The Autobiography of Malcolm X*, Harmondsworth 1968, pp. 41, 85, 276–7; ed. S. Epps, *The Speeches of Malcolm X*, London 1969, pp. 61–2, 77, 168–9. Alex Haley, *Roots*, London 1979 for an ambitious and very successful attempt to make the Afro-American the basis for a family history. Alice Walker's novel *The Color Purple* is a brilliantly successful fiction in this vein.

5. Michael Wallace, 'Professionalizing the Past, Reflections on the History of Historic Preservation in Benson et al.; Charles E. Peterson, 'The Historic American Buildings Survey: Its Beginnings', in *Historic America, Buildings, Structures and Sites*, Washington 1983 pp. 7–21.

6. For a splendid account of the role of this in the cultural politics of the 1790s, B. Deloche and J.-M. Leniaud, *La Culture des sans culottes, le premier dossier du patrimoine 1789–1798*, Paris 1989. Daniel Hermant, 'Destructions et vandalisme pendant la révolution française', *Annales*, July–August 1978.

7. Marcel Maget, 'A Propos du Musée des arts, 1935–44' *Genèses*, IV, 1992.

8. A sinister reminder of what this meant – and of its potential appeal – comes in the chapter on 'Lessons from other Countries' which Lord Howard of Penrith contributed to Clough Williams-Ellis's 1938 rural preservationist volume *Britain and the Beast*. It quotes with approval the law for protecting the natural beauties of the Reich passed by the National Socialist Government on 26 June 1935, 'signed by the Führer and Chancellor of the Realm Adolph Hitler', and countersigned by General Goering and other ministers.

Today as formerly Nature in Wood and Field is the object of the desire, the joy, and the recreation of the German people. The landscape of the countryside has however been completely changed in these latter years, its garb of trees and flowers owing to intensive agriculture and afforestation, to narrow minded cleaning up of meadows and to the cultivation of conifers has been in many places completely altered. Many species of animals which inhabited wood and field have disappeared with the disappearance of their natural haunts. . . . The protection of objects of natural interest (*Naturdenkmalpflege*) which has been growing for centuries could be carried out with but partial success, because the necessary political and cultural conditions were lacking. It was only the transformation of the German man which created the preliminary conditions necessary for an effective system of protection of Natural Beauty.

Lord Howard of Penrith comments:

Whatever we may think or feel about Nazi political philosophy all must I think acknowledge that in this introduction to a Law, which I hope will in many things become a model for the rest of the world, its draughtsmen have expressed a deeply felt sense of the beauties of their country and of the necessity of preserving these for the 'desire, the joy, and recreation' of future generations. We who share their views in this matter can at least applaud the effectiveness of the measures they are taking to attain their laudable object.

9. Michael Wildt, 'History Workshops in Germany', in R. Samuel, ed., *History Workshop, A Collectanea, 1967–1991*, Oxford 1991.

10. R. Bahro, *The Alternative in Eastern Europe*, London 1979. *Building the Green Movement*, London 1986.

11. Hillier Parker research. *Market Briefing*, June 1992. I am grateful to Robert Thorne for a copy of this document.

12. I have argued this in 'Mrs Thatcher's Return to Victorian Values' in T.C. Smout, ed., *Victorian Values*, Oxford 1992.

13. Bailly, *The Architectural Heritage of European Cities*, Cambridge, Mass. 1979, pp. 97–8. English Heritage, says a former member of the GLC Historical Buildings Department, 'is now the only strategically effective body for London … The only form of public interest property men will listen to.' Robert Thorne in discussion, January 1994.

14. *British Architectural Design Awards*, Macclesfield 1984.

15. *Architectural Review*, 'Outrage', June 1955; 'Counter-Attack', December 1956.

16. Peter Hall, *Great Planning Disasters*, London 1980; Alice Coleman, *Utopia on Trial. Vision and Reality in Planned Housing*, London 1985.

17. 'Free to Save a Traditional Cornish Craft', *Independent*, 10 January 1994.

18. Raymond Williams, *The Country and the City*, London 1975.

19. Martin J. Wiener, *English Culture and the Decline of the Industrial Spirit 1850–1980*, Cambridge 1981.

20. Lord Eversley (G.J. Shaw-Lefevre), *English Common and Forest, the Story of the Battle during the last Thirty Years for Public Rights over the Commons and Forests of England and Wales*, London 1894; *Commons, Forests and Footpaths*, London 1910; W.H. Williams, *The Commons, Open Spaces and Footpaths Preservation Society, 1865–1965, A Short History of the Society and its Work*, London 1965; J. Rawlett, 'Checking Nature's Desecration; Late Victorian Environmental Organisation', in *Victorian Studies* 22, 1983, pp. 197–222. On C.R. Ashbee's role as Council member of the National Trust, National Trust Archives Acc. 42/25–6 lectures to be delivered in the USA by Canon Rawnsley and C.R. Ashbee 1899–1900. 'Sydney Olivier is on the Executive Committee of the Commons Preservation Society', runs a notice in *Fabian News*, May 1893, '… Members are specially requested to inform him of any cases of enclosure of Commons, roadside strips, or footpaths which may come under their notice.'

21. Robert Hunter, *Preservation of Commons*, London 1880 for some of his battles with railway companies and property owners. Christopher Helm, *Founders of the National Trust*, London 1987 for a not very illuminating collective profile.

22. Eleanor F. Rawnsley, *Canon Rawnsley, An Account of His Life*, Glasgow 1923.

23. National Trust Archives, Acc. 6/4, letter of William Morris to Canon Rawnsley, 10 February (1887?). Morris did not take part in the foundation of the National Trust, but C.R. Ashbee, in some sort his successor on the anarchist and community-building aesthetic wing of English Socialism, did. Cf. National Trust Archives, Acc. 42/25–26 for the prospectus of the lectures he delivered for the Trust in the USA in 1900; and Acc. 1/30 for a letter to Ashbee in 1897.

24. G. Naylor, *The Arts and Crafts Movement, A Study of its Sources, Ideals and Influence on Design Theory*, London 1990. Fiona MacCarthy, *The Simple Life; C.R. Ashbee in the Cotswolds*, London 1981. Elizabeth Cumming and Wendy Kaplan, *The Arts and Crafts Movement*, London 1991. For the community-building side of Arts and Crafts, cf. Jan Marsh's excellent *Back to the Land, the Pastoral Influence in Victorian England from 1880 to 1914*, London 1982; Dennis Hardy, *Alternative Communities in Nineteenth Century England*, London 1979; W.H.G. Armytage, *Heavens Below, Utopian Experiments in England, 1560–1960*, London 1961.

25. M.H. Baillie Scott, *Houses and Gardens*, London 1900; Raymond Unwin and M.H. Baillie Scott, *Town Planning and Modern Architecture at the Hampstead Garden Suburb*, London 1909; James D. Kornwolf, *M.H. Baillie Scott and the Arts and Crafts Movement*, London 1972.

26. Cecil Sharp House, Sharp Correspondence, Box 2, Correspondence with William Kimber.

27. John Bird, *Percy Grainger*, London 1982.

28. On Dartington there is Michael Young's excellent and loving *The Elmhirsts of Dartington*, London 1982; cf. also Maurice Punch, *Progressive Retreat, A Sociological Study of Dartington Hall School, 1926–1957*, Cambridge 1977; Victor Bonham-Carter and W.B. Curry, *Dartington Hall, the History of an Experiment*, London 1958; Anthony Emery, *Dartington Hall*, Oxford 1973.

29. Clough Williams-Ellis, *England and the Octopus*, London 1928; (ed.), *Britain and the Beast*, London 1938; *Architect-errant*, London, 1971, for his autobiography.

30. Lansbury's support of the National Trust was of a piece with his lifelong attention to environmental issues, his promotion of farm colonies and – as Minister of Works in the

1929–31 Labour government – his championship of open-air lidos. Raymond Postgate, *The Life of George Lansbury*, London 1951.

31. Nicholas Davenport, *Memoirs of a City Radical*, London 1974 for the place of Hinton Manor in the XYZ Club where the young Hugh Gaitskell cut his political teeth.

32. Modern Record Office, Warwick University, Mss. 74/6/2/105, Letter of Countess of Warwick to Ben Tillett, 21 December 1936 is a poignant reminder of what Easton Lodge had once meant.

33. Vita Sackville-West, *English Country Houses*, London 1941; Jane Brown, *Vita's Other World, a Gardening Biography of V. Sackville-West*, London 1985; Suzanne Raitt, *Vita and Virginia, the Work and Friendship of V. Sackville-West and Virginia Woolf*, Oxford 1993 for a hostile though interesting account.

34. John Sheail, 'The Concept of National Parks in Great Britain, 1900–1950', *Trans. Inst. of British Geographers*, 66, 1975; *Rural Conservation in Inter-War Britain*, Oxford 1981.

35. Ruth Adler, *A Family of Shopkeepers*, London 1985, Ch XVIII for the rambling craze among young Stepney Jews.

36. C.E.M. Joad, *A Charter for Ramblers*, London 1934; Joad, who became a national figure during the Second World War when he emerged as one of the stars of the BBC 'Brains Trust', was chosen to compile the BBC's 50th anniversary tribute to the National Trust – see National Trust Archives, Acc. 45 'The National Trust. Past Achievements and Present Activities', script to BBC Third Programme 10 August 1947.

37. For a splendid new account of the Woodcraft Folk in relation to the nature mysticisms of the 1920s, Derek Edgell, *The Order of Woodcraft Chivalry 1916–1949 as a New Age Alternative to the Boy Scouts*, 2 vols, Lampeter 1992. Also D. Prynn, 'The Woodcraft Folk and the Labour Movement, 1925–1970', *Journal of Contemporary History*, 1983, vol. 8, pp. 79–95.

38. Howard Hill, *Freedom to Roam*, Ashbourne 1980. Ewan MacColl, *Journeyman, An Autobiography*, London 1990 for the young motor mechanic whose 'I'm a Rambler' written for the mass trespass became, thirty years later, one of the unofficial anthems of the folk club movement. John Lowerson, 'Battles for the Countryside' in Frank Gloversmith, ed., *Class, Culture and Social Change*, Brighton 1980.

39. Josephine Poole, *The Country Diary Companion*, London 1984, p. 12.

40. Arthur Holden, Edith's father, a paint and varnish manufacturer, was 'in financial difficulties', and about the time she may have been compiling the diary, the family had been forced to move to a suburban house in a fast-growing commuter village, though 'Edith was still within cycling distance of her beloved childhood scenes', ibid., p. 20.

41. The CPRE, as the monthly *Reports* show, worked in tandem with such organizations as the National Housing and Town Planning Council, and took a full part in parliamentary pressure for land use legislation, planning powers and access to the countryside. For an interesting memoir on the founding of the CPRE and its early campaign for the Derbyshire Peak, North West Sound Archive, interview with Garard Haythorn Thwaite, 17 December 1991. 'Skeffington-lodge's spiritual home was the Fabian Society, in which he was exceedingly active until his late eighties', runs an obituary on the former MP for Bedford. 'He was chairman and president for many years of the Brighton and Sussex branch, which is among the most active in the country. He was very friendly with John Parker, Arthur Blenkinsop, and Arthur Skeffington (no relation), all Fabians deeply concerned about the countryside. This led him to give vigorous support to the Council for the Protection of Rural England, of which he was chairman of the Brighton district committee, the Royal Society for the Protection of Birds and the Friends of the Lake District. He was an ecologist long before it became fashionable.' Tam Dalyell, 'Tom Skeffington-lodge', *Independent*, 26 February 1994.

42. John Cornforth, *The Inspiration of the Past, County House Taste in the Twentieth Century*, Harmondsworth 1985, pp. 146–7.

43. W.R. Lethaby, *Home and Country Arts*, London 1924; *Form in Civilisation*, London 1938; R.W.S. Weir, *William Richard Lethaby*, London 1938; Godfrey Rubens, *Richard Lethaby, His Life and Work*, London 1986.

44. For an account of this campaign by the leader of its latest and most successful phase, Steve Peak, 'The Battle on the Beaches Since 1945', in his *Fishermen of Hastings; 200 Years*

of the Hastings Fishing Community, Hastings 1985.

45. J.M. Richards, *The Functional Tradition in Early Industrial Buildings,* London 1958, p. 165.

46. Peter Mandler 'John Summerson, the Architectural Critic and the Quest for the Modern', in S. Pendersen and P. Mandler, eds, *After the Victorians; Private Conscience and Public Duty in Modern Britain,* London 1994, pp. 229–46.

47. Georgina Boyes, *The Imagined Village,* Manchester 1993, pp. 72–86, 94–5, 155–6 for Mary Neal and the Espérance Club – the most determined, if controversial, attempt to translate the principles of the Revival into elementary school practice. Roy Judge, 'Mary Neal and the Espérance Morris', *Folk Music Journal,* V: 5, 1989, pp. 545–91. Cecil Sharp, *Folk Singing in Schools,* London 1912.

48. For progressive ideas in English education between the wars, R.J.W. Selleck, *English Education and the Progressives, 1914–1939,* London 1972; Trevor E. Blewitt, ed., *The Modern Schools Handbook,* London 1934; W. Boyd and W.T. Rawson, *The Story of the New Education,* London 1965.

49. S. Clements, J. Dixon and L. Stratta, *Reflections,* Oxford 1963; and *Things Being Various,* Oxford 1967; John Dixon, *A Schooling in English; Critical Episodes in the Struggle to Shape Literary and Cultural Studies,* Milton Keynes 1991, pp. 150–54 for a retrospective account. In *Things Being Various* black-and-white photographs were introduced in the same spirit as folk-songs had been in *Reflections.*

50. Barrie Trinder, 'A Philosophy for the Industrial Open-Air Museum', in Claus Ahrens, ed., *Report of the Conference of the European Association of Open-Air Museums,* Hargen-Detmold 1985, pp. 87–95.

51. Anita Roddick, *Body and Soul,* London 1991; Gilly McKay and Alison Corke, *The Body Shop, Franchising a Philosophy,* London 1986.

52. Richard Boston, *Beer and Skittles,* London 1977. I am grateful to Mr Boston for letting me read the file of his weekly articles. Apart from their interest for the progress of CAMRA, they are a fascinating commentary on changing mores.

53. Letter to the writer from Malcolm MacEwan, 10 October 1987. For some of MacEwan's other activity in this field, see his autobiography, *The Greening of a Red,* London 1991.

54. 'Pleasing Decay', the subject of a justly famous chapter in John Piper's *Buildings and Prospects,* London 1949.

55. For the RSPB reserve at Minsmere, see Simon Barnes, *Flying in the Face of Nature; A Year in Minsmere Bird Reserve,* London 1992,

56. Alessandro Triulzi, 'A Museum of Peasant Life in Emilia', *History Workshop Journal,* 1, Spring 1976, pp. 117–20 for an account of the origins of the museum. I am drawing on memories and notes of a visit there, with one of the museum's founders, in 1983. Interestingly the one room really crowded with visitors was the kitchen, where there had been no attempt to caption the objects or even, in any museological way, to display them. My guide seemed irritated that the local Italian people were more interested in domestic and culinary bric-à-brac than the story of agricultural change carried in the main panels.

57. Robert Aickman, *The River Runs Uphill, A Story of Success and Failure,* Burton-on-Trent 1986, for a personal account. Robert W. Squires, *Canals Revived, the Story of the Waterways Restoration Movement,* Bradford-on-Avon 1979, for a history.

58. George Ewart Evans, *The Strength of the Hills, An Autobiography,* London 1983; *Ask the Fellows Who Cut the Hay,* London 1956, for the first of his ethnographies.

59. Kenneth Hudson, *The Archaeology of the Consumer Society; the Second Industrial Revolution in Britain,* London 1983, for the Thirties turn in industrial archaeology.

60. Dan Cruikshank points to the interesting parallel to the early development of the English seaside, when, in Regency times, ramshackle fishing ports, such as Bright-ensholme, were turned into fashionable resorts, cultivating 'views' and 'prospects' that looked out to sea, rather than turning its back on them.

PART V

Old Photographs

The Eye of History

I can still remember the shock of seeing my first nineteenth-century photograph. Or rather I think I can, but since my recollection involves two quite separate occasions, and two quite different sets of prints, memory, in one case or both, must be playing tricks. The first occasion (or it may be the second) was at a seminar where, in 1965, a number of us had grouped together to raise a flag for 'alternative history' in Oxford. At one of our sessions somebody brought in some mug-shots of nineteenth-century convicts which Keith Thomas had come upon by chance in the Bedfordshire County Records Office. The faces which stared out at us were startlingly modern, with nothing except for the captions – and the criminal record – to indicate that they belonged to the nineteenth century rather than our own. The men were clean-shaven with not a sideburn to be seen. The women (I think there were two of them) were bonnetless. The faces were disconcertingly 'human' – or to put it more precisely, vulnerable. It was difficult to think of them as cosh-carriers – the role assigned to them in Dickens – still less as the 'dangerous classes', that outcast poor, or lumpenproletariat which so fascinated the apprentice social historians of the 1960s, and which Louis Chevalier had taught us to see as a pathology of the nineteenth-century city.[1] I did not know then that the prison commissioners had been systematically photographing prisoners from the 1850s, and that mug-shots were already an established part of forensic practice. The Bedfordshire photos seemed, rather, to be miraculous survivals, giving us a rare glimpse into realities which had been 'hidden from history' in the past.

My second Victorian photograph – or, as I now remember it, the first – was in the summer of 1965. I had been travelling the record offices and presbyteries of northern England in search of the nineteenth-century Irish Catholic poor, and immersing myself by day in riot depositions, visitation returns and priests' books. In the Harris library at Preston, where I passed the evenings when the record office closed, I chanced

315

upon some reproductions from Thomson and Smith's *Street Life in London* (1877)[2] and this led me to their source: a book then hardly known, but subsequently reprinted, and today one of the sources of those atmospheric prints to be found on the walls of the 'period' pub. The faces were, if anything, even more human than those in the Bedfordshire mug-shots, and were as different as it would be possible to imagine them from the spectral figures of Gustave Doré and Blanchard Jerrold's *London: A Pilgrimage* (1872) – a book which was acquiring a vogue following among nineteenth-century historians.[3] The figures did not lurk in the shadows, but stood out boldly in the foreground. In place of the flaming gin palaces of Doré's chiaroscuro there were two compelling pictures of the 'regulars' at a Whitechapel pub – a mixed group of men, women and children chatting amicably to each other in the sunshine, seated on an outside bench. The photographs were printed in soft-focus sepia, or what I now know to be Woodburytype; Doré's phantasmagoric engravings were executed in black-and-white. Thomson's figures were highly individualized, often no more than two or three to a print. His bowler-hatted street entertainers had real-life musical instruments – a violin, a harp, a cello, a trombone; his 'hokey-pokey' or ice-cream man, scooping out the tub, looked a near relative of the tricycled 'Stop Me and Buy One' ice-cream sellers of my earliest childhood. The man who propped up the doorway in one of Thomson's Seven Dials pictures, photographed in what looked like a trilby hat, might have stepped out of a George Raft movie. No less disconcerting were Thomson's glimpses of London. The street-sellers, so far from wildly gesticulating at the masses, as they did in nineteenth-century word-pictures of Saturday night market, were quietly attending to individual customers, very much in the manner of more contemporary West End barrow boys; the secondhand furniture dealer photographed in Monmouth Street – that ultimate emporium of shabby gentility, immortalized in the pages of *Boz* – was selling some very solid sticks which would not have looked out of place in one of the new stripped-pine shops. Thomson's figures looked solemn, even melancholy, but there was nothing of menace about them, nor – with the exception of 'the Crawler' – abject poverty. It was difficult to imagine that they belonged to the same universe as *The Wilds of London* (James Green-wood's melodramatic explorations of 'low-life deeps' which so fascinated 1870s readers of *The Daily Telegraph*); General Booth's *Darkest England* (which had the London poor living below the level of a cart-horse); or Jack London's *People of the Abyss*.

My excitement at the new discovery was crossed with guilt and shame. Here was I, who was supposed to know something about the nineteenth century, who had studied it for three years at university and who had even begun to teach it. Yet I had not so much heard of Fox Talbot and indeed thought of photography, if I thought of it at all, as a purely twentieth-century phenomenon. Worse (I remember thinking guiltily), it had not even occurred to me to wonder what nineteenth-century people looked like. Nothing had prepared me for any resemblance to ourselves.

With hindsight I can see that both my excitement and my disarray were predictable. Like other social historians of my generation I was completely pre-televisual and indeed remained so until, seven years ago, I married a modern. I had been brought up in a bookish, religiously Communist family; one which, though my mother was (in her spare time) a musician, had no space for visual pleasure. Our own home was bereft of it, and by the standards of the present day unbelievably bleak. There were the Van Goghs and the Renoirs which I bought my mother for Christmas or for birthday presents. There was the bust of J.V. Stalin on the kitchen mantelpiece, and one of Beethoven in my mother's room. Otherwise, nothing: not a single ornament. I revered libraries – in the Communist homes of my childhood 'the library' (even if it were no more than a couple of shelves in a bed-sit) was a sacred object – but I suspect that, as a committed atheist, I would have thought any indulgence in imagery a throw-back to magic and superstition. (My historical mentors seem to have been formed in a similar school, and in their books I find a singular absence of reference to the visual, even when prints and drawings might have been the most vivid illustrations of what they had to say.) At university, the documents I studied for gobbets were legal and constitutional, while my special subject – England in the 1840s – drew heavily on the Corn Law debates and the writings of the political economists. Intellectually, the *vade mecum* of my undergraduate studies was G.M. Young's *Portrait of an Age*, a book which captivated us by asking us to listen to the Victorians (he meant their writings) until we could hear them speak[4] (the idea of the real-life spoken word – oral history – was not yet on the horizon, though when it did come, in 1968–9, some of us seized on it with the same eagerness as we did photography, and for very much the same reason, a belief that without it history was dead).

My notions of the Victorian were entirely literary. They owed much to childhood reading of *Oliver Twist, David Copperfield* and *Great Expectations* and this was being reinforced, in 1965, by a first-time engagement with the 'dark' Dickens of *Our Mutual Friend* and *Dombey and Son*. I was completely ignorant of Victorian painting, something which in our young historians' self-help group in Oxford we were attempting to remedy by engaging with the Pre-Raphaelites. But this break-out from the cramp of the literary did not extend to popular art (I don't think I had even heard of Cruikshank, though I must have seen his illustrations to *Boz*).

I was thus quite unprepared for a history which involved 'ways of seeing', and which took the world of appearances as its point of departure. Then there was the difficulty of reconciling the candid camera and intimate portraits I was beginning to see with either melodramatic notions of the 'dangerous classes' or Marxian ones of 'the masses'. Other photographs which I saw at this time increased my disarray – a picture of the *fusillés* of the Paris Commune, face upwards, eyes open, in their coffins;[5] an alarming piece of Evangelical motto art scrawled in bold black lettering on a farm-yard gate (a photograph in *Hardy's Wessex*[6]); the gypsies camped on Hackney Marshes in G.R. Sims's *Living London*. Each in its own way was a vivid reminder of histories which I had somehow missed out on, and which it was not easy to assimilate to history with a capital 'H'.

On the other hand I cannot have been quite as visually illiterate as I now think myself to have been. As a child, from the age of ten, I was a fanatical cinema-goer (I can't think why), going to the Everyman, Hampstead for the 'poetic realism' of Jacques Prévert, Marcel Carné and Marcel Pagnol; to the Academy, Oxford Street for the Italian neo-realists (they made so deep an impression on me that I still find it difficult not to think of that country as a gigantic film-set); and Hollywood movies at the Odeon, Swiss Cottage, and the Gaumont, Camden Town. A childhood reading of *Picture Post* (we had a big store of them in the cellar) no doubt prepared me unconsciously to associate photography with social realism and to expect of it 'positive' images; while a visit to the *Family of Man* exhibition in 1956[7] (I still have the catalogue) must subliminally have prepared the way for a wider association of photography with notions of the 'human'. It was in this spirit that, when we began *Universities and Left Review* in 1957, one of our star articles, by Lindsay Anderson, was a defence of the exhibition against its detractors.[8] We were ourselves, at the time, fierce partisans of 'Free Cinema' – Lindsay Anderson and Karel Reisz's revival of the British documentary – and we also drew heavily on the Notting Hill street photographs of Roger Mayne.[9]

In my historical studies I must have come upon Victorian photographs. I was certainly familiar with Mr Gladstone's face and I knew (from O.F. Christie's *The Transition to Democracy*, which I read in the sixth form) that the Northumberland miners had been in the habit of putting postcards of him on the mantelpiece. More recently, immersed in Mayhew's *London Labour and the London Poor* (1851) I had seen numerous daguerreotypes (I thought of them as nineteenth-century engravings with a funny name). Finally I should mention that, perhaps as a result of the Labour propaganda of the day, I had had a morbid fascination, from early childhood, with the idea of a slum, so that anything which, voyeuristically, promised a glimpse of the lower depths, was immediately seductive. Thomson and Smith's sombre pictures, however disconcerting, were then, also, very *à propos*.

Ignorance did not inhibit me from responding with enthusiasm to the new source, and buying whatever I could lay my hands on. Like others I was particularly excited by Gordon Winter's *Country Camera* (1966), the book which perhaps first caught the public imagination in the matter of Victorian photography, and I suspect that it shaped the whole direction of early History Workshop work. Our first informal seminar, in 1966, was called 'The English Countryside in the Nineteenth Century'; our third national Workshop, in 1968, was held under the same title; and our first published book, in 1975, was *Village Life and Labour*. From our discovery of Henry Taunt,[10] the Oxford photographer whose work we used in our 1972 History Workshop pamphlet, Sally Alexander's *The Industrial Revolution and St Giles's Fair*, we were also seized with what photography might do for popular publication, and in the History Workshop series of books a great deal of time and energy was devoted to the plates.

One of the disconcerting things which led me to work on the present essay was a belated realization that, in our ignorance of the artifices of Victorian photography, much of what we reproduced so lovingly and annotated (as we believed) so meticulously, was fake – painterly in origin and intention even if it was documentary in form. Thus (I now see) the group of harvesters, reproduced (in sepia) on the book-jacket of *Village Life and Labour*, picturesquely grouped around the corn-sheaves, had been carefully arranged to resemble a genre scene, while the picture of a Northumbrian scytheman is clearly an exercise in the poetics of labour. My friend Gareth Stedman Jones (or his picture editors) seem to have been susceptible to the same dupe. The hardback edition of his *Outcast London* had one of Doré's engravings on the book jacket; the Penguin edition, in 1978, had Rejlander's hugely popular 'Poor Jo', an alleged photograph of a shivering street boy, in which every last detail was bogus (Rejlander paid a Wolverhampton boy five shillings for the sitting, dressed him up in rags and smudged his face with the appropriate soot).[11]

For new-wave social history as a whole, the discovery of photography was overdetermined and it is not surprising that it was so widely and so immediately taken up. It corresponded to the search for 'human' documents – one of the watchwords of 'living history', then as now. It also seemed to answer to our insatiable appetite for 'immediacy', allowing us to become literally, as well as metaphorically, eyewitnesses to the historical event. It also promised a new intimacy between historians and their subject matter, allowing us if not to eavesdrop on the past (a role soon to be assigned to oral testimony) at least to see it, in everyday terms, 'as it was'. Another of our aims which it seemed to bring within reach was that of giving names and faces to the hitherto anonymous crowd – the 'masses' whom it was the object of new-wave social history to rescue from the 'enormous condescension' of posterity. With its heterogeneous variety of settings and its preference for the private over the public sphere, photography was also particularly attractive to those of us who wanted to escape the world of riot and disturbance – the grand terrain of E.P. Thompson's *The Making of the English Working Class* – and give greater salience to what was called (not without a trace of condescension) 'ordinary' people and 'everyday' life.

The *annus mirabilis* of the photographic revival, the point at which, both institutionally and aesthetically, it is said to have come of age, is 1972, the year when the Arts Council appointed its first photographic officer, and the National Portrait Gallery the first photographic curator in the country. But so far as historic postcards and *cartes de visite* are concerned, a market seems to have been growing up from the early 1960s, and, for 'railway interest' photography, even earlier. Amongst professional historians, the discovery of old photographs was prefigured in a series of small stirrings which brought the idea of the visual to the fore. At Leicester, the one university to have extended a helping hand to English local history, Professor Hoskins had been vigorously arguing a case for 'visual history', though his point of address was to material culture and landscape rather than the visual representation of them; one of his colleagues, Professor Jack Simmons, launched a multi-volume *Visual History of England*, of which eight titles appeared, by various hands, between 1963 and 1968.[12] In a quite other sphere, the British Printing Corporation, encouraged by A.J.P. Taylor, the first senior historian to argue photography's cause, was assembling a vast array of prints for its *History of the Twentieth Century* part-series publication.

The first book to use old photographs not as illustrations or as a peg for authorial commentary, but as substantial texts in their own right, with the power to make their own narrative, was Gordon Winter's *Country Camera*, published by *Country Life* in 1966 and later reprinted, first by David & Charles and then by Penguin. It owed something to the romantic circumstances of the writer's discoveries – as the preface told us, he had rescued some of his glass slides from a lettuce bed where a gardener was using them for frames[13] – and rather more to a new appetite for the visual which by the mid 1960s was manifesting itself in every sphere of national life. Winter's book was published at a peculiarly opportune time. It coincided with the birth (or rebirth) of what Ronald Blythe (who was himself to make no mean contribution to it) witheringly described as 'the national village cult';[14] the crystallization of a new pastoral, in relation to the environment (what was later to be called ecology); and the rise of a new rusticity in commodity marketing and design. The counter-culture though in one of its platforms promoting the idea of the 24-hour city was in another turning ecological and opening the door to the emergence of 'organic' farming and wholefood fanatics. Laura Ashley, who opened her first boutique in 1968, projected the milkmaid look as a kind of alternative national dress; while Julie Christie's ravishing performance as Bathsheba, in the film version of *Far from the Madding Crowd* (1967), turned broderie anglaise into the latest thing. Thus it was, perhaps, that Winter's book had numerous epigones (among them, two further albums from the writer himself) whereas its two forebears (or elder cousins), Peter Quennell's *Victorian Panorama* (1937)[15] and O.J. Morris's *Grandfather's London* (1956),[16] had disappeared from public view.

Schools,[17] under the influence of pedagogies which exalted 'iconic representation', were far more hospitable to the reception of photography – and far more critical and self-aware in their use of it – than university historians, who lent their dignity and authority to coffee-table books and Sunday colour supplement articles, but showed no sign of incorporating old photographs into their teaching materials or primary sources.

But it was above all in the localities that, in the 1970s, the taste for historical photographs took root, leading both to the discovery of the work of forgotten local photographers, and to the animation of the meticulously preserved, but hitherto unused, caches in the public libraries. It corresponded to a sea-change in research interest from early modern times – the original heartland of the post-war renaissance of English local history – to the nineteenth and twentieth centuries, and from manuscript to oral sources. The flood of 'We Remember' books which poured out of the local and community presses, or sometimes the public library, opened the contents of family albums to public view, as for example those published by Manchester Studies,[18] Centerprise in Hackney and Queensspark in Brighton. The Batsford Victorians and Edwardians series is well known, but in many ways more interesting, prefiguring the massive town-by-town project being undertaken in the present day by the Alan Sutton company of Gloucestershire, was that of the Hendon Publishing Company, a one-man business with premises in a disused family mill. Starting in the high Pennines with an album on the proprietor's home town of Colne, it spread ecumenically over the whole country, though mainly north of the Thames. The series, printed in demi-octavo, depended almost entirely on local sales; it drew on local sources and enlisted the energies of both local historians and borough and city librarians. Publication started in 1971 with a single title. In the next year they published 13 new titles, and sales rose to a peak in 1976, when they published 24 new titles and 13 reprints; by 1981 reprints were as high as 37 a year; though, with a backlist of 147 by this time, new titles were trailing off.[19]

When historians first turned towards old photographs, it was as a way of modernizing the subject, of bringing the outside in and bridging (or vaulting) the gap between past and present. It promised to turn our subjects, metaphorically speaking, into contemporaries, physiognomically recognizable as likenesses of ourselves, whatever the contrasts in comportment and dress. It was a way of seeing the nineteenth century with twentieth-century eyes, or, as a historian of photography has put it, seeing that 'then can also be now'. Matters changed with the historicist turn in British culture and the growing disenchantment with the promise of modernism, a reversal which can retrospectively be dated to the late 1960s. Images came to be chosen – not least by historians themselves – not for their intimation of the shape of things to come, or as an exemplification of those larger unities which transcend mere temporal division, but for their aura of 'pastness'. The history which accompanied this, as it appeared in school projects, museum displays and exhibitions, Sunday colour supplements and coffee-table books, turned on a dialectic of 'now' and 'then' rather than – as in more traditional historical narrative, with its sequence of events or developmental laws of change – 'before' and 'after'. Instead of the past being a prelude to the present it was an alternative to it, a reverse image of the way we live now, and 'period' photographs were chosen accordingly.

One reason why the showing of old photographs was adopted with such enthusiasm in the primary schools, as a way of initiating younger children to the historical idea, was because of the graphic representation of otherness.[20] A similar inspiration seems to have animated the compilers of local history albums and pictorials. Sometimes this is made explicit – as it is also when old photographs are published in the local newspapers with two contrasting sets of images titled 'now' and 'then', exemplifying the opposition between past and present. Even without this, the caption writers seem to find it difficult to resist making the point, sometimes with the aim of listing casualties (as in John Betjeman's *Victorian and Edwardian London*),[21] sometimes to astonish the reader, by illustrating the magnitude of recent change. 'Liskeard Cornwall, *c.* 1914', runs one, a companion to the writing of family history, 'A picture very evocative of the period. Note the hatter's shop and the absence of traffic.'[22] 'The pre-bikini age', runs another, captioning one of Paul Martin's 'candid' shots of canoodling couples on Yarmouth sands.[23] The caption to a 1930s picture of a playground fight draws out another set of dualities which, while genuinely perceptive, seems to owe as much to contemporary fears about law-and-order, as to an effort to reconstruct the past. 'One of the most noticeable contrasts with our time', runs the caption, 'is the comparative formality of those watching a wrestling match, as is the organisation of the children forming an orderly ringside for young (and gloved) boxers, a most improbable sight today.'[24]

If such photographs focus, as they often do, on the 'ordinary' and the 'everyday' it is because, with the subsequent metamorphoses over time, they have become, retrospectively, curiosities. The street in which there is not a car to be seen, but only the occasional bicycle or children bowling hoops, is an adventure playground, a promenade, or else is the crooked original of what is today a six-lane highway. The shop with the rough lettering in the window and the proprietor in the doorway becomes an emblem of individualism, the trade enamel to Mazawette Tea is a memorial to vanished commodities. The seaside views recall the time when Brighton beach was crowded from pier to pier, and there was barely a pebble to be seen; when Torquay ('The English Naples') was queen of the resorts; when package holidays were unknown and when instead of Sony Walkmans on the beach there were pierrots. For children growing up today, accustomed to television – and to technicolor – from the earliest age, old photographs, even if they are presented in the name of 'living history', must often seem inconceivably remote. The very fact that they are stills marks them out as the creatures of another age, while their colours, whether black and white or sepia, brand them indelibly as 'period'. The faces in the studio photograph – distant, reticent and withholding, as of those not used to the camera's eye – may seem those of another race. The brake party, with serried ranks of day-trippers drawn up for the group photograph, could hardly be more anachronistic in a time when the August Bank Holiday is becoming little more than a historical souvenir.

The cumulative effect of these discoveries, at least in the popular imagination and, albeit subliminally, in that of historians, was to create an iconography of the national past (at any rate the recent past) in which lifestyle rather than politics or economics became the subject of history's grand narratives. Old photographs also offered a whole new gallery of national characters, personifying family fortunes and occupational types. Fishermen, who because of the peculiarities of their industry and their way of life figure not at all in mainstream economic and social history, here take pride of place with their sou'westers, their seaboots and their guernseys, the most photographed (and the most painted) class of working men in nineteenth-century Britain, and the subject of one of photography's founding texts, the Hill/Adamson Newhaven pictures of 1843. More space is given to the munitions workers of the First World War than to the much less exotic female 'typewriters'. On the one hand, these photographs gave a new visibility to the world of rank and fashion, or those whom the Victorians called the Upper Ten Thousand (one might imagine that the rich spent their entire time playing croquet, so faithfully do the reprint albums follow the conventions and chore-ography of society portraiture). On the other hand, in a manner of speaking, they emancipated the poor, giving due space to household servants and staff – the largest single occupational category in mid Victorian times – and in the search for the old-fashioned and the picturesque returning to the figure of the street trader almost as obsessively as did Henry Mayhew.

So far as nineteenth-century Britain is concerned, the effect of these images has been profoundly revisionist, bearding history and literature in their lairs, undermining existing stereotypes and putting novel ones in their place. Nineteenth-century commercialism, denounced by high Tories and socialists alike for its shoddy and its shams, looks altogether more appealing when we see it in period dress (even the 'puffs' of pill millionaires, making their fortunes out of rubbish and trading on fears of illness, can look momentarily benevolent when we see the vernacular of their advertisements decorating the knife-board of a horse-drawn bus). The shopkeeper, too, is retrospectively, or at any rate pictorially, rehabili-tated. In the person of the high-street butcher – a favourite illustration in the books of local views – he is a Napoleon of trade, flanked by a small army of assistants, and backed by mountains of produce, with Christmas turkeys jammed up to the very eaves of the shopfront.

Likewise in industrial photography, a genre enthusiastically taken up by Victorian employers and one which answered perfectly to the gospel of work, backbreaking tasks appear as honest toil. Pictured, if only because of the difficulties of lighting, in open-air and outdoor settings, Victorian work, under the camera's eye, seems retrospectively heroic, and those who engaged in it, if only because of the positioning of the camera (photographers stooped to their work) indomitable. In place of the bow-legged tailor, sitting at his board; the tubercular Sheffield grinder coughing out his lungs; or the seamstress, toiling away for dear life in the attic, we have the sturdy blacksmith, a Vulcan at the forge; the colliers assembled for a works photograph, demonstrating their determi-nation to work; the broad-shouldered navvies performing – or resting from – miracles of toil. In place of the coffin ships we have a forest of masts and derricks and loading bays; wizened old sea-dogs seated on the harbour wall; helmsmen looking masterfully out to sea. Women workers as pictured by the Victorian photographers are, if anything, even more robust – pit-brow lasses, arms akimbo, photographed in the dignity of the Wigan studios;[25] Scots herring girls, standing proudly by their baskets.

Photography gave Victorianism a human face, and it is possible that in doing so it helped to rehabilitate 'Victorian values', in public taste if not in the public mind, by associating it with brake parties and picnics rather than the workhouse and the Poor Law. A term of opprobrium from the 1890s onwards, and in the discourse of Bloomsbury progressivism a by-word for the claustrophobic and the repressed, 'Victorian Values' appeared in an altogether more benevolent light when seen through the camera's eye. Eminent Victorians no longer looked preposterous when photographed in the quiet dignity of the studio portrait, least of all when it was executed, as in the now well-known work of Julia Margaret Cameron, in the best manner of romantic portraiture.[26] Victorian patriarchs lost their terror when pictured – a favourite setting in *plein air* photography – presiding over the family picnic or looking out over the lawn. Instead of the little piecers panting after spinning mules, the much-reproduced lithographs illustrating the factory inquiries of the 1840s, or the pathetic pictures of children down the mines, we are faced with row upon row of aproned artisans staring out at us, in frozen dignity, from the works photographs; navvies standing at ease building the Crystal Palace; needlewomen bent over their sewing, patient as Griselda. Even the little factory children are transformed. In one book of reproductions a very small factory girl is photographed with her family in a portrait of 1861: 'Despite the meagreness of their clothes', the knowing caption tells us, 'all bespeaks virtuous and hard-won respectability.'[27]

In the case of the Depression Years, the 1930s, another *locus classicus* in the current rediscovery and recycling of period photographs, positions are in some sort reversed. It is history here which is revisionist, photography which is hegemonic. The first maps the progress of modernization, the rise of new industries, advances in public health, the extensions of the welfare idea, the convergence of 'middle opinion', the new faith in planning and spread of a leisure culture in which class distinction was relegated to a secondary plane. Imaginatively these cannot compete with a visualization of England, which – for reasons which have to do more with the photographers than their subjects – fixes obsessively on the insignia of class, which sticks to the back streets while ignoring the out-county estates and the suburbs. Nor can it dislodge those icons derived from the documentary photography of the time which have imprinted themselves on the national consciousness, in Britain as in the United States and France, and which have become part of the international repertoire of art – the way in which, visually speaking, in popular publications and on television, the Depression years are returned to us – the worried faces of Humphrey Spender's Worktowners, gazing on life's meagre chances and going uncomprehendingly about their daily tasks;[28] the somnambulist figures who haunt

Holiday souvenir photographs seem to have gravitated at an early date to the comic, the sentimental and the grotesque. The glamorous, make-believe settings invite semiotic (or psychoanalytical) analysis in terms of fantasy and excess: they could also be used as an index to the visual sensations of the day. The example above is taken from a vast collection of family albums gathered by Audrey Linkman and available at the Manchester City Records Office.

The family photograph, though posed, is arguably more 'natural' than those 'candid camera' shots (much favoured as documentary illustrations) where the photographer catches the subject unawares. The family may look stilted, but they are posing not for the viewer but for themselves, projecting an image, however fantasized, of what they believe themselves to be. In the one above, the father, with his eyes averted from the camera, appears to be communing with himself, and the boy on his right arm to be enjoying a quiet smirk.

This picture, one of 20,000 recently deposited by the Manchester Ship Canal Company, introduces us to a class of labour that has hitherto escaped historical notice: boy navvies. Unlike the abject children of the factory engravings, these boys are positively cocky. Hands nonchalantly folded or thrust into their pockets, they are perhaps acting out the part of adults, and look more like apprentice Isambard Kingdom Brunels than exploited wage slaves.

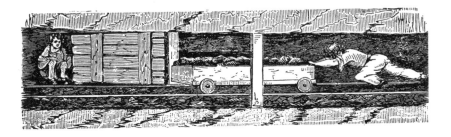

The martyr-child was a potent figure in the factory agitation movement of the 1830s and 1840s. The engravings printed in the Royal Commissions on children's employment in the mines and mills have long been a favourite illustration in school textbooks. Nineteenth-century industrial photography – much of it promoted by the employers – carries a very different narrative.

the midnight streets of Brassaï's Paris;[29] Bill Brandt's down-and-out, the
unemployed man avoiding the children's stare at the corner of the
street, head bowed down, shoulders hunched, feet shuffling, as the mist
and the fog crowd in;[30] the itinerant pea-picker of Dorothea Lange's
'Migrant Mother' series, with a child on either shoulder crying into her
neck, her face set – as it might have been in a Victorian narrative
painting – in a gesture of magnificent defiance.[31]

Historians, like anyone else, expect a photograph to tell a story and so
we are ill prepared for those which tell not one story but two, or worse,
in the case of the unidentified family snapshot – perhaps for that reason
conspicuously underused in the recycling of old photographs – none.
When choosing illustrations we are apt to plump for the iconic – the
image which will stand for a larger whole. Ideally it should be transparent, an objective correlative of truth. We have little patience with
pictures which keep their secrets: the whole point of using them is to
show history 'as it was'. Exegesis is typically a matter of close reading to
bring out the last details, not of identifying repressed narratives. Ideally
the photograph, if it is well chosen, should – like oral testimony or, for
that matter, the archive document – speak itself.

Matthew Brady, the American photographer who persuaded the
Federal government to support a visual record of the Civil War,
described photography as the 'eye of history'. He was invoking history in
a Thucydidean sense as a commemorative act, preserving an account of
deeds which would otherwise be forgotten, laying up a record for the
future, and it is in this sense that the matter is usually discussed – whether
in present-day debates over 'realism' and 'representation', or the more
ancient ones (as old as photography itself) of whether or not the camera
can lie. But the 'discovery' of old photographs, and the widespread
exploitation of them for actuality-effect, whether in popular illustration,
television backdrops, museum displays or teaching packs, poses an
entirely different question, one concerned with the meaning which a
picture acquires *retrospectively*, in the course of its subsequent career,
turning something which may have been taken for quite mundane
purposes – the photograph of a bicycle meet in July 1914, say – into a
source of aesthetic (and reflective) excitement. The power of these
pictures is the reverse of what they seem. We may think we are going to
them for knowledge about the past, but it is the knowledge we bring to
them which makes them historically significant, transforming a more or
less chance residue of the past into a precious icon.

The 'eye of history' left to itself will be at the mercy of what it sees, and
in the absence of even a rudimentary critical method an old photo is
only too liable to be used as though it were a transparency, showing us,
in lifelike detail, history 'as it was'. If we are not to be at the mercy of

these images, and if we are to use them to construct new narratives or pursue different problematics, we need to be able to take a critical distance. Genre analysis would be a help, not only in identifying, or attempting to identify, the imaginative complexes which structure photography's narratives, but also in showing the archetypal images underpinning them – the massacre of the innocents, as in those May 1945 pictures of Bergen-Belsen which, as Susan Sontag[32] and Theodor Adorno among others have recorded, changed the historical consciousness of a generation; the horrors of war, as in the Biafran child suckling a withered breast, or a hand reaching out from the field of corpses at Gettysburg; the freedom of the streets, as in Paul Martin's hugely popular 'candid camera' shots of London children, gambolling in the wake of the watercarts or swinging on the lamp-posts.[33] Attention to ideology would be a help too. The Victorian cult of genius, and even perhaps phrenology, would help to explain the power of Julia Margaret Cameron's portraits, since what she set out to do, from her magnificent Tennyson onwards, was to convey the essence of greatness in her sitters; likewise aristocratic or Byronic romanticism might be helpful in accounting for her shock-headed Herschel or the free-flowing tresses of her Ellen Terry. In more recent times, what might be called 'urban pastoral' – descending in one line from the collaboration of Utrillo and Atget, a painter and a photographer joining forces to make a carousel of the Paris streets; and in another from music hall and cabaret – might help to account for some of our most enduring photographic images of the city, such as those which sell, in pirated editions, at late-night stands in Covent Garden, or which hang as period prints in the pubs.

It is a curious fact that historians, who are normally so pernickety about the evidential status of their documents, are content to take photographs on trust and to treat them as transparent reflections of fact. We may caption them to bring out what – for our purposes – is tell-tale detail;[34] but we do not feel obliged to question, or for that matter to corroborate, the picture's authenticity, to inquire into its provenance, or to speculate on why some figures are there and others, who might have been expected to be present, are not. We do not even follow the elementary rules of our trade, such as asking the name of the photographer, the circumstances in which the picture was taken, or its date. Consequently, we do not have a way, as we would when making use of a manuscript or printed source, of putting quotation marks, metaphorically speaking, around old photographs; nor, even if we are using them to pursue an argument, of footnoting and referencing them. All that appears is a mere credit – 'Mansell Collection' 'Mary Evans Picture Library', 'Museum of English Rural Life' – as though a depository had the same authority as a source. Thirty years on there are not even the rudiments of an agreed scholarly procedure which would allow photographs to be treated with the high seriousness accorded to much less problematical sources. As one curator puts it caustically, most of them are treated as 'eye-wipes'.[35]

In museums, to follow the argument of Gabriel Porter, the use of photographs is no less cavalier. While material artefacts will be lovingly classified, according to age, genre and provenance, photographic back-ups or blow-ups dramatizing 'the look of the past', and recreating, perhaps, some workplace or domestic interior, are treated as self-explanatory. 'In the object *collection* [her italics] each item is identified; production and use are recorded; acquisition by the museum is registered with a transfer document; contextual materials are sought ... On the other hand in the photographic *archive* ... the image speaks by, and for, itself'.[36]

Photographs, if we are to use them as historical illustration, or as empirical evidence about the past, need historical criticism. Formal analysis, in terms of composition, lighting and frame – the grammar of photography – could tell us something of what the camera is up to in, say, the carefully choreographed works photograph, the comic holiday snapshot, the stylized child portrait. Record linkage, illuminating the visible by the evidence of things unseen, and focusing on what the frame excludes, might help us piece together the original contexts, as has been done, wherever possible, in the case of the Manchester collection of family albums. Criminal records, or medical ones, could surely give a whole new meaning to nineteenth-century mugshots. Genre analysis, such as would routinely be applied to a literary text, might be used to pinpoint the aesthetic choices, closed or open, to the photographer, in say high street 'views' (a great favourite in current reproduction), or – one of the great absences – those of natural history. Above all, if we are not to be at the mercy of the optical unconscious, such a criticism would have to extend to the here-and-now, asking why a photograph is, in contemporary terms, appealing.

Photographs in the nineteenth century, or at any rate those which have been reprinted in recent years, were quite self-consciously fabri-cated with a view to narrative or visual effect. In the case of outdoor photographs, the sitters or subjects had often to be bribed or paid for their complaisance; and they might be dressed up for the occasion – rather as Curtis was to dress up his American Indians – to make them look more traditional. As one 1872 cameraman put it:

> Some days ago I had a grand opportunity offered me of getting some haymaking pictures, of which I was not slow to avail myself. I took a great deal of trouble to drill the men, arrange waggons and horses, and other

accessories, so that they should compose well, and waiting until that time of the day arrived when I thought the best effect of light and shade occurred, I photographed the scene.[37]

A rather more difficult subject – reported in *The Photographic News* for 9 October 1885 – was that of a political bootmaker:

> My model ... happened to be passing my studio door, and, looking very dirty, it struck me it was possible to make a picture of him if I could get him to sit. I managed to make his acquaintance, and soon found out his profession was a bootmaker, and his great weakness was politics. After a lot of trouble, I managed to get him into the studio; but directly I ventured to suggest to him to sit for a photograph was the sign for his making for the door. Beer soon made that right, and to get an empty packing case, an old box, some string, and cardboard, was the work of two or three minutes.
>
> The greatest difficulty of the lot was to make him more untidy than he was; and when I asked him to take off his coat he jumped up and said, 'No; my friends will not know me like that.'
>
> I got the expression by making him excited over the latest speeches (political), and at the last moment asked him if he had heard of the defeat of the Government, and the dissolution of Parliament, upon which he strained his neck, and said, 'Government defeated! where?' – and then I got him. The next job was to build a shoemaker's shop; which I did in my printing room, and then printed in the picture.[38]

The social realists, or documentary photographers, of the 1930s, though making much of spontaneity and informal or natural settings, were in the grip of conventions quite as limiting and quite as demanding as those of their nineteenth-century predecessors. In Humphrey Spender's 'Worktown' photographs, his contribution to Mass Observation's 1937 survey of Bolton, figures are typically seen from the rear or sideways. The people look preoccupied and withdrawn. Faces, where they are seen in close-up, are lined with worry. Images of entrapment abound, nowhere more so than at the pub, where the drinkers are literally cornered. Whippet-like men fill the stands at the greyhound racing track. A long shot of a woman whitening the doorstep has her face – and that of a watching child – a mere blur. A bird's-eye view of Blackpool beach has all the faces out of focus, as though even on holiday relaxation was a forbidden luxury.[39]

Walker Evans has his people – the dungareed share-croppers, or poor white trash, of Alabama – stare accusingly, in mute protest, at the camera. He lines them up against the planks, impaled, as it were, on the rough-hewn walls of their homesteads. They are cancerous figures, with skin stretched tightly over their cheekbones, and not an ounce of superfluous flesh. Like the native Americans of Edmund Curtis, they are modern primitives, living in conditions of Shaker-like simplicity. With only one exception they appear before the camera barefoot, treading the rough-hewn floorboards, and pose for Walker Evans in the shabbiest states of undress. Each picture is an icon of suffering. Nobody moves a muscle. Nobody works. Nobody laughs.[40]

It is often the accidental (or incidental) detail in a picture, unnoticed by the original photographer and by subsequent publishers or exhibi-tors, which will be of capital interest to the historian – the *Défense de Fumer* notice on a hay-rick (a reminder, Le Roy Ladurie tells us in his commentary on the photographic self-portrait of an Aveyron village, of the ever-present risk of fire in the Occitan countryside); the positioning of a man on horseback; the tricolour flag at a public ball.[41] Let me give a British example of a remarkable discovery in the royal archives at Windsor: a photograph of the Kennington Common demonstration of the Chartists on 10 April 1848 – one of the best known dates in nineteenth-century political history.[42] Picturing, as it does, a thin and scattered crowd, it proves beyond doubt that the fiasco of April 10 – effectively the end of Chartism – was due not to some failure of nerve on the part of the Chartist leader, Feargus O'Connor, but rather to the small turnout. The picture also bears centrally on the question (currently a matter of hot dispute among historians) of whether or not Chartism was a social movement. Draped around the platform, pointing both to a Chartist political economy, and to a labour theory of value, some thirty years before the Marxist version of it has been heard of, is the single, striking watchword 'Labour is the Source of all Wealth'.[43]

Deconstruction, using photographs in conjunction with oral testi-mony and written documents, splicing together different classes of evidence, or using one to expose the silences and absences of the other, is one procedure which historians can bring to bear on the explication and interpretation of old photographs. Family historians, by force of necessity, are past masters at this. Faced with unattributed *cartes de visite* or cabinet portraits, they have to learn to date 'heirloom' photography by reference to adult fashions, children's clothes, photographers' props and backdrops, and not least the quality of the paper and print and the developer.[44] As the inquiry extends from genealogy and family trees, to family fortunes, an astonishing number of different funds of knowledge can be brought into play around an apparently limited set of images.[45]

It would be a great pity if old photographs were merely used as a further source of information about the small details of everyday life. As the example of the 1848 Chartist photograph may suggest, they can bear on questions of high politics, even on epistemology and the history of ideas. School photographs, if they were illumined by comparative analysis, might be equally serviceable for the study of corporate loyalties and pedagogic ideals. Exercises in Swedish drill (a great favourite in board school photographs of the 1880s and 1890s) and mass assemblies might be contrasted with the highly individualized portrait which passes for a school photograph today. More obliquely, by looking at school displays of the Union Jack, old photographs might serve as a reminder of those pre-1914 patriotic occasions where, in Britain as no doubt in France and Germany, participation in the Great War was in some sort prefigured and prepared.[46]

Photography, if we were to call on it as a primary source, or as a principal point of address, might subvert those compartmentalizations of inquiry which consign our subjects to separate spheres. The whole idea of body politics, or what Tom Laqueur calls 'bodily theatrics' – a growth area in current publication and research – would look a great deal less hermetic if it were approached not through medical treatises, or notions of surveillance and control, but through the fantastic wealth of imagery in which notions of masculinity and femininity, or male and female beauty, are refracted through notions of family and community, youth and age, culture and class.

Notes

1. Louis Chevalier, *Classes laborieuses et classes dangereuses à Paris pendant la première moitié du XIX siècle*, Paris 1958, was the seminal text here, though the parallel rise of 'deviancy' studies in West-coast America and of a fascination with the Victorian Underworld in 1960s Britain, suggests that 'dangerous classes', a term which Chevalier had plucked from the 1820s and 1830s, had a particular resonance and appeal for cultural dissidents.

2. John Thomson and Adolphe Smith, *Street Life in London*, London 1877. The volume was reprinted by E.P. Publishers of East Ardsley, Wakefield, Yorkshire, in 1973.

3. In 1970 it was reprinted with an excellent introduction by Millicent Rose, by the Dover Publishing Company of New York.

4. G.M. Young, *Victorian England: Portrait of an Age*, Oxford 1953; first published as a chapter in a two-volume collaborative work, edited by G.M. Young, in 1936.

5. The photograph was reproduced in Jean Bruhat et al., eds., *La Commune de 1871*, Paris 1960, p. 273.

6. Hermann Lea, *Thomas Hardy's Wessex: Illustrated from Photographs by the Author*, London 1913. The photographs, being almost contemporary with the writing of *Jude* and *Tess* have exceptional interest.

7. The exhibition was the occasion of a pioneering essay in deconstruction by Roland Barthes; see 'The Great Family of Man' in his *Mythologies*, London 1970, pp. 100–103.

8. Lindsay Anderson, 'Commitment in Cinema Criticism', *Universities and Left Review*, vol. 1, no. 1, Spring 1957.

9. These photographs began to appear in *Universities and Left Review* – one of their early public platforms – from issue no. 5. They have recently been published in *The Street Photographs of Roger Mayne*, London 1993, a collection based on the V & A exhibition of 1986.

10. Like Frank Sutcliffe of Whitby and other local photographers of the late nineteenth century, Henry Taunt is now continually reproduced. *The England of Henry Taunt*, ed. Bryan Brown, London 1973; *The Thames of Henry Taunt*, ed. Susan Read, London 1980; are attractive selections of some of his prints.

11. Edgar Yoxall Jones, *Father of Art Photography, O.G. Rejlander, 1813–1875*, Newton Abbot 1973, p. 27; Beaumont Newhall, *The History of Photography*, London 1972, p. 74; Helmut and Alison Gernsheim, *The History of Photography*, London 1969, pp. 246–7. There is an excellent detailed discussion of this image in Stephanie Spencer, 'O.G. Rejlander's Photographs of Street Urchins', *Oxford Art Journal*, Vol VII, No. 2, 1984 and a more general one in Roger Taylor. 'The Victorian London Photograph: Realities Recorded?', *London Journal* VII, No. 2, Winter, 1982, pp. 205–7. Rejlander, a Swede, had been a painter before he took up photography and his pictures were composed as exercises in narrative art.

12. The series, 'designed to give a comprehensive pictorial presentation of modern British history', drew heavily on lithographs and engravings for its illustrations. W.H. Chaloner and A.E. Musson's volume, *Industry and Technology*, published in 1963, uses photographs only for twentieth-century factory labour.

13. Gordon Winter, *A Country Camera, 1844–1914*, Harmondsworth 1973, p. 9.

14. Ronald Blythe, *Akenfield, Portrait of an English Village*, London 1964, p. 16.

15. Quennell's book, subtitled 'a survey of life and fashion from contemporary photographs', opened with a chapter on 'The Beginnings of Photography'.

16. O.J. Morris, *Grandfather's London*, London 1956. This is a puzzling book. The photographs were apparently taken in Greenwich in the 1880s to illustrate a lantern-slide lecture on the conditions of the poor. The Baptist minister who commissioned them contrives to appear in some of the photographs, and both in subject matter and style they are remarkably similar to Thomson and Smith's 1877 *Street Life in London*. O.J. Morris, the compiler of the volume, was a transport historian. Aided by Annie M. Bell of Norwood, 'my principal guide to a period . . . which she vividly remembers', and drawing on other local sources he was able to put in some remarkable detective work on the individual pictures and to produce a quite exceptionally informative commentary. *Grandfather's Greenwich*, ed. Alan Glencross, London 1972, is a later selection from the same set of negatives.

17. On the take-up in the schools, see P.J.H. Gosden and David Sylvester, *History for the Average Child*, 1968, pp. 62–3, who make the point that pictorial education is more used in primary than in secondary education; P.J. Rogers, 'The Power of Visual Presentation', in A.K. Dickinson et al., eds., *Learning History*, London 1984; D.J. Steel and L. Taylor, *Family History in Schools*, Chichester 1973, pp. 85–96; R. Unwin, *The Visual Dimension in the Study and Teaching of History*, Historical Association, 1981.

18. The Manchester Studies 1982 exhibition, 'Family Albums', detailing contents, date and occasion of each photograph, and drawing liberally on holiday occasions, was the original nucleus of the now formidable 'Documentary Photography Archive', drawn mainly from family albums in the Manchester district. It was founded in 1985 and is now housed with Manchester City Records. See Audrey Linkman, 'Today's Photographs, Tomorrow's History' in *Rewriting Photographic History*, ed. Michael Hallett, Birmingham 1989, pp. 33–5.

19. Information from Henry Nelson, the owner of the firm. Numbers of these booklets – e.g. 'Vintage Middlesborough', 'Darlington as It Was' – are now in their fifth, sixth, seventh or eighth impressions. The first booklet – on Colne – was prepared by Wilson Spencer, the town librarian, and librarians were the compilers of many of the subsequent volumes. Many of the Alan Sutton volumes come from the same source. Reference should also be made to E.P. of Wakefield's 'Old and New' series. An overview of these reprints is David Viner, 'Is There Life and Tradition Yet?', *Social History Curators Group Journal*, 18, 1990–91.

20. '*Photo-antithesis* . . . has long been used by teachers to make vivid contrasts – e.g. past and present, town and country, different social classes', Steel and Taylor, *Family History in Schools*, p. 93.

21. John Betjeman, *Victorian and Edwardian London from Old Photographs*, London 1969.

22. Don Steel, *Discovering Your Family History*, London 1980, p. 125.

23. Nicholas Bentley, *Victorian Scene*, London 1968, p. 267.

24. Boys boxing. Reference mislaid.

25. For photography at Wigan, John Hannavy, *Pictures of Wigan*, Wigan 1978; *Working in Wigan Mills*, Wigan 1987.

26. See the very interesting discussion of Julia Margaret Cameron's work in Michael Bartram, *The Pre-Raphaelite Camera: Aspects of Victorian Photography*, London 1985.

27. Alan Thomas, *Time in a Frame: Photography and the Nineteenth Century Mind*, New York 1977.

28. Humphrey Spender, *Worktown People: Photographs from Northern England, 1937–38*, Bristol 1982. These were the photographs taken as part of the Mass Observation inquiry into Bolton. See also Spender's autobiography, *'Lensman', Photographs 1932–1952*, London 1987.

29. There is an accessible if miniaturized collection of Brassaï in the Thames & Hudson 'Photofile' series.

30. Bill Brandt's pictorial inventions – his stage-managed groupings and choreographed scenes; his use of expressionist high-key lighting and his melodramatic preference for nocturnal (or twilight) scenes – are becoming more and more apparent with each retrospective. For the most recent exhibition and appraisal, Ian Jeffrey, *Bill Brandt: Photographer, 1928–1983*, London 1993. The well-known TV series 'Upstairs, Downstairs' was apparently based on his 1939 *The English at Home*. *The Story of Popular Photography*, ed. Colin Ford, London 1989, p. 26.

31. For the 'migrant mother' series, see Carl Fleischhauer et al., eds., *Documenting America, 1935–1943*, Berkeley 1988, pp. 8, 16–17, 20, 25–6, 30, 34, 36, 41–4, 68–70.

32. Susan Sontag, *On Photography*, Harmondsworth 1979, p. 19.

33. Bill Jay, *Victorian Candid Camera: Paul Martin, 1864–1944*, London 1973.

34. Captioning of photographs is often very *knowing*, suggesting that we are on familiar terms with the subject and are privy to their innermost feelings and thoughts. As Michael Baxandall points out, in another context ('Exhibiting Intention' in Ivan Kard and Steven D. Lavine, eds., *Exhibiting Cultures; The Poetics and Politics of Museum Display*, Washington 1990, pp. 35–6) such labels are not 'in any normal sense' descriptive; they are acts of interpretation masquerading as verbal aids.

35. Roger Taylor in conversation with the writer, September 1992.

36. Gaby Porter, 'The Economy of Truth, Photography in Museums', *Ten/8*, 34, Autumn 1989, pp. 20–33.

37. 'Useful to Artists', by 'Only a Photographer', *Photographic News*, 19 July 1872.

38. Ibid., 9 October 1885, p. 642. The photograph in question, 'Strengthening the Understanding', won an award at the annual exhibition of the Photographic Society and is reproduced in the 9 October issue of *Photographic News*. I am very grateful to Audrey Linkman for both of these references.

39. The interview with Humphrey Spender, which prefigures the 1982 collection of his 'Worktown' photographs, returns again and again to the 'Lensman's' sense of intrusion and embarrassment in his 1937 work.

40. In a now rich and splendid range of commentary on Walker Evans's work, reference might be made to J.A. Ward, *American Silences: The Realism of James Agee, Walker Evans and Edward Hopper*. Baton Rouge 1985; *Walker Evans: The Hungry Eye*, ed. Gilles Mora and John T. Hill, London 1993; *Documenting America, 1935–1945*, ed. Carl Fleischhauer et al., Berkeley 1988. It is instructive to compare the now reprinted contact prints with the pictures chosen for James Agee and Walker Evans, *Let Us Now Praise Famous Men*. The first has Lucille Burroughs, a young girl in a sunhat, picking cotton and – in one striking print – looking quite pastoral in the fields. In the book, one of the most famous of Walker Evans's prints, she is pictured against the clapboarding of the family shack.

41. I have taken my examples from Le Roy Ladurie's commentary in Bernard Dufour, *La pierre et le seigle, histoire des habitants de Villefranche-de-Rouergue racontée par . . . les albums de famille, 1860–1950*, Paris 1977.

42. 'Found – The World's First Crowd Photograph', *Sunday Times*, 5 June 1977.

43. Gareth Stedman Jones, 'Rethinking Chartism', in *Languages of Class*, Cambridge 1983, puts forward a bold reconceptualization of Chartism, arguing that its inspiration was political rather than social, drawing on popular constitutionalism rather than political economy. For some variant readings, Dorothy Thompson, 'The Language of Class', *Bulletin of the Society for the Study of Labour History*, 52, 1987; Joan Scott, 'On Language, Gender and Working-Class History', *International Labour and Working-Class History*, 31, 1987; Ellen Meiksins Wood, *The Retreat from Class: A New 'True' Socialism*, London 1984, Chapter 7.

44. Robert Pols, *Dating Old Photographs*, Newbury 1993; 'Can You Date Heirloom

Photographs from Children's Clothes?', *Family Tree Magazine*, March 1990.

45. Steel and Taylor, *Family History in Schools*, pp. 93–4.

46. *The London Borough of Hackney in Old Photographs*, ed. David Mander, Gloucester 1989, p. 149: Berger Road Girls' School celebrating Empire Day in May 1909. See Le Roy Ladurie's interesting remarks on pre-1914 patriotic manifestation in Dufour, *La pierre et le seigle*.

The Discovery of Old Photographs

There was no such thing as a market in old photographs before the 1970s, and such collections of them as existed (as it turned out a large number) had been lying fallow for half a century and more. In the antiques boom of the 1960s, and the discovery of new classes of collectables, photographs, by comparison with, say, period graphics, were latecomers to the scene. There is not so much as a mention of them in Violet Wood's 1960 *Victoriana: A Collector's Guide*, though Valentines ('now so scarce as to cause quite a stir should an album come to light during the sale at a . . . country house'), theatre programmes, invitations to balls, and 1850s fashion plates ('highly decorative . . . they . . . often bear the names of famous houses') were all thought worthy of an entry.[1] At Portobello Road, the nursery of the antiques boom, loose-leaf folders of photographs could at this time (according to legend) still be picked up 'for a song', while Victorian *cartes de visite* – the photographic miniatures of the 1860s – were only bought on account of their frames.[2] A few years later the photographs themselves began to attract a following among the dealers, while adventurous bargain-hunters began to snap them up and use them for make-believe Victorian panels and screens. But it was not until 1971, with the sale of Julia Margaret Camerons at Sotheby's, that Victorian portrait photography was given the accolade of recognition by the fine-art auctioneers.

Period photographs were also a latecomer to pub Victoriana, though today the two are inseparable. A 1965 London pub guide gives only one example – a newly installed blow-up of Victorian London, which served as a mural at The Coleherne, Old Brompton Road, then as now a famous homosexual meeting place.[3] The 1973 edition of this guide mentions only one other – The Nashville, West Cromwell Road, where, incongruously for a pub which made a speciality of country-and-western music, the landlord had installed a panoramic view of Westminster and the Houses of Parliament behind the public bar.[4]

The make-believe Victorian print – vignetted in the manner of the 'cabinet' portraits of the 1870s, with the head and shoulders set in a gradually fading surround – perhaps did as much as anything to recommend period photography to popular taste. One original here – an exercise in high camp which at the time seemed more like a throw-back to the bright young things of the 1920s than a portent of the shape of things to come – was Cecil Beaton's 1965 'Victorian picnic', a photographic *tableau vivant* featuring the leading model of the day, Jean Shrimpton.[5] Twiggy, the seventeen-year-old who became fashion's 'Girl of the Year' in 1966, was photographed in a similar frame, sepia-tinted and dressed up as a Victorian Miss, in the manner of a Kate Greenaway illustration – a *Vogue* cover picture which is also remembered as an advertising poster.[6] The record sleeve of *Sergeant Pepper's Lonely Hearts Club Band* (1967) famously had the Beatles dressed up in Edwardian regimentals; while that of Clive Dunn's egregiously sentimental ballad, 'Grandad', Top of the Pops in 1969, had the actor togged up as a late Victorian worthy. The example caught on, and within a very few years the fairground and seaside photography booths were offering a choice of period costume – mid Victorian bonnets for the demure, feather boas for the more daring. By the mid 1970s there was even a salon at the *Daily Mail* Ideal Home exhibition.[7]

It seems possible that a taste for old photographs was cultivated not only by the pioneers of retrochic but also by some of the leading spirits of 1960s modernism – the architects of 'new English' in the schools, for instance, who used social realist photography, drawn from the 1930s to give their publications street credibility.[8] The graphic designers of the velvet underground, though by their own lights futurist, dabbled in old film stills, putting Clara Bow on the cover of the *International Times* (drug culture's earliest and best-known contribution to British journalism) and using the fashion plates of the 1920s, or the stars of the silent screen, for those figures of mystery who peered out from the backdrop of such alternative clothes shops as Granny Takes a Trip and Biba. In a more necrophiliac vein, appealing more perhaps to adolescent melancholia than to middle-aged nostalgia, the most brilliantly successful of the underground posters, reproduced on countless medallions and T-shirts, and a best-seller in the shops – the 1967 death's head of Ernesto Che Guevara, a martyr-portrait drawn from the photograph of his corpse, and closely modelled, it seems possible, on Mantegna's 'Death of Christ'[9] – anticipated and possibly served as one of the originals for those curious 1970s cults, still very much in evidence in the card shops and poster galleries today, which found their heart-throbs in dead movie stars and turned a succession of newly deceased pop singers into cultural icons – Jimi Hendrix, Buddy Holly, Janis Joplin, Jim Morrison.

Pop art's engagement with old photographs, those 'second generation' photographs which by dint of constant repetition had become visual clichés, was continuous. It called on them as an image-bank for its cut-outs; as a source of visual jokes when cocking a snook at the Academy; as an invitation to visual pleasure; and not least, when translated into record sleeves and posters, as a way of reaching a mass public. Old film stills, fashion ads, 'girlie' pictures were all grist to its mill. By treating the contemporary as memorabilia, and depicting commercial ephemera as art, it executed a dance of death on the pretensions of high culture. Andy Warhol's Marilyn Monroe, playing with polyphoto imagery – a 1950s craze – has some claim to being a morning star of necrophilia. Roy Lichtenstein seems to have been among the very first to have redis-covered the delights of Art Deco.[10]

The new-wave fashion photographers of the 1960s, though apparently traditionless and impatient of anything beyond the thrills of the moment, may, however inadvertently, have done something to create an appetite for period photographs. Exchanging Venice and St Tropez for East End and Thameside settings, taking Chelsea girls down to Rother-hithe and Wapping, using lamp posts, grimy walls and waste lots for their location settings, they created, or traded in, a kind of 'metropolitan picturesque' (to adapt a phrase of David Mellor's[11]), a visual idiom which, in its addiction to the old, the decayed and decrepit, formed a kind of London counterpart to the Northern pastoral of new-wave cinema realism. Male fashion models, as one can see from the features in *Man About Town*, were pictured in no less vernacular settings – the crowded, smoke-filled bar of a Dublin pub, in one of Terence Donovan's pictures,[12] the Roundhouse, Chalk Farm (still, then, a railway engine-house), in one of Brian Duffy's fashion photographs.[13] Even a story about evening dress, with its model in full regalia, seems to have been photographed in one of the back alleys of Southwark. It was then fitting that Antonioni's *Blow-up*, which treats the cockney-born fashion photog-rapher as an epitome of Swinging London, should have taken its opening sequence from the Rowton House in Camden Town – a hostel for homeless working men, then on its last legs.[14]

The discovery of old photographs was of a piece with a heightened awareness of the visual which, in the course of the 1960s, invaded every sphere of national life – from mass communications, where the eclipse of radio by TV turned Britain, in the space of ten years, from a nation of listeners into a nation of viewers, to body politics, where picture windows, plate-glass doors and open-plan layouts gave offices and shops a see-through look. In costume and dress one could linger on that expressive revolution which led to the discarding of school uniform in favour of teenage gear, and the advent of such novelties as see-through blouses and slogan-bearing T-shirts which served as advertisements for the self. In education one could refer to the riot of colour in the new adventure playgrounds, little oases of freedom planted in the urban waste; or to the display of children's paintings in the corridors and classrooms of the primary school; or to the role of the visual in curriculum innovation where, under the influence of liberal and progressive educators, 'education by seeing' challenged the hegemony of the written word. The gravitational pull of the visual was also a force for change in high politics where political leaders were packaged for public consumption, very much in the manner of TV personalities, and success or failure in party leadership was measured in terms of photo-opportunities and airtime rather than decibel counts of applause.

The appetite for the visual was nowhere more apparent than in commodity design where, under the influence of the packaging revolution, and with the aid of silk-screen printing, the look and feel of things came to count for as much as the quality and price. In the music industry record covers, which had previously been a visual blank, serving the purely utilitarian end of keeping off dust, were replaced by eye-catching, high-gloss sleeves, picturing the stars in the act of performance or dissolving them in the atmospherics of a light show (the 'incredibly modern' cover of the first Rolling Stones LP dispensed with lettering entirely, even the group's name, substituting a photograph of the five bathed in a kind of half-light).[15] In publishing, the paperback revolution of the 1960s not only multiplied the number of imprints but also brought specially commissioned artwork to the covers – in the case of Pelicans, abstract designs or, for sociological works, old photographs and industrial prints. In shop design, the spread of self-service stores, with their free-standing racks or open-access shelves, introduced a whole new language of 'front' display, dispensing with the mysteries of bureaux, boxes and drawers, and introducing a battery of eye-catching devices to promote impulse-buying and break down customer reserve. Goods which previously would have been laboriously weighed on scales, or tied up with string in brown paper parcels, now came pre-packed in cellophane wrappers (or, in the case of food, cling-film) and were carried away in gaily-coloured shopping-bags or gift-wraps. In the new boutiques – 'Kleptomania' was the expressively chosen name of one of them – gigantic blow-ups and multiple mirrors invited the customers to gaze narcissistically on idealized projections of themselves. At the gift shops, where gonks and hummel figures served as mascots and T-shirts as souvenirs, the shopping experience was transformed from an exercise of discrimination into a kind of potlatch, with a range of rainbow-coloured knick-knacks in place of utility goods.

Photography was the cutting edge of these new developments, glamorizing the new lifestyles, aestheticizing consumption, degentrifying politics, desublimating sexuality. Like pop music it bridged the gulf between high culture and low by offering a language that, in principle, was common to both. The new breed of streetwise photographers used it to undermine the pretensions of *haute couture*, the pop artists to make a poetics of advertising and packaging. In the schools, progressive teachers seized on it as a talisman of 'relevance'. In the quality press photography invaded the space previously reserved for newsprint (or, in *The Times*, for the 'agony' column) and the announcement of births, marriages and deaths. Another influential example would be the new charities, such as Oxfam, which were the nether side of 1960s opulence. Aided in some cases by the photo-journalists and the fashion photographers, and adopting the sales strategy of the record sleeve, they abandoned the discreet appeal to *noblesse oblige* in favour of visual sensation, playing on harrowing 'up-front' pictures of suffering, and creating a new iconography of disaster in which the naked child with swollen belly and splindly legs became as familiar a figure as the Holocaust victim in striped pyjamas or the mushroom cloud over Hiroshima.

If at the beginning of the 1960s photography was an avatar of modernism, by the end of the decade, in line with the rise of conservationist sentiment and the back-to-nature turn in the counter-culture, it was proving no less serviceable to retrochic. The advertisers adopted it for what Judith Williamson calls 'memory ads',[16] an increasingly popular sub-genre in which sepia-tinted vignettes or period images, juxtaposed against the product label, served as a gauge of old-fashioned quality. The evolution of the Beatles' record sleeves, like the increasingly wistful character of their lyrics, bears the imprint of the new turn. The cover of *With The Beatles* (1963), their second LP, using a black-and-white photograph of the group taken by the fashion photographer Robert Freeman, was starkly simple and discreet, while *A Hard Day's Night* (1964), using polyphoto portraits, in the manner of Andy Warhol, was still determinedly modernist. Peter Blake's cover for *Sergeant Pepper* (1967) belongs to another world, a democracy of entertainment in which old-time showmen – in massed array – are leavened by a sprinkling of the newly dead. Clara Bow and Jean Harlow, the glamour girls of the 1920s, compete for attention with Marlene Dietrich and Diana Dors; Karl Marx rubs shoulders with Laurel and Hardy; Oscar Wilde with Marlon Brando. For sound, the brass band drum, the clarinet and the coronets have taken the place of electronic amplifiers. The stars themselves are dressed as Ruritanian soldiers, and their name, instead of being blazoned on the rostrum, is picked out in the flowers of a wreath. Drawing its colours from the circus and the fairground, and its pop-up figures from Madame

Tussaud's, the sleeve resembles nothing so much as a requiem for the dead.

The 1970s saw photography, in Britain as in the United States, climbing towards a new pinnacle of esteem,[17] but whereas in the latter country this was bound up with a recognition of contemporary excellence, in Britain it seems rather to have turned on a belated recognition of the camera's historicity. It was the famous Hill/Adamson controversy of 1971–72, a national debate over the fate of some 1840s photographs of Newhaven fisherfolk, which led the National Portrait Gallery to appoint Colin Ford as photography curator, the first in the country. It was a series of mainly nineteenth-century retrospectives, starting with 'Today Painting is Dead', which established photography's claim to retrospectives in the art galleries. The 1970s saw a series of monographs on the great Victorian masters; a new interest in the 'naturalistic' photographers of the 1880s and 1890s, whose work had become popular in reproduction prints – Frank Sutcliffe and P.H. Emerson; and the beginnings of work on photography's unknown history. *The Camera and Dr Barnado* (1974), one of the first fruits of the Arts Council's new interest in photography, exhumed the detail of a once-celebrated forgery.[18] Likewise in the salesrooms it was the work of the great Victorian photographers which set off an inflationary price spiral.[19] It is perhaps indicative of this historicist turn that Bill Jay, one of photography's 'new wave' in the late 1960s and a founder-editor of *Creative Camera*, should have turned his attention, in the early 1970s, to excavating the half-forgotten chapters of photography's past.[20] *Victorian Cameraman* (1973) was written in conjunction with Rothman's purchase of that 'unique record of Victorian England', Frith's 'views' photography; while *Victorian Candid Camera* celebrated the work of Paul Martin and helped to win his work a new public at the V & A. The 1970s also brought the discovery of numbers of forgotten local photographers and the reproduction in book or album form of their work. Frank Meadow Sutcliffe's Whitby,[21] Henry Taunt's Oxford, Robert French's Dublin,[22] Charles White's London[23] became as familiar, at least to the picture editors, as the work of Fenton, Fox Talbot or Julia Margaret Cameron; while for the aficionado – or the local historian – such lesser luminaries, brilliant lights in their own locality, as William Whiffen of Poplar became names to conjure with.

Perhaps the most remarkable of the decade's discoveries, from the point of view of the recycling of old photographs, was the Francis Frith collection – a quarter of a million negatives, 'all painstakingly dated and filed', including views of almost every town and village in the United Kingdom, taken over a period of a hundred years by the great Victorian photographer and his successors. Identified as the result of an initiative by Bill Jay, and re-established, as a kind of 'retro' firm in 1977, it supports today a vast industry in the dissemination of Victorian and Edwardian views; offering 'accurately dated and titled' prints for over four thousand villages: framed photographs, wall murals ('giant sepia enlargements ... for spectacular impact') and table mats. Phillimore, the local history publishers, have produced approaching a hundred book-albums on the strength of them; there is a guild of Francis Frith collectors; book clubs make use of them for 'incentive marketing'. They also provide the local views which festoon such fast-food chains as Pizza Hut (the Oxford Street branch offers a gallery of old-time London scenes), or lend an identity to high-street banks, such as Barclays and Lloyds, and corporate insurance companies such as Canada Life and Sun Alliance.[24]

The discovery of old photographs was the work of many different hands – connoisseurs and collectors, totters and dealers, museum curators and local librarians, historians (especially local historians) and archivists, schools officers and county education committees, community arts groups and WEA branches. Picture researchers were the invisible hands behind such 1960s blockbusters as the BBC's *World at War* and the British Printing Corporation's part-work, published over a 97-week period, *The History of the Twentieth Century* – a new breed of mainly freelance professionals, often with an art or art historical background, called into being by the explosive 1960s growth of the visual media.[25] Typically the discoveries came from individual enthusiasts whose profession lay elsewhere – for instance Kieran Hickey, whose discovery of the work of the Dublin photographer Robert French, lying half-forgotten in the archives of the National Library, produced a sumptuous pictorial account of Irish life at the turn of the century, *The Light of Other Days*. At the *Sunday Times Magazine*, the colour supplement which, over a twenty-year period, did so much to popularize the new discoveries, the invisible hand from 1965 to 1975 was that of David King, a young typographer who had been trained at the London School of Printing. Appointed art editor at the age of twenty-two, he made a point of printing nineteenth-century photographs whenever they came his way because 'big plate photographs' were 'infinitely better' than anything else coming into the office 'except for Don McCullin'.[26] Bruce Bernard, who followed him, served his picture researching apprenticeship when employed by the British Printing Corporation on their historical part-works.[27]

Among local enthusiasts a precocious recovery project, reported in an early issue of *The Amateur Historian* under the title 'Village History: A Photographic Record', was that of Edward Heymer, a London man who, retiring to Hawkhurst, Kent in the early 1950s, found 'a wealth of unrecorded history that was crying out to be gone into'. Cycling round the village with his camera in the manner of the record and survey movement of the 1890s, he began systematically to photograph the built environment; then he issued an appeal for old photographs, sketches and engravings. Encouraged by the response, and with the aid of an epidiascope and amplifying equipment, he put on a village show, in conjunction with the Committee of the Coronation Festivities. 'This attracted enough people to collect £5 which went to aid our bombed-out Church Funds.' The next stage of his research took him to the maps, charters and perambulations in the County Record Office and at the PRO in London, while local residents forwarded, along with old photographs, estate and tithe maps, and copies of local wills. The publicity brought to light 'one of the most outstanding discoveries ever made in local history': 'a collection of old photographs, sketches, etc. of our village as it was about 100 years ago'. This he put in a further village show. 'We packed the Hall and had to turn others away. A silver collection was made and realised £5. This could only mean one thing, the screen show would have to be repeated.'[28]

A more representative case, though still an early one, is that of Malcolm Seaborne, a young and idealistic schoolmaster, 'keen on old buildings', who was working in Corby, a then rapidly expanding town of steelworkers which had been grafted on to a very old village. He interested himself in the fate of a street of seventeenth-century ironstone cottages, then falling into decay and threatened with clearance. The residents showed him their old photographs, among them Edwardian street photographs ('Some chap would come round with a horse and cart and the word would get round that there was a photographer in the village'). These photographs proved serviceable, indeed decisive, when the fate of the cottages came before a public inquiry and they also turned out to be an exciting addition to classwork. Through the medium of the local records section of the Corby Natural History Society ('founded chiefly by birdwatchers'), a local records section was set up which issued an appeal to old Corby residents: 'Lend us your old photographs – and your memories – so that the story of your village can be preserved for future generations.... We want to collect as many photographs, souvenirs, posters, books, plans, maps, legal documents, and other relics of Old Corby which still exist with a view to a public exhibition.' The response was 'tremendous', Latvian and Scots newcomers being even more interested than the native villagers, and the exhibition packed some three thousand people into the Town Hall. The example was adopted by the Northamptonshire County Local History Committee and the County Record Office, which set about encouraging the systematic collection of old photographs, and it was also followed by lectures and exhibitions 'often in association with other village events' in other parts of Northamptonshire: 'Every lecture has produced more pictures from the audience.' 'For readers not familiar with this rich source of pictorial history', Mr Seaborne wrote in *Amateur Historian* in 1961, 'it may be helpful to indicate briefly the subjects usually covered by old photographs':

> First, there are the picture postcards, commercially produced, usually depicting street scenes. Quite often buildings are shown which have since been demolished, a record which exists nowhere else. I have been astonished at the amount of detail shown: with the aid of a magnifying glass it is frequently possible, for instance, to read the date stones and inscriptions on houses. Apart from houses and streets, one can obtain photographs of windmills, smithies, wheelwrights' shops and so on … Another group of old photographs is more difficult to classify, but in some ways provides the most interesting pictures of life half a century or more ago. One imagines that local firms sent out photographers to take pictures of men and women going about their ordinary daily tasks. The great merit and charm of these photographs lies in their informality; there is no posing and they bear the stamp of authenticity in many small but important details. One finds, for example, a picture of a group working in the hay harvest, often showing farming implements and carts no longer in use; or one sees a group of people working in a village smithy or digging in a local mine. In the Corby area, it is possible to trace from this source the gradual introduction of machinery for the open-cast mining of ironstone, and George Freeston of Blisworth has a superb collection of photographs of every ironstone pit in his area.[29]

Gloucester museums in 1965 were making a more specific appeal for negatives or stocks of picture postcards:

> The practice of sending picture postcards reached one of its greatest peaks of popularity towards the end of the nineteenth century. Local photographers throughout the country produced views of town and village in great quantity. Not only did they make cards of the obvious subjects such as the village street, the church, and the 'pub', but they also attended local events to record them and to sell the cards to those taking part, for the day of the almost universal ownership of the cheap camera was yet to come. In this way such occasions as village feasts, processions, ceremonies, even local funerals came to be recorded. A photograph of a funeral at Brimscombe Fort which was brought to a Gloucester Museum recently shows in the background a dockside crane, the sort of thing which the industrial archaeologist is anxious to record. There is a wealth of incidental detail of this kind to be discovered in the study of old postcards.
>
> Street scenes in towns frequently show early public transport, horse drawn trams and buses for example, and there is scarcely an aspect of local history which cannot be furthered by studying local postcard views. There may well be small shops in towns and villages throughout the county which have stocks of old postcards tucked away in store cupboards – it has been said that it is still possible to buy pre-1914 views over the counter in the post office of a village

in the north of Gloucestershire! It is even possible that the stocks of negatives taken by photographers still exist. The pictures could prove most informative about life in town and village sixty or seventy years ago. That is why the Museums in Gloucester have made their plea for postcards.[30]

The curious thing about the discovery of old photographs is that, notwithstanding some sensational finds – as, for example, A.J. Munby's voyeuristic portraits of mid-Victorian working women[31] – most of the prints circulating in reproduction today already had some prior institutional home, even though it is only in recent years that they have entered the public domain. The Imperial War Museum, to take an extreme example, has some five-and-a-half million negatives, though before the 1960s their use was largely confined to next-of-kin and to regimental historians. The Francis Frith collection, which provides so many pubs and restaurants with their period prints, and so many stationers with their historic views, are drawn entirely from that firm's century-long existence in the postcard trade, and from the work of its founder. Borough librarians have in many cases been systematically collecting local photographs from the earliest days of the public library movement; libraries were the chief depository chosen for the work of the Record and Survey movement which, from the 1890s onwards, set itself the task of keeping a systematic photographic record of the built environment.[32] The Library Association was setting out a programme for the rescue of old photographs as early as 1961 and it seems fitting that in the current spate of reprints, compilation, and sometimes publication, should be in the hands of borough librarians.[33]

Victorian 'art' photography had always had its connoisseurs and admirers. Contrary to common belief, the first major show was not the Hill/Adamson exhibition of 1972 at the National Portrait Gallery, but the V & A's 'Masterpieces of Photography' in 1951. Earlier, a curator at the V & A had taken down the memoirs of Paul Martin, which were published, together with some plates, in *A Victorian Snapshot* (1939). The V & A also held a large collection of Paul Martins, though it was only in the 1970s that it began to reprint them. Many of today's enthusiasms are remarkably prefigured in Peter Quennell's *Victorian Panorama* (1939), 'A Survey of Life and Fashion from Contemporary Photographs'. The book was built on the collection of Charles Fry, second in command at Batsford, and undertaken at his suggestion. The selection is a splendidly catholic one, as one might expect from such an author, ranging from the dramatic (Edward Southern as Lord Dundreary) to the ultra-domestic, and including some of today's favourite prints, for example Thomson's photographs in *Street Life in London*. Yet *Victorian Panorama* had no successor.[34] *History Today*, the illustrated journal of which Quennell was a founder-editor in 1951, made very little use of photographs, and those it did call on – for the most part head-and-shoulders portraits or modern topographical views – it used in quite conservative ways.

There is slightly more continuity in historical postcards, the substantial basis of the 'As It Was' series of reproduction photographs which the Hendon Publishing Co. began to produce, town by town, in 1971. Collecting postcards is as old as picture postcards themselves, and is said to have enjoyed a very large following in Edwardian times. But according to Anthony Byatt, one of the historians of the movement and himself a leading dealer, postcard collection 'almost died out' in the 1920s, and 'during the thirty years that followed many publishers' records were lost or destroyed'.[35] There seems to have been a certain following for sporting prints, as for instance old cricketing XIs, and vintage sports cars; and in Cecil Court off the Charing Cross Road there were some well-known houses specializing in theatrical prints. In the 1950s, under the influence of the preservation movement, 'railway interest' cards seem to have had a fillip, and it is perhaps indicative of their continuing pull on the market that in the catalogues transport issues are more highly sought after than any other.

There is no reason to suppose that discovery of old photographs is at an end: on the contrary, like the location of prehistoric settlements it may barely yet have begun. The twenty thousand photographs of the Manchester Ship Canal recently deposited at the City Record Office have far outpaced the capacity of the institution to deal with them, and will take some five years for even a minimum inventory (the pictures of cargo – including the first oil tankers – show twentieth-century industry in a new and unfamiliar light, as well as giving individual portraits of thousands of company employees). The 1.3 million pictures in the *Daily Herald* archive recently deposited with the National Photographic Museum at Bradford remain, says the curator, 'quite unused, though people come from time to time for a Gracie Fields illustration'. Butlin's holiday camp photography – and indeed seaside photography generally – is only just beginning to make its way into the archives (the Manchester Record Office has a fine collection). The collection of film footage is in a very early stage: the remarkable health propaganda films from 1930s Bermondsey which have been given a public viewing at the National Film Theatre give some indication of its historiographic potential and excitements.[36]

Notes

1. Violet Wood, *Victoriana: A Collector's Guide*, London 1960, pp. 161, 163.

2. Jeremy Cooper, *Complete Guide to London's Antique Markets*, London 1974, pp. 103–4. By 1992 Art Nouveau photographic frames were fetching up to £250 in the auction rooms: *Miller's Collectables Price Guide*, 1992–3, pp. 348–9.

3. On The Coleherne, Martin Green and Tony White, *Guide to London Pubs*, London 1965, p. 42, have the following note: 'The present landlord, a former Yorkshire League cricketer, arrived in 1951: two years later, the interior was completely altered, partitions removed, and new lighting and furniture installed. The cricketing murals and photos, as well as the cricketing prints by Watkins Taylor have now been replaced by 'blow-ups' of Victorian London, in keeping with the leisurely Saloon Bar, with its grandfather clock, mirrors, armchairs and (in winter) log fire. The Coleherne which now has a handsome restaurant (open till midnight) gets pretty crowded even in the week – almost exclusively male clientele – but really comes into its own as a musical pub on Sunday mornings with the appearance of a dynamic West Indian Band.'

4. Martin Green and Tony White, *Evening Standard Pub Guide*, London 1973, p. 93. Pub Lotus in Regent's Park Road, NW1 – then a 'theme' pub devoted to motor racing – had racing photos in its showcases. Ibid., p. 107.

5. Cecil Beaton. Barbican Art Gallery, 16 May–20 July 1986. From *Vogue* July 1965, 'Picnic Fashion Group Including the Models Jean Shrimpton and Celia Hammond'.

6. 'The walls boast more Blakes and a sepia-tinted photograph of him and Twiggy in Victorian clothes', 'Return of the Sixties Svengali', *Evening Standard* 19 August 1992.

7. The make-believe period photograph has become one of the routine excitements of the great British holiday. At the Trocadero, Piccadilly, opened in 1992, 'Old Times Portraits' offers customers a choice of period: 'Victorian' ('military' or 'top hat and tails' for the men; 'hoop dress, high-neck or off-the-shoulder' for the ladies); 'Western' ('military' or 'cowboy' for gentlemen; 'saloon dresses' for the ladies); or '1920' ('Al Capone with machine gun' for gentlemen; 'flapper dress' for the ladies)'. An enterprising Watford photographic saloon has extended the principle to juniors – 'Soldier-cadet', 'Bandsman', 'Office Boy', 'Delivery Boy', 'Barnado Kid', 'Little Lord Fauntleroy' ('they even supplied the wig'), was one fourteen-year-old's haul from an afternoon of sittings.

8. Simon Clements, John Dixon, Leslie Stratta, *Reflections, An English Course for Students 14–18*, Oxford 1963, with photographs by Roger Mayne, 'whose work especially has helped to educate us in the possibilities of such photography'.

9. John Berger, 'The Legendary Ché Guevara is dead', *New Society*, 26 October 1967.

10. Roy Lichtenstein adopted Art Deco, in 1966, as a populist alternative to what he thought of as the elitism of functional architecture. Janis Hendrickson, *Roy Lichtenstein*, Cologne 1987, pp. 62–6.

11. David Mellor, 'Phantasms', in Mark Haworth-Booth, ed., *Bill Brandt Behind the Camera: Photography 1928–1983*, Oxford 1985, pp. 78, 89.

12. *Man About Town*, vol. 3, no. 11, November 1962, p. 78. This magazine – later entitled *Town* and later still amalgamated with *Queen* – was one of those enterprises which helped to make the fortunes of the Conservative politician, Michael Heseltine.

13. *Man About Town*, vol. 3, no. 9, September 1962, p. 70.

14. Of the 'new-wave' fashion photographers, David Bailey had a particular eye for the murky, or what he calls, in relationship to one of his East End townscapes, 'dark, sombre tonality' (*Bailey's Book of Pin-Ups*, London 1965, p. 6). Particularly striking is his *NW1* (London 1982), a book of Camden Town, compiled over a twenty-year period of residence, when it was being systematically gentrified. The book was said 'to evoke the air of urban decay which permeates this largely 19th century area of London'. Martin Harrison, *David Bailey*, London 1984, p. 61. Similarly, in Don McCullin's photography (*Man About Town*, vol. 3, no. 7, July 1962, pp. 28ff), the Stock Exchange crowd under high-exposure lighting looks like nothing so much as a Bill Brandt or Worktown scene.

15. On record sleeves, Nigel Whiteley, *Pop Design: Modernism to Mod*, London 1987, pp. 108, 165–6, 212–13; Simon Frith and Howard Horne, *Art into Pop*, London 1987; John

A. Walker, *Cross-Overs: Art into Pop, Pop into Art*, London 1987.

16. Judith Williamson, *Decoding Advertisements*, London 1986, pp. 162–6.

17. For a useful overview, Gerry Badger et al., eds., *Through the Looking Glass: Photographic Art in Britain, 1945–1989*, London 1989, pp. 22–34. The decade brought three dazzling aesthetic and theoretical reflections on the subject which remain the natural starting point for any critical discussion today – John Berger's *Ways of Seeing* and *About Looking*; Susan Sontag's *On Photography*, and, best of all, Barthes's *Camera Lucida*.

18. Valerie Lloyd, *The Camera and Dr Barnado*, London 1974.

19. The prices at first were modest. In 1971 Julia Margaret Cameron's photograph of the scientist Herschel made £260; in early 1972, a photograph of Tennyson by Lewis Carroll was sold for £220. Ronald Pearsall and Graham Webb, *Inside the Antique Trade*, Shaldon 1974, p. 190.

20. After founding *Creative Camera* Bill Jay went on to be the first director of photography at the Institute of Contemporary Arts. *Negative/Positive: A Philosophy of Photography*, Iowa 1979, consists of his interesting retrospections.

21. Michael Hiley, *Frank Sutcliffe: Photographer of Whitby*, London 1974.

22. *The Light of Other Days, Irish Life at the Turn of the Century in the Photographs of Robert French*, ed. Kieran Hickey, London 1973.

23. Benny Green, *The Streets of London: Moments in Time from the Albums of Charles White and London Transport*, selected by Lawrence Edwards, London 1983.

24. 'Francis Frith Collection', *Amateur Photographer*, 16 October 1982; *Landmarks*, newspaper of the Francis Frith Collectors Guild, 3, 1992; 'Special Services for Designers', 1992. I am grateful to John Buck, managing director of the collection, for this information.

25. I am grateful to Jennie Pozzi, who worked on the *History of the Twentieth Century* project, for information about the development of picture research.

26. I am grateful to Dave King for these recollections.

27. Bernard's recent selection of photographs from the Hulton-Deutsch collection, 'All Human Life', at the Barbican, did not do justice to the audacity of his use of photography.

28. *Amateur Historian*, vol. 2, no. 2, pp. 42–3.

29. M.V.J. Seaborne, 'Pictorial Records', *Amateur Historian*, vol. 5, no. 5, pp. 151–2, for a brief description. 'The Corby Story: Group to Put it On Record', *Corby Leader*, 28 March 1958, for a fuller one. I am grateful to Mr Seaborne for correspondence, cuttings and memories of this project.

30. *Amateur Historian*, vol. 6, no. 8, Summer 1965, p. 287.

31. Michael Hiley, *Victorian Working Women: Portraits from Life*, London 1979.

32. For the Record and Survey movement, started by Sir Benjamin Stone in the 1890s and enthusiastically pursued by librarians for some twenty years, H.D. Gower, L. Stanley Jast, and W.W. Topley, *The Camera as Historian; A Handbook to Photographic Record Work For . . . Survey or Record Societies*, London 1916. This covers both town and country surveys and carries an elaborate and fascinating classification of the subjects the Record and Survey movement aimed to cover.

33. *Amateur Historian*, vol. 5, no. 5, p. 154.

34. I was fortunate to collect Peter Quennell's memory of this episode shortly before he died.

35. Anthony Byatt, *Picture Postcards and Their Publishers*, Malvern 1978.

36. Elizabeth Lebas, 'When there was a cinema in every street', *History Workshop Journal* no. 39, Spring 1995.

Dreamscapes

It is an interesting testimony to the aesthetic appeal of the time-warped that, at the very moment when the family album threatens to pass into the limbo of history and the still-life snapshot to be replaced by compact discs or video, it is staging something of a comeback, or enjoying a new incarnation, in the arts. In photography itself the snapshot, with its eye-level naturalism, artless framing and spontaneous action, is finding its belated partisans and defenders, as a form of modern folk-art,[1] and even its self-consciously avant-garde practitioners. In the wake of Roland Barthes's *Camera Lucida* it is also beginning to receive critical commentary, though hardly as yet even rudimentary periodization or chronology.[2] Social historians, if more belatedly, have begun to recognize its challenge as a form of representation and documentation which can take on whole new meanings when other forms of knowledge and understanding are brought to bear on it.[3] Interestingly the major effort to collect family photographs *organically* – in relation to time, circumstance and photographer – has come from a group of working historians.[4]

In cinema, the idea of using the family album as a framing or location device might speculatively be traced back to the 'Rosebud' sequence in *Citizen Kane* (1941). Another possible progenitor is *Meet Me in St Louis* (1944), where 1900s picture postcards were used to frame the action and reaffirm the worth of small-town America. But it was in the Hollywood nostalgia films of the 1960s, with their new-style credit sequences – dissolving views of what was to follow – that the snapshot came into its own. *Bonnie and Clyde* (1967) was an influential example, opening (to the click, click of the camera) with a series of framed, tinted and faded photographs of the gun-toting *dramatis personae* (there was a real-life original here, since Bonnie was in the habit of taunting the police by sending them snapshots of the gang). Another influential example, and one to which we arguably owe the association of sepia with vintage chic, was *Butch Cassidy and the Sundance Kid* (1969) – another outlaw film, though this time staged in the Wild West of the 1880s. True to its period, it gave extended coverage to the film credits and introduced the characters in the full-frontal conventions of Victorian portrait photography, before fading the director himself into the honeyed glow of the prairie.

In a more modernist (or postmodern) mode – deconstructing the still-life photograph rather than (or as well as) animating it – avant-garde and experimental film-makers have been using a similar framing device, taking up arms against the seductive powers of the snapshot image, and counteracting the icons of family life with its dark underside. Thus in Jane Campion's *An Angel at My Table*, a Madonna-like cameo of mother and child used in the credit sequence provides a savage and ironical prelude to what becomes a three-part chronicle of the descent into madness. In Terence Davies's narrative *Distant Voices, Still Lives*, a prolonged leave-taking of the director's Liverpool Catholic childhood, a family photograph prefaces each of the sequences in freeze-frame, leaving the characters to stare back at the camera's lens, still and silent, while from somewhere outside the frame – separating image and sound – an indistinct hubbub can be heard. Only when the camera begins to move in on them do the snapshots begin to move. *The Close of the Day*, the final film of the trilogy, though adopting the cinema rather than the family album as its leading visual metaphor, is, if anything, even more iconic, with little in the way of action or speech to distract the viewer's gaze. The film's director of photography prepared for it by immersing himself in the idiom of 1950s Kodak camerawork. The monochromatic 'period' look of the film was sustained by using 1950s colours which were then 'desaturated' to provide the greyness requisite for the subject and the period.[5]

The family photograph has long been used as a narrative device in autobiography. A more complex use of it, as a means of distancing the author from the remembered self, has more recently come to the fore. Ronald Fraser, in his *In Search of a Past*, uses it in a series of flashbacks to rediscover a repressed and buried self;[6] Roland Barthes in *Camera Lucida* argues that precisely because of its artifice it is truer to reality than reality itself could be.[7]

A much more straightforwardly nostalgic use of the family album is in oral history, which has used them as a device for family reconstitution and opening up memory lanes. In popular publication, such as the hundreds of reminiscence books and booklets issued by do-it-yourself oral history projects, local museums and local presses, the format of the family album is adopted. Desk-top publication and offset-litho have made it possible here to turn words and pictures into each other's interlocutors. The dozen or so booklets of 'The People's Autobiography of Hackney', with titles like *Coronation Cups and Jam Jars*, are a well-known case in point. More recently, and more remarkably, one might point to those photo-biographies of neighbourhoods and streets which are beginning to appear, such as Jimmy Forsyth's *Scotswood Road*, the by-product of a Tyne-Tees television feature, or Shirley Baker's *Hulme*.[8]

Old photographs – albeit for the most part reproductions rather than originals – play an increasing part in domestic culture, and there must nowadays be very few homes without them. As panelled insets, they may form the pictures on tea-towels and T-shirts, mugs and plates, calendars and yearbooks. In the form of scenic views, comic figures or stars of the silver screen, they plop through the letterbox as greetings cards, or come wrapped up with the presents. Children's toys may make use of them; the adolescent's bedroom may be lined with them.

Another new or relatively new phenomenon in the home is the 'restored' family photograph, previously half-forgotten in some drawer or tucked away in an album, but now, enlarged and framed, mounted on the mantelpiece or hung on the wall. It may owe something to the vogue for multiplying decorative and period effects; rather more to the current enthusiasm for family history and the anxiety, particularly marked among the geographically mobile and the sociologically orphaned, to reaffirm family roots. Typically it seems to involve relatives who are long since dead and gone, not so much perpetuating a memory – as in the days when the funeral was the great occasion for distributing souvenirs of the deceased – but rather creating a symbolic and visual space in which one can begin to materialize, making a living and daily presence of one who before was no more than a distant and occasional name. 'Ninety per cent are old grannies', according to one East London restorer, adding that some of them went back as far as the 1890s. He attributed the origins of the trade to the ingenuities of the tallymen and clubmen ('knocker boys') who used the lure of restoring pictures to get their foot in the door of target customers. ('Any old pictures you want framing?') Its more recent prosperity has been encouraged by the manufacture and marketing of 'Victorian-style' picture frames, by the multiplication of picture framers (there are no fewer than three of them in Romford High Street), and by the new facilities for what the photography studios call 'enhancement' – i.e. removing cracks and blemishes from old photographs. Not least is the demand for the period look: 'Some people ask them to be done in sepia to make them look even older.'[9] Second cousin to the 'restored' family photograph, mounted on the wall, is the make-believe one. In *Signs of the Times*, BB2's snobbish dissection of period and modern interiors (only the aristocracy got off scot-free), the would-be 'Victorian' mother and daughter had no modern family photos except for one taken in period costume, at the *Daily Mail* Ideal Home Exhibition. But they had some half-a-dozen 1860s *cartes de visite* arranged as though they were family pictures.[10]

Historic photographs also play some part in gift culture though they can hardly compete with the giant blow-ups of animals and pets. 'Ready to frame real photograph gift cards' (as the Harrogate manufacturer of one series calls them) make up the classier (and pricier) end of the market in the card shops.[11] Some stay quite close to seaside motto art (e.g. riding a donkey on the sands); some seem to recommend themselves by age value (as, say, in the sepia portrait of an Edwardian football team); others, more daring, draw their images from quite bleak urban and industrial settings, offsetting the gloom by love interest (e.g. a Bert Hardy picture of romantic coupledom in a slum), or by the addition of a sentimental caption.

The photographic poster – the king-size blow-ups of black-and-white photography which figure so largely in the Athena shops, the art stationers and the picture and poster galleries, as also, in pirated editions, in the street markets (there is a whole bank of them on Sunday mornings at Petticoat Lane) and at late-night West End stands – ministers to an altogether more sophisticated public: youthful and culturally dissident, ultra-modernist (even though many of the posters are the work of the French humanist photographers of the 1940s and 1950s), conversant with futurist work in the arts (Manhattan experimentalists such as Mapplethorpe figure alongside Doisneau, Izis and Brassaï). The pictures themselves are a kind of upmarket equivalent of the rock stars who decorate the bedroom walls of the pubescent. Realist in form and plebeian in their settings, the spirit of these photographs is by turns Blakean and Byronic, with a special appeal, one might have thought, to the melancholic. They linger lovingly over the cobbled streets of the old revolutionary quarters of Paris, Montmartre, Belleville and Ménilmontant; press up hard against the windows of the brasseries and bars; and take midnight walks along the Seine. The market for these pictures is international, though it seems that their production and distribution is largely a London and Paris affair. According to Michael Bowmer of the Art Group, one of the distributors, a taste for these posters goes hand in hand with 'black ash furniture' and tubular steel chairs.[12] But in fact the public seems at least as likely to be female as male. Doisneau's 'Le Baiser à l'Hôtel de Ville' is apparently the 'all-time best-seller' among them, while such other favourites as 'Lost Dreams' or 'Goodbye My Love' (a girl wandering disconsolately in a misty park) are hardly likely to appeal to Iron Men.[13]

'Views' photographs – the greatest single source of 'historic' postcards, as indeed of reproduction work of all kinds – have nothing in common with the blow-up, ministering to a much more traditional public and an inconceivably more heterogeneous one. Their interest is historical and topographical rather than sentimental and romantic; their style determinedly documentary, concerned to cram the maximum amount of visual information into a minimum of space. When they picture the high street – a favourite view – they are more concerned with the names of the shops than with atmospherics. Children line up dutifully to face the camera, rather than – as in Doisneau – clambering over the fountains or turning hand-stands in the gutter. Yet their subject matter, even more determinedly than the Paris of the Popular Front, is a world that has been irretrievably lost – one in which knife-board omnibuses and trams compete for urban space, where haystacks and hedges frame the scenic view, where terraces are unbroken and there are real live fishermen on the quays.

Historical 'views' are not only popular with the general public; they are also very serviceable to business, and in particular to retail trade. There is indeed a whole industry with a computerized back-up which supplies pubs, restaurants and hotels with old photographs of their locality, ideally featuring the premises themselves (facsimile reproductions of Victorian maps are apparently supplied on the same terms, and by the same firms). Hoteliers make a feature of them, rather as in the old days they would have put antlers in the hallway or fishing-rods on the walls. Supermarkets use them, more occasionally, for blow-ups. On the A-roads, the Little Chef restaurants, ruthlessly standardized when it comes to appointments, furniture and menu, festoon the walls with local scenes. In pubs the choice of historical photographs is systematic, taking a cue sometimes from the name of the pub, sometimes from the location, but often it seems from the fancy of the licensee or the shopfitter. Thus The Edinburgh Castle, Camden Town, a pub which except for the name has no known associations with Scotland, has ravishing turn-of-the-century pictures of the Edinburgh Wynds, and shows Princes Street and the Scott monument romantically swirled in the mists. The East End pubs seem to have been persuaded that the most appropriate display is one which illustrates old-time slum scenes – albeit, in the case of The Owl and Pussycat, Redchurch Street, taken from Edwardian (or 1920s) Salford rather than Shoreditch or Bethnal Green. The Woodin's Shade, a 'vintage' inn at the corner of Middlesex Street and Bishopsgate, has a harrowing panel: 'Time for "Lights Out" at Salvation Army Barracks Blackfriars' (a picture of a roomful of men in their coffin-beds); 'Women Cycle Factory Workers' (bent double to their toil); 'East End Tailor's Sweatshop' (a picture possibly reproduced from the Sweated Industries Exhibition of 1906); 'Waiting for Work in East End'; 'Waiting for Food Parcels'. The panel on the adjacent wall is scarcely more cheerful, one image showing a tenement block; another, Smith and Thomson's melancholy street traders.

The pictures of old-time high-street scenes at the supermarket check-out seem to be functioning as the photographic equivalent of a blue plaque, commemorating some prehistoric activity which took place, possibly on the same site, before modern retailing was heard of. The Club Row mural at the Bethnal Green Tesco's – a blow-up of a street scene photographed in 1930 – is a very antithesis of modern business, with not a mall or a trolley to be seen, but a sea of faces. Instead of shops, there is an open-air market, and it has all the peculiarities of a fair. Customers (if that is what they were) are far outnumbered by the bystanders gathered in almost impenetrable number at the road junction. The crowd is almost exclusively male, with a plentiful attendance of dogs both on and off their leads (Club Row was then the great pet market for East London, as well as the assembly point for an army of secondhand dealers).[14]

The same negative dialectic might be suggested for the relationship of 'views' photography to the spirit of place. It is as memorials to the departed rather than as living links to the present that they seem to be most highly prized. Thus the topographical cards on sale at the flea markets and the car boot sales, auctioned at the collectors' fairs, exchanged in the collectors' clubs, and rifled through by Saturday visitors to the concourse at London Bridge station – 'real' photos as they are called in the trade – are valued according to how radically the scene has changed. 'If the railway has ceased to exist, and the station has changed to another use, that will make an original picture of it more valuable.'[15] Streetscapes are valued on the same lines: the more completely the environment has been destroyed, the higher the going rate. Thus, to follow a writer in *Picture Postcard Monthly*, churches, stately homes and public buildings – unless they have been providentially destroyed – are a drag on the market, while 'anything that is no longer with us', including quite recent buildings 'either totally destroyed or greatly altered by the developer', are a snip.[16]

The choice of pictures in local albums follows similar lines, showing the suburb in the days when it could still claim to be a village, and, in the case of a village, one in which weekend commuters were unheard-of, and country folk ruled the roost. The compilers of the town album – often borough or city librarians – seem to be animated by a kind of municipal nostalgia, fondly recalling the days when 'local authorities had greater powers than they do in the late twentieth century'. The photograph of an electricity showroom and of a generating plant serves to remind readers that not so long ago boroughs produced their own power: the open-air lido recalls the time when they brought the pleasure principle into public health policy. They linger lovingly on such monuments to civic pride as the Art Nouveau swimming baths and the public reading-rooms, reproduce the glories of the stone-laying ceremony in the days when it was attended by thousands, show the Sunday schools assembling for their Whit Walk, the fire brigade exhibiting their newest engine or pump. They are equally alert to anything which, because of its subsequent disappearance, can be labelled 'picturesque' – the open-fronted shops with stalls sprawling out over the pavement; the Wake Monday crowd or the Methodist chapel parade.[17]

A subtext in many of these albums is that of lost sociability – those 'scenes of animation'[18] so highly prized by the picture postcard collectors and so conspicuously lacking in an increasingly home-centred and privatized society. The 'many lovely postcards associated with rural life', as one collector fondly terms them, seem often to have to do with the field full of folk at haymaking and at harvest time. The school photograph, 'the most characteristic souvenir', acquires an antique quality in an age which has, in many places, abolished school assembly and substituted a coloured photograph of the individual child for the mass collective portrait; the 'ranks of attentive and well-behaved scholars sitting at their desk'[19] seem equally remote from a pedagogy which has the boy or girl ideally peering down the microscope or sitting at a keyboard. One of the visual shocks, and no doubt visual pleasures, in these albums is the spectacle of crowds gathering in, by today's standards, unimaginable number. Derided at the time as manifestations of the herd instinct, they have become, retrospectively, as alien as creatures from outer space. One might instance – to take a photograph which is a great favourite in the albums and scrapbooks – the sea of upturned faces on Tower Hill when the dockers assembled, a hundred thousand strong, lifting their hats when Ben Tillett called on God to strike Lord Devonport (chairman of the port employers) 'dead'; or the scarcely less crammed Butlin's holiday campers, seated (as a 1946 photograph suggests[20]) in their hundreds at the breakfast tables.

Nostalgia, or homesickness, is famously not about the past but about felt absences or 'lack' in the present. It can locate itself in the blue remembered hills of adolescence or childhood but, as the example of nineteenth-century medievalism (or nineteenth-century Hellenism) may remind us, it can find its historical homeland in times that are inconceivably more remote. What seems to be involved in the case of old photographs is not so much getting back to the past – anyway the remembered past – still less, as the compilers of local albums sometimes suggest, hanging on to it as it disappears before our eyes, but rather of creating a lost Eden. As in the case of family history, where the geographically mobile and the sociologically orphaned, researching their 'roots', discover ancestors inconceivably more glamorous or interesting than their immediate forebears, old photographs here are not so much kindling memories as creating an allegorical space and allowing us to people it with our imaginings. For some it may be a time when people enjoyed more 'natural' ways of living; when pleasures, though few, were those which people made themselves; when children were childlike; work, if laborious, dignified. For others, looking at pictures of carriage folk or supping on country-house photography – no less characteristic a feature of the current revival than the albums of back-street snapshots – it may be rather a time of lost plenitude, when big families were flanked by a loyal band of retainers (group and individual portraits of household staff are often the most striking images in such books: *The Servants' Hall* is given over to them entirely[21]) and when tradesmen and their assistants, assembled expectantly outside the shop doorway, were only too anxious to attend to the customer's needs. In a more Dionysiac vein, the viewer is offered images of workers' playtime, Coronation or Armistice Day street parties, village festivities, Victorian picnics and regattas, and, in the case of the British diaspora, scenes of proconsular luxury.

Being photography, these images can never abdicate their claim to represent, if not to be, the real. Their otherness, too, is very often mediated by intimations of the shape of things to come. What seems often to be at work in period reprints is a double dialectic, in which the past is made to seem simultaneously more and less remote. Thus there is an enormous interest in public transport, but a no less distinct preference for the horse-drawn or steam-driven variety, and for such dinosaurs as the tram. Advertisements, so insistent a presence in period views that it is difficult not to think that they forced themselves, albeit subliminally, on the attention of the compilers, seem perfectly to represent this double dialectic. On the one hand, they are prototypes of modernity, with railside advertisements (for Bovril or Virol or Carter's Little Liver Pills) assailing the traveller rather as the hoardings do on the motorways and flyovers today; and familiar names often appearing on the panels of the horse-drawn omnibus, as say, 'Quaker Oats' in some favourite late-nineteenth-century photographs of traffic jams. On the other hand, the brand images, and still more affectingly the products themselves, are usually extinct. The Latinate (or Greek) neologisms of the pharmaceutical manufacturers have acquired a surreal quality with the passage of time; the housetop-high hoardings covered with eye-catching bills, the wall enamels advertising meat extracts and ointments, shoe blackings and hair oil, and not least the arresting black-letter shop signs, covering, it seems, every inch of a tradesman's premises, suggest an anarchy of puffery which makes today's commercial, by comparison, seem positively restrained.

Not familiarity but distance, the lure of the mysterious and the exotic

EARLY START

MOTHER'S PRIDE

– and not least the magic of Paris and New York – would be needed to explain the popularity, anyway among the young, of the black-and-white blow-ups. Their romanticism is not that of simple lifeism but of decadence – in one idiom *Weltschmerz* (world-weariness and melancholy); in another fantasies of male omnipotence and female ecstasy. In the present these photographs transport the viewer to the hot-spots of Manhattan or the wide-open spaces of Nevada, showing us sexual rapture in the shadow of the skyscrapers, or lovers on Harley-Davidsons speeding off in a desert-like swirl. In another they transport us to a dreamscape which, though set in the 1950s, is as different from the modern-day metropolis as it would be possible to imagine. The railway stations photographed here are not the destination of commuters, but rather a trysting-place for urgent meetings and even more desperate farewells.

In popular taste, as the advertisers well know, for they have taken to exploiting it ruthlessly, old photographs owe their appeal, in the first place, to period icons. A Doisneau picture, printed in sepia, and showing a cellist in a Parisian working man's bistro, is currently advertising a cognac;[22] a Jack Daniels whisky advert, on show in the London underground, is printed in period grey and pictures a Walker Evans-like weatherboarded still-room; while Foster's, the Australian lager manufacturers, fill the hoardings with a gigantic black-and-white photograph of the Last Days of the Raj – with, for good measure, a steam train thrown in.[23] This is not a matter of what the art historian, Alois Riegl, called 'age value', nor of the price which an old photograph can fetch as an antique. A copy is as good as an original in conveying period feel, indeed it could be argued – as the colour supplement editors seem sometimes to have believed – more so when, by dint of enlargement, blow-up and selection, it is possible to give prominence to the half-hidden. Nor does it attach to any particular subject. Colour and tone, to judge by the photographs currently on display as period prints in the pubs, seem to matter more than topic. From this point of view as the more astute greetings-card manufacturers seem to have realized, a sepia-tinted print of a 1906 football team (on sale at the stationers for the royal price of £2.50) is quite as serviceable as women demonstrating for the suffrage or children bowling hoops (to take the example of two well-known Edwardian favourites).

Pictures seem to recommend themselves for reproduction because they are, in some ineffable sense, 'atmospheric'; blurring the hard lines of detail in some more generalized aura of pastness. It follows from this that they must bear the tell-tale marks of time. Whence, it may be, in the current enthusiasm for reproducing 'views' photography, the strong preference for peopled landscapes and the systematic exclusion of those which depict wild nature in its aboriginal state. It is not mountains we want to see in a period photograph, but villages or farmhouses; not stormy seas but promenades, piers and pierrots. Whence, too, it may be, the preference for the high-street scene over the residential street or suburb: the first, whatever the particular date, is necessarily filled with a heteroglossia of period signs; the second – unless, fortuitously, there is a hand-cart or fire engine in the foreground – may look almost indistinguishable from the same scene today.

In the early days of the discovery of old photographs it was the Victorian which seemed to be picturesque. But, as in other fields of contemporary resurrectionism, the earlier past has been overlain by a more recent one, and there has been a persistent updating of the notion of period. Ever since the Hovis advertisements of the 1970s, filmed in the cobbled streets of Shaftesbury though pretending to be Yorkshire, and following the fortunes of a 1920s delivery round, the inter-war years have been as plausible a period setting as high Victorian England. More recently, in the vogue for *Picture Post* photography of the austerity years, the 1940s and the 1950s have moved easily into this symbolic space. Factory girls in their scarves, workmen on their bicycles have become as familiar figures as the fisherman in his sou'wester, or the harvesters and gleaners with their arms full of sheaves. 'Mother's Pride' is the caption given to one such picture, offered for sale as a ready-to-frame print. It is a genre scene of a Lancashire ginnel which might have been taken from any period but, being a photograph, it gets its detail right – the pinnied working-class mums with their arms akimbo, the backyard palings, the upturned face of the post-war child full of eagerness and hope.[24]

The discovery of old photographs coincided with the advent of the faded look in the fashion trade and the vogue for 'granny clothes' and stonewashed jeans. The adoption of the old and used in preference to the new also had its counterpart in the 1960s craze for stripped-pine furniture and the bleaching out, by caustic soda, of the faintest hint of gloss. Mention might be made, too, of the early stirrings of that taste for faded elegance which in the 1960s, 1970s and 1980s was to become mandatory for the 'restored' (i.e. newly created) 'period' interior, and which was supported not only by architectural salvage – a trade which traces its origins to the late 1960s – but by a variety of 'distressing' and 'ageing' technologies which allowed the newest products to bear the mark of the venerable and the decrepit.

The faded look was possibly anticipated by new-wave fashion photography's taste for soft-focus images and deep shadows; its choice of urban detritus as background props and its taste for scenes of urban decay. TV commercials took this up, using misty interiors for their memory ads ('vague enough to allow us a place in that very undefined place') and using blurred or bleached images to promote products which could lay some claim to being vintage or old-fashioned. With the aid of 'dream filters' (putting Vaseline over the lens can, it seems, soften the hard edges of even the most angular building), the faded look was also to leave its mark on the picture-postcard trade, where the hard, bright colours and high gloss finish of the standard offering were challenged by a new breed of 'art' products – dominant in many card-racks today – which made a speciality of misty mornings, evening streets, timeless vistas, and blurred and out-of-focus images which could transform even the most unpromising material (such as the modern city of Oxford) into dreamscapes. When, in his most recent film, Terence Davies set about using the 'bleach by-pass process' in order to drain the colour from the work, he may have believed he was recreating an Austerity look, and indeed gave his cameraman sepia photographs of 1950s Liverpool to work from; but both the technology and the artistic ambition might be seen as a child of the opulent sixties.[25] (The self-consciousness about photography is, of course, very sixties too.)

It was very much of a piece with this that the first old masters to be rediscovered, the first photographers to fire the enthusiasm of the professional historians, and the first to win a public following, so far as reproduction was concerned, should have been the impressionist-naturalistic photographers of the 1880s and 1890s with their predilection for 'atmospheric' effects; Frank Meadow Sutcliffe[26] and P.H. Emerson,[27] the Whitby and East Anglian 'pictorialists'. The 'fuzzy' school, as they were derisorily labelled by their more orthodox late Victorian rivals – 'hazing' out the background – they enveloped their subjects (or so it was alleged) in perpetual mist. Sutcliffe himself, as Michael Hiley records in his fine monograph, believed that fine weather was to be avoided like the plague, and that the best time for finding pictures was either twilight or evening, 'when the shadows are long', or in the early morning, 'before the sun has driven off the mist'.[28] He also believed that England, and in particular his native coast of East Yorkshire, was blessed with a climate that was peculiarly sympathetic to the photographer. 'To this vile weather we owe our most charming effects. If there was no bad weather there would be no clouds and no gales, no rain and no snow. If there is one time more than another when the country smiles the most, it is during rain.'

Notes

1. Brian Coe and Paul Gates, *The Snapshot Photograph: The Rise of Popular Photography, 1888–1930*, London 1977, p. 14.

2. Peter Turner, *A History of Photography*, London 1987, pp. 81–7; Graham King, *Snapshots as Art*, London 1978; *Say 'Cheese': The Snapshot as Art and Social History*,

London 1984; 'Snapshot Chic' in *Say 'Cheese'*, Jo Spence and Patricia Holland, eds., *Family Snaps, The Meaning of Domestic Photography*, London 1991; Jonathan Green, ed., *The Snapshot*, New York 1974; Julia Hirsch, *Family Photographs: Content, Memory and Effect*, Oxford 1981.

3. Michael Ignatieff, *The Russian Album*, London 1987, pp. 1–7; Georges Perec. *W. ou le souvenir d'enfance*, Paris 1975 (I am grateful to Lucy Morton for this reference); Estelle Jussim, 'From the Studio to the Snapshot: an Immigrant Photographer of the 1920s', *History of Photography*, vol. 1, no. 3, July 1977, pp. 183–9.

4. My reference is to the Manchester Studies photographic archive, on which see A.E. Linkman, 'Today's Photographs, Tomorrow's History: The Work of the Documentary Photography Archive', in Michael Hallett, ed., *Rewriting Photographic History*, Birmingham 1989, pp. 33–5.

5. John Caughie, 'Halfway to Paradise St', *Sight and Sound*, vol. 2, no. 2, May 1992, pp. 11–12; Pat Kirkham and Mike O'Shaugnessy, 'Designing Desire', *Sight and Sound*, vol. 2, no. 2, p. 13.

6. Ronald Fraser, *In Search of a Past: The Manor House, Amnersfield, 1933–1945*, London 1984.

7. Roland Barthes, *Camera Lucida: Reflections on Photography*, London 1984.

8. Jimmy Forsyth, *Scotswood Road*, Newcastle-upon-Tyne 1986; Shirley Baker, *Street Photographs: Manchester and Salford*, Newcastle-upon-Tyne 1989.

9. Information from Clapton Colour Services, E5, and Harlequin Studios, Bethnal Green Rd, E2, August 1992.

10. *Signs of the Times*, BBC2, 28 August 1992. Nicholas Barker, *Signs of the Times*, London 1992, is the book of the series.

11. The photographs in question, to judge by the little shelf of samples in a Bethnal Green stationers, continued to appeal to both the sportsman and the paedophile – a manly picture of a 1900s football team rubbing shoulders with some Edwardian child nudes.

12. Oral information, Michael Bowmer, of Poster Art International, July 1992.

13. On Doisneau, *Un Certain Robert Doisneau, la très véridique histoire d'un photographe racontée par lui-même*, Paris 1986; there is a 1980 Gordon Fraser gallery album of his photographs. Sadly, the couple in 'Le Baiser' have been revealed to be actors (Obituary, *Independent*, 2 April 1994).

14. The Tesco superstore at Abingdon, Berks, has 'Stevens Boatyard', a river scene photographed in 1885; a picture of a cycle shop in 1911; and one of some 1880s timbered houses. Tesco's High Wycombe has old high-street scenes and a huge blow-up of 1900 slums.

15. Anthony Byatt, *Collecting Picture Postcards*, Malvern 1979, p. 9.

16. *Picture Postcard Monthly*, June 1980.

17. 'The Picturesque Open Butcher's Shop', David Mander and Jenny Goulder, *The London Borough of Hackney in Old Photographs, 1860–1960*, Stroud 1991.

18. Martin Willoughby, *A History of Picture Postcards*, London 1992, p. 83; *Picture Postcard Monthly*, June 1980.

19. Colin and Tim Ward, *Images of Childhood in Old Postcards*, Gloucester 1991, pp. 43–4.

20. Reproduced in the *Observer*, 30 August 1992.

21. Merlin Waterson, ed., *The Servants' Hall, A Domestic History of Erddig*, London 1980.

22. *Evening Standard*, 25 August 1992.

23. Advertising hoarding, July–August 1992.

24. 'The Premier Collection', printed in sepia on the wrapping is the only clue to their provenance.

25. Kirkham and O'Shaughnessy, 'Dangerous Desire'.

26. Michael Hiley, *Frank Sutcliffe, Photographer of Whitby*, London 1974; *Frank Meadow Sutcliffe*, Oxford 1979.

27. Peter Turner, *Emerson*, London 1974; Ellen Handy, 'Art and Science in P.H. Emerson's Naturalistic Vision', in Mike Weaver, ed., *British Photography in the Nineteenth Century: The Fine Art Tradition*, Cambridge 1989; M. Hiley, 'The Photographer as Artist', *Studio International*, July–August 1975. For Emerson's programmatic statement, P.H. Emerson, *Naturalistic Photography for Students of Art*, London 1989.

28. Hiley, *Frank Sutcliffe*, pp. 54, 74. An 1890 reviewer of Sutcliffe in *The Amateur Photographer* wrote: 'Lately Mr Sutcliffe has thought fit to "haze off" the distance, until in some that he exhibits Whitby is completely enveloped in fog, although there is a bright light upon the men and women on the jetty', quoted in Hiley, *Frank Sutcliffe*, p. 125.

Scopophilia

Any photography, whether or not it aspires to the status of art, has a hidden aesthetics. Framing is necessarily theatrical, and, as on the proscenium stage, what it leaves out, accidentally or by design – not least the photographer, sometimes the missing interlocutor and always the impresario responsible for the *mise-en-scène* – may be more germane to the progress of the drama than what is offered to the viewer's gaze. Objects, however seemingly fugitive, tell their own narrative, sometimes wildly at variance with the ostensible point of the story, and it is for this reason, among others, that wide-awake local historians have taken to using a magnifying glass when reading high-street scenes. Lighting, as well as giving high exposure to some figures while leaving others in the shade, will also determine the mood of the whole – whence the preference for twilight (according to Victorian aesthetics the ideal hour for numinous thoughts) in photographs of 'timeless' landscapes; for brilliant sunlight when portraying the open-air assemblies of the rich, as, say, in 1930s pictures of Eton and Ascot, or 1900s ones of Rotten Row; and for cloud-laden skies when picturing landscapes, or townscapes, which are intended to be sombre – for example, the moorland scene from Top Withens (the supposed original for *Wuthering Heights*), or the snicket of an old-time northern mill.[1] By the same token any grouping – whether 'spontaneous', as in 'candid camera' shots, or carefully arranged, as in that cliché of nineteenth-century country house photography, the picnic party assembled on the lawn – is choreographed and stylized according to the intended effect. One might instance the children paying rapt attention to the teacher in photographs of the nineteenth-century schoolroom or scenically arranged to give an air of animation to the town 'view'; the aged patriarchs gazing out to the far horizon or pulling on their pipes; the women caught in profile hanging out the washing, whitening the steps or gossiping over the courtyard pump.

Likewise captions, even those attached to the snapshots in family albums, have a rhetoric, telling us what we are to see and how we are to see it. Often they set out to tell a story, using the conventions of motto art or, in nineteenth-century work, narrative painting. However spare, they are never purely referential. Thus a place name, though seemingly no more than descriptive and locating a particular scene, doubles in the role of a signifier, allowing the single image to stand for a larger whole – a mere back alley in the Bill Brandt picture which he chose to label 'Limehouse'. Like other texts too, both verbal and visual, captions change in their connotations over time. 'Gorbals' may have struck a chill in the heart of 1948 *Picture Post* readers, anyway those who had supped on stories of Glasgow razor gangs; today, for those who buy 'Gorbals 1948' – the Bert Hardy photograph of two scruffy, carefree boys which is currently a bestseller on the card-racks at W.H. Smith's and Menzies – it may look more like a paradise lost. (It is a great pity that in current reproduction work, the original captions are so often doctored, replaced or still worse – as in the sumptuous reproduction of Frank Sutcliffe's Whitby photographs – relegated to footnotes at the back of the book.)

What is called documentary photography, so far from being insulated from aesthetic influences, might be said rather to exemplify their hidden hand. Setting out, in Moholy-Nagy's words, to provide 'a truthful record of objectively determined fact',[2] they nevertheless carry an unspoken narrative, an invisible point of address. A street scene, if it is filled with people or traffic or (like Robert Venturi's Las Vegas[3]) a forest of competing signs, is thought to reflect the 'frenetic urgent pace' of modern living. If, on the other hand, the streets, like those of Atget's Paris (a very *beau idéal* of avant-garde photographers),[4] are empty, they inevitably wear a desolate air and serve as a symbol for alienation or distress. (For this reason the slum courts of the 1880s and 1890s whose pictures appear at the back of Medical Office of Health reports usually look inexpressibly melancholy.)

A comparison of Bill Brandt's 1948 'Gorbals' with that of Bert Hardy's is particularly instructive on this point, since both photographers were sent out by *Picture Post* on the same mission, and it was a matter of some moment, for the subsequent course of British photography, that the editor chose to highlight the second at the expense of the first. Brandt bathed his Gorbals in Stygian gloom, picking out long rows of tenements and picturing the streets, as was his wont in *plein air* working-class photography, empty of people but with sinister de Chirico shadows. Bert Hardy, on the other hand, dispatched to Glasgow when the editor was worried by Brandt's prints, produced a series of eye-level portraits in which the tenements were relegated to the background, while local characters or children came to the fore.[5]

For those brought up on, or influenced by, the 1960s cult of authenticity – the imaginative complex in which the taste for old photographs was born, and the early retrieval projects carried out – 'informality' is a gauge of authenticity, a rough-and-ready principle of selection in subsequent reproduction. The more informal the pose, the more confidence we have in it. But a critical review of the period photographs which are in vogue today, whether as sources of visual pleasure, to hang up as prints on the wall, or to leaf through in books and journals, may remind us that nothing is more contrived than the natural, or more carefully prepared than the spontaneous shot. Indeed we have many accounts from the documentary photographers themselves to remind us of how carefully the ground was staked out beforehand. Bill Brandt must have needed all his tact to persuade a miner to appear with coal-black face at the supper table, or – a startling image for a working-class home – to persuade the family to continue eating their dinner while, in the foreground of the picture, a chair, apparently mortally wounded, was lying on its side.

From the point of view of historical veracity, though not of visual pleasure, the posed photograph, even though it might involve, as it often did in the nineteenth century, clasping the sitter's face in irons and providing a group with a paraphernalia of hand-rests to keep the image steady, was arguably a great deal more 'natural' and objective than those seemingly more spontaneous *cinéma-vérité* ones where the photographer seizes on the decisive moment and catches the subjects unawares. One might compare here the family grouping as it appears in Victorian or Edwardian studio photography with those favoured by the 'social realist' documentary. In the first the family, dressed in their Sunday best and photographed against a studio backdrop – an aspidistra in a pot, a sideboard or a column to serve as hand-rest – are arranged in a decorous group: the father and mother behind, presiding over their brood and looking upright; the older children standing to attention as young cadets; the toddlers respectfully scattered on the floor. To modern eyes they may look stilted. But they are posing not for the viewer but for themselves, projecting an image, however idealized, or fantasized, of what they believed themselves to be. It is unlikely that the photographer's studio was the only occasion when such appearances were required. It would be mandatory if they attended church or chapel, and conventional at the family dinner-table or on family outings. The paterfamilias might well have comported himself in the same spirit when he was accosted by a stranger, or when he travelled to work, or when he took a stick or a belt to his children. One cannot think that the mother only appeared as a Madonna figure when sitting before the camera, nor that the children were careless of seniority rules in the more everyday phases of their life.

In documentary, on the other hand, the family is photographed to exemplify their social position. If they are rich they must look like the lords of mankind, with not a furrow of anxiety or self-doubt. If they are poor they ought to seem careworn. If they are suburban they should look ordinary. In slum photography, where human beings rather than the buildings are the objects of attention, the camera's eye, though a compassionate one, cannot allow the sitter to move or speak – even if they are taken unawares, they must be a *tableau vivant* of despair. Thus in the East End photograph (taken in 1922) which bizarrely illustrates Orwell's 1937 *Road to Wigan Pier*,[6] the family is a picture of misery, staring vacantly at the camera, and it requires an effort of imagination to see that the next moment the children might be tumbling on the floor, or going out into the street to play, or that the mother and father might be having a laugh or sitting down to a cup of tea.

In Humphrey Spender's 'Worktown' photographs, the only one of a domestic interior has the father clutching desperately at his knee while the mother, a blank figure with bowed head, bathes the baby in a tin bath.[7] A Liverpool photograph from the same epoch has the father cloth-capped, with hunched shoulders and downcast eyes, communing with his feet.[8] If one were to be asked what such families were doing one could only reply, 'being miserable'. Edwardian social documentary, though much more melodramatic, and following the style of low-life scenes on the stage, is even more despairing. The children typically cling to their parents for protection, or comfort each other as best they can, the older ones carrying little ones in their arms. The father, sometimes pictured sullenly in the doorway, is a living monument to defeat. 'An East End family, 1912', runs the caption to one such picture, 'In spite of the impressive array of china and glass these children have nothing to eat.' Perhaps this is what the photographer wanted us to think. There is indeed a baby, yelling its head off in the mother's arms; an older sister appears to be sobbing convulsively, on the table: a brother comforts her while another sucks hungrily at his thumb. But the room is festooned with lace, the baby has a spotlessly white – and immensely long – robe, the mantelpiece is a picture of domestic order, the shelves have space not only for a fine tea-set and a liberal display of glassware but also for decorative vases of all kinds.[9]

In the nineteenth century these painterly inspirations were open and avowed. Studio portraiture, whether in the hands of 'art' photographers such as Julia Margaret Cameron or commercial high-street photographers, was modelled on the old masters – most obviously in those Rembrandtesque head-and-shoulders cabinet portraits where the background was kept as a dark blur to give the sitter's physiognomy – the eyes especially – high exposure. 'Views' photography followed the inspiration of genre painting and landscape art.[10] Thus Hill, who served his artistic

The only domestic interior in Humphrey Spender's 1937 'Worktown' photographs. The father is a picture of desperation, the mother invisible.

apprenticeship by executing engravings for an illustrated edition of Sir Walter Scott, was an admirer of the painter Wilkie: the casual arrangement and informal setting of his Newhaven fisherfolk, as well as representing a pioneering essay in social documentary, were also an attempt to make life imitate art.[11] Emerson was no less indebted to Millais,[12] and his atmospheric vistas of life and labour on the Norfolk Broads have obvious affinities to the 'dreary landscape' school of art.[13]

A more rewarding influence or affinity to consider, if only because it has received so much less commentary, would be with cinema. Bill Brandt's debt to and fascination with the films of Alfred Hitchcock are well known, and help to explain some of the more uncanny groupings which appear in his *London by Night*.[14] Atget's Paris has the closest affinities to Vigo's *L'Atalante*, and one may wonder whether the second did not take its location, as well as its spirit, from the first. Likewise the Paris-based humanist photographers of the 1930s and 1940s – Doisneau, Izis and Kertesz – seem to haunt the same quarters as the poetic realist films of Marcel Carné and Jean Renoir. They are, as it were, still-life versions of *Le Million*, or *Le Jour se Lève*. The romantic young couples who figure so largely in current reproductions of their work, might be thought to take their cue from the working-class heart-throbs of Popular Front cinema.

As well as the artistic influences (richly documented in recent work on the early history of photography) there are also more archetypal images and myths, lodged, as it were, in the visual unconscious, which spring to life at the camera's bidding. This is often true of those pictures which by dint of constant repetition have become in recent years iconic. One might instance the *rus in urbe* of Paul Martin's well-known picture of back-street children making a merry-go-round of the lamppost for all the world as if it were the village maypole;[15] or the image of lost innocence in his no less well known pictures of slum children turning somersaults in the gutter or tumbling in the wake of the watering-carts. They take their place in a long line of little ragamuffins, descending perhaps from Victorian sentimental art, famously personified in the Bisto kids of the gravy advertisements, and well represented, in the black-and-white reproductions currently on sale at the poster galleries and card-shops, by the cheeky *gamins* of Robert Doisneau's Paris, by the children performing street pantomime against a background of graffiti in Izis's 'Montmartre, 1949', and by the *Just William* figures, with their scruffy shorts and muddy knees, of Bert Hardy's 'Gorbals'.[16] In a more sombre register there are those pictures of suffering which draw on the iconography of Christian art. Dorothea Lange's 'Migrant mother, Nipomo, California', 'camped on the edge of a pea field when the crop had failed in a freeze' – perhaps the best-known image of Depression Years America – is an

influential example, a *Mater Dolorosa* crossed with a *virgo lactans*, caught (or composed) in a moment of despair when (as Dorothea Lange's field-notes tell us) 'The tyres had just been sold from the car to buy food'. The woman, pondering her troubles, has a child on either shoulder, one of them sobbing into her neck, and a baby asleep on her lap; her strong face is puckered with lines of worry and fatigue, her worker's arm is raised in what might become a gesture of defiance, though all it can provide her with is a temporary head-rest. Like Henry Fonda at the wheel in the ramshackle jalopy of *The Grapes of Wrath* she is gazing out on a road to nowhere.[17]

It is a commonplace of contemporary criticism that meaning is in the eye of the beholder: that a picture will tell different stories, depending on how it is framed; and that the after-image, subject to multiple and dissonant appropriations, will diverge radically from the original. Even so, it is astonishing to observe some of the reversals which take place when pictures taken at the time for their actuality or topicality are exhibited as trophies of the past or recycled as period prints. The mean and shabby streets of the 1940s, photographed for their melancholy and dishevelled air and often at the terminal point in a long life, take on an altogether more hopeful character when they are reproduced on greetings cards or marketed as 'ready to frame' pictures. Thus Bert Hardy's 'Elephant and Castle, 1949', though picturing a comfortless basement, with neither carpet nor curtains, nor (save for a tin opener and tea cups) cutlery or crockery, seems to be selling as an illustration of young love, the light streaming in through the windows while the husband and wife gaze fondly, if anxiously, into each other's eyes. 'Early Start' is the cheery caption given to another such print – a rear view of factory girls on their way to work, currently on sale at £1 a print in the open-air markets. The corner shop, with the morning papers furled like banners in their rack, and the *Tit-Bits* hand-bill, stands as a kind of neighbourhood sentinel, framing the journey to work. The cyclist on one side of the street, and the bikes propped up on the kerbside of the other, call back memories of yesteryear's car-free streets; while the mill chimney in the far distance, so far from belching out smoke, seems rather to be wreathed in mists. And it does not seem fanciful to think of the young women, with their purposeful tread, as marching towards a new dawn.

Walker Evans's famous photographs of the Alabama sharecroppers, chosen (as a recent study of his contact prints has shown) to exemplify hardship and deprivation, are enjoying an even stranger after-life, being sold as Americana at the 'retro' stores, mounted in frameless frames in the Manhattan studios, and adopted as cultural icons by the fashionable. The dungareed clothes of the sharecroppers, which fifty years ago denoted 'coarse' materials and rough and poorly paid work, have taken on a new look in an age when stonewashed jeans are a universal leisurewear, or even (as the current Levi's advert has it) an invitation to strip. The faces which stare out at us, eyes riveted on the camera, have also taken on a new meaning when the plain boards which so insistently frame them, so far from mirroring worry and fatigue as they did for Walker Evans (he is evidently fascinated by the boards – some of his photographs are given over to them entirely), are on the contrary, in the distressed idiom of today's designer-led interiors, the height of chic. The ramshackle, weatherboarded farmsteads are as different from the 'flash' of New York as they were when the Farm Security Administration sent out its photographers in 1935, but in the light of today's vogue for Shaker furniture and old pine, the stark interiors radiate vernacular charm. Likewise the impromptu storefronts, with their hand-blocked lettering and scrawled notices, seem to be the ancestors of that vernacular signwriting which Robert Venturi and the postmodernists celebrate in the gambling casinos of Las Vegas. Reference might be made finally to those simple virtues, much insisted on by Walker Evans and James Magee, which retrospectively make their human subjects appear less the symbolic victims of oppression, but rather (the character which

Yesterday's icons of poverty – today's vernacular style.
Walker Evans, Alabama 1936.

had brought their forebears into the region), heroic pioneers. Passing, in short, from the realm of politics and economics to that of history, Walker Evans's sharecroppers are in some sort reabsorbed into the American past.

One way of approaching the current vogue for the reproduction and display of period photographs would be in terms of what Freud called 'scopophilia' – the desire to see.[18] Avant-garde film theorists, attempting to come to terms with the universal appeal of Hollywood films, have produced a critical commentary on this, using Freudian notions of ego-identification (and Lacanian ones of the 'mirror-stage') to account for the enduring popularity of such major genres as the weepie, the thriller and the western. The pleasures of the gaze, they argue, release libidinal desires and correspond to those of primary narcissism and identification – that stage of infantile self-absorption which gives rise to impossible longings (the desire to return to the mother's womb), and feeds on regressive fantasies. As a theory of the mechanics of viewing it has the great merit, like 'reception' theory in literary criticism and the study of iconography in art history, of focusing on the consumption rather than the production of images. It forces us to reflect on the ways in which the spectator is positioned by the camera's eye. In the hands of feminist critics it has been used both to foreground issues on the representation of womanhood and to unravel the secrets of such 'women's films' as the melodramas of Douglas Sirk. It is no less relevant to the 'poetic realism' of the documentary, and the ways in which lighting, composition and tonality can turn the empirical and the factual into objects of desire – a matter which, whether or not we acknowledge it, puts realist enterprises of all kinds, including that of the historian, in question. More generally, by focusing on the *compulsive* character of viewing, it opens up inquiry into the nature of visual sensation.

The scopophiliac pleasures of old photographs are in principle no less open to this kind of analysis than those of film. 'Voyeurism', to take the most familiar and the least problematical of its psychic mechanisms, has an obvious purchase on the revelatory sense of *disclosure*, which has been a leading excitement in the discovery of old glass slides – the recovery of what had hitherto been secreted, and the public exposure of private worlds. More precisely, it might help to account for the talismanic importance attached to 'informality' and 'spontaneity', a leitmotiv in the reprinting and recycling of old prints. We are invited to become the visual equivalent of eavesdroppers. In the record of great events, we are taken behind the scenes – whence perhaps the special regard for Roger Fenton's Crimean War photography, showing officers and men in their relaxed moments, the war-wounded in their impromptu stretchers and beds. In celebrity portraiture a special value is attached to those rare photographs which capture the subject off-duty – as, famously, Isambard Kingdom Brunel in the easy-going pose which has made Robert Howlett's photograph such a firm favourite, both with the professional historian and the viewing public – shoes scuffed, coat untidy, hand stuck jauntily into his waistcoat pocket, a cigar playing nonchalantly from his mouth. In documentary photography, reproducing, in some sort, the original excitement of the 'candid' hand-held camera, a special value is attached to pictures which have succeeded in capturing their subjects unawares – as, say, harvesters taking a break for their 'elevenses' or 'fourses', a couple canoodling in the grass or on the sands, even (to take the example of one of documentary photography's most famous coups) the soldier caught in the act of dying. Still more pertinent perhaps – a kind of ultimate in voyeurism, and one in which the most committed of historians, and the most avant-garde of aesthetes have been very much to the fore – would be the current enthusiasm for breaking open the family album, and turning the impromptu occasions and intimacies of family life into what is in some sort a public spectacle. Visually stunning when the original snapshot is turned into a framed print, the plate-sized blow-up of an octavo volume, or a double crown spread in a colour supplement, these pictures are exhibited as raids on the historically inarticulate, trophies of the otherwise invisible: the viewer's pleasures are those of a Peeping Tom.

In a more speculative vein, akin to a long-standing explanation given to the star system in the cinema, it would be possible to align scopophilia, in the shape of 'narcissistic ego-identification', with some of the prints currently in vogue. Robert Doisneau's 'Le Baiser à l'Hôtel de Ville', the 'all-time favourite' in the poster blow-ups, might serve as some kind of contemporary equivalent to the enthusiasm shown by the cinemagoers of 1940 for Rhett Butler and Scarlett O'Hara. But the pleasure principle, even if it is defined as generously and as dialectically as it is in Freud, while it might accommodate them, could hardly account for an old photograph's power to take one unawares. Projection, rather than (or as well as) identification, might help to explain, or at any rate to problematize, that hallucinatory sense of oneness with the past which old photographs seem so often to induce – fostering the illusion that, as Salman Rushdie puts it in an autobiographical essay, we are more at home in it than we are in the present.[19] 'Oceanic feelings' – Freud's term for the effect of an encounter with the numinous and the ineffable – might help to account for the revelatory power of a particular image and of those strong emotions which well up seemingly from nowhere. Freud's 'family romance', the child's rejection of real-life parents in favour of imaginary and more glamorous others – a recurring fantasy which seems very germane to the current enthusiasm for family history, and the discovery of 'roots' – could also be used to explain such contemporary clichés as the display of 1860s *cartes de visite* in the manner of ancestral portraits.

This line of inquiry might help to explain the strong identification which photography, like film, can establish with a past that never was, but which corresponds to what we would have liked it to be. It would allow for those identifications which we establish, as it were, vicariously or by proxy, not because of lived experience but because of the power of visual representation. If for instance we feel immediately at home with a picture of a pierrot show, it will not be because we spent our childhood holidays on Brighton pier or Margate sands but, perhaps, because Joan Littlewood's *Oh What A Lovely War* turned the pierrot show into a last post for pre-1914 England.

Freud's 'Mourning and Melancholia' is an essay which seems particularly pertinent to the pathos of old photographs, even if – particularly if – we have never known their subject; it underscores that valedictory note of leave-taking which turns the photographic album into a kind of elegy for the dead. It also bears on the role of photography as a commemorative art – the quality which brings it closest to the spirit of the historian's project. Freud's arguments here are complex but the capital point – and it is one which distinguishes the old photograph from that whole family of keepsakes, souvenirs and tokens with which it is so often bracketed – is that the loved object no longer exists, that the original bond, or relationship, has been irretrievably shattered. Under this optic old photographs could be seen as a play on the irrecoverability of the past, the impossibility of bringing the dead to life. The keeping of the photograph here is a grasping after shadows; it is a closing of the stable door after the horse has bolted.

Necrophilia, though generally regarded as beyond the pale, a latter-day expression of decadence, shares with history (and with the exhibitors of period photography) the aim of establishing a new intimacy with the dead. In its strong version it bears on 'the beauties of the horrid'; in its weaker one it could apply to the morbid appetite for the spectacle of pleasing decay. Photography has long been one of its natural constituencies. Disaster scenes – not only pit explosions, shipwrecks and fires but even such parochial dramas as the fatal fall of a horse – were a magnet to the 'views' photographers of the 1900s, and command much the highest price in the 'historic' postcard market today. Earlier it was quite normal in the nineteenth century for the family album to have photographs of the infant dead, choreographed so that, with eyes open, they still seemed to be alive.

Scopophilia, with its focus on psychical phenomena, leaves little conceptual space for such matters, crucial to reception theory in photography and in the visual arts generally, as changes in exhibition space, revolutions or reversals in public taste, style wars, fashion revivals – in sum the concurrence of different causes in which an appetite for the visual takes shape. Nor can narcissistic self-identification explain what Barthes calls photography's 'punctum'[20] – the power to astonish, amaze and disconcert.

There is a case for considering history as a source, if not of photography's visual pleasures, then certainly of its visual excitements. Retrospectively it can charge with foreboding and significance pictures which might otherwise go unremarked, as for instance – to take an example which I find moving – a summer 1914 photograph of an Oxford cricket XI. Indeed it is arguably the presence of the terminal other – the banks of the Somme and the mud-flats of Flanders – which may help to account for the extraordinary appeal of the Edwardian in the photographic revival of the last thirty years, something not matched by any comparable vogue in architecture or *objets d'art*. Likewise the enormous critical attention lavished on August Sander's mug-shots – which in television documentary serve as a kind of visual shorthand for the social background to Nazism – is entirely a matter of retrospective readings, and of the special value which attaches to pictures which can be read as portents and signs. No less historical in origin would be the taste for dying cultures and disappearing worlds, a leitmotiv of photography as a commemorative art, and one never so apparent as in the current revival. Here the pleasures of the look would need to be related to their social conditions of existence, and to such historical particulars as geographical and occupational mobility, innovations in the built environment, changes in the domestic order, and revolutions in public taste. But it would also need to engage in the field of representation, addressing itself to such more ineffable questions as 'period charm' and notions of the 'photogenic' – a term coined by Fox Talbot in 1843, which has exhibited such astonishing reversals in its subsequent career. Above all it would need to engage with the irrecoverability of the past: the central pathos of retrieval projects, as of any kind of historical enterprise which also – by one of those mysterious alchemies of taste which it is beyond the reach of history to explain, even though we are among its prime beneficiaries – transforms subjects of study into objects of desire.

Notes

1. All these examples are taken from Bill Brandt, *Photographs, 1928–1983*, Barbican Art Gallery 1983.

2. L. Moholy-Nagy, foreword to Mary Benedetta, *The Street Markets of London*, London 1936, p. vii.

3. Robert Venturi, *Learning from Las Vegas*, Cambridge, Mass. 1986.

4. *The Work of Atget*, ed. John Szarkowski and Maria Morris Hambourg, vol. 4: *Modern Times*, London 1985.

5. The story is told in David Mellor, 'Phantasms', in Mark Haworth-Booth, ed., *Bill Brandt, Behind the Camera, Photography, 1928–1983*, London 1985, pp. 85 ff.

6. George Orwell, *The Road to Wigan Pier*, London 1937. There is a good discussion of this in John Taylor, 'Imaginary Landscapes', *Ten: 8*, 12, 1983, p. 17.

7. Humphrey Spender, *Worktown People: Photographs from Northern England, 1937–38*, Bristol 1982.

8. Robert Westall, *Children of the Blitz*, London 1985, p. 139.

9. Jenni Calder, *The Victorians and Edwardians at Home from Old Photographs*, London 1979.

10. Early photographs were famously concerned to ape and emulate the fine arts, scouring nature for any scene that would show off their artistic powers, and in their portraits imitating the chiaroscuro effects of the old masters. Michael Bartram, *The Pre-Raphaelite Camera: Aspects of Victorian Photographs*, London 1985, pp. 8, 73–4, 178, 186 and passim; Peter Galassi, *Before Photography: Painting and the Invention of Photography*, New York 1981.

11. Sara Stevenson, *David Octavius Hill and Robert Adamson*, Edinburgh 1981, pp. 13–14; see also *An Early Victorian Album, The Photographic Masterpieces (1843–1847) of David Octavius Hill and Robert Adamson*, ed. Colin Ford, New York 1976.

12. John Szarkowski, *Looking at Photographs*, New York 1974, p. 40; Peter Turner, *History of Photography*, p. 69.

13. Howard D. Rodee, 'The "Dreary Landscape" as a Background for Scenes of Rural Poverty in Victorian Paintings', *Art Journal*, vol. 36, no. 4, Summer 1974, pp. 307–13.

14. Bill Brandt, *A Night in London: The Story of a London Night*, London 1938; David Mellor, 'Phantasms', in Mark Howarth-Booth, ed., *Bill Brandt Behind the Camera: Photography, 1928–1983*, Oxford 1985.

15. 'Lamp-post swinging, 1892'. This sells in huge quantities at the V&A and figured in *Victorian Snapshots*, London 1939, a precocious reproduction of some of Paul Martin's work. See Roy Flukinger et al., *Paul Martin, Victorian Photographer*, London 1978.

16. Rejlander's street urchin sequence of photographs, best known for 'Poor Jo', included numbers of more smiling tumblers and ragamuffins. Unlike Paul Martin's subjects, they had been carefully groomed for their part. Stephanie Spencer, 'O.G. Rejlander's Photographs of Street Urchins', *Oxford Art Journal*, vol. 7, no. 2, 1984, excellently relates such photographs to their fine-art predecessors.

17. 'Dorothea Lange: Migrant Workers' in C. Fleishhaver and B.W. Brannan, eds., *Documenting America, 1935–1943*, Berkeley 1988, pp. 114–27; see also Lawrence W. Levine, 'The Historian and the Icon', in ibid., pp. 16–17, 25–6, 31–2, 34, 36. 'Characteristically', writes Levine, commenting on the Protean, double-edged character of such icons, '*Life* magazine had no difficulty in perceiving in Dorothea Lange's photo of a grizzled, impoverished migrant farmer the visage of a traditional American pioneer' (p. 36). See also Karin Becker Ohrn, *Dorothea Lange and the Documentary Tradition*, Baton Rouge 1980; Milton Meltzer, *Dorothea Lange, A Photographer's Life*, New York 1978.

18. G. Malanga, ed., *Scopophilia: The Love of Looking*, New York 1985; Laura Mulvey, 'Visual Pleasure and Narrative Cinema', in *Visual and other Pleasures: Collected Writings*, London 1989.

19. Rushdie, reflecting on a photograph of his childhood, begins by quoting L.P. Hartley, 'The past is a foreign country, they do things differently there' and comments: 'But the photograph tells me to invert this idea; it reminds me that it is my present that is foreign and that the past is home, albeit a home in a lost city in the mists of time', Salman Rushdie, *Imagined Homelands, Essays and Criticism 1981–91*, London 1991.

20. Roland Barthes, *Camera Lucida: Reflections on Photography*, London 1984, pp. 26–7, 42, 47, 51, 93.

PART VI

Costume Drama

Modern Gothic:
The Elephant Man

Gothic, literary critics argue, allows us to indulge a taste for the uncanny, to play with fantasies of impossible desire, and to explore the extremes of the human condition. It leads us into the dark passages of the unconscious. It descends to the lower depths. Stephen Sondheim, in his ballad-opera version of *Sweeney Todd* (1979), used it to make a phantasmagoria of commerce, evoking the most primitive of horrors – the fear of being eaten – and using cannibalism as a metaphor for trade. The demon barber himself, in a socially conscious up-date of what in the 1840s was an unexplained horror, becomes the victim of unjust imprisonment; Mrs Lovett the cockney pie-maker, and the lecherous judge who was the original architect of Sweeney's fall, represent a principle of pure evil.

David Lynch's *The Elephant Man*, which appeared a year later, was a more conservative essay in Gothic. It earned a lot of attention and praise. Its 'good taste' and 'sensitivity' were generally admired, and John Hurt's performance as the elephant man, Joseph Merrick (the film wrongly calls him 'John' Merrick) has been endorsed as 'moving', 'touching' and 'courageous', despite a hideous mask. The National Film Theatre, when it screened *The Elephant Man*, described it in a programme note as 'One of the most original and perfectly realized films of recent years'.

I came out of the film with mixed feelings; resentment at the way it travestied history, and at the same time an uneasy sense of its power. I also found myself wondering how it was that an obscure episode, plucked from 1880s Whitechapel, and relatively unknown even in its own time, should suddenly become the subject of a Broadway hit, two bestselling paperbacks, and one of the more highly regarded films of recent times – certainly one with a devastating emotional impact. A second viewing suggests some possible answers, and if they are right – the argument is necessarily speculative – they may perhaps suggest some of the ways in which our understanding of the historical past is constructed not so much in the light of the documentary evidence, but rather of the symbolic space or imaginative categories into which representations are fitted.

One obvious strength of *The Elephant Man* is that it satisfies our expectation of what the past should look like. The settings are those which British cinema has accustomed us to accept as 'realistic' so far as nineteenth-century England is concerned. The townscape is thoroughly 'Dickensian', with narrow, dripping alleys, and cobbled, gas-lit streets. The horrors of industrialism are evoked (somewhat oddly for a district like Whitechapel, where a system of domestic out-work prevailed) by factory chimneys belching out smoke, and the throb of steam-powered machines. The characters (with one notable exception, to be discussed later) speak in those stilted tones which scriptwriters seem to regard as 'period'. *The Elephant Man*, moreover, is based on an original substance of fact and follows (more or less faithfully) Sir Frederick Treves's autobiographical account of it. John Hurt's mask is a replica of an 1884 photograph. The film is shot on location in East London, and the 'period' realism is further enhanced by the use of monochrome film. As Mel Brooks, one of the executive producers put it, 'black and white gives you a more authentic look . . .'

Yet, for all the surface realism of its effects, this film is mythopoeic, and its narrative is structured around a well-worn fairy-tale motif. In the course of it Merrick, the hero, is miraculously translated from the lowest to the highest spheres. From being the most despised of outcasts – a performing human animal, flogged by his showman captor, and exhibited to the fairground crowds – he is elevated into a figure of national celebrity. His true worth is recognized first by Treves, the surgeon who befriends him, then by Carr Gomm, the head of the London hospital, and finally by Queen Victoria herself. Mrs Kendal, the Society actress, discovers that he is a prince in disguise. In a scene which cannot fail to stir memories of *Beauty and the Beast*, she visits him in his chamber and they rehearse together a passage from *Romeo and Juliet*. The drama comes to a crescendo when (to the accompaniment of lyrical sounds from the orchestra) she places a kiss on his cheek. 'Oh, Mr Merrick', she cries, with eyes radiant and voice melting, 'You are not an elephant man at all . . . You are Romeo.'

From another vantage point, *The Elephant Man* is an evangelical tract, bearing marked resemblances – not least in its capacity to draw tears – to those 'moral and improving' stories which used to be given away as Sunday School prize books. In all the hideous circumstances of his life – speechless, deformed, outcast – Merrick maintains an inner grace. His humanity is established, and his sanctuary in the hospital secured when, to the amazement of his interlocutors, he recites the twenty-third psalm ('The Lord is my Shepherd . . .'). His creativity is expressed when, to a

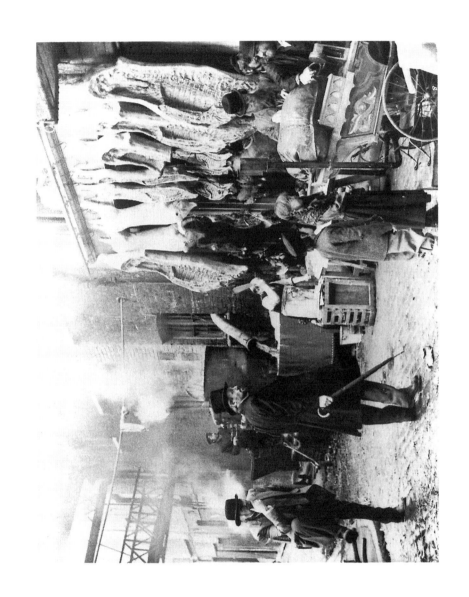

background of sacred music on the soundtrack, he makes a model of a cathedral. The death-bed scene which closes the film also draws heavily on Christian imagery, with a voice-over (that of his mother) promising eternal life. As a hospital patient, Merrick is a very incarnation of that favourite subject of the nineteenth-century evangelical imagination – the moral and deserving poor. In distress, he is a very monument to patient suffering. In comfort, he is effusively grateful to his benefactors, and rewards their little presents with transports of child-like joy. As Treves wrote in the memoir on which this film is based: 'His troubles had ennobled him. He showed himself to be a gentle, affectionate and lovable creature, as amiable as a happy woman, free from any trace of ... resentment, without a grievance ... without an unkind word ...' If an upper-class evangelical of the 1880s had possessed a cine camera, this is the film they might have made. (The idea is not so fanciful as it might seem. Dr Barnardo was a skilled hand at photographing orphans in such a way as to make them look pitiable; missionaries made use of the magic lantern to show the primitive ways of savages, temperance advocates to show the horrors of drink.)

Merrick is not only morally uncontaminated by the atrocious circumstances of his life, he is also miraculously unmarked by the proletarian, or sub-proletarian, character of his associates. Socially, as well as spiritually, he bears an inner grace. Even as a pariah, in the opening sequences of the film, his deportment is indefinably aristocratic. John Hurt plays him to look tall and imposing (in real life he was only five foot two inches tall). He bears his sufferings with dignity – a kind of battered Lear – looking upright even when he walks with a limp, and holding his arm, though it is paralysed, in an elegant crook. (By contrast, Bytes, his showman-captor, shuffles about the set, while his ragged-trousered boy is forever crouching and cringing.) In the sympathetic environment of the hospital Merrick's social capabilities blossom. His voice, once he has a chance to exercise it, is refined. His manners, when he sits down to tea, are excellent. He takes to wearing a frock-coat with aplomb. He is in short, that very English version of the Noble Savage, so dear to generations of snobs: 'one of nature's gentlemen'. Like Oliver Twist, his good breeding is ineradicable.

One favourite evangelical theme which the film could be said to reproduce is that of the little boy lost. As in so many children's books of the last century – or for that matter *Oliver Twist* – the fundamental drama is that of the friendless orphan cast adrift in a heartless world. What makes Merrick a figure of pathos, it could be argued, is not so much his physical disfigurements – those hideous deformities which make him a fairground wonder – but the fact that he is motherless. Throughout the film, he suffers the torments and reproduces the gestures of an innocent, persecuted child. Orphanhood, in short, could be seen as the leitmotiv of the film, turning a bizarre subject into a universal one. The film begins with a dream sequence about childbirth. Wild elephants stampede across the screen; tropical creatures writhe; the orchestra screeches out menacing notes of discord. Only the words of the mother – voice-over – speak a message of calm. In the film's closing sequence, the elephant man faces death. He gazes wistfully at his mother's portrait, framed in a bedside photograph, and the film fades out with her sadly grave voice beckoning him up to the stars. The mother theme also underpins the film's most tender moments. 'She was so beautiful', he tells his aristocratic visitors, fondling her portrait, and the film offers us a flashback to underscore the point. 'She had the face of an angel', he tells Mrs Treves, reducing her, instantaneously, to uncontrollable sobs.

Great play is made of Merrick's love for 'beautiful' women, and he is overcome with emotion when he meets them. But in each of these encounters, it is the likeness to the mother which is in question and his enthusiasm is devotional rather than amorous. As in an evangelical children's book, there is not the slightest hint of sexual desire. Conversely, when female sexuality does make a momentary appearance in the film, it is immediately represented as disgusting, and the worst of the horrors inflicted on Merrick is when he is forcibly kissed by two whores. Merrick's mother is the upper-class mother of the Victorian drawing-room – spiritualized, aloof and uncontaminated not only by sexuality (no reference is made in the film to a father), but by any bodily or social function at all; hers is the idealized femininity of the locket-portrait – the bourgeois madonna queening it in outer space. Merrick too is thoroughly de-sexed, in spite of the fact that in real life (according to Treves's medical examination) his genitalia remained untouched by his deformities, and his great passion was the reading of love stories. The film thus offers us, like the evangelical tract, an escape from, or sublimation of, sexuality, a return to the lost innocence of childhood where the nurturing mother prevails.

The Elephant Man could also be said to be structured – albeit uncon-sciously – by class mythology. As very often in British cinema's representa-tion of the past, the poor are a mindless mob, brutalized by the poverty of their existence. In one scene, screaming harridans fight it out in the hospital waiting room; in another, maudlin extras stagger about drunk-enly in a pub; in yet another, ragged street Arabs turn bullies. The proletarian extras are a gallery of grotesques, and the nearest they come to acquiring an individual identity is aptly indicated by the credits – 'First Fighting Woman', 'Second Fighting Woman', 'First Whore', 'Second Whore' – which appear at the end of the film. In a horrific sequence, the denizens of the slums invade the hospital and violate the elephant man's peace. They trample his fragile cathedral underfoot and fling his mother's portrait to the floor. The men pour gin down his helpless throat; the women (half-fearful, half-giggling) sexually assault him. Finally, they carry him round the room, faint and swooning, to lead a *danse macabre*. It is a sustained metaphor of pollution, culminating in an act of symbolic rape, a blazingly sincere, if melodramatic, representation of what, to an upper-class evangelical of Merrick's time, would have seemed the ultimate horror.

At the other end of the social scale, wealth and beauty prevail. If cruelty and ugliness are with the poor, civilization and refinement are with the rich, and there is a chasm of sensibility between them. The film makes some perfunctory gestures in the direction of a more modern ambiguity. At one point Merrick's upper-class visitors are likened to the fairground crowd ('he's only being stared at all over again'); at another, Treves is momentarily troubled at a possible analogy between his own conduct and that of Bytes, the showman ('You wanted a freak . . . to make a name for yourself'). But the comparison is merely rhetorical, and it is utterly overborne by a tide of countervailing images showing upper-class benevolence at work. Treves, for all his occasional moments of self-doubt, never ceases to be the handsome young doctor (he is played by Anthony Hopkins), whereas Bytes, the showman, is a seedy old drunk. Like any decent Englishman, Treves keeps his feelings on tight rein, but his eyes brim surreptitiously with tears when he first catches sight of the elephant man's deformities, and in the later passages of the film he addresses him in tones of reverent kindness. The stiffly authoritative Carr Gomm (Sir John Gielgud) – paternalism personified – bends the hospital rule to give Merrick sanctuary. The crusty matron (Wendy Hiller), overcoming an initial repulsion, looks after his interests with tender, dutiful care. Mrs Kendal is a lady bountiful; Princess Alexandra a fairy godmother, coming to Merrick's rescue when his place at the hospital is threatened by a cabal of local tradesmen, and sitting alongside him in the royal box at the theatre. Finally, in the climactic scene of the film, upper-class London, symbolized by the audience at Drury Lane, recognize his true worth and, prompted by Mrs Kendal, rise to their feet to applaud him. 'My life is full, I know that I am loved', says Merrick, as he is taken, dying, to this triumph of warm-hearted charity.

These class contrasts are amplified by the film's use of black and white. Visually, the poor are shrouded in darkness, epitomizing both moral and physical squalor. They are the animal-like inhabitants of a nether world which only comes to life at night. The dream sequence with which the film opens is full of jungle imagery, and we are then taken, in the first narrative episode, to the labyrinthine interior of the showman's booth – here represented not by funfair music and garish lights (the alternative filmic cliché) but by a heavy, impenetrable gloom. The showman's den, scene of a later episode, is no less claustrophobic – a decrepit shanty at the end of a cul-de-sac, positively dripping with grime. The night porter, a sinister figure who haunts the elephant man's dreams, has his lair in the hospital basement, emerging at the witching hour to pace the deserted corridors, and cast a shadow of fear. When the Whitechapel mob invade the hospital, they pick their way across an expressionist wasteland, with frightened clouds scudding across a menacing night-time sky. In the more deliberately symbolic sequences – mysterious interludes which provide a kind of visual counterpoint to the narrative – the factory (filmed, of course, at night) is a dark inferno and the boiler-room (an allegory of danger) a Gothic dungeon of barbarous noise and pipes.

In the reverse image, all is light and space. Whereas the poor only come on to the scene at night, the rich are photographed in broad daylight. The London hospital rises like a celestial city from out of the sordid streets, a pool of light set in the darkling sea. The clouds clear when Treves steps out on the pavement. The underground boiler stops throbbing when the day staff and matron take command. The governors meet in a spacious boardroom. Carr Gomm receives his visitors in a vast executive suite. Mrs Kendal, the Society actress, is filmed as a radiant presence; Mrs Treves, the surgeon's wife, glows, and the drawing-room of her Wimpole Street home, when Merrick takes afternoon tea there, is filled with a tranquil light. In the theatre at Drury Lane – the one sequence in which the rich appear at night – chandeliers glitter in the auditorium, and the pantomime on stage is filmed as though it were a light show, with gossamer figures floating through the air, in a fantasia of shooting stars.

These are the visual contrasts which, ever since Gustave Doré's *London* (1872), we have been accustomed to accept as symbolizing the rich and the poor, while the scenes of mob frenzy have an evident kinship with the age-old ruling-class nightmare of the poor as a 'swinish multitude'. Superimposed on this older class mythology, however, the film explores the possibilities of an altogether newer one – that which represents the working class not as downtrodden and outcast, but rather as cynical, greedy and materialistic. The real devil in the film is not the shambling showman – a Dickensian grotesque – but the night porter at the hospital, who runs a small racket on the side and ends up as a small-time torturer. Played by Michael Elphick, an actor who has made a speciality of 'cockney' character parts, he is a disconcertingly modern figure, a kind of shop steward to the underworld. Like the cockney heroes of 1960s 'new wave' British films – or Bob Hoskins in *The Long Good Friday* – he is sexually alert, emancipated in his bearing, and unmistakably 'sharp'.

A cheroot plays sensually about his lips. His speech, unlike that of the rest of the cast, is recognizably colloquial. His manner is friendly, but his temper is short, and when he finds himself crossed he adopts the stance of a bully. 'You should be more sociable, mate, you'll get yourself disliked', he says to the terrified elephant man, as he tries to force him to drink. 'You look beautiful, darling', he says, as he hurls him into the dance. In the pub he introduces himself to potential customers as 'Your very own Sonny Jim'. In the hospital, when his evil has been exposed, he shouts back defiantly 'We were only having a laugh'. Elphick seems to conflate within a single *persona* a whole number of contemporary middle-class folk devils: – 'bovver boys', street-corner soccer hooligans, flying pickets – and when one remembers how closely the film followed the 'winter of discontent', that is, the public service workers' strikes of January 1979, one wonders whether, insensibly, he may not have taken on the complexion of the NUPE 'yobbo'.

I do not think one needs to allege class prejudice to account for the presence in the film of such stereotypes (the director is an American, and if his grasp of present-day British reality is as uncertain as it is for 1880s Whitechapel, it is unlikely that conscious intention is at work). Rather it is a matter of a whole set of categories, drawn from the visual and verbal unconscious, which slip into the film, as it were, unobserved. There are stock scenes which have established themselves as realistic by dint of continuous repetition; there are costume drama clichés which have become formulaic because they correspond to stylized and cine-matically established notions of what history is about. They have little to do with documentary record, which itself, so far as 1880s Whitechapel is concerned, is extremely difficult to separate from melodramatic repre-sentation. *The Elephant Man* is based on a real-life episode, but neither the invading mob nor the hospital porter have any place in Treves's original record, and the fact that they can be added to touch up the 'realism' of the film might make us pause to wonder what other atrocities are passed off in the name of authenticity.

The Elephant Man is not a genre film, but a pastiche of different styles, a horror film laced with a dash of mysticism, a weepie pretending to be emotionally restrained, a fairy tale in the documentary mode. Its symbols are drawn sometimes from Christian imagery, sometimes from cinema realism, sometimes from Gothic romance. Ideologically it is no less promiscuous, reproducing, more or less uncritically, a conventional upper-class view of how the other half lives, yet tempering this with a touch of populism (in one scene, Merrick is rescued from a cage by his fellow fairground freaks), and a moment of liberal self-doubt. It is possible, in the manner of *Cahiers du Cinéma*, to compare the film with its cult predecessor *Eraserhead*, and to discuss the director's work as a unified and developing whole. But if one wants to account for the film's emotional hold on contemporary audiences, it might be more rewarding to look at the subliminal play of much more ancient motifs, such as those of the fairy tale; to consider the enduring vitality of that iconographical tradition – so powerfully embedded in European culture – which equates darkness with animality and reason with light; and to identify those archetypal figures whom Merrick successively embodies; the tall, dark, mysterious stranger of Gothic romance; the helpless child of the Christian parable; the well-born foundling whose parentage is unknown; Frankenstein's monster seeking out love.

The particular effectiveness of the film must also lie, however, in the way it speaks to our present-day needs and condition. In the Year of the Disabled, it allows us to measure the humanitarian progress we have made, and to recognize our own good taste. Instead of being titillated by the spectacle of a freak, we are moved with compassion towards him, identifying his triumphs as our own, and recognizing the nobility which lies beneath the surface disfigurements. Allied to this, the film offers us the reassurance of historical contrast. Conveniently forgetting our own more contemporary version of the flesh show (striptease acts; magazine and film pornography), the film invites us to consider the penny exhibition as a symbol of old-time barbarism, and the gawping crowd as a world we are lucky to have lost. The film thus flatters our sense of moral superiority towards the past, moving us sentimentally to tears at the thought of our own benevolence, and allowing us, at very little cost, to celebrate our own humanity.

Note

For some critical endorsements of *The Elephant Man*, see *Sight and Sound*, Winter 1980–81; *Cahiers du Cinéma*, April 1981; *Jeune Cinéma*, July–August 1981. For a historical reconstruction of the episode, Michael Howell and Peter Ford, *The Elephant Man*, London 1980; for Tom Horman, the showman original of Bytes, see *The Era*, 26 October 1901; and for his activity in Shoreditch, where in 1895 he was exhibiting 'the celebrated and only Russian giantess', *Bethnal Green News*, 23 March 1895.

Doing the Lambeth Walk*

When Mass Observation, those pioneer ethnographers of the 'beliefs and behaviour of the British Islanders'[1] produced their book on *Britain* (a Penguin Special published in January 1939), they devoted a whole chapter to the phenomenon of 'The Lambeth Walk', monitoring its impact as a song hit (41 per cent of those they questioned had first heard it on the wireless), charting its progress as a dance craze, and recording memories and opinions in Lambeth, the old London borough from which the dance, or 'walk', allegedly derived. *Me and My Girl*, the musical which launched the Walk on its career, opened at the Victoria Theatre, Westminster, at Christmas in 1937 and was to play for the following four years. The Walk came a little later, introduced as a 'novelty dance' at the Locarno, Streatham, and popularized by instructors at the great public dance halls. Tom Harrisson and Charles Madge, the founders of Mass Observation, socialists by conviction though at least in intention impartial observers, believed that it was the working class who had taken up the Lambeth Walk 'with more enthusiasm than anybody'. They claimed – though it was a claim in which the wish was possibly father to the thought – that in the East End of London anti-fascists had used it to break up Mosleyite demonstrations, and in their private capacity they seem to have urged both the Labour Party and the Communist Party to take note of its phenomenal success.[2] But they were bound to admit that its popularity was a cross-class phenomenon: 'You ... can ... find them doing the Lambeth Walk in Mayfair ballrooms, suburban dance halls, cockney parties and village hops.' The success of the Lambeth Walk was an international phenomenon, 'the first contemporary dance from this country that has put the world on its feet'.[3] Abroad, as in England, its popularity transcended political and social divides. The Nazis, relieved, apparently, that the dance did not derive from Negroes, nor the libretto from a Jew, permitted it to be broadcast on German radio; while in Italy, Mussolini took instruction in its steps.

*The co-author of this chapter is Alison Light

390

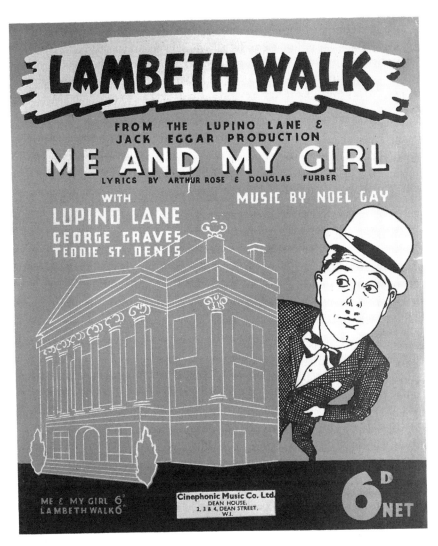

It was no less popular in Czechoslovakia, hitting Prague about the time of the Munich crisis in September 1938, as the war clouds gathered.

The current success of *Me and My Girl* – voted 'Musical of the Year' in 1985 and still playing to packed houses at the Adelphi in the Strand – hardly yet ranks with that of the original production.[4] But, like that other long-running West End hit, *No Sex, Please, We're British*, it seems to have caught on with the tourists, and at the time of writing is no less popular than Agatha Christie's *The Mousetrap* with the organizers of charabanc outings. One of *Me and My Girl*'s numbers, 'The Sun Has Put His Hat

On' (a revival of a separate 1920s hit which in the new production serves as curtain-raiser for Act II), has already appeared in the song-charts; if the *Daily Mail* is anything to go by, the play's success has begun to attract the notice of the moralists. Any play which can get an audience stomping and clapping in the rigid seating of a West End theatre is worthy of respect. Moreover like other 'revivals', this one tells us as much about the present as the past, and the ways in which the original 'book' has been reworked for the current production provides some interesting clues about conservative appropriations of 'tradition'. It also tells us something about the tricks which memory plays on itself.[5]

Me and My Girl, with the exception of a Lambeth scene and one in a village pub, is played out in a stately home, but the sets are transparently cardboard, the props jokey (in the library scene, the ancestral busts come alive and perform song-and-dance routines) and the luxury motor which opens the show – to our untutored eyes a Rolls or a Daimler – turns out to be made of collapsible panels. In short, despite the country house there is little of the mellow dignity normally evoked by Loamshire settings, nor yet of the mystifications of class and birth of *Brideshead Revisited*, both in its original version as a novel or the still more glamorized register of the recent TV serial. The aristocracy in the musical, though wealthy, are absurd; neither power brokers nor landed gentry, but a completely idle rich (whisky-drinking Sir John – a Colonel Chinstrap figure – is a sentimental old buffer; young cousin Gerald a flannelled fool). The real force of the humour and the dramatic energy of the performance lie in Bill and Sally, the London cock-sparrow and his Lambeth pal, and in their own ways of living and loving. Against the starched tones of the upper-class characters, they are at once vulnerable and open, their speech and movements flamboyantly expressive, theatrical and self-assured. Left alone for the first time in the lofty vestibule of Hareford Hall, Sally looks forward to making the place more cheerful and less like 'the bleedin' Odeon', whilst Bill (the improbable heir to an ancient title) starts giving away the objects he now owns in a mad rush of generosity.

Me and My Girl is a kind of pantomime of class; one which, by exaggerating social differences, robs them of their pain. The cockneys can't speak the King's English and don't know where to put their coats. They can't keep still for a moment. The aristocracy, though wealthy, are absurd.

The basic appeal of the original production, to judge by the rehearsal script, was that of the 'world turned upside-down'. It re-enacted, albeit in the setting of the theatre rather than that of the market place or village green, the enthronement of the Lord of Misrule. In the folk festivals and feasts (in Garrett Town, Wandsworth, a gypsified London

suburb, they survived down to the 1860s), the meanest of beggars would
be dressed in regalia and treated for the day as king. Here, it is the
low comic – Bill Snibson, the Lambeth wide boy and coster, who inherits
a great estate. The comedy offers us a reverse image of the social order:
instead of shop-girls imitating debutantes – the fashion leaders of the
day – it is the high-born who, in the original production, are revitalized
from below. At the end of the first act, when Lambeth invades the stately
home en masse – with pearlies dressed in their regalia, and Sally the
Lambeth heroine in flaming Bank Holiday dress – the social breakdown
is complete; footmen, majordomo, maids, and eventually the aristocrats
themselves succumb to cockney vitality: 'everyone joins in and shouts
"oi" and Duchess goes in to dinner wearing Bill's bowler on her head.'
(In the original production the finale was repeated at the end of
Act II.)

Role reversal, in *Me and My Girl*, extends from social position to
character and gait. It is not the rich but the poor who behave like
aristocrats. Emotionally, sartorially, verbally, it is the working class of
Lambeth who dominate the play – at least in its original 1937 production. They swagger. They show off. They behave with reckless self-
assertion. They comport themselves on stage with complete
self-confidence. They provide the play with its songs, with its dance, with
its wit, with its highly individualized hero and heroine. The sensuality
and intelligent affection of Bill and Sally's love affair is contrasted – as
in the duet which gives the musical its title – with the mercenary
onslaughts of the gold-digger Jacqueline and her miserable follower, an
archetypal young noodle who believes that to do a day's work would be
to bring disgrace on the family name. Bill absolutely refuses to learn
composure, and is forever running to excess. He disrupts and subverts
every well-meaning attempt to teach him good manners, because he
cannot be physically contained. He clowns, he somersaults, he puns, he
mimes, he transgresses. It is excess itself which gives him power, the
energy to be vulnerable and even, as the larking about on stage
demonstrates, the freedom to make a fool of himself; excess which
makes the very idea of gentrification absurd. He will carouse with whisky-
drinking Sir John, turn somersaults on his would-be patrons, and mock
their titles.

Sally, his pal, is if anything even more resistant to the aristocratic
embrace – save for one crucial moment to which we will return later in
this essay. Confronted with Bill's unexpected fortune, her mind runs not
to entering a great inheritance but to setting up 'in a little dress shop'
and exchanging the one-and-threepenny seats at the local cinema for the
three-and-sixpennies. She wants no part in the pageantry of wealth, and
only allows herself to be made into a lady for the sake of her man – an

expression not of social ambition but of true love. In the original production, the transformation is brief and it is no sooner effected than Lambeth reclaims her.

Bill and Sally are the representatives of a working-class great estate – the world of costers and pearlies which produced the Lambeth Walk. The plot may be in the hands of the aristocracy, but the moving force in the play is theirs. Their love of display is not the conspicuous consumption of the moneyed classes but making accessible and public the pleasures of being human – they are the people who, however humble their walk in life or lowly their social station, know how to have a good time; how to be true in love. They can defy social convention and make the stuffed shirts dance. The generosity and the self-assertion is irresistible. 'Do as you damn well pleasey' – a favourite line from the Lambeth Walk – is hardly a revolutionary injunction, but in *Me and My Girl*, contrasted to the starched voices and anxious stratagems of the upper-class characters, it certainly seems liberatory. And like the defiant 'oi' which brings song and dance to a climax it is completely transgressive. The truly social act of communication which the song and dance embodies galvanizes the audience and unites them in the make-believe solidarity of an auditorium.

Me and My Girl was based both on real-life and stage originals. The 1937 star, Lupino Lane, 'an alert little cockney, on his toes the whole time like a boxer', had already created the stage character of Bill Snibson in the previous year when he appeared in Arthur Rose's *Twenty to One* at the Coliseum. It was then too that he invented (or re-invented) the Lambeth Walk which was to serve him for many years as a classic piece of stage 'business'. An earlier lineage which irresistibly suggests itself, though denied by the putative ancestor, is that with Lambeth's most famous comic son, Charlie Chaplin. Lupino Lane's 'cocky grey bowler' is second cousin to Charlie Chapin's still more famous hat; and his rolling gait – 'half lilting, half swaggering' – has obvious affinities to Chaplin's crab-like walk (Chaplin himself, in a 1938 letter to Mass Observation, attributed his walk not to 'Lambeth' but to 'the necessity of wearing ill-fitting shoes').[6] The Lambeth Walk Song was even more antique. Under the same name – though with a different tune – it had been a smash-hit of 1903. (Mass Observation suggests that it may have been based on the 'Cake Walk', a 'coon dance' that came to England from the United States in a minstrel show.)

There were also, as the admirably comprehensive inquiry of Mass Observation documents, real-life originals. Lupino Lane, 'a cockney born and bred', attributed the 'walk' – aggressive, hips swaying, arms out at the side – to one he had known all his life, 'just an exaggerated view of how the cockney struts'. Douglas Furber, the Cambridge-educated composer of the song, claimed to have drawn his inspiration from the singing of the factory lasses of his Yorkshire boyhood. A spontaneous talent for dancing and song, Mass Observation argues, was a Lambeth tradition, surviving at Saturday night house parties if not in the streets:

> For the men it is a swagger, arms out from the sides, like a boxer playing for position; for the women it is more of a lilt, with hips swaying. The two get mixed, though, when the men dress as women and behave like them . . . which is part of the tradition. Also, men dance with men and women with women quite freely.

There was – and is – a real-life Lambeth Walk, still a street market, as it was in the days when it was described by Mayhew though surrounded in 1938 by what appeared as 'huge blocks' of LCC flats. Mass Observation did not find it difficult to find denizens of Lambeth who claimed to have been familiar both with the original song and the 'walk', and it may be that it continued to linger on.

The 'Lambeth Walk' really belonged, however, to very much earlier times, and by 1938, even after an August Bank Holiday booze-up, it was almost certainly archaic. 'Things', as the old timers did not fail to inform Mass Observation, were not what they used to be. Some referred back to the long-lost days – the time of their great-grandparents – when there had been public dancing in Vauxhall Gardens (closed on grounds of indecency in the 1850s and built over by early property developers). Others referred to the days of the bare-knuckle fighters (a breed already extinct in the 1880s, when professional boxing became established as a legal sport);* yet others to the old-time 'Harmonic' meetings in the pubs (there is a fine description of them in Dickens's *Bleak House*). The term 'free and easy', which is the motif of the Lambeth Walk, also derives from the pre-music hall pub, though it was one which still lived on in late Victorian times. Above all – the one point on which Mass Observation have surprisingly little to say – there was the tradition of street dancing, a mass phenomenon of the later nineteenth century, associated on the one hand with children's play – that of girls especially – and on the other with the ubiquitous presence of barrel-organs. There is no reason to suppose this tradition was more rampant in Lambeth than in other parts of London, but it is from Lambeth that we have a classic description of it, in Somerset Maugham's first novel – the fruit both of observation as a young doctor at Guy's hospital, and of romantic fiction – in *Liza of Lambeth* (1896). Here is his account of the scene:

> The organ-man was an Italian, with a shock of black hair and a ferocious moustache. Drawing his organ to a favourable spot, he stopped, released his shoulder from the leather straps by which he dragged it, and cocking his large

soft hat on one side of his head began turning the handle. It was a lively tune, and in less than no time a little crowd had gathered round to listen, chiefly the young men and maidens ... There was a moment's hesitation ... then one girl said to another:

'Come on, Florrie, you and me ain't shy; we'll begin, and bust it!' The two girls took hold of one another, one acting gentleman, the other lady; three or four more pairs of girls immediately joined then, and they began a waltz.

Liza, Maugham's tragic heroine, joins in, but the dance is too slow for her, and she gets the 'Italian' to produce something more abandoned:

She ... swayed about, manipulating her skirt ... then, the music altering, she changed the style of her dancing, her feet moved more quickly, and did not keep so strictly to the ground. She was getting excited at the admiration of the onlookers, and her dance grew wilder and more daring. She lifted her skirts higher, brought in new and more difficult movements ... kicking up her legs she did the wonderful twist, backwards and forwards, of which the dancer is proud ... Her dance became gayer; her feet scarcely touched the ground, she whirled round madly ... and she went on, making twists and turns, flourishing her skirts, kicking higher and higher, and finally, among a volley of shouts ... turned head over heels in a magnificent catherine-wheel; then scrambling to her feet again, she tumbled into the arms of a young man standing in the front of the ring.

The 'Lambeth' of *Me and My Girl* thus drew on venerable tradition, and was already, in 1937, a throw-back to Edwardian and even late Victorian times. Yet for all its archaism, *Me and My Girl* was evidently in tune with its time. As a catchy number 'Lambeth Walk' was the hit song of 1938. As a social dance 'full of vitality and movement' it offered itself as a universal antidote to shyness, saving young people the embarrassment of having to make overtures to each other. As a comedy, or fantasy of class, the musical offered a make-believe world, in which benevolence ruled supreme: class differences did not have to be negotiated, for when tested against the claims of common humanity, they collapsed. Its popularity may have owed something to reassurance: the working class – however rough their ways – were harmless; the aristocracy, however apparently stuck up, benevolent; the English a race of lovable eccentrics. If the working class was the 'coming class', as it appeared in the play, it was neither because of its spending power nor on account of its industrial might, still less of its politics, but because its people were pleasure-loving, in the words of Mass Observation, 'the class who knew how to have a good time'.

Me and My Girl perhaps captured, or anticipated, something of the mood with which working-class England entered the Second World War – not with the clenched fist of their more politicized counterparts in occupied Europe, but with the downbeat stoicism of 'smiling through'. 'Knees up Mother Brown', an old cockney favourite, appeared in sheet music for the first time in 1939, and by 1940, when Mass Observation produced *Britain at War*, it had outrivalled the Lambeth Walk as a song-and-dance number. *Me and My Girl* rehearses what was to be a major theme of war-time propaganda – cross-class fraternization – 'all in it together', and the pleasing illusion that 'ordinary people' had come into their own. It could also be said to prefigure the terms of Labour's 1945 victory; on the one hand, it appeals to a democratic sense of being English, a patriotism which is dependent upon a dream of classlessness, whilst on the other, deriving its specific force and passion from a version of distinctly working-class community – an informing belief that it was the working class who were really the backbone of the nation.

The 1980s production of *Me and My Girl* at the Adelphi, though claiming to be a faithful rendering of the original, is a self-conscious play with nostalgia, and a whole pastiche of 'period' effects. A new scene in the servants' basement clearly owes more to *Upstairs Downstairs* than to the original, though an Electrolux fridge is offered as a gauge of authenticity. Memories of the silver screen are insistently involved. Sally, originally played in this production by cockney actress Lorraine Chase (she of the Campari ads and *Blankety Blank* fame), is given a number to herself: its force and poignancy, however, owe more to a Brecht–Weill Jenny than to any jollier London prototype.

More tellingly, though, the whole social balance of the show has been tilted in favour of gentrification. In the original production, the cockney hegemony was uncontested: it was not only Bill who spoke rhyming slang but also – because it was so catching – the aristocrats. The Lambeth Walk not only brought the first act to a climax, it also served as the opening of the second act, and at the end brought the play to a grand finale.

In the original production, the opening scene of the second act has Bill instructing his aristocratic listeners on how to play the mouth-organ and learn the notes of the Lambeth Walk. The new production scraps this scene and replaces it with a kind of celebration of the bright young things. Instead of the Lambeth Walk we have 'The Sun Has Got His Hat On' – a number imported from a very different musical, and it becomes the occasion for the aristocratic house-guests to disport themselves and in some sort to match the vitality of Lambeth with their own. Instead of being stuffed shirts they blossom out in leisure wear, toting tennis rackets and croquet mallets, all blazers and charming frocks. If there are Labour supporters in the audience with tears in their eyes at the Lambeth Walk with all its memories of the days when ordinary people (at least in make-believe) could be kings, there must be quite as many old-time Tories fondly remembering *Salad Days*.

The second half of the current production seems to be a class revenge in which it is the working class rather than the aristocracy who are consistently outwitted. Sally, in her loyalty to Bill, is persuaded by Sir John to undergo a transformation, Pygmalion-like, into a 'real' lady in order to be a fit consort for the new earl. This twist features in both versions but in the 1985 version the change is for real. And the second addition to the show's song sheet marks a further shift. George Formby's 'Leaning On A Lamp Post' is crooned mildly and elegiacally by Bill – its original quirky edginess and rough and ready humour transposed into a kind of misty 'fifties' lyricism. This is followed by a dream sequence in which Bill and Sally become Fred Astaire and Ginger Rogers gliding over the stage suitably swathed in silk and dry ice.

Running parallel to this shift is a scene in the Hareford library in which Bill's own specific class of masculinity is threatened and absorbed by an appeal to Englishness, to a universal heritage – his 'lineage' not just as the new Earl, but, it is implied, as a 'freeborn Englishman'. In the 1937 production, at least in the eyes of Mass Observation, this scene was a kind of send-up of the Coronation, but here the comic business is firmly subordinated to a reassertion of tradition. His statesmen and warrior ancestors descend from their portraits in a pageant-like procession and the absurdity of this is forgotten in the solemnity of the music and ritualistic splendour. No doubt meant as a moving reassertion of Englishness, the anthem of *noblesse oblige* is shown to have the superior claims.

The aristocratic counterpoint is even more insistent in the last scene, when Bill is reunited with his Sally – no longer a Lambeth girl, but, at least in outward appearances, carrying herself like a duchess. This magical moment is crucial to both productions but it is handled very differently, and the differences are revealing. In the original production, her transformation is only skin-deep; reunited in the semblance of Lord and Lady, Bill and Sally revert to cockney, mocking the lah-dee-dah:

Bill: Ger cher! Oi-oi, Sal!
Sally: Wot cher, Bill!
Bill: Ssh. Don't let the ancestors hear us. I think we'll return.
Sally: Well, we'll nevah forget old Lambeth.
Bill: No, not the Lambeth Walk.

They do the Walk together and the curtain descends on the whole cast joining in; the coming class, whatever assaults are made upon it, seems here to stay.

The current production runs otherwise. The above dialogue is absent and the dignity and pathos of Sally's earlier characterization is replaced by the smooth elegance of a mannequin. Bill still speaks cockney –

'Where the bloody 'll 'ave you bin?' he asks. But Sally takes the change seriously. She speaks with the voice of a queen, and the crowd of aristocratic bystanders cheer her on with grey toppers waving and morning coats bobbing, in anticipation of a society wedding. Against this background the Lambeth Walk, though sounding again from the orchestra pit, sounds more like a dying fall.

Me and My Girl conforms to the traditional conventions of the pastoral in which the 'natural' behaviour of plain folk is contrasted to the artificial glitter of the salons. It offers an anti-heroic view of national character, in which the men of whatever class are philanderers, and it is the women who keep them up to the mark. But in the current revival it has been given a conservative twist. The workers are no longer the coming class; the cockneys no longer know how to be true to themselves. Energy may be with the masses, but it is no match for the guile of their betters and even when it comes to having a good time it seems the upper classes can teach them a thing or two.

What has perhaps shifted in the forty years since the first production along with the terrain upon which working people might find some sense of collective self-regard and enthusiastic purpose, is also the confidence with which transgressing class boundaries can be seen as a brave and correct impulse, one which might be politically productive or even generate some happiness.

Part of the effect of this shift is to suggest that romance within working-class life is a contradiction in terms – it has to take place elsewhere; partly it signals a much more thorough move in the later production whereby the power of traditional heterosexual romance is used to take over and subsume the claims of class solidarity.

Doing the Lambeth Walk – or rather watching it done in a West End theatre – like any other trip down memory lane – is certainly not a short cut to some unmediated and untarnished haven of authentic working-class culture. But it does encompass some of the compassionate collectivity which is the basis for a solidarity across social difference. *Me and My Girl* might seem a bit of a meagre celebration even if you remember shouting 'oi' with the best of them, but it is still heartening to hear that finale when you consider the odds now militating against any form of collective engagement. If the point of celebration of popular working-class culture appears so often at the point also of its disintegration (a comment which might be made about the fantastic community of the contemporary television *EastEnders*), then this makes the recognition of the positive potential of those class forms *more*, not less, urgent. The last line in *Me and My Girl* remains a Lambeth line – 'if only Lambeth could continue to have the last laugh.'

*This was an attempt to explain Lupino Lane's aggressive posture. Another possible derivation worth exploring would be that of 'the Hooligan', a journalist's fiction created in 1899 round the figure of a real-life Lambeth original, a cockney Irish boy called Patrick Hooligan.[7]

Notes

1. Mass Observation, *First Year's Work, 1937–8*, London 1938, p. 8.
2. Mass Observation, *Britain*, Harmondsworth 1939, p. 175.
3. Ibid., p. 184.
4. It was still playing when this piece first went to press, in summer 1989.
5. The original script is in the Lord Chancellor's papers which have now been deposited at the British Museum, BM, Add MSS, 1937/43c.
6. David Robinson, *Charlie Chaplin, His Life and Art*, London 1985, pp. 152–3.
7. See *The Nineteenth Century*, May 1899, for the article which launched the term 'hooligan' on its world career; and Geoff Pearson, *Hooligan*, London 1983, for its aetiology. Alexander Patterson, *Across the Bridges*, London 1912, is a temperate account of adolescent gang life in Lambeth; Clarence Rook's *Hooligan Nights* a more highly coloured journalist's one.

Docklands Dickens

Dickens's work was never far distant from the idea of performance. He was a lifelong amateur actor and, as is well known, in his later years a great public reader. His earliest writings were for the stage. He conceived novels themselves as a species of performance art in which the characters were actors. As he put it in a well-known passage, 'every good actor plays direct to every good author, and every writer of fiction, though he may not adopt the dramatic form writes in effect for the stage'. In the early novels in particular the stage analogies are inescapable. Pickwick was modelled on the comic monologues of Charles Mathews, the leading comedian of his youth. The capering, grimacing Quilp (Dickens's own anarchic ego, some critics suggest) was a figure taken from pantomime; Ralph Nickleby, the wicked uncle, corresponds to the villains of melodrama. *Little Dorrit*, the most restrained and complex of Dickens's novels, is not less melodramatic than its predecessors, whether in the play of mystery, the build-up of guilt, or the dialectic of good and evil.[1]

Dickens's cinematic qualities have been less frequently discussed, though they were handsomely acknowledged by D.W. Griffith, the father of the American cinema, who proclaimed Dickens as his master, while the structural similarities between Dickens's narrative and avant-garde film-making is the subject of a brilliant essay by Sergei Eisenstein.[2] Both declared that Dickens was the pioneer of montage, as also of that animistic view of the universe in which landscape and setting were living protagonists of the drama: 'settings that reflect the characters' states of mind'. *Little Dorrit* – the novel but not, alas, the film – provides plenty of examples, where London itself becomes a metaphor for imprisonment: 'Nothing to see but streets, streets, streets. Nothing to breathe but streets, streets, streets.'

This 'optical' quality of Dickens (as Eisenstein called it) is very much to the fore in David Lean's *Great Expectations* (1946) and his *Oliver Twist* (1948). Each is a visual translation of the plot, making an expressionist use of the background to secure stunning dramatic effects – most memorably in the desolate scene on the marsh which provides the shock opening of *Great Expectations*, a scene which older readers may remember as the most frightening of their childhood. Lean's films were important not only as landmarks of British *film noir*, but also for fixing a notion of the Victorian as a time of oppression and fear. They represented a social democratic as well as a Gothic imagination, the summit of some three decades of modernist revolt. In Miss Havisham, a death-in-life figure, festooned in cobwebs, was a witch-like emblem of nineteenth-century claustrophobia, while the settings of *Oliver Twist* helped to fasten the epithet 'Dickensian' to slum housing. *Oliver Twist* is played for the most part in the dead of night; *Great Expectations* is shadowed by marshland mists. Mental states, in either case, are projected by visual terrors. Both films end in the most basic of melodrama's forms, the chase. Coming at a time when cinema attendances were at an all-time high, these films were hugely influential in stigmatizing the Victorian era as a time of captivity.

Imaginatively as well as cinematically Christine Edzard's *Little Dorrit*, which opened to critical acclaim on 11 December 1987, belongs to a different world, one in which 'Victorian', so far from being a term of opprobrium, as it was in the 1940s, has been assimilated to notions of 'heritage' and serves as a signifier for *objets d'art*. Where David Lean, a practitioner of the Gothic, set out to astonish and shock, pivoting his film on sensation scenes and underlining disturbing effects, *Little Dorrit* soothes. The lighting is flat rather than, as in David Lean's Dickens, theatrical; the frames are regular; the camera perspective is fixed, a succession of eye-level shots which never disturb the viewer's gaze. Where Lean worked in the sinister shadows, using black-and-white photography to create a landscape of fear, *Little Dorrit* bathes its characters in colour, with soft focus images when there is a romance afoot, and the sombre rendered as mellow. The musical score – orchestral selections from Verdi – amplifies these effects. It does not evoke the ghostly presences which haunt the Dickens plot, nor create a tense expectancy. It is used rather to underline the film's lyrical moments – for example sunny afternoons in Twickenham – or to sound a positive note.

London, in the intervening years between Lean's and Edzard's films, even it seems the malodorous London of *Little Dorrit*, has been spring-cleaned. The Thames is no longer a 'deadly sewer' running through the heart of the city, but rather a quiet retreat, not an industrial highway but the resort of sailing boats and seagulls. The air is no longer polluted, but fresh. The 'penitential garb of soot' has been stripped from the buildings; the 'old blasted and blackened forest of chimneys', when they appear in the film (painted in as backdrops), miraculously emit no

smoke. The 'poor mean shops' of Borough High Street, the subject of a whole series of shots in this film, now look quietly prosperous: the brickwork has been newly pointed and sand-blasted, it seems, to give a honeyed glow. Bleeding Heart Yard, the slum court off Gray's Inn Lane, is rendered here as quaint, a kind of *rus in urbe* with old-time pantiles. Industry, too, has been given a face-lift. At Doyce and Clennam's workshop, the machinery positively glistens, with not so much as a speck of oil or a trace of iron filings. The brass wheels are spotless, the engine no longer frantically throbs. The inscription on the door-posts has become an artistically lettered fascia, 'DOYCE AND CLENNAM. PRESSURE GAUGES'. (The treatment of Chivery's, the tobacconists, is even more quaint, with Egyptian Gothic lettering and a doorbell which tinkles to the customer's touch.)

The weather too has improved out of all recognition and there are none of those atmospherics which we are accustomed to think of as Dickensian. The fog has lifted; the skies have cleared; in all the six hours of the film there is hardly a drop of rain. In most of the scenes the sun (or its studio lighting equivalent) is shining, its rays penetrating to what in the novel are lightless depths. At night 'equinoctial gales' no longer sweep in on the metropolis, plunging down the chimneys and blackening the walls with rain; nor are there 'wild clouds' chasing across the skies: when Little Dorrit and Maggie are forced to walk the streets, the sky deepens to a Mediterranean indigo. Not until some five hours into the film is there a serious break in the weather, but even then, after a premonitory roll of thunder, the storm dies away.

The *dramatis personae* of the film have also been spruced up. All of the cast are tastefully dressed; cottons have been hand-sewn for the production; linens have been well laundered. Pancks, the rent collector, sports a brilliant show of cuff, and his 'dirty broken hands' and 'dirty broken fingernails' have apparently been manicured. Amy Dorrit's 'old worn dress' has become a powder-blue gown; Maggie, the idiot girl she befriends, is no longer in rags: she appears to be dressed in a Laura Ashley print and her bonnet – 'monstrous' and 'black' in the Dickens original – is now gaily coloured primrose. The poor of Bleeding Heart Yard are no longer the Great Unwashed but look for the most part in the pink of condition, well-fed, with ruddy countenances, good complexions and colourful clothes. Mrs Plornish alone looks pinched, but her children are rosy-cheeked; while the urchins of the yard, acting as look-outs for the rent man, look more like Little Lord Fauntleroys than street Arabs: there is not a smudge to be seen on their faces, nor a rent or a patch on their clothes.

If the poor have been sanitized, with well-scrubbed faces and no trace of physical deformity, the rich have been glamorized, an Upper Ten

Thousand not imprisoned by their wealth, as in Dickens, but a world of rank and fashion. They are pictured as living in palaces – literally so in the Italian scenes, metaphorically in London. The Merdle establishment in Harley Street is a court; the Circumlocution Office, with its marble halls, Palladian. Tite Barnacle is no longer an aristocratic nincompoop – the windbag of the Meagles' wedding – but a genuinely imposing authority figure, radiating patrician charisma. The parasitic Henry Gowan is invested with a handsome figure and good looks. Mrs Merdle, the Bosom of Dickens's satire, is played by Eleanor Bron as a dazzling society lady, an object of envy and admiration rather than scorn. If low life glows in this film, high society glitters.

The shabby-genteel, too, have been upgraded, their threadbare clothes forgotten, their tattered dignity repaired. At the Marshalsea they are by no means down at heel. The needlework teacher, with her RADA voice and brilliant dress, though notionally a seamstress, is every inch a lady. The dancing master looks like a fashion plate. Tip, Little Dorrit's brother, dresses like a dandy and looks like Dorian Gray. William Dorrit, the Father of the Marshalsea, is a figure of dignity rather than pathos. In the novel he is a shambling figure, weak and self-deluded, a 'shabby old debtor' with trembling lips and irresolute hands, feebly bursting into tears when his pretensions are ignored. In the film, played by Alec Guinness, he looks positively majestic, moving about the set with stately grace, gesturing regally, and dressed in silks and satins. His talk, fragmentary and disjointed in the original, taking refuge in circumlocution and periphrasis, is serene rather than agitated, and always clear as to where it is going. Translated into the world of high society, his dignity is unimpaired. Even his breakdown – the great scene where his mind gives way, and he addresses a Society banquet as though the guests were fellow-prisoners – is played as a kind of triumph. In the novel he looks confusedly about him and makes a rambling speech, punctuated by pauses and collapsing in self-pity. In the film he is grandiloquent.

Visually, *Little Dorrit* in this film has been robbed of its potential terrors. The streets, photographed by day rather than by night, are neither menacing nor claustrophobic but picturesque. They are represented not by high, imprisoning walls, as in Phiz's original illustrations to the novel, but by make-believe 'period' shopfronts, remarkably similar to those which are now to be found in Covent Garden. Domestic interiors, too, so far from being prison-like, are emblems of sweetness and light; one admiring critic has likened them to the genre paintings of Vermeer. In the novel, the Marshalsea prison is an 'oblong pile of barrack building, partitioned into squalid houses standing back to back'. In the film, it is a loose assemblage of period cottages (one of them weather-boarded); the windows are leaded lights and the panes are dust-free; in the courtyard – improbably for a scene supposedly set in the 1820s – there is a brand new Victorian street-lamp.

The 'dark horrors' have also been eliminated from Mrs Clennam's house. In the novel it is a 'debilitated old house ... wrapped in its mantle of soot, and leaning heavily ... on crutches'. In the film it is a splendid Georgian mansion. The 'ugly old chairs without any seats' have been upholstered; the 'threadbare patternless carpet' has been replaced by Persian rugs; the 'maimed table' has given way to a Chippendale piece; even the copperware in the kitchen has been polished. The dark, airless room where Mrs Clennam imprisons herself – a kind of prototype for Miss Havisham and her cobwebs – has become a handsome morning-room, with sunlight playing on the window-seats. The ceilings, with their ornate mouldings, are spotless. It comes then as something of a surprise when in what should have been one of the dramatic climaxes of the film, as it is in the Dickens original, the house collapses.[3]

It is not only the photography which has been purged of its Gothic element, but also the narrative. The story no longer opens, as it does in Dickens, with a Dantesque vision of hell: a Marseilles dungeon. It begins in the altogether more reassuring setting of a coffee-house on Ludgate Hill. Rigaud, the satanic figure who haunts the novel – there is a terrifying engraving of him by Phiz – has been eliminated from the plot. So has the 'enigmatic and perhaps lesbian Miss Wade', a truly subversive feminine figure. The surviving figures of evil have also lost their terrors; Mrs Clennam is no longer a vengeful fury, but, as played by Joan Greenwood, she is more of a queen than a witch. The more melodramatic passages in the narrative have disappeared. Merdle, the millionaire financier, commits suicide offstage. Flintwinch's 'dreadful end' (he is buried alive in the house fall), is hardly less invisible, without so much as a glimpse of his mutilated body, or the sound of his dying groans. Acoustically, too, the film dispenses with shock effects. No heavy footfalls echo on the staircases, as they would do in *film noir* versions of Dickens; doors do not creak on their hinges, even when they are being opened by sinister characters; nor does the musical score become agitated. The most that is attempted, in the way of extraneous sound, is an occasional background buzz.

The rationale for these transformations is an aesthetic of ordinariness. The film-makers have wanted, it seems, to make *Little Dorrit* more believable to moderns. Where Dickens caricatures, the film tries to make its characters lifelike, eliminating their more extravagant tropes and returning them to the world of everyday behaviour. Thus Mr Merdle, the millionaire swindler, is no longer at sixes and sevens with his body (in the novel his hands and feet are perpetually disappearing), but plods about the set. At the other end of the social scale Mrs Plornish, the fantasist of

Bleeding Heart Yard, with her make-believe Arcadia, becomes a hard-pressed mother. Above all, everything is done to diminish Little Dorrit's otherness. Her speech is invested with a faint London twang, as if to offer assurances that she is made of the common clay. She busies herself with domestic chores even when offering love. She is also in some sort despiritualized, no longer the subject of a drama of suffering and redemption, but rather – in the film's reworking of the narrative – the woman who gets her man. The 'strong passivity' which Dickens saw as the noblest aspect of the truly womanly disappears; so does the theme of the 'Martyr-daughter'. Where Dickens's plot thickens, building up suspense, here it is simplified to the symmetries of romance – a story to be understood in contemporary terms. *Little Dorrit*, the film's editors have decided, 'is a love story'.[4]

The film-makers' approach to *Little Dorrit* is reverently mimetic. Truth to the original rather than dramatic invention has been their guiding star. The lines of the original dialogue have been faithfully reproduced, foreshortened but without embellishment. Incidents and events have been transcribed literally and re-enacted as though in answer to stage directions. Significant moments are paused upon to allow them to have their true weight. In one aspect the film resembles nothing so much as a series of cameos in which the chapters of the book are replayed as scenes. Speech, mannerism and posture too have been imitated, as for example Flintwich's 'crab-like' walk or Flora Finching's flounces.

Closely related to, but consorting uneasily with this, is the concern for historical verisimilitude. Verdi's music, for instance, was chosen for 'period' reasons, 'an almost obvious accompaniment to Dickens's work' (the programme notes tell us) because he was born within a year of Dickens and shared (the film-makers believe) Dickens's 'romantic quality'. The sets have been lovingly antiqued – hand-grained panels, for instance in the Clennam household, designer-craftsman chairs at Mr Merdle's, both of them on show, along with the film's costumes, at an exhibition in the Museum of London. The film-makers have lavished a vast amount of attention on the costume, and it says something of the production values of the company that Olivier Stockman, the co-script-writer and film editor, also designed the hats. Coats and gowns have been copied down to the last buttonhole, individually hand-made to guarantee an absolute authenticity, and following the pattern books of the 1830s and 1840s. A host of talents were mobilized for the task – some twenty-five designer-craftspeople working for a period of two years – and they were rewarded by being given exhibition space at the Museum of London. Here the costume and artefacts of the film have been reverently labelled, as though they were real-life antiques, with a set of colour plates by Lord Snowdon to serve as mementoes. The organizers of the

exhibition, untroubled by blood on the needles or memories of *The Song of the Shirt*, celebrate the seamstresses' art as one of England's glories:

> The three hundred or so costumes for the film were entirely made by hand, as they would have been at the time, with the greatest attention to the shape and cut of the period, and to every possible detail. For over two years, dresses and coats were cut and fitted and sewn, waistcoats were embroidered, buttons were made, straw bonnets were plaited, petticoats, shirts, corsets were stitched up, gentlemen's hats, ladies' shawls and even jewels were made in the workshops of Sands Films, the work of some twenty-five people.

The historicity of the film and the fetishization of period effects are inseparable from the claim that it is 'intensely real'. As the film-makers put it: 'A very large amount of work and affection and care have gone into making every part of it ... as richly detailed and authentic as possible.'

The film's preoccupation with period effects is singularly at variance with Dickens himself, who was notoriously cavalier in his treatment of history and contemptuous of notions of heritage.[5] In his autobiographical novels, *David Copperfield* and *Great Expectations*, the past – the remembered past of his childhood – is a prison-house, a time of cruelty and oppression; in his historical novels, *A Tale of Two Cities* and *Barnaby Rudge*, it is a theatre where his phobias have free play. In *Little Dorrit* it is a nightmare weight on the living which the protagonists desperately try to escape. Dickens had a radical contempt for the past and his *Child's History of England* is the very reverse of reverential: James I is 'his Sowship', Henry VIII a 'Pig', George III 'that swine-headed anointed of the Lord'. In the battle of Ancients and Moderns he was uninhibitedly on the side of the latter. Among the false book-backs with which he decorated his study at Gad's Hill was a set, Humphry House tells us, called: 'The Wisdom of our Ancestors: I. Ignorance, II. Superstition, III. The Block, IV. The Stake, V. The Rack, VI. Dirt, VII. Disease'.[6] When antiquarianism makes a brief appearance in *Little Dorrit*, it is an object of scorn, 'scratching up the driest little bones' (he writes of Mrs General in Rome) '... and bolting them down whole'; and he is no more respectful of Mr Meagles's picturesque souvenirs.

Dickens was not a period novelist in the way in which, say, Thackeray was in *Henry Esmond* or *Vanity Fair*. Even when a story seems to be taking place at one moment, the characters may be drawn from another. In *Little Dorrit* itself he cheerfully conflates entirely different epochs: the Marshalsea of his 1820s childhood, where his father briefly served a term of imprisonment, and the administrative scandals and financial swindles of the 1850s. The story is set, like many of his novels, 'thirty years ago', but the Circumlocution Office and the Tite Barnacles were the campaigning targets of the day. The film-makers have compounded this difficulty by drawing their costume from originals which belong to neither time: to judge by the credits at the Museum of London, the *Journal des Desmoiselles* of 1839 was a leading model. The period effects in this film are not only pedantic; in relation to *Little Dorrit*, a novel which belongs, chronologically speaking, nowhere, they are by definition misplaced.

Dickens was not a realist in the way the film-makers want him to be. His Victorian England has only the most accidental relation to that of the historians who, by and large, have found it prudent to ignore him. Alienation, the great theme of his 'dark' novels, has little or no place in accounts of the Age of Equipoise; nor do the shabby-genteel, one of his basic points of social reference and the very subject of *Little Dorrit*, have even a walk-on part in the Age of Improvement. Dickens's realism was a grotesque realism; his genius was in caricature; he made a fantasy of Victorian England and peopled it with creatures of his own invention. The attempt, then, to make the characters of the novel lifelike – whether by playing down or, as in the treatment of Amy Dorrit, by eliminating the symbolic – seems self-defeating. The film is in fact most successful when it breaks from the reality frame, and allows the actors to be theatrical. A wonderful performance by Miriam Margolyes translates Flora's verbal flounces into pantomime, casting sly oeillades at her former paramour, frantically smoothing his hat, acting out the words rather than – or as well as – speaking her lines. Emelda Brown is comparably illuminating in the part of the spoilt little rich girl, Fanny, shifting gear emotionally from one moment to the next, now in tears, now ingratiating.

Film requires a different aesthetic from conservation, and *Little Dorrit* illustrates some of the difficulties of attempting to marry the two. The sets, so lovingly reconstructed, take on a life of their own. The period costume, with its high arm-holes, turns the actors and actresses into clothes-hangers. Hats depersonalize, disastrously so in the case of Little Dorrit who for much of the time is invisible by reason of her enormous poke bonnet. The beautiful copperware makes even the Clennam kitchen cosy; the simple table in the Dorrit garret, even if intended to signify poverty, cannot fail to look like a period piece.

The contrived authenticities of this film undermine the narrative. The dialogue, though faithfully drawn on the original, often sounds stilted, with long silences which underline the laboured effect ('Time for your oysters', Flintwich at one point improbably says to his mistress). The 'period' music, however chronologically apt, is totally at variance with the murky world which Dickens is describing, one which, if the musical score were to be taken from a composer of the time, might more fittingly be Wagner rather than Verdi.

The Marshalsea here may be truer to the historical original than to the phantasmagoria conjured up by Dickens and by Phiz; but as depicted in the film it is not so much a closed world as a theatre of comings and goings. The look of the film, in short, continually belies the words. A house can hardly function, symbolically, as a morgue, when it looks like the *World of Interiors*; nor the city as a prison – a guiding metaphor of Dickens's novel – when it is full of inviting shops.

The past can never be transcribed, but has always to be re-invented. In the case of Dickens, it seems, this necessarily involves an attitude to Victorian values. The discovery of the 'dark' Dickens, as much a phenomenon of the 1940s in literary criticism, with the new attention to the later novels, as in the films of David Lean, was intimately bound up with the revolt against Victorianism in politics and the arts. Victorianism, then, was freely associated with injustice and oppression, the 'Dickensian' with Poor Law and the slums. Edzard's *Little Dorrit* might speculatively be explained by the rehabilitation of Victorian values which has been such a feature of recent years. In one aspect it reflects that urban pastoral which emerged in the wake of modernization and slum clearances; in another the aestheticization of dying industries. One could note here the representation of the slum as an Arcadia and of machinery as pretty – no longer the monstrous engines of *Hard Times* but, as in the industrial museums, historical monuments. In another aspect the film reproduces the enthusiasms of conservation, in which the past is not a dead weight to be thrown off but a heritage to preserve, and here it seems no accident that Sands films should be located – and the film should have been made – in that temple of conservation-led redevelopment, London Docklands.[7]

Notes

1. For a biographical account, J.B. Van Amerongen, *The Actor in Dickens: A Study of the Histrionic and Dramatic Elements in the Novelist's Life and Work*, London 1926. Among later works, William F. Axton, *Circle of Fire: Dickens' Vision and Style and the Popular Victorian Theatre*, Lexington 1966. For melodrama, Peter Brooks, *The Melodramatic Image*, New Haven 1976.

2. Sergei Eisenstein, 'Dickens, Griffith and the Film Today' in *Film Forum*, London 1951. A.L. Zambrano, *Dickens and Film*, New York 1977, is a critical account which includes detailed discussion of Dickens adaptations on both stage and screen.

3. The rationale for this astonishing transformation, argued by John Carey, the Oxford literary critic, in the film brochure is that we are seeing the house, in the second part of the film, through Little Dorrit's eyes. In fact the house is quite as elegant in Part I, where the narrative is supposedly Arthur Clennam's. Carey, in any event, celebrates the transformation. 'It is, we realize, a stately and beautiful house, with its polished woods and ornate moulded ceilings.'

4. The romance is not that of Arthur Clennam and Little Dorrit, whose encounters lack any of the tensions or electricity of desire, but of the camera and Derek Jacobi, the actor who takes Arthur's part. He plays it in a way that seems to be deeply appealing to women. He is given the opening scene of the film, as a Little Boy Lost, a child-adult with neither mother nor home; and he is pictured through the film in becoming settings – seated

majestically at his desk in one moment, in another ostensibly locked up in the Marshalsea with romantically dishevelled hair (whereas Little Dorrit is distanced throughout the film by her bonnet, Jacobi is generally hatless). He does not say much; he does not do anything. *He looks.* The camera plays about his face lasciviously. (People who have wanted to highlight the fact that the film has a woman director have speculated on some possibly feminist reading of Amy Dorrit. It would be more rewarding to consider the way in which the script has elevated Clennam from a narrative cipher into a romantic lead, and the way in which the camera transforms him into an object of filmic desire.)

5. For an excellent early discussion of Dickens and history, see G.K. Chesterton's introduction to the Everyman edition of *A Child's History of England* (London 1912). Later discussion takes its cue from the splendid chapter on 'History' in Humphry House, *The Dickens World*, Oxford 1950. There is a chapter on the historical novels in Michael Hollington, *Dickens and the Grotesque*, London 1984; Andrew Sanders, *The Victorian Historical Novel: 1840–1880*, London 1978, discusses the transformations in the genre.

6. Humphry House, *The Dickens World*, p. 35.

7. For an admiring account of the making of the film 'amidst the yuppification of London's docklands', *Films and Filming*, December 1987.

'Who Calls So Loud?'
Dickens on Stage and Screen

I read *Little Dorrit* for the first time on honeymoon. It seemed a good occasion to make up for a long-standing neglect. Both Alison, my companion, and I are Dickens-lovers, and reading out passages from *Our Mutual Friend* (I remember particularly Silas Wegg instructing Mr Boffin in the mysteries of *The Decline and Fall of the Roman Empire*) had played quite a part in the early days of our courtship. But neither of us had read *Little Dorrit* and the honeymoon gave us time to enjoy it (as also each other). You can't sunbathe in Shetland, which is where we were staying, and though there are rocky promontories to walk on, a wildlife sanctuary and windswept cliffs, there were no beaches to lie on, anyway on our island. So we spent a good deal of time with our new Dickens.

It was a sombre experience. *Little Dorrit* is a novel of alienation with an underlying melancholy – Christian pessimism, according to some – which makes it a disturbing read. The narrative advances by circumlocution. The plot, even by nineteenth-century standards, is labyrinthine. The settings, with only one partial exception, are oppressive. The messages of the novel are severe. Poverty and wealth mirror one another's cupidities. Society is a swindle, government a cheat. Marriages are loveless – in those of Flintwich and Henry Gowan, a mere convenience for designing males. The family is a site of imprisonment, not so much a refuge from the world as a place where its cruelties are anticipated. Even the benevolent characters are malignant, if not in their intentions, at any rate in their effects. The 'patriarchal Mr Casby' is a pious old fraud who makes his livelihood from rack-renting. The amiable Pancks succumbs to speculative mania. The well-meaning Mr Meagles, a doting father and kindly employer, spoils his child, 'Pet', infantilizes his servant, Tattycoram, and grovels at the feet of the aristocracy. William Dorrit, though based in some sort on Dickens's own father, is no longer the good-natured Mr Micawber, waiting for something to turn up, but rather a self-serving parasite, levying emotional blackmail on his daughter and exploiting the gullibility of his fellow prisoners. His female

413

counterpart, Mrs Clennam, is even more warped, a cruel mother – one of a long line in Dickens – nursing her hatreds and making a religion of her fears.

I cannot pretend to have understood the novel, but I found, as often with Dickens, that the pictures grew in the mind even when I had not fathomed the intricacies of the text. There were the London streets, where the opposing rows of houses 'were very grim with one another'. There was the Marseilles dungeon on which the novel opens – a place of torment taken, one may imagine, from Dumas's Chateau d'If, a prison terror which had stayed with me from one of the radio serials of my childhood. There were the mists and shadows and darkness of Great St Bernard Pass, the scene which opens Book Two – the miasma of London, as it were, pursuing the escaped inmates of the Marshalsea when they go on their Italian travels. In a lighter vein – there are not many which the book offers – we found ourselves recognizing the insistently coquettish Flora in one of our friends; and more discomfortingly had to acknowledge a likeness between Mrs Plornish's make-believe Arcady in Bleeding Heart Yard and our own terraced cottage in Spitalfields.

The film of *Little Dorrit* was our idea of a Christmas treat, as it was, evidently, of the many other Londoners who crowded the Curzon cinema in Shaftesbury Avenue in December 1987. I waited in pleasurable expectancy for familiar scenes and hoped perhaps that it would help to clear up some of the novel's mysteries. The film, we learnt, was a labour of love, which had taken some five or six years to prepare, and the six hours of screen-time seemed a fitting response to a dense and difficult text. Coming so recently from a reading of the text, my companion and I could hardly fail to be riveted by the film. It was only walking home that doubts began to appear. Why, we asked, had it all been so clean? Why was the light so bright? Had not much of the original narrative been enacted in darkness; Little Dorrit wending her way through the midnight streets of the metropolis? Why did the film have a happy ending – in fact, not one happy ending but *two* – the union of the two lovers at the end of Part One, their marriage at the end of Part Two? How could the film have closed on a wedding ceremony, a joyous procession with cheerful music, rather than the sombre scene with which Dickens closed his book – the roaring streets 'where the noisy and the eager, the arrogant and the forward and the vain fretted and chafed and made their usual uproar'?

What disturbed us most of all, and puzzled us, was that we had been moved neither to laughter nor to tears. Like the rest of the audience, we watched the film in absolute stillness. Even the death of William Dorrit – surely the longest death-bed scene in the history of British cinema – left us dry-eyed and unbelieving. It seemed that we had been witness to a

spectacle rather than engaged by a drama.

A visit to the Museum of London cast light on one of the film's inspirations, historical realism. Here one saw assembled, in an exhibition timed to coincide with *Little Dorrit*'s West End run, a display of the film's 'amazingly authentic' costumes. They were hand-made, visitors were told; as though the seamstress's work, in the age of *The Song of the Shirt*, had been one of England's glories. They were copied from the fashion plates of the period (we were shown some of the originals). And they had taken twenty-five people some two years to sew. Alongside the costume was a range of designer-made props, including the panelling of the Clennam home. The exhibition threw light on the film's guiding aesthetic, a notion of 'realism' in which truth to the Dickens original had somehow been conflated with achieving a 'period' look. It also gave a clue as to why the film had looked so clean. There was not a rent or a patch in the garments and, except for Mr Plornish's working smock, not a single stain.

A second viewing of the film provided some clues about why it had been so undisturbing. The looks of the film constantly belied the words, delighting the eye even when they were supposed to be emblems of poverty. The weather, astonishingly for Dickens's London, was for the most part fine; the chimneys in the painted backdrops miraculously emitted no smoke. The shops, with their picturesque small-paned windows seemed (to follow those shown on the film's opening credits) to be selling prints and antiques. High society – the object of Dickens's satire – glittered. The shabby-genteel had been spruced up (Alec Guinness as William Dorrit looked regal); the poor had been sanitized. Even the flies in the gallipot, bathed in Old Master colours, looked as though they were being marinated in brandy.

What was most disabling about the film was its *flatness*. It practised, towards both the period and the Dickens text, precisely that form of 'everyday' realism which is the common currency of the new social history, in the process (it seems to me) cruelly exposing its limitations. It made a fetish of the ordinary. Dickens's powerful sense of evil has been systematically excluded. 'Melodramatic' incidents have been eliminated; sinister characters dropped. The dialogue, though faithful to the original, was spoken rather than acted, as though any gesture to the histrionic would undermine its 'natural' character. The costumes were insistently true to life, so that for instance, Little Dorrit is quite often invisible to the viewer by reason of her enormous bonnet. 'Realistic' settings have been substituted for Gothic ones – disastrously so in the case of the Clennam residence: in the Dickens original it is a house of guilty secrets 'wrapped in its mantle of soot, leaning heavily on crutches', and as we learn in one of the book's climatic moments, on the point of terminal collapse; in the film it becomes instead 'a stately and beautiful house, with its polished woods and ornate moulded ceiling'. The objects of fantasy and satire have been scaled down to those which might appear in 'everyday' life: Mrs Plornish is no longer the fantasist of Bleeding Heart Yard, building a make-believe Arcadia, but a pale and careworn housewife. Mrs Merdle is no longer the Bosom of Dickens's satire but a brilliant Society lady.

The filming of Dickens seems to arouse passionate feelings, as I discovered after publishing a critical article on *Little Dorrit* in the *Guardian*. A friend of some twenty-five years wrote to say that he thought my piece 'a disgrace' and he has refused, ever since, to have any communication with me. Derek Malcolm, the paper's film critic, writing under the heading 'Duel at the Watershed', hoped that Olivier Stockman, the film's co-director (with Christine Edzard), would run a sword through me when we met in debate. David Lean, by contrast, whose *Great Expectations* (1946) and *Oliver Twist* (1948) I had used as a point of comparison, was a conservative whom no one on the left had any business to praise. The debate at Bristol – as also a subsequent one at the Birmingham Film Festival – certainly did confirm the radical intention of the film-makers, and it also cast light on the particular version of realism which had been their guiding aesthetic: one in which truth to period and fidelity to the text had been treated as equivalents.

My implicit point of reference and contrast when writing about *Little Dorrit* was the Royal Shakespeare Company's *Nicholas Nickleby*, an eight-hour, two-part production, a filmed version of which was being serialized on Channel 4. I found it intensely moving, often hilarious. I marvelled at how it created a 'Dickensian' atmosphere without any of *Little Dorrit's* studied effects. There is no pretence here at realism in any archaeological sense. Props and scenery are perfunctory, often no more than a backdrop or a screen. The costume is unobtrusive. Kate Nickleby is vulnerably bare-headed, as befits the part if not the period, since she is subject to humiliation on the part of her employers, and the torments of her would-be seducers. The music is designed to match mood rather than period, ranging from Christmas carols and sub-madrigals to squeaky modern dissonances. Donizetti is used for the opera scene; a jazz-age number, played on the alto sax, serves as the Mulberry Hawk theme in the aristocratic gambling hell of St James's.

The RSC *Nicholas Nickleby*, unlike Christine Edzard's *Little Dorrit*, takes continuous liberties with the text, changing the sequence of events, introducing new scenes, altering the plot, amplifying the characters. Peg Skilderskew, the grotesque servant, is made into a Glaswegian hag; Arthur Gride, the usurer, rubbing his hands hebraically, is turned into a kind of Jew. The dialogue is invented rather than reproduced and much of it seems to have come from translating Dickens's observations and thoughts into actorly lines. Kate Nickleby, as David Edgar (the adapter and scriptwriter) tells us in his recently published commentary, was transformed by being given words which in the novel are the author's; as a result she emerges as a character in her own right – a spirited young girl rather than, as in the Dickens original, a blushing Victorian maiden. The most remarkable of these inventions – and a key to the success of the production – is the virtual reinvention of Smike. Having decided at an early stage that Smike was a kind of alter ego to Nicholas, they gave him a centrality which was lacking in the original plot, and transformed him from a crushed boy of nineteen into a kind of Titan of stuttering, a cripple who writhes monstrously with his every uttered word, and whose words are the more eloquent in that each one has to be so strenuously fought for – above all, that object of his impossible desires, spoken long and loud to rhyme with 'moan'; 'HOME'.

Yet, for all its many inventions, *Nicholas Nickleby* seems extraordinarily faithful to the *spirit* and the *sentiment* of the original. In the manner of Dickens it is digressive, giving extended attention to such relatively minor characters as the Keniwigs; adding, where it seems opportune, to an already crowded canvas by inventing fresh incidents (a hilarious performance of *Romeo and Juliet* by the Vincent Crummles Company is a kind of actorly revenge for generations of having to strut about the stage with swords). It is faithful to the Christian humanism of the original – the drama of sin and redemption – and it also contrives to be true to the extremely ambiguous sexuality of the novel. Instead of pairing Nicholas off with his eventual bride, it gives him in some sort four lovers and four separate romances – most powerfully that with his sister Kate; most interestingly the male bonding with Smike, whom he carries with him on his ways, and Newman Noggs, the sensitive, shabby-genteel alcoholic (beautifully played by Edward Petherbridge) who protects him from the powerful. Most striking of all, *Nicholas Nickleby* returns us to those sentiments of tenderness and compassion which constituted one of Dickens's leading appeals to the Victorian reading public. Here, in the doomed life and eventual death of Smike – the pivot of the eight-hour drama – one sees in miniature that 'exquisite pathos' which marked the delineation of the long line of martyr-children who did so much to win Dickens the affections of his readers, even though they alienated the highbrow critics. The death of Smike – a brilliant invention of David Edgar's – reverses a century of hard-boiled cynicism; allowing, indeed forcing us, to weep at precisely the point where (commenting on the death of Little Nell) Oscar Wilde said that one would need a heart of stone not to laugh. Edgar has Kate join her brother for Smike's end, turning the morality of death into the pathos of unrequited love. 'Who calls so loud?', says Smike, urgently but painfully mouthing the words he has spoken in the Crummles's *Romeo and Juliet* – the only line he has ever learnt. 'Who calls so loud?', he repeats, as the Angel of Death draws near.

The RSC *Nicholas Nickleby* is also avowedly theatrical. It opens with the company announcing themselves, the actors and actresses play the part of the narrative voice; props and scenery are moved hither and thither before our eyes. In the manner of alternative theatre – the crucible in which David Edgar forged his art – it is very much an ensemble production, with no stars but actors and actresses doubling in their parts; indeed at moments the production looks like nothing so much as the performance of a group of strolling players, like the Vincent Crummles Company with whom Nicholas's fortunes are briefly and hilariously joined. Moving with great speed from scene to scene, and sometimes intercutting between them, to restore the simultaneity of the text; changing in mood from the indignant or the exuberant to the pathetic, the production, for all its great length – eight and a half hours in the original RSC staging – hardly gives you moment's pause to take a breath.

The characters in this production are larger than life, memorable rather than believable, and owing their force as much to theatrical as to literary (or real-life) originals. There is the pantomime figure of Mr Mantalini; with his waistcoat and his Turkish trousers, the philanderer who married on the strength of his whiskers and keeps his wife at bay with elaborate compliments to his 'jewel'. Squeers, the schoolmaster, is alternatively pantomime and Grand Guignol, wearing his face like a mask; thanks to a livid make-up, the lines of cruelty positively glow. The wicked uncle Ralph is pure melodrama.

My other point of comparison with *Little Dorrit* had been David Lean's *Great Expectations* (1947) and *Oliver Twist* (1948), the Dickens films of my childhood. It had seemed to me that the power of Lean's films lay in his capacity to find visual metaphors for key moments in Dickens's narrative – most memorably in the desolate scene on the marshes which provides the shock opening of *Great Expectations*; and in the Gothic horror of Satis House, where the witch-like Miss Havisham presides and eventually burns to death. As well as being true to Dickens's animistic vision, these films also corresponded, it seemed to me, with a stigmatization of the Victorian era which had been gathering strength since the turn of the century, and which reached some kind of apogee in Labour's election victory of 1945.

A second viewing of *Great Expectations* brought back some of the visual excitements which had riveted themselves on me as a child. It also showed up some of these films' more obvious weaknesses – the absence, for instance, of comedy; or in a 'Dickensian' sense, characters (the treatment of Mr Wemmick and his Walworth castle is particularly disappointing). By abbreviating the childhood scenes and particularly Pip's relation to Biddy, we cannot measure the force of his later betrayal of Joe Gargery, nor the strength of Joe's eventual pull on him. (The voice-over narrator is not a success.) The camera consistently takes Pip's view of himself – not the un-illusioned middle-aged Pip who is the narrator (a voice-over in the film) but the personable man about town.

John Mills, playing Pip, looks like a tennis club blade, and it is difficult to credit him with a change of heart, while Valerie Hobson, with her haw-haw voice, makes Estella into the Head Girl type (Jean Simmons, by contrast, playing the pubescent Estella, is – as the narrative requires – mysteriously erotic).

The great success of the film is that it is, as the director intended, a fairy story, at one level a Victorian up-date of the Dick Whittington legend, the poor boy making good; at another, a kind of male version of Cinderella. Miss Havisham, played by Martita Hunt, is a witch; Magwitch an ogre or giant, albeit one who turns out to have a heart of gold; Estella – at least as played by Jean Simmons – a siren.

The really startling discovery of my second viewing, was a realization that the ending of *Great Expectations* which, like the opening sequence, has engraved itself on my memory, was Lean's invention. Dickens's original end was to have been a melancholy one, in line with his deeply depressed mood at the time. Under pressure from Bulwer Lytton he modified this to allow a middle-aged Pip to meet up again with Estella, the object of his childhood desire. But whether or not they will stay together is left in doubt. The film, by contrast, ends in an epiphany. A still youthful Pip returns to Satis House where to his horror he finds Estella sinking into the shadows. She is visibly becoming the death-in-life figure of Miss Havisham. Pip begs her to come away with him: 'Leave this house. . . . It's Miss Havisham's. It's a dead house. No one can live here.' Estella insists that it is her house, the one in which she was brought up: 'I have come back home.' 'Then I defy her', says Pip in desperation, trying to exorcise Miss Havisham's ghost. To break the spell he dashes at the windows, tears down the curtains and begins smashing the panes. 'Look, Estella, nothing but dust and decay. Come with me, out into the sunlight.' On one view the film ends in a conventional romantic clinch, but it does not seem fanciful to align it to the social-democratic vision of 1945, a dream of light and space.

Dickens, as Orwell remarks in a well-known essay on him, 'is one of those writers who are well worth stealing'. This is certainly true of the commentators and critics, who have shown themselves past masters at fashioning Dickens in their image, whether as a humorist, a moralist or a social critic. Bernard Shaw, one of Dickens's champions at a time when his literary reputation was waning, claimed that *Little Dorrit* made him a socialist; Eisenstein that Dickens had taught him montage. The 'dark' Dickens of the 1940s was very much a creation of highbrow critics, attempting to reclaim the novels – the later novels in particular – from a sentimentalized popular taste and assimilate them to the canon of modernism. Dickens, on this view, was second cousin to Dostoevsky, and the progenitor of Kafka and Joyce; a tormented soul 'inwardly hostile to the age which acclaimed him and seeking relief from the strain of his double life in fantasies of crime and violence'. The contrast with the genial Dickens of G.K. Chesterton – 'the one living link between the old kindness and the new' – could hardly be more complete.

What is true of literary commentary is even more true of popular entertainment, where adaptation and dramatization – a feature of Dickens's writings ever since the publication of *Sketches by Boz* – seem to have been closely related to shifts in sensibility and changes in public taste. Victorian theatre audiences seem to have wanted and expected to be harrowed. Nancy was the leading character in the stage version of *Oliver Twist*, and her murder by Bill Sikes the accepted dramatic climax (Henry Mayhew, in *London Labour and the London Poor*, describes the gallery at the Vic yelling their abuse as Bill dragged Nancy round the stage). Later, *The Only Way*, a dramatization of *A Tale of Two Cities* in which 'for a generation' Sir John Martin-Hervey interpreted Sidney Carton, was to prove Dickens's most lasting stage success. In his own public readings, Dickens showed a very strong penchant for the morbid, stirring his audiences to a frenzy of pity over such scenes as the death of Paul Dombey.

The Dickens of the 1930s, popularized in letters by J.B. Priestley and George Orwell – played on the music-hall stage by Bransby Williams, with his much-loved impersonations of Dickens's 'characters'; and on the screen by W.C. Fields as Mr Micawber – was essentially benevolent, a messenger of good cheer offering to the public, as in the Hollywood version of *David Copperfield*, a gallery of lovable eccentrics. He was a radical, albeit of an undoctrinaire kind, combining humanitarian sentiment with a Chaplinesque irreverence for authority; it may be indicative of this that the most widely circulated Complete Works of the decade was that distributed by Odhams Press as part of its promotion campaign for Labour's *Daily Herald*. (It was in this guise that Dickens arrived in the Labour home of Raymond Williams's childhood.)

Lean's *Great Expectations* and *Oliver Twist* were very much films of their time. They have obvious resemblances to such period melodramas as *Fanny by Gaslight*, *Dead of Night* and *Hatter's Castle* as well as the 'Gothic' films of Gainsborough Studios. With their expressionist angles, atmospheric darkness, and theatrical high-contrast lighting, if not in their subject-matter, they could also be seen as a kind of English counterpart to the Hollywood *film noir*. Dispensing with Dickens's humour whilst amplifying his spookier moments, these films were hugely influential in popularizing the notion of the Victorian as a time of darkness and fear.

Oliver!, Lionel Bart's hugely popular musical of 1968, belongs to a period in which attitudes to the Victorian were becoming much more ambiguous. The very idea of producing a musical of Dickens's novel suggests that we are in a different world. Lionel Bart the librettist, an East

Londoner himself, had already produced *Fings Ain't What They Used to Be*, a requiem for a world that was being lost; in *Oliver!* he brings something of the same kind of imagination to bear on London's old-time artful dodgers and treats street life itself as colourful and interesting rather than squalid. He gives some of his most tuneful numbers to Fagin, the king of the pickpockets – a bad father, but still a father, whispering words of endearment to his juvenile flock and tucking them up to sleep. When he counts his shekels he is more comic than frightening. Yet, even as a musical, *Oliver!* still has the quality of nightmare. The flower girls, making a harmony of the old London street cries, turn by degrees into sinister outriders of the underworld, laying their snares in the outer suburbs. Bill Sikes, the only leading character who is not redeemed by having a song, remains a figure of evil, brutalizing his dog, and turning viciously on his mistress. Above all, as a figure of fear, there is Oliver the little boy lost, that recurring figure of Dickens's nightmare, the orphaned child of the respectable, cast off into the lower depths.

The RSC *Nicholas Nickleby* marked a further stage in the rehabilitation of the Victorian, and as a matter of fact – though it is not one which has yet got through to the university literature departments – the rediscovery of the un-dark Dickens. The RSC had set out, in the manner of Edzard, to research the 'period' background, and they had discovered real-life historical horror stories to match those of Dickens's narrative. They had also decided that the unifying theme of the novel – at any rate in their own reading of it – was cash nexus and the advent of a society where cupidity ruled. Yet, whatever the radical, critical intentions of the company, and of the writer, it is a joyous production and it was indeed its 'life-enhancing qualities' – in the words of its earliest champion – which, in face of critical indifference or hostility, eventually won it tremendous acclaim. For one thing the epic quality of the production itself – an eight-and-a-half hour show with actors and actresses doubling in the parts and also serving as narrators and scene-shifters – it was (like Timberlake Wertenbaker's *Our Country's Good*) a celebration of theatre itself. Then, like the 'promenade' productions at the National Theatre which preceded it (for example, Bill Bryden's *Lark Rise to Candleford*) and David Edgar's own more recent *Entertaining Strangers*, the spirit is exuberant and zestful even when the subject-matter is grim. Finally, like *Nicholas Nickleby* it is picaresque, a 'life and adventures' which takes us through a kaleidoscope of swiftly changing scenes. In place of claustrophobia it gives us a magical mystery tour where fugitives elude their captors, and oppressors receive their comeuppance. In the manner of Dickens himself, the RSC *Nicholas Nickleby* is inclusive, giving interest and even humanity to some of its worst characters and allowing even the most wicked – Ralph Nickleby – to experience a change of heart. Squeers may be a monster, but his gluttony somehow contrives to keep him within the pale of human society; the usurer, as played here, never rises above the comic; the aristocratic roué is a fop. There are no figures of absolute evil to match Bill Sikes.

So far as dramaturgy is concerned, one crucial issue raised by these films – *Little Dorrit* in particular – is the relationship of the verbal to the visual. A film can show one thing while apparently saying another, and in this respect the long and sinister shadows which are such a feature of the Lean version of Dickens are more eloquent of his notion of the Victorian than the buzz of surface happenings. Conversely, the critical and radical intentions of Edzard's *Little Dorrit* are continually betrayed by the prettiness of the scenic properties. This is not (if the argument of the foregoing is correct) a matter of artistic failure but rather of an imaginative revolution which has taken place in perceptions of the Victorian past, and the altogether new value conservationism has given to 'period' setting. It is difficult to imagine how anyone would go about remaking a David Lean-like version of Dickens today. Jacob's island, the scene of the terrifying chase in *Oliver Twist*, would be a yachting marina; Fagin's den a 'restored' cottage. The desolate marsh on which *Great Expectations* opens would no doubt be a wildlife sanctuary, with tastefully lettered National Trust notices to keep one from going astray. The gibbets would have been taken off to a theme park; Joe Gargery's forge for an open-air museum. Pip must still be told off for being an 'uncommon bolter' but Mrs Gargery, so far from locking her meat pies in the pantry, would enjoy a brisk trade with passing motorists in farm-fresh country snacks. Satis House, Miss Havisham's mysterious residence, would, of course, be a listed building; possibly on account of the gargoyles classified as Grade I. Pip could hardly set about destroying it, as he does in the closing sequence of David Lean's film. 'Watch the dado, darling', it is not difficult to imagine Estella crying out as he moves to rip down the curtain, 'and do be careful of the panelling'.

Another issue raised by recent film versions of Dickens is the gulf between intentionality and effect. Christine Edzard may have had a 'steely eye' on Mrs Thatcher when making her film, and she may have intended *Little Dorrit* to serve as a tract for our times, but the artefacts so lovingly assembled turn the London of her film from a prison-house – Dickens's guiding metaphor – into a showcase of period delights. Conversely, David Lean may have been a conservative, but his *Great Expectations* and *Oliver Twist* were made in the wake of some two generations of modernist revolt against Victorianism. *Oliver Twist*, which includes a stunning scene of the orphan boys peering down at the rich man's feast, clearly belongs to the 'social conscience' films of the period, and the sentiments of outraged and benevolent paternalism which helped to give Labour its landslide victory in 1945.

Great Expectations might now also be seen to have the elements of a social-democratic fable. The film contrasts the heartlessness of high society with the unselfseeking generosity of the humble. It offsets the drama of social mobility with a parable of the dignity of labour. The salience given to Magwitch, a convict strapped in irons, might be seen to be representing one of Labour's ideal objects of compassion; the noble savage Joe Gargery himself, played here by Bernard Miles (a Labour man and a 'progressive' who specialized in 'country' parts), is a very epitome of male working-class decency, of the kind to which 1945 Labour was making its appeal. The sympathy which he expresses for Magwitch's plight ('We wouldn't have you starve to death, poor, miserable creature'), like Pip's action in smuggling meat pies to him, might speculatively be said to give us a glimpse of the emotionality which underpinned Labour's 1945 ideology of 'fair shares'. (If, as Gareth Stedman Jones has argued, the Labour government of 1945–51 represented a 'late flowering' of Victorian philanthropy, then Dickens – represented here in the fullness of benevolent paternalism – has some claim to be one of its fathers.) What is not in doubt is that Lean's nightmare vision of the Victorian is thoroughly in line with the progressive consensus of the time.

The gulf between intention and effect might be even more rewarding to consider in the case of the RSC's *Nicholas Nickleby.* It was a product of the radical counter-culture of the 1970s and conceived on Brechtian lines. The actors and actresses were at pains to locate the play in the economic and social reality of the 1830s, and they were delighted when they discovered a real-life historical original for the Yorkshire horror of Dotheboys Hall. They identified money as the key nexus in the narrative and decided to play up the affinities between Ralph Nickleby the financier and such small-time operators as Squeers. As good radicals, they were no doubt also on the lookout for signs of protest, and when the original failed them, they interpolated an invention of their own (in the novel, the pupils of Dotheboys Hall are silent when Nicholas beats Squeers insensible: in the RSC version, they riot). Yet what they produce is a Victorian morality, and one moreover of a decidedly conservative hue. Money may be the root of all evil, but in the right hands – that of the Cheerybles – it is a power for good. Parents may be bad parents, as they usually are in Dickens (those who appear in *Nicholas Nickleby* are without exception dreadful), but in the RSC production Nicholas and Kate contrive to make the idea of filial duty genuinely moving, cleaving loyally to their twittering mother even though she is ready to sell them into slavery. The families in the RSC *Nickleby* stick together like glue – not only the Keniwigs and the Crummles (complete with the Infant

Phenomenon, who becomes the star of their shows) but also the Nicklebys and the Squeers: in the end, family spirit redeems even Ralph, the wicked uncle. The Victorian cult of the home is also endorsed by the negative example of the orphan boys cast out of the magic circle, and forced to fend for themselves alone.

The RSC *Nickleby* toys with some High Tory imagery. By making Roger Rees a wholly plausible romantic lead – generous in indignation, tender in compassion – it does something to rescue the idea of a 'gentleman'; a concept much insisted upon in the Dickens original, but difficult to make plausible today. There is too a Tory Arcadia, the Devon home of Nicholas's nativity to which at the end of the play he returns – a 'good' countryside to contrast with the brutal one of Dotheboys Hall.

The RSC *Nickleby* is not a celebration of Victorian values in Mrs Thatcher's sense of the term – it is too respectful of Dickens for that – but it could be said in some sort to exemplify them. The techniques may have been drawn from agitprop, Brecht or 'fringe' theatre, but the sentiments are those of Dickens and the dramatic form is in some sort analogous to that of the Victorian parlour ballad – grand emotion on a small scale. Death is a point of reconciliation as well as the great destroyer. Virtue triumphs over cupidity. Honest worth receives its just reward. The Victorian cult of the home, which was of course Dickens's own obsession, is endorsed by both negative and positive examples – most memorably in the plight of the orphan boys, cast out on a friendless world.

The closing scene of the play – another of Edgar's genial inventions, drawing on the spirit of the original, but giving it a new choreography – was apparently intended as an irony. The Nicklebys, returned to their Devon Arcady, are observing the family Christmas, while a new Smike – token of the outcast poor – hovers in the wings. But the ancient words of the wassailing – 'God rest you merry gentlemen/Let nothing you dismay' – impose themselves. It is simultaneously a celebration and a lament, the melancholy of the music undermining the ostensible good cheer of the words. It apparently moved the playwright himself to make a last gesture of reconciliation, for he has Kate steal away from the family circle to take the little-boy-lost by the hand.

Afterword

Hybrids

The idea that the past is a plaything of the present, or, as postmodernist theory would have it, a 'metafiction', is only now beginning to impinge on the consciousness and disturb the tranquillity of professional historians. But it has been for some twenty years or more a commonplace of epistemological criticism, and a very mainspring of experimental work in literature and the arts. It is also a leitmotiv in commodity marketing and design, where a vast amount of ingenuity is devoted to giving brand-new products a look of instant oldness. In the novel, 'magic realism', intercutting past and present, juxtaposing fact and fantasy, simultaneously using history and calling its authenticity into question, has made time-travelling into an international style, a *lingua franca* as familiar in the samizdat publications and writings of Eastern Europe – and now it seems the Indian subcontinent – as it is in the novels of Márquez and Borges.

These fictions come to us peppered with epigraph and quotation. They criss-cross between historical research and invention; they will sometimes incorporate chunks of what scholars would recognize as original documents, duly footnoted or acknowledged in the afterword. But the purpose is not to establish the real but to make it phantasmagoric, and to suggest that history, like reality, is a chimera. Typically these fictions inhabit a no-man's-land where the rules of time and space, as well as those of narrative, are suspended. Narrators double in the role of Methuselah, taking the action back, it may be, to the earliest times and carrying it forward to such indeterminate times as what one recent fiction calls 'the near future'. Characters pass their hundredth birthday without so much as a nod or a wink, so that a single life can serve as a thread on which to hang a family saga. A sense of period is no sooner established than it is rudely disturbed by authorial intervention or the invasion of some creature from outer space. Chronological sequences are deliberately disrupted; the action takes place in an imaginary space where the normal limitations of time and space are suspended.

The idea of playing with the past – whether by animatronics, dressing up in period costume, or historical re-enactment – is deeply offensive to the historian, while the attempt to abolish or suspend temporality seems to put the historian's vocation into question. Our practice presupposes the existence of an objectively verifiable body of knowledge, while a commonsense realism – showing the past 'as it was' – is not the least of our inheritances from the nineteenth-century revolution in historical scholarship. According to conventional wisdom, historians, if they are to be true to their vocation, should keep their imagination on a tight rein. Ethically they should be neutral, avoiding the needless utterance of opinion, eschewing value-judgement and cultivating an air of detachment. 'Our scheme requires that nothing shall reveal the country, the religion or the party to which the writers belong', wrote Lord Acton, when outlining his scheme for the *Cambridge Modern History*. 'The disclosure of personal views would lead to such confusion that all unity of design would disappear'.[1] Methodologically, too, historians are told to be self-effacing, allowing documents, so far as possible, to speak for themselves. We are not masters but servants of the evidence. Our first duty is to be objective, making no statement which cannot be verified from the sources; and using sources, ideally, which are free of bias. The integrity of history should be respected, too. Subjects should be studied on their own terms, or, as Bishop Stubbs put it, 'historically',[2] rather than in ways which might be suggested by the language and thought of the present day. Indeed, for the more extreme advocates of a return to the 'traditional' school syllabus, like Sheila Lawlor, the deputy director of the Policy Studies Institute, the merest touch of the contemporary contaminates.

Despite these cautions, we are in fact constantly reinterpreting the past in the light of the present, and indeed, like conservationists and restorationists in other spheres, reinventing it. The angle of vision is inescapably contemporary, however remote the object in view. Even when we reproduce words and phrases verbatim, the resonances are those of our time. However faithfully we document a period and steep ourselves in the sources, we cannot rid ourselves of afterthought. However jealously we protect the integrity of our subject matter, we cannot insulate it from ourselves.

History is an argument about the past, as well as the record of it, and its terms are forever changing, sometimes under the influence of developments in adjacent fields of thought, sometimes – as with the sea-change in attitudes which followed the First World War[3] – as a result of politics. Historical research, in the hands (quite often) of self-proclaimed revisionists, is continually putting old and established markers into question. Explanations, greeted at the time as 'authoritative', now

appear as contrived or beside the point. The plot thickens with fresh
characters and previously undeveloped motifs. Forgotten episodes are
exhumed. Old stories are given a new twist. Attention is drawn to
hitherto unnoticed clues. What previously seemed momentous may now
appear as no more than a passing interlude. Conversely, apparently
trivial events are elevated to the status of precedents and treated as
portents and signs.

The immaculate conception of knowledge – with its insistence on
keeping inquiry within the boundaries of the discipline, and its refusal
to countenance any traffic between the imaginary and the real – is
impossible, in practice, to sustain. There are to begin with the silences
and gaps in the written record which only inference can fill: the
statements to be ventured, if only for the sake of a continuous narrative,
which a thousand different instances would not prove. Even when we are
immersed in the minutiae of empirical research, we are continually
having to abandon the world of hard, verifiable fact for the more pliable
one of interpretation and conjecture, 'an unsatisfactory world peopled
with rogue elements', as Linda Hannas writes in a fascinating account of
her attempt to piece together the underworld of mid-Victorian popular
art.[4]

In folk cultures – those which depend on the storyteller for knowledge
of the past – the distinction between the ordinary and the fabulous is
difficult to maintain. 'The lives of living men turned into legend,' writes
Edwin Muir of his Orkney boyhood:

> A man I knew once sailed out in a boat to look for a mermaid, and claimed
> afterwards that he had talked with her. Fantastic feats of strength were
> commonly reported. Fairies, or 'fairicks', as they were often called, were
> encountered dancing on the sands on moonlight nights. From people's talk
> they were small, graceful creatures about the size of leprechauns, but pretty,
> not grotesque. There was no harm in them. All these things have vanished
> from Orkney in the last fifty years under the pressure of compulsory
> education.[5]

The earliest historians were forgers – or, to use a less loaded term,
inventors. They put words into the mouths of their subjects – as Caesar
did with Vercingetorix in *De Bello Gallico*, and Tacitus with Boadicea.
Indeed the composition of historic speeches – such as Pericles' oration
to the Athenians – was the first of Clio's arts. History, under this optic,
was an exercise in rhetoric. It was also regarded as a branch of literature
– albeit, according to Aristotle's *Poetics*, an inferior one. What distinguished the historian from the annalist was literary ambition. Where
the latter, such as the local historians of Attica,[6] were concerned with
collecting genealogical information or topographical facts, the historian

constructed a complete narrative.[7] Herodotus, 'the father of history', has always been to his critics, from Thucydides onwards, 'the father of lies', filling his narrative with miraculous and extraordinary stories.[8] But even Thucydides, the historians' historian, who eschews the wondrous and the picturesque and cleaves to what he claims he actually witnessed, had no compunction about imputing motives to the protagonists of his drama, or composing speeches for them to utter. F.M. Cornford in *Thucydides Mythistoricus*[9] (1907) argued that speeches were more promi-nent in Thucydides than in Herodotus because he was an Athenian; and that they had been dramatically conceived by the author, in line with Aeschylean tragedy, to express character and ideals. Thucydides himself was quite open about his rhetorical strategy: 'As to the accounts given of themselves by the several parties in speeches, either on the eve of the war or when they were already engaged, it would be hard to reproduce the exact language used, whether I heard it myself or it was reported to me by others. The speeches as they stand represent what, in my opinion was most necessary to be said by the several speakers about the matter in question ... and I have kept as closely as possible to the general sense of what was said.'

Arguably the true architects of record-based research – and certainly among the first to make a fetish of manuscript sources – were those medieval forgers, who used their writerly skills and their historical knowledge to create ideal pedigrees and produce the documents which ought, by rights, to have been there but which, perhaps because of over-reliance on oral tradition, were not. 'The figment was hardly dis-tinguished from the reality', writes Gurevich. 'What seemed "due" or "fitting" was readily preferred to what was.'[10]

Both lay and clerical institutions had recourse to forgery when their antiquity needed to be established; when their privileges were in question; or when their title to property had to be defended against would-be predators. It seems to have been the monks who practised the most elaborate frauds, though when it came to claims to an impossible antiquity the universities were not far behind.[11] In England, M.T. Clanchy argues in *From Memory to Written Record*, the growth of legal documentation went hand in hand with a multiplication of mythical charters. The years after the Norman conquest, when old titles of every kind were in question, was also the golden age of the forger; and it seems that, so far as monastic charters are concerned, authentic documents may have been the exception rather than the rule.[12] Bede's *Ecclesiastical History of the English People* provided them with a convincing historical background. 'They did not appeal to it to provide specific precedents relevant to the points at issue', writes Antonia Gransden. '... Indeed, had they been able to do so, they might not have considered forgery necessary ... rather they borrowed phrases with the intention of making the style of their spurious documents appropriate to the time when they were supposed to have been written.'[13]

One of the most ambitious of these forgeries, and certainly the one with the greatest influence on our own day, because without it the New Age travellers and the eco-freaks would be without their central shrine, was that perpetrated by the monks of Glastonbury. Lacking both a detailed foundation story and famous relics, they commissioned William of Malmesbury, the finest of the twelfth-century scholars, to provide them with a pedigree. By dint of remarkable quasi-archaeological exploration, he was able to date the foundation of the abbey to the seventh century, and to claim that St Patrick, the patron saint of Ireland, was among its early visitors. The monks, not content with this, set about embellishing the story, first by converting Glastonbury into St Patrick's burial place; then, in 1191, by exhuming the supposed bodies of King Arthur and Queen Guinevere, using them as proof that Glastonbury had been Camelot; finally, and most enduringly, discovering that it had a pre-history in New Testament times, and that in AD 63 it had been visited by Joseph of Arimathea.[14]

Historical illustration is another field in which forgery, or knowledge-based invention, could be said to have set the pace. Francis Haskell in *History and Its Images* pays tribute to the 'remarkable quality of many of those forgeries', in the case of the spuriously Roman coins on which Renaissance numismatists called when initiating the study of classical antiquity. Seventeenth-century historical portraits, sometimes engraved from medals and coins but quite often, it seems, an artist's impression drawn from surviving word pictures, are also (Haskell shows) after their own fashion testimonies to historical knowledge, even if they can be technically classed as fakes. 'In the sixteenth and seventeenth centuries many publishers of grandiose and apparently fanciful portrait collections went out of their way to emphasise the meticulous nature of their researches and to make clear that it was "not without the expense of great labour, trouble and money" that they had explored "seals, monuments, statues, paintings and books" in their determination to reproduce genuine likenesses.'[15]

Historians today don't knowingly forge documents. But by the nature of our trade we are continually having to fabricate contexts. We may not construct imaginary speeches in the manner of Thucydides, but by selective quotation we can make subjects give expression to what we believe to be their innermost being. We make extravagant claims for the importance of our subject, and strain interpretation to secure the maximum effect. Footnotes serve as fetishes and are given as authorities for generalizations which a thousand different instances would not prove. We suppress the authorial 'I' so that the evidence appears to speak for itself. We improve on the original, making connections to cover the gaps in the story, the silences in the evidence. Our pictures, apparently seamless, are so artfully framed and carefully composed, that the historian's gaze imposes itself. We may not go in for hagiography, as our medieval predecessors did, but we are not averse to touching up our portraits; giving a star turn to hitherto unnoticed characters; and crediting our heroes or heroines with genius. Like the Anglo-Norman monks we are adept at simulating antique effects, using the language and idiom of the original documents even though the template of analysis and the descriptive categories are our own – as when a seventeenth-century rhetoric of order and degree is used to illustrate twentieth-century understanding of class.

History is an allegorical as well as – in intention at least – a mimetic art. Where others, such as antiquarians or archaeologists, *collect* facts, we pride ourselves, as our predecessors did, on *arranging* them.[16] The lifelike detail on which we pride ourselves is there not so much as documentary proof but rather as a gauge of authenticity. Real events double in the character of turning points, symbolic moments when all things are made anew. Like allegorists, historians are adept at discovering a hidden or half-hidden order. We find occult meanings in apparently simple truths, revelations in seemingly mundane happenings. We claim the right to treat relics as emblems and thought as paradigmatic. We use numbers in magical ways, to give form and shape to our tale-types, turning dyads into romantic contraries, and triads into totalities.[17] We also exercise the allegorist's freedom in drawing promiscuously on whatever materials come to hand. The historian's reading of the evidence is necessarily an act of interpretation, abstracting nuggets of information and relocating them in novel surroundings. Often it involves juxtaposing wildly different orders of evidence to establish a problematic, as in those *crises de subsistence* which a Depression-bred generation of historians hypothesized as the progenitor, or catalyst, of phenomena as various as the religious wars of the seventeenth century, the outbreak of the French Revolution, and the fiasco of the 1848 Chartist Demonstration on Kennington Common.[18]

In another way of looking at it, the historian's 'reading' of the evidence could be seen as an essay in make-believe, a way of dressing up fragments to make them look like meaningful wholes – rather as animatronics produces a *tableau vivant* of the museum exhibit. Or it could be seen as an exercise in the story-teller's arts, relying heavily on the expectation of continuity and using a battery of devices to heighten what Roland Barthes calls the 'reality effect'.[19] The art of historical writing is that of making a master narrative out of chaos. The synthesis by which we set such store, when sketching in a background, aims to cover the entire work in the field. Our classifications and taxonomies – the bedrock of the social-science history of the 1960s, as of the economic history which preceded it – are all-inclusive. Our categories make individuals into representative types. We give an ordered sequence, with a beginning, a middle and an end, to events which to the participants themselves may have seemed quite random.

The language of history, so far from being a simple medium for the transmission of fact, intercepts meaning, giving fixity and definition to what in the documents is elliptical or opaque. It animates description, conjuring evocative detail from unpromising sources. It reifies figures of speech. It anthropomorphizes the historian's own categories. Period labels (referring more, in their current usage, to the past of interior decorators than to monarchical reigns) are used to personify eras. Abstractions such as 'the nation' or 'women' masquerade as real-life historical actors and are credited with a mind and will of their own – the historian's equivalent of that pathetic fallacy which John Ruskin identified in mid-Victorian art. Age cohorts, in the hands of historical demographers, also acquire individual characteristics – now wreaking a Malthusian revenge on their straightened conditions of existence by delaying marriage or limiting family size; now breaking out in Dionysiac frenzies, as in that spectacular rise in the bastardy rates in eighteenth-century Europe which so fascinates students of the family.

Economic historians, perhaps to atone for the bleakness of their preoccupations, seem particularly prone to anthropomorphize their subject matter, adopting an 'ages and stages' view of the life-cycle, and picturing a whole series of genetic transformations which carry the economy from a state of childhood innocence to one of world-weary senescence. At one end of the time-scale there is a new attention to the 'birth' of consumerism (variously ascribed to the 1590s, the 1730s and the 1880s), at the other there is a morbid awareness of the symptoms of decay. 'Climacteric', when referring to women a euphemism for meno-pause, is annexed to the scholarly lexicon, and given the symbolic space which was occupied by 'watersheds' and 'turning points' in the school textbooks of yesteryear. 'Proto-industrialization', the subject of a rich literature in the past twenty years, becomes a kind of adolescent or teenage stage of a nation's life-cycle.[20]

Our time-reckonings, too, though apparently adopted for purposes of expository commonsense, occupy an imaginative as well as a chrono-logical space. Dates, as well as offering mnemonic devices to the teacher, and precise locations to the stickler for accuracy, also serve as choreo-graphic devices; investing events with dramatic and historical pattern; characterizing and ordering what might otherwise seem formless; and creating the space in which notions of linear progression can have free play.[21]

One might think of those three- and four-stage models of human development which from the time of the ancient Greeks have provided narrative history with its symbolic framework[22] and in particular the tripartite division between 'ancient', 'medieval' and 'modern' history which, appearing first in the 1470s, with the term *medium aevum*, has been seemingly untouched by subsequent development.[23] (Such neologisms as 'early modern', a coinage which is now routinely applied to the entire stretch of history which separates the Renaissance and the French Revolution, have helped to keep it intact.) In another register, where history deals in millennia rather than centuries or decades, geological time, with its story of how man became a giant, inescapably supports the notion of history as a forward march.

Historians may no longer subscribe, as their Evangelical and Catholic forebears did, to a doctrine of the Fall, but a secularized version of it might be thought to underpin a whole series of dualisms which oppose past and present, or before and after, in terms of some prelapsarian social state. The idea of theodicy, of some large design which the individual event illustrates, also enjoys a vigorous after-life. We are continually fastening on symptoms of decline or precocious instances which foreshadow the shape of things to come.[24] Current enthusiasm for the study of the transgressive, and in particular those carnivalesque occasions when the world turns upside down, encourages a quest for moments when the social order is apparently dissolved and, as in the revolutionist's utopia, all things have to be made anew.

Some of history's key terms are theological in origin. The division of historical time into centuries was, it seems, the invention or discovery of some Lutheran pastors of the 1530s.[25] Quite apart from numbers-mysticism – an inescapable component of history's classificatory schema – it might be chastening to monitor the continuing influence of the medieval Christian idea of 'the great chain of being'. Arthur Lovejoy has shown how this influenced the heavenly city of the eighteenth-century philosophers;[26] it might be no less germane to our taken-for-granted notions of trends, patterns and processes.

Residues of Judeo-Christian theology, with its eschatological sense of a final end, could be seen as the ghostly presence in historical notions of destiny and ideas of historically inevitability; and in those unspoken teleologies which see a progress from lower to higher things, or, more pessimistically, a free fall from an originally virtuous state. History may no longer serve expressly prophetic purposes as it did in the Middle Ages,[27] or in early Protestant propaganda,[28] but it does not seem fanciful to see evidence of its continuing imaginative appeal in our liking for portents, albeit retrospective, of the shape of things to come, in our 'idolatry of origins' and in our penchant for discovering eternity in a grain of sand. Thus, to take some examples of prolepsis from recently influential work, a cat massacre in 1730s Paris becomes, in Robert Darnton's extravagant treatment of it, a dress rehearsal for the French Revolution;[29] the 'Machiavellian moment' of Lucrezia Borgia's Florence prefigures the public service ethic and even the coming of the Welfare State;[30] sixteenth-century magic precociously anticipates modern science.

The first history of the English people – Bede's – was an ecclesiastical one, a narrative of missionaries and saints rather than monarchs, and having as its climacteric not some mighty battle or famous conquest but a synod of the Church. In the historical establishment's hiving off of 'Roman Britain' into a subject of separate study – or, in the case of the Oxford history syllabus, its elimination – it is possible to see Bede's original perception at work: the English only became English when they converted to Christianity.[31] In a more Protestant vein one might wonder whether there are not residues of ancient religious battles in the fact that, in all the received versions of the national past, 'modern' Britain begins at the time of the Reformation. Religion has left its mark on apocryphal history too. It seems that one of the most famous incidents in national history – the story of King Canute and the waves – was a monkish parable, designed to prove that kings were made of the common clay; the story of Alfred and the burnt cakes has apparently a similar origin.[32]

Record-based history – with its famous names and dates, causes and effects, and progression from point to point – has always had to compete with rival narratives which attempt to tell the story of the past in different ways. There is to begin with the timeless past of tradition; the 'once upon a time'; the 'good old days' (or 'hard times') of popular memory. Then there are the legendary histories dramatized in the folk-play, the dressing-up games, the public pageants and rituals. In a no-man's land, epistemologically speaking, are those parables which, by dint of constant repetition, have come to be accepted as true, and which indeed furnish many of the high points in our island story, from fables about the likely burial place of Boadicea to that of Dunkirk, and the alleged rescue of the British army by a flotilla of pleasure-boats. Here are the stories that had graved themselves in the memory of an early-twentieth-century Stockport hat-maker:

JOHN BARRATT   I know very little of jovial John's career at Canal Street. I know he was here as warehouse boy with my father a short time. If one thinks of a person living or dead of this age or any other, we always fancy some personal appearance and action. Julius Caesar crowned with laurel and his baton in his hand, or else at the head of his Romans, sword in hand just landing on our shores; Wm. Tell has his bow, and is about to shoot at the apple on the head of his son; or else he is leaping from the boat at Altorf; Huss and others are being unpleasantly roasted; Napoleon is standing with folded arms at Helena, or he is on horseback leading his soldiers over the Alps; and lastly John Barratt when at Canal Street always appears to me with a brush in his hand sweeping the old warehouse floor under the very clock which is now hung on J. Fox's room! For years he has now been our head-traveller![33]

It seems likely that notions of the olden days have always been made up of promiscuous elements, with words and things, perhaps, pulling in opposite directions, local traditions and family lore marking their own narrative, and so far as 'our island story' is concerned, a mixture of real-life and apocryphal events. So far as the learning process is concerned, the young Samuel Bamford cannot have been alone in reading the penny history chap-books as though they were true; in believing in 'boggarts' (the Lancashire word for ghosts); and in putting legendary figures on a par with historically recognized ones.[34]

Sacred history, as it was taught in nineteenth-century Bible classes, had the closest affinities, pedagogically speaking, to national history, using mnemonic devices to enable children to learn the Kings of Israel off by heart, much as if they had been Tudors and Plantagenets, making constant reference to maps of the Holy Land (sacred geography), and even – under the influence of nineteenth-century social Romanticism – making a feature of scenes from everyday life. 'Places', 'Customs', 'Arts', 'Antiquities', 'Natural History' and 'Poems on the Subjects of History' figures alongside Holy Writ in Charles Baker's 1860 *Bible Class for Schools, Teachers and Families*, with upwards of a hundred wood-cuts, 'chiefly referring to the manners and customs of the Orientals' to explicate the text. A chronological index preceded the text, and a general index to the notes and poems followed.[35]

Joseph Barker, a sometime Chartist and later an independent minister in the West Riding, has left an autobiographical account of how, as a boy, he negotiated these different histories:

The first book I remember to have read was the Bible. I read it chiefly as a book of history, and was very greatly delighted with many of its stories. The effect which it had upon my mind at this early period I can scarcely recollect, but one effect was to lead me to regard miracles as nothing improbable, and another was to impress upon my mind the doctrine of one God, the creator, upholder, and governor of all things, the ruler, the judge, and the rewarder of mankind, and to strengthen in my mind the sense of right and duty.

The next book that I remember to have read was Bunyan's Pilgrim's Progress. I regarded that book also as a history. I had no idea that it was a parable or an allegory. My impression was, that the whole was literal and true,

– that there was, somewhere in the world, a real City of Destruction and a New Jerusalem, and that from the one to the other there was a path through some part of the country, just such a pathway as that which Bunyan represents his pilgrim as treading. And, as I have said before, I often used to wish that I could find that way to heaven. One of the next books that I read was a History of Joseph, a work written in a similar style to that of Klopstock's Messiah or Milton's Paradise Lost, being partly fiction and partly truth. But I regarded that also as a true story. I had no idea at that time that people could write and print anything in the form of a history, that was not real matter of fact. I was naturally a firm believer in all that was gravely spoken or printed ...

Some time after this I began to be fond of another kind of book. I read with great greediness all the fairy tales I could get hold of, and any kind of wild and foolish romances. I also read the tales of Baron Munchausen, A Thousand Notable Things, The Oddest of all Oddities, and a number of similar productions. I read all, in fact, that came in my way, and that with great greediness. I then got hold of the Life and Adventures of Robin Hood, Blind Jack of Knaresborough, Eugene Aram, Mary Bateman, and some other stories of remarkable persons or great thieves and highwaymen. A little earlier than this, perhaps, I read Robinson Crusoe. But that also I regarded as a true story. I had no idea at the time I read Robinson Crusoe, that there were such things as novels, works of fiction, in existence. I liked Robinson Crusoe very much till I came towards the latter part, and then I began to be weary.[36]

In Elizabethan England, at the dawn of record-based research, there were some half-a-dozen alternative versions of the past on offer. There was to begin with the legendary history of Geoffrey of Monmouth and the *Brut* Chronicles which, until the 1590s and notwithstanding the damaging criticism of Polydore Virgil, remained the received version of the national past.[37] Then there were the ecclesiastical histories, notably Foxe's *Acts and Monuments*, chained to the pulpit alongside the *Book of Common Prayer*, and Knox's *History of the Reformation*, which were at once key texts for Protestant propaganda and also in some sort paradigms for the philosophical histories of the Enlightenment.[38] In a quite different imaginative realm were the 'chorographies', devoted to the descriptions and delineation of place. Those who read them (Helgerson writes) had a much better grounding than those who relied on the chronicle histories. The chronicle was 'almost by definition', the story of kings. The chorographers told of locality. 'In them England is Devonshire, Stafford, and York; Stratton Hundred, Cripplegate Wood, and the Diocese of Rochester ... loyalty to England here means loyalty to the land, to its counties, cities, towns, villages, manors, and wards, even to its uninhabited geographical features.'[39] In yet another sphere, there were the chap-book histories, and the 'artisan' novels of Thomas Deloney,[40] which introduced such male Cinderellas as Jack of Newbury, the supposed wool brogger, and Dick Whittington, the apprentice boy who became Lord Mayor of London – a new type of hero, the poor boy made good, to replace the giants and giant-killers of ancient lore. Lastly, reference might be made to history on stage, both the chronicle plays of Shakespeare and Marlowe, and the mummers' plays which, according to some recent scholars, began life as adaptations of the chap-books.[41]

In the nineteenth century there were any number of competing histories on offer, ranging – if war and peace were to be the measure – from such ultra-bellicose, and hugely popular, 'drum-and-trumpet' histories as Edward Creasy's *Fifteen Decisive Battles of the World* (a book which seems to have been continually in print from its publication in the 1850s down to the First World War) to such expressively-named primers as G. Pitt's *History of England with the Wars Left Out*, which reached a third edition in 1893. The cribs themselves were by no means all of a piece, but might be written in as many as half a dozen voices, with the history of manners and morals serving as some kind of counterweight to that of constitutional developments or genealogical descent.[42] Likewise in the school anthologies and readers, heroic lays, such as those of Lord Macaulay and Mrs Hemans, with their invitation to an epical sense of the past, were printed cheek-by-jowl with word-pictures of old-time country life.

The notion of history as a self-contained 'discipline', or separate subject, is a comparatively recent one, dating perhaps only from the professionalization of writing and research between the wars. Local history – a term which seems only to have entered common usage in the 1920s – was in its nineteenth-century development quite largely in the hands of ecclesiologists studying the fabric of the church, and naturalists monitoring flora and fauna. Likewise the history of everyday things, adopted as a flagship of 'learning by doing' in the progressive ped- agogies of the 1970s, was in its earlier phases the province of Jonathan Oldbuck-like antiquarians. When, for instance, William Francis Collier, a prolific author of mid-Victorian school histories, wanted to follow the example of Macaulay's Chapter III and offer passages on *mores*, he drew on the researches of 'eminent antiquarians like Thomas Wright';[43] following this up, in 1865, with a fully-fledged *Tales of Old English Life, or Pictures of the Period*, which combined real-life characters and fictional narratives, using imaginary dialogue but drawing on 'the most recent results of antiquarian research' and making a feature of minuteness of commonplace detail.[44]

In the nineteenth century, history was conventionally regarded as a branch of literature, inferior indeed to poetry, but on a par with oratory and definitely superior to the mere entertainment of the novel or the comedy of manners. Sir Walter Scott, the great architect of historical realism, drew his characters and his leading incidents – even the most melodramatic of them, like the wedding night of *The Bride of Lammermoor* – from living memory and family lore, making a great point, in the prefaces and the annotations, of how they corresponded to oral tradition. His dialogue was no less beholden – even in its archaisms – to living speech.

'Literary' historians – those men of letters, scholar–radicals and Victorian sages who cut such a great figure in the columns of the periodical press – began to come under attack in the 1870s, when history schools established themselves in the ancient universities and the subject was marked out as an apprenticeship in statecraft.[45] The attack was renewed in the 1930s when a generation of hard-nosed professionals took on the 'Whig' interpretation of history and set about waging war on the gentleman-amateur. It was carried to new heights in the postwar turn to cliometrics: for the economic historians of the 1950s, virtually any non-quantifiable class of evidence was liable to be given the pejorative label of 'literary' and 'impressionistic'. Yet the 'literary' remains an inescapable component of history's appeal and of its practice. It is not difficult, for instance, to see the influence of modern Gothic in the current scholarly enthusiasm for the study of the marvellous,[46] while the beauties of the horrid may be not the least of the reasons for the vast new historical literature on thanatology, the renewed scholarly (and feminist) interest in witchcraft,[47] and the spate of writing on such saturnalian occasions as public hangings.[48] In another register, micro-history and today's insistence on the small detail of everyday life might be aligned to the grainy realism of new-wave writing and photography in the 1960s or even to an Audenesque excitement in juxtaposing the epic and the everyday.

When Jean Bodin, in 1566, set out his *Method for the Easy Comprehension of History* – still an attractive read – he distinguished three classes of narration: the first concerned man, the second nature, the third God.[49] Natural history tended to be subsumed in what came to be called 'natural philosophy' or 'natural theology', and when it entered the schoolroom it was apt to appear under the label of biology – though a minority of county historians, following the example of Robert Plot's *Natural History of Staffordshire* addressed themselves to flora and fauna. The field clubs and natural history societies of the nineteenth century – liberal it seems in outlook, where the antiquarians were Tory – had a prosperous local following; as did the museums movement, which put natural curiosities on display.[50] But history with a capital 'H', even the social history of J.R. Green and Lord Macaulay, took off in quite other directions.

Today, natural history is a growing point in both archive-based and archaeological research, and it is possible to imagine a state in which the historical study of man and that of nature will once again be, as it was apparently in Bodin's time, coeval. Keith Thomas's *Man and the Natural World* (1983), a book which, from the point of view of history as a specialist discipline, came from nowhere, put the matter on the agenda of scholarly inquiry.[51] Still more pertinent would be the rise of conservationist sentiment, and the new awareness of the natural world as an environment at risk.

As with any new departure in higher research, the turn to natural history – or the return of it – was no doubt over-determined. It owed something to the new arboriculture of the 1960s, and indeed Oliver Rackham, the most widely read of the new ecologically minded historians, has been a leading figure in the campaign to rescue ancient woodland.[52] Animal rights campaigners could claim the credit for creating a climate of opinion in which the study of the horse-drawn society of nineteenth-century Britain,[53] or of the demographic explosion among fourteenth-century rabbits[54] can be accepted as a legitimate, indeed innovative, subject for higher research. Friends of the Earth, and such newly-formed organizations as the Soil Association, are giving a new lease of life to that study of the landscape which professors Hoskins and Beresford established in the 1940s as the very basis for local history. And it is possible – the matter is necessarily speculative – that hunt saboteurs may have been indirectly responsible for that horrified fascination which historians of the British Empire are currently giving to the murderous field-sports of the empire-builders in Africa and British India.[55]

It is arguable that myth, or what F.M. Cornford called 'Mythistoricus' – a history cast in a mould of conception, 'whether artistic or philosophic', which, 'long before the work was contemplated' was already 'inwrought into the very structure of the author's mind'[56] – is immanent in any historical work. Typically we conflate a great mass of evidence to illustrate or to exemplify relatively simple truths – the classical procedure of the allegorist. Our whole effort is to discover a logic or pattern in seemingly quite fortuitous associations; to give meaning and draw lessons from what might otherwise be a quite random sequence of events. In the terms proposed by Vladimir Propp in his morphology of folk-lore, our narratives conform to 'tale-types'.

The nineteenth century, which saw the growth of the idea of 'scientific' history,[57] was also a prolific source of new historical legends. One might refer to the frequency of those two-, three-, four-, or (in Marx's case) five-stage theories of historical development which offered a modernist update of the medieval and pre-medieval Four Ages of Man. Or one might look at nineteenth-century popularizations of apocrypha, such as the story of William Tell, in Sunday School prize books. In France the *mythe celtique* – memorably represented, for radical readers, in

Eugène Sue's *Histoire d'une famille prolétaire à travers les ages* – would be worth attending to. In Britain the idea of Merrie England, which appears in the pages of Cobbett and Carlyle as a paradise lost, and in graphic art as a bucolic alternative to the severities of a commercial civilization, has a large documentation waiting to be pieced together in the manner of the cult of chivalry in Mark Girouard's *Return to Camelot.*

Closely related to this one might instance the nineteenth-century discovery of such figures of national myth as Boadicea, who disappeared from the records for a thousand years and who only really came into her own in Victorian times,[58] or (one of Michelet's additions to the democratic pantheon) Joan of Arc.[59] In another sphere, drawing on the word-books of the county dialect societies, or the 'Notes and Queries' corners in the provincial newspapers, one could look at the legends which grew up around place names; the rise of the workplace ghost (the Victorian coalface seems to have been full of them); and the diffusion of those newly-minted local traditions which arose in the wake of environmental and social change. The popularity of *The Ingoldsby Legends* – a Victorian bestseller, with a strong cult following – might be interesting here, drawing as it did on Kentish lore, and offering a kind of Home Counties version of Sir Walter Scott's *Minstrelsy of the Scottish Borders*, while at the same time laying claim to that rib-tickling space which in the 1840s and 1850s seems to have been reserved for comic histories.[60]

> The World, according to the best geographers, is divided into Europe, Asia, Africa, America and Romney Marsh. In this last named and fifth quarter of the globe, a Witch may still be occasionally discovered in favourable, i.e. stormy, seasons, weathering Dungeness Point in an egg-shell, or careering on her broom-stick over Dymchurch Wall.

History has always been a hybrid form of knowledge, syncretizing past and present, memory and myth, the written record and the spoken word. Its subject matter is promiscuous, as the almanacks printed as a frontispiece to this volume may suggest. In popular memory, if not in high scholarship, the great flood or the freak storm may eclipse wars, battles and the rise and fall of governments. As a form of communication, history finds expression not only in chronicle and commentary but also ballad and song, legends and proverbs, riddles and puzzles. Church liturgies have carried one version of it – sacred history; civic ritual another. A present-day inventory would need to be equally alert to the memory work performed (albeit unintentionally) by the advertisers, and to the influence of tourism, home tourism especially. As a self-conscious art, history begins with monuments and inscriptions, and as the record of the built environment suggests, not the least of the influences changing historical consciousness today is the writing on the walls. The influence of video-games and science-fiction would be no less pertinent in trying to explain why the idea of chronological reversal, or time travelling, has become a normal way of engaging with the idea of the past.

History owes much of its vitality to parallel movements in literature and politics. In Renaissance France, as in Jacobean England, its fortunes were closely bound up with those of jurisprudence and indeed to follow the researches of Donald R. Kelley, it seems that discussion of the origins and nature of feudalism goes back to scholarly debates among sixteenth-century lawyers. In the schools, history has often been associated with what was called, in Edwardian Britain, 'civics'. In the 1920s, when there was a determined attempt in the schools to promote One Worldism, it was closely bound up with League of Nations Union idealism; while in its new-found enthusiasm for the history of everyday things it was no less beholden to a kind of Thames Valley, or Cotswolds, Little Englandism.

Beyond such cultural borrowings, or syncretism, there is the matter of the politics of history which, by a kind of return of the repressed, is now an inescapable element in any discussion of pedagogy or research. The influence of feminism which, in the space of twenty years, has driven a sociology from the field, destabilized, or destroyed, Labour history, and put all our taken-for-granted social categories into question, hardly needs arguing, though in the field of political history it still seems possible for all-male platforms of academics to assemble. Particularly subversive, and particularly fruitful, at the time of writing, is gay history, which takes the whole of the human condition for its province and finds as much sustenance in the Dark Ages as in modern times. Its intuitive feel for, and interest in, the world of appearances, and readiness to take this seriously, makes it peculiarly a scholarship of our time, as does its natural sympathy for the forbidden and the transgressive.

At a time when numbers in higher education are expanding; when whole new constituencies of research are forming outside the academy; and when questions of individual and collective identity are making history a front-line subject in the schools, it would be absurd for historians to abandon the field of moral and political argument; to attempt to return to history with a capital 'H' – i.e. a single master narrative – or to try to retreat to the cloistered seclusion of a library carrel.

Notes

1. Lord Acton, Letter to Contributors to the Cambridge Modern History, 12 March 1898, in William H. MacNeill, ed., *Essays in the Liberal Interpretations of History*, Chicago 1967, pp. 397–9.

2. W. Stubbs, *Two Lectures on the Present State and Prospects of Historical Study*, Oxford, 1876.

3. There is some discussion of this in my 'Continuous National History' in R. Samuel, ed., *Patriotism*, London 1989, vol. I.

4. Linda Hannas, *The English Jigsaw Puzzle: 1760–1890*, London 1972.

5. Edwin Muir, *An Autobiography*, London 1954, p. 14.

6. Lionel Pearson, *The Local Historians of Attica*, American Philological Association, 1981.

7. G.A. Press, *The Development of the Idea of History in Antiquity*, Montreal, 1982, p. 45.

8. M.I. Finley, 'Myth, Memory and History', *History and Theory*, IV, 1964–5, pp. 281–302; John Gould, *Herodotus*, London 1989, is an excellent introduction. J.A.S. Evans, *Herodotus, Explorer of the Past*, Princeton 1991; and Rosalind Thomas, *Oral Tradition and Written Record in Classical Athens*, Cambridge 1990, for the relationship of Herodotus to eye-witness and oral testimony. 'Herodotus and the Invention of History', *Arethusa*, vol. 20, nos 1 & 2, 1987, for the relation to legend and epic.

9. F.M. Cornford, *Thucydides Mythistoricus*, Oxford 1907. Anthony Grafton, *Forgers and Critics; Creativity and Duplicity in Western Scholarship*, Princeton 1990, pp. 8–15 is a more simple-minded discussion of this phenomenon.

10. A. Gurevich, *Categories of Medieval Thought*, London 1985, p. 179.

11. Oxford claimed King Alfred as its founder; Cambridge the legendary King Arthur. Ibid., pp. 177–8.

12. M.T. Clanchy, *From Memory to Written Record: England, 1066–1307*, London 1979, pp. 248–9.

13. A. Gransden, 'Bede's Reputation as an Historian in Medieval England', in *Legends, Traditions and History in Medieval England*, London 1992, p. 15.

14. A. Gransden, 'The Growth of the Glastonbury Traditions and Legends in the Twelfth Century', in ibid., pp. 152–79. William of Malmesbury's *De Antiquitate Glastoniensis Ecclesiae* did come up with some remarkable visual evidence about seventh-century church-building on this site, which twentieth-century excavation has confirmed. Ibid., p. 160, quoting a 1963 paper by Joan and Harold Taylor. See *Glastonbury: Ancient Avalon, New Jerusalem*, ed. Anthony Roberts, London 1978, for a modern zodiacal account.

15. Francis Haskell, *History and Its Images: Art and the Interpretation of the Past*, London 1993, pp. 21, 31–5, 46, 53, 59.

16. The distinction and contrast was made by Thomas Hodgkin in an address to the Historical Section of the Archaeological Institute in 1891. Philippa Levine, *The Amateur and the Professional: Historians and Archaeologists in Victorian England, 1838–1886*, Cambridge 1986, p. 91.

17. On numbers mysticism, Umberto Eco, *Art and Beauty in the Middle Ages*, New Haven 1986, p. 35.

18. Originally a medical term, 'crisis' was first adopted as a way of characterizing the social and political order in the aftermath of the 1914–18 war. Winston Churchill, in *World Crisis*, his extended history of the war, used the term as a metaphor for the break-up of the old Empires, and the appearance in the East of an alien force. Lenin, in his prophetic *Imperialism* (1916) saw the war as heralding a 'general crisis' of capitalism. Imperialism was not only the highest stage of capitalism, it was also the last. The Communist International sat out the 'relative stabilization' of the 1920s, waiting for 'the final crisis' to take its bow. The great crash of 1929, the rise of fascism, and the renewed threat of war, seemed to confirm these apocalyptic imaginings. Huizinga's *Waning of the Middle Ages*, published in the very shadow of the Great War – a dazzling account of chivalry in its decadence – was perhaps the first work by a professional historian to take crisis (the 'decay of overripe forms of civilisation') as the theme of its narrative; in the 1930s, his insights were complemented by a new awareness, among economic and social historians, of the Malthusian elements in the population crisis of the fourteenth century; a little later K.B. MacFarlane in England and Edouard Perroy in France related the Hundred Years War to a supposed crisis in seigneurial revenues. By 1946, when Robert Boutruche's *Crise d'une société* was published – a study of the late-medieval Bordelais – all the elements were in place for the historical discovery of a 'feudal crisis'. It was the work of Ernest Labrousse on the economic collapse

which allegedly precipitated the downfall of the *ancien régime* which implanted the word 'crisis' in the historian's lexicon. In the 1950s it was adopted by the journal *Past and Present*. Eric Hobsbawm, in the lead article of what proved to be a sustained controversy, argued that there was a 'general crisis' in seventeenth-century Europe, representing for late feudalism an analogous set of contradictions to those which (Marxists believed) were hastening the decay of capitalism. Hobsbawm drew together under a single optic the English Civil War of 1642–49, the French Fronde, and the near contemporaneous Wars of Religion in Germany. The thesis won support from a formidable group of historians, though Hugh Trevor-Roper shifted the emphasis from the economy to religious fanaticism, while East European contributors argued that, east of the Elbe, the seventeenth-century 'crisis' had been followed by a *strengthening* of feudalism. Lawrence Stone's monumental *Crisis of the Aristocracy 1540–1640* – a kind of dance of death over England's *ancien régime* – is perhaps the most enduring English work written in a crisis idiom; Gareth Stedman Jones's much more sophisticated *Outcast London* (1973) – the 'crisis' of unskilled labour in 1889 – is arguably a late echo of it.

19. Roland Barthes, 'The Discourse of History', reprinted and translated in *Comparative Criticism* vol. 3, Cambridge 1981; 'L'Effet de réel', *Communications*, 2, 1968.

20. E.H. Phelps-Brown, 'The Climacteric of the 1890s; A Study in the Expanding Economy', *Oxford Economic Papers*, N.S., vol. 4, no. 3, October 1952; L.A. Clarkson, *Proto-Industrialisation, the First Stage of Industrialisation*, Basingstoke 1985, for a summary; Hans Medick, 'The Proto-Industrial Family Economy', in J.A. Chartres, ed., *Pre-Industrial Britain*, Oxford 1944; F. Mendels, 'Proto-industrialisation' in D.R.T. Jenkins, ed., *The Textile Industries*, Oxford 1994.

21. G.J. Whitrow, *Time in History: Views of Time from Prehistory to the Present Day*, Oxford 1990; G.J. Whitrow, *The Natural Philosophy of Time*, Oxford 1980; D.S. Landes, *Revolution in Time*, Cambridge, Mass. 1983; Norbert Elias, *Time: An Essay*, Oxford 1993; Stephen Hawking, *A Brief History of Time*, London 1989; Martin Heidegger, *A History of the Concept of Time*, Indiana 1985; R. Kosellek, *Futures Past: On the Semantics of Historical Time*, Cambridge, Mass. 1985.

22. Ronald Meek, *Social Science and the Ignoble Savage*, Cambridge 1976.

23. G.S. Gordon, *Medium Aevum and the Middle Ages*, Society for Pure English, Tract 19, London 1925, is a splendidly detailed aetiology; see also Peter Burke, *The Renaissance Sense of the Past*; E. Breisach, *Historiography; Ancient, Medieval and Modern*, Chicago 1983.

24. Raphael Samuel, 'Reading the Signs: 2', *History Workshop Journal*, 33, Spring 1992.

25. Denys Hay, *Annalists and Historians, Western Historiography from the VIIIth to the XVIII Century*, London 1977, p. 123.

26. Arthur Lovejoy, *The Great Chain of Being*, Cambridge, Mass. 1972.

27. R.W. Southern, 'Aspects of the European Tradition of Historical Writing: 3. History as Prophecy', *Transactions of the Royal Historical Society*, 5th series, 27, 1971, pp. 159 et seq.

28. *Foxe's Book of Martyrs*, that monument of Elizabethan historical scholarship, and for a century and more afterwards a primary medium of popular education, was, according to William Haller, the first 'Whig' history, picturing England as an 'elect' nation moving towards its appointed destiny, and substituting for medieval (and classical) notions of endless flux an altogether more modern one of progressive development. A similar affinity has recently been suggested between Knox's *History of the Reformation* and the Scottish 'philosophical' historians of the eighteenth century.

29. Robert Darnton, *The Great Cat Massacre*, Harmondsworth 1983; for some critical commentary, Harold Mah, 'Suppressing the Text', *History Workshop Journal*, 31, Spring 1991; Raphael Samuel, 'Reading the Signs. 2', *History Workshop Journal*, 33, Spring 1992; and the articles in *Journal of Modern History*, vol. 57, 1985, pp. 682–99; vol. 58, 1986, pp. 218–34; vol. 60, 1988, pp. 95–112.

30. J.G.A. Pocock, *The Machiavellian Moment: Florentine Political Thought and the Atlantic Republican Tradition*, Princeton 1975, has bred a vast number of epigones.

31. I am grateful to Professor Janet Nelson for this suggestion. Peter Hunter Blair, *The World of Bede*, Cambridge 1991, pp. 11–40, for Bede's view of England.

32. See the interesting discussion of this in Robert Birley, 'The Undergrowth of History', in *History*, 1961.

33. *The Chronicles of Canal Street*, Stockport 1922, pp. 14–15. For a nineteenth-century example, *The Royal Readers*, London 1872, vol. IV–V.

34. Samuel Bamford, *Early Days*, London 1849.

35. Charles Baker, *The Bible Class Book for Schools, Teachers and Families*, 2nd edn, London 1860.

36. *The Life of Joseph Barker, Written by Himself*, London 1880.

37. F.J. Levy, *Tudor Historical Thought*, San Marino 1967; Denys Hay, *Polydore Vergil*, Oxford 1952; *Annalists and Historians: Western Historiography from the VIIIth to the XVIIIth Century*, London 1977, pp. 118–22.

38. Mary Fearnly-Sander, 'Philosophical History and the Scottish Reformation: William Robertson and the Knoxian Tradition', *Historical Journal*, vol. XXXIII, no. 2, 1990, pp. 323–38.

39. Richard Helgerson, *Forms of Nationhood: Elizabethan Writing of England*, Chicago 1992.

40. Laura Caroline Stevenson, *Praise and Paradox: Merchants and Craftsmen in Elizabethan Popular Literature*, Cambridge 1984.

41. Ronald Hutton, *The Rise and Fall of Merry England: The Ritual Year, 1400–1700*, Oxford 1994, is a detailed new account.

42. J.C. Curtis, *A School and College History of England*, London 1960; W. Longman, *Lectures on the History of England*, London 1860–61.

43. William Francis Collier, *The History of England with a Sketch of Our Indian and Colonial Empire*, London 1864, p. v.

44. William Francis Collier, *Tales of Old English Life, or Pictures of the Periods*, Edinburgh 1868; Thomas Wright and Richard M. Dorson, *The British Folklorists: A History*, London 1968, pp. 61–6; *C.R. Smith's Retrospections*, Vol. I, London 1883, pp. 76–84.

45. Rosemary Jann, *The Art and Science of Victorian History*, Ohio 1986, p. 218.

46. Jacques Le Goff, 'The Marvelous', *The Medieval Imagination*, Chicago 1988. Ed. Joy Kenseth, *The Age of the Marvelous*, Chicago 1992.

47. Lyndal Roper, *Oedipus and the Devil, Witchcraft, Sexuality and Religion in Early Modern Europe*, London 1994.

48. Thomas W. Laqueur, 'Crowds, Carnival and the State in English Executions, 1604–1868', in A.L. Beier et al., eds., *The First Modern Society*, Cambridge 1989. Peter Linebaugh, *The London Hanged: Crime and Civil Society in the Eighteenth Century*, London 1981; V.A.C. Gattrell, *The Hanging Tree: Execution and the English People*, 1770–1868, Oxford 1994.

49. Jean Bodin, *Method for the Easy Comprehension of History*, New York 1945.

50. Philippa Levine, *The Amateur and the Professional*, p. ; Lynn Barber, *The Heyday of Natural History, 1820–1870*, London 1980, is an attractive introduction to the subject.

51. Keith Thomas, *Man and the Natural World; Changing Attitudes in England, 1500–1800*, Harmondsworth, 1984.

52. Oliver Rackham, *The History of the Countryside*, London 1986; *Trees and Woodland in the British Landscape*, London 1990.

53. F.M.L. Thompson, *Victorian England, the Horse-Drawn Society*, London 1971.

54. Harry Thompson and Carolyn King, *The European Rabbit; History and Biology of a Successful Coloniser*, Oxford 1994.

55. J.M. Mackenzie, *Empire of Nature; Hunting, Conservation and British Imperialism*, Manchester 1990.

56. F.N. Cornford, *Thucydides*, p. viii.

57. Donald R. Kelley, 'Mythistory in the Age of Ranke', in George C. Iggers, ed., *Leopold von Ranke*, credits Ranke's 'scientific history' with a complete ascendancy and suggests that it is only in contemporary postmodernism that its hegemony has been disturbed.

58. Raphael Samuel, ed., *Patriotism: The Making and Unmaking of National Identity, Vol. III: National Fictions*, London 1989.

59. For Michelet's discovery of Joan of Arc, Gabriel Monod, *La vie et la pensée de Jules Michelet*, Paris 1923; and the delightful essay by Roland Barthes.

60. Richard Harris Barham, *The Ingoldsby Legends*, London 1961. The legends were originally published by Dickens in *Bentley's Magazine*. Illustrated by Cruikshank, Leech and Tenniel, they were constantly reprinted in book form.

Index

Note: Most references are to England, unless otherwise indicated.

Abbey Mills 276
Abbeydale 188
Abercrombie, Sir Patrick 229, 233, 300
Aberdeen 174
Abingdon 64, 362
Aborigines 288, 308
Accrington Stanley 101
acting *see* re-enactments; theatre
Acton, John E.E.D., Lord 430, 444
Adam, Robert and James 70, 205
Adamson, Robert 323, 342, 346
Addyman, Peter 178, 198
Adler, Ruth 311
Adorno, Theodor 329
advertisements
    living history 194
    old photographs 339, 341, 357, 359
    property 55
    retrochic 93–5, 107
    television 56, 93, 95
aesthetics
    hidden, of old photographs *see*
        scopophilia
    of light and space 51–9, 76
    objections of aesthetes to heritage
        259–73
Afro-Americans 289
Agee, James 335
Aickman, Robert 200, 304, 312
Ainsworth, Harrison 5
Aitken, Jonathan 201
Albeck, Pat 304
Albert Docks (Liverpool) 125–6, 179, 264,
    300
Albert Hall 126
Aldeburgh Festival 214, 300
Aldermanbury 225

Aldermaston 277, 298
Alderson, Stanley 153–4, 167
Alexander, Sally 319
Alexandra, Princess 386
Alfred the Great 34, 35, 437, 444
Allan, Mea 44, 255
Allen, David Elliston 239
Allingham, Helen 234
Altick, Richard 45, 182, 200
Amberley Chalk Pits Museum 147
Ambrus, Victor 45
American Retro 87
Americana 99–100
    see also United States
Amos, Adrian 254
Amsterdam 102
ancestors *see* family history
ancient Britons *see* archaeology
ancient buildings 147, 163, 186, 227, 231,
    288
Ancient Monuments Act (1882) 229, 232
Anderson, Lindsay 267–8, 318, 333
Anderton, James 108
Anglo-Saxon period 4, 17, 23, 35, 170,
    174–5, 227
animals *see* wildlife
Anson, Brian 254
anti-fashion *see* retrochic
anti-heritage 242, 259–73
antiquaries/antiquarianism
    Elizabethan 439, 447
    see also Aubrey; Scott; Percy; Stukeley;
        Thoms; Wright
antique collecting 92, 95–6, 152, 164, 235,
    337
Antonioni, M. 339
Appleford 248–9

apples, English 155
appliances 66–7
Aram, Eugene 439
Arbus, Diane 263
archaeology, industrial *see* industrial
    archaeology
archaeology and prehistory 27–8, 47
    heritage and 210, 229, 275, 277, 282
    resurrectionism 140, 143, 144, 145,
        150–52, 156, 169, 201
    see also megaliths
Architectural Association 247, 302
architecture *see* buildings and architecture
Argyll 151
Argyll, Duke of 215
Ariès, Philippe 29, 46
Aristotle x, 431
Armada, Spanish 176
Armytage, W.H.G. 310
Arnold, Matthew 161, 267
Arnold, Thomas 46
art *see* Art Deco; Art Nouveau; Arts Council;
        Arts and Crafts; Dada; graphics;
        literature; music; old photographs;
        pop art; theatre
Art Deco 111, 158
    revival 21, 89, 96–7, 98, 103, 194, 205,
        277, 339
art galleries *see* museums and art galleries
Art Nouveau 91, 98–9, 355
Arthur, King 229, 433, 444
artificial materials *see* synthetic materials
Arts Council 263, 320, 342
Arts and Crafts movement 91, 164, 278
    brick 124, 128
    heritage concepts 211, 216, 294, 296,
        297, 299
Ascherson, Neal 262, 265, 267, 272
Ashbee, C.R. 91, 310
Ashley, Laura 60, 62, 80, 92, 116, 189, 194,
        321
Ashmolean Museum 20
Ashton, John 46
Astley's amphitheatre 7
Aston, Margaret 40
Atget, Eugène 211, 329, 365, 369
Atholl, Katherine M., Duchess of 297
Atkinson, Frank 147
Atkinson, Rowan 17
Attlee, Clement 41, 242, 288
Aubrey, John 11, 22
Audley End 172
Augustine, St vii
Austen, Jane 111, 215
Australia 131, 179, 288–9, 308
authenticity 197, 388, 434
    and informality 366, 373

irrelevant 112–13
autobiography and biography 8–11, 84–5
Automobile Association 238
Avebury 11
Axton, William 411

Bacon, David 222
Badger, Gerry 349
Baez, Joan 306
Baglee, Christopher 167
Bailey, David 348
Baillie Scott, M.H. 296, 310
Bakelite Museum 152
Baker, Charles 438, 447
Baker, Kenneth 153
Baker, Shirley 352
Baldwin, Stanley 231, 239, 288
Ball, A. 167
Ball, Joanne 116
ballads *see* songs
Balliol College 125
Baltimore 179
Bamford, Samuel 31, 34, 46, 438, 447
Banbury 213
Banham, Mary 116
Bann, Stephen 8
Barber, Lynn 81, 239, 447
Barbury Castle 145
Barham, Richard Harris 447
Barho, Rudolph 289, 309
Barker, Joseph 41, 438
Barker, Nicholas 362
Barker, Theo 201
Barley, Maurice 29, 46
Barmouth 216
barn conversions 129, 230
Barnardo, Dr Thomas 184, 342, 384
Barnes, Simon 199, 312
Baroque music 23, 139
Barratt, John 437–8
Barrowclough, Susan 43
Bart, Lionel 421–2
Barthes, Roland 333, 349, 350, 351, 362,
        376, 377, 434, 446, 447
Bartók, Béla 206
Bartram, Michael 334, 377
Bateman, Mary 439
Bath 212
bathrooms, modernized 52, 70, 71–2, 76
Battersea 55, 70, 93
Battle 152, 170, 174
Battlefields Society 221
battles *see under* wars
Baudrillard, Jean 113, 118
Bauhaus 57, 63, 129
Bawden, Edward 30, 165
Baxandall, Michael 335

Baxter, Cyril 45
Bayeux tapestry 23, 28, 32, 33
Bazalgette, Sir Joseph 276
Bazell, Rev. C. 47
BBC *see* radio; television
Beale, John 86, 115, 117
Beamish Museum 146, 160, 173, 264
Beatles 95, 97, 101, 153, 190, 205, 338, 341
Beaton, Cecil 21, 109, 338, 348
Beaufort, Cardinal 15
Beddoe, Stella 44
Bede 432, 437
Bedford Park 63
Bedfordshire 315
Beeching, Richard, Lord 185
Beecroft, Roger 171
Beeston Castle 175
Bell, Annie M. 334
Bellamy, Liz 166, 239
Benedetta, Mary 376
Benn, Tony 140, 165
Bennett, Arnold 276
Bennett, Tony 309
Bentham 192
Bentley, Nicholas 334
Benzie, William 43
Beresford, Maurice 169, 188, 305, 442
Bergen-Belsen 329
Berger, John 348, 349
Berkshire 149, 173, 251–2, 362
Bermondsey 347
Bernard, Bruce 343, 349
Best, George 97
Bethnal Green 184, 355
Betjeman, John 21, 209, 322, 334
Bevan, Aneurin/Bevanism 262, 297
Bevin, Ernest 262
Bewick, Thomas 165
bibliographers 19
Billericay 209
Binney, Marcus 254
Binns, G. 286
biography 8–11, 84–5
Birch (archaeologist) 47
Bird, John 310
birds 156, 171, 227, 228, 234, 293, 311
Birley, Robert 178, 446
Birley, Robin and Pat 198, 199
Birmingham 8, 64, 102, 265, 299, 417
Bisley 58
black consciousness 289
Black Country Museum 147, 181, 199, 280,
    283
Black Death 29, 156
Black Prince 28
black-and-white photography 359, 386
Blackburn, Julia 239

Blackburn (town) 160
Blackpool 180, 268
Black's (literary club) 87–8
Blaize, Bishop (festival) 28
Blake, Peter 95, 341
Blandford steam traction fair 249, 283
Blenkinsop, Arthur 311
Blight, J.T. 30
Blind Jack of Knaresborough 439
Bloch, Marc 24, 269
Bloomsbury 212, 325
Blunden, John 254
Blythe, Ronald 320, 334
Boadicea 431, 437, 443
Bodin, Jean 441, 442, 447
Bodleian Library 21
Bodmin Moor 143
Body Shop *see* Roddick
Bogart, Humphrey 13, 95, 273
Bolan, Marc 90
Bologna 304
Bolton 160, 331
Bonham, Mary 80
Bonham-Carter, Victor 310
books *see* documents; literature
Booth, Michael 45
Booth, General William 184, 316
Borges, Jorge Luis 429
Borgia, Lucrezia 437
Borlase 30
Bossy, John 43
Boston, Richard 81, 312
botany *see* plants
Bott, Alan 118
Bottomley, Horatio 6
Boulton, Sir Harold 23
Bourdieu, Pierre 264
Bourne, George 167
Boutruche, Robert 445
Bow, Clara 338, 341
Bowman, Marion 117
Bowmer, Michael 353, 362
Boy George 104
Boyd, W. 312
Boyes, Georgina 44–5, 222, 241, 312
Bradford 75, 102, 347
Brady, Matthew 34, 328
Bramwell, R.D. 48
Branagh, Kenneth 197
Brando, Marlon 99, 341
Brandt, Bill 328, 335, 365, 366, 369, 376,
    377
Brassaï 328, 353
Braudel, Fernand 243
Brecht, Bertold/Brechtianism 266, 425
Bredeln 276
Breisach, E. 446

brewery 279
brick 63, 66, 119–35
Brick Development Association 132
'Brideshead' effect see under country
   houses
Briggs, Asa 164
Brighton 64, 223, 302
   brickwork 121
   'Engineerium' 249
   Museum 20, 44
   old photographs 321, 323
   Pavilion 227
Brimscombe Fort 345
Bristol 174, 417
British Architectural Design Awards 63
British Museum 100, 245
British Printing Corporation 320, 343
British Rail see railways
Brittain, Vera 225
Britten, Benjamin 300
Bromley 148
Brontë family 209, 264, 364
Brooking, Charles 64
Brooks, Mel 382
Brooks, Peter 411
Brooks, Roy 55, 92, 116
Brown, Emelda 410
Brown, Hablot Knight see Phiz
Brown, Jane 311
Brown, Shirley Ann 46
Bruisyard Hall 172
Brunel, Isambard Kingdom 79, 125, 174,
   220, 327, 374
Brunskill, R.W. 134
Bryden, Bill 192, 422
Buck, John 349
buildings and architecture
   ancient 147, 163, 186, 227, 231, 288
   brick 119–35
   cleaning 126, 246
   clearance see demolition; salvage
   DIY see do-it-yourself
   heritage concepts 210
      genealogies 227, 230, 231, 233–5,
       238
      politics 290–92, 293, 300–302, 304
   large firms see housebuilders
   modernization see retrofitting
   owner-occupancy 76, 128, 237, 291
   unofficial knowledge 7, 37, 39
   see also ancient buildings; country
      houses; domestic sphere;
      gentrification of buildings; kitchens;
      listed buildings; urban areas
Bunyan, John 16, 438–9
Burdett-Coutts, Angela G. 215
Burford 92, 134, 192

Burke, Edmund 7
Burke, Peter 40, 446
Burroughs, Lucille 335
Burton, Neil 118
Burton on Trent 279
Busby, Matt 99
Bute 151
Butterfield, William 125
Byatt, Anthony 347, 349, 362
'bygones' and 'memorabilia' 27, 209, 215
   see also antiques; collecting; ephemera;
      museums; retrochic
Byron, George, Lord 215

Caesar, Julius 431, 437–8
Cain, P.J. 286
Caldecott, Randolph 44
Calder, Jenni 377
Cambridge 148, 157, 213
   Camden Society 230–31
   University 19–20
Cambridgeshire 64
Camden 22, 74, 184, 339, 354
Camden Lock 141, 298
   retrochic 91, 98, 102, 103, 117
Camden Passage (Islington) 92, 190
Camden Society of Cambridge 230–31
Camelot 11, 229, 433
Cameron, Isla 222
Cameron, Julia Margaret 325, 329, 334,
   337, 342, 349, 367
camp 96
Campaign for Real Ale 65, 302
campaigns see pressure groups and
   campaigns
Campbell, John 215
Campbell, Malcolm 220
Campion, Jane 351
canals 157, 189, 304–5
   restoration 141–2, 185, 247–8, 304–5
   trips 141–2, 184
candles 60
Cannadine, David 261, 272
Canning, George 7
Canonbury 126
Canterbury 23, 179
Canute, King 437
car ownership see under roads
Cardiff 64
Carey, John 208–9, 224, 411
Carlisle Castle 175
Carlyle, Jane Welsh 41
Carlyle, Thomas 22, 269, 443
Carnaby Street 96, 298
Carné, Marcel 318, 369
Carroll, Lewis 35, 349
Carruthers, Mary viii

Carter, Howard 111
Carver, Derek 223
Casaubon, Isaac 444
Caudrey, Adriana 199
Caughie, John 362
central heating 62, 65–6, 76, 244
Central School of Arts and Crafts 300
ceremonial occasions 219–20
Ceres (wholegrain shop) 237
Cerne Giant 172
Chafford Hundred 106, 127
Chaloner, W.H. 334
Chamberlain, Neville 164
Chambers, Robert 37
Chancellor, Valerie 40, 43
chap-books 31, 439
Chaplin, Charlie 190, 394
Chaplin, Peter H. 200
Chapman, Eddie 105
Charing Cross 30
charities 102, 150, 341
Charlemagne 34
Charles I 8
Charles Edward Stuart, Prince ('Bonnie
    Prince Charlie') 23, 32
Charles, Prince of Wales 120, 132
Chartism 164, 223, 332, 335, 434, 438
Chase, Lorraine 397
Chase, Malcolm 287
Chassy-Poulay, Pierre-Arnaud de 179
Chatham 179
Chatham, William Pitt, Earl of 7
Chaucer, Geoffrey 35
Cheal, David 117
Cheesewring 143
Chelsea 55, 154, 300
Chepstow Castle 178, 270
Cherry, Gordon E. 254
Cheshire 175, 190, 276, 282, 304
Chester 190
Chesterton, G.K. 412, 421
Chevalier, Louis 315, 333
Chichester 214
children/childhood 29
    childhood cult 93
    education see pedagogies
    learning and participating see
        pedagogies
    literature 140, 185, 223
    and living history 177, 196
    nostalgia 356
    radio for 235
    ragamuffins 369
    rooms for 54
    toys 93
    working 327
    see also youth culture

Chinese taste 110
Choay, Françoise 224
chorography 29
Chrimes, S.B. 40
Christensen, Terry 254
Christian Socialism 295
Christianity/theology viii
    costume drama 382, 384, 388, 413, 418
    forgery 432–3, 436–9
    heritage concepts 215, 227, 229–31
    iconography 36
    memory keeping 230–31, 245, 246
    unofficial knowledge 6–7, 24, 37
Christie, Agatha 391
Christie, Julie 96, 321
Christie, O.F. 318
Churchill, Winston 445
churchyards 29, 215–16, 234, 275
Cicero vii, 7
cinema buildings 132–3
    see also films
cities see urban areas
City of London 182, 190, 200, 214–15, 291
Civic Amenities Act (1967) 68, 155, 237,
    248
Civic Trust 74, 155, 194
Civil War, American 34, 328
Civil War, English 31, 270, 445
    antiquarian effort 19, 30, 44
    living history 174, 178, 199, 281
Civil War, Spanish 207, 297
Clanchy, M.T. 24, 42, 47, 432, 445
Clapton, Eric 104
Clare, John 46, 295
Clare (place) 209
Clarion League 297
Clark, Carol 132
Clark, Sir Kenneth 21, 30
Clarke, Basil F.L. 224
Clarke, Norma 41
Clarkson, L.A. 446
class differences 128
    costume drama 385–7, 390, 392–3,
        396–9, 404–5, 413, 416, 424
    heritage concepts 242, 246–7
    heritage-baiting 264–5, 267–8
    old photographs 324
    resurrectionism 150, 163
    retrochic 93
    retrofitting 56, 57, 72
    see also country houses; gentrification;
        slums
classicism see Greece, ancient;
        neo-classicism; Roman period
Clayton, Ian 133
Clean Air Act (1958) 76, 79, 129
cleaning buildings 126, 246

Clements, Simon 312, 348
Cleveland 175
Cliff, Clarice 21, 152, 167
Clifford, H. Dalton 79, 80
Clifton suspension bridge 125
Clio vii, 18, 19, 23, 431
clothes and fashion trade
    costume drama 404, 405, 407–9, 410,
        415–16, 417
    photography 338, 339, 348, 360, 371
    retrochic 85–7, 89, 91, 92, 94, 96–8, 103,
        104, 107, 109
Coalbrookdale 220–21
Cobbett, William 22, 223, 295, 443
cobblestones 73–4
Cobden, Richard 44
Cockley Cley 169
Cockrill, Pauline 115
Coe, Brian 361
coins 139, 152, 433
Coke, Sir Edward 231
Cole, J.W. 45
Colefax, Sybil 111, 297
Coleman, Alice 80
Coleman, Fitzroy 222
Coley, Hilda 217, 225
collecting
    flea markets 83, 91, 96–7, 103–4
    heritage concepts 209, 235, 252, 274,
        278, 337
    resurrectionism 139, 149, 152, 164
    retrochic 92, 95–6, 113
    unofficial knowledge 19–22, 27
    see also gift culture
Collier, William Francis 440, 447
Collingwood, R.G. 43
Colman's (museum and shop) 153
Colne 321, 334
colour 83, 340, 402
Commission Internationale d'Eclairage
    180
commodification of past 259–60, 266
    see also retrochic; heritage-baiting;
        shopping; theme parks
Common Ground 155
Commons, Open Spaces and Footpaths
        Society 295
Communism 223, 245, 317, 390, 445
    London march of 1936 207–8
concrete 124
Conran, Terence 58
conservation 25
    brick 119–20, 125–7, 128
    heritage concepts 276
        genealogies 227–9, 232, 237
        politics 288–307
        semantics 209–11, 217, 221

sociology 244, 245, 248, 252–3
    legislation 227, 228, 229, 237
    living history 186, 188, 190, 195
    resurrectionism 145–6, 151, 159, 163
    retrofitting 63, 68, 76–7, 78
    see also environmentalism; nature;
        preservationism; pressure groups
Conservative Party 162–3, 264, 281,
        290–91, 297, 302, 324, 425
    see also Thatcher
conspiracy theory of heritage 242, 264
Constable, John 151, 266
construction see buildings and architecture
consumerism see advertisements;
        commodification; retrochic
containerization see docklands
'contemporary' designs see modernistic
Conwy 63
Cook, Brian 216, 225
Cook, Ian 225
Cook, Captain James 159
Cooke, Alison 81
Cookson, Catherine 159, 161
Cooper, Jeremy 115, 116, 348
Co-operative Movement 301
Cope, Wendy 202
Copenhagen 301
Copper family 306
Corbridge 175
Corby 209, 344–5
Corke, Alison 117, 312
Corner, John 253
Cornford, F.M. 432, 442, 445, 447
Cornforth, John 199, 311
Cornish, Vaughan 232
Cornwall 110, 178
    heritage concepts 216, 249–50, 285,
        295
    old photographs 322
    unofficial knowledge 11, 30
corporate image-building 214–15, 225
Corpus Christi procession 28
Cosgrove, Stuart 272
Cossons, Neil 173, 201
costume drama 96, 103, 105
    Dickens on stage and screen 401–25
    Elephant Man 381–9
    Lambeth Walk 390–400
    see also re-enactments; theatre
Cotswolds 56, 92, 235
    Cotswold Way 145
'cottagey' look see 'country' style
Council for British Archaeology 201
council housing 63, 67, 72
Council of Industrial Design 56, 300
Council for Preservation of Rural England
        212, 221, 229, 236, 299–300, 311

Council for Small Industries in Rural Areas 146
counter-culture 91, 237, 264, 321
    see also retrochic
country houses
    'below stairs' 160
    'Brideshead' effect 58, 233, 260, 281
    decline of 58–9
    in films 58, 139
    heritage concepts 224, 227, 233–5, 242, 246, 297, 302
    heritage-baiting 260, 265
'country' style 65, 66, 77–8
countryside see birds; Council for Preservation of Rural England; nature; rural areas; wetlands; woodlands
Countryside Act (1979) 269
Countryside Commission 145, 238, 241
County Councils Act (1888) 228
courtyard developments 130, 134
Coutts 214–15, 225
Covent Garden
    brick 132
    heritage concepts 246–7, 250, 293, 302
    living history 194
    old photographs 329
    retrochic 88, 100, 104
    retrofitting 73, 74, 405
Coventry 189, 214
Coward, Noël 23, 218, 219, 391
Cox, Harry 306
Cox, Margaret 285
CPRE see Council for Preservation of Rural England
Crabtree and Evelyn 88, 103
crafts revival 245, 296, 301
    see also open-air and industrial museums
Crane, Walter 165
Cranks 92, 237, 298
Crawford, Joan 87
Crawford, Marion 224
crazes 110
    see also retrochic
Creasy, Edward 440
Crich (tram museum) 264
Crichton, Michael 48
Crimean War 27, 373
crisis, the idea of 434, 445–6
Critics Group 306
Crompton, Richmal 208
Cromwell, Oliver 8, 207
cross-dressing 98, 109
crowds 356
    mob 385, 387
Crozier, Michael 82
Cruden, Alexander 229

Cruikshank, Dan 110, 118, 134, 312
Cruikshank, George 47, 317, 447
Crystal Palace 125, 234, 325
Cullen, Gordon 82, 155
Culloden, battle of 23
Cumbria 175, 296, 311
Cumming, Elizabeth 310
Cunard, Nancy 297
Curl, James Stevens 45
Currie, Nigel 254
Curry, W.B. 310
curtains see windows and curtains
Curtis, Dr 133
Curtis, Edmund 330, 331
Curtis, J.C. 447
Curtis, Ray 116
Czechoslovakia 391

Dada 110
Dallas, Karl 223
Dalton, Hugh 308
Dalyell, Tam 311
Dalziel, Eleanor 43
dance 296, 301
    Lambeth Walk 390–400
Daniel, Glyn 44, 47
Darnton, Robert 437, 446
Dartington Hall 296–7
Dartmoor 64
Dartmouth, Lady (Countess Spencer) 302
Dartmouth 189
Darvill, Timothy 222
Darwinism 216
dates in history 12, 435–6
Davenport, Nicholas 311
Davidson, T. 225
Davie, W.Galsworthy 235
Davies, Philip 240
Davies, Terence 351, 361
Davis, Ben 81
Dawber, E.Guy 235
Day, John 34
D-Day 23
Dean, James 99
death see necrophilia
debates and history teaching 7–8, 41
decadence 261
decorative style see neo-vernacular
Defoe, Daniel: Robinson Crusoe 5, 15, 439
Degh, Linda 40
Deloche, B. 309
Deloney, Thomas 439
Democratic Party (USA) 289
democratization of history 160–61
demolition
    clandestine 151
    slum clearance 67–8, 130, 153–5

see also salvage
Denby 183
Denmark Street 88
Denny, Brian 223
Denselow, Robin 223
Depression, Great 325, 445–6
Derbyshire, Sir Andrew 63, 81
Derbyshire (county) 64, 104, 122, 186, 210, 264
    Peak District 11, 147, 311
Derwent County Park 145
Design Council 74
Design and Industries Association 300
Devon 110, 323
Devonport, Lord 356
Dewey, John 38
Dewsbury 209
Dibner, Fred 245
Dickens, Charles 401–25, 447
    Bleak House 395
    David Copperfield 317, 409, 421
    'Dickensian' surroundings 51, 67, 114, 124, 129, 247, 382, 402
    films and theatre 58, 381–425
    heritage concepts 213, 247, 276
    Nicholas Nickleby 401, 417–19, 422–3, 424–5
    Old Curiosity Shop 213
    old photographs 315, 317
    resurrectionism 192, 201
    Tale of Two Cities 421
    'Week' in Rochester 192, 201
    see also Great Expectations; *Little Dorrit*; *Oliver Twist*
Dietrich, Marlene 341
Diggers 19
Dimbleby, Jonathan 241
Dimbleby, Richard 236
Dinas Oleu 216
direct action *see* pressure groups and campaigns
disclosure 373
Disneyland *see* theme parks
Ditherington 220
Dixon, John 312, 348
DIY *see* do-it-yourself
Dobson, R.B. 45
Dobwalls' Theme Park 178
Docklands Development Corporation 281
docklands and warehouses 126, 128
    Liverpool 125–6, 179, 264, 300
    London 66, 131, 132, 134, 174, 281–2
    docklands Dickens 401–12
Doctorow, E.L. 268
documentaries
    photographic 331, 365, 366–70, 374
    television 13, 139, 192

documents
    forgery 432–3
    historians' concern with 3–5, 268–70, 274
Doisneau, Robert 353–4, 359, 362, 369, 374
do-it-yourself
    history
        heritage concepts 230, 248–51
        resurrectionism 150, 162, 176, 187, 191
        unofficial knowledge 5, 24–5, 27
        see also family history
    in home 51, 52, 56, 72–3, 76, 154
Domesday Book 170, 174, 175, 177, 187
domestic sphere emphasized 277, 286, 352
    resurrectionism 161–2, 186–7, 192, 196–7, 198
Donizetti, Gaetano 417
Donovan, Paul 240
Donovan, Terence 339
Doré, Gustave 35, 316, 319, 387
Dore, J.N. 198
Dors, Diana 341
Dorset 13, 42, 111, 157, 172, 249, 283, 285
Dorson, Richard M. 47, 447
'double-coding' 130–31
double-glazing 76, 77
Doubleday, H.A. 44
Douglas, David C. 44, 46
Dover 153, 177
drama *see* theatre
dreamscapes 350–63
dressing-up *see* clothes; re-enactments; role play
Druids 30, 229
du Maurier, Daphne 40, 200
Dublin 339, 342, 343
Dudley *see* Black Country Museum
Duff, David 224
Duffy, Brian 339
Dufour, Bernard 335
Dugdale, Sir Thomas 29
Dulwich 121, 152
Dumas, Alexandre 414
Dundee 174
Dungeness 234
Dunkirk 437
Dunn, Clive 338
Dunnett, H.McG. 81
Durham 146–7, 156, 157, 159, 179, 263
    see also Beamish
Durr, Andy 255
Dylan, Bob 306

Ealing 161
Earl, Tracey 225
Earth Liberation Front 143

East Anglia 66, 179, 217, 231, 361
    see also Norfolk; Suffolk
East India Company 232–3, 291
Easterbrook, L.F. 225
Eastern Europe 307, 391, 429, 445
Eastlake, Charles Locke 133
Easton Lodge 297
EC (European Community) 307
ecclesiastical history see Christianity
Eco, Umberto 201, 243, 445
ecology see environmentalism
economic historians 244, 435, 441
Eden Camp 264
Edgar, David 417, 418, 419, 422, 425
Edgell, Derek 311
Edinburgh, Duke of 174, 185
Edinburgh 154, 172, 196, 354
Edmonds, Chris 255
education see pedagogies
Edward I 162, 184
Edward III 35, 281
Edward VII 6
Edwardian period and style 396
    evoked 66–7
    heritage concepts 209, 266, 297, 298–9,
        301
    living history 177, 184, 192
    old photographs 266, 347, 359, 366,
        367
    retrofitting 70, 71
Edwards, Anne 224
Edzard, Christine 402, 411, 417, 422–3
Eglington Tournament 181
Egypt 21, 28, 110, 111
Eisenstein, Sergei 401, 411, 420
Eleanor Cross 30
Elephant Man, The 381–9
Elgar, Edward 263, 266
Elias, Norbert 446
Eliot, T.S. 215, 223
Elizabeth II 134, 219
Elizabethan Stage Society 247
Elizabethan and Tudor period and style 72,
        111, 130, 155
    heritage concepts 247
    historians 439, 447
    living history 176, 177, 182, 184
    theatres of memory 4, 11, 22, 29, 50
Ellesmere Port 147
Elmhirst, Leonard 296–7
Elphick, Michael 387–8
Elton, G.R. 4, 40, 197
Elwin, Verrier 240
Emerson, P.H. 342, 361, 362, 369
Emery, Anthony 310
Emett, Rowland 55
Emilia, Museum of Peasant Life 304, 312

Endangered Species Act (1976) 308
English Heritage 75, 78, 159, 210, 271, 275,
        291
    living history 172, 174–5, 195, 281, 291
English Nature (earlier Nature
        Conservancy) 221
English Tourist Board 248
'Enterprise Neptune' 146
Enthoven collection 250
environmentalism and ecology 61, 140,
        143–8, 149, 158
    see also conservation; nature
Environmentally Sensitive Areas 210, 260
ephemera 19–21, 83, 91, 96–7, 103–4, 113
    see also collecting; old photographs
Epping Forest 196, 295
Ermine Street Guard 191–2, 193
Essex 68, 106, 127, 134, 173
estate agents 71–2, 121, 127
Eton 74, 364
eugenics 206
    urban 130
Eurodisney 102
Europe 57, 65, 307, 429
    see also Czechoslovakia; Greece; Eastern
        Europe; France; Germany; Italy;
        Netherlands; Norway; Russia; Sicily;
        Sweden; Spain
European Architectural Heritage Year 180,
        190, 244, 248, 302, 308
European Community 307
European Conservation Year 307
Euston station and arch 67, 124, 125, 234,
        237
Evans, David 239
Evans, George Ewart 165, 188, 201, 241,
        305, 312
Evans, J.A.S. 445
Evans, Walker 331–2, 335, 371–3
Evelyn, John 228
Evens, Eunice 240
Evens, J.Bramwell ('Romany') 235, 240
Eversley, G.J., Lord (Shaw-Lefevre) 310
Exmoor 216

Fabians 163, 296, 297, 311
fabrics
    cotton see Ashley
    retrofitting 51, 60, 66
facsimile reprints 191
Fairholt, Frederick William 45, 239
fakes see forgeries and fakes
Falklands War 290
family
    in Dickens 413, 424–5
    England as 218
    history and genealogy 25, 27, 205, 332,

356, 374–5
   resurrectionism 148–9, 158, 160–61,
      167
motherhood 161, 385
photographs 210, 326, 328, 334
   dreamscapes 350, 351, 352
   scopophilia 364–7, 374, 375
resurrectionism 161–2, 163
Faringdon, Lord 297
Farjeon, Eleanor 32, 42, 46
farmers and farming 88, 248–9
Farrer, Francis 202
Fascism 207
fashion *see* clothes; retrochic
Fatboy's Diner 100
Faulkner, William vii
fauna *see* birds; fisheries; wildlife
Faversham 209
Fawcett, Henry 295
Fawkes, Guy 29
Fearnly-Sander, Mary 447
Feaver, William 116
Fells, Richard 201
femininity
   amanuenses and helpers 18
   living history 188–9
   nature feminized 161
   of neo-vernacular 59
   see also domestic sphere; gift culture
feminism 373, 444
Fenton, Roger 342, 373
Fentress, James 42
Ferguson, A.B. 40
Ferrier, Kathleen 235
Festival of Britain
   heritage concepts 219–20, 244, 247
   resurrectionism 154, 184
   retrochic 92, 93, 98
   retrofitting 55–6, 69–70, 73, 78
fiction *see* films; literature; myths
Fielding, Sir John 34
Fields, Gracie 347
Fields, W.C. 421
films
   country houses in 58, 139
   of Dickens 403–9, 410–11, 414–17,
      419–24
   Elephant Man, The 381–9
   heritage concepts 208, 218, 219, 223,
      233–4, 243
   living history 192
   old photographs
      discovery of 338, 339, 341
      dreamscapes 350–51, 361
      eye of history 318, 321
      scopophilia 369, 373, 374
   propaganda 208

resurrectionism 139
retrochic 96, 103, 105, 114
unofficial knowledge 13–14, 25
wartime 208
see also television
Fine Arts Commission 78, 291
Finley, M.I. 445
Firestone factory 158, 277
First World War 219, 430
   aftermath *see* inter-war period
   old photographs 323, 333, 376
   resurrectionism 158, 164, 185
Fisher, Chris 239
fisheries 227, 228, 229, 238–9
Fishman, Bill 184
Flaherty, Robert 211
flea markets 83, 91, 96–7, 103–4
Flogging a Dead Horse (exhibition and book)
   263–7
floodlighting 179–80
flowers 217, 228
Flukinger, Roy 377
folk music 112, 206–7, 222, 233, 235,
   296–7, 301, 305–6
Fonda, Henry 370
food 92, 103, 152, 155, 237
Foot, Michael 272
Ford, Colin 342
Ford, Henry 289
Ford, Peter 389
Forest of Dean 231
Foresters' demonstrations 29
Forestry Commission 155
forests *see* woodlands
forgeries and fakes
   medieval 432–3
   posed photographs 319, 326, 330–31,
      335, 337–8, 348, 352
Formby, George 398
Forsyth, Ian 222
Forsyth, Jimmy 352, 362
Fortescue, G.K. 44
Fortress Study Group 221
Forty, Adrian 118
Foucault, Michel 264
Fowler, John 60, 111, 194
Fowler, Peter 287
Fowler, Simon 167
Fox, B.P. 287
Fox, J. 438
Fox, Ralph 223
Fox Talbot, W.H. 317, 342, 376
Foxe, John 34, 46, 47, 439, 446
France
   brickwork 131, 135
   heritage concepts 210–11, 224, 264,
      289–90

historians 442–3, 444, 445
     living history 179
     old photographs 318, 325, 329, 353–4,
          359, 365, 369, 374
     retrochic 83, 102, 103
     Revolution 289, 434, 437
     theatres of memory 23, 32
franchises 102–3
Frankfurt 102
Frankum, Wynne 251–2, 255, 287
Fraser, Frankie 105
Fraser, Kennedy 116
Fraser, Ronald 351, 362
Freeman, Robert 341
Freeston, George 345
French, Robert 342, 343
Freud, Sigmund 373, 374, 375
Fridenson, Patrick 200
Friel, Brian 196
Friends of the Earth 140, 210, 230, 308, 442
Friends of the Lake District 311
Frith, Francis 342–3, 346, 349
Frith, Simon 348
Frith, W.P. 22
frivolity see fun
Froebel, Friedrich W.A. 38
Froude, J.A. 273
Frow, Eddie and Ruth 255
Fry, Betty 251
Fry, Charles 346
Fry, Henry 250–51
Fuentes, Nick 201
Fulham 129
fun and frivolity 95–6, 113
     see also retrochic
functionalism see modernistic style
Furley, O.W. 45
furniture 54, 55, 97, 406
     see also sets
Furnivall, F.J. 18, 43
futurism 156, 294

Gaia 230
Gaitskell, Hugh 311
Galassi, Peter 377
Galliano, John 83
Gambier, Royston 166
Game, M. 222
Game Laws 229
Gance, Abel 23
gardens 60
     Garden Festivals 62, 307
     heritage concepts 209, 211, 212, 219,
          235
Gardner, B. 287
Gardner, James 116
Garibaldi, Giuseppe 208

Garnett, Jane 41
Garrad, L.S. 286
Garsington 297
Gates, Paul 361
Gateshead 102, 145, 173
Gatrell, V.A.C. 447
gay community 82, 98, 99
     Pink Festival 109
gay history 444
     see also cross-dressing; masculinity
Gaynor, Anthony 198
Gaze, John 288, 308
gaze, pleasure of see scopophilia
GCSE examinations 193
Geddes, Sir Patrick 300
Geffrye Museum 182, 190, 194, 286
gender see femininity; masculinity
genealogies
     of families see family history
     of 'heritage' 227–41
Gentleman, David 30, 46, 140, 165–6
gentrification
     of buildings 70–71, 127, 128, 149, 164,
          290
     of people 397–8
          degentrification 246
     see also class
Geoffrey of Monmouth 229, 439
geography 29, 40, 46, 439, 446
geology 24, 44, 228
George III 6, 409
Georgian Group 211–12, 227, 300
Georgian period and style 179
     brickwork 120, 126, 130
     heritage concepts 211–12, 227, 300,
          301
     retrochic 87, 114
     retrofitting 71, 74, 77
Germany 78, 102, 178, 290, 445
Gernsheim, Helmut and Alison 334
Gettysburg, battle of 29
Gibbon, Edward 29
Gibraltar, Siege of 28
Gielgud, Sir John 386
Gifford, Denis 240
gift culture of women 98–9, 100, 267, 340,
          353
     see also collecting
Gilbert, Bob 168
Gilbert, John 22
Gillam, J.P. 198
Gilliatt, Mary 58, 79, 80
Girouard, Mark 32, 45, 46, 181, 200, 443
Gisborough Priory 175
Gissing, George 18, 44
Gittings, Robert 200
Gladstone, W.E. 318

Glasgow 146, 159, 179–80, 215, 292, 365, 369
glass 132, 134
Glastonbury 107–8, 140, 433
Gliksten, Malcolm 115
Globe Theatre 214, 233, 247
Gloucestershire 152, 192, 321, 345–6
Goering, Hermann 309
Goff, Jacques le ix, 447
Gog and Magog 28, 231
Goldcrest (films) 103
Gomm, Carr 382, 386, 387
Gomme, Lady 12
Gomme, Richard 115
Gooch, G.P. 44
Goode, David 221
Gordon, G.S. 446
Gordon, Jean 165
Gorham, John 116
Gorham, Maurice 81
Gorman, John 150, 167, 255, 286
Gorman, Jon (son of John) 255, 287
Goscinny, R. 47
Gosden, P.J.H. 166, 334
Gosling, Ray 199
Gothic and horror style 441
    brickwork 119, 124–5
    Elephant Man, The 381–9
    heritage concepts 213, 227, 284–5
    neo-Gothic 77, 119
    pedagogies 276
    resurrectionism 139, 197
    retrochic 108, 110, 111, 112
    retrofitting 79
    theatres of memory 30, 31, 32, 37
    unofficial knowledge 16, 21
Gottingen 17
Goubert, Pierre 40
Gough 21
Gould, John 445
Goulder, Jenny 362
Goultry, George A. 238
Gower, H.D. 349
Goyder, J. 241
Gradidge, Roderick 65, 81
Grafton, Anthony 445
Grainger, Percy 296
Gramsci, Antonio 223
Grand National 225
Granny Takes a Trip 89, 98, 338
Gransden, Antonia 42, 432–3, 445
graphics viii, 433–4
    retrochic 91–2
    unofficial knowledge 21–2, 23, 27–39
    see also old photographs
Graves, Robert 44
gravestones see churchyards

Great Exhibition (1851) 111
Great Expectations 317, 401–3, 409, 417, 419–20, 421, 423–4
Greece, ancient 7, 110, 328, 431–2, 433, 436
Green, Benny 349
Green, E.Curtis 235
Green, J. 201
Green, J.R. 441
Green, Martin 348
'green' attitudes
    green consumerism 106–7
    'greening' of city 62, 205, 208
    see also conservation; environmentalism; preservationism
Green Belts 124, 288
Greenaway, Kate 338
Greenfield Village (USA) 289
Greenpeace 230, 293
Greenwich (London) 334
Greenwich Village (New York) 131
Greenwood, James 316
Greenwood, Joan 406
Greg family 276, 304
Grégoire, Abbé Henri 289
Grey, Lady Jane 31
Grieg, Elizabeth 256
Grierson, John 211
Griffin, Leonard 167
Griffith, D.W. 401
Grigson, Geoffrey 154, 167
Grimes Graves 145
Grimsby 179
Groome, Francis 244, 254
Grosvenor Estate 291
Guevara, Ernesto Che 338
Guides (Girl) 301
Guillaume, Marc 224
Guinevere, Queen 433
Guinness, Alec 405, 416
Guise, Hilary 45
Gunnersbury Triangle 205
Gurevich, A. 432, 445
Gurr, Andrew 254
Guthrie, Woody 206

Hackney 134, 191, 277
    Empire 131
    Geffrye Museum 182, 190, 194, 286
    old photographs 318, 321, 351
Hadrian's Wall 152, 169, 172, 179, 229, 284
Halbwachs, Maurice ix
Hales, J.E. 225
Haley, Alex 14, 309
Halifax 176
Hall, Brian 225
Hall, Peter 310

Hall, Richard 198
Hall, S.C. 37, 47
Hallam, Paul 87, 115
Hallazz, Piri 115
Haller, William 47, 446
Hamilton, Stanley B. 201
Hamilton, Sir W. 111
Hammond, Celia 348
Hampshire 149, 165, 173, 195, 217
Hampson, Frank 47
Hampson, Robert 240
Hampstead 63, 295
Hampton Court 179
Handy, Ellen 362
Hannas, Linda 46, 431, 445
Hannavy, John 334
Harbige, Sarah 287
Hardy, Bert 353, 365, 369, 371
Hardy, Dennis 310
Hardy, Oliver 153, 341
Hardy, Thomas 318, 333
Hardyment, Christine 286
Hare Krishna cult 97
Harker, David 222
Harlow, Jean 341
Harman, Claire 43
Harradine, Archie 44
Harral, Horace 28
Harris, Jennifer 201
Harrison, Brian 41
Harrison, George 97
Harrison, Martin 348
Harrison, Molly 182, 200, 286
Harrison, Tony 192
Harrisson, Tom 390
Harrogate 353
Harrop, Wendy 199
Hart, Cyril 238
Hartlebury 281
Hartlepool 252
Hartley, Dorothy 217, 225
Hartley, L.P. 377
Harvey, Sylvia 253
Haskell, Francis 433, 445
Haskell, Harry 165
Hasler, Charles 116
Hasted, John 222
Hastings (town) 251, 300
    battle of 23, 28, 32, 33, 170, 174–5, 193, 270
Hawkesbury 189
Hawkhurst 343–4
Hawking, Stephen 446
Hawkings, David T. 167
Haworth 209, 264
Hay, Denys 446, 447
Hayes, Charles 201

Head, Sir George 228
Headington Quarry 296
Hearne, Thomas 20
Heath, Peter 75, 82
heating of houses 62, 65–6, 76, 244
hedgerows 147–8, 156, 187, 217, 221
Heere, Lucas de 28
Heidegger, Martin 446
Helgerson, Richard 40, 46, 439, 447
Hell-fire Club 181
Helston 178
Hemans, Felicia 41, 440
Henderson, George 47, 118
Henderson, Lesley 43
Hendon 321
Hendrickson, Janis 348
Hendrix, Jimi 90, 104, 338
Henige, David 40
Henry IV 40
Henry VII 229
Henry VIII 6, 8, 162, 274, 409
heraldry 37
Hereford 179
Herefordshire 281
heritage 205–312
    genealogies 227–41
    heritage-baiting 242, 259–73
    pedagogies 274–87
    politics 288–312
    semantics 205–26
    sociology 242–56
    see also living history; old photographs;
        'period' design; resurrectionism
'Heritage Coast' 285
Hermant, Daniel 309
Herodotus 432, 444
Heron, Liz 202
Herschel, Sir John 329
Hertfordshire 56, 157
Hewison, Robert 242, 253, 261, 263, 272, 295
Heyer, Georgette 111
Heyerdahl, Thor 179
Heymer, Edward 343–4
Hickathrift, Tom 15
Hickey, Kieran 343
hiking see walks
Hiley, Michael 349, 361, 362–3
Hill, David Octavius 323, 342, 346, 367, 369
Hill, George 271
Hill, Howard 311
Hill, Octavia 225, 295–6
Hiller, Wendy 386
Hillhouse, James 174
Hillier, Bevis 44, 65, 80, 81, 116, 201, 244, 253
Hillingdon 63, 127

Hillman, Judith 254
Hilton, R.H. 239
Hinton Manor 297
hippies 97
    see also New Ageism
Hirsch, Julia 362
historians 430–41
    and documents 3–5, 268–70, 274
    as forgers and inventors' invisible hands
        17–27
    and heritage-baiting 261, 268–71
    impecunious 245
    and unofficial knowledge 3–5, 41
    see also history
Historic Buildings Commission 174
Historic Scotland 262
Historical Association 38
Historical Monuments Commission 126,
    275, 277
historiography 3–39, 429–44
    see also Heredotus; Hoskins; Ranke;
        Stubbs; Thucydides; Whig
        interpretation
history
    dramatized see costume drama
    heritage concepts see heritage
    illustrated see old photographs
    'on the ground' 158–9, 186, 187–8, 190
    resurrection and revival of past see
        brick; living history;
        resurrectionism; retrochic;
        retrofitting
    see also archaeology; crisis; debates;
        economic historians; local history;
        Middle Ages; National Curriculum;
        natural history; oral history;
        pedagogies; 'Public History'
History Working Party 261
Hitchcock, Alfred 369
Hitler, Adolf 291
Hobley, Brian 45
Hobsbawm, Eric 16, 446
Hobson, Valerie 420
Hodge, Alan 44
Hodgkin, Thomas 445
Hodgkinson, Anthony W. 223
Hodnett, Edward 34, 45, 46
Hogarth, William 27, 88, 114
Hogg, Min 199
Hoggart, Richard 268, 272–3
Hokne 221
Holden, Arthur 311
Holden, Edith ('Edwardian Country
    Lady') 298–9, 311
Holden, Effie 299
Holding, Norman 167
holiday industry see tourism

Holland House (Whiggery) 21
Hollington, Michael 412
Holly, Buddy 338
Hollywood see films
Holt, J.C. 43
Holy Island 276
Holy Loch 306
home see buildings; domestic sphere
Home Counties see south-east England
Hone, William 37, 47
Hood, Robin 22, 29, 35, 439
Hood, Thomas 164
Hooligan, Patrick 400
Hoover factory 305
Hopkin, Mary 90
Hopkins, A.G. 286
Hopkins, Anthony 386
Hopper, Edward 335
Horman, Tom 389
Horne, Howard 348
horror see Gothic
Horseguards Parade 126
Hoskins, Bob 105, 387
Hoskins, W.G. 132, 305, 320, 442
    and resurrectionism 156–7, 158, 167,
        186–8, 200
    and retrofitting 58–9, 80
Hospital Sunday demonstrations 29
Houndsditch 291
House, Humphry 412
housebuilders, quantity 65–6, 91, 106,
    120–21, 134
Houses of Parliament 28, 102, 111, 153,
    220–21, 242, 337
housing see buildings and architecture
Howard, Leslie 219
Howard of Penrith, Lord 309
Howell, Michael 389
Howkins, Alun 44
Howlett, Robert 374
Hoyau, Philippe 224, 264, 272
Hoyles, Martin 19, 44
Hudson, Derek 43
Hudson, George 6
Hudson, Kenneth 199, 200, 201, 224, 286,
    312
Huguenots 11
Huizinga, Johan 445
Hulanicki, Barbara 201
Hull 147
Hulme, Jack 183
Hunt, Martita 420
Hunter, Robert 295, 310
Hurt, John 381, 382, 384
Huss, John 438
Hutt, Christopher 81
Hutton, Ronald 447

Hyde, Pippa 224
Hyde, Sarah 201
'hyper-history' 263

Iceni 284
Icknield Way 145
identification 374–5
Ignatieff, Michael 362
illustration *see* graphics; photography; film;
       television; museums
imaginary history *see* living history
Imperial War Graves Commission 229–30
Imperial War Museum 159, 178, 346
India 86, 232–3, 240, 429
Indians, American 330
industrial archaeology 125, 345
     heritage concepts 220, 226, 235, 267,
         275–6, 301
       politics 290, 303–4, 305
       sociology 244, 248–51
     living history 188, 189
     resurrectionism 139, 146–7, 150–51,
         156–7
     see also Ironbridge; open-air
Industrial Monuments Record 157
industrial museums *see* open-air
industrial photography 324–5, 327
Industrial Revolution 220–21, 275–6
informality 366, 373
Ingrams, Richard 240
Inland Waterways Association 184, 185,
       189, 304–5
inner city *see* urban areas
Innes, Jocasta 85, 115
Inns of Court 130
Institute of Historical Research 5
intentionality and effect, gulf between
       423–4
inter-war Britain 227, 300, 325, 445
interactive displays 192
interiors *see* retrofitting
international conservation 307–8
International Convention of Wild Flora
       and Fauna 308
International Genealogical Index 27
International Health Exhibition of 1884
       182
inventors, historians as 431–3
Inventory of Ancient Woodland 145
inversion 85, 392–3
Ireland 196, 306
     old photographs 339, 342, 343
iron 125
Ironbridge 30
     heritage concepts 238, 245, 264, 282,
         301
     resurrectionism 139, 169, 173, 199

Isle of Man 276
Islington 71, 92, 126, 132, 133, 190
Italy 245, 304, 312, 390
ivy, demonization of 211, 212–13, 224
IWA *see* Inland Waterways Association
Izis 353, 369

Jack of Newbury 10, 439
Jack the Ripper 284–5
Jack-the-Giant-Killer 15
Jackman, Brian 255
Jackson, John 45, 47
Jacobi, Derek 411–12
Jacobins 289
Jacobites 22
Jacobs, Jane 80
James I 409
James, Alex 215
James, John 141–2
James, Louis 41, 44
James, Mervyn 239
Jameson, Fredric 140, 165
Jann, Rosemary 447
Japan 65, 153
Jarman, Derek 234
Jason's Trip 141–2, 184
Jast, L.Stanley 349
Jay, Bill 335, 342, 343, 349
Jeesebhoy, Sir Jamsetjee 233
Jeffrey, Ian 335
Jekyll, Gertrude 216, 235
Jencks, Charles 130, 134
Jennings, Humphrey 208, 223
Jermyn Street 178
Jerrold, Blanchard 316
Joad, C.E.M. 236, 311
Joan of Arc 16, 34, 443, 447
Johns, Captain W.E. 140
Johnson, John (ephemera collection)
       20–21
Johnson, Richard 223, 253, 272
Johnson, Stephen 198
Jones, Barbara 116, 234
Jones, Edgar Yoxall 334
Jones, Gareth *see* Stedman Jones
Jones, L.E. 43
Jones, Michael 287
Jonson, Ben 295
Joplin, Janis 338
Jorvik 87, 114, 170, 178, 182, 198, 282, 284,
       287
Joseph of Arimathea 433
Jourdain, Margaret 111, 118
Jousting Federation of Great Britain
       174
Judge, Roy 312
Jussim, Estelle 362

Kaplan, Wendy 310
Kean, Charles 22, 117
Keble College 125
Keeting 249
Keith, Crispin 286
Kelley, Donald R. 447
Kemp, Jim 81
Kendal, Mrs 382, 386, 387
Kendrick, T.D. 40, 46
Kennington Common 332, 434
Kensington, Royal Borough of 102, 119,
    182, 284
    see also Portobello Road
Kent 443
    heritage concepts 209, 217, 234, 235,
        259, 285
    living history 148, 153, 177, 179, 192,
        201
    old photographs 343–4
    see also Hastings
Kentwell Hall 177
Keyworth, John 225
Kinderscout (mass trespass on) 298
King, Carolyn 447
King, Christine 116
King, David 343, 349
King, Graham 361
King George's Square (Richmond) 121,
    129
King's Cross station 125, 133
Kipling, John Lockwood 233
Kipling, Rudyard 5, 40, 240
Kirchen, Alf 215
Kirk, John L. 182
kitchens 152
    modernized 7–12, 52, 53, 58, 69, 76,
        77–8, 82
Klopstock, Friedrich G. 439
Knight, Charles (nineteenth century) 35
Knightley, Charles (twentieth century) 201
Knox, John 439, 446
Kornwolf, James D. 310
Kosellek, R. 446
Kristiansen, Kristian 239

labour history 150, 161, 211, 250–51
Labour Party in Australia 289
Labour Party in Britain 318, 390, 424
    heritage concepts 238, 242, 262, 288,
        292–3, 297, 298, 301
    resurrectionism 154, 163, 164
    victory in 1945 288, 397
Labrousse, Ernest 445
Lachaise, Père 29, 90
Ladurie, Emmanuel Le Roy 40, 332, 335,
    336
Laing, Dave 223

Lake District 296, 311
Lambeth 126, 395
    Walk (song) 390–400
Lamy, Yvon 224
Lancashire 282, 305, 438
    heritage concepts 244, 252, 262, 263
    old photographs 315, 321, 324, 331,
        354, 360
    resurrectionism 146–7, 160, 180
    see also Liverpool; Manchester
Lancaster, Osbert 297
Landes, D.S. 446
Land's End 143
landscaping see gardens
Lane, Lupino 391, 394, 400
Lang, Jack 211
Lange, Dorothea 328, 360–70, 377
language 435
    semantics 205–26
Lansbury, George 297, 310–11
Laqueur, Thomas W. 44, 333, 447
Larner, Sam 306
Laslett, Peter 38, 40, 148, 166
Laurel, Stan 153, 341
Laurie, Joe 255
Lawes, Eric 254
Lawlor, Sheila 430
Lawrence, D.H. 299
Lawrence, M. 115
Lawrie, Jo 287
Lawson, Mark 273
Le Corbusier 67
Le Goff, Jacques ix, 447
Le Mesurier, Peter 239
Lea, Hermann 333
Lean, David 401–2, 411, 417, 419, 420, 423
Leavis, F.R. 215, 267
Leavis, Q.D. 272
Lee, Arthur H. 232
Leeds 28, 80–81, 126, 298
Leek tapestry 175
Lees-Milne, James 302
Left 390, 424
    heritage concepts 238, 242, 288
        heritage-baiting 259, 260, 262, 268
        politics 292–4, 296–8, 300, 301, 303
    old photographs 318, 324
    resurrectionism 154–5, 162–3, 164
    see also Communism; Labour Party;
        Marx; socialism
legends see myths and legends
legislation
    ancient monuments 229, 232
    Australia 289
    civic amenities 68, 155, 237, 248
    conservation 227, 228, 229, 237, 269,
        308

countryside 269
county councils 228
endangered species 308
France 210
game 229
Green Belts 124
local government 166
military remains 205
National Parks 155, 210, 288
nature conservancy 237
planning 68, 124, 308
against pollution 76, 79, 129
Leicester Square 73
Leicestershire 185, 209, 284, 320
Leland, John 182
Leniaud, Jean-Michel 224, 309
Lenin, V.I. 445
Lennon, John 97
Letchworth 63
Lethaby, W.R. 300, 311
Levant Beam Whim 249–50
Levellers 19
Levine, Philippa 41, 45, 47, 445, 447
Levy, F.J. 40, 447
Levy, Mike 202
Lewes 64
Lewis, John 255, 286
Lewisham 250
Lhuyd, Edward 29–30
Liberal Party 295, 296, 297
librarians 19
Lichtenstein, Roy 339, 348
Liddell, Billy 215
Light, Alison 40, 118, 390n, 413
light and lighting
    aesthetics of 51–60, 76
    in films 386, 402, 414, 416
    floodlighting 179–80
    lack of 211, 386–7, 402, 414
    old photographs 364
    street 67–8, 74, 82
Lillington Gardens 127, 132, 133–4
Lincoln, Abraham 208
Lincolnshire 155, 157, 173
Lindisfarne 276
Linebaugh, Peter 447
Linkman, Audrey 326, 334, 335, 362
Linquist, Svante 199
Linquist, Sven 200
Lippiard, Lucy 86, 115, 116
Liskeard 178, 322
listed buildings 68, 125, 126, 139, 153, 154,
    244, 260, 291, 305
literature viii, 317
    for children 140, 185, 223
    heritage concepts 206, 209, 223, 231–2,
        266–7

historical romance 5, 6, 16, 159, 161–2
history as 431–2, 434–41
unofficial knowledge 41, 43
    invisible hands 17, 18, 21, 24
    popular memory 4–5, 7, 15–16
    see also theatre
litho-printing 83
Little Dorrit
    book 401, 409, 413–14, 420
    film 402, 404–9, 410–11, 414–17, 423
'Little Englandism' 261, 290–91, 301, 307
'Little Germany' (Bradford) 75
Littlewood, Joan 375
Liverpool 67, 153
    docklands 125–6, 179, 264, 300
    heritage concepts 205, 215, 259
    old photographs 351, 361, 367
Liverpool Street station 78–9, 83, 85, 115
Livesey Museum 196
living history 149, 153, 169–202
    see also open-air; resurrectionism
'living memory' 205
Llewellyn, Roddy 81
Lloyd, A.L. 206, 233, 235, 241, 305
Lloyd, David 200
Lloyd, Harold 93
Lloyd, Nathaniel 134
Lloyd, Valerie 349
Lloyd Webber, Andrew 105
Lloyd-Jones, Bob 132
Local Government Act (1964) 166
local history 4, 11–12, 147–8, 277–9, 321–3,
    440
    see also family history; living history;
        open-air and industrial museums;
        re-enactment
London, Jack 316
London
    Appreciation Society 184
    brickwork 119, 121, 124–7, 129, 131–4
    films and theatre set in 58, 381–425
    heritage concepts 246–7, 250
        politics 288, 291, 292, 295, 298, 300,
            302, 305, 307
        semantics 205, 214–15, 219–20, 225
        sociology 246–7, 250
    living history 169, 172, 174–82 passim,
        184–6, 190–91, 200
    march by Communist Party 207–8
    Museum of see under museums
    old photographs
        discovery of 337, 342–3, 347, 348
        dreamscapes 351, 352, 353, 354–5
        eye of history 315, 318, 319, 321,
            325, 329, 332, 334
        scopophilia 365, 367, 371
    pedagogies 275, 276, 281–2, 284–5

resurrectionism 141–2, 143, 152, 154, 156, 158, 160–61, 162
retrochic 83, 87–9, 91–3, 94, 96–8, 102–5, 110, 111
retrofitting 51, 55, 64, 66, 67, 70–75, 78–9
theatres of memory 36
Tower 162, 172, 356
underground 30, 133, 220
wartime 218
woodlands 168, 196, 295
see also Dickens
London Bridge station 355
Long Melford 177
Lord, Albert Bates 40
Louis XIII 29
Love, Harriet 89
Lovejoy, Arthur 436, 446
Lovel 6, 40
Lovelock, James 239
Lovesey, Peter 17, 43
Lowe, P. 241
Lowell (USA) 289
Lowenthal, David 118, 271
Lowerson, John 311
Loxley, John 255
Lumley, R. 240
Lunn, Mark 168
Lutyens, Sir Edward L. 128, 235
Lyall, Sutherland 134
Lynch, David 381
Lynn, Vera 23, 178
Lyons, Eric 76
Lytton, E.G.L.Bulwer 420

Mabey, Richard 144, 166, 198, 222
Mabo judgement (Australia) 308
macabre *see* Gothic
Macaulay, Thomas B., Lord 20, 265, 440, 441
MacCarthy, Fiona 310
MacColl, Ewan 222, 235–6, 241, 305, 306
MacColl, James 81
McCullin, Don 343, 348
McEwan, Malcolm 312
    quoted 302
MacFarlane, K.B. 445
MacGregor, John 144
McKay, Gilly 81, 117, 312
McKee, Alexander 285
Mackenzie, J.M. 447
Mackersey, Ian 200
McLaren, Malcolm 85–6, 112
Maclise, Daniel 34
Macmillan, Harold 246
McMillan, Margaret 182, 200
Maddox, Richard 165

Madge, Charles 390
Madrid 102
Magee, James 371
Maget, Marcel 309
magic 143–4, 229
Major, John 208, 209, 223
Malcolm, Derek 417
Maldon, battle of 22
Malraux, André 179, 210
Malton 264
man-made materials *see* synthetic materials
Manchester 28, 31, 298, 303
    Science and Technology Museum 250
    old photographs 321, 327, 330, 334, 347
    Pink Festival 108–9
    'Studies' 238
Mander, David 250, 362
Mandler, Peter 300–301, 312
Manet, Edouard 279
Mannix, Daniel 200
Manpower Services Commission 238
Mansfield, Nick 255
Mantegna, Andrea 338
mapping 29
Mapplethorpe, Robert 353
Marchant, Hilda 226
Margolyes, Miriam 410
Marian, Maid 29
Maritime Trust 174
Market Harborough 185, 209
Marley, Bob 90
Marlowe, Christopher 440
Márquez, Gabriel Garcia 429
Marsden, John 47
Marsden, Peter 251, 254
Marsh, Jan 310
Marshall, Howard 236
Marshall, Mick 115
Marston Moor, battle of 221, 270
Martello towers 205
Martin, Kingsley (pseud. Mr Park) 298
Martin, Kit 254
Martin, Paul 322, 329, 342, 346, 369, 377
Martin-Hervey, Sir John 421
Marx, Karl/Marxism 17, 149, 442, 445
    heritage concepts 207, 246, 276, 301
    old photographs 318, 332, 341
Mary, Queen, Queen Mother 212, 224
Mary Queen of Scots 7, 8, 16, 196
Marylebone 97, 119
masculinity
    of modernizing aesthetic 57
    in retrochic 99–101
Mason, Norman 222
Mass Observation 331, 390, 394–5, 397, 398
Massingberd, Hugh 254
Masson, David 44

Mathews, Charles 401
Matthew, Colin 41
Matthews, Janet 286–7
Maugham, Somerset 395–6
Maurer 12
Mayfair 154, 291, 297, 390
Mayhall, John 12
Mayhew, Henry 191, 318, 324, 395, 421
Mayne, Roger 318, 348
Me and My Girl 390–400
Medick, Hans 446
medieval England *see* Middle Ages
Medmenham Abbey 181
Meek, Ronald 446
megaliths 143, 229, 282
Meisel, Louis J. 167
Mellor, David 46, 240, 339, 348, 377
Meltzer, Milton 377
'memorabilia' *see* 'bygones'
memory
    art of vi–viii
    mnemonic devices vii, viii, 36, 438
    popular 3–17
    and religion 230–31, 245, 246
    theatre of viii–ix
        see also history
Mendels, F. 446
Mentmore 308
Merchant-Ivory 103, 139
Merrick, Joseph 381–9
Merrifield, Ralph 43
metal detectorists 274
Metro Centre 102
Michel, John 44, 166
Michelet, Jules viii, 41, 197, 447
Middle Ages viii–ix, 156, 436
    forgeries 433
    heritage concepts 205, 213, 231
    living history 169, 176, 182
    theatres of memory 23–4, 28, 29, 32, 36,
        37
    unofficial knowledge 21, 36
'middle class radicalism' *see* pressure
    groups and campaigns
Middle East 103
Middlesbrough 159
Midlands 26, 27, 189, 209, 214, 319, 344–5
    Black Country Museum 147, 181, 199,
        280, 283
    see also Birmingham; Derbyshire;
        Leicestershire
Miles, Bernard 234, 424
Military Remains Act (1986) 205
Mill, John Stuart 295
Millais, Sir John E. 369
Mills, John 419–20
Milne, Kirsty 199

Milton, John 207, 208, 439
Minsmere 171
Mitchell, G. 240
Mitchenson 250
Moberley, J.C. 228, 239
Modern Movement 300
modernistic style/modernization 51–9,
    123–4, 154, 294–9, 322, 338
    reaction against *see* brick;
        neo-vernacular; retrochic;
        retrofitting
Moholy-Nagy, L. 365, 376
Molleson, Theya 285
monarchy attacked 246
Monmouth 70
Monmouth Street 316
Monod, Gabriel 447
Monroe, Marilyn 13, 95, 339
Montfort, Simon de 207, 223
Moorhouse, Geoffrey 58, 80
Moorse, Kate 42–3
    quoted 13
More, Sir Thomas 295
Morley, Andrew 167
Mormons 27
Morrah, H.A. 41
Morris, O.J. 321, 334
Morris, William 262
    designs 18, 60, 80, 92, 194
    and National Trust 296, 310
    utopianism 156
    see also Arts and Crafts; Society for
        Protection of Ancient Monuments
Morrison, Jim 90, 338
Morton, A.L. 241
Morton, Lucy 362
Mosley, Sir Oswald 390
motherhood 161, 385
Mowlem, John 111
Muir, Edwin 431, 445
Munby, A.J. 43, 346
Munich 178
Munro, Ailie 222
Murray, Elizabeth 43
Murray, James 18
museums and art galleries
    Australia 289
    England as one gigantic 260, 262
    heritage concepts
        genealogies 233, 238
        heritage-baiting 260, 262, 263, 264,
            265, 267
        pedagogies 274, 278–83
        politics 289, 290, 301, 303–4, 312
        semantics 209, 210–11, 215
        sociology 242, 243, 244, 245, 250–53
    Italy 304, 312

living history 169–73, 176–7, 181–2, 189, 190, 192, 194
  Museum of London 169, 175, 178, 194, 251, 407, 410, 415
  old photographs 102, 320, 330, 342, 346
  railway 139, 147
  resurrectionism 139, 146–7, 149, 153, 159, 166
  retrochic 93, 100, 102
  war 159, 178, 346
  see also open-air and industrial; theme parks
music 18
  Baroque 23, 139
  film 402, 407, 410
  heritage concepts 206, 208, 222
  musicals 390–400, 421–2
  theatre 214, 410
  see also folk music; pop and rock; songs
Mussolini, B. 390
Musson, A.E. 334
Muthesius, Stefan 167
Mystery plays 93, 192
myths and legends 436, 437–8, 439, 442–3
  costume drama 382, 385
  unofficial knowledge 11, 15, 28–9

Nadeau, Maurice 118
Nairn, Ian 294, 302
Nairne, Lady 22
Napoleon 27, 28, 32, 110, 438
Napper, Arthur 248–9
narcissism 374, 376
Nash, John 22, 227
National Association of Re-enactment Societies 174
National Building (later Monument) Record 201
National Curriculum 279
National Film Theatre 347, 381
National Heritage, Department of 210
National Housing and Town Planning Council 311
National Land Fund 308
National Museum of Photography 102
National Parks
  heritage concepts 288, 297, 300, 308
  legislation 155, 210, 288
National Portrait Gallery 320, 342
National Record of Industrial Monuments 157, 189
National Theatre 152, 192, 214, 422
National Trust 39
  founded 295–6, 308
  gardens 209
  gift shops 93, 100, 267
  heritage concepts 276

genealogies 6, 227, 228, 233, 238
  heritage-baiting 260, 271
  politics 288, 295–7, 302, 304, 308, 310
  semantics 208, 216
  sociology 242, 250, 253
  living history 185, 194
  pedagogies 275, 276, 277, 282, 285
  resurrectionism 139, 146, 156, 160, 162
  retrofitting 60
  of Scotland 253
nationalism see patriotism
natural history 158, 228, 441–2
  see also nature
'natural' and 'organic' 60–62
nature 11
  'back to' 237, 298
  conservation
    heritage concepts 209–10, 217, 221, 227–9, 232, 234, 237, 288, 307, 309
    resurrectionism 143–6, 148, 155–6, 168
    see also Nature Conservancy; wildlife
  feminized 161
  heritage concepts 145, 171, 216, 218, 221
  reserves 145, 155, 160, 171, 205, 210, 228, 237, 260, 288, 303
  trails 171, 283, 284
  see also birds; environmentalism; gardens; hedgerows; wildlife; woodlands; Wordsworth
Nature Conservancy (now English Nature) 105–6, 144–5, 148, 209, 221, 234, 288
Nature Conservancy Act (1970) 237
Nature Detective Trails 145
'Nature's Heritage' 144
Naylor, G. 310
Naylor, John 225
Nazis 219, 290, 309, 376, 390
  see also Second World War
Neal, Mary 296, 301, 312
necrophilia 339, 341, 375
  dead pop stars 89–90, 338
Neeson, Jeanette 231, 239
Nelson, Henry 334
Nelson, Horatio 164–5, 179, 214
Nelson, Janet 446
neo-classicism 111, 124, 213, 215
neo-Georgian style 65, 120–21
neo-Gothic style 77, 119
  see also Gothic
neo-vernacular 91
  bricks 120, 123, 124, 127, 129, 131
  retrofitting 59–67

Netherlands 102, 179
Nevinson, J.L. 46
New Ageism 229, 285
    Glastonbury 107–8, 140, 433
    resurrectionism 140–43, 144
    retrochic 82, 86, 97
    vegetarianism 92, 237
New Brutalism 63, 68
New Deal 289
New English 301
New Lanark 304
new replacing old *see* old
New Right 260, 264, 289
    see also Conservative Party
New York 86, 89, 102, 122, 131, 359
Newbold, R. 104
Newcastle 63
Newcastle, Duke of 15
Newcomen, Thomas 189
Newcomen Society 189, 226
Newgate 197
Newhall, Beaumont 334
Newhaven 342, 369
Newman, Oscar 59, 80
Newport 223
Nicholas Nickleby 401, 417–19, 422–3, 424–5
Nicholas, T.Islwyn 223
Nicholls, Ann 224
Nicholson-Lord, David 167
Niesewand, Nonie 115
Nightingale, Florence 27, 214
nineteenth century *see* Victorian period
Nohl, Johannes 29
Nora, Pierre 11, 42
Norfolk 145, 153, 169, 250, 322, 369
Norman, E.R. 47
Norman period 17
    see also Hastings
North, Richard 271
north-east England 63, 102
    heritage concepts 220, 276
    living history 169, 172, 173, 175, 178,
        179
    old photographs 318, 319, 321, 334, 352
    resurrectionism 145, 146, 159, 160
Northamptonshire 209, 344–5
Northern England
    Northerners denigrated 264, 267–8
    see also Cumbria; Lancashire; north-east;
        Yorkshire
Northern Mill Engine Society 250
Northumberland 175, 276, 318, 319
Norway 179
Norwich 153
nostalgia industry *see* retrochic
Notting Hill 176, 318
Nottingham 122

novels *see* literature

objet trouvé 110
objectivity of historians 430
O'Connor, Feargus 332
Odeon cinemas 132–3
Odham's Walk 132
office development 64, 121, 151
Ohrn, Karin Becker 377
Okey, Thomas 46
old, new replacing *see* modernistic;
        neo-vernacular; retrochic;
        retrofitting
old photographs 315–77
    discovery of 328, 337–49
    dreamscapes 350–63
    eye of history 315–36
    heritage concepts 210, 211, 215, 217,
        248
    living history 183, 186, 190, 192
    resurrectionism 163–4
    scopophilia 271, 364–77
    unofficial knowledge 25, 35–6
Oldbuck, Jonathan 440
Oliver, Michael 249
Oliver, Paul 206
Oliver! 421–2
Oliver Twist 35, 317, 384, 401, 402, 417, 419,
        421–2, 423
Oliver's Wharf 132
Olivier, Laurence 233
Olivier, Sydney 310
Oman, Sir Charles 8, 41, 269, 273
Oodles 92, 237
open-air and industrial museums
    heritage concepts 238, 264
        pedagogies 280–83
        politics 290, 301, 303–4
        sociology 244, 245
    major *see* Beamish; Black Country
        Museum; Ironbridge
    resurrectionism 139, 146–7, 151, 157,
        160
        living history 169, 172–3, 176–7,
            189, 199
    see also industrial archaeology
'Operation Groundwork' 146
Operation Neptune 209
Opie, Iona and Peter 12, 40, 93
Opie, Robert 152
oral history 235, 351
    Oral History Society 191
    resurrectionism 140, 161, 188, 191, 192
    unofficial knowledge 4, 5–6, 42–3
Orford Ness 277
organizations, major *see* Council for
        Preservation of Rural England;

National Trust; pressure groups
Orkneys 431
Orpington 148
Orrell, John 254
Orton, Clive 198
Orton, Joe 190
Orwell, George 190, 218, 219, 367, 377, 420, 421
Orwin, C.S. and C.S. 38, 48
Osborne, John 268
Otter Trust 308
Otterton Mill 147
Owen, Robert 304
owner-occupancy 76, 128, 237, 291
Oxfam 150, 341
Oxford 20–21
    brick 124–5, 132
    heritage concepts 206, 222, 273, 276, 302
    Inspector Morse 260, 271
    museums 177
    old photographs 315, 317, 319, 333, 342, 376
    resurrectionism 152, 184
    retrochic 86, 102
    University 8, 124–5, 152, 184, 222, 302
Oxfordshire 134, 145, 213, 248–9, 297
Oxleas Wood 143–4, 259, 293
Oxo tower 305

Pabst, G.W. 34
Paddington Basin 134
Page, Christopher 165
pageants and spectaculars 176, 179, 191, 207
Pagnol, Marcel 318
painting 234
Panizza, Mario 254
Papworth, Martin 172
Paris 102, 131, 437
    Commune 23, 318
    exhibition 32
    old photographs 318, 329, 353–4, 359, 365, 369
Paris, Matthew 36
Parker, Charles 236
Parker, John 311
Parker, Roszicka 18, 44
Parkin, Frank 247, 254
Parliament
    Acts *see* legislation
    buildings *see* Houses of Parliament
parody and retrochic 95–6
Parrot, Richard 249
Past Times 86–7, 98–9
pastoralism *see* rural areas

Pate, David 221
Patrick, St 433
patrimoine 210–11, 289–90
patriotism and nationalism 208, 212, 218–19
    'Little Englandism' 261, 290–91, 301, 307
Patterson, Alexander 400
Pattison, Bruce 222
Paulin, Tom 260
paving 74–5
Peak, Steve 255, 311
Peak District 11, 147, 311
Pearce, David 239
Pearman, Hugh 272
Pears, Peter 300
Pearsall, Ronald 116, 349
Pearson, Geoff 400
Pearson, Lionel 445
Peate, Iorweth C. 205, 222, 224
Peck, Lady 46
pedagogies 274–87, 438, 440–41
    heritage concepts 216, 220, 223, 232, 235, 252, 261, 265, 301
    living history 176–7, 182, 190, 193–4, 196
    old photographs 321, 322, 338, 340, 341, 356
    resurrectionism 147–9
    unofficial knowledge 34, 40, 42, 46
        graphics 31, 37–8
        popular memory 5, 6–7, 12–13
    see also school
Peet, Stephen 191, 235
Penhaligon's 59
Peninsular War 35
Pennant, Thomas 21
Pennines 321
    Pennine Way 175, 186, 238, 298
People of the Dragon 143
'People Show' 26, 27
Peplow, Mary 167, 224
Pepys, Samuel 19–20
Percy, Bishop Thomas 205
Perec, Georges 362
Pericles 431
'period' design 65–6, 71
    see also brick; heritage; neo-vernacular; periods; retrochic
periods and styles, major *see* Anglo-Saxon; Edwardian; Georgian; Gothic; Middle Ages; Regency; Roman; Victorian; Vikings
Perroy, Edouard 445
Peterborough 159
Peters, Ellis 17, 43
Peterson, Charles E. 309

Petticoat Lane 353
Pevsner, Nikolaus 116, 125, 133–4, 244,
    253, 300
Phelps-Brown, E.H. 446
Philip, Duke of Edinburgh 174, 185
Phiz 405, 406, 411
photography
    denigrating heritage 263–7
    see also graphics; old photographs
Pickles, Sheila 59
Pickles, Walter 167
pictures 234
    see also graphics; photography
Pidoux, Rev. C. 47
Piggott, Stuart 28, 40, 45, 46, 222, 239, 286
Pike, Royston 201
'Pilgrim's Way' 186
Pimlico 127, 133–4
Pimlott, Ben 308
Pink Festival 108–9
Pinnock 7
Piper, John 30, 116, 234, 240, 312
Pitt, G. 440
place-names 11–12
planning 120
    'blight' 67
    heritage concepts 293, 299, 300, 308,
        311
    legislation 68, 124, 308
    see also listed buildings
plants 228, 299
    see also ivy; woodlands
Platt, John 222
play see re-enactments; role play; theatre
Pliny 42
Plot, Robert 12, 42, 441
Pocock, J.G.A. 239, 446
Poel, William 247
politics 288–312, 430
    see also Communism; Conservative
        Party; Labour Party; Liberal Party;
        Marx; socialism
Pollard, Michael 199
Pols, Robert 335
Poole 157
Poole, Josephine 311
pop art 95, 110, 195, 338–9, 341
pop and rock music 22, 23–7
    heritage concepts 206–7
    memorabilia 85, 159
    record sleeves 338, 340, 341, 348
    resurrectionism 139, 140, 143, 153
    retrochic 85–6, 88, 89–91, 104–5, 107
    shrines 89–90, 140, 153, 338
    see also Beatles
Pope-Hennessey, Una 41
Poplar 342

Popular Front (France) 290
popular memory 3–17
Porter Benson, Susan 82
Porter, Gabriel 330, 335
Porter, Jimmy 55
Portland stone 119, 124, 128
    Quarrymen 231
Portobello Road 73, 152, 278
    old photographs 337
    retrochic 83, 91, 92, 96–8
ports see ships
Portsmouth 164, 173
post-colonialism 308
postcards 345–7, 353–4, 355, 356
posters 215, 353, 374
postmodernism 35, 63, 95, 146, 195, 266,
    351, 429
Potter, Beatrix 93
Potter, Sally (Orlando) 114
Potteries area 20, 111, 157, 276
Powell, Michael 186, 234
Powell, W.R. 44
Power, John 273
Pozzi, Jennie 349
prehistory see archaeology
present, nostalgia for 140, 192
preservationism
    canal 141–2, 185, 247–8, 304–5
    railway 139, 184–5, 191, 236, 245,
        249–50, 259, 302
    steam traction 249–50, 283
    woodlands 144–5, 155–6, 168, 228, 229,
        232, 442
    see also conservation; resurrectionism
Presley, Elvis 116
Press, G.A. 445
Pressburger, Emeric 186, 234
pressure groups and campaigns 68, 237,
    247–8, 292–3, 295–6, 297, 299, 306
    see also organizations
Preston 315
Preston, Andy 88
Preston, Mr 115
Prévert, Jacques 318
Priestley, J.B. 124, 133, 218, 236, 240, 268,
    272, 273, 421
Primrose League 180
printing 25, 83, 191
private sphere see domestic sphere
Prochaska, Alice 285
Proctor, John 252
propaganda films 208
property
    boom 65, 71, 78
    see also buildings and architecture
Propp, Vladimir 442
Provence 131, 135

Prynn, D. 311
'Public History' 278
public housing *see* council housing
Public Record Office 177
publishers
    heritage concepts 215–16, 217, 232, 278
    old photographs 321–2, 340, 343, 347
    unofficial knowledge 34, 35, 38
pubs 395
    mirror craze 83
    music 206, 207
    old photographs 337, 348, 354
    Victorianized 65, 75, 81, 83, 112, 337
Pugh, R.P. 44
Pugin, August W.N. 18, 22
Punch, Maurice 310
Purbeck 231
Putney 176, 208

Queen Anne's Gate 75, 110
Queen's Acre 121
Quennell, C.H.B. 216, 286
Quennell, Marjorie 182, 216, 286
Quennell, Peter 321, 334, 346–7, 349

Rackham, Oliver 145, 158, 166, 168, 442,
        447
radicalism *see* pressure groups and
        campaigns
radio 219, 235–6, 339, 343, 352
railways
    museums 139, 147
    preservation 139, 184–5, 191, 236, 245,
        249–50, 259, 302
    stations 125, 126, 133, 355
        see also Euston; Liverpool Street
    underground 30, 133, 220
Raitt, Suzanne 311
Raleigh, Carew 11
Raleigh, Sir Walter 11, 45
Ramblers' Association 186
rambling *see* walks
Ranger, Terence 16
Ranke, Leopold von 3, 15, 41, 42, 197, 274,
        447
Ravilious, Eric 30
Rawlett, J. 310
Rawnsley, Eleanor F. 310
Rawnsley, Canon H.D. 216, 225, 296, 310
Rawnsley, Stuart 285
Rawson, W.T. 312
Read, Benedict 45
Read, Herbert 300
Reading 173, 251–2
Reagan, Ronald 166
realism/reality 338, 414
    allegories of real 429–47

effect 434
'hyper-reality' 243
'magic' 429
Reas, Paul 267, 272
record societies 19, 22
Red House 63
Reece, Gordon 209
Reed, Talbot Baines 45
re-enactments 7, 28, 265, 270–71, 280, 437
    for children *see* role play
    living history 174–6, 178, 180, 182,
        191–2, 194
Rees, Roger 425
Reformation 437, 439
Regency period and style 21, 71, 77, 111,
        128, 227, 300
Regent Street 70, 227
Regent's Park and Canal 141–2, 230
Reid, Forest 45
Reigate 250
Reilly, Paul 56
Reisz, Karel 318
Rejlander, O.G. 319, 334, 377
religion *see* Christianity/theology
Renoir, Jean 369
'rescue' archaeology 150–51
restoration *see* conservation; 'period'
        design; preservationism;
        resurrectionism; retrofitting
resurrectionism viii, 139–65, 197, 294
    living history 169–202
retrochic 83–118, 429
    heritage concepts 208, 209, 245
    living history 194
    old photographs 338, 341, 371
retrofads 110
retrofitting 39, 51–82, 360, 405
    aesthetics of light and space 51–9
    living history 194–5
    modernization in disguise 67–79
    neo-vernacular 59–67
    see also modernistic
revivals *see* restoration
Reydon Wood 145
Reynolds, Jack 285
rhetoric 431–2
Rhondda Heritage Park 146
Richard Coeur de Lion 28, 35
Richards, Jeffrey 240
Richards, J.M. 116, 125, 133, 300, 312
Richardson, Ruth 29, 46
Richmond 121, 129, 132, 175
Rickards, Maurice 253, 255
Rickmansworth 56, 157
rides in museums 169, 184, 200, 282, 284
        see also transport
Ridgeway, Peter 44

Ridley, Nicholas 291
Riegl, Alois 359
Rigby, A. 298
Right 162–3, 324, 425
    heritage concepts 264, 281, 290–91,
        297, 302, 303
        heritage-baiting 259, 260, 262, 265
    see also Conservative Party
rights, hereditary 231
Riverside development (Richmond) 121
Rix, Michael 157, 220, 226
Roach Smith, Charles 25, 37, 45, 47
roads and streets
    building and widening 67, 69, 143–4,
        217, 221, 236
    car ownership 236, 243, 244
    cobbled 73–4
    dancing in 395–6
    lighting 67–8, 74, 82
    motorway box opposed 236, 247, 302
    old photographs 323, 324, 329
    paving 74–5
    protests about 143–4
    resurrectionism 143–4, 157, 181
    shopping 181–2, 354–5, 357, 360, 365,
        370–71
Robertshaw, Andrew 287
Robertson, E.Arnot 200
Robertson, Martin 166, 199
Robin Hood 29, 35, 439
Robinson, David 400
Robinson, Henry Russell 198
Robson, Graham 200
Robson-Smith, R.W. 200
Rochester 177, 192, 201, 259
Rochfort-Smith, Teena 43
rock music see pop and rock
Rockefeller 289
Rocks (Sydney, Australia) 179
Roddick, Anita: Body Shop 61, 81, 98, 100,
        112, 117, 302, 312
Rodee, Howard D. 377
Rodgers, Frank 183
Roehampton 51
Rogers, P.J. 334
Roland Way 119
Rolling Stones 207, 340
Rolt, Tom 200, 233, 248, 255, 304, 305
Roman period and style 431, 433
    heritage concepts 205, 221, 229, 263,
        297
    living history 169, 172, 175, 176, 179,
        192
    pedagogies 284, 437
    resurrectionism 139, 152, 159
    retrochic 87, 110
    unofficial knowledge 25, 29

    see also Hadrian's Wall
Roman Way 192
Romanticism vii, ix, 22, 31, 229, 234
    see also Wordsworth
Romany 235, 240
Romford 352
Ronan Point 67
Roncevaux, battle of 22
Ronis, Willy 211
Rook, Clarence 400
Room, Adrian 42
Roper, Lyndal 447
Rose, Arthur 394
Rose, Millicent 333
Rose, Tony 222
Rose Theatre 230
Rosicrucians ix
Ross, W.S. 40, 43
Rotherhithe 281
Rothesay 151
Round, J.H. 18, 44
Rowntree, Kenneth 234
Rowse, A.L. 40
Royal Albert Hall 131
Royal Commission on Historical
    Monuments see Historical
    Monuments
Royal Historical Society 19
Royal Institute of British Architects 63, 302
Royal Shakespeare Company see Nicholas
    Nickleby
Royal Society for Protection of Birds 171,
    234, 237, 293, 311
Rubens, Godfrey 311
Rubin, Miri 45, 200
Rubinstein, W.D. 275, 286
Ruffins, Faith Davis 309
Rugby School 46
Rule, Margaret 285
rural areas 88
    heritage concepts 248–9, 295–9
    old photographs 319–21, 331–2, 335,
        369–72
    see also country houses; nature
Rushdie, Salman 374, 377
Ruskin, John 18, 44, 119, 231, 296, 435
Russell, Gordon 56
Russia 307
Ruston 276
Ryder, Charles 271
Rymer, Edward 20

Saalburg 178
Sachs, Leonard 21
Sackville-West, Vita 199, 206, 222, 297, 311
sacred history see Christianity
sailing see ships and boats

Sainsbury's 106–7, 117, 127
Saint, Andrew 81
St Augustine's Priory 23
St Crispin's Day celebrations 28–9
St Fagan's 178, 205
St Katherine's Dock 174
St Mary's Square 121
St Pancras station 124, 125, 126, 133
St Paul's 126, 179
St Thomas's Hospital 214
Salford 354
Salisbury 64, 157
salvage trade 64–5, 110–11, 121–2, 127, 245
Sander, August 370
Sanders, Andrew 412
Sanitarian movement 213
Saunders, Gill 46, 240
Savage, Jon 115
SAVE Britain's Heritage 150, 246, 254, 308
'Save Our Orchards' 155
Saxon, A.H. 41
Saxons *see* Anglo-Saxon period
Scandinavia 178–9
    design 154, 301–2
scenery *see* nature
Schama, Simon 197
school
    as museum 251–2
    photographs 332–3
    see also pedagogies
Schools Council 147, 176
Schwarz, Bill 223, 253
Schweizer, Klaartje 117
Science Museum 177, 244
'scientific history' 197–8, 442
scopophilia 271, 364–77
Scotland 292, 431, 443
    conservation 228
    heritage concepts 209, 215, 228, 234,
        253, 262
    living history 174, 179–80, 196
    old photographs 365
    resurrectionism 144, 146, 151, 154, 159
    songs 22–3, 306
    see also Aberdeen; Dundee; Edinburgh;
        Glasgow
Scotney Castle 285
Scott, Amoret 116
Scott, Sir Gilbert 125
Scott, Joan 335
Scott, M.H.Baillie 296, 310
Scott, Paul 139
Scott, Peter 307
Scott, Ridley 93
Scott, Robert F. 174
Scott, Sir Walter vii, 16, 21, 24, 28, 31, 35,
    42, 309, 440–41, 443

Scottish Natural Heritage 209
Scouts (Boy) 301
Sea Birds Preservation Act 228
Seaborne, Malcolm V.J. 344–5, 349
Sealed Knot 191–2, 199, 281
Sear, Roy 223
Sebba, Anna 80, 201
Second World War 1, 23, 437
    costume drama 391, 396–7
    heritage concepts 205, 208, 218, 219,
        221, 233, 234, 235
    old photographs 329
    pedagogies 277, 281, 284
    resurrectionism 153, 158, 159, 178
second-hand materials *see* salvage
Secord, Anne 239
Seifert, Colonel 64
Selborne 228
Selleck, R.J.W. 312
Severs, Denis 88, 114
Shaftesbury, Anthony A.C., Lord 230
Shaftesbury (town) 360
Shakespeare, William ix, 7, 15, 22, 197, 440
    theatre (Globe) 214, 233, 247
Shankland, Graeme 67, 81
Shankly, Bill 215
Sharp, Cecil 206, 222, 296, 310
Shaw, Bernard 420
Shaw, Christopher 287
Shaw, Norman 63, 124
Shaw, Paula 286–7
Shaw-Lefevre, G.J. 310
Sheail, John 311
Sheffield 12, 58, 188, 214, 298
Shelley, Percy B. 223
Shelter 150
Shelton, Robert 223
Shepard, Leslie 42
Sheratsky, Rodney E. 223
Shipley, Debra 167, 224
ships and boats
    heritage concepts 245, 251, 274, 284,
        285, 287
    resurrectionism 173–4, 178–9, 185
Shooter's Hill 143–4
shopping 159–60, 340
    heritage concepts 211
    precincts 73, 88, 194
    shopkeeper 161
    streets 181–2, 354–5, 357, 360, 365,
        370–71
Shrewsbury 43, 220
Shrimpton, Jean 338, 348
Shropshire 43, 220
    see also Ironbridge
Sicily 308
Silver, Jeremy 240

Simmons, Jack 320
Simmons, Jean 420
Simonides of Ceos vii, viii
Simple Lifeism 301
Sims, G.R. 318
Sir John Soane's Museum 300
Sirk, Douglas 373
Sitbon, Martine 116
Sites of Special Scientific Interest *see* nature
    reserves
Skansen 178
Skeffington, Arthur 311
Skeffington-lodge, Tom 311
skiffle 206–7
Slater, Montagu 223
slums
    clearance *see* demolition
    improved *see* gentrification
    photographs 318–19, 367, 368, 371
Smail, Mr 253
Smedley, John 87
Smigielski, Konrad 82
Smiles, Samuel 16, 164
Smith, Adam 146
Smith, Adolphe 316, 319, 333, 334, 354
Smith, Charles Roach 25, 37, 45, 47
Smith, Greg 201
Smith, Gypsy Lee 240
Smith, Henry 41
Smith, Ivan 172
Smith, Paul 104
Smith, Stevie 224
Smyth, Bob 239
Snape Maltings 214, 300
Snibston 284
Snowdon, Lord 407
Snowdonia 184
Social Democrats (Germany) 290
socialism 162–3, 262, 324
    heritage concepts 262, 288, 296, 297,
        300
    see also Communism; Labour Party;
        Marx; Morris
Society of Antiquaries 32, 227
Society of Friends 250
Society for Protection of Ancient Buildings
        147, 162, 186, 227, 231, 288
Soho (London) 74, 75, 87–8, 133
SoHo (New York) 131
Soil Association 442
Sokemen 231
Somerleyton 224
Somerset levels 171
son et lumière 179–80
Sondheim, Stephen 381
songs and ballads
    heritage concepts 206, 222, 235–6, 296,

301, 305–6
'Lambeth Walk' 390–400
unofficial knowledge 7, 11, 15, 19, 22–3
    see also pop and rock
Sontag, Susan 329, 335, 349
South Downs Way 145
South Kensington 119
South Molton 110
South Shields 159, 169, 178
South Woodham Ferrers 127, 134
south-east England 149, 232, 315
    see also Berkshire; Essex; Kent; London;
        Oxfordshire; Surrey; Sussex
south-west England *see* West Country
Southall, Brian 167
Southam, Brian 215, 225
Southampton 195
Southern, Edward 346
Southern, Richard 45
Southern, R.W. 23, 446
Southey, Robert 28, 140
Southgate, Walter 250–51
Southwark 156, 190, 292, 307, 339
Southwold 145
space, aesthetics of 51–9, 76
Spain 102
    Civil War 207, 297
Spencer, Countess 302
Spencer, Stephanie 334, 377
Spencer, Wilson 334
Spender, Humphrey 325, 331, 335, 367,
        377
Spielberg, Stephen 273
Spitalfields 11, 100, 114, 190, 225, 275, 284
Sports Council 174
Sproule, Anna 199
Spufford, Margaret 43, 46, 269, 273
Squire, Sir John 232
Squires, Roger W. 200
SSSI (Sites of Special Scientific Interest) *see*
        nature reserves
Staffordshire 20, 111, 157, 276, 441
Stamford 155
Stamp, Terence 96
stamps, postage 30, 140, 165–6
Stanley, Dean 46
Stapleton Hall 134
Starkey, David 272
stately homes *see* country houses
stations *see under* railways
steam traction and fairs 249–50, 283
    see also railways
Stedman Jones, Gareth 319, 335, 424, 446
Steedman, Carolyn 16, 42
Steel, Don 149, 168, 334, 336
Steele, Tommy 207
Stenton, Sir Frank 12

Stephen, King 17
Stephenson, George 220
Stevenson, Laura C. 447
Stevenson, Sara 377
Stewart, Geoffrey C. 309
Stockholm 178
Stockman, Olivier 407, 417
Stone, Sir Benjamin 349
Stone, Lawrence 446
stone buildings 119, 124–5, 127–8
Stonehenge 229, 282
stories *see* literature; myths
Storrington 130
Stothard, Charles Alfred 21, 32, 44
Stothard, Thomas 44
Stow, John 184
Stratford and Avon Canal 185
Stratta, Leslie 312, 348
Stratten, Michael 254
Streatham 390
Street, G.E. 133
streets *see* roads; shopping
Stretham 189
Strickland, Agnes 7, 41
Stuarts *see* Charles Edward
Stubbes, Philip 267
Stubbs, Bishop W. 430
Stukeley, William 30, 206, 229
Styal Mill 276, 304
suburbia 152, 164, 208–9, 212
Sudbury Hall 196
Sue, Eugène 443
Suffolk 58, 122, 156
    heritage concepts 209, 224, 277
    living history 171, 172, 177, 188
    pedagogies 277, 284
Summerson, John 300, 312
surrealism 110
Surrey 56, 121, 129, 132, 161, 235
Sussex 64, 130, 214, 235, 249, 306, 342, 369
    see also Brighton
Sutcliffe, Frank Meadow 333, 342, 361, 363,
    365
Sutcliffe, Tom 117
Sutton, Alan 334
Sutton House and Square 134, 277
Sutton Windmill 147
Swanage 111
Sweden 178
Swindells 31
Swing, Captain 295
Switzerland 307
Sydney 179
Sykes, Christopher 44, 118
Sylvester, David 149, 166, 334
Symonds, Richard 240
synthetic materials 51, 52, 56–7

rejected 60–63
systems-building 127
Szarkowski, John 377

Tacitus 431
Tagore, Rabindranath 232, 240, 297
Tahran, Su 87, 115
Tait, Simon 255
Taithe, Bertrand 135
Tal-y-llyn railway 184
Talbot, W.H.Fox 316, 342, 376
Tanner, Alain 268
tape recorders 191
Tarrant Place 119
Tasmania 289
Tatton Park 282
Taunt, Henry 319, 333, 342
Tawney, R.H. 22, 269
Taylor, A.J.P. 320
Taylor, Alan 115, 117
Taylor, B.J. 134
Taylor, E.G.R. 40
Taylor, J. 45
Taylor, Joan and Harold 444
Taylor, John 377
Taylor, Lawrence 149, 334
Taylor, Lou 115, 116
Taylor, Malcolm 222
Taylor, Roger 335, 336
technology 39
    buildings 123, 127, 131
    living history 171–2, 182
    printing 25, 83, 191
    retrochic 83–4
teddy bears 85, 115
Teddy Boys 112
television
    advertisements 56, 93, 95
    documentaries 13, 139, 192
    heritage concepts 235, 260, 263, 267,
        275
    living history 191
    old photographs 339, 343, 352
    retrochic 105
    studios 153
    unofficial knowledge 13–15, 17, 25, 35
    see also films
Telford, Thomas 174
Telford (town) 122, 131, 139
Tell, William 438, 442
Tenniel, Sir John 35, 140, 447
Tennyson, Alfred, Lord 329, 349
Terry, Ellen 329
Terry, Quinlan 119, 121
Terry, Sonny 206
Tesco 127
Thackeray, W.M. 409

Thames 228, 234, 241, 292
Thatcher, Margaret 121, 166, 261, 290
    cabinet 224, 246
    degentrification of Conservative Party
        246
    'Victorian values' 160–61, 163–4, 208,
        291, 310, 325, 425
Thaw, John 260
theatre
    heritage concepts 214, 233, 247
    Me and My Girl 390–400
    music 214, 410
    musicals 390–400, 421–2
    Mystery plays 93, 192
    retrochic 93, 114
    in the round 192
    'Theatre in Education' 193
    unofficial knowledge 28, 36
    see also Nicholas Nickleby; pageants;
        re-enactments; Shakespeare
theme parks 242
    heritage-baiting 260, 263, 265, 267
    resurrectionism 153, 169, 177–8
    see also open-air and industrial
        museums; museums
theology see Christianity/theology
Thetford Forest Park 145
Thirties Society 277
Thom, J. 42
Thomas, Alan 335
Thomas, Keith 42, 148, 158, 166, 168, 315,
        442, 447
Thomas, Sir Miles 220
Thomas, Milton 250
Thomas, Rosalind 42, 445
Thomas Aquinas, St vii
Thomason, George 19, 44
Thompson, Dorothy 335
Thompson, Edward J. 232, 240
Thompson, E.P. viii, 38, 223, 232, 240, 320
Thompson, Flora 40, 189
Thompson, F.M.L. 447
Thompson, Harry 447
Thompson, Paul 238–9
Thoms, W.J. 45
Thomson, John 316, 319, 333, 334, 346,
        354
Thorne, Robert 309, 310
Thornton, Andy 102, 117
Thrupp, Sylvia 36, 47
Thucydides 328, 432, 433
Thurloe, Charles 287
Thwaite, Garard Haythorne 311
Tillett, Ben 311, 356
Tilley, Roger 45
Tin Pan Alley Association 88
Tintagel 216

Tintern Abbey 172
Tocqueville, A. de 41
Tonkin, Elizabeth 40
Top Withens 364
Topley, W.W. 349
topographical illustration 29–30
Torem, Dorothy Hehl 116
Torquay 323
'total' history 444
tourism 159, 248
    see also museums; theme parks
Tower of London and Tower Bridge 162,
        172, 356
Town and Country Planning Act (1947)
        124, 308
towns see urban areas
trade unions see labour history
Tradescant family 20, 250
Trafalgar, Battle of 28, 164–5
Trafalgar Square 111
tramways 185–6, 357
transport 345, 357
    see also canals; railways; rides; roads;
        ships; tramways
Trease, Geoffrey 223
trees see woodlands
Trerice Museum 152
Tressell, Robert 71
Trevelyan, George M. 233
Treves, Sir Frederick 382–8 passim
Treves, Mrs 387
Trevithick Society 250
Trevor-Roper, Hugh 446
Trigari, Ivano 304
Trimley Nature Reserve 171
Trinder, Barrie 169, 198, 301–2, 312
Triulzi, Alessandro 312
Trory, Ernie 223
Tudor Church Music Project 18
Tudors see Elizabethan and Tudor
Tuner, Bruce 222
Turner, Michael 44
Turner, Peter 361, 362
Turpin, Dick 7
Tussaud, Madame 24, 341–2
Twiggy 338, 348
Twydell, David 99
Twyford 143, 144, 151
Twyman, Michael 45, 46
Tylden-Wright, David 42

Uderzo, A. 47
Ulysses 22
United Arab Emirates 103
United Nations World Heritage Site see
        Ironbridge
United States 34, 307

brickwork 131
Civil War 34, 328, 329
heritage concepts 264, 272–3, 289, 302,
    305–6
milk-bars 272–3
old photographs 335, 342
    dreamscapes 350, 359
    eye of history 325, 328, 329, 330–32
    scopophilia 365, 369–73
resurrectionism 149, 150, 154, 179
retrochic 85–6, 89, 97–8, 99–100, 102,
    103
retrofitting 57
salvaged materials for 65
songs 206, 305–6
theme parks from 268
unofficial knowledge 3–48
    graphics 27–39
    invisible hands 17–27
    popular memory 3–17
Unstead, R.J. 45
Unwin, Raymond 63, 296, 310, 334
urban areas
    'greening' of city 62, 205, 208
    inner city colonized see gentrification
    resurrectionism 146, 149, 153, 159–60,
        163
    town photographic album 322, 334,
        355
    see also buildings; roads and streets and
        in particular London
'Utility' schemes 300
utopianism 156, 292
Utrillo, Maurice 329

Van Amerongen, J.B. 411
Vanbrugh, Sir John 297
Vansina, Jan 40
Varah, Chad 47
Vaughan, Richard 47
Vaughan Williams, Ralph 208, 222, 223
Vaughan Williams, Ursula 223
Vauxhall Gardens 395
Venturi, Robert 80, 365, 371, 376
Vercingetorix 431
Verdi, Giuseppe 402, 407, 410
Vermeer, Jan 405
vernacular 68
    see also neo-vernacular
Victoria and Albert Museum 242, 246, 250,
    342
Victoria Line 133
Victoria, Queen 250, 382
Victorian period and style 291, 382, 435
    brickwork 119, 120, 125–7, 128, 129
    heritage concepts 211, 231, 244, 250,
        291, 295–6, 305

historians 440–41, 442–3
living history 176, 182, 184, 186, 189,
    193–4, 196
pedagogies 275, 276, 279–80
resurrectionism 152, 153, 154, 155, 159,
    164
retrochic 82, 83, 86, 87, 92, 93, 96–7,
    100, 102, 103, 109, 111–12
retrofitting 51, 54, 58, 60, 62, 65, 67,
    70–77, 80
street dancing 395–6
theatres of memory 17, 21, 24, 27–9, 35,
    37
unofficial knowledge 16, 18, 44
    see also Dickens; old photographs
Victorian Society 125, 126, 133, 186, 200
'Victorian values' see under Thatcher
'views' photography 353–4, 355, 359
Vigo, Jean 369
Vikings 27, 86, 179
    see also Jorvik
Vindolanda 178, 284
Viner, David 334
Vinogradov, Sir Paul 20
Virgil 439
visual themes see films; light; old
        photographs; television
Volkskunde 290
voyeurism 373–4
Voysey, Charles Francis 215

Wailes, Rex 157, 189, 201
Wainwright, David 167
Wake, Roy 149, 166
Wakefield 103
Wakeman, Geoffrey 47
Wales
    Folk Museum 178, 205
    heritage concepts 216, 223, 270
    living history 146, 184
    popular memory 30
    retrofitting 63, 64
Walker, Alice 309
Walker, John A. 348–9
walks
    historical 182, 184, 186, 190, 200, 245,
        248, 284
    long-distance 145, 175, 186, 238, 298
    nature 171, 283, 284
    rambling 298, 300
Wallace, Michael 82, 309
Wallas, Graham 216, 225
Walsall Museum 26, 27
Walton Hall 228
Wandsworth 176, 392–3
Wapping 132
Warburg, Abby 301

Ward, Colin 81, 362
Ward, J.A. 335
Ward, Tim 362
warehouses *see* docklands
Warhol, Andy 195, 339, 341
Warrham Percy 169
wars 28, 434
   battles, major 22, 23, 28, 221, 270, 329, 440
      see also under Hastings
   Crimean 27, 373
   Falklands 290
   films 208
   glorified 28
   graves 229–30
   and history writing 445
   museums 159, 178, 346
   old photographs 346
   Peninsular 35–6
   see also Civil War; First World War; Second World War
Warwick, Countess of 297, 311
Warwickshire 8, 26, 27, 29, 265
Waters, Muddy 206
Waterton, Charles 228
Watkin, David 134
Watkins, Alfred 166
Watlington 41
Watson, Pat and Howard 167
Watts, Michael and Christopher 167
Watts, Ruth 287
Waugh, Evelyn 58, 233, 242
Wayne, John 95
Weaver, John 199
Webb, Graham 116, 349
Webb, Philip 63, 288
Wedgwood, Josiah 111
Wedgwood Visitor Centre 147
Weedon, Geoff 116
Wegee 263
Wellbeloved, Horace 45
Wellcome Institute 177
Wertenbaker, Timberlake 422
West, Benjamin 34
West, Bob 245, 254, 286, 287
West Country 11, 30, 110
   heritage concepts 212, 229
   living history 152, 171, 174, 178, 192
   old photographs 321, 345–6
West Ham 276
West, Richard 251
Westacott, Hugh D. 166
Westall, Robert 377
Westland, Ella 255
Westminster 291, 390
   Abbey 153, 179, 264
   heritage-baiting 260

old photographs 337
Palace of 246
Queen Anne's Gate 75, 110
see also Covent Garden; Houses of Parliament; Soho (London)
Weston-super-Mare 185
Westwood, Jennifer 43, 166
Westwood, Vivienne 112
wetlands 156, 171, 228
Wheal Martyn 283
Whiffen, William 342
'Whig' interpretation of history 205, 441, 446
Whitby 159
   old photographs 333, 342, 361, 363, 365
Whitcombe 192
White, Hayden 8, 41–2
White, James F. 224, 239
White, John 45
White, Tony 348
Whitechapel 93, 316
   portrayed *see Elephant Man*
Whiteley, Nigel 348
Whiteread, Rachel 39
Whitrow, G.J. 446
Whittington, Sir Richard (Dick) 9, 15, 182, 420, 439–40
Wicken Fen 228
Wickham, Chris 42
Wickham, Glynne 45, 200
Wiener, Martin 225, 295, 310
Wigan 324
   Pier 244, 262, 263
Wigston Magna 187
Wild Flower Society 228
Wilde, Oscar 114, 341, 418
Wilder, John 249
wildlife reserves 155, 159, 205, 210, 228, 237, 260, 288
   see also birds; nature
Wildt, Michael 309
Willett, Henry 20, 44
William the Conqueror 23, 174
William of Malmesbury 433, 444
Williams, Alfred 11, 42
Williams, Bransby 421
Williams, Gwyn 239
Williams, James 40
Williams, Raymond 90, 295, 310, 421
Williams, W.H. 310
Williams-Ellis, Clough 297, 301, 309, 310
Williamsburg 178, 289
Williamson, Judith 341, 349
Williamson, Tom 166, 239
Willoughby, Martin 362
Wilson, Angus 240
Wilson, David M. 46

Wilson, Elizabeth 95, 97, 115, 116, 201
Wilson, Roger J.A. 198
Wilson, Roy 58
Wiltshire 64, 66, 145, 157
Winchester School 8
Winckelmann 110
Windett, Peter 117
windows and curtains 52, 54–5, 58, 60, 72, 77
Windsor 121, 212
Winter, Gordon 150, 319, 320–21, 334
Winwood, Steve 104
wireless see radio
Wirksworth 210
Wise, Douglas 132
Wolstencroft, H.P. 225
women see femininity
Wood, Ellen Meiksins 335
Wood, Robert 252–3
Wood, Tony 287
Wood, Violet 337, 348
Woodcraft Folk 297–8, 301
Wooden, Warren J. 47
Woodham, Dai 245, 254
Woodland Trust 146
woodlands 98, 144–6, 155–6, 168, 228, 229, 232, 442
Wookey Hole 196
Woolf, D.R. 42
Woolf, Virginia 212, 224, 297
Worcester 263, 266
Worcestershire 281
Wordsworth, William and Wordsworthianism vii, ix, 161, 172, 216, 296
working museums see open-air and industrial
World Heritage Convention 308
World Heritage Site see Ironbridge
World Wars see First World War; Second World War
World Wildlife Trust 307
Worsley, Giles 254
Wray, Christopher 102
Wright, Basil 240
Wright, Brian 225
Wright, Frank Lloyd 296

Wright, Lawrence 286
Wright, Patrick 43, 46, 233, 240, 242, 253, 261, 263, 272, 274, 285, 295, 302
Wright, Thomas 37, 41, 47–8, 440, 447
Wrightson, Keith 166
Wyld, Peter 134

X, Malcolm 309

Yarmouth 306, 322
Yates, Francis A. vii, viii–ix, 36, 47
Yates, Mark 100
York 302
    Cathedral 179
    living history 160, 170, 178, 179, 181, 188, 194, 195, 198
    museums 147, 160
        Castle 160, 182, 194
        see also Jorvik
    Mystery plays 93
    public lavatory 260
    son et lumière 179
York stone 74–5
Yorkshire 12, 28, 126
    heritage concepts 209, 214, 223, 228, 264, 298, 305
    living history 175, 176, 188
    old photographs 102, 333, 342, 347, 353, 361, 363, 365
    pedagogies 282
    resurrectionism 146, 147, 157, 159
    retrochic 102–3
    retrofitting 56, 58, 66, 75
    see also York
Young, G.M. 317, 333
Young, Michael 310
youth culture see Camden Lock; children; New Ageism; pop and rock; retrochic
Youth Hostels Association 298
Youth Training Schemes 238
Yoxall Jones, Edgar 334

Zambrano, A.L. 411
Zukin, Sharon 135, 272, 273
Zuleika Dobson 271
Zurich 307